Philip J. Franceschini

EDUCATIONAL PSYCHOLOGY

EDUCATIONAL PSYCHOLOGY

William A. Kelly, Ph.D.

REVISED EDITION

THE BRUCE PUBLISHING COMPANY • MILWAUKEE

Library of Congress Catalog Card Number: 65–19752

MADE IN THE UNITED STATES OF AMERICA

(21/65)

TO MARGARET REUTHER KELLY
WITHOUT WHOSE AID AND
ENCOURAGEMENT THIS BOOK
COULD NOT HAVE BEEN WRITTEN

Foreword to the Revised Edition

The purpose and function of this text remain unchanged from earlier editions. Designed for use primarily in Catholic colleges and teacher-training institutions, the text is intended to meet the needs of students in an introductory or fundamental course in educational psychology. Accordingly, the aim throughout has been to present simply, clearly, and concisely the principles, facts, and techniques which constitute a sound basis for teaching procedure.

This revision is based on a thorough survey of courses in educational psychology and of teachers' reactions to previous editions. Each chapter has been completely revised and supplemented by the best available research. All materials have been brought up to date, and several new illustrations in the form of figures and graphs have been added. The bibliographies and exercises have also been entirely revised.

The most striking revisions concern the background material from general psychology and the addition of four new chapters. Chapters II to XIII of the previous edition have been condensed into one chapter (Chapter II) on the backgrounds from general psychology in accordance with the recommendations of those in the field. This compression permitted the inclusion of four new chapters — namely, "The Elementary School Child," "The Adolescent," "Efficiency of Learning," and "Measurement and Evaluation."

The abundance of content in this revision makes EDUCATIONAL PSYCHOLOGY readily adaptable to different classroom and curriculum situations. Instructors may select and order the topics according to their individual requirements.

The author would have wanted to acknowledge his debt and gratitude to the following: to his fellow staff members of the Division of Educational Psychology, Measurement, and Guidance, the School of Education, Fordham University; in particular, to Dr. Francis J. Crowley, Dr. Barbara W. Lake, Dr. Genevieve Hunter Loughran, Dr. John M. Skalski, Dr. Irene Impellizzeri, and Rev. Thomas Hennessy, S.J.; to the editorial staff of The Bruce Publishing Company, especially Dr. John P. Treacy; to Dr. William G. Kelly, College of Physicians and Surgeons, Columbia

University; to Rev. James B. McGoldrick, S.J., Seattle University; to Margaret Reuther Kelly, for her understanding and encouragement; and to the many authors and publishers who graciously permitted the use of various quotations and illustrations from their copyrighted materials.

BRUNO B. WOLFF

Shorewood, Wisconsin

How is the child equipped to learn.

i.e. faculties, memory, intell, environ.

(every child does not learn at the same rate)

Contents

part V MEASUREMENT AND EVALUATION

part VI GUIDANCE AND ADJUSTMENT

part I

THE FIELD OF EDUCATIONAL PSYCHOLOGY

chapter 1

The Nature and Functions of Educational Psychology

The Purpose of Educational Psychology. The major activities of the school are *learning* and *teaching*. Other activities, including administration, curriculum construction, guidance, and methodology, likewise play important roles in the process of modern education. However, their purpose is fundamentally and primarily to facilitate and to render more effective the major activities of learning and teaching. Both of these major activities are by their nature complex and in the school situation are necessarily coordinated. Moreover, both are essentially mental processes. *Learning* is the mental activity by which knowledge and skills, habits and attitudes, virtues and ideals are acquired, retained, and utilized, resulting in the progressive adaptation and modification of conduct and behavior. Learning requires motivation, direction, guidance, control, and evaluation. The process by which these essentials are provided is *teaching*. Hence learning is the ultimate purpose of the teaching process and the true measure of its success. In turn the teaching process concerns itself with the activities which will promote and facilitate learning. To provide the necessary motivation and direction, effective guidance and control, and likewise to evaluate the outcomes of learning activity, the teacher must have an understanding of the basic laws and principles which govern the development of the growing child. Furthermore, it is essential that the teacher be familiar with the applications of these laws and principles to the situations and problems arising within the educational process. In order that a knowledge of these laws and principles may be available to the teacher, they have been embodied in a normative professional subject designated *educational psychology*. This subject endeavors to present the relationship of the science of the mind to the art of teaching.

Psychology is a science while teaching is an art. The art of teaching involves *creativity* which is dependent upon a knowledge of effective techniques and also upon the application of these techniques. An art is learned primarily by doing. Hence, it is not possible for one to become a good teacher merely through a process of reading books on psychology. There is no doubt, however, that good teaching can become better through an acquaintance with the principles of psychology for these furnish many of the rules of teaching. In fact a sound psychology furnishes the *rationale* of good teaching. A teacher who understands the science upon which the art of teaching is based will be able to avoid many errors in teaching. Accordingly, the primary purpose of educational psychology is to place the work of the teacher upon a scientific basis.

The purpose of educational psychology is not confined merely to presenting facts and techniques, to imparting laws and principles. More important is the emphasis which it places upon the application of these to the problems, materials, and methods of the educational process. Consequently, educational psychology should enable the teacher to understand the nature, the abilities, and the activities of the child. While it is concerned primarily with the guidance of mental growth and development, educational psychology necessarily takes into consideration other phases of the processes of growth and development, including the physical, the moral, the emotional, and the social. Thus it should, likewise, aid the teacher to realize the significance of the various changes accompanying growth and development. It should enable the teacher to understand the laws governing learning, thereby helping him to teach effectively and efficiently. It should afford the teacher a fundamental background in terms of which to estimate the value of the means employed in the educative process to guide mental development and to promote the formation of character. Thus *the major purpose of educational psychology is to provide the teacher with a background of practical information concerning the problems of growth and development of the child, not only mental but also physical, moral, emotional, and social, and in addition to provide the principles and laws which function as effective guides in the solution of these problems.*

The Meaning of Education. The term *education* has been derived from the Latin word *educare,* which means "to rear, to nourish, to bring up, to train." It may also have been derived from *educere* which means "to draw out" or "to lead out." Modern writers have assigned many and varied meanings to this term. It has been described as a "process of adjustment," as "a means of developing social efficiency," as "the progressive remaking of environment," as "the formation of habits," as "a way of life," or merely as "life," as "reconstruction of experiences," as "a process of change," as "development of personality," "a modification of psychological tendencies," "a reorganization and rearrangement of activity patterns," and in some instances as a combination of several or all of these.

Each of these descriptions contains an element which is recognized as important in the process of education; but each, or even all of these together, lacks the completeness which should be characteristic of the definition of this process, because each fails to impart a correct understanding of man's intrinsic nature, of his purpose and destiny.

The following definitions, representative of the Catholic point of view, are characterized by such completeness:

> Education is the deliberate and systematic influence exerted by the mature person upon the immature through instruction, discipline, and the harmonious development of all the powers of the human being, physical, social, intellectual, aesthetic, moral, and spiritual according to their essential hierarchy, by and for their individual and social uses, and directed toward the union of the educand with his Creator as the final end.[1]
>
> Education is the organized development and equipment of all the powers of a human being, moral, intellectual and physical, by and for their individual and social uses, directed towards the union of these activities with their Creator as their final end.[2]
>
> To the Christian, education is that culture of the mind, the will and the emotions which, whilst adapting a man for the exercise of a particular calling, disposes him to achieve an excellent personal and social life within the framework of that calling.[3]

An analysis of these definitions indicates that education involves the training, instruction, guidance, and direction of children and youth in order to effect the harmonious development of all their powers, capacities, capabilities — spiritual, moral, mental, physical, social, and emotional — to prepare them to live honorable, upright, useful, happy lives in this world and to attain in the next the end for which they were created. Such

---

[1] J. D. Redden and F. A. Ryan, *A Catholic Philosophy of Education,* rev. ed. (Milwaukee: The Bruce Publishing Co., 1956), pp. 23–24.

[2] W. J. McGucken, S.J., *The Philosophy of Catholic Education* (New York: The America Press, 1944), p. 7.

[3] Edward Leen, C.S.Sp., *What Is Education?* (New York: Sheed & Ward, 1944), p. 1.

education depends primarily on the nature of the one to be educated. Human beings are composed of body and soul, made in the image and likeness of God. Hence, to educate a child means the development, naturally and harmoniously, of all the powers and capabilities of body and soul.

Education consists of building up in the individual an organization of knowledge and skills, of habits and attitudes, of values and ideals which will aid in fulfilling life's purposes. Education is an active process; it is the doing of something; it is the cultivating and fertilizing of human minds. It is concerned with the growth and development of the child, for education cannot create or endow; it must develop. It is the development of the child's potential powers into actuality.

The fundamental aim of education is to help each individual to make of himself all that it is possible for him to become. Everything the teacher does and everything pupils do should lead to one end, the harmonious development of all the God-given powers and capacities of a human being.

The true goal and ultimate objective of Christian education have been formulated as:

> The proper and immediate end of Christian Education is to cooperate with Divine grace in forming the true and perfect Christian. . . . For precisely this reason, Christian Education takes in the whole aggregate of human life, physical and spiritual, intellectual and moral, individual, domestic and social, not with a view of reducing it in any way, but in order to elevate, regulate and perfect it, in accordance with the example and teaching of Christ.
>
> Hence the true Christian, product of Christian Education, is the supernatural man who thinks, judges and acts constantly and consistently in accordance with right reason illumined by the supernatural light of the example and teaching of Christ; in other words, to use the current term, the true and finished man of character. . . .
>
> The true Christian does not renounce the activities of this life, he does not stunt his natural faculties; but he develops and perfects them, by coordinating them with the supernatural. He thus ennobles what is merely natural in life and secures for it new strength in the material and temporal order, no less than in the spiritual and eternal.[4]

The Meaning of Psychology. The term *psychology* has been derived from two Greek words, ψυχή and λόγος, which mean the study or the

[4] Pope Pius XI, *Encyclical on Christian Education of Youth* (New York: The America Press, 1936), pp. 32–33.

science of the soul. In the broadest meaning of the term, it is that branch of philosophy which studies the soul and its operations. The soul is the substantial form of the body, the principle of life and the principle of thought. Fundamentally, soul and mind are conceived as one. The term *mind,* however, is used to designate the animating or vital principle as the subject of mental or conscious operations and activities, the principle by which man knows, wills, and feels. The term *soul* is used to designate the source of all vital activity, the principle by which the body is animated. *Psychology,* then, in its broadest meaning, is that branch of philosophy which embraces all that knowledge which concerns the soul, its manifestations and processes, its origin and nature, its destiny. In this broad sense it is usually termed rational or philosophical psychology or the philosophy of man.

Psychology, in the restricted meaning of the term, is the *study of human personality*. It is the organized, systematic, scientific study of human beings. It involves the study of how man knows, thinks, reasons, wills, feels, and how he adjusts himself to his environment. It involves the scientific investigation of the nature, the attributes, the powers, and the activities of the mind. It seeks to analyze, classify, and explain; to describe, interpret, and evaluate the facts concerning human personality in order to determine the laws which govern its operation.

The Meaning of Educational Psychology. Educational psychology derives its meaning, its purposes, and its functions from two disciplines, psychology and education. It is that aspect of applied psychology in which facts, theories, and hypotheses of the science of psychology are presented with reference particularly to their application and implementation in the school situation. The insights which scientific psychology has provided through research resources constitute a framework of concepts, facts, principles, and values concerning human nature which endeavor to explain man's mental life, behavior, and personality as well as his relations to his fellowmen and to his environment. The significance of scientific psychology, however, is dependent not alone upon research carried on and results produced in experimental laboratories; for research is not wholly complete when reported, data do not speak for themselves, facts gathered are not meaningful *per se.* The technical knowledge acquired through research and investigation must be interpreted, translated into useful practice, and made widely available. The major field for applying psychological knowledge has always been education. In fact the first branch of psychology definitely to have flourished in America was educational psychology.

The primary concern of educational psychology is the application of the scientific knowledge concerning human personality to the process of teaching, that is, to the motivation, direction, control, and evaluation of learning. Accordingly, it seeks to provide an understanding both of the learner and of the process of instruction and training by which the growth and development of the learner are guided and directed. This involves the selection, organization, interpretation, and integration of the facts, materials, techniques, and principles within the entire field of psychology which have a practical bearing upon the process of education. Educational psychology, then, embodies those aspects of psychology which will provide for the teacher a correct and thoroughly scientific understanding of the child, an insight into the nature and conditions of learning, an appreciation of the significance of individual differences, a knowledge of maturation, an awareness of the importance of adjustment, and a recognition of the necessity for the proper formation of character. Thus, it seeks to provide for the teacher the fundamental principles which will be of service in meeting the problems which arise in the classroom and in evaluating the means to be employed to achieve the objectives of the educational process. In order to fulfill these functions educational psychology has adopted and has endeavored to present in systematic fashion the basic psychological principles applicable to the educative process; has formulated a technical vocabulary; has developed through research a body of objective data concerning personality, growth and development, learning, and adjustment; and has devised precise instruments of measurement and evaluation.

The Methods of Obtaining Data in Educational Psychology. There are definite ways which are utilized to study and investigate the problems involved in learning and teaching. Educational psychology derives its data from many sources including the following: introspection, observation, experimentation, psychometrics or measurement, the case study, the genetic method, and the normative survey.

Introspection. The oldest and most fundamental method of obtaining data in psychology is *introspection.* Literally introspection means to look within oneself. It is a process of controlled self-observation which involves examination by the person himself of his own mental activities and experiences. It is then the reflective observation of one's own mental operations and activities together with the report of this observation. As a method of obtaining data introspection has serious limitations. It is purely subjective or personal in character; it cannot be used with young children or with the mentally retarded; the findings which it yields cannot be verified by another observer. As the tendency toward experimentation in psychology developed during the early years of the twentieth century, some systems of psychology, notably Behaviorism and Connectionism, rejected completely introspection as a means of studying human behavior. Yet introspection affords the only means of direct access to mental phenomena and constitutes a primary source of information concerning such subjective states as feelings, emotions, and thoughts. Moreover, if utilized carefully, introspection is of value as an aid in the interpretation and evaluation of objective data. However, introspection must be employed with caution and must be supplemented by other data.

Observation. In its general meaning *observation* involves intentional scrutiny in order to acquire information concerning some thing, or person, or situation. In psychology it has a similar meaning. It involves a methodical examination of the conduct and behavior of individuals or of groups, together with inferences regarding and interpretations of the factors which influence conduct and behavior. Among the types of observation which are of significance as means of deriving data in educational psychology are the following:

Incidental observation, which is also designated as informal, is the process of viewing and recording behavior as it occurs in natural situations, within the home and school and also on the playground without any attempt on the part of the observer to control either the behavior or the conditions under which it occurs. This type of observation has obvious limitations including the following: the field of behavior is not delimited; the observer may attend only to certain phases of activity and neglect others; the observer may not be entirely objective, or may be biased or may be inaccurate in observing and reporting.

Systematic observation, which is also designated as formal, involves methodical, purposeful, structured, and controlled observation of conduct and behavior. The accuracy of observation is insured by defining clearly the behavior to be observed, by selecting beforehand the particular situation or series of situations in which it is to be observed, and by specifying definitely the population to be observed. In addition, the reliability and objectivity of observation will be increased by making provision for repeated observations by the same observer or by different observers. An important factor in this method is the development of adequate techniques whereby the observations may be collated and recorded systematically and accurately.

In order to increase the reliability and objectivity of observation the *time-sampling* technique has been devised. This involves observation of the number of situations and the types of behavior episodes in which an individual or a group engages during a specified time, usually a definite short period at the end of which the reactions of the subjects are recorded immediately. Many variations of this technique are possible. The reporting of such observations may be facilitated by the use of checklists or tables of behavior or rating scales. Likewise, the tape recorder and motion-picture camera have been utilized to enhance the accuracy of observation in situations in which it is possible to employ these devices.

Anecdotal records usually involve a series of objective, systematic observations which in their accumulated form constitute a partial basis for an appraisal of the conduct and development of the individual child. Anecdotal records are narrative accounts, usually in chronological order, which describe significant and interesting items of conduct or events in which the pupil has participated. If significant episodes are reported in a truly objective manner, anecdotal records will aid the teacher in understanding and appraising the pupil's conduct and development.

Experimentation. The most precise and reliable way of obtaining data in educational psychology is experimentation, which is the basic scientific method. *Experimentation* involves observation made under conditions which the experimenter arranges carefully and controls adequately for the purpose of examining and testing the factor being studied in order to solve a problem or answer a question in the field. The experiment must be conducted by a trained worker who has isolated the situation or factor to be observed and studied; has brought under control all variables or conditions except the one which is being investigated; has arranged and recorded procedures so that the experiment could be repeated exactly, in order that results may be verified. A great many experiments which have been conducted in the classroom setting have produced considerable data in the field of educational psychology. Likewise, the findings of experiments carried on in psychological laboratories have been adapted for use in school settings. However, considerable caution must be exercised in applying the results of laboratory experiments to classroom situations.

Experimentation involves five distinct steps as follows:

1. Definition and limitation of the problem, which includes a statement of the questions for which answers are sought;

2. Formulation of an hypothesis, that is, the setting up of the problem within a conceptual frame of reference;

3. Collection of the data pertinent to the investigation. Here the matter of control is important;

4. Organization, analysis, and interpretation of data in order to present the findings of the investigation. Here statistical techniques are utilized for purposes of analysis;

5. Drawing of inferences and conclusions in order to answer the relevant questions in an adequate and feasible manner.

The experimental method has been used in educational psychology for evaluating the materials and methods employed in the processes of learning and teaching in order to improve educational practice. Experimentation may be of many designs. The technique most frequently employed in educational psychology is the *equivalent* or *parallel* group method. In this technique two groups of subjects are studied and compared. The two groups are selected in such a manner that they are as equivalent as possible in all relevant aspects, except the variable being studied. This process is designated as *matching* or *equating* groups. One group is termed the *experimental group,* the other, the *control group*. The experimental group is given special training in the method, materials, or technique being investigated. The control group, however, does not participate in or even know about the special training given to the experimental group. It serves as the standard of comparison. At the end of a definite training period both groups are given the same final test, and on the basis of the results obtained conclusions are drawn. Certain advanced research procedures make it possible to effect statistical control without actually matching groups.

Experimentation has played an important role in educational psychology. Through careful and persistent experimentation valuable data have been acquired. Through it, also, problems which might have otherwise remained obscure have been cleared up and explained. Furthermore, experimentation has been of assistance in determining precise limitations for various phases of the field and for ascertaining specific and exact meanings for many aspects of the subject.

The Method of Measurement or Psychometrics. This method has resulted in valuable contributions to the data in the field of educational psychology. It consists of the use of psychological and educational tests for research purposes. These instruments, which have been carefully constructed, are objective in form, are standardized, and yield scores which can be interpreted uniformly. They provide quantitative data of a precise and valid nature. Devised primarily to measure individual differences, they are predictive and diagnostic in nature. They include measures of mental ability, scholastic achievement, aptitudes and special abilities, aspects of personality and character, as well as attitudes and interests of various kinds. In experimental research they are employed, subject to adequate statistical treatment, to determine the status of experimental and control groups, particularly in the process of equating groups. Likewise they are used to ascertain the extent of progress made under experimental conditions by individuals and groups. They have been especially helpful in the solution of a wide range of problems particularly in the areas of learning, motivation, transfer of training, guidance, and evaluation of the effectiveness of teaching procedures and methods.

The Case-Study Method. This method involves a comprehensive and intensive study of the child and his environment for the purpose of collecting, organizing, and presenting pertinent information in the form of a *case history*. This is actually a summary of a large number of descriptive characteristics and includes materials concerning family background, growth and development, health, home life and environment, socioeconomic status, school experiences, social and emotional adjustment, together with a record of mental ability, scholastic achievement, interests, attitudes, and aptitudes. This procedure emphasizes the interview technique in gathering the necessary information. The function of the case history usually is to provide information which will be helpful in discovering the sources and causes of maladjustment, learning difficulties, misconduct, and undesirable behavior, and also in planning methods of adjustment, remedial services, and the like. At one time case studies were concerned with problem and maladjusted children. However, as an outcome of the universal adaptation of guidance and student personnel work, there seems to be a trend at present toward the study of the developmental background and abilities of all schoolchildren in order that data concerning the mental ability, scholastic progress, social and emotional adjustment, physical health, and other factors may be available at any time during the child's school life. As such data are accumulated and are checked by objective means whenever possible, the understanding of many problems in the various areas of growth and development will be greatly increased.

The Genetic Method. This is also designated as the developmental method. It involves intensive longitudinal studies of individual children over relatively long periods of time. This method is based upon the fact that the development of each child is a unique process, and therefore should be studied in terms of the growth of the individual. The *genetic* method consists of a series of measurements or controlled observations or both of the same child or of a small group of children repeated over a period of years, usually throughout the school career of the child, in order to observe the sequence of growth as it occurs and to ascertain relationships which exist between environment and development, including the mental, physical, social, and emotional aspects.

The Normative Survey. Some research in educational psychology has been directed toward the ascertainment of prevailing conditions and involves essentially a quantitative description of the general characteristics of a group. This type of research has been designated as the *normative survey* and the instruments employed in this method to gather data include questionnaires, checklists, rating scales, and interviews, as well as more objective approaches.

The questionnaire is a device which has been employed in educational psychology primarily for the purpose of collecting, classifying, and interpreting information, belief, and opinion. In form it consists of a list of questions which should be formulated very carefully in order that the answers may be sufficiently simple to tabulate satisfactorily. The questions should be so phrased that they will avoid suggesting a definite type of answer and also avoid making an appeal to bias. In most cases only a certain percentage of the questionnaires are returned and inferences are drawn from these limited returns. The principal drawbacks in the use of the questionnaire method are the impossibility of checking upon the ability and sincerity of the respondents, and also the difficulties usually experienced in securing an adequate and accurate sampling. However, the results obtained by the questionnaire method often suggest aims and methods for later and more carefully conducted surveys, and also indicate problems for further investigation. While recognized as having limitations, the questionnaire method may occasionally, when the proper statistical techniques are applied, yield results which are of value in educational psychology.

An improvement in the questionnaire technique is the *checklist*. This device provides a list of well-phrased questions which can be answered by *Yes* or *No,* or contains a list of items to which answers may be made by placing a check mark (✓) opposite the appropriate items. The checklist has been employed in many observational and evaluative studies, and in investigations of leisure-time activities, interests, study skills practiced, and the like.

Another technique similar in nature to the questionnaire and the checklist is the *rating scale*. This is a checklist to which has been added the dimension of quantitative judgment. This device has been employed in making appraisals of behavior, personality, character, and citizenship—which do not lend themselves to direct measurement. Several types of rating scales have been developed. Some forms list traits to be checked for possession or nonpossession; other forms provide spaces for qualitative estimates, such as superior, good, average, poor. There are also graphic rating scales on which the rater checks along a line extending from zero to one hundred the amount or percentage of the characteristic he believes the child possesses. These ratings are connected by lines which yield a trait profile or graph that portrays the child's strong and weak points. There are also self-rating scales which the child is expected to apply to himself. While rating scales are used frequently, the ratings thus obtained are always subjective and usually low in reliability.

The *interview* as employed for research purposes involves the collection of data directly in a face-to-face situation rather than by the use of questionnaires or checklists. By means of the interview technique it is possible to obtain data which cannot be secured through the use of less personal procedures. In addition this technique permits the interviewer to gain a general impression of the person giving the information or facts, and to form a judgment concerning the truthfulness and seriousness of the replies made.

Historical Backgrounds of Educational Psychology. Although educational psychology is considered a relatively new field, it has become a most important basic subject in the professional education of teachers. The origin of the term *educational psychology* seems to be somewhat vague. According to a statement[5] attributed to a former dean of Teachers College, Columbia University, James E. Russell, the term was coined when Edward L. Thorndike was appointed to the staff of Teachers College in 1898. However, it has also been stated that DeGarmo[6] offered a course designated Educational Psychology at the University of Illinois in 1890. Likewise, a small booklet of less than one hundred pages by Louise Hopkins, entitled *Educational Psychology,*[7] appeared in 1886. This was actually an outline of the application of psychological principles to education. With regard to the subject matter of educational psychology, American educators[8] are inclined to give credit to Thorndike for the formulation of its content. The reason for this is that previous to 1900 educational psychology consisted largely of descriptive and theoretical analyses of teaching and learning, while after that date, due chiefly to Thorndike's influence, it became concerned with the application of experimental and statistical methods to educational data.[9] In this connection frequent reference is made to his three volumes entitled *Educational Psychology,* which were published in 1913. Likewise, American educators have often considered John Dewey as a pioneer in this field because of his insistence upon scientific analysis in education.[10]

Historians of education usually maintain that several educational theorists of the nineteenth century, notably Pestalozzi, Froebel, Spencer, and particularly Herbart, were among the first to recognize and to develop the psychological foundations of the educational process. In addition, there seems to be a noticeable trend to stress the work of Ebbinghaus and Meumann, who introduced experimental methods and thus supplied the foundations for scientific study in the field. Wilhelm Wundt (1832–1920), who established the first psychological laboratory at the University of Leipzig in 1879, is likewise frequently referred to as having given the

[5] P. M. Symonds, "A New Meaning for Educational Psychology," *Journal of Educational Psychology,* 30:33–37, 1939; A. I. Gates, "The Department of Psychology at Teachers College, Columbia University," *The New York State Psychologist,* Vol. 7, No. 2, p. 3, October, 1954.

[6] G. M. Blair, *Educational Psychology, Its Development and Present Status,* University of Illinois Bulletin, Vol. 46, No. 13 (Urbana, Ill.: Bureau of Research and Service, College of Education, 1948), p. 9.

[7] A. A. Robach, *History of American Psychology* (New York: Library Publishers, 1952), p. 378.

[8] L. W. Webb, "Some Trends in Educational Psychology," *Educational Trends,* 3:20–27, 1934.

[9] D. Starch, H. M. Stanton, and W. Koerth, *Psychology in Education* (New York: Appleton-Century-Crofts, Inc., 1941), pp. 5–6.

[10] A. A. Robach, *op. cit.,* pp. 378–379.

impetus to experimental work. Moreover, American writers often pay tribute to William James, to G. Stanley Hall, and to James McKeen Cattell as pioneers in the introduction of experimental procedures in educational psychology.

It might be well to point out here something which may not be generally realized. Long before Herbart or Thorndike or anyone else had devised a systematic presentation of educational psychology, good teachers everywhere and always applied the laws and principles of psychology to their work, whether as a result of previous training in philosophy and psychology or by virtue of what is ordinarily called "common sense" and their own experiences in meeting classroom problems.

Especially noteworthy is the fact that several writers have discovered a Catholic tradition in educational psychology, antedating considerably the contributions of Herbart and the others previously mentioned. De La Vaissiere[11] has credited Raymond Lully (Ramon Lull) with formulating the directive principles of child study in the thirteenth century. He has also called attention to the fact that, in the sixteenth century, Juan Luis Vives devised a plan of research and experimentation which would be considered thoroughly modern in educational psychology. Likewise, Kane has pointed out that Vives' *De Anima et Vita* was an empirical treatise which made use of inductive methods in psychology for the first time and first applied psychological principles to educational practices. In fact it has been asserted that, "all the authors who have studied Vives show that he was the real founder of educational psychology."[12] In addition Blair[13] has stated that educational psychology really dates from the founding of the early normal schools and has noted that possibly the first such school for the training of teachers was founded by St. John Baptist de La Salle in 1685.

Furthermore, even the development of the "Psychological Tendency in Education" during the nineteenth century was not without a Catholic influence, although that influence has not received the general recognition which it deserves. An Italian priest, Antonio Rosmini-Serbati, the founder

[11] Jules De La Vaissiere, S.J., *Educational Psychology*, translated from the fifth French edition by S. A. Raemers (St. Louis: B. Herder Book Co., 1930), pp. 24–25.

[12] W. T. Kane, S.J., and J. J. O'Brien, *History of Education* (Revised Edition; Chicago: Loyola University Press, 1954), p. 208. See also W. A. Daly, *The Educational Psychology of Juan Luis Vives* (Washington, D. C.: The Catholic Education Press, 1924).

[13] G. M. Blair, *op. cit.*, pp. 5–6. See also E. A. Fitzpatrick, *La Salle, Patron of All Teachers* (Milwaukee: The Bruce Publishing Co., 1951).

of the Institute of Charity, set forth the fundamental psychological principles underlying education. These principles closely resemble those of Froebel. The essential difference in the work of Rosmini consisted in the nature of the religious and moral training and guidance of the child. His principal contribution to educational psychology has been translated into English under the title of *Ruling Principle of Method Applied to Education.*[14] This work has been characterized as "an astonishingly shrewd application of psychology to methods."

Functions of Educational Psychology. Because of the strategic position which educational psychology occupies as the foundation science upon which all educational practice rests, the course in this subject as presented in the Catholic college must include the best and most progressive data derived from scientific experimental research to reinforce the principles drawn from rational psychology, and must synthesize the teaching of Catholic philosophy and the sound contributions of scientific psychology. At the same time "the postulates, principles, and ideals of Faith must be kept inviolate." This imposes upon the Catholic college the obligation to meet alike in the course in educational psychology "the demands of science and the demands of religion."

In order to meet this obligation the course in educational psychology must serve certain functions, must stress certain aspects of the field. These functions are eight in number and indicate that the introductory course should be extensive and descriptive rather than intensive and technical. The first three functions are basic. They are concerned with the application of Christian principles, which present the true and valid concept of human nature and human destiny as well as the nature and aim of education; and with the interpretation of scientific procedures in terms of time-tried principles which consider the whole child and not merely his physiological and biological processes. The remaining five functions involve the presentation and application of the laws and techniques which will be of use in directing the experiences by which knowledge and skills, habits and attitudes, ideals and virtues are acquired; in solving the problems that arise in the educative process; and in determining and evaluating methods of instruction.

The *first function* is to afford a thorough knowledge of the nature of the child. By virtue of his human nature, the child is composed of body

[14] A. Rosmini-Serbati, *The Ruling Principle of Method Applied to Education,* translated by Maria G. Gray (Boston: D. C. Heath and Co., 1889).

and soul, endowed with intellect and will, destined for an eternal life. This function is especially significant, since in the last analysis every system of education is based upon some theory of the nature and destiny of the child. Consequently, when the teacher's interpretation of the nature and destiny of the child is false, his work is bound to be faulty and even harmful.

The *second function* is to provide an understanding of the nature, aims, and purposes of education. For the Catholic, education is the complete formation of the whole child, the development of all his powers and capacities to enable him to fulfill life's purposes and to achieve the end for which he was created.

The *third function* is to acquire familiarity with the technical vocabulary and to further an understanding and an appreciation of the scientific procedures by which the data of educational psychology are obtained, leading to the development of a scientific attitude. This involves both the acquainting of the student with the best work of this kind done in the field and also the inculcating of an awareness of the importance of drawing correct conclusions from scientific data. Likewise, it involves the interpretation, the evaluation, and the application of both data and conclusions in terms of true and unchanging philosophical principles.

The *fourth function* is to provide a significant knowledge of the developmental process with particular emphasis upon the promotion, guidance, and control of mental and moral aspects in order that the nature of man may be better understood and his original endowments may be used to develop his latent possibilities.

The *fifth function* and, at the same time, the core of the course in educational psychology, is to provide an understanding of the principles governing learning, together with a knowledge of the techniques for guiding improvement in learning and their application to the practical problems of the classroom. To accomplish these purposes it is essential that the following phases and topics be presented adequately and considered thoroughly:

a) Individual differences
b) The learning process
c) The motivation of learning
d) The factors and conditions which influence the efficiency of learning
e) Transfer of learning
f) Development of effective study habits and skills.

The *sixth function* is to present the theories underlying the measurement and evaluation of mental abilities, aptitudes, educational achievements, interests, and personality organization.

The *seventh function* is to present the principles and conclusions regarding the prevention of all types of maladjustments together with the approved practices for achieving satisfactory adjustments. This will involve a consideration of: *the principles of mental hygiene,* with particular emphasis upon the necessity of establishing emotional stability and volitional control; *the principles of guidance.*

The *eighth and culminating function* of the course in educational psychology is to inculcate in the prospective teacher the realization that the most essential purpose, the most important objective, and the primary consideration throughout the entire educational process from the kindergarten through the university is *character formation.* Consequently, definite consideration must be given to the principles, processes, and techniques involved in character training. The best and most efficacious means of forming character must be presented as an essential part of the teacher's preparation. Character is the intelligent direction and purposeful control of human conduct under the influence of *morally correct principles.* These principles must be converted into standards of action and applied consistently in the activities of life. It must be emphasized, furthermore, that there can be no true formation of character without religion.

Finally, the course in educational psychology, although the basis of the sequence of professional courses in preparation for teaching, must be something more than merely a vocational subject which will help the student to meet certification requirements. It must bridge the gap between learning theory and realistic learning experience in the classroom by providing a broad and functional understanding of the child, of his nature, of his development and adjustment, of how he learns, and it must do so in the light of true principles.

Relationship With Other Fields. A major task of educational psychology has been to determine the psychological knowledge which is essential to the teacher and to make it available in organized, systematic form. Accordingly, in the development of educational psychology many related fields have provided fundamental laws, principles, facts, and techniques. It has been the aim of educational psychology to integrate these effectively. The areas of psychology from which basic facts and information, principles and laws, vocabulary and classifications, methodology and scientific evaluation have been derived include the fields of *general, experimental, child, adolescent, differential, social, clinical,* and *abnormal psychology* as well as *mental hygiene* and *counseling psychology.* In addition, contributions have been made by fields other than psychology. Materials concerning heredity, the structure and functions of the physical dynamisms, the laws governing the data and theory concerning physical growth and development have been supplied by the sciences of *biology* and *physiology.* The methods employed in the tabulation, analysis, and interpretation of data have been borrowed from *statistics.* Likewise, the results of medical and psychiatric research as well as findings in the areas of sociology and cultural anthropology have influenced the interpretations given to various problems and aspects of educational psychology.

However it should be noted that, although educational psychology has borrowed much material from other fields, it has also developed its own areas of research. The areas in which impressive contributions have been made include learning, individual differences, teacher-pupil relationships, diagnosis of learning difficulties and disabilities, remedial teaching, counseling and guidance, "readiness," attitudes, values, the development of criteria and technique for evaluating educational procedures, audio-visual methods, programed learning, and teaching machines.

Point of View: A Summary Statement. It is recognized by many within the field that educational psychology is not and cannot be strictly and purely a factual science but must be cultivated within a "frame of reference," that is, a framework of philosophical background and theory. Accordingly, to affect profoundly educational practices and procedures, educational psychology needs and must have the proper orientation and continuous guidance afforded by a true and sound philosophy of education. This philosophy of education must supply *correct, universal, unchanging principles* by which to establish the objectives of education. The basic factor in such a directive philosophy of education must consist of a true understanding of both the origin and nature of man and also of the meaning and purpose of life. Every system and process of education is based in the last analysis upon some theory of man's nature and destiny. The fulfillment of the main function of educational psychology, that is, the guidance and direction of growth and development in all their aspects, depends wholly upon such an understanding. Consequently, it is essential that the Catholic concept of the dignity and worth of man permeate the course in educational psychology. The Catholic concept of man is that of a being composed of body and soul, "made in the image and likeness of his Creator," endowed with an intellect and a free will, responsible for his actions, destined for an eternal life. The purpose of Catholic education is to make present life an effective preparation for future life. For this it is necessary to take into consideration the relationship of the individual to the primary cause and ultimate end of his existence — Him in whose image and likeness he is made. No guidance and direction of the growth and development of the child can be wholly successful unless inspired by an awareness of the destiny of man. The most important and essential function of the teaching process is the guidance of the spiritual, moral, intellectual, and volitional development of the child for the formation of the *complete man.* Catholic philosophy of education has always maintained that the subject of education is the *whole child,* body and soul cooperating in the performance of every act. "The subject of Christian Education is man, whole and entire; soul united to body in unity of nature, with all his faculties natural and supernatural, such as right reason and Revelation show him to be."[15]

Hence educational psychology must consider the whole being of the child. It cannot consider the child as other than a being endowed not only with body, nervous system, and senses, but also with a soul, intellect, and will. The whole child cannot be educated if his spiritual soul and immortal destiny are ignored. Consequently, educational psychology must be concerned with the guidance and direction of the full range of the child's nature, his physical, emotional, and social powers; his mental, moral, and volitional capacities. Educational psychology cannot be content merely to present facts and principles for the material guidance and instruction of the child, for his social development, for the attainment of his physical well-being, for the achievement of emotional balance.

EXERCISES

1. Outline this chapter.
2. List and define the terms which you have learned from your study of this chapter.
3. *a*) What purposes does educational psychology serve in the training of the teacher?
   b) What is implied in "understanding the child"?

[15] Pope Pius XI, *op. cit.,* p. 19.

4. Distinguish between:
   a) Learning and teaching;
   b) Art and science;
   c) Systematic observation and experimentation;
   d) Experimental and control group;
   e) Questionnaire and checklist.
5. *a*) Why are not all educators in agreement concerning the meaning of *education?*
   b) Examine six recent textbooks in educational psychology in order to determine how *educational psychology* is defined in each. What common elements appear in the definitions? In what ways is it possible to account for the differences in definitions? Note the differences in the amount of space devoted to the various areas of the field. In what ways is it possible to account for this?
6. Describe the historical backgrounds of educational psychology.
7. Discuss the following statements:
   a) "The major field for applying psychological knowledge has always been education."
   b) "All psychologists have a personal stake in educational psychology."
   c) "Experimental results are useful only insofar as they relate to actual purposes and conditions within the school."
   d) "In the last analysis every system of education is based upon some theory of child nature."
   e) "Psychology is not and cannot be strictly and purely a factual science but must be cultivated within a large framework of philosophical theory."
9. Discuss the functions of the course in educational psychology. Compare those listed in this chapter with similar statements in other textbooks.
10. What point of view is presented in this book? Why is it of definite significance to know the point of view underlying the principles of educational psychology?

SELECTED REFERENCES FOR STUDY AND READING

Bachrach, A. J., *Psychological Research: An Introduction* (New York: Random House, 1962).

Barzun, J., *The House of Intellect* (New York: Harper & Row, 1959).

Best, J. W., *Research in Education* (Englewood Cliffs, N. J.: Prentice-Hall, Inc., 1959).

Borg, W. R., *Educational Research: An Introduction* (New York: David McKay Co., Inc., 1963).

Brown, C. W., and Ghiselli, E. F., *Scientific Method in Psychology* (New York: McGraw-Hill Book Co., 1955).

Burton, W. H., *The Guidance of Learning Activities,* 3 ed. (New York: Appleton-Century-Crofts, Inc., 1962).

Conway, P., *Principles of Education* (Washington, D. C.: Thomist Press, 1960).

Donceel, J. F., *Philosophical Psychology,* 2 ed. (New York: Sheed & Ward, 1961).
Good, C. F., *Introduction to Educational Research* (New York: Appleton-Century-Crofts, Inc., 1959).
Mandler, G., and Kessen, W., *The Language of Psychology* (New York: John Wiley & Sons, Inc., 1959).
McAshan, H. H., *Elements of Educational Research* (New York: McGraw-Hill Book Co., 1963).
McCall, R. J., *A Preface to Scientific Psychology* (Milwaukee: The Bruce Publishing Co., 1959).
McCluskey, N. G., *Catholic Viewpoint on Education* (Garden City, N. Y.: Hanover House, 1959).
Misiak, H., *The Philosophical Roots of Scientific Psychology* (New York: Fordham University Press, 1961).
Mouroux, J., *The Meaning of Man* (New York: Sheed & Ward, 1948).
Postman, L., *Psychology in the Making* (New York: Alfred A. Knopf, Inc., 1962).
Renard, H., *The Philosophy of Man,* revised and enlarged by M. Vaske, 2 ed. (Milwaukee: The Bruce Publishing Co., 1956).
Roback, A. A., *History of American Psychology* (New York: Library Publishers, 1952), Chap. 17 and 18.
——— ed., *Present-Day Psychology* (New York: Philosophical Library, 1955) Chap. 12.
Royce, J. E., *Man and His Nature* (New York: McGraw-Hill Book Co., Inc., 1961).
Rummel, J. F., *An Introduction to Research Procedures in Education* (New York: Harper & Row, 1958).
Seagoe, M. V., "Educational Psychology," in *Encyclopedia of Educational Research,* C. W. Harris, ed., 3 ed. (New York: The Macmillan Co., 1960), pp. 403–407.
Watson, R. I., *The Great Psychologists: From Aristotle to Freud* (Philadelphia: J. B. Lippincott Co., 1963).

part II

THE NATURE OF THE LEARNER

chapter 2

The Nature and Fundamental Equipment of the Learner

A. THE NATURE OF THE LEARNER

Basically, educational psychology is considered to involve the application of the facts, methods, laws, and principles of psychology to the process of education. Psychology has been defined as the study of human personality. The true notion of the human individual is not the soul only, not the body only, but the composite subject of soul and body which constitutes the *human person*. One aspect of man, the person, consists of a corporeal substance which is alive and grows, which experiences sensations, which feels pleasure and pain. The other aspect is a spiritual substance which is the principle of spiritual acts, thc source of intellectual abstraction, the source of self-reflection, the origin of free rational volitions. The sentient body and the rational soul by their union form one single substance, one nature, one person, one self. The soul and body exist in mutual dependence. Since both soul and body enter into the constitution of human personality, it is essential that the teacher have an accurate fundamental knowledge of both.

The Soul. The soul is the ultimate internal principle by which the body is animated. It is the principle by which man thinks, feels, and wills. It is the principle by which man lives and moves, perceives and understands. The soul does not differ from the mind, for they are one and the same reality. The term *soul* is more comprehensive than the term *mind.* The term *soul* is used to designate the principle and substantial form of vital activity. The term *mind* is used to signify the source of mental activity. Mind is the ultimate internal principle considered as the subject of conscious or mental states. The mind is considered as the source of conscious life, while the soul is considered as the principle of life itself.

The soul is a simple, spiritual form substantially united to a particular body forming together with that body an integrated, unique personality. The soul is the substantial form of the body and communicates to the body its very subsistence. The soul is so united to the body that through it the body receives and possesses subsistence and life. It is the cause of life and the functional activities of the body. From this union of soul and body there results a single substance. The union of soul and body does not mean a confusion of the two, but signifies only that they complete each other. The single substance that results from the union of soul and body constitutes an individual of rational nature; that is, a human personality.

The term *faculty* is derived from the Latin word *facultas,* which means "a power" or "an ability." The faculties are the principles of action, the instruments by means of which the powers of the soul are manifest. One mind, the principle of all conscious states, has a multitude of capabilities. So the faculties may be defined as the capabilities possessed by the mind for engaging in a particular kind of activity or the powers to perform certain actions.

There exists among modern psychologists a considerable misunderstanding of the term *faculty*. Likewise, the position of the Scholastics regarding the faculties has been misrepresented. The chief difficulty is that most educational psychologists are *monists,* that is, they do not recognize any distinction between physical capacities and spiritual powers. So when the term *faculty* is used by psychologists other than Scholastics, it means not "a special mode of action through which the mind acts"; not a spiritual power but merely a physical function; a material part of the mental machinery.

The faculties are classified as follows:

A. Cognitive Faculties
   1. Sensuous and Organic
      a) External Senses:
         Sight, hearing, touch, taste, smell
      b) Internal Senses:
         Instinct, imagination, memory

2. Spiritual and Inorganic
   a) Acts of the Intellect:
   Concept, judgment, reasoning

B. Appetitive Faculties
   1. Feelings and Emotions
   2. Rational Will

The Body. The body is the means of communication between the outside world and the mind. Through the body the outside world acts on the mind; through the body the mind adjusts to the outside world. However, the body is something more than a passive intermediary between mind and matter; it is one of the active determining factors of mental states. It is necessary for the teacher to have a knowledge of the organization of the body which is so intimately connected with mind. Hence, it is essential that educational psychology study bodily conditions under which mental life actually functions.

The reception of impressions from the outside world, the organization and integration of nerve impulses, their combination and distribution, their facilitation and inhibition, are effected by the nervous system. The nervous system is comprised of two divisions, the *cerebrospinal* or *central* and the *autonomic,* consisting of two groups of nerve centers and two groups of nerves. To the cerebrospinal division belong primarily the functions of animal life, while to the autonomic division belong chiefly the control of vegetative life, the nervation of the viscera, blood vessels, and glands. The cerebrospinal division constitutes the bodily machinery for mental states. The autonomic division provides for the functioning of bodily organs. These two divisions do not constitute two independent systems; they are mutually related and interdependent. Both divisions of the nervous system are composed essentially of neurons. Each neuron is composed of a unit of living matter called *protoplasm.* The neuron consists of a *cell body* containing a *nucleus.* From the surface of the neuron project many short branching outgrowths or *fibers,* called *dendrites,* and a single long process incased in a fatty sheath, called an *axon.* At intervals the axon gives off side branches, known as *collaterals.* Usually there is only one axon in each cell, but each has a number of dendrites. Nerve impulses pass from a dendrite through the cell body to the axon and collaterals. Dendrites are used as receiving stations or as the points of entrance for a nerve impulse which is conveyed *to the cell body.* Axons serve as distributing channels along which the nerve impulse is conducted *away from the cell body.*

Neurons are classified according to function into three groups: *sensory; motor;* and *associating neurons.* Sensory neurons carry the nerve impulse from a *sense organ,* or *receptor,* and transmit the impulse to the spinal cord and brain. Motor neurons conduct impulses from the brain and spinal cord to the *reacting organ,* or *effector,* that is, to a *muscle* or *gland.* Associating neurons transmit impulses between sensory or motor neurons from one side of the spinal cord to the other. They lie wholly within the brain and spinal cord. Neurons have two characteristics, *sensitivity* and *conductivity.* Sensitivity is the capacity to respond quickly to a stimulus when an excitant has been applied to a nerve at the end organ. *Conductivity* is the capacity to transmit the impulse along the nerve fibers from the point of stimulation to the nerve center. The process by which a stimulus is received and transmitted is termed a *nerve impulse.* The exact nature of this nerve impulse which is transmitted over the neurons is unknown. Several interesting and ingenious theories of its nature have been proposed. It has been described as a chemical substance which diffuses the length of the nerve and also as a form of electrical energy which originates at the site of stimulation and is propagated to the site of reaction. The impulse is initiated by a stimulus acting on a sense organ and is transmitted over the neural pathway to the natural outlet of all nerve impulses, the muscles or the glands.

Physiologically each neuron is closely related to other neurons, but anatomically the relationship is one of contiguity. The axons of all except motor neurons end in masses of fine branches or fibrils known as *end brushes* or *telodendrions.* These end brushes are in contact with the branching dendrites of some other neuron. This arrangement may be compared to that of two trees, one growing alongside the other, with their branches intermingling and touching but obviously not continuous. The place of contact between the end brush of one neuron and the dendrites of another is a tiny space or gap known as a *synapse* or a *synaptic connection.* This transmission of the impulse across a synapse is always in one direction, from the end brush of one neuron to the dendrites of another.

In order that a nerve impulse may pass from one neuron to another it must cross the synapse. Usually each neuron has connections with several other neurons, but the nerve impulse crosses only one or perhaps a few of these synapses. At some synaptic connection great resistance may be offered to the passage of the impulses, while at others relatively little resistance may be offered. The tendency is for the impulse to cross where the resistance is low. This resistance in the synapse determines the course of the impulse. However, the more frequently the synaptic pathway is used the weaker becomes the resistance.

The Cerebrospinal Division of the Nervous System. The chief nerve centers of the cerebrospinal division of the nervous system are the *spinal cord* and the *brain masses.*

The spinal cord is a cylindrical structure made up of a bundle of nerve fibers and connections which form a pathway to and from the brain.

The brain masses consist of those parts of the cerebrospinal division of the nervous system which are contained within the cavity of the skull. The chief parts are the *medulla,* the *cerebellum,* and the *cerebrum.*

The *medulla* is a direct continuation of the upper end of the spinal cord, where the cord thickens on entering the skull. The medulla contains nerve centers which control and regulate the rhythmic processes of such vital reflex functions as respiration, digestion, and the circulation of the blood. It serves also as the correlating center for the movements of the muscles of the tongue and for those muscles in the back part of the throat which function in swallowing.

The *cerebellum* or little brain lies back of and above the medulla. The functions of the cerebellum include the coordination of muscular movements, the maintenance of proper muscular tone, and possibly also the maintenance of equilibrium. The activities of the cerebellum do not enter consciousness.

The *cerebrum* or large brain exceeds in size all other parts of the brain. It occupies about two thirds of the cranial cavity and forms one half of the weight of the brain. The cerebrum is composed of white and gray matters. The white matter consists mainly of nerve fibers and constitutes the inner layer of the cerebrum. The gray matter, which is made up of nerve cells, constitutes the outer layers and is termed the *cortex.* The cortex contains three groups of areas which have been assigned definite functions. To the sensory area are transmitted neural impulses stimulated in the sense organs. In the motor area are initiated the movements of skeletal muscles. In the associating areas are made the inner connections between sensory and motor neurons.

Reflex action, which is the simplest action of the nervous system, is an involuntary and automatic production of activity in response to the stimulation of sensory nerve fibers. The basis of reflex action is the *reflex arc.* This is a neural mechanism which secures a definite and immediate response to a given physiological organism. A stimulus acts on a receptor and an impulse is generated. This impulse is transmitted along the sensory neuron to a motor center: the motor center is stimulated and a motor impulse is transmitted along the motor neuron to a gland or muscle. The individual may be conscious of the stimulus, or of the response, or both; but consciousness does not enter into reflex action as an essential factor. Reflex action is an immediate response to a stimulus without the intervention of any conscious effort. In reflex action, movement follows promptly with mechanical necessity upon the excitation by the stimulus. The reflex possesses a definite purpose, that is, to serve to coordinate the muscles of the body to enable the organism to respond effectively and immediately to external stimuli and at times to protect the organism from harm.

The Autonomic Division of the Nervous System. The *autonomic division* of the nervous system is composed of groups of nerves essentially similar in construction to those in the brain masses and in the spinal cord. It is made up of a series of neurons, the cell bodies of which lie wholly outside of the cerebrospinal division. It includes nerve centers in the cervical, thoracic, and lumbar regions, and a chain of ganglia, that is, aggregations of nerve cells bound together by connective tissue, located on either side of the spinal cord. It is made up of these ganglia, the communicating branches which they send out and the *plexuses* which they form, the most important being the solar, hypogastric, and cardiac plexuses. Nerve fibers branch out from the ganglia to the muscular coating of the blood vessels, of the viscera, and of the glands; that is, the autonomic division governs such human functions as breathing, digestion, contraction of smooth muscles, heartbeat, excretion. The autonomic division serves an important purpose in mental life, since it is concerned largely with the control of the vital processes of the body and is closely connected with emotional response.

Relation of the Nervous System to the Muscles and the Glands. The cerebrospinal division of the nervous system governs the operations of the *skeletal muscles. Smooth muscles* and the *glands* are directly controlled by the autonomic division.

The Muscles. The muscle tissues play a large part in human life and conduct, for they are the main motor organs of the body. There are two classes or types of muscles. The *skeletal* or *striped* muscles, which constitute a considerable part of the body, and vary in size from the large muscles in the shoulders and legs to the small ones attached to the eyes and vocal organs. They are attached to the skeleton and can, by alterations in form, bring changes in the arrangement and position of nearly all parts of the body. The skeletal muscles function, usually, in voluntary action, and their activities are regulated by the cerebrospinal division.

The *smooth* or *unstriped* muscles function in the operation of the vital organs. They are not affixed to the skeleton, but surround cavities or tubes in the body, as the blood vessels or alimentary canal, and by their movements control the passage of substances through these tubes.

The characteristics which enable muscles to perform the function of motion are:

Irritability or *excitability,* that is, the power to receive and respond to stimuli. *Contractibility,* that is, the power which enables the muscles to change shape so as to become shorter and thicker when they receive impulses transmitted to them through the motor nerves. It is the power to contract involving the shortening of the muscle and its fixation in a new form. *Extensibility,* that is, the power which enables the muscle to be stretched and or extend its form. *Elasticity,* that is, the power which enables the muscle to return to its original form.

The Endocrine Glands.[1] These glands secrete chemical substances which play an important part in mental life and general behavior as well as in growth, development, and physiological functions. These chemical substances are termed *hormones.* A hormone is a chemical substance, produced by a specialized group of cells, which is transported to some other area of the body where it has a specific effect on a specific tissue. The usual mode of transportation is the blood. The group of cells which secrete the hormone generally compose endocrine tissue or an *endocrine gland.* The specific tissue on which the hormone acts is referred to as the *target organ.* Although the mode of action of the hormones is not known, they modify the rate of various biochemical reactions occurring in the

[1] A. Garbman and H. Bun, *A Textbook of Comparative Endocrinology* (New York: John Wiley & Sons, Inc., 1962); C. H. Best and N. B. Taylor, *The Human Body: Its Anatomy and Physiology,* 4 ed. (New York: Holt, Rinehart, and Winston, Inc., 1963); R. N. Williams, *Textbook of Endocrinology,* 3 ed. (Philadelphia: W. B. Saunders Co., 1962).

body. They do not initiate reactions which are not already occurring. Thus they function as chemical regulators.

The more important of the endocrine glands are the *thyroid,* the *parathyroids,* the *adrenal,* the *pituitary,* the *gonads* or sex glands, and the *Isles of Langerhans* in the pancreas.

The *thyroid* is a butterfly-shaped gland located in the neck near the larynx. This gland secretes two hormones: *tri-iodothyronine* and *thyroxine.* These hormones are unique in that they are among the few biologically occurring organic compounds which contain iodine. The thyroid hormones regulate the rate of metabolism throughout the body and in addition have a poorly understood effect on body development. Hyposecretion of thyroid hormones results in a slow rate of metabolism and retarded development. Mental function may also be impaired. If hyposecretion is present at birth both mental and physical development are impaired. This condition is called *cretinism.* It may be treated by the administration of thyroid hormones and the individual will develop normally as long as the treatment is maintained. Hypothyroidism can result from a deficiency of iodine in the diet. Hypersecretion of thyroid hormones is characterized by a rapid rate of metabolism and by emotional tenseness and irritability. Both hypothyroidism and hyperthyroidism can result from a variety of defects in either the thyroid itself or in the pituitary.

The *parathyroid glands* usually consist of four small bodies located in the general area of the thyroid. Little is known concerning the chemical nature, biological activity, and control of the secretion of the hormone, *parathormone* which these glands secrete. The function of this hormone is the maintenance of the concentration of calcium in the blood. It also controls the metabolism of calcium and plays a role in the proper formation and maintenance of bone structure.

The *adrenal glands* are located one on each side of the body directly above the kidneys. Each is composed of two distinct parts: the outer area or *cortex* and the inner area or *medulla.* The secretions of these two sections are very different and perform distinct functions. The adrenal cortex secretes three types of hormones, *glucocorticoids, mineralocertoids,* and *adrenal androgens.* The primary glucocorticoid is *cortisol.* Its presence is required by almost every organ of the body and its effects are subtle and diffuse. Its particular effect is to increase the amount of glucose made at the expense of protein. It plays a vital, but poorly understood, role in the adaptation of the body to physiological and emotional stress. *Aldo-*

sterone is the primary mineralocorticoid. Its major function is the control of sodium excretion by the kidneys. The function of the adrenal androgens is not yet known.

The several congenital disorders in the production of cortisol are known collectively as the *androgenital syndrome*. All forms of this disease are characterized by excessive secretions of adrenal androgens with masculinization in girls and early puberty in boys. In certain forms of this disease there may also be hypertension, inability to conserve sodium, or deficiency in the secretion of cortisol. Children with the adrenogenital syndrome are usually normal mentally but may have emotional problems secondary to the symptoms of the disease. Other adrenal cortisol disorders include *Addison's disease,* which is characterized by hyposecretion of all adrenal corticol hormones and *Cushing's syndrome* which is characterized by hypersecretion of cortisol. Hypersecretion of cortisol can sometimes result in emotional irritability, aggressive behavior, and even mental illness.

The chief secretions of the adrenal medulla are *epinephrine* and *norepinephrine.* Extra quantities of these hormones are secreted in immediate response to stress, fright, or anger. The physiological functions of epinephrine are to mobilize glucose and to increase blood pressure. Deficiency of epinephrine during infancy and early childhood may cause emotional maladjustment and mental retardation; an excess may produce a state of chronic exhaustion.

The *pituitary* is a small gland located at the base of an area of the brain called the hypothalmus. It is divided into three distinct regions: the *anterior,* the *posterior,* and the *intermediary* lobes. Each of these parts secretes its own group of hormones. The function of the secretion of the intermediary lobe in man is unknown. Proper secretion of *somatotropin* or *growth hormone* by the anterior lobe of the pituitary is necessary for growth in general and for growth and development of the skeleton in particular. Hypersecretion of this hormone during childhood will result in overgrowth of the bones or *pituitary giantism.* If such hypersecretion occurs after the individual has attained adult size, a disharmonious growth evident in face, hands and feet will produce marked changes in the individual's appearance. This condition is known as *acromegaly.* Hyposecretion of the growth hormone results in *pituitary dwarfism,* a condition in which skeletal structures reach maximum development in early life and no longer continue to grow, thus producing a miniature person whose bodily proportions and mental ability are usually normal. The anterior lobe of the pituitary also secretes *thyrotropin,* a thyroid-stimulating hormone. Hypersecretion of thyrotropic hormone by the anterior pituitary causes hypersecretion of thyroxine by the thyroid and hyposecretion thyrotropin results in hyposecretion of thyroxine. Hyposecretion of thyrotropin can result in cretinism and other disorders characterized by low thyroid hormone secretion. The *adrenocorticotropic hormone* (ACTH) stimulates the adrenal glands to secrete cortisol and has a less stimulatory effect on the secretion of adrenal androgens. Several *gonadotropins* are also produced, the most important of which are the *follicle-stimulating hormone,* the *lutenizing hormone* and *prolactin.* In the female, the follicle-stimulating hormone stimulates the secretion of estrogen. The functions of the lutenizing hormone are to stimulate the secretion of *progesterone* and the formation and maintenance of the corpus luteum. All of these gonadotropins are necessary for ovulation. In the male the gonadotropins regulate the production of androgens by the testes and they are also necessary for spermatogenesis or production of sperm.

The secretions of the posterior lobe of the pituitary are oxytocin and vasopressin. The function of *oxytocin* is not known but one of its effects is the stimulation of uterine contractions. *Vasopressin* has two effects: it maintains blood pressure at the proper level and is also the *antidiuretic* hormone which controls the excretion of water by the kidneys. A lack of antidiuretic hormone results in a disease known as diabetes insipidus.

The *gonads* or sex glands are the *ovaries* in the female and the *testes* in the male. Relatively inactive during childhood they begin to secrete their hormones either just before or at the beginning of puberty. The hormone in the male is *testosterone* and its function is the development at puberty and the maintenance thereafter of the secondary sex characteristics. The female sex hormones are the *estrogens* and *progesterone.* The estrogens are responsible for the development at puberty and the maintenance thereafter of secondary female sex characteristics. Progesterone also is necessary for the development and maintenance of the secondary female sex characteristics and in addition is necessary for the maintenance of pregnancy. The secondary sex characteristics involve the bodily changes which occur at puberty. In the female they include the distribution of hair, the general bone structure and disposition of adipose tissue, both of which result in the female form and walk. In the male the secondary sex characteristics include the masculine muscular development, change of voice, and growth of beard. The secretions of the gonads are likewise considered responsible for other differences between males and females in bodily and muscular development.

The *Isles of Langerhans* are groups of various types of cells located in the pancreas. They produce the hormone *insulin,* the function of which is the regulation of the utilization of carbohydrates. Deficiency of insulin results in the inability to metabolize carbohydrates. This condition is known as diabetes mellitus and can be controlled by supplying the lacking hormone medically and by regulating diet. The Isles of Langerhans also produce a hormone called *glucagon.* This hormone stimulates the conversion of glycogen to glucose by the liver and its subsequent release into the blood.

Control of Hormone Secretions. After secretion, the hormones, like other bodily components, are metabolized and excreted. Thus the hormones must be continuously secreted to balance the loss by degradation. Furthermore, certain situations require the secretion of greater amounts of hormones than are normally required. It is evident that some mechanism must operate whereby the rate of secretion of the hormones is regulated. In general these mechanisms are not well understood. The control of the secretion of vasopressin, growth hormone, oxytocin, parathormone, and aldosterone is not known. The secretion of the adrenal medullary hormones is believed to be under the direct control of the nervous system. As implied earlier, the anterior lobe of the pituitary secretes a number of tropic hormones which stimulate specific glands to secrete specific hormones. In each of these cases, the hormone itself acts upon either the anterior pituitary or the hypothalamus to inhibit the secretion of the tropic hormone. This is referred to as the *negative feedback mechanism.* Thus thyrotropin stimulates the thyroid to produce thyroid hormones which in turn inhibit the secretion of thyrotropin.

The negative feedback mechanism operates in the control of secretion of cortisol, testosterone, estrogen, progesterone, as well as thyroid hormone. However this is not the only mechanism which regulates the secretion of these hormones. For example, the rapid increase in secretion of epinepherine in response to acute stress stimulates the secretion of ACTH which in turn stimulates the secretion of extra amounts of cortisol by the adrenal. Unfortunately little is known about these secondary regulations and how they operate.

B. THE FUNDAMENTAL EQUIPMENT OF THE LEARNER

Sensation. Sensation may be described as the conscious response resulting from the stimulation of a sense organ. Sensation is the elementary unit of mental experience. It is the first and simplest mental process. It is the first mental process because mental life begins with sensation; the first contact of mind with matter is sensation. It is the simplest form of mental life because all other mental states are based upon and presuppose sensation. Mental content is dependent upon what is received through the senses. Through the senses contact is made with the external world which exists apart from and independent of the mind. The Scholastics formulated this principle: *Nihil est in intellectu quod non prius fuerit in sensu:* "There is nothing in the intellect which was not first in some manner in the senses."

Sensation is the conscious reaction of the mind to the stimulation of the sense organs. This reaction makes known the existence and properties of the objects that stimulate the senses to action. Sensation is defined as *the conscious processes which are the immediate results of the stimulation of sense organs, by means of which man becomes aware of existence and properties of particular objects which stimulate the senses to action.*

A sense organ, often termed a receptor, is a specialized end organ of a sensory neuron endowed with the property of reacting to a particular type of stimulus. A sense organ includes three essential elements; namely: (1) sensory receptory apparatus, (2) a sensory nerve connecting this receptory apparatus with (3) a sensory area in the cortex of the cerebrum.

A sensation takes place when a *stimulus,* that is, a physical force or substance, acting upon a *sense organ,* initiates a *neural impulse* which is transmitted by the *sensory neuron* to the *sensory area* in the *cortex of the cerebrum* in which the sensory neuron ends. This resulting activity or reaction is the *sensation.* The *physiological bases* of sensation are the *sense organs* and the *cerebrospinal division of the nervous system.* The necessary conditions of sensation are: (1) *physical,* that is a *stimulus* acting upon a sense organ; (2) *physiological,* that is, a *receptor* or *sense organ* especially sensitive to its own form of stimulus; a *sensory neuron* which conducts the neural impulse to the cortex; (3) *psychological,* that is, the arousing of the mind to *consciousness.*

The attributes of sensation are three, namely, *intensity, quality,* and *duration.*

The *intensity of sensation* denotes the vividness or strength of the sensation. Every sensation occurs with a certain degree of intensity which influences the kind of effect that the sensation produces. The difference between a bright and a dull light, between a loud and a soft sound are differences of intensity. When the sensation is so weak or so fine that it is just barely perceptible, it is said to be at the threshold; when it increases in vividness or strength to the point where further increase is impossible or is unnoticed, it is said to be at the maximum. Between the threshold and the maximum a number of degrees of intensity may be noticed. Among the conditions which may modify the intensity of sensations are: the force of the stimulus, the sensitivity of the receptor, the condition of the nervous system, expectant attention, and inattention or concentration elsewhere, duration, and rate of change.

The *quality of sensation* signifies the characteristic kind of reaction made to specific stimuli. Quality is the most prominent attribute by which sensations of the same or different senses are distinguished from each other. Each shade or color is a different quality of visual sensation, that is, a different response of the sense of sight to some variety of light. Each pitch or timbre is a different quality of auditory sensation. Differences in the quality of sensation are due primarily to differences in the susceptibility of the sense organs, and to differences in the form of the stimulus.

The *duration of sensation,* which is really self-explanatory, indicates how long the sensation actually exists. Thus the duration of a sensation of sound is from the time of its commencement to the time that it ceases. Every sensation has a certain duration, being either momentary or persistent for an appreciable time.

Sensations are classified into five divisions according to the sense organs which give rise to them. They are in order of their importance for learning: visual, auditory, tactile, gustatory, and olfactory. However, tactile sensation involves four forms of consciousness: (1) sensations of *contact and pressure,* that is, *tactile sensations* really so called; (2) *temperature* or *thermal sensations;* (3) *kinesthetic* or *muscular* sensations; (4) *organic* sensations.

The senses may also be classified according to the source or location of stimulation into: (*a*) *exteroceptors* when the stimulus is external to the body; (*b*) *interoceptors* when the stimulus is within the body cavity; (*c*) *proprioceptors* when the stimulus is between the body cavity and the outer surface of the body. The exteroceptors yield knowledge of environment; the interoceptors, of the general welfare of the body; and the proprioceptors, of movement, balance, and bodily performance.

Imperfections in the functioning of the sense organs are likely to impair effectiveness in learning. All defects in the sense organs affect in various ways and degrees the character and range of sensations and consequently the ideas derived from them. The organs of sight and of hearing are the senses of most importance for the service of the mind. These sense organs often become partially or wholly incapable of performing their normal functions because of defects of structure, or as a result of disease.

Sensation is the first source of all knowledge, for by means of his sensory equipment the individual becomes aware of the objective world which exists apart from and independent of the mind. Without sensation there would be nothing to be converted into knowledge. In school the pupil comes into contact with books, with subjects of study, with teachers, by means of his sense organs. Through the organs of hearing, he becomes accustomed to and identifies various kinds of sound. Through the organs of sight, he becomes aware of distance, size, form, color, and movement of objects. Through the organs of touch, he acquires much information about shape, texture, and temperature. To a much lesser extent he acquires information through the organs of taste and smell. Thus the sense organs play a most significant part in the acquisition of knowledge.

Perception. Sensations never occur as isolated factors; for example, the color blue is always the color of some object. They are always related to other sensations. The present sensation has to be associated and compared with past sensory experiences. If the mind is lacking in these past experiences, as in the case of very young children, the sensation has little effect from the educational point of view. After the mind has associated and compared the sensation with past experiences, that sensation has been interpreted and given a meaning. *Perception* may be defined as the *mental process of interpreting* and *giving a meaning to sensation of a particular object.* It is a mental process but, nevertheless, is associated closely with bodily activities; that is, with the activities of the sense organs and of the nervous system. In perception sensations acquire a meaning.

The mind is stored with records of past experiences. Every incoming sensation is an accretion and carries with it suggestions of some portion or other of past experiences. The result is that any impression made on the sense organs does not evoke merely its immediate conscious response, that is, a simple sensation; but it awakens and revives also experiences which in the past have been associated with such sensations. The nature of perception is then a compound result of a sensation aroused by a stimulus and supplemented by revivals and associations of former sensory experience. Perception equals S + s + s + s + s + s + s. The S designates the actual sensation aroused by the stimulus acting upon the sense organ. The s + s + s + s + s + s signifies the revival and association of sensations which have been stimulated on previous occasions by the same or similar objects. Perception is by its nature synthetic and coordinates several sensations.

The basis of every perception consists in present or past experiences. The perception is always of some definite thing or condition affecting one or more of the sense organs. It may be the perception of an object, such as a writing desk, or it may be the perception of a bodily condition, such as a headache. It may be the perception of a melody, or it may be the perception of the representation of an object such as a model, a picture, or a statue. It may be the perception of a symbol, such as a word, a map, a number, or a formula.

There are three aspects or phases of the process of perception, namely: (*a*) the sensation; (*b*) the discrimination and identification of sense impressions; (*c*) the unification of present sense impressions with past sense impressions.

At times a separate term has been employed in order to distinguish the unifying phase of the perceptive process from the mere reception of sense impressions. To this phase the term *apperception* has been applied. Apperception is not a separate process nor is it a special mental function. It is merely a statement of the way in which one phase of the perceptive process functions.

Perception is not a separate process that occurs after the sensations have been received, as digestion occurs after eating, but it is the way in which sensations are received. There are no sensations except perceived sensations. There is no perception without sensation, and (after the first few months of life) no sensation without perception.

Perception may be defective or inaccurate due to any of the following causes: (1) defects in sense organs, for example, color blindness; (2) inaccurate report due to carelessness, haste, or difficulty in getting the sensation as well as to lack of attention; (3) errors of interpretation designated as illusions, for example, the mirage, or camouflage, the function of which is to disorganize the perceptions; (4) emotional strain.

Each sense represents the stimulating object according to its character. Sight represents objects as colored; hearing, as sounds; smell and taste, as agreeable or disagreeable; touch, as hard or soft, warm or cold, etc. Hence, perceptions are usually named according to the class of impressions that predominate. Perceptions are the outcome of visual, auditory, tactual, gustatory, and olfactory experiences with things and events. The most prominent are the visual, the auditory, the tactual, and the mixed. The most important perceptions are those of sight; touch also contributes greatly to the other senses, and hearing is important. Smell and taste occupy the lowest place.

The meaning of an object present to the senses is the awareness of the thing plus all one's associated previous experiences as far as the present experience recalls them to mind. To see the roundness or smoothness of an object, to see a friend, to see that another person is ill or sad or joyful, signifies that here the object or qualities are not perceived directly by the sense of vision to which they are attributed, but are inferred by habitual association.

The reliability and efficiency of perception depend upon the completeness and accuracy of the sensation, the association of sensation with past sense experiences, and the fullness and correctness of this association.

Children are lacking in the richness, in the definiteness, and in the detail of sense perception. They have only a very limited amount of experience from which to draw. They also lack the power of fine discrimination. They lack also maturity of judgment necessary for interpretation of their experiences. There is a marked difference between children and adults in the ability to make use of sustained attention. These are important facts for learning and teaching, since it is a well-known tendency of the child with his limited experiences to fall back on pure fancy for the meanings that he gives to new experiences.

Perceptions become more and more perfected with age, education, and mental development, because they embody a more accurate and complete knowledge of perceived objects. The more accurate and extensive the individual's observation is and the more faithful his interpretation of it, the better his opportunity to remember and use the materials presented to his senses.

Imagination. Imagination may be described as the mental power of reproducing past sensory experiences of objects not actually present to the senses and of recombining elements of past sensory experiences into new forms. By means of his imagination man has the capacity not only to view the past as though it were present but also to construct images outside of his specific previous experiences. *Imagination is,* then, *the mental power of forming representations of material objects which are not actually present to the senses.* The mental representation so formed is designated the *image,* which term is derived from the Latin word meaning a likeness or picture. In the popular meaning of the term, imagination is often considered to deal only with the fanciful or to consist wholly of daydreams or reverie. In the more technical and scientific meaning of the term, imagination signifies the mental power by which man reproduces and constructs images.

Imagination presupposes sensation and perception, for the imagination can utilize only those materials which have reached it in some way through the senses. It is evident that where a sense is defective or lacking, the corresponding images will be defective or lacking.

The stages of the imaginative process may be classified as: (1) the *reproduction* or the *revival* in part, at least, of sensory experiences; (2) the *modification* or *transformation* of elements of these revived images into new combinations; and (3) the *construction* of these combinations into new wholes to form the image of something which has not come within the field of one's experiences or which may never even have existed. Into this new product not a single element has entered which was not familiar in the form of an image of one kind or another. Nothing can be imagined which has not been experienced in some way through the sense organs. Past sensory experiences furnish the materials out of which imagery comes. The *form* is new, the *material* is old. Hence there is one limitation to the imaginative activity. While it may combine elements of materials furnished by former experiences into an almost endless variety of forms, it cannot produce new elements.

It is possible to distinguish between two functions of imagination, namely, the *reproductive* and the *constructive.* Neither works independently or entirely by itself, for there is always an overlapping.

The *reproductive imagination* involves the reviving of past sensory impressions in their original form and in the order in which they originally occurred, though not in the same exactitude with which they were first experienced. It consists of the power of forming images of objects and events which have been previously perceived and the revival of such images in unaltered form. The *constructive imagination* signifies the power of producing images of objects not previously perceived. This is accomplished by isolating elements of objects separately perceived. Some elements are retained; others, rejected. The elements of previous experiences are modified, transformed, recombined, elaborated. However, this requires the presence of certain materials. These materials are supplied ultimately by previous sensory experiences.

Imagination must be cultivated on account of its utility and controlled on account of its dangers. The imagination should be regulated by reason and prudently directed by the will. The imagination plays a very important part in the life and education of man, since it furnishes his intellect with materials for its operations. It is necessary so to regulate the imagination that it may be of great service in the acquisition of truth and that it may make man's senses the useful servants of his rational nature. It should never be allowed wholly to rule the other powers and activities or to guide human actions and behavior. It must remain always under the guidance of reason and the control of the will.

During the school life of the individual the imagination must be guided and directed most carefully. The imagination, particularly the constructive imagination, is necessary for the understanding of schoolwork, for the interpretation of history, literature, art, music, geography. Increased appreciation of literature, art, music, drama depends upon training of the imagination. The training, direction, and guidance of the child's imagination is one of the teacher's most important tasks. While everything that motivates the imagination should be made use of, there is also the important task of avoiding anything in the process of training that might lead to disordered imagination or to overextravagant activity of the imagination which is termed *hyperphantasy*. This hyperphantasy shows itself in the pathological lie, and in hysteria.

The pupil who is lacking in imagination does not learn, he merely imitates. Project and other similar types of methodology are valuable in that they provide an opportunity for planning, imagining, and constructing new situations out of the materials at hand. Such simple activities as drawing a map or composing a story involve imagery. Were it not for the ability to imagine, art would lose its effectiveness. A keen, fertile imagination, well organized toward definite ends, is a great help to the student.

Memory. Memory is the power of the mind by which past mental acts and states of consciousness are retained, recalled, and recognized. It is the capability of the mind to preserve conscious processes, that is, to retain representations of past experiences and to reproduce them later with the recognition or awareness that they are past experiences. Moore has defined memory as "the conservation of past experience and its later utilization as the occasion may arise." The mere recall of a past experience is only one phase in the process of memory. There must be added to recall, the recognition that what has been recalled is something which has been known or experienced previously at some time. Memory always implies a reference to the past, and in this respect differs from imagination which is not thus limited but refers to the present or the future. Memory includes recognition while imagination does not.

Memory is an essential condition in the assimilation of knowledge, for the simplest judgment and the most involved reasoning process depend upon and imply the retention, recall, and recognition of past experiences.

There are two divisions of memory; namely, the *sensory* and the *intellectual.*

The *sensory memory* preserves and recalls impressions acquired through the senses and reproduces the sensible images with a knowledge or awareness of their perception at a previous time. Sensory memory does not retain, recall, and recognize sensations, but rather does it retain, recall and recognize representations or sensory images of past sensations. It is, then, the power to receive and preserve any impression of an event or other experience acquired through the senses and also to recall the experience with the knowledge that it has taken place at a past time.

The *intellectual memory* is the capacity which the intellect possesses to retain and to reproduce intellective cognitions that have already been acquired. Man not only acquires, retains, and reproduces sensory impressions, but he has the power to acquire, retain, and reproduce rational cognitions which implies essentially the intellect. He has, then, the capacity to recall past acts both sensory and intellective. While sensory memory retains and recalls that which has been perceived through the senses, intellectual memory retains and recalls abstractions and generalizations.

Memory involves three functions or basic operations: namely, the *retention, recall,* and *recognition* of past experiences.

Retention is based on the theory that experiences, both sense and intellective, persist in some form, while not realized in consciousness. *Retention* depends upon the *vividness,* the *frequency,* and the *recency of impressions.* The improvement of retention may be accomplished by meaningful repetition, and by multiple sense appeal, by interest, and by concentration of attention.

Recall is the actual reproduction or revival of past experiences in consciousness. Memory not only retains sensory impressions and ideas, but it also brings them back to consciousness. Recall is of two types, *spontaneous* or *immediate,* and *voluntary. Spontaneous recall* involves the memory of familiar objects and persons. It depends upon association with or suggestions from present perceptions or images. The efficient recall of past experiences is governed by the laws of association, i.e., by contiguity in time and space, by similarity, and by contrast, which provide facilitation in the acquisition of meaning. *Voluntary recall* of past mental experiences is usually termed *reminiscence* and involves *reflection, comparison,* and *choice,* or the acceptance or rejection of a selected line of thought.

Recognition is the reference of the present recalled experience to the past. It involves the recollection and placing of recalled experiences and requires a background of meaning and a familiar setting. Recognition is of two types. *Vague recognition* implies some recognition but little more than a general feeling or awareness of familiarity, that is, somewhere at some time one has had the experience. *Definite recognition,* that is, *recognition* properly so called, occurs only when the attention is directed to the past. It implies a conscious recognition of past experience. It means the identification, with varying degrees of perfection, more or less accurately and completely, of the present percept, image, or idea with its corresponding original previously formed. Very definite recognition produces confidence in the accuracy of recall.

Recognition is purely mental. The improvement of recognition is accomplished by the well-organized systems of ideas. Improvement of recognition depends upon improvement of associations. This is brought about by repeating the association until it has been firmly fixed, by substituting logical associations for mechanical and ingenious connections, and by converting isolated types of associations into logical systems of thought. A rich background of familiarity, a clear understanding and interpretation of all related facts will aid in proper association and hence in recognition. Hence, it may be stated as a principle that any idea that is definitely and positively committed to memory in a clear and forceful connection with the associated ideas with which it should function will be as clearly and positively recognized when recalled.

It is possible also to classify memory into two general types, *rote* and *logical. Rote memory* is frequently called mechanical memory or is described as "learning by heart." It refers to the ability to repeat verbatim materials previously learned or mastered. It should mean repeating exactly what the intellect has mastered, but too frequently it is only the unthinking rattling off of words by means of contiguous association. As such words are recalled merely by mechanical repetition, both the process and the result are bad. There is the additional danger that pupils may remember words and never get the meaning. One may have a good rote memory without understanding, since words rather than ideas are memorized. This type of memory requires little mental activity.

Logical memory implies understanding. For logical memory the pupil must first comprehend the significance and meaning of the material. This involves an analysis of the material, a recognition of significant features and their relation to one another as well as to wider experience. Logical memory calls into play the reasoning powers; it strives for the thought rather than for the mere word; it stresses the similar and essential relations of things as well as their place in a system of thought. It has been found that there is a very high positive correlation between logical memory and intelligence. The pupil who comprehends significant facts as such and can recall and use them is intelligent. The pupil who remembers well ideas which are logically related is the pupil who is attentive, who grasps the significance of schoolwork, who organizes his work.

Memory cannot exist without association which is the mental process in which past ideas and experiences are brought into consciousness by means of their connections with others in it. It is the mental process of relating two or more experiences to each other. When two or more ideas or experiences have occurred together in consciousness in the past, the recurrence of one idea or experience will tend to suggest or to revive the other or several others. Association, however, does not mean a process of combination by which several ideas unite to become one. It accounts for the succession of ideas in the mind and means that ideas are not revived independently, but that their recall depends upon the presence of other ideas in the mind. Ideas, perceptions, and experiences are grouped together so that the recall of one tends to bring about the recall of another or several others. Sometimes the individual is clearly aware of the association, is able to follow the train of ideas, and to note the connections and relationships. In other cases the person is unable to understand why an idea is recalled; it seems to flash into the mind without being related to any other idea. Frequently, in such cases after some reflection the individual is able to discover a hidden relationship which binds together the ideas.

The process of forming associations is always going on, and it is worthy of note that these connections are by no means made at random. The process by which associations are formed is subject to an ordered control, and associations are made under definite conditions. They are not formed arbitrarily but according to certain laws which indicate how related groups of experiences and ideas are formed and how one experience or idea suggests another. These laws are designated as the *primary and secondary laws of association.* The *primary laws of association* are those of *similarity, contrast,* and *contiguity*. The *secondary laws of association* are those of *recency, frequency,* and *vividness.*

The *law of similarity* expresses the principle that present actions, sensations, emotions, or thoughts may be facilitating factors in reviving and reproducing their like among previous impressions or states. Things which resemble each other tend to reappear together in the mind; thus a photograph recalls the person; a story or a song tends to remind one of similar experiences in the past. To be similar, two things must have something in common. Frequently, it is difficult to determine just what is common between two objects, but nevertheless the common characteristic is there. The similarity may be total or it may be partial; the common features may be more or less numerous.

The *law of contrast* states the principle that present actions, sensations, emotions, or thoughts may be facilitating factors in reviving and reproducing their opposites among past impressions and mental activities. The mind recalls images and ideas that represent experiences of an opposite character, as, north, south; dwarf, giant; rich, poor; virtue, vice; young, old. Mere contrast, however, is not invariably sufficient to establish relationships, even though contrasting objects do impress themselves easily and deeply on the memory. There is involved also the perception of difference and the fact of discrimination.

The *law of contiguity or propinquity* formulates the principle that present action, sensations, emotions, or thoughts occurring together in a time or space relationship have a tendency to evoke one another. Probably the major portion of associations are made according to the law of contiguity.

In addition to the primary laws of association, there are several *secon-*

dary laws which involve principles of establishing and strengthening associations. *The law of recency* states the principle that the more recently experiences have occurred together, the more likely are they to recur together. The *law of frequency* formulates the principle that the more frequently the connection has been made the more thoroughly the association is formed. This is probably the most important factor in determining associations. Permanent associations usually cannot be established without frequent repetitions.

The *law of vividness* expresses the principle that objects and events which make the most vivid impression at the time of observation are most likely to be recalled. Events which have occurred in so striking a manner as to transfix the attention are usually impressed indelibly upon the mind. Vividness depends objectively on the force of the stimulating objects and subjectively on the energy of the attention of the individual. Hence, the more attention one centers on an associated series of experiences, the less frequently will it be necessary to repeat the experiences to make them permanent possessions of the mind.

Attention. Attention may be described as the direction of the cognitive powers toward one object or a group of objects; or toward a thought; or toward an activity to the exclusion, more or less completely, of all others. *It is the concentration or focusing of consciousness upon a specific object, situation, activity, or mental process, to the more or less complete exclusion of all others for the purpose of understanding its nature or knowing its qualities.*

There are two forms of attention, the *spontaneous* and the *voluntary.*

Attention is *spontaneous* or involuntary when the mind is acted upon by the mere force of the stimulus presented; that is, the stimulus is strong enough to force itself into the focus of consciousness regardless of all other conditions that obtain at the moment. Such stimuli as flashing lights, loud noises, moving objects, and brilliant colors will produce this mental state. Spontaneous attention is given naturally and easily without effort of will. Attention of this type is clearly manifested by the child from the very beginning of his life.

Attention is *voluntary* when there is a deliberate and purposive focusing of the mind upon an object. This type of attention is determined chiefly by the motives that influence the will. It is termed *voluntary* because it requires effort of the will; it is "activated by the will." The individual is aware of the effort put forth and of the energy expended. Voluntary attention comes with the growth and development of the child. The child learns to recognize the importance of attending to what is not immediately interesting, because of its future value. This becomes increasingly true when he begins to live in a world of thoughts and ideas as contrasted with a world of perceptions. This type of attention makes possible expulsion of the unimportant and gives place and value to the significant and important. This power of voluntary attention is the key to self-control.

The important laws of attention are those of *intensity, duration,* and *extent.*

Intensity of attention is the degree of concentration of the mind upon its object. The intensity of spontaneous attention is determined by the *strength of the stimulus* which arouses attention and by the *comparative attractiveness* of the objects presented to the mind.

Duration of attention is the degree to which attention is sustained. It involves the factors of *constancy* and *fluctuation,* for voluntary attention and spontaneous attention are essentially variable in character. Attention does not remain constant in the same direction for a long period of time, but gradually decreases and disappears unless its object changes or some new aspect of the object is discovered. Attention does not flow on in a constant level stream, but has a tendency to fluctuate. When an individual is said to keep his attention fixed for a long time on a single object, he really follows out a train of ideas related to the object present to the mind.

The *extent* of attention is the number of objects attended to at one time. It is the *scope* of attention and refers to the efficiency of mental energy. The direction of attention is limited in range as well as in duration. The extent of attention is usually inversely proportional to its intensity. The extent of attention is always a single idea or unit of thought.

The primary effect of attention is the *intensification* of the mental state, that is, of the sensation, emotion, or thought, on which one concentrates. As a result, this state is impressed more deeply on consciousness. Another very important effect of attention is the increased *distinctness* of the mental state. The object on which attention is focused becomes clear and prominent. It is discerned from all other objects. The prominence of all or of a part of the object is increased, and likewise the clearness of the mental state is also increased.

Attention also brings about the establishment of many relations and associations of one object with others and also aids in bringing about relationships of similarity, contrast, contiguity, and cause and effect. This is the *unifying effect of attention.* When the individual attends to one object of thought, the mind makes use of this object as a central core of thought and brings into relation with the object the things that belong with it.

A further effect of attention is an *increased retentiveness.* In order that ideas may be faithfully retained and accurately recalled, it is essential that the objects which attract attention be impressed more quickly, more surely on the memory. Evidence of this effect of attention is presented by the fact that important experiences in life to which attention has been given may be recalled accurately with details after long periods of time.

The direction of attention is largely determined by *interest.* Some objects attract man's attention because they afford him either pleasure or pain of a particular kind. Hence, interest is identified with a peculiar attraction exerted by objects in virtue of the pleasurable or painful experiences with which these objects have been associated in the past. It is the feeling side of attention. Interest may be defined as the *pleasant or unpleasant feeling produced by an idea or an object with the power of attracting and sustaining attention.* It involves usually a liking for and a tendency toward an object which attracts the individual's attention, is valued by him, and results in his satisfaction. It is the means by which the mind is attracted to an object and constitutes a most important factor in the acquisition of knowledge. Interest secures economy in learning and efficiency in response, since it implies not only a favorable disposition toward an object but also a tendency toward making further responses.

Interest may be *native* or *acquired.* Some objects arc natively interesting while in others an interest must be built up gradually. Native interest is that value which an object has in itself to attract attention. Acquired interest is derived from the association of an object with others in which an interest already exists.

Although attention is in part a natural mental endowment, no other power of the mind is more susceptible to training. The secret of the development of attention lies in its use. *The only way to train attention is by attending.* No amount of theory or of resolution can take the place of practice in the actual process of attending. *To pay attention consists in keeping the desired object at the center of consciousness and in keeping the distractions in the background.*

Intellect. The intellect is the cognitive power of the mind. The term *intellect* is derived from the Latin word *intelligere* (*intus,* "within," and *legere,* "to read"), which means to discern. As the name indicates, the intellect is the power which discerns or recognizes the inner nature of things or the essence of things. It is the power by which human knowledge is acquired. The function of the intellect is *intellection* or *thought,* which consists of three mental processes; the formation of ideas, judgment, and reasoning.

The intellectual process may be described as follows: A material object first stimulates the external senses. The resulting impression passing from the external senses to perception and imagination gives rise to a percept and to an image of this individual material object. The percept and the image represent the object with the sensory and concrete conditions which make it that object and no other object. When the sense representation, that is, the percept or image, is formed, the intellect adverts to it and calls into exercise its abstractive power which constitutes what is termed the *active* or *agent intellect.* This strips the representation of its sensible and individual conditions, thus manifesting the essence of the material object. In this way the object becomes *actually intelligible.* Then the *intellect proper,* called the *potential* or *passive intellect,* forms the concept out of the elements abstracted from the sensory representation. The further activity of the intellect consists in the comparison, identification, or discrimination or concepts.

The acts of the intellect consist in the forming of concepts or ideas, of judging, and of reasoning. In the first process the intellect forms universal ideas. This is called *conception.* In the second operation the intellect discerns the identity or diversity of two concepts. This is termed *judgment.* The third act is that by which the intellect derives a new judgment or a conclusion from two other related judgments which were previously known. This is designated *reasoning.* For every process of reasoning several judgments are required, and every judgment demands the apprehension of two concepts.

The most elementary of the intellectual processes is *conception,* which may be defined as the operation of the intellect in abstracting from representations of concrete objects and qualities the essential elements or substantial nature or essence of the object. This power of abstraction constitutes *conception,* and the product is designated *concept* or *idea.* By means of this process of abstraction the concept represents only those features which are absolutely essential to the object and therefore common to all objects of the same kind, leaving out the unessential, particular, distinctive, and individual features of the object. Concepts are the coins of thought and are expressed in words.

The second operation of the intellect is *judgment* which is essentially the affirming of the relationship between things or concepts. This relationship may be one of agreement or disagreement. Judgment may be defined as the mental act by which man discerns the agreement or disagreement between two concepts. By means of judgment, the intellect makes use of its concepts. Human thinking essentially takes the form of judgment which alone has meaning, and to which truth and falsehood in the strict sense belong. The process of judgment consists of three elements. The first is the presence in the intellect of two concepts; the one is the subject about which something is affirmed or denied, the other is the predicate or attribute which is affirmed or denied of the subject. The second element is the comparison of these two concepts. The third element is the affirmation of the agreement or disagreement, which is the judgment proper. Hence, judgment implies two concepts or groups of concepts and a discernment of their relationship. A judgment is expressed in a sentence.

The third operation of the intellect is *reasoning*. Like judgment, reasoning is an act by which the intellect discerns the agreement or disagreement between two concepts. However, it differs from judgment in this respect, that in reasoning the intellect discerns that agreement or disagreement between two concepts through the medium of a third idea. Hence, reasoning may be defined as that act of the intellect by which the agreement or disagreement of two concepts is discerned through a comparison between them and a third idea.

The act of reasoning is based upon the law of identity and the law of difference. The law of identity states that things which are identical with the same thing are identical with each other. Upon this principle rests every affirmative conclusion in reasoning. The law of difference states that two things, one of which agrees with a third thing, and the other of which disagrees with the same third thing, disagree with each other. Upon this principle rest all negative conclusions in reasoning.

The elements of the reasoning process are four. The first element consists of three concepts. The second element is the comparison of two of the concepts with the third. The third element consists of the recognition of the agreement or disagreement between these two concepts and the third idea which involves the formation of two judgments. The final element consists of the discernment of the agreement or disagreement with each other of the two concepts thus compared with the third. The method employed to express reasoning is the syllogism.

Reasoning assumes two general forms, *induction* and *deduction. Induction* is the method of reasoning which consists in forming judgments about a number of particular cases and then deriving from these cases a general rule or principle by discovering the common qualities presented by these cases. Induction is a process of reasoning from particular to universal, from effect to cause, from phenomenon to law. Its purpose is to generalize, to find uniformities, and to arrive at a knowledge of general truths. Induction is an analytic process involving the resolution of the complex into that which is more simple. *Deduction* is the method of reasoning which consists in the application of a general principle or law to particular facts. It is a process of reasoning from the universal to the particular, from what is true of all to what is true of one, from cause to effect. Deduction is essentially a synthetic process, combining simple elements into something more complex.

Another form of reasoning and perhaps the process used earliest in schoolwork is reasoning by *analogy*. By means of this process resemblances between things are noted. This process is based upon the principle that when two things resemble each other, a certain proposition true of one is true also of the other. If the points of likeness are few, this process of reasoning may be false, but if the points of resemblance are many, this process will probably be true. It is used very frequently in the school. Pupils look back through textbooks in search of a problem similar to the one under consideration, for the purpose of solving the new problem. This process should be guided very carefully, since the certainty of the process depends on the extent and number of resemblances. At most it should be applied only so far as the resemblances actually exist between the given objects.

Intellectual training is bound to be meager and deficient if the teacher does not understand the nature and the operations of the intellect. If the spiritual nature of the intellect is denied, then the rules, systems, and methods for training the intellect are of little value; for if the intellect were not spiritual in nature, man would be guided and dominated by his impulses. If the operations of the intellect are functions of any but a spiritual faculty, then man is in no higher category than the brute. However, human intellect, together with the use made of it, places man at an immeasurable distance from the brute, in fact, constitutes him man. This fact must be kept unobscured, for it determines the function of education in the training of the intellect.

The Will. The will is man's rational appetitive power. It is the tendency to desire, to seek, and to enjoy that which is apprehended by the intellect as good.

Man's will, more than any other of his powers, has a direct practical bearing upon the problems of education. The will is the guiding force which molds and directs the life of man, and as such it is the chief integrating force in man's character. Without the function which the will contributes to his life, man would be not a person but merely an animated organism. Yet modern psychological literature treats the will very inadequately, and educational psychology neglects it almost entirely. Nevertheless, despite this tendency among modern psychologists to discredit the use of the term *will,* insofar as it is employed to signify a single and simple mental power or faculty, practically all psychologists admit the existence of experiences which as a whole deserve the name of volitional processes. Hence, there is a universal agreement that the capability, which man possesses, to decide upon and to determine his conduct is of particular importance in the affairs both of mind and of life. *Nothing is willed unless it is first known.* Thought must precede the deliberation of the will. An object is willed as it is known by the intellect and proposed to the will as desirable and good. Hence, the *formal* and *adequate object of the will is good as apprehended by the intellect.*

Acts of the will are performed under the influence of motives. A motive is the reason why an act is performed and includes whatever influences the will in any degree. Since whatever is done voluntarily is done on account of some good to be derived from the action, the motive is always the idea of some good, that is, of something useful, noble, pleasurable, beneficial, advantageous, desirable, or gratifying which the individual wishes to obtain. Motives may be highly diversified, ranging from the most fundamental sensory objects to the most lofty ethical ideals, but they all have the common character of goodness.

The motives actuating the will act upon it either as means or as ends. The reasons for choosing one end rather than another, and when the end has been selected, the reasons for using some means in preference to others are examined, weighed, and compared with one another. This examination of motives is termed *deliberation.* This deliberation is followed by *choice or decision,* which is the acceptance or rejection by the mind of an object or a course of action after the motives for and against the selection of the object or course of action have been considered.

Freedom of the will is the capacity for self-determination, implying the absence of external force and of internal necessity. The essential feature in freedom of the will is the *element of choice,* which is the culmination of the exercise of freedom. To will freely is to choose freely. Freedom of the will is the power of determining which motives will prevail in the mind to influence selection by the will, but without the will being necessitated by these motives. Therefore, freedom of the will means that when an individual is confronted by two or more possible motives, he may choose one and reject the others, after having weighed the motives for selection and having considered the motives which militate against it. Even then, after having recognized the *good,* he may act or not act because he is free to determine his actions.

When it is stated that the will of man is free, it is by no means asserted that all the acts of man are free. The freedom of the will means only this, that, when all the conditions for an act of the will are present, the will is endowed with the power to choose among various motives intellectually apprehended as good, to act or to abstain from action. Furthermore, there are actions which are not free, over which the individual has no control and for which he is not responsible. Free will does not imply that man is constantly exerting this power. By far the larger part of man's life is administered by reflex acts, by the automatic working of the organism, and by acquired habits.

The theory which denies the freedom of the will is termed *determinism.* There are various types of determinism, according to the nature of the antecedents which are held to account for man's actions. The first type is *mechanical determinism* or *fatalism* which maintains that whatever man does is predestined by the laws of nature. According to the various aspects of this theory, man's thoughts, his character, his external actions are merely the inevitable outcome of his circumstances. They are inexorably predetermined in every detail by events in the past over which he has no control. The second type is *psychological determinism,* which holds that choice invariably follows what is presented as the greatest good. The third type is *biological determinism* in which volition is likened to reflex action, since conduct is considered to be the necessary outcome of biological structure and function. Man is regarded not as a free agent but as a machine which is automatically adjusted to its environment and is therefore freed from blame for his unworthy acts as well as undeserving of praise for his good behavior.

Self-control involves the capability of directing and restraining one's own thoughts, emotions, and actions by means of conscious and deliberate choice. Self-control does not mean the crushing of the human powers here brought into play, but the guiding and training of them. The ultimate end of self-control is a perfect integration of man's powers, a coordination of the powers of intellect, emotion, and will. The individual who exercises self-control is master of himself. He does not follow blindly the example of others or his own impulses, but first examines these in order to determine whether they are worth following. He is able to check the natural impulse to act until he has reached a prudent decision based on calm judgment.

The principal means of training the will consist in presenting to the intellect worthwhile motives, in teaching the child to evaluate them and to appreciate these motives, in guiding the child to make them permanent possessions, in preventing less worthy motives from superseding them. These motives which influence the will must be integrated harmoniously in the form of purposes which are desirable to the child, which are in accord with his nature. These motives must have true subjective value in addition to being objectively good. The fundamental motives for building ideals are formed during the years of childhood. During this period, instruction in religion, in history, and in literature offers abundant opportunities for inspiring ideals.

Training of the will must be essentially self-training. The habit of yielding to impulse results in the enfeeblement of self-control. The power of inhibiting urgent desires, of concentrating attention on more remote good, of reenforcing the higher but less urgent motives undergoes a kind of atrophy through disuse. Habitually yielding to any vice, while it does not lessen man's responsibility, does diminish his ability to resist temptation. Likewise the more frequently man restrains impulse, checks inclination, persists against temptation, and steadily aims at virtuous living, the more does he increase his self-control, and therefore his freedom. To have a strong will means to have control over the will, to be able to direct it despite all contrary impulses.

Good will is as necessary as strong will. Good will involves moral excellence, righteousness, benevolence, and the earnest striving after ends worthy of human energy and of human life. Mere strength of will is not sufficient. The will must be made strong for doing the good. Will becomes inclined toward the good by performing successfully good acts inspired by worthy motives and by experiencing the satisfaction resulting from such actions.

The Affective States. The mental activities which are characterized by feeling and emotion are designated *affective states*. These play a very important role in life, for to some degree they enter into practically all behavior. They furnish many dominant motives, interests, and standards of value. Intrinsic in most activities of life are feelings and emotions. One rarely has an experience entirely devoid of feeling. With most people conduct is more a matter of feeling than of intellect. Knowledge is bound up with the feelings regardless of whether or not the person is aware of these feelings. The very meaning which anything in the whole field of knowledge has for an individual is indicative of his feelings and emotions toward it. Since all thinking and doing are colored by the affective states, these states are important both for the individual himself and for his relations with others. These states give to life its tone, its happiness or unhappiness. They constitute an important part of the motive power of life.

In the broad sense of the term, *feeling* denotes the states of consciousness described as pleasant and painful, agreeable and disagreeable, satisfactory and unsatisfactory, which result from the manner in which objects affect man. In a more restricted use of the term, feeling denotes only the elementary processes of affective life; namely, pleasantness or unpleasantness. Feeling is the awareness or perception of the pleasantness or unpleasantness that accompanies mental processes and bodily actions. Every conscious state has its feeling aspect which gives it color and life. Feeling is an essential element of consciousness, for without feeling there is no consciousness.

Emotions are accompanied and followed by marked changes throughout the entire organism. These accompaniments and effects consist of glandular secretions, muscular strain, and mental disturbance.

a) *Glandular Effects.* Many investigations, particularly those of Cannon, have demonstrated that the secretions of some glands are stimulated by emotional excitement, while the activity of others is inhibited. Intense unpleasant emotions, such as fear, anger, hatred, or grief, are accompanied by an inhibition of the glandular processes involved in digestion and excretion. The flow of saliva and the secretion of gastric juices are inhibited. During strong emotional excitement the adrenal glands pour their hormone, adrenalin, into the blood stream in large quantities. This affects the action of the liver and causes an increase in blood sugar. As a consequence there is an improved muscular contraction, a restoration of fatigued muscular activity, and a hastening of the coagulation of the blood mobilizing the body for action. Prolonged emotional excitement increases the activity of the thyroid gland which produces a continuance of the emotional state. However, during pleasant emotional states, such as joy and contentment, the salivary and gastric secretions are speeded up, thus aiding digestion, and at the same time rapid heartbeat is inhibited.

b) *Muscular Effects.* The smooth muscles are greatly affected by intense emotion, chiefly as a result of the glandular changes. These accompaniments lead to acceleration in breathing, to an increase in rate of heartbeat, and to a rise in blood pressure. The skeletal muscles also are affected by strong emotions. One of the chief indications of emotion is muscular tenseness and activity. It is possible to determine by facial expression the nature of the emotional state, for the muscles of the face are associated with the various forms of emotion. Other physical effects also accompany the emotions. In anger the teeth are set, the fists are clenched, the posture is rigid. In fear, the muscles collapse, the joints tremble, the tendency for flight is stimulated. Pride, joy, surprise, scorn, and grief all have their evident forms of physical expression. Some of these are easily noted, such as smiling, trembling, and weeping, while others have been described as "the tingling glow of pleasure, the blush of shame, the cold sweat of fear, the taut muscles of anger." Usually the energy supplied to the muscles is greater than is actually used, and the diffusion of this energy results in trembling. Intense emotions are ordinarily followed by periods of depression, the chief characteristic of which is fatigue.

c) *Mental Effects.* Emotion of the right type, in moderation, is stimulating to mental activity. However, strong emotion is always highly distractive and interferes with intellectual efficiency. At times in the display of an intense emotion like anger the restraints and inhibitions of civilized life may give way and impulse will dominate.

One of the most important as well as one of the most difficult problems of education is the control of the emotions. Emotions in themselves are not evil. It is only when the emotion becomes excessive, becomes unmanageable, becomes sufficiently strong to disturb the functioning of the organism and to affect the power of decision and choice that it becomes evil. It is impossible to deprive a normal person of his emotional experiences, and it would be most unfortunate to do so even if it were possible. The problem is for each individual to secure a proper balance between emotional expression and control. To be healthy and happy the emotions must be kept under control. The individual must rule his emotions rather than be ruled by them.

The term *emotion* is much more inclusive than that of feeling. It is derived from the Latin word *emotus,* which signifies a movement outward and implies an action or tendency toward action which arises from some inner need and is directed toward the outside world. *Emotion* consists of one or more simple feelings along with sensations, images, ideas, and tendencies to action. These are closely interwoven and form a very complex and intricate state of mind. Though the pleasant and unpleasant elements are usually very pronounced, emotion is more complex than feeling, for it is the way in which the mind is affected by a complex situation which it apprehends. Emotion may be described as *a composite of feelings complicated with sensations, images, ideas, tendencies to action,* characterized by physiological changes or "stirred-up" bodily conditions, and directed toward a specific object or situation.

The nature of the emotional process is not simple, but rather it is very complex. This complexity has caused much controversy concerning the exact nature of emotion. The traditional and most widely accepted explanation of the nature of emotion is that the perceived object or idea causes the emotion which in turn causes the physical expression. This is known as the *cause theory*. The *effect theory,* or "James-Lange theory," states that the emotion is due not to the perceived object and its influence on consciousness, but that when the object is perceived, the physiological changes take place and then emotion follows. This theory has been disproved by later studies. The acceptable explanation may be stated thus: Emotions are due first to the awareness of the perceived object, which is followed by the incipient emotion, after which comes the physiological expression, and finally the intensified and fully rounded emotion. The physiological expression does not cause the emotion but does increase it.

Human experiences include a wide range of emotions. There are personal or self-regarding emotions, social or altruistic emotions, intellectual and aesthetic emotions. However, these forms are not mutually exclusive.

The *personal emotions* refer to and center around the self, and their central emphasis is the personal welfare of the individual. These emotions are based on the innate tendencies of self-preservation, self-assertion, and development not only of the body but also of the mental powers, reputation, and character. The personal emotions include some that produce pleasure, such as self-esteem, self-reliance, self-love, and others which are unpleasant in their effects, such as pride, self-pity, remorse, shame, fear, anger.

The *social emotions* center around the nonselfish and benevolent aspects of man's nature. Since man is made to live in society, he is also endowed with certain feelings that refer to his fellowmen. The fundamental social emotion is sympathy. Literally, sympathy means to feel with others. Hence, sympathy connotes an understanding and a sharing of the pleasures and pain, the joy and sorrows of others. These sympathetic feelings take several forms, including love, friendship, family affections, patriotism, and philanthropy.

The *intellectual* and *aesthetic emotions* are based on higher needs and depend to a large extent on education. The basis of the intellectual emotions is love of truth. These emotions include novelty, surprise, and wonder. The bases of the aesthetic emotions consist of love of the sublime, the beautiful, and the harmonious. These emotions include admiration, awe, and elation.

As a rule the personal emotions tend toward excess and require considerable direction and control, while the social, intellectual, and aesthetic emotions tend to deficiency and should be developed and stimulated. A certain amount of suppression is essential and is not in any way harmful to the individual. In fact, suppression keeps the emotions as helpful servants and prevents them from becoming masters.

The modification and control of emotions may be accomplished either through the control of the conditions causing the emotions, or through the control of the expression of the emotions. The conditions causing the emotions may be controlled through the supremacy of the intellect. The idea or image which is in part the source of the emotion is subject to change through the redirection of attention. If the individual concentrates on other things which have sufficient interest to keep his attention, if he becomes engrossed with another situation, the emotion tends to fade away. A fundamental principle for the control of the emotions is the avoidance of the occasions and causes for violent emotions. The removal of the improper stimulus or the substitution of a worthy object also aids in the control of the emotions.

An effective method of controlling the emotions is to sublimate the emotional impulses, that is, to refine and elevate them by the redirection of the emotions into higher and better channels. This is accomplished by the substitution of a wholesome expression. For example, one should not cease to hate, but he should learn to hate evil and meanness; fear should be developed into the spirit of respect for things worth while, into a deference for superior wisdom and worth, into a fear of God. The diversion of the outer display of the emotion also serves as a check to the inner force, and if there is no expression the emotion will quickly disappear.

The use of the will to control the emotions constitutes the most effective method. The control of emotions by the will is self-control. The way is direct and consists first in setting clearly before the mind the desirability of acting from thought, principles, and purposes rather than from impulses. This decision having been made, persistent and faithful adherence to it is required.

Another method of control of the emotions consists of a psychological analysis of emotion. This process has been described in the following manner:

> If we attempt to make a psychological analysis of an emotion, to bring the emotion before the focus point of consciousness, not its cause but the emotion itself, it melts away like wax in front of a hot fire. Emotional states, as such, cannot be brought to the focus point of consciousness, and any attempt to do so makes them dwindle away at once.
>
> We have, therefore, a certain possibility of emotional control. Attend to the cause of the emotion and you strengthen it. Attend to the emotion itself, analyze it as such without reference to its cause, and you weaken it. It takes, however, considerable ingenuity in the pilot of the human mechanism to make a psychological analysis of any violent emotion, or to turn the mind away from a consideration of the facts that brought about the emotional outburst.[2]

Habit. The term *habit* has been derived from the Latin verb *habere,* which means "to have," that is, to acquire something which one did not have originally. Habit is an acquired mode of behavior; that is, it is a learned reaction, involving the tendency to repeat and to reproduce certain

[2] T. V. Moore, *Dynamic Psychology* (Philadelphia: J. B. Lippincott Co., 1924), pp. 316–317.

actions frequently and consistently; that is, to act in the same general way under the same or similar circumstances. The real usefulness of habit lies in the fact that it provides a reasonable variability in response to situations which are basically similar. It is the tendency, common to all human beings, to acquire relatively fixed ways of reacting to particular situations. Habit formation involves the learning to perceive, to imagine, to remember, to feel, to think, to act in a particular manner under special circumstances, as one has done in the past. It implies facility in the performance of an action combined with a persisting inclination toward the repetition of the action. All mental and physical activities are subject to the laws of habit. Thus the range, the application, and the influence of habit include every aspect of human life. The effect of habit is to give to man, who is free to act in one way or the other, a tendency to react readily and easily in a particular way, in a given situation.

The physical basis of habit lies in the mechanism of the nervous system. The reason for man's acquired aptitude of action is the plasticity of the nervous system. Plasticity means that the nervous system is endowed with the capacity for being molded and fashioned. The excitability and conductivity of neural substance makes possible a connection between the sense organ receiving the stimulus and the central nervous system. A theoretical explanation is that this connection leaves some trace or impression in the nervous system, and habits are formed by repeated impressions on the nervous system while it is still plastic. The psychological basis of habit lies in the law of association by contiguity; namely, that any group of mental states which had occurred together or in succession tends to be reproduced simultaneously or in the original order. In its psychological aspect habit may be said to be the association of mental states which recall one another. Psychologically habit signifies the acquired facility of conscious processes.

The main factors in the formation of habit are uniform, meaningful, and frequent repetition of activity, an interest which motivates, and satisfaction accompanying either the performance or the result.

Habit plays such an important role in everyday human life that it is of utmost importance to form good physical, mental, and moral habits in an efficient, effective, economic manner, and to avoid the trial-an-error method of acquiring such abilities. For this reason guidance in habit formation is necessary. The following laws are of great value in this respect:

1. Make automatic and habitual as early as possible as many useful actions as we can.
2. In the acquisition of a new habit or the leaving off of an old one care must be taken to launch the project with as strong and decided initiative as possible.
3. Never suffer an exception to occur until the new habit is securely rooted in your life.
4. Seize the very first possible opportunity to act on every resolution you make and on every emotional prompting you may experience in the direction of the habits you aspire to gain.
5. Keep the faculty of effort alive by a little gratuitous exercise every day.[3]

Habits can be broken or changed or modified just as surely as they are formed or established. Any habit may disappear through misuse just as anything is forgotten, but the difficulty is to start the disuse. Since habits decrease in strength through lack of exercise, the first way to break a habit is a negative one; namely, to abstain from exercising it. This usually requires strenuous effort both of will and of attention. The will to resist is effective according to the strength of the habit and the amount of effort expended. To eliminate a habit by letting it disintegrate through disuse requires constant watchfulness and persistence, for the habit may be secure and does not disappear readily. Then, just as a habit may be formed by repeatedly practicing an activity, so it can be broken by ceasing at once to permit it to function and by never permitting an exception to it.

A second way to break a habit is to develop another habit as positive and as satisfying as possible in place of the one to be eliminated. Whenever possible this should be a habit which is antagonistic to the old one. This means that, in order to form a counterhabit, some management is necessary. Consequently attention must be centered on the new habit rather than on the one which is to be discarded. This counterhabit must be practiced diligently and with determination. The habit to be eliminated must not be permitted to come back in disguised forms, nor must transgressions be condoned or ignored. Annoyance should attend any tendency to revert to the old habits. Once the desirable substitute activity has been devised, it should be practiced with many satisfactory repetitions.

Habit is important because the range of its application and influence includes every aspect of human life from the most ordinary actions such as walking and writing to the highest mental functions of thinking and

[3] William James, *Talks to Teachers* (New York: Henry Holt and Co., 1899), pp. 66–76.

judging. Habit formation lies at the basis of education. Without habit, learning would be impossible, since education consists largely of the processes of habit formation varying from the comparatively simple to very complex habits. It is almost impossible to overestimate the importance of habit.

EXERCISES

1. List and define the terms which you have learned from your study of this chapter.
2. Explain why it is necessary for the teacher to have a knowledge both of the soul and of the body.
3. What processes and capacities are included in the fundamental equipment of the learner?
4. Distinguish between:
   a) Cognitive and appetitive powers or faculties;
   b) Autonomic and cerebrospinal divisions of the nervous system;
   c) Sensation and perception;
   d) Constructive and reproductive imagination;
   e) Recall and recognition;
   f) Spontaneous and voluntary attention;
   g) Rote and logical memory;
   h) Percept and concept;
   i) Feeling and emotion;
   j) Judgment and reasoning;
   k) Inductive and deductive reasoning.
5. Discuss the following topics:
   a) The importance of the nervous system;
   b) Relationship of the laws of association to the process of teaching;
   c) The dependence of the intellect upon the senses in the process of conception;
   d) The functions of the endocrine glands;
   e) The basic operations in memory;
   f) The laws of association;
   g) The effects of attention;
   h) The laws of habit formation.
6. Describe the intellectual process of conception, judgment, and reasoning.
7. Explain the nature and function of the will. What is determinism? How may the will be trained?
8. Explain:
   a) The nature and types of emotions;
   b) The methods of controlling the emotions.
9. Discuss the following statements:
   a) "A complete explanation of education must take into account both the body and the soul."
   b) "Imperfections in the functioning of the sense organs impair the effectiveness of learning."

c) "The child's understanding of anything new depends upon his past experiences."
d) "The effectiveness of attention determines the amount and quality of learning."
e) "The basis of conception is full and accurate perception."
f) "Nothing is willed unless it is first known."
g) "Emotions are not evil in themselves but become so through excess."
h) "Habit has been called a second nature and man termed a mere bundle of habits. Although such expressions, like all aphorisms may be open to criticism if taken too literally, yet they contain much truth."

10. What is the educational significance of each of the following:
    a) The will?
    b) Habit formation?
    c) Emotion?

SELECTED REFERENCES FOR STUDY AND READING

Arnold, M. B., *Emotion and Personality,* 2 vols. (New York: Columbia University Press, 1960).

Bittle, C. N., *The Whole Man* (Milwaukee: The Bruce Publishing Co., 1945).

Brennan, R. E., *General Psychology,* 2 ed. (New York: The Macmillan Co., 1952).

Donceel, J. F., *Philosophical Psychology,* 2 ed. (New York: Sheed & Ward, 1961).

Dunbar, H. F., *Emotions and Bodily Changes,* 4 ed. (New York: Columbia University Press, 1954).

Gannon, T. J., *Psychology: The Unity of Human Behavior* (Boston: Quinn and Co., 1954).

King, B. G., and Showers, M. J., *Human Anatomy and Physiology,* 5 ed. (Philadelphia: W. B. Saunders Co., 1963).

Klubertanz, G., *The Philosophy of Human Nature* (New York: Appleton-Century-Crofts, Inc., 1953).

Lindworsky, J., *Training of the Will* (Milwaukee: The Bruce Publishing Co., 1929).

Maher, M., *Psychology,* 9 ed. (New York: Longmans, Green and Co., 1930).

Moore, T. V., *Cognitive Psychology* (Philadelphia: J. B. Lippincott Co., 1939).

Plutchik, R., *The Emotions* (New York: Random House, 1962).

Renard, H., *The Philosophy of Man,* 2 ed. (Milwaukee: The Bruce Publishing Co., 1956).

Royce, J. E., *Man and His Nature* (New York: McGraw-Hill Book Co., 1961).

Schneiders, A. A., *Introductory Psychology* (New York: Holt, Rinehart and Winston, Inc., 1951).

Sullivan, D. J., *An Introduction to Philosophy,* rev. ed. (Milwaukee: The Bruce Publishing Co., 1964).

Walters, Sister Annette, and O'Hara, Sister Kevin, *Persons and Personality* (New York: Appleton-Century-Crofts, Inc., 1953).

part III

GROWTH AND DEVELOPMENT OF THE LEARNER

chapter 3

The Processes of Growth and Development

Growth, Development, and Maturation. The term *growth* as employed here means the progressive increase and continuous advancement of the child from birth to maturity. It refers primarily to the increment of the bodily tissues, organs, and structures. It is used also to designate changes which occur with time. Growth is evidenced not only in an increase in quantity or in size but also in enlarged capacity and changing proportions, either of the organism as a whole or of its parts. Growth then implies more than increased dimensions; it involves also structural and functional changes.

The term *development* means the gradual and orderly unfolding of the characteristics of the successive stages of growth involving the emerging and expanding of the capacities of the individual to provide greater facility in functioning. It means essentially progress toward a goal. It involves changes from simplicity to complexity and implies an increasingly progressive maturity of behavior as well as organization of personality and character. It connotes a continuous, gradual progress in the powers of functioning as well as in coordination between body and mind leading toward maturity. It signifies progressive emergence of capacities, powers, and attributes as well as greater complexity and organization. Development is then the process in the life of the human being by which the "individual's potentialities unfold and appear. . . . Development implies a progressive change of an individual's pattern of reaction."[1] For all practical purposes many psychologists and educators at the present time accept the terms *growth* and *development* as synonymous.

[1] J. Pikunas and E. J. Albrecht, *Psychology of Human Development* (New York: McGraw-Hill Book Co., 1961), p. 22. Used by permission.

Another basic term which is of fundamental importance in the discussion of growth and development has been borrowed from the science of genetics. This term is *maturation*. However, there has been lack of agreement within the field of educational psychology concerning the exact meaning and connotations of this term. In its simplest connotation it designates the natural ripening or growing-up process, the culmination of which is maturity. Likewise, the term has been employed to designate a process of internal growth, consisting chiefly of structural changes and coordinations within the nervous system together with a level of development of the mental functions, which is indicated by a state of readiness to engage in a definite type of learning activity or to perform a specified type of behavior. It has two effects, the first of which is to increase efficiency in learning, and the second, to increase efficiency of performance. A simple and clear description of the term has been presented by Harmon:

> By *maturation* psychologists mean the process of attaining a level of development at which some specified mental function or type of behavior ordinarily appears. Generally speaking, maturation connotes growth or development that is intrinsically rather than extrinsically determined, that is to say, it is supposed to be essentially independent of exercise.[2]

Actually maturation involves development of all aspects of personality, not alone the physical and mental but also the social and emotional. The term *psychological maturity* is used to designate such maturation, and psychological maturity involves response on the part of the individual to situations in ways which are appropriate to his degree of development and which are likewise proportionate to the demands of the situation.

The significance of maturation for the educator consists in the fact that the placement of many aspects of the school curriculum is determined by the maturational status of pupils.

There is a natural order of the growth of both body and mind, and also of the development of physical powers and mental capacities. Since the years from the child's birth to his maturity witness a remarkable series of changes — physical, mental, social, emotional, and moral — it is evident that growth and development occur in all of these areas. However, all of these phases are interrelated, for the child grows and develops as a whole.

However, in considering the successive phases in the growth and

---

[2] F. L. Harmon, *Principles of Psychology*, rev. ed. (Milwaukee: The Bruce Publishing Co., 1951), p. 103. See also Sister Barbara Geoghegan, Sister Marie Baptista Pollard, and W. A. Kelly, *Developmental Psychology* (Milwaukee: The Bruce Publishing Co., 1963), p. 20.

development of the child, it is essential to remember that no two children are exactly alike and hence that the rates of growth and the degrees of development of the various aspects or phases vary a great deal in different children. The ideal is an adequate balance between the physical and mental growth and development of the child as he advances from birth to maturity.

The importance of a knowledge of the process and the conditions which influence growth and development has been realized generally. It is most essential that the teacher understand how the body and the mind of the child grow and develop and how he progresses socially, emotionally, and morally, in order to meet intelligently the problems of the child, to comprehend adequately the causes of his behavior. The whole child goes to school, hence, the educational process must be concerned with the child in his entirety, with what he is, and with what he may be. However, the primary concern of the school is the mental growth and development of the child. No teacher is equipped for his or her work until he has adequate knowledge of the nature of mental growth and development and of the ways in which these processes may be influenced and directed.

Mental growth and development consist in a steady increase in the fullness, richness, and variety of mental activities, and in the perfection of control over, correlation and interpretation of, mental content. Mental growth and development are evident in the child's behavior and conduct, and the changes which take place in these as he progresses from infancy to adulthood. They manifest themselves in various ways at different times. Very early in child life mental growth and development are evident in increased motor control, and a little later language ability becomes an evident manifestation of growth and development. The most important indication of mental growth and development is, however, capacity for abstract thinking and reasoning. Mental growth and development are measured by means of tests of mental ability and of level of achievement attained in school skills and subjects. Since these measures of mental ability and of achievement will be treated in subsequent chapters, no further description of them will be presented here.

The teacher of necessity, however, has interest also in the physical growth and development of the child, because these are so closely related to many factors in the child's welfare. Failure to grow and to develop normally is very frequently suggestive of poor nutritional status, of glandular maladjustment, of other undesirable conditions. Furthermore, the physical is intimately bound up with the mental, and, likewise, influences the social adjustment of the child. The physical growth and development of the child are evident in the modifications, chiefly in dimension, which his body undergoes. These modifications can be observed readily and can be measured objectively. It should be noted that while physical growth is a very complex process, involving different rates for various body structures, yet there are available for purposes of comparison numerous data concerning physical growth and development. The most commonly used measures are height and weight as compared with norms listed on standard weight-height-age tables. Other indices of physical growth and development include dentition, or number of permanent teeth erupted, extent of bone ossification — usually of the carpal or wrist and hand bones — and onset of pubescence.

Many studies have been made of the various aspects of growth and development. These studies have been of two types. The first type has employed the method of measuring or testing large groups of children of both sexes at different chronological age levels and at various stages of development and then deriving averages or norms and standards for these ages. Such norms as mental abilities at various age levels, vocabulary, height and weight, interests, and the like have been derived in this way. This method is known as normative *cross-sectional* analysis. In order that the results obtained by the method may be of value it is essential that the groups studied should contain sufficiently large numbers of children at various ages to secure representativeness and also to minimize the influence of individual variations. The advantage claimed for this method is that it permits comparison of a child with the characteristics of children of the same sex and age level. The second type of study consists of a series of measures or tests of the same child or of a small group of individuals, repeated over a period of years and through successive stages of growth. These measures or tests, if reliable, will detect elements of change and of speed of growth and also the consistency or lack of consistency of patterns of development. This is termed the *genetic longitudinal* method.[3] Many research centers have used the longitudinal method in studying child development. Among the studies which have utilized this method are the Berkeley Growth study, the Harvard Growth study, and

[3] A. A. Stone and G. C. Onque, *Longitudinal Studies of Child Personality* (Cambridge, Mass.: Harvard University Press, 1959).

the studies conducted at the Institute of Child Welfare, University of Iowa. At the present time the tendency is toward the use of the longitudinal method because it provides a more accurate representation of the process of growth and is a more reliable method of establishing growth norms.

The teacher's interest in the process of growth and development is not confined only to the physical and mental aspects but extends also to the social, emotional, and moral phases. Since the child is by nature a social being, he progresses in ability to understand and to get along with others; to cooperate, to follow, to lead, and to adjust to others; to recognize that he is a member of various groups and to assume progressively responsible membership in continuously expanding groups. The home and the family provide much of the environment that affects social development; and the school, by providing group experiences, broadens social consciousness and aids in the development of social attitudes and values. The social aspect of growth and development is more difficult to appraise than are the physical and mental phases. At the present time, despite the great importance attached to social development, adequate tests to measure this phase are lacking. Emotional growth and development consist of the changes which occur in affective responses and in the manner of expressing these responses as the child progresses from birth to maturity. These changes involve a gradual process of transition from the basic, simple affective responses characteristic of infancy to the complex patterns of responses in adolescence, which determine to a large extent the attitudes of the individual toward his experiences. Techniques for the measurement of emotions are at the present time in a state of imperfect development. Moral growth and development reflect the progressive expansion of the intellectual and volitional capacities, which provide increased capability to understand and to apply correct moral standards for directing conduct. Thus, the process of moral growth and development implies understanding and acquisition of, and also adherence to, moral principles, values, and ideals. It implies advancement in self-control and improvement in the extent to which conduct conforms to the rational nature of the individual, considered in all of its relations, including the individual himself, his fellow human beings, the world about him, and God. Tests of moral knowledge and information are available, but the measurement of the application of moral principles is still in the initiatory stage.

The principles of growth and development which are of significance for the teacher may be summarized briefly as follows:

1. The processes of growth and development are continuous, gradual, and orderly, that is, follow a genetic sequence.
2. Development progresses from the simple to the highly complex.
3. The various aspects of the processes of growth and development are interrelated and interdependent.
4. The processes of growth and development are influenced by heredity and environment.
5. Individual differences occur in the rate of growth and also various parts, functions, and structures of the body seem to have different developmental rates.
6. Growth and development may be accelerated or retarded.
7. The rate of growth is more rapid in the early years of life.
8. Generally girls mature more rapidly than boys.

THE FACTORS INFLUENCING GROWTH, DEVELOPMENT, AND MATURATION

The growth and development of the child depend at any time in his life on three factors: on what he has inherited, on what he has acquired, and on the use he makes of both. This means that the principal factors influencing growth and development are three: namely, *heredity, environment,* and *will or human freedom.*

1. The Factor of Heredity. Concerning heredity and its role in child growth and development, there are many misconceptions and much controversy. For the purposes of this book a lengthy description of the biological mechanism of heredity is not necessary. Rather such facts of human heredity have been selected as will provide a background of knowledge concerning the child's natural environment.

Heredity[4] *involves organic resemblance based on descent.* It refers to

[4] "Heredity concerns only the physical constitution *directly,* because it is only the body that develops from the germ plasm. The soul of each individual is created immediately by God. Since, however, the soul is dependent upon the body in its operations, it is affected indirectly by heredity. Defective cells may result, for example, in an imperfectly developed brain. The consequence is feeble-mindedness. But this condition does not prove any inferiority in the soul itself. It merely manifests a deficiency in the instrument through which the soul must receive its impressions of the outside world, and through which it externalizes its own internal states. The soul of an idiot is hampered by an imperfect tool. The case is analogous to that of a man who uses a telescope with a broken lens. He sees little or nothing at all, but his failure is not due to any defect in his own vision: it is the result of the defective instrument he is using."

R. C. McCarthy, S.J., *Safeguarding Mental Health* (Milwaukee: The Bruce Publishing Co., 1937), p. 38.

the sum total of characteristics biologically transmitted through the parents to offspring and directly determining physical constitution and traits. It is that which inheres in the nature of the child and is often termed *original nature.* It is nature's way of passing on to children the actual and potential characteristics of parents. It is the relationship between generation and generation. It sets for each individual a general pattern of possible development. It consists of the transmission to, and reproduction in, the child of ancestral traits, both actual and potential. These traits and characteristics include bodily structure, skin color, the nervous system capable of a certain range, capacity, and intensity of response, the basic rates and patterns of growth which are fixed for each individual.

Every human being is composed of two types of cells, the body or somatic cells, and the germ or reproductive cells. Heredity is concerned with germ cells. Each of these cells has a nucleus which contains chromosomes which are microscopic particles of protoplasm.

Chromosomes are the agents by which traits are transmitted. Encased within the chromosomes are aggregations of exceedingly minute tightly coiled strands of chemical particles which are arranged much as beads on a string. These are termed *genes.* Geneticists maintain that the genes constitute the chemical mechanism of inheritance. They are the actual elements or direct carriers of hereditary potentialities and are important determinants of the various physical traits which characterize the individual, including color of skin, hair, and eyes; height; facial features; blood type; general physical structure; and rate of maturation. The chemical material of which the genes are composed is termed *deoxyribonucleic acid* or DNA[5] for short. This is believed to be responsible for the transmission of hereditary characteristics from one generation to another. Recent research in the field of biochemistry has resulted in considerable progress toward the elucidation of the structure of DNA. It is now regarded as a double helix, spiraling ladderlike in appearance, bound together by chemical bonds. DNA embodies the genetic code of all living organisms. It consists of four bases or chemical substances which are nucleic acids, namely, adenine, thymine, guanine, and cytosine. These are conveniently denoted by the letters ATG and C. The way in which these substances are assembled and bonded together into complex and varied

[5] See B. J. Gardner, *Principles of Genetics* (New York: John Wiley & Sons, Inc., 1960); J. L. Fuller and W. R. Thompson, *Behavior Genetics* (New York: John Wiley & Sons, Inc., 1960); M. W. Nirenberg, "The Genetic Code: II," *Scientific American,* 208:80–95, 1963.

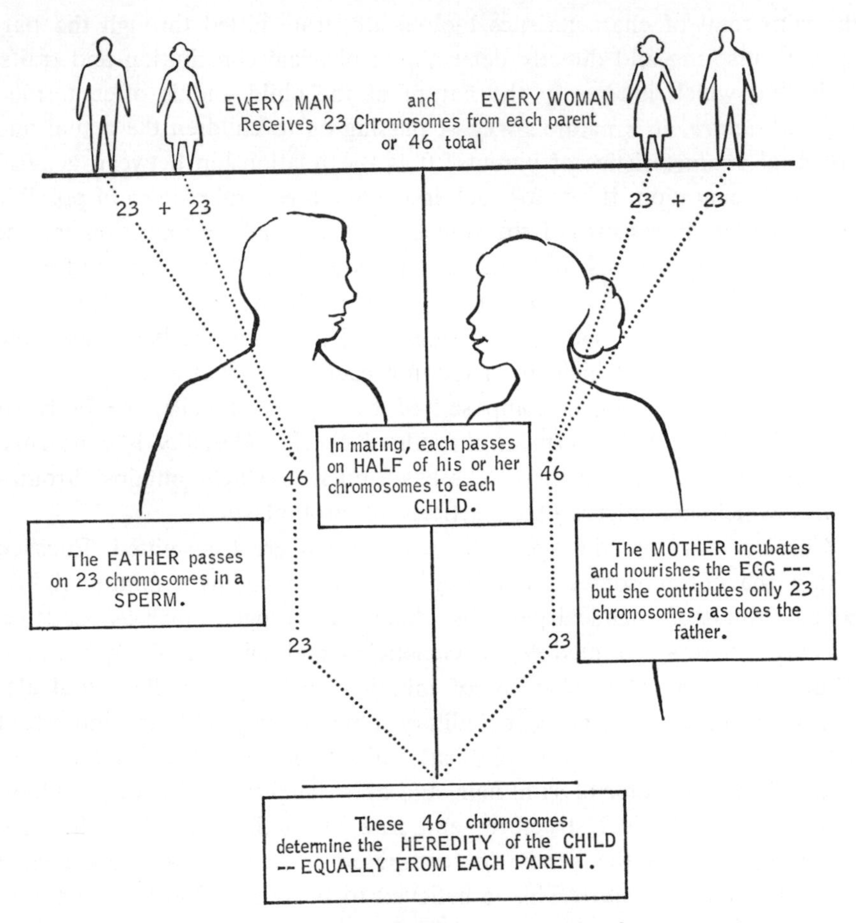
EVERY MAN and EVERY WOMAN
Receives 23 Chromosomes from each parent
or 46 total
23 + 23
23 + 23
In mating, each passes on HALF of his or her chromosomes to each CHILD.
46
46
The FATHER passes on 23 chromosomes in a SPERM.
The MOTHER incubates and nourishes the EGG --- but she contributes only 23 chromosomes, as does the father.
23
23
These 46 chromosomes determine the HEREDITY of the CHILD -- EQUALLY FROM EACH PARENT.

Fig. 1. The pattern of heredity.[6]

combinations makes a particular individual unique and different from every other person. One of the major problems of research is the determination of how DNA does its vital work, that is, how the chemical units which make up DNA molecules are "coded" so that they can through chemical mechanisms pass on hereditary characteristics.

Inheritance is determined at conception by the fusion of the particular maternal and paternal germ cells which unite to form the fertilized cell or zygote. This fertilized cell receives from each parent 23 chromosomes

[6] From M. E. Breckenridge and E. L. Vincent, *Child Development*, 4 ed. (Philadelphia: W. B. Saunders Co., 1960), p. 65.

or a total of 46 in all. These unite in pairs, one of each pair coming from the mother, the other from the father. Each chromosome contains vast numbers of genes. The genes like the chromosomes are paired, one of each pair coming from each parent. In general each member of each pair is equipped for the same function, for example, the determination of color of the eyes. The fertilized cell carries within it all the potentialities that the developed individual can ever have. The single fertilized cell must be multiplied countless times in order to produce a fully developed person. This is accomplished by the process of division and redivision which is known as mitosis. In ordinary cell division as in the growth of the embryo each chromosome duplicates itself as the cell divides so that each daughter cell comes to possess a complete set of 46 chromosomes.

The sex of the child is determined by the chromosomes. In the reproductive cell women have two special chromosomes, occurring in pairs and designated as X-chromosomes. When cell reproduction and division takes place at fertilization the ovum keeps one X-chromosome which it transmits and discards the other. Men, however, have only one X-chromosome paired with a smaller Y-chromosome. When the sperm cell is reduced before fertilizing the ovum, the X-Y pair split, one of the pair being transmitted and the other lost. If the sperm cell retains and transmits the X-chromosome to join the X-chromosome of the ovum, there will result an X-X pair and the offspring will be female. If, however, the sperm cell retains and transmits the Y-chromosome, forming an X-Y pair in the zygote then the child will be male. Statistics indicate that 106 boys are born for each 100 girls. However, because of the differential death rate of males and females during childhood, the females gradually overtake the males in numbers by the age of twenty years and after that their numbers exceed those of the males.[7]

The basic law of heredity was discovered and formulated by Gregor Johann Mendel (1822–1884), a monk of the Augustinian Order, Abbot of Königskloster, a monastery in Brünn, Austria. Abbot Mendel was professor of physics and mathematics at the Realschule connected with the monastery. Between the years 1857 and 1859, when Darwin's theories were attracting attention, Mendel became interested in the phenomena of heredity, which he believed must be understood thoroughly before a final verdict could be reached on the theory of evolution. He planned a

[7] See J. Pikunas and E. J. Albrecht, *op. cit.*, p. 39; E. L. Vincent and P. C. Martin, *Human Psychological Development* (New York: The Ronald Press Co., 1961), p. 39.

set of systematic experiments to be made with peas growing in the monastery garden. These experiments were continued over a period of eight years. Then the results were presented in a treatise which was published in the *Proceedings* of the Natural History Society of Brünn, in 1866. Unfortunately, the *Proceedings* had only a local circulation, and so the treatise did not come to the attention of the scientific world generally until thirty-four years later, in 1900, when within a few months of each other three prominent biologists rediscovered it.

A simple explanation of one of Abbot Mendel's experiments will serve to illustrate the law of heredity. Mendel crossed two varieties of garden peas, one of which had a tall stem, the other, a short or dwarf stem. When the resulting seeds were planted, they all grew into tall plants and there was no indication that one of the parents had been a dwarf plant. However, these seeds were *hybrids;* that is, they had inherited both tallness and dwarfness, for, when the seeds of this hybrid generation were planted, one fourth of the offspring of these tall hybrids were dwarfs. Evidently, then, dwarfness had still been present in the seeds even though the plants that bore the seeds gave no indication of it. Mendel designated the character of tallness which prevailed, the *dominant characteristic,* while the character of dwarfness which was suppressed or apparently suppressed, he termed the *recessive characteristic.* When two dwarf seeds were combined, the resulting plants were all dwarf. When two hybrids were crossed, the outcome was one fourth tall plants, one half hybrids; that is, plants in which tallness is dominant and in which dwarfness is recessive, while the remaining one fourth were dwarf plants.

Abbot Mendel's observations made in his monastery gardens have proved, after rigorous investigations, to apply generally to all living things. Scientists have tested Mendel's theory thoroughly, and now it constitutes the basic principle of heredity, which may be stated thus: *In every case where the inheritance of an alternative pair of characters*[8] *was concerned, the effect of the crossing in successive generations was to produce three types of offsprings; namely, dominants which bred true, dominants which gave both dominant and recessive offsprings in the ratio of three to one, and recessives which bred true.*

This explanation of the law of heredity is of value in showing the manner in which some human traits are inherited. Despite this it is very

---

[8] By *character* here is meant any distinguishing feature, trait, or property of an organism.

difficult to draw definite conclusions regarding human heredity, because of the complexity of the organism, because human traits are for the most part not simple units, and therefore possible combinations are difficult to trace. In spite of these difficulties, studies have been made with the result that certain human traits appear to be inherited in accordance with Mendelian proportions. It has been ascertained that certain physical traits are dominant over other traits and may be expected to appear in the offspring. These traits include color of eyes, that is, brown is considered to be dominant over blue; and hair characteristics, that is, curly is dominant over straight, dark over light. Moreover, certain abnormalities also seem to be inherited as dominants, including digital malformations, polydactylism, and presenile cataract. Likewise certain abnormalities appear to be inherited as *sex-linked recessive characteristics*. These include hemophilia, baldness, and color blindness.

The general principles of heredity may be stated as follows:

1. Heredity is determined at the moment of conception.
2. Like begets like; that is, men do not gather grapes of thorns, nor figs of thistles. There is a tendency for children to resemble their parents in physical appearance.
3. Variations occur, for within the species there are differences. No two individuals are exactly alike.
4. Inheritance is not merely from the father and mother, but also from the two lines of ancestry of both families.
5. All hereditary qualities are not apparent at birth.
6. Heredity involves a general capacity to do certain things rather than a specific ability; that is, what is inherited is the total of *potentialities*[9] which can manifest themselves only in the course of development under suitable conditions.
7. Acquired characteristics are not inherited.

The practical application by the teacher of the facts of heredity must be directed toward the discovery of native capacities worthy of cultivation, of native limitations which need compensating through the cultivation of other traits, and toward providing for an environment which will furnish the most favorable opportunities for healthy development. The question of human development is not one of heredity alone nor one of environment only; both are necessary and must work hand in hand. However, the bodily structure, the nervous system, the native endow-

[9] By *potentiality* is meant an inherent capacity for development.

ment of capacities for knowledge and feeling will determine to some extent how the child will react to the experiences which environment presents.

2. The Factor of Environment. Environment, which is often referred to as *nurture,* is the descriptive term applied to the factors, surrounding conditions, influences, and forces which modify and exert an influence on growth and development from the instant of conception. It refers to the sum total of external conditions and factors potentially capable of influencing an organism.[10] These external conditions and factors which may modify and influence growth and development include the physical, mental, and moral agencies which surround the child; the domestic, educational, and social influences with which he comes into contact. Environment is the field in which the child's hereditary traits and capacities are developed. Heredity supplies the raw materials upon which environment acts. Heredity accounts for the general native equipment of the child, while environment provides the opportunity for growth and development of these hereditary traits and capacities. The child possesses numerous potentialities which may or may not manifest themselves and become actualities depending upon the environment surrounding the growing child.

The child's heredity is determined at the moment of conception when the germ and sperm cells with their respective hereditary determiners unite to form the new individual. During the prenatal period many environmental forces are operating to affect growth and development. Important as prenatal environmental influences undoubtedly are, the teacher is concerned with providing through the school a definite type of surrounding influences in order that potentialities may be realized. Inherited traits and tendencies, both physical and mental, may be accentuated, altered, controlled, and perhaps even definitely eliminated by environment. Heredity determines limits and tendencies within which the child will grow and develop. To heredity the child owes his possibilities. However, to environment he owes the realization of these possibilities. The child is able to realize his highest possibilities only if his environment be such as to draw them forth. All school training is based upon his fact. In addition, juvenile courts, child-guidance clinics, child-labor laws, and other provisions for the welfare of the child are based upon the assumption that hereditary effects are not immutable and do not predetermine the child's destiny.

---

[10] H. B. English and A. C. English, *Comprehensive Dictionary of Psychological and Psychoanalytical Terms* (New York: Longmans, Green & Co., 1958).

The study of the processes of growth and development is properly concerned with all of the changes which take place in the individual as he progresses from infancy to adulthood. Control and guidance of these processes is essential from birth to maturity, but such control and guidance must be thoughtful and must lead to intelligent self-control and self-guidance. It is well to remember that all child training is either positive or negative, that it cannot be indifferent. During the school age, as well as before and after, the child is passing through a series of changes in interests and in capabilities. Therefore, it is the teacher's task to use methods of guiding the child which keep pace with these changes in interests and capabilities. The teacher's purpose is essentially to guide growth and development, for hereditary characteristics fix the limits beyond which the individual cannot grow. Education provides the means by which the inherited capacities and potentialities are transformed into actualities. Education must provide a select and ideal environment which not only permits the expression of growth and development, but also improves these processes.

A knowledge of both heredity and environment, then, is essential to the teacher, for neither can be defective or faulty without influencing, more or less seriously, the growth and development of the child. Heredity and environment do not operate independently. They do not oppose each other in a struggle for mastery. There is an interaction between them; they are cooperative influences; they are so intimately united that one cannot properly be thought of without the other. To draw a sharp line showing where heredity leaves off and environment begins is impossible. The two factors supplement each other in every phase of growth and development. They are mutually interdependent and complement each other. It is necessary to recognize the influence of both. No two individuals possess the same heredity and no two individuals react to the same environmental factors in the same way. While the role played by heredity is important and must therefore be respected, nevertheless any fatalistic attitude which makes heredity all important retards a true understanding of the process of growth and development. Without minimizing the importance of heredity, emphasis must be placed on environment as the factor of greater significance in the educative process.[11]

---

[11] Historically the relative influence of heredity and environment of the individual has been the subject of much controversy. One extreme position, *environmentalism,* maintained that environment (nurture) constituted the determinant of behavior. The other extreme position, *hereditarianism,* stressed the influence of

Consequently in the process of education both heredity and environment must be taken into account. However, environment supplies the experiences necessary for the most advantageous development of the intellectual capacities of the pupils. The environmental influences of the child are provided chiefly by the home, the school, and the church. Since growth and development in all stages and periods are subject to modification by environmental forces, the home, the church, and particularly the school must provide suitable environment, regulate and use it for a definite purpose. Furthermore, each subject in the curriculum should represent a special phase of the past experiences of mankind in order that the experiences of others may form part of the developmental influences. Great care must be exercised at all times to secure for the child an environment which is thoroughly imbued with wholesome influences. It is the school's task to provide for the proper expression of good traits and to ward off wrong forms of incitement and chances for harmful expression. Hence, education in determining the kind of training which the child should receive must take account of his inborn capacities and traits, but in calculating what the final result of his development is to be, it must take into account more particularly the influence both of his formal education, and of his environment outside of school. Environment provides opportunity and plays the greater part in the education of the child. Hence, the teacher must learn as much as possible of the child's environment, must supply directive and corrective as well as preventive treatment, must supply a classroom environment of highest type possible.

3. The Factor of Volition. Heredity bestows capacity, while environment provides opportunity, but the power of self-determination or the capacity to choose both realizes the inherited capacity and utilizes the environmental opportunities. The intellect enables the individual to interpret situations, and the will enables him to control situations. Volition weaves into their fitting parts in life the factors of heredity and environment by striving to overcome conflicts, by seeking to attain perseverance, by avoiding vacillation. The will, which is man's controlling and sovereign power, functions as the guiding force of his life and the integrating

---

genetic factors. In the light of present knowledge both of these extreme positions are untenable. The middle of the road position, that is, *interaction* of biological equipment and environmental forces is most widely accepted. See Sister Barbara Geoghegan, Sister Marie Baptista Pollard, and W. A. Kelly, *op. cit.*, pp. 39–42.

factor in his character. The will is man's capacity to direct and to restrain thought, emotion, and action. By means of the will purposes are pursued steadily and attention is centered on tasks. Since the influence of the will extends to all the capacities of man, it is thus the controlling factor in the direction of conduct and the affairs of life. This has been stated in the following manner:

> A child's self-directive powers liberate him from original innate inclinations and from environmental factors; the self when developed constitutes a pivot for integration of everything important that has occurred up to the present time. It establishes an order of priority in responding to various stimuli, sentiments, ideals and goals. It becomes a final arbiter.[12]

Since the decision of the will is determined by motives, the capacity to choose from among motives must determine how the individual will react in any specific situation. This means that it is the will which realizes or neglects the capacity which heredity bestows, which improves or disregards the opportunities which environment presents.

The Periods of Growth and Development. While the rate of growth and the degree of development may be either accelerated or retarded within limits, the tendency is for the child to grow physically and mentally, and to develop the powers and capacities of body and mind gradually and regularly. The teacher should know the general sequence of growth and development through which the individual progresses. From a helpless, wholly dependent infant, the child progresses through a long period of immaturity to a self-directed, mature personality. While this progress is gradual and regular, for purposes of convenience the process of growth and development has been divided into periods covering certain years of child life which may be considered as stages in the continuous process. It must be remembered at all times that each stage merges into that which follows. Infancy merges into childhood which in turn merges into adolescence. There are no clearly defined boundaries between one stage and another. Also, it must not be assumed that the child is distinctly different mentally or physically during each of these periods. The placement of the age limits for these periods is a very artificial procedure. The only reason for making such divisions at all is the fact that the entire process is so long and so involved that it is not possible to obtain a clear, definite, and full knowledge of it unless the process is divided up in some manner and studied a little at a time. In making such

[12] J. Pikunas and E. J. Albrecht, *op. cit.*, p. 51.

divisions it is customary and convenient to use as the division point the average age or time at which it has been observed that certain events in the process of growth and development, such as rapid or slow physical growth, entrance into school, and the like, take place. The division employed here consists of five periods:

1. *Infancy,* which extends throughout the first two years of life.
2. *Early childhood,* which includes ages three, four, and five, and is frequently designated as the *preschool age.*
3. *Middle childhood,* which comprises the years from six to nine or ten and is ordinarily referred to as the *primary school age.*
4. *Preadolescence,* or the *prepubertal stage,* which begins at the age of nine or ten and continues until puberty is attained. This period involves the *intermediate school age* and merges into the *junior high school age.*
5. *Adolescence,* which extends from puberty to maturity or roughly throughout the teen years, approximately from ages thirteen to twenty.

In presenting a summary of the process of growth and development, it must be remembered that no two children are exactly alike, and hence that the rate of growth and the degree of development may vary greatly in the case of individual children.

A brief consideration and description of the periods of infancy and early childhood is presented here in order to serve as background information which seems essential for a complete understanding of the processes of growth and development as these take place later during the periods of middle childhood, preadolescence and adolescence. Separate chapters will be devoted to the elementary school child which include accounts of the periods of middle childhood and preadolescence, and also to the adolescent.

Infancy. This term has been derived from a Latin verb which means "not speaking." The period extends throughout approximately the first two years of life, or from birth to the time when the child has developed speech sufficiently to express himself purposively by using very simple words to connote thought and feelings. Infancy is by far the most formative stage in the entire process of growth and development. No other phase possesses more significance for the future than these first years of life. During infancy the foundations are established for all future growth and development. The characteristics of infancy are rapid physical growth, unfolding of the mental powers, acquisition of motor skills, development of language. Rapid physical growth is the principal feature of infancy. This growth is manifested by considerable gain in weight and increase in height. Birth weight is ordinarily trebled within the first year, and height is increased by eight or nine inches while bodily proportions become more symmetrical. Muscular tone and vigor are evident through the development of motor ability, and progress is made through the motor sequence leading to walking. The eruption of the deciduous or baby teeth takes place.

Mental growth and development are, likewise, very rapid during infancy. With the exception of the basic physical reactions necessary to sustain life, the infant must learn all else required to adapt to the physical and social world about him. This learning begins at birth and is exceedingly rapid during the first two years of life. It is dependent upon maturation; that is, how and what the infant learns depends upon his state of readiness to react, or the level of maturation reached at the time. The primary adaptations which the infant must make to the physical and social environment are walking and talking. Control over bodily movements and organs in the activities of sitting, creeping, standing, walking, and talking involve not merely growth of bone and of muscle and coordination of neural structures, but also development of the mental powers by means of which the child learns, including the perceptual process, imagination, memory, and intellect. The primary characteristic of mental development during infancy is the acquisition of language and its use as a means of expression and communication. The child at birth possesses the necessary physical apparatus for vocalization and the mental potentialities for the acquisition of speech. However acquisition of speech is at once a function of maturation involving motor control and auditory development, and also of learning stimulated by the interest and attention of parents and other members of the family who make up the environment of the infant. The language which the child speaks must be learned very largely through imitation of sounds in environment, through the process of association, and memory, through the process of abstraction and the formation of ideas. Language development involves comprehension first, and is followed by speech or oral vocalization. During the first year the child progresses from crying to babbling, to imitation of sound, to articulation of one or two syllables, to the combination of these into words, and then to the comprehension and use of these words. Through differentiation and imitation of sounds and under continuing stimulation, the infant may, by the end of the first year, have evolved a small vocabulary, perhaps of seven or eight words. The child comprehends a considerable number of words before he can use them, that is, his listening vocabulary will be very much larger than his speaking vocabulary. Vocabulary growth is slow in the beginning, but during the second year there is a rapid expansion both in understanding and purposive use of language. Names of familiar persons and objects are learned and speech is used purposively. The rate at which speech develops varies considerably. As a rule girls talk two to four months earlier than do boys. Likewise mentally superior children usually talk about three months before average children.

Social development during infancy is slight, but there is an expanding awareness of other people as separate from himself and a widening of interests beyond himself. Since it is the foundation period of life, infancy inevitably influences all later personality development. A fundamental aspect of emotional development during infancy is security, which bears a direct relationship to future ability to adjust to life situations. Security includes parental love, affection, care, interest, and understanding, leading to recognition by the child of personal worth as an individual, accepted by and belonging within the family group, and eventuating to the development of self-confidence.

Early Childhood. This period includes the interval between the time when the child has developed language sufficiently to express himself purposively and his entrance to school. Ordinarily this interval includes the years three, four, and five, since the child usually enters school at the age of six. During this stage the rate of physical growth is slower than it was in infancy. Considerable progress is made in the acquisition of motor skills, which is evident in self-care activities, such as dressing, feeding, and washing self, picking up toys and the like, which are developed into habits. Likewise, this period is marked by increased physical vigor and muscular control, exhibited in the greater ease and confidence with which such activities as running and climbing are performed. During this period there is a gradual change from the chubbiness of babyhood to a more slender and muscular appearance.

Mental growth and development are rapid during this period. There is considerable improvement in perceptual ability, which is manifested in capability to distinguish differences in color, size, shape, and weight. The constructive imagination is vivid and is an evident factor in dramatic imitative play activities as well as in stories liked. Rote memory is functioning excellently. The attention span of the child during this stage is likely to be very brief, and depends largely upon interest in the activity or task in which he is engaged. Progress in intellectual development is evident from the fact that the child is beginning to acquire concepts of time and number, is aware of relationship between ideas, can make simple generalizations from experience. Judgment and reasoning are demonstrated by adaptations made to new situations encountered in play, in the selection of materials, in planning what to build or to make or what activities in which to engage, and in determining what to do first and at definite times. The predominant characteristic of the period is curiosity, and for this reason it is usually designated at the *questioning age.* The child seeks to know the what, why, where, when, and how of everything. These questions are indications of the child's eagerness to learn and to acquire new experiences. Usually, this eagerness leads to an expansion of vocabulary as well as improvement in understanding and using language. Other indications of development in language ability are the disappearance of infantile pronunciation, the use of complete sentences and mastery of pronouns, and, to some extent, past tense. The child during this period understands many more words than he uses. However, he can usually define by use, purpose, or example most of the words which he employs, and some few he can define by general terms or description.

Social development in the preschool period is manifested by extending the range of contacts with other children in play groups. This interaction with other children through association with them in play marks the beginnings of group activity, a widening field of experiences, and the beginnings of cooperative behavior. Although the preschool child cannot read, he has a keen interest in hearing stories which feature sense impressions and actions, which are characterized by rhythm and repetition.

Among all of the influences on growth and development during the first six years of life the home is the most significant. During these years the child is completely dependent upon the home. Accordingly, its influence is profound and extensive. It constitutes the child's first environment and influences all activities and interests. In the home are established the foundations for all growth and development, for the formation of personality. There the child acquires his first and, in many cases, his most lasting impressions. There he has his first contacts with life, meets his first problems, learns his first lessons. There he acquires his fundamental ideas of right and wrong. There, through the processes of imitation, precept, example, and training, are formed also the basic habits, attitudes, emotions, and ideals upon which all future conduct will be built.

EXERCISES

1. Outline this chapter.
2. List and define the terms which you have learned from your study of this chapter.
3. Explain the nature of growth and development.
4. List the principles of growth and development which are of significance for the teacher.
5. Distinguish between:
   a) Heredity and environment;
   b) Growth and development;
   c) Potentiality and character;
   d) Chromosome and gene;
   e) Maturation and learning;
   f) Cross-sectional and longitudinal.
6. Explain the factors which influence growth and development. Designate the ways in which each factor exercises its influence in the process.
7. Discuss the following statements:
   a) "Heredity determines the limits within which an individual can develop."
   b) "No two individuals possess the same heredity and no two individuals react to the same environmental factors in the same way."
   c) "The placement of age limits for periods of growth and development is a very artificial procedure."
8. Since growth and development constitute a continuous process, justify the practice of dividing this process into periods each of which is described as though it were a well-defined stage in itself.
9. Describe the physical and mental growth and development which take place during infancy.
10. Describe the physical, mental, and social development of the preschool child.

SELECTED REFERENCES FOR STUDY AND READING

Almy, M., *Child Development* (New York: Holt, Rinehart and Winston, Inc., 1955).

Baller, W. R., *Readings in the Psychology of Human Growth and Development* (New York: Holt, Rinehart and Winston, Inc., 1962).

Breckenridge, M. E., and Vincent, E. L., *Child Development,* 4 ed. (Philadelphia: W. B. Saunders Co., 1960).

Carmichael, L., ed., *Manual of Child Psychology,* 2 ed. (New York: John Wiley & Sons, Inc., 1954).

Dennis, W., *Readings in Child Psychology,* 2 ed. (Englewood Cliffs, N. J.: Prentice-Hall, Inc., 1963).

English, H. B., *Dynamics of Child Development* (New York: Holt, Rinehart and Winston, Inc., 1961).

Geoghegan, Sister Barbara, Pollard, Sister Marie Baptista, and Kelly, W. A., *Developmental Psychology* (Milwaukee: The Bruce Publishing Co., 1963).

Goodenough, F. L., and Tyler, L. E., *Developmental Psychology* (New York: Appleton-Century-Crofts, Inc., 1959).

Gordon, I. J., *Human Development* (New York: Harper & Row, 1962).

Havighurst, R. J., *Human Development and Education* (New York: Longmans, Green and Co., 1953).

Hurlock, E. B., *Child Development,* 3 ed. (New York: McGraw-Hill Book Co., 1956).

——— *Developmental Psychology,* 2 ed. (New York: McGraw-Hill Book Co., 1959).

Kuhlen, R. G., and Thompson, G. C., *Psychological Studies of Human Development,* 2 ed. (New York: Appleton-Century-Crofts, Inc., 1963).

Lane, H., and Beauchamp, M., *Understanding Human Development* (Englewood Cliffs, N. J.: Prentice-Hall, Inc., 1959).

Mussen, P. H., *A Handbook of Research Methods in Child Psychology* (New York: John Wiley & Sons, Inc., 1960).

Mussen, P. H., Conger, J. J., and Kagan, J., *Child Development and Personality,* 2 ed. (New York: Harper & Row, 1962).

National Society for the Study of Education, Sixty-Second Yearbook, Part I, *Child Psychology,* 1963.

Pikunas, J., and Albrecht, E. J., *Psychology of Human Development* (New York: McGraw-Hill Book Co., Inc., 1961).

Stone, A. A., and Ongue, G. C., *Longitudinal Studies of Child Personality* (Cambridge, Mass.: Harvard University Press, 1959).

Strang, R., *An Introduction to Child Study,* 4 ed. (New York: The Macmillan Co., 1959).

Thompson, G. G., *Child Psychology,* 2 ed. (Boston: Houghton-Mifflin Co., 1962).

Thorpe, L. P., *Child Psychology and Development,* 3 ed. (New York: The Ronald Press Co., 1962).

Vincent, E. L., and Martin, P. C., *Human Psychological Development* (New York: The Ronald Press Co., 1961).

chapter 4

The Elementary School Child

The age limits of the elementary school period are determined by modern educational practice. Customarily the child enters school at the age of six years and progresses through Grades 1 to 6 at the rate of one grade per year. Accordingly, by the time he has completed the six grades of the elementary school the child has reached the age of twelve. Thus in the present discussion of the elementary school child the age limits under consideration extend from the sixth to the twelfth year, even though elementary schools extend through Grade 8. Actually these years constitute two periods in the process of development. The first three years of the span, ages six to nine, include the period of middle childhood while the latter three years, ages nine to twelve, constitute the period of later childhood or preadolescence. The developmental sequences of each period will be considered separately.

The years from six to twelve constitute a time for learning and are characterized by activity, eagerness, interest, and to some extent creativity. These are the first six years of the child's school life, first not only in time but also in importance. It is essential that the teacher understand the development which takes place during these years; what the child does; what he is capable of accomplishing; something of the causes of motivation as he progresses in learning.

DEVELOPMENT DURING THE PERIOD OF MIDDLE CHILDHOOD

The period of middle childhood extends from age six to nine or ten. Because it corresponds with the progress of the child through the early grades in school, it is frequently designated as the primary school period. Development is not as spectacular during these years as it was during the previous periods of infancy and early childhood. Physical growth is relatively slow. At the beginning of the period, however, the child is considered to have achieved a sufficient degree of maturity to enable him to profit from formal education. Customarily he enters school at the age of six years. This constitutes a critical stage in development because the child moves from the smaller simple and sheltered milieu of the home into the larger, complex, and less protective environment of the school. It means also the beginnings of contacts with groups of peers or contemporaries, and participation in the activities of such groups. These in turn involve competition with and getting along with others as well as being accepted by and attaining status within the group. Thus entering school involves learning to make new adjustments; to accept the authority of the teacher in place of the parents; and to accept discipline as a necessary component of school life; to assume responsibilities; to attain satisfaction in doing things for himself. The six-year-old is the product of the first five years of life spent within the home. These basic personality patterns have been formed during these earlier years. Entering school tests this previous development. If the child's earlier experiences and training within the home have been adequate, he should adjust satisfactorily to the environment and requirements of the school.

Physical Development. During this period physical growth has begun to level off to a slower, more consistent rate than was apparent during the earlier periods of infancy and early childhood. Thus the years from six to nine are not marked by rapid changes. Physical growth proceeds gradually, slowly and in a relative uniform fashion. The child seems to be consolidating gains made during the preschool years. By the age of six the child will have doubled his birth height and have attained approximately two thirds of adult height. Likewise, the child will have increased his birth weight five or six times. During this period the average yearly gain in height will be one to two inches and in weight three to five pounds. However, since the development of each child is unique, considerable variation occurs. For this reason each child should be evaluated in terms of his own rate of growth rather than through comparison with so termed "averages."[1] Much depends upon the general body type. Some children are slender while others are broader; some children are small-boned while others are large-boned. Some will always

[1] R. Strang, *Introduction to Child Study,* 4 ed. (New York: The Macmillan Co., 1959), pp. 264–267.

be "big for their age"[2] while others will always seem small. This seems to depend largely upon biological and family background. The physical growth and development of the child will be influenced by various factors including: race, family health history, economic status, diet, sunlight, play, rest and sleep, physical defects, birth conditions, illnesses, endocrine balance, and emotional conditions which affect the child's well-being.

During this period there are sex differences in physical growth and development. Boys tend to be slightly taller and heavier than girls and also to be more muscular and stronger. However, by the sixth year the girls are about twelve months more mature in bone structure than are the boys. This differential continues to increase until the time of puberty when the girl is usually two years ahead of the boy of the same age in general development.

Improvement occurs in bodily proportions because of skeletal development involving growth in size and change in the basic muscular structure, which is evident particularly in the lengthening of arms and legs. All strictly infantile characteristics including the last vestiges of baby looks are lost. By the age of six the basic motor skills involving the large muscles have been established. By that age most children can run well and generally can jump, skip, and climb. During the period an increased smoothness and efficiency in these activities as well as the development of better balance, becomes evident. Speed and coordination increase and many motor skills involving the large muscles are perfected. This coordination is utilized in many forms of games and play including climbing, jumping rope, games of chase, and the like which call for precise muscular adjustment. In addition to improvement in motor skills there is also an increase in strength. Middle childhood is a period of great activity, when energy and exuberance are expressed.

As the child's neuromuscular system matures there is an increasingly steady gain in coordination and control of the fine muscles. Gradually the eyes, hands, fingers, feet, and body posture come to work together in closer harmony. This is particularly evident in the development of manual dexterity as well as hand and eye coordination to the extent that it becomes possible for the child to utilize these in writing, in drawing, and in play activities. During the early part of this period the child attains discrimination of size, depth, movement, and distance, which

[2] H. Lane and M. Beauchamp, *Understanding Human Development* (Englewood Cliffs, N. J.: Prentice-Hall, Inc., 1959), p. 240.

requires the coordinated activity of both eyes as well as the maturation of the optic nerve. When this occurs the child is physically ready to learn to read, that is, he is ready to perceive symbols and signs on the printed page which he will recognize as words. At the age of six, handedness is well established and by the end of the period or about the ninth year, dominance of either the left or right eye is established. Permanent dentition begins at about the sixth year with the appearance of the six-year molars and gradually the first or deciduous teeth are replaced by permanent teeth. By the end of the period the child will have ten or eleven permanent teeth.

During the period of middle childhood the child gains in symmetry and balance. The physical activities of the school program should be in keeping with the child's stage of development. Boys and girls differ in this development during the period, and this difference influences achievement in the acquisition of many competencies and skills in the field of sensorimotor behavior.

Mental Development. The period of middle childhood is marked by extensive mental development. During the years from six to nine the child's perceptional abilities are remarkably acute. This is significant because upon that acuity of perception, the amount and correctness of ideas are dependent. It is evident that the child who has many visual, auditory, and tactile experiences will have a richer source of specific percepts from which to derive generalizations. The more numerous the specific experiences, the more materials the child has from which to abstract and generalize. So also is there an increase in the ability to utilize memory, particularly verbal memory, which becomes more active as the child acquires ideas, increases vocabulary, and expands experiences. The imagination, particularly the make-believe, is still functioning strongly. The world of fantasy holds consuming interest during this period and even before the child is able to read for himself, he projects himself into stories read to him, and also identifies himself with characters and situations witnessed on television or in the comics or the movies. Toward the end of the period, however, images become grounded more in reality and less fantastic in nature. Utilization of constructive imagery is evident both in play activities and in schoolwork. The span of attention improves and the child is able to concentrate for longer periods of time. It should be noted that the span of attention is dependent upon interest in an activity. The child is capable of persistence and concentra-

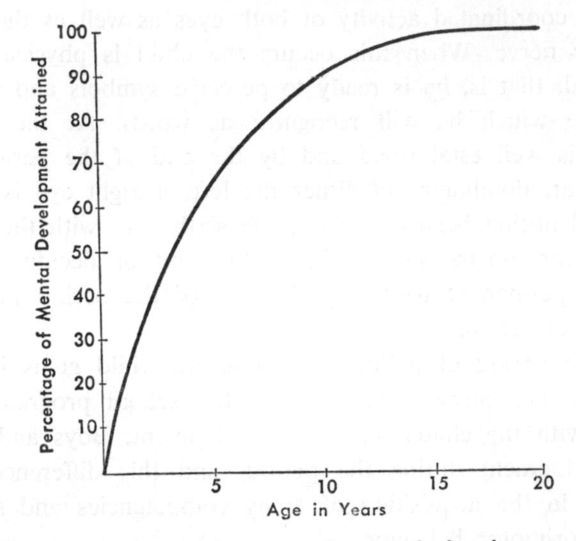

Fig. 2. Theoretical curve of mental development.[3]

tion and will work for a long period of time on something which is really of interest to him. The improvement in the ability to grasp meaning and to form concepts, however, is the basic factor in mental development. This phase is evident primarily in the command and usage of language employed by the child. During this period the child's concepts of time and space become more accurate and clear-cut. It is only after the age of ten, however, that more complex ideas of time, such as centuries, and unclear concepts of distance have much meaning for the child. Although the child at this time has some awareness of the past, historical sequences remain somewhat vague to him. The concept of spatial relationship becomes quite realistic as is evident in the drawings of children in this period. This development constitutes evidence that the child is ready to begin formal learning.

The child of six brings to the new environment of the school an accumulated body of experiential information derived from many sources within the home and the neighborhood during his preschool years. This experiential information constitutes a rich supply of raw material for in-

[3] G. M. Blair, R. S. Jones, and R. H. Simpson, *Educational Psychology*, 2 ed. (New York: The Macmillan Co., 1962), p. 52; see also F. L. Goodenough, "The Measurement of Mental Growth in Childhood," in *Manual of Child Psychology*, 2 ed., L. Carmichael, ed. (New York: John Wiley & Sons, Inc., 1954), pp. 477–479.

tellectual development and provides a source for the formation of ideas and expression of judgments. The child's reasoning powers improve as his experiences at school increase, as his ability to sustain attention for longer periods grows, as he becomes capable of forming orderly associations between and among experiences and ideas. Children of seven years are usually able to apply general principles to specific situations and, at the level of their own experiences, to detect logical fallacies. Because some slight growth in critical thinking may be expected during the period, the child should be encouraged to evaluate and to apply critical judgments in terms of his experience and in keeping with his developing ability.

In this period a gradually increasing portion of time is devoted to the acquisition and utilization of symbols, both verbal and numerical. The child becomes able to develop categories and to recognize both likenesses and differences. He is curious about natural phenomena and exhibits an interest in cause and effect. He seeks to add to his store of knowledge and likewise to organize and integrate experiences within that knowledge. The mental development of the child in this stage is best indicated by his attainment of "readiness to learn" or sufficient maturity to profit from formal instruction in the school situation. Although not all children who enter school at the age of six are equally ready, the majority of children are ready for certain learning experiences at approximately the same time. That is why it is possible to develop a basic curriculum from which to work. Readiness to learn involves the attainment of sufficient physical, mental, and emotional development, an adequate experiential background, interest, and willingness to learn. For the school this readiness involves recognition of and cooperation with the development of the child, by offering appropriate experiences. Accordingly when readiness is attained the child learns to read, to write, and to use numbers; that is, he acquires the basic skills upon which all later education will be based. Throughout the primary grades he gains in ability to employ these skills.

The most evident indication of mental development during this period consists in the command and usage of language, since it is closely bound to the ability to form ideas. The child should speak with a noninfantile articulation. Improvement in language ability is manifested primarily by increase in size of vocabulary, and also by the length and structure of sentences used, effectiveness in the expression of ideas, and correct

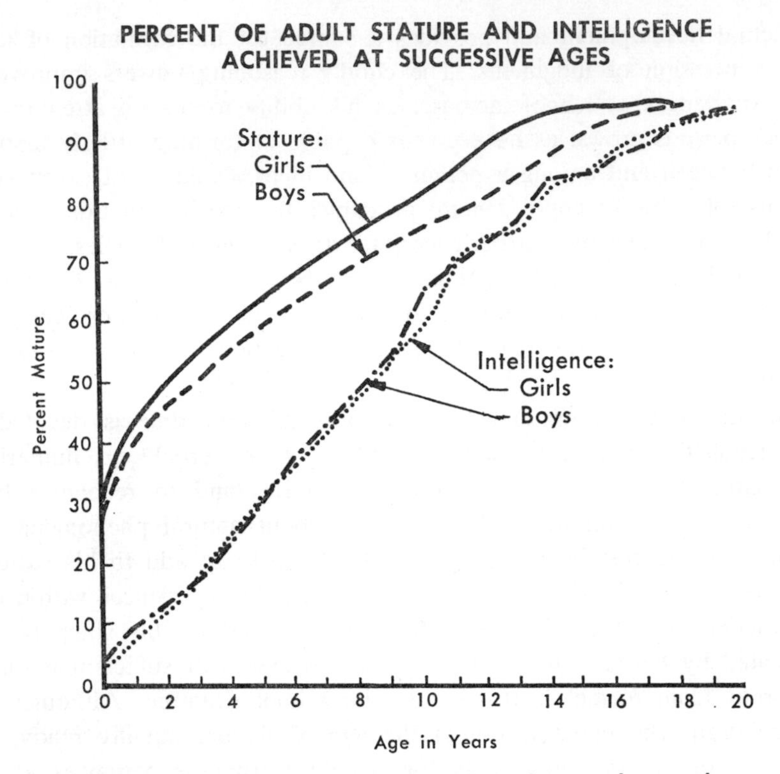

Fig. 3. Sex difference in physical and mental growth.

usage of words. The recognition vocabulary of the child generally surpasses the use vocabulary. The child understands more words than he actually uses. Not only does the child's vocabulary change in quantity, but there are in addition marked qualitative changes. Before the age of five the child is rarely able to define words; yet early in the period of middle childhood he will be able to define objects in terms of use or of description and often to distinguish attributes of an object for the general classification. As the developmental level increases, explanations of words are given and use of synonyms occurs more frequently. The child's vocabulary provides many clues to the level of his thinking as well as indications of the range of comprehension and information and also something concerning his interests. The use of vocabulary in conversation and in connected accounts of experience increases markedly. Hence it is essential that the child be provided with many experiences which encourage him to increase and enrich his vocabulary. This is especially important because reading ability is built upon the foundation of language development. Various estimates have been made of the vocabulary of children in this period. Such estimates, however, are dependent upon the methods of investigation employed. One study[4] indicated that by the age of six the average child can recognize about 24,000 words. Another study[5] reported 14,700 basic words as the estimated vocabulary at age six with a continuous increase occurring in size during the period of middle childhood, so that at the age of ten the estimated vocabulary was reported as 34,300 words.[6]

Emotional Development. During the period of middle childhood the child develops the ability both to experience an increasing range of emotions and also to react to stimuli which are more subtle than those experienced during the previous periods. The major emotional needs, that is, to be loved, valued, wanted, and approved, must continue to be met primarily by the parents and secondarily by the teacher. During the latter part of the period, however, some satisfaction of these needs will be offered by the peer group. School experiences during the period should exercise a healthy influence upon personality development. Yet, if during the period children are exposed to unhappy, irritating, and disquieting environmental influences in the home or in the school, they tend to absorb easily and to imitate frequently these experiences in their own emotional reactions. The undesirable emotional reactions of the child during this period seem to be centered very largely in fear, which is expressed in the forms of worry and timidity. Usually such fears center around the child's self. Frequently, entering the new world of the school with its unfamiliar surroundings and in which the teachers and other children are strangers to him may cause fear. As he progresses through the primary grades fear may develop as a result of failure to achieve some goal, particularly success in school experiences. It may also result from not being liked or accepted by companions, and likewise from rejection by the teacher, whether the rejection is real or is only imagined.

---

[4] M. K. Smith, "Measurement of Size of General English Vocabulary Through the Elementary Grades and High School," *Genetic Psychology Monographs,* 24:311–345, 1941; see also R. Strang, *op. cit.,* pp. 277–278; H. B. English, *Dynamics of Child Development* (New York: Holt, Rinehart and Winston, Inc., 1961), p. 316.

[5] R. H. Seashore, "A New Light on Children's Vocabulary," *School and Society,* 66:163–164, 1947.

[6] From National Society for the Study of Education, Sixty-first Yearbook, Part I, *Individualizing Instruction,* 1962, p. 133.

Particularly, the child during this early stage of his school life fears anything in the school situation which offers a threat to his status or security. Failure, ridicule, loss of prestige, and feeling of inadequacy are causes of fear reactions. Because the demands made upon the child by the new environment of the school are complex, he will require aid and guidance in meeting these demands. Approval of parents and teachers is important for his self-esteem, and yet not the least of his emotional problems at this time may arise from the fear of having his fears become known, especially by his peers, who may use them to ridicule him. These fears may find widely different forms of expression. They may be masked by aggressive behavior or may be expressed in less obvious ways such as withdrawal from social contact, overdependence upon parents, or even physically in lack of appetite, restlessness, and other forms.

Investigations[7] which have been conducted in classroom situations have provided evidence that children tend to reflect the emotional status not only of their parents but also of their teachers. Teachers with anxieties may influence many pupils adversely, tending to cause these children to become fearful and insecure. Teachers who are relaxed and cheerful seem to influence their pupils favorably since the studies reported that in their classrooms a preponderance of the children do not display emotional problems attributable to the school climate. Inconsistency in the emotional behavior of parents and teachers is bound to be reflected in the emotional reactions of the child, and constitutes an important source of fear reactions in children of this age.

Anger reactions[8] during the period of middle childhood may be attributed to a wide variety of causes. It is possible that temper tantrums, characteristic of the preschool period, may still occur. When such is the case the child is probably uncertain of himself and perceives in the anger-provoking situation a threat to his self-concept, of which he is not yet sure but which he feels he must protect from assault in the only way which he knows how to use. As the child progresses through the period, the violent anger reactions which were characteristic of the preschool period tend to be replaced by less spectacular forms of emotional reaction. Such forms include fighting, pushing, jostling, and verbal reactions such as

---

[7] D. G. Ryans, *Characteristics of Teachers* (Washington, D. C.: American Council on Education, 1960).

[8] Sister Barbara Geoghegan, Sister Marie Baptista Pollard, and W. A. Kelly, *Developmental Psychology* (Milwaukee: The Bruce Publishing Co., 1963), pp. 308–315.

name-calling. At the end of this period most children have learned to exercise a fair amount of control over the expression of anger. However, some may substitute sulking, pouting, or crying for the more violent earlier responses.

Jealousy is also an emotional reaction commonly found in children during this period. It involves the fear that something which means much to the child, especially the affection of a parent, will be transferred to another. It involves also a type of anger reaction to a threat to security. The jealous child is usually extremely self-centered. Sibling jealousy is the most usual type. Jealousy may be overcome by encouraging the child to be interested in the welfare of others. He should be encouraged to consider himself an integral part of the group, with duties toward others, particularly the other members of the family and more especially the younger children in the family. Parents and teachers can do much to prevent jealousy by being fair and impartial to all children and by not making unfavorable comparisons among members of a family.

In order to be most effective in her work with primary school children the teacher should be aware of and sensitive to the varied emotional needs of each child. Some of these children require affection more than anything else. Others should be so guided and directed that they acquire a less antagonistic attitude toward authority. Still others should be helped to become more independent. There are many effective ways of dealing with individual emotional reactions. These include frequent checks on physical condition; correction of misbehavior without losing temper; recognition of the child's needs without giving him everything he demands; training in self-reliance; respecting the child as a person with real interests of his own; reasoning with him to the extent that this is possible at this particular age.

Social Development. The years of middle childhood, during which the child makes the transition from the home to the broader world of the school and neighborhood, represent a very important fundamental phase of the process of social development. Necessarily, social development is bound up with and dependent, to no small extent, upon the degree of physical, mental, and emotional development which the child has attained during the first six years of his life. Entering school is an experience which is universally anticipated by children, perhaps because in the school the child enters more fully into the world of children. Family security, which was so important in the preschool period, becomes secondary to the needs for belonging to a group and for forming close friendships.

There is a growing individualization and an increasing independence of the home.

When the child enters school, however, he faces new and formidable problems of a social nature, particularly the problems of belonging and of maintaining status become complex. During the primary school period the child develops a group consciousness, which is expressed primarily in the desire to participate in the group activities of his peers. Consequently, he begins to identify himself with groups of increasing size and complexity, and he seeks the companionship of children of his own age. In this way he becomes part of a peer group, that is, a group of individuals who are approximately his equals in age, size, and status. In this group he will spend a great part of his day, and in the activities of this group, his abilities and social adjustment will be tested and challenged. From his participation in the activities of this group he learns to develop new feelings of adequacy and worth as well as of acceptance and belonging. It is during this time that he learns to get along with others, to share, to take turns, to be courteous, and to assume responsibility. He gains in self-confidence and self-reliance. Friendships with other children occupy a large share of his time and attention. Best friends are likely to be of the same sex. Friendships are usually brief in duration and shift rapidly from one individual to another. Choice of friends is not influenced by social or economic status. The child has learned by this time something concerning the existence of prejudices and is frequently puzzled by them. Ordinarily attitudes of discrimination against other races, nationalities, creeds, and social classes are not characteristic of the period unless such attitudes are emphasized in the immediate environment, particularly in the home. Although the age group is becoming more important than adults to the primary child, nevertheless he is still sensitive to adult criticism and vulnerable to ridicule and excessive teasing. Likewise he does not know how to accept loss of prestige. He is still in need of adult support and tenderness.

Many of the child's social attitudes and concepts are acquired in play activities. Frequently acceptance in the peer group is dependent upon skill in the approved play activities and games of the group. In the early stage of the period free activity games involving running and chasing but lacking in organization and rules are characteristic play activities. The epitome of these games is "tag." The interest of both boys and girls in games of chase continues to be strong throughout the period. In addition, as he becomes ready the child will learn from his playmates the skills necessary for ordinary play activities: to throw, to catch, to ride a bicycle. These are particularly important to the boy because failure to achieve such skills brings indifference and disdain from age-mates. During this period the child is extremely active and seems to be interested in movement or activity rather than the form of activity. Dramatic initiative play representing the experiences of daily life is characteristic of the child during the greater part of this period. In their dramatic role-playing, children take the parts of "Mother," "Father," "Teacher," and the like. At about the eighth year a transition is noticeable. The child grows more self-assertive and becomes more interested in play activities which involve competition and self-testing. Thus, at this time, the child participates both competitively and cooperatively in small-group activities. Although boys and girls still participate in group play activities together, their interests are really divergent.

Educational Provisions During the Primary Grades. The development of the child in the period of middle childhood is best indicated by the attainment of readiness to learn or sufficient maturity to profit from formal instruction in the school situation. Although not all children who enter school at the age of six are equally ready, learning can take place only when readiness has been attained. This involves proper physical, mental, and emotional development, adequate experiential background, interest and willingness to learn. Thus both maturational and motivational factors are involved in readiness. When readiness is attained the child learns to read, to use numbers, to write; that is, he acquires the basic skills upon which all later education will be based, and throughout the primary school period he gains in ability to employ these skills.

The most fundamental skill taught in the school and the activity most frequently engaged in throughout life is reading which is the indispensable basis of all education. In the primary grades the essential mechanics of reading are acquired. Just as there are preparatory stages for walking and talking, so also is there a preliminary stage during which the child becomes ready to learn to read. Many complex factors are involved in readiness for reading.[9] The mental factors are of primary importance because reading

[9] R. Strang, *op. cit.,* pp. 276–282. See also J. A. Fitzgerald and P. G. Fitzgerald. *Methods and Curricula in Elementary Education* (Milwaukee: The Bruce Pub-

y a mental process. These include: a mental age of six and ... years, an adequate memory span, ability to focus attention, some knowledge of word meanings, an adequate speaking vocabulary, and a desire to read. In addition there are also significant physical factors which include: reasonable accuracy in visual and auditory acuity, ability to recognize differences in formation and shape of letters, adequate health and vigor. Language factors are likewise very important. These include: word fluency, pronunciation, enunciation, and length and structure of sentences used. Emotional adjustment constitutes a factor also since there is usually a definite relationship between reading difficulties and emotional problems. The factors in the social development of the child during this period which influence reading readiness include: ability to adjust to school situations; experiences in the home, the nursery school, and the kindergarten; and the previous guidance of parents as well as the range and intensity of the child's interests. It is to be noted that ordinarily nursery school and kindergarten experiences promote readiness for learning, particularly since such experiences help the child to develop a sense of security in school and a cooperative and willing attitude toward other children.

The stages in learning to read during primary grades are, in addition to reading readiness, accomplishment of word recognition and usually rapid progress in perfecting the fundamental skills, habits, and attitudes necessary for comprehension. In the primary grades the desire to read, reading habits, and reading interests are established. The aim of instruction in reading in these grades is to train the child to become aware of the meaning of the printed word and then to develop habits of reading wisely for information and for enjoyment. In the primary grades the child particularly enjoys stories about children of his own age, where experiences are similar to his own. This is the period also in which the child becomes interested in reading about child life in other lands. Interest in simple historical and travel stories as well as informational nature study is beginning to develop. Yet parallel with this high degree of interest in reality, the child retains his interest in fantasy, for the peak of interest in fairy tales is reached at about the age of eight and may continue for the next two or three years. Likewise interest in comics begins almost as soon as the child can read.

---

lishing Co., 1955), pp. 246, 260, for discussion of reading readiness and methods of teaching reading.

Not only must the child be able to employ reading skills efficiently in order to enhance his understanding of the world, but also he must acquire and be able to utilize arithmetic skills. Upon entering school the child ordinarily has some slight knowledge of quantities and of numbers. Because of preschool experiences in life situations he is usually aware of the size of objects as large or small, few or many, heavy or light; he may also recognize groups of three or four objects and in some instances he may be able to count, perhaps to ten. There is a relationship between degree of mental maturity and capacity to master concepts in arithmetic. Just as was the case in reading, children will manifest different degrees of readiness for arithmetic. During the primary grades number concepts and space relationships such as length, height, and width are grasped rapidly. Likewise, during these grades the child learns minutes, hours, and days as measure of time and also learns to read the calendar as well as to tell time to the quarter hour. An important fundamental aspect of arithmetic learning during the primary grades is the acquisition of vocabulary for expressing quantities. Usually within the first two grades the child attains comprehension of abstract number concepts such as "fiveness" and "nineness." However, it may happen, as in reading, that the child may recognize the arithmetical term or symbol, may pronounce it properly but have little or no idea of its meaning. For this reason, frequent testing of meanings which the child associates with terms and symbols will be necessary in addition to practice and drill in using terms and symbols correctly. An important part of the work of the primary grades is to impart the fundamentals of arithmetic, the techniques of addition, subtraction, multiplication, and division. In the second grade simple addition and subtraction are acquired, followed in the third grade by the acquisition of multiplication and division. Facility with number combinations, involving these techniques, involves mastery of a wide variety of combinations and such mastery is the result of practice and drill.

The curriculum of the primary grades has also been broadened in scope to include a wide variety of activities with the arts and crafts. The purpose in introducing these activities is not to teach techniques but rather to develop understanding and appreciation. In the primary grades, class periods and exercises are brief and parallel as closely as possible the developing interests of the child. In addition, psychological research involving study of the learning problems of the child has improved methods of teaching at the primary level.

DEVELOPMENT DURING THE PERIOD OF LATER CHILDHOOD OR PREADOLESCENCE[10]

This period has been designated as later childhood and is perhaps more properly referred to as the period of preadolescence. It is a transitional stage in development between the years when the child "finds" himself as an individual in the home, in the school, and in the small social group, and those years which mark his entrance into the last stage of immaturity, the long period of adolescence. Customarily the period of preadolescence is considered to include the years between the age of nine or ten and the onset of puberty. Thus the boundaries of the period are flexible, since the end is determined by the physical changes which mark the beginnings of puberty. Also, there seems to be increasing evidence that puberty tends to occur earlier in the present generation than was the case in preceding generations. However, the span of the period is roughly the three or four years during which the child passes through Grades 4, 5, and 6 in the modern school system. For this reason, the period is sometimes referred to as the *postprimary* or the *elementary school period.* It is an aspect of the developmental process which was for a long time the neglected or forgotten phase of child study. Only recently have the preadolescent years become the subject of investigation and research commensurate with that devoted to both the preceding and the following periods.

Preadolescence is a real formative period, marked by characteristics of individualism, a growing independence, and self-assertion. It is likewise the time when the fundamentals of team work and cooperation are learned, and has been described as the period of "competitive socialization." It is marked by considerable mental and social development and characterized by broadened interests and new activities. If many of the characteristics ascribed to the period seem to have been found, at least to some extent, previously during the early and middle stages of childhood, it should be remembered that this period is the culmination of all of the stages of childhood. Characteristics previously attained function during this period as truly influential life factors.

Physical Development. During the early part of the period physical growth, particularly in height, is slow but continuous and is more steady

[10] See A. W. Blair and W. H. Burton, *Growth and Development of the Preadolescent* (New York: Appleton-Century-Crofts, Inc., 1951) and M. J. Loomis, *The Preadolescent: Three Major Concerns* (New York: Appleton-Century-Crofts, Inc., 1959).

than during any previous period. Growth increments are the smallest of all periods of child life and changes in bodily proportions occur very gradually. There may be a plateau extending over six months or a year during which only very slight gains are made in height and weight. The average annual increase in height is about two inches, and the average annual gain in weight, about six pounds. Considerable structural development takes place, however, and is evident in improved muscular coordination which makes it possible for the child to engage in activities involving the use of the fine muscles leading to the acquisition of skills. Among such skills are those involving manual dexterity including improvement in handwriting, learning to play a musical instrument, learning to swim, and the like. There is, likewise, a notable increase in strength and capacity for endurance which is especially evident among boys, who are likely to be more active than girls. The resulting abundance of energy and vigor which is frequently manifested in restlessness is probably responsible for many of the disciplinary problems which occur during the elementary school period.

Permanent dentition, which began with the appearance of the six-year molars at the beginning of middle childhood, continues throughout this period and at its close the child should have twenty-four permanent teeth. Generally preadolescence is a healthy period during which the child is freer from disease than ever before, has a high degree of physical energy and greater resistance to fatigue.

During the later part of the period of preadolescence the rate of physical growth is accelerated, sometimes rather rapidly but unevenly as the boy and especially the girl approach puberty. Since gains in height and weight usually do not take place simultaneously, the child at this time may seem out of proportion. To this is attributed the ungainly and awkward appearance of many preadolescents, particularly girls of eleven or twelve. This acceleration occurs in girls at the eleventh year or even earlier and in boys usually after the twelfth year. Thus it is evident that boys and girls mature at different rates. Physiologically girls are usually one year or more ahead of boys in this aspect of development. This difference in maturing may influence school achievement and adjustment, both emotional and social. However, individual differences are very marked at this stage of development, for each child grows at his own unique rate in relation to his own constitutional makeup. The longitudinal studies of development have demonstrated very clearly that the course of development is not uniform for all individuals; that each child has his own pattern of growth. Thus variations in growth patterns are both natural and normal. It is to be noted that growth in size may be retarded by severe illnesses, malnutrition, prolonged poor health, and unfavorable living conditions.

Mental Development. The manifestations of mental development during the period of preadolescence are many. During these years the child will acquire a great deal through perceptional experiences, and so he needs an enriched experiential background. He is keenly observant of details, and this is the time to make full use of audio-visual aids in the classroom. The constructive aspect of imagination is well developed and realistic while the reproductive phase is likely to be vivid, concrete, and predominantly visual. Span of attention has improved and continues to increase, with the result that class periods may be lengthened accordingly. While memory is still better for concrete rather than for abstract materials, yet the boy particularly demonstrates rather frequently that logical memory is also functioning quite well. During this period, concepts of time become more definite, and toward the end of the period most children have developed a clear understanding of time in the historical sense. Strong language interests and wide reading activities lead to expansion of vocabulary so that the preadolescent may be expected to have attained a recognition vocabulary of between 45,000 and 50,000 words. Ordinarily the preadolescent is curious and eager to learn, with the result that he makes tremendous gains in the acquisition of knowledge during this period.

TABLE 1. Size of Vocabulary at Different Grade Levels[11]

GRADE	BASIC	DERIVED	TOTAL
1	16,900	7,100	24,000
2	22,000	12,000	34,000
3	26,000	18,000	44,000
4	26,200	18,800	45,000
5	28,500	22,500	51,000
6	31,500	18,000	49,500
7	35,000	20,000	55,000
8	36,000	20,000	56,000

[11] M. K. Smith, "Measurement of Size of General English Vocabulary Through the Elementary Grades and High School," *Genetic Psychology Monographs,* Vol. 24, 1941, pp. 311–345. See also E. B. Hurlock, *Child Development,* 3 ed. (New York: McGraw-Hill Book Co., 1956), p. 188.

Moreover, abilities in the areas of generalization, reasoning, and volitional capacity are developing rapidly. The preadolescent may be expected to manifest ability to plan ahead, to demonstrate the beginnings of critical thinking, to evaluate his own actions. The eleventh year usually marks the turning point in the ability to do logical thinking. The preadolescent is able to understand abstractions such as "pity," "justice," and "honesty"; to make effective use of judgment and to manifest an understanding of causal relationships with respect to physical, mechanical, and natural phenomena. The period is, thus, a time for accumulating a great deal of factual information, and for applying the problem-solving approach to increasingly complex situations. Customarily, the preadolescent displays a deeper insight into social situations with a consequent expansion of interests in history, geography, and science. Intellectually he is ready for more complex curricula.

Emotional Development. During the period of preadolescence, emotional development presents a fluctuating pattern. The child at this time has attained better insight into social situations, and displays loyalty to the group and enthusiasm for its activities. He gives evidence that much of his conduct is well motivated and also that there is an increasing responsibility for behavior. He is not devoid of feeling for others, or incapable of appreciation or irresponsive to sympathy, although he finds it difficult to express these emotions. In his actions he frequently manifests respect, reverence, and even gratitude. He is very much concerned with "fairness" on the part of adults. Yet the period is also marked by such characteristics as an increase in noncompliant behavior, "freshness," defiance, and disrespect for both elders and authority. Carelessness about appearance, slovenly personal habits, bad manners, a tendency to "explode" — to have outbursts of anger — as well as verbal aggressiveness and bullying are also characteristic of many preadolescents. Among boys there is a noticeable tendency toward restlessness and boisterousness, and among girls a tendency toward "giggling" which adults find very annoying.

Although childish fears decrease and caution increases, the most characteristic emotional reaction is likely to be anxiety caused by the demands of the period. Such anxiety is the outgrowth of failure to develop feelings of personal adequacy. It may be due also to failure, either real or imagined, to make adequate adjustment to school requirements or to meet the expectations of the peer group for accomplishment. Within the school difficulties in learning, particularly in reading, and the setting of standards which are beyond the child's competency to attain, frequently cause anxiety which the preadolescent may endeavor to cover up by being inattentive, by an apparent lack of interest, by daydreaming, or even by expression of a "fresh" attitude. Anxiety may also be caused during this period by the fact that the child develops physically either ahead of or later than his companions.

Social Development. The most marked phase of development during the period of preadolescence is social. This involves a very definite social consciousness as well as an increase in and expansion of group activities. The term "gang spirit" is frequently employed to indicate this natural and necessary stage in development. To most preadolescents the group or the "gang" may become the very core of life since security during this period comes from being accepted by the group. It seems at times that they identify themselves so completely with the group that they lack their own individuality. For the most part, preadolescents seek membership in groups composed of members of their own sex. During the period there is very little association between the sexes. Preadolescents, particularly boys, tend on their own initiative to associate themselves together in spontaneous groups usually composed of eight or ten or more. These groups are designated as spontaneous in order to distinguish them from adult-directed groups. The factors which bring a particular group of boys together are: (1) *propinquity,* the primary criterion, that is, they usually live in the same neighborhood and in large cities ordinarily in the same block or in the same housing development; (2) *age* likewise is an important factor since most groups restrict their membership to a given age range; (3) the same stage of *physical* and *mental development;* (4) the same degree of *social maturity;* (5) similarity with respect to *interests* and also to *moral standards.* Some of the spontaneous groups become highly structured with formal requirements for membership, rituals for conduct of meetings, passwords, secret codes and sometimes having a definite meeting place such as a "shack" or the like. The group spirit is also present among preadolescent girls but to a lesser degree and a less marked extent. The loyalty of the preadolescent girl is directed toward a small group in the form of a clique or set or club which, though the purposes are less well defined, are quite similar to the boys' gang in motivation and in effects exercised upon behavior and attitudes. However, the boys' groups tend to be better organized and to have greater stability in membership than do the girls' groups.

By means of participation in group activities the preadolescent learns the necessity for cooperation; attains a sense of personal worth, that is, learns what makes him acceptable to others of his own age; acquires such characteristics as loyalty, responsibility, consideration for others. Likewise, he learns much about honor, friendship, and unselfishness. In addition, he gains in self-reliance and in perseverance in effort. The mentally superior child is frequently rejected by preadolescent groups and the shy child is likely to be overlooked. Among boys lack of certain skills in games, particularly in playing ball, may be reasons for rejection. During the preadolescent years children are cruel and not likely to be considerate of those who do not measure up to group standards. Another characteristic manifested during the preadolescent years is a strong tendency among both boys and girls toward hero worship, which leads the child to idealize and to imitate in his conduct those whom he considers to be heroes. Both boys and girls admire intensely the leader and the adventurer whether these be characters of literature, of history, of legend, or of real life.

Recognition of the possibilities latent in the preadolescent spontaneous group has led to the formation of adult-directed groups such as the Boy and Girl Scouts and similar organizations. These organizations endeavor to organize and standardize group interests and activities under the direction of skilled adult leaders who can help the preadolescent to plan and carry out group activities in an efficient manner.

Interests During Preadolescence. The interests of preadolescents reflect their progress toward maturity, and also demonstrate that boys express preferences for activities which are typically masculine, and girls for those which are typically feminine in nature. During this period a number of new behavior patterns appear. Both boys and girls become increasingly interested in their own play groups and activities. In keeping with the social development characteristic of the period, the most conspicuous play interests of the preadolescent boy consist of group activities in the form of organized play and team games. About the eleventh year these activities feature well-organized, competitive games such as baseball and football, in which fixed rules and teamwork are stressed. Through these team games the boy learns the necessity for cooperation and develops traits of self-reliance and perseverance. The preadolescent boy retains his interest in two types of toys, electric trains and constructive or scientific toys such as chemistry sets, model planes, rockets, spaceships, and the like. The boy toward the end of the period also manifests interest in using tools. Also, boys during this period seem interested in building some kind of meeting place with whatever material the environment offers. This is a group project and takes the form of a tree hut, shack, cove, wigwam, or the like.

Preadolescent girls have usually put aside dolls and dramatic, imaginative play seems to have disappeared entirely from their activities. While the "team sense" is not strong in girls it exists to some extent, usually involving small groups, and is manifested in such games as field hockey and basketball. The chief play interests of girls during this period seem to be centered in dancing, both folk and social, in music, and in some outdoor activities such as tennis, skating, and jumping rope. Cooking, sewing, and other homemaking activities also form part of their play interests.

During preadolescence collecting reaches its peak. Almost all preadolescents collect some "prized possessions" such as stamps, coins, match folders, records, pictures of athletes and movie stars, nature objects, and the like. What is collected depends somewhat upon convenience as well as attractiveness. Girls' collections are more likely to be more aesthetic than those of boys and many include such objects as dolls from foreign countries, figurines, shells, and the like. As the child grows older the collections tend to become more specialized. Usually preadolescents vie with others and strive to surpass in the number of objects, and in the arrangement or organization of the collection. Likewise, a great deal of trading activity usually takes place. Collecting may become a real educational experience.

Although the period is marked by a great number of physical interests and activities, the preadolescent has also developed intellectual interests, principally reading interests. Having learned to read, that is, having mastered the techniques of reading during the primary grades, the preadolescent reads to learn. He will continue to acquire considerable skill, efficiency, and speed in reading during the elementary grades. The preadolescent should read for enjoyment and as a wise use of leisure. In fact, preadolescence is the time where free reading reaches its peak. Reading interests will touch many fields of literature and there is a notable increase in the reading of newspapers and magazines. The foundations are laid for the reading habits and interests which will last a lifetime. The preadolescent's intellectual development enables him to comprehend increasingly difficult material and also to read selectively for different purposes. In a period which is characterized by strong hero-worshiping tendencies, biography and historical narratives featuring heroic qualities are preferred, especially by boys. Through his reading the preadolescent becomes familiar with problems of human relationships outside of the family, the immediate neighborhood, and the peer group. He also learns something concerning the objects, forces, and ideals which motivate conduct. Boys' interests center in science fiction, factual stories, biography, and stories featuring adventure, action, and mystery. Girls manifest interest in stories of romance, devotion, sacrifice, and home life. During preadolescence girls also make their first contacts with adult fiction. Girls read more books than boys do but not necessarily better books.

One of the strongest free-time interests during preadolescence is the comics, Interest in comics begins as soon as the child learns to read and they continue to exercise an unusual appeal during the period of preadolescence because of the action, adventure, and extravagant imagination which characterize them. Interest in movies is manifested by the fact that most preadolescents attend movies at least once a week. While there has been a decline in radio-listening activities since the advent of television, preadolescents usually spend at least twenty hours per week listening to radio programs and watching television. As was the case in reading, there are sex differences in radio and television interests. Programs featuring comedy, variety, and crime drama are popular with both boys and girls. Interests in adventure, westerns, and sports programs are predominantly masculine, while preference for programs featuring popular music and dramas of love, private life, and glamor are more typically feminine. While interest in television is seasonal, nevertheless the preadolescent devotes at least two hours per day, and twice that time on the weekends, to television programs. With the use of educational television this medium may contribute to a greater extent to learning experiences.[12]

Educational Provisions During Preadolescence. During this period the child will pass through Grades 4, 5, and 6, the elementary grades. By the time he enters Grade 4 the child should have acquired sufficient skills to provide a solid foundation upon which to build. He should be able to utilize well the basic processes of reading and arithmetic. Likewise he should be able to write legibly, and, because of growth both in use and in understanding vocabulary, he should be able to express his thoughts clearly. The elementary grades constitute a critical time in reading development because it is during these grades that the child must learn

[12] W. E. Schramm, *Television in the Lives of Our Children* (Stanford, Calif.: Stanford University Press, 1961).

to analyze what he reads, to read for facts, to detect relationships, to follow a line of reasoning in order to increase knowledge. He also must learn to read for appreciation. Reading disabilities reach their peak during the elementary grades. The incidence of such disabilities is greater among boys than among girls. As has previously been noted, emotional problems often constitute a factor in reading disabilities. In turn, lack of achievement in reading may lead to emotional problems. Other factors which contribute to reading difficulties during preadolescence include: bilingualism in the home, poor cultural background, and a high incidence of childhood diseases.

Arithmetical understanding involving competency both in use of computational skills and in problem-solving must be acquired in the elementary grades. Mathematical concepts such as "decimal," "fraction," "product," and the like must be developed. Spatial concepts become increasingly important in learning to apply basic knowledge to situations which become more and more complex. The mental development which is evident in increased ability to utilize abstract ideas, to judge, to reason, and to comprehend cause and effect should enable the child to become aware of interrelationships among various areas of knowledge. During the elementary grades the child acquires the ability to make the discriminations of time and space required for the study of geography and history. During these grades also the child should acquire and continue to develop effective study skills.

In addition to stress upon improvement of the basic skills previously mastered, the curriculum of the elementary school is designed to provide materials, contents, and experiences which have not only immediate but also permanent values. The broad curriculum of the present-day elementary school through selected subject matter and directed experiences in the areas of the language arts, the social studies, science, arts, physical and health education seeks to develop communication and computational skills, critical thinking and creative expression, social relationships and scientific understanding, appreciation and worthwhile interests.

DEVELOPMENTAL TASKS FOR THE PERIODS OF MIDDLE CHILDHOOD AND PREADOLESCENCE

As the child progresses from birth to maturity there are certain learnings, adjustments, and achievements which he must master if this progress is to be normal. According to Havighurst, who introduced the concept of developmental tasks into the psychological and educational literature, each period of growth and development is accompanied by certain tasks which are appropriate to the physical, mental, and social development of the individual. He has defined *development task* as

> . . . a task which arises at or about a certain period in the life of the individual, successful achievement of which leads to his happiness and to success with later tasks, while failure leads to unhappiness in the individual, disapproval by society and difficulty with later tasks.[13]

The concept of development tasks aids the teacher in the timing of educational efforts. Ideas, techniques, and skills are more easily learned when they come at the teachable moments. Developmental tasks arise mainly from physical maturation. However, there are some developmental tasks which arise primarily from the cultural premise of society, and others which originate in the personal value and aspirations of the individual.

For the periods of middle childhood and preadolescence — roughly from six to twelve years — the following developmental tasks have been listed:

1. Learning physical skills necessary for ordinary games.
2. Building wholesome attitudes toward oneself as a growing organism.
3. Learning to get along with age-mates.
4. Learning the appropriate masculine or feminine social role.
5. Developing fundamental skills in reading, writing, and calculating.
6. Developing concepts necessary for everyday living.
7. Developing conscience, morality and a scale of values.
8. Achieving personal independence.
9. Developing attitudes toward social groups and institutions.[14]

EXERCISES

1. Outline this chapter.
2. List and define the terms which you have learned from your study of this chapter.
3. Describe the development — physical, mental, emotional, and social — which takes place during the period of middle childhood.
4. What are the most significant effects of the transition from home to school which the child must make at the beginning of the period of early childhood?
5. What essential factors are involved in reading readiness? Discuss the importance of each.

---

[13] R. J. Havighurst, *Developmental Tasks and Education* (New York: Longmans, Green & Co., Inc., 1953), p. 2.

[14] *Ibid.*, pp. 25–46.

6. What are the stages involved in learning to read? Discuss the importance of each.
7. Describe the development — physical, mental, social, and emotional — which takes place during the period of preadolescence.
8. Discuss the interests of preadolescents.
9. Discuss the following statements:
   a) During the primary grades improvement in language ability is manifested primarily by increase in size of vocabulary.
   b) The boy learns civics from his teacher and democracy from the gang.
   c) During preadolescence collecting reaches its peak.
   d) Having learned to read in the first three grades, the child from that time on reads to learn.
   e) During the elementary grades the child should acquire and continue to develop effective study skills.
10. What educational provisions are made for:
    a) The child from 6 to 9 years;
    b) The child from 9 or 10 to puberty.

SELECTED REFERENCES FOR STUDY AND READING

Ausubel, D. P., *Theory and Problems of Child Development* (New York: Grune & Stratton, 1958).

Baller, W. R., *Readings in the Psychology of Growth and Development* (New York: Holt, Rinehart and Winston, Inc., 1962).

Bayer, L. M., and Bayley, N., *Growth Diagnosis* (Chicago: The University of Chicago Press, 1959).

Beller, W. R., and Charles, D. C., *Psychology of Human Growth and Development* (New York: Holt, Rinehart and Winston, Inc., 1961).

Blair, A. W., and Burton, W. H., *Growth and Development of the Preadolescent* (New York: Appleton-Century-Crofts, Inc., 1951).

Breckenridge, M. E., and Vincent, E. L., *Child Development,* 4 ed. (Philadelphia: W. B. Saunders Co., 1960).

Davis, D. C., *Patterns of Primary Education* (New York: Harper and Row, 1963).

English, H. B., *Dynamics of Child Development* (New York: Holt, Rinehart and Winston, Inc., 1961).

Fitzgerald, J. A., and Fitzgerald, P. G., *Methods and Curricula in Elementary Education* (Milwaukee: The Bruce Publishing Co., 1955).

Geoghegan, Sister Barbara, Pollard, Sister Marie Baptista, and Kelly, W. A., *Developmental Psychology* (Milwaukee: The Bruce Publishing Co., 1963), Chaps. 9 and 10.

Gesell, A., and Ilg, F. L., *The Child From Five to Ten* (New York: Harper & Row, 1946).

Gordon, I. J., *Human Development* (New York: Harper & Row, 1962), Chaps. 8–13.

Havighurst, R. J., *Human Development and Education* (New York: Longmans, Green and Co., Inc., 1953).

Hawkes, G. R., and Pease, D., *Behavior and Development From 5 to 12* (New York: Harper & Row, 1962).
Hurlock, E. B., *Developmental Psychology,* 2 ed. (New York: McGraw-Hill Book Co., 1959).
Hutt, M. L., and Gibby, R. G., *The Child: Development and Adjustment* (Boston: Allyn and Bacon, Inc., 1960).
Lane, H., and Beauchamp, M., *Understanding Human Development* (Englewood Cliffs, N. J.: Prentice-Hall, Inc., 1959), Chaps. 10 and 11.
Loomis, M. J., *The Preadolescent: Three Major Concerns* (New York: Appleton-Century-Crofts, Inc., 1959).
Martin, W. F., and Stengler, L. B., *Child Behavior and Development,* rev. ed. (New York: Harcourt, Brace & World, 1959).
Millard, C. V., *Child Growth and Development in the Elementary School,* rev. ed. (Boston: D. C. Heath and Co., 1958).
Millard, C. V., and Rothney, J. W., *The Elementary School Child: A Book of Cases* (New York: Holt, Rinehart and Winston, Inc., 1957).
National Society for the Study of Education, Sixty-Second Yearkbook, Part I, *Child Psychology,* 1963.
Norvell, G. W., *What Boys and Girls Like to Read* (Morristown, N. J.: Silver, Burdett Co., 1958).
Odenwald, R. P., *Your Child's World* (New York: Random House, Inc., 1958).
Olson, W. C., *Child Development,* 2 ed. (Boston: D. C. Heath & Co., 1959).
Pikunas, J., and Albrecht, E. J., *Psychology of Human Development* (New York: McGraw-Hill Book Co., 1961), Chaps. 12 and 13.
Prescott, D. A., *The Child in the Education Process* (New York: McGraw-Hill Book Co., 1957).
Russell, D. H., *Children Learn to Read,* 2 ed. (Boston: Ginn and Co., 1961).
Sarason, S., Davidson, K. S., Lightall, F. F., Waite, R. R., and Ruhlbush, B. K., *Anxiety in Elementary School Children* (New York: John Wiley and Sons, Inc., 1960).
Seidman, J. M., *The Child: A Book of Readings* (New York: Holt, Rinehart and Winston, Inc., 1958), Selections 18, 33, 38, and 65.
Stern, C., and Gould, T., *Children Discover Reading* (New York: Random House, Inc., 1963).
Stone, L. J., and Church, J., *Childhood and Adolescence* (New York: Random House, Inc., 1957), Chaps. 8 and 9.
Thorpe, L. P., *Child Psychology and Development,* 3 ed. (New York: The Ronald Press Co., 1962).
Vincent, E. L., and Martin, P. C., *Human Psychological Development* (New York: The Ronald Press Co., 1961), Chap. 6.
Watson, R. I., *Psychology of the Child* (New York: John Wiley & Sons, Inc., 1959).

chapter 5

The Adolescent[1]

There is in the life of every human being a significant segment, approximately eight or more years in duration, when he is no longer a child and when he has not yet become an adult. During this time of transition, the characteristics of the child are being exchanged for those of the adult. The very expressive term *adolescence* has been employed to designate this period. It is then that many significant and distinctive changes take place in the individual. These changes occur gradually rather than suddenly, for adolescence is the last stage of the continuous process of growth and development which has been going on since birth. Thus, the boy and the girl pass by imperceptible degrees from infancy, through childhood and preadolescence, to this final phase. As a result of the changes which occur during adolescence new thoughts, new interests, new experiences, and new strengths become evident. The adolescent becomes self-conscious, social conscious, and sex conscious. It is during adolescence also that the vigor and energy, the enthusiasm and self-assertiveness, the devotion and the daring which are so characteristic of youth manifest themselves in thought, word, and action.

As a consequence adolescence involves the necessity of adapting to new emergencies, of measuring up to new demands, of assuming new responsibilities. The adolescent is faced with the necessity of making strenuous efforts to adjust to many and complex phases of life. These efforts give rise to numerous problems and difficulties which make adolescence a critical period in psychological development.

---

[1] The materials presented in this chapter have been derived from *Developmental Psychology* by Sister Barbara Geoghegan, Sister Marie Baptista Pollard and W. A. Kelly, Chapter 11.

It is during this period that ideals become set, that character is determined, that future success or failure is almost invariably decided. The realization of this has led to a universal recognition of the fact that at no other time in life is there greater need for providing thoughtful counsel, understanding guidance, and prudent direction in order that a youth may achieve that self-control and self-sufficiency which will enable him to take his place in the adult world; which will help him to adjust to that world; which will aid him in performing the tasks necessary both to live his life and also to make his living.

If a youth passes through this period of adolescence simply and normally, the proper foundations for a wholesome successful adult life will have been laid. However, preparation is required during the earlier periods of growth and development in order that he may meet adequately the problems arising during adolescence. The adolescent is dependent upon the experiences and relationships of his earlier years and how he was prepared before adolescence. Striking and distinctive as are the problems of adolescence, they have their foundations in the early life of the child. In fact there exists no characteristic of adolescence, good or bad, the germ of which may not be found in childhood and the consequences of which may not be traced in adulthood. Adolescence is the culmination of all that has gone before, for it is then that the effectiveness of preparation, either adequate or faulty, becomes so dramatically evident. The period of adolescence, then, must be considered in context as related to the past and as preparation for the future; that is, adolescent development is dependent in many ways on childhood experiences, while what transpires during adolescence influences maturity.

The Meaning of Adolescence. The ways in which adolescence has been described and defined are as many and as varied as are the approaches to the study of human development. It has been considered in terms of a biological process which begins with puberty and ends with maturity. It has been described in terms of chronological age as extending from the twelfth to the twentieth year, that is, through the "teen years." It has been characterized as a social-cultural transition from childhood to maturity. It would seem that any inclusive definition of adolescence should contain all of these notions, that is, the process of growing up, the time during which this process ordinarily occurs, and the transitional nature of the process.

The term *adolescence* has been derived from the Latin verb *adolescere,* the basic meaning of which is "to ripen," that is, "to grow to maturity." Actually it has been derived from the present participle, *adolescens,* denoting the process of growing up or growing toward or into maturity. In its broadest sense adolescence is the transitional period between childhood and adulthood. It is the last stage of immaturity during which a gradual physiological and psychological transition is made from one important phase of life to another of equal importance, that is, from the dependency which is characteristic of childhood to the independence which is indicative of maturity. It involves a gradual, continual, and complex process of growth and development during which the appearance and behavior of the child are replaced by the appearance and behavior of a mature person. It is the time during which the boy and the girl are in the process of completing their physical, mental, social, emotional, and moral preparation for maturity.

While the time during which the process of growing up takes place is often considered to correspond approximately to the "teen years," extending from the thirteenth to the nineteenth years, nevertheless, adolescence cannot readily be limited to the precise span of these years, or described in terms of time alone. The age limits assigned to this period are relative and arbitrary. Chronological age is a poor measure to choose in determining the limits of the period. Actually there is no definite year which may be considered as marking the beginning or the end of the period. There is a wide range of individual differences in the age at which adolescence begins and ends. Adolescence may and frequently does begin shortly before or after the age of thirteen. Some individuals may become adolescent at the age of ten or twelve, others at the age of fifteen or sixteen or even later. There are "early" and "late" maturers. Likewise, in certain individuals adolescence undoubtedly extends beyond the nineteenth year. That which distinguishes the adolescent is not so much his age as the fact that he is a person who is passing through a stage of transition. He is passing from childhood to maturity, and during the transition he is not firmly established in either category. He is no longer a child but yet he is not quite mature. Adolescence involves a process of development and adjustment during the social-cultural transition between childhood and maturity.

It is customary, because of the length of the period and because various forms of development occur at different times, to divide the period of adolescence into two stages, designated as early and later adolescence. The early stage of adolescence consists of the first four years, from the ages of twelve or thirteen to sixteen or seventeen, and is considered as the time when the boy and the girl are growing out of childhood. The later stage of adolescence extends from the ages of sixteen or seventeen to the early twenties and is considered to be the time when the individual is growing toward maturity.

Puberty. Usually the limits of the period of adolescence have been described in terms of physical development, involving changes in structure and function. The boundaries of the period are considered to be puberty, which marks the onset or beginning, and maturity, which designates the end of the period. The term *puberty* has been derived from the Latin word *pubertas,* which denotes the physical changes characteristic of the beginning of the process of sexual maturation. It is applied to the earlier stage of physical development at which a person becomes functionally capable of producing offspring. It is the earliest stage at which the generative powers become established; the time during which the reproductive functions become operative. The term *pubescence* is employed to indicate the time during which certain physical changes accompanying sexual maturation occur. These physical changes involve chiefly the emergence of the primary and, more particularly, of the secondary sex characteristics.

The exact time at which puberty begins is difficult to establish and is subject to individual variations. The age at which puberty is attained appears to vary according to sex, racial background, climatic conditions, socioeconomic background, nutritional status, the physical condition of the individual, and general intelligence. Thus puberty does not begin at the same age for all individuals, nor do the physical changes occur in the same sequence in all individuals.

In girls the *menarche,* that is, the occurrence of the first menstrual period, is generally accepted as the criterion of the attainment of puberty. Various studies have indicated that in the United States the average age at which the first menstruation occurs is approximately thirteen, with the range extending from ten to sixteen or even later. In boys, however, no such conspicuous or recordable change presents specific evidence of the attainment of puberty. Accordingly the exact time of its advent in the boy is difficult to determine. However, such physical signs as the appearance of hair on the face of the boy, the presence of pubic hair, the change of voice and other secondary sex characteristics are usually accepted as approximate indices of the attainment of puberty. The best evidence seems to indicate that puberty tends to occur from one to two years later in boys than in girls.

The development of the genital organs and the reproductive system constitutes the primary sex characteristics of puberty. In addition, a variety of bodily changes which occur gradually constitute the secondary sex characteristics. These serve as indices of masculinity and femininity. They include the development of the breasts, enlargement of pelvic breadth, and widening of hips in girls; the appearance of pubic and axillary hair, changes in bodily shape and contour, changes in voice and in the activity of the sweat and skin glands in both sexes. The secondary sex characteristics are usually considered to be of greater significance psychologically than are the primary characteristics for the reason that they are more readily observable, and also because these secondary characteristics play an important role in the determination of the physical attractiveness of the individual as a male or female person.

It is customary to describe the advent of puberty, and the physical changes which take place during and consequent to puberty, in terms of the average. This is done because most individuals experience essentially similar patterns and sequence of bodily growth. However, as has been noted previously, variations exist both with respect to the onset of puberty and the sequence of physical growth. There are individuals in whom the onset of puberty occurs earlier than the average and in whom the changes in physical growth occur more rapidly. Likewise there are some in whom the advent of puberty occurs later than the average and in whom the changes take place more slowly. In each case problems of adjustment, both social and emotional, may arise, depending upon the extent and conspicuousness of the acceleration or retardation. In many ways and in numerous situations the individual whose maturation is slow or late may be placed at a greater disadvantage, while early maturation may often constitute an advantage.

Physical Development. The first step toward maturity involves physical and physiological growth and development. In order to attain an adequate understanding of adolescence it is essential to have a knowledge of the physical changes which take place, and particularly of the relationship of these changes to the psychological functions. Throughout the period, physical development has important psychological and social implications and also constitutes a contributory factor, either favorable or adverse, to the process of adjustment. Behavior, particularly in the early stage of adolescence, is dependent in no small part on the physical changes which occur in the individual.

As has previously been indicated the advent of puberty, which is part of the normal growth process, marks the beginning of adolescence. Puberty involves physical growth, physical changes, and corresponding development of physical functions. A considerable amount of research has been devoted to ascertaining exactly what physical growth and development, what changes in structure and in function, take place during adolescence. During the early stage of the period the rate of physical growth is accelerated rapidly and to some extent suddenly, leading to what has been designated as the *pubertal growth spurt.* Among the earliest indications of this growth spurt is the evident increase in height, which is followed by an increase in weight. The increase in height is due to skeletal growth in the long bones of the body while the increase in weight is due largely to the development of muscles, particularly the large muscles, which grow in size, firmness, and power. This muscular development is more apparent in boys than in girls. The Harvard Growth Study[2] reported that the age of greatest increase in height occurs among girls at the age of 12.56 years, and among boys at the age of 14.78 years. The increase among boys may range from 6 to 12 inches, and among girls it is slightly less. The duration of the rapid growth in height is usually about one year. In another study[3] it was established that the period of rapid growth in girls is closely associated with the menarche or the onset of puberty. It is to be noted that, since puberty begins earlier in girls than in boys, the accelerated rate of growth also occurs at an earlier age. Thus, at the beginning of adolescence there is a period of approximately two years when girls grow faster than boys both in stature and in weight. Eventually the boys catch up and grow not only faster but for a longer period of time. Girls ordinarily attain full height approximately at the age of eighteen, while boys as a rule tend to continue to grow until they have

---

[2] F. K. Shuttleworth, *The Physical and Mental Growth of Girls and Boys, Age Six to Nineteen, in Relation to Age at Maximum Growth,* Monograph of Society for Research in Child Development, Vol. IV, No. 3, 1939.

[3] F. K. Shuttleworth, *Sexual Maturation and Physical Growth of Girls, Age Six to Nineteen,* Monograph of Society for Research in Child Development, Vol. II, No. 5, 1937.

reached the early twenties. However, growth in boys slows down considerably after the eighteenth year.

As a concomitant of the growth spurt which characterizes early adolescence, changes take place in bodily proportions. The various parts and organs of the body do not grow and develop uniformly or at the same rate of speed.[4] In fact growth seems to take place in segments. Particularly affected by the uneven rate of growth are the arms, legs, hands, feet, and nose. In both boys and girls much of this growth is centered in the extremities, that is, in the legs, arms and neck rather than in the trunk. During early adolescence the individual seems to shoot upward, legs and arms stretch out; hands become too large, feet too long; and as a consequence the boy or girl is likely to appear somewhat "gangling" or "gawky." As a result of this rapid, erratic, and uneven growth the adolescent is sometimes unable to coordinate and to control muscular responses. This may account in part for the temporary awkwardness often evident in the lack of poise, and the clumsiness which may be so embarrassing to the adolescent. Since the finer muscles which govern growth of movement develop slowly, muscular coordination and bodily control require time. However, most psychologists are of the opinion that much of the so-called awkwardness of early adolescence stems not so much from uneven rate of growth as from emotional tension caused by ridicule or fear of criticism, which results in a feeling of physical inadequacy and may arouse deep resentment. Thus the physical clumsiness may actually be due to embarrassment and self-consciousness rather than to uneven rate of growth. As Goodenough and Tyler have stated:

> The adolescent who is so clumsy and awkward that disaster seems to follow wherever he goes may show surprising dexterity of hand in his workshop when no one is watching him and splendid body control on the athletic field. His awkwardness is not due to lack of motor skill but is the result of embarrassment and self-consciousness.[5]

Changes occur in the size and functioning of practically every part and organ of the body. During early adolescence disproportion of facial features often occurs. The nose seems to grow faster than the other features and this may be disconcerting to the individual. Other changes

---

[4] This tendency of the body's various organs to grow at separate rates is termed asynchrony. See L. J. Stone and J. Church, *Childhood and Adolescence* (New York: Random House, Inc., 1957), p. 301.

[5] F. L. Goodenough and L. E. Tyler, *Developmental Psychology* (New York: Appleton-Century-Crofts, Inc., 1959), pp. 388–389.

include considerable growth of the thorax, with the result that the chest cavity and lungs enlarge and the respiratory capacity is increased. The circulatory system also participates in the acceleration of growth, involving a rise in blood pressure, in pulse rate, and in basal metabolic rate.

Change of voice, which is characteristic of early adolescence, is due to the enlargement of the larynx and elongation of the vocal cords. This change of voice is more evident in the boy than in the girl. The boy's voice deepens perceptibly, becomes an octave lower in pitch, more masculine in texture and volume, pleasanter in quality. Ordinarily it requires two years for the boy to acquire complete control of his voice. During this time the lack of control over the lower tones is frequently evidenced by the so-called "broken voice" which may at the most inappropriate moment fluctuate treacherously from "basso profundo" to a "squeaky soprano," much to the discomfiture of the boy, since this may become a source of ridicule. Most boys in the early stage of adolescence seem to experience the "breaking voice," but in some, however, the change seems to be gradual, or the individual seems to acquire control quickly and thus prevent noticeable difficulty with the voice. The girl's voice changes also, but to a lesser extent. The change is not one of pitch but rather involves a moderate lowering of the voice, a gradual increase in tonal quality, which becomes fuller and richer.

While many of the physical changes which occur during early adolescence are obvious, some others of equal, if not greater, significance are less evident because they take place within the body. Among the most important of these is the increased activity of the endocrine glands, which influence to a great extent the growth, metabolism, and emotions of the individual. The pituitary increases production of *somatotrophin* and *gonadatotrophin.* The former influences general physical growth, the latter the functional maturation of the sex glands.[6] The hormones of the gonads or sex glands (the testes in the male and the ovaries in the female), known as estrogen and testosterone, in turn influence the development of the secondary sex characteristics which differentiate the sexes.

An increase also occurs in secretory activity of the sweat glands, particularly in the armpits and in the genital regions. The sebaceous or oil-producing glands also become more active so that both skin and hair may become more oily. Overactivity or malfunctioning of these glands

[6] J. Pikunas and E. J. Albrecht, *Psychology of Human Development* (New York: McGraw-Hill Book Co., 1961), pp. 174–175.

frequently leads to skin eruptions and blemishes, particularly acne, which are common among both boys and girls during the early years of adolescence.

During later adolescence, that is, from the ages of sixteen or seventeen to the early twenties, the body becomes perfected in structure and integrated in functions. By the beginning of this stage the individual has attained nine tenths of adult height and about two thirds of adult weight. During later adolescence the body becomes better proportioned. Through continuous muscle growth the individual acquires greater coordination, increased strength, and the motor ability essential for the acquisition and development of skills. The peak of physical coordination is reached. By the end of later adolescence both sexes have attained maximum growth in height, but in weight considerable variation exists. The physical equipment of the individual is practically complete both in growth and in control. The build and carriage of the body will become those of an adult. The awkwardness and ungainliness which may have marked the early years of adolescence give way by degree to ease of movement and grace of form. Facial features become better proportioned. The activity of the skin glands becomes stabilized, with the result that acne and other skin blemishes decrease to a marked extent and eventually disappear. The rate of respiration stabilizes, the change of voice is completed and the qualities of the mature voice are developed. Physical vitality is high and health is good.

Mental Development. During adolescence mental development is not so readily observed or so easily appraised as is the physical. Since the early years of the present century considerable attention has been focused upon ascertaining the extent of mental development. During that time numerous investigations have been conducted in which endeavors have been made to ascertain the rate of mental development. The means employed to determine this rate have been tests of mental ability or of general intelligence administered at successive age levels. These investigations have indicated that great variations exist in both the rate and the pattern of mental development. However, there seems to be agreement among the investigators that during the early stage of adolescence the growth curve shows a continuous steady gain or improvement in general intelligence and tapers off gradually in the later stage of adolescence, becoming less marked until ultimate growth is attained, probably during the early twenties. It is to be recognized that this is the general picture of mental development, and that there are many variations among individual adolescents.

There seems to be considerable agreement that during the period of adolescence, mental development is characterized by an expanding of the mental powers, which is evident in a broadening and deepening of thought, and in the improvement of judgment and reasoning as well as the capacity to perform increasingly difficult mental tasks. As a result of this development, improvement in performance is evident in the whole field of mental activity. This improvement is demonstrated in a more effective and efficient utilization of the processes of perception, imagination, logical memory, and attention; and particularly in the ability to form abstract ideas, to judge, to reason, to formulate decisions, to acquire knowledge, to learn.

A fundamental characteristic of mental development during adolescence is "heightened sensitivity," that is, an increasing awareness of and sensitivity to various aspects of environment as apprehended by the senses, involving changes in the manner of interpreting and reacting to these. During adolescence sensory impressions are interpreted and given meaning in terms of a wide background of experience and knowledge, which has been acquired both incidentally and as a result of training during the previous periods of childhood and preadolescence. This enrichment of experience, together with more intensive and accurate use of observation, enable the adolescent to utilize in better fashion the process of perception which is basic in all learning, and important also in various aspects of adjustment.

Because of the increasing sensitivity to various aspects of his environment, the adolescent's world becomes larger in space and in time. Because he has acquired a more impressive background of experiences to recall, the imagination, that is, the capacity of representing past experiences and also of combining elements of these experiences into novel forms, is often rich, vivid, colorful, and sometimes unrestrained. This development of imagination is frequently evidenced in an increased appreciation of literature, music, and art. The richness and vividness of the imagination during adolescence may be expressed, often very skillfully, in the form of poetry and in artistic productions of various kinds while even commonplace writing and speech are likely to be embellished by descriptive adjectives, often superlatives. Likewise, in the early stage of adolescence, there is a tendency for imagination to be expressed in the form of exaggeration.

Daydreaming is a universal form of self-expression and escape during adolescence, probably because of the increase in problems of emotional adjustment. Daydreaming involves solving difficulties in fantasy by creating imaginary situations in which the individual is the center of attention. Frequently this involves a wish for approbation and success. Daydreaming becomes a genuine danger if it is indulged in excessively, and when it becomes a substitute for real accomplishment. It should be noted, however, that not all daydreaming is unhealthy or harmful. It may be a constructive way of dealing with problems as well as a means of evading them. It may actually be helpful, for if it keeps in touch with reality, it may be a spur to enterprise. Few individuals would accomplish anything noteworthy if they did not daydream about it beforehand. The adolescent should have an active but realistically controlled imagination. Usually from about the age of sixteen on, or during the later stage of adolescence, there is evident in most individuals an increase in the ability to control the functioning of the imagination.

Many research studies have indicated that throughout adolescence considerable development takes place in logical or intellectual memory. This aspect of memory involves the capacity to retain, to recall, and to recognize past experiences and ideas not as discrete impressions but as items which are associated and linked together in a logical connection or system. Logical memory implies understanding and comprehension of the significance and relatedness of materials. It depends on the ability to recognize, analyze, understand, and organize experiences, ideas, and judgments into a functioning whole. Because of the development of the logical memory, routine repetition and drill which ordinarily involve rote memory are likely to be considered irksome and annoying by the adolescent. It is worthy of note that as a rule logical memory tends to be better developed among boys than among girls of the same age.

The span of attention increases gradually with age. During adolescence the capacity for voluntary or sustained attention continues to develop and is strengthened considerably. Voluntary attention involves purposive focusing or concentration upon a specific object, situation, activity, or mental process for the purpose of understanding its nature and knowing its qualities. This type of attention makes possible the exclusion of the unimportant, and gives place and value to the important. Voluntary attention is influenced by many factors including emotional responses, attitudes, ability to discern relationships and especially values. The direction of attention is largely determined by interest, and consequently successful concentration is linked with the interests of the individual.

Most noteworthy, however, is the progress which is made during adolescence toward intellectual maturity. This progress is due both to the continuance of mental growth and the expansion of experience. It involves an increase in the ability to think in general terms, to understand, and to apply abstract ideas; to comprehend meaning with a resultant expansion of vocabulary; to weigh values objectively in the forming of judgments; to grasp new relationships; to group ideas into logical and coherent systems; to reason clearly and constructively for the purpose of achieving insight into increasingly complex situations. Thus intellectual development during adolescence involves improvement in the ability to perform increasingly difficult mental tasks; to engage in more complex and exact thought processes; to utilize symbolization; to be aware of complex meanings and interrelationships; to detect shades of meaning and to be discriminative; to make generalizations from specific facts and to make applications of rules and principles, that is, to apply problem-solving techniques to complex situations, and to utilize experiences in meaningful ways.

While the ability to make decisions has not been studied to any great extent from a developmental point of view, nevertheless the adolescent may be expected to manifest increasing maturity in this aspect of intellectual development also. The primary element in making decisions consists of weighing motives and values in the form of judgments and choosing the motive or value upon which to act in a particular situation. The significance of improvement in making decisions during adolescence is evident, since during that period many important choices which will affect the whole life of the individual must be made.

Intellectual development during adolescence is evidenced in the learning process through better organization, arrangement, analysis, and classification of knowledge. Since learning ability is potentially as great as it will be in adult years, adolescence is probably the optimum period for learning. Accordingly, the adolescent may profitably be subjected to learning experiences which are greater in amount, increasingly difficult in type, and challenging to his capacities. In addition, the adolescent may be expected to exercise initiative in thinking in an orderly, discriminative, systematic fashion; to be critical and to some extent original in his thinking, as well as to be able to express and to communicate thoughts adequately and well. Intellectual development is conditioned by native capacity, by environmental opportunities, by training and education, together with the conscious desire and effort to learn.

Emotional Development. Generally the outstanding characteristic of development during adolescence is considered to be the emotional aspect. This is due primarily to the idealism and enthusiasm, the self-assertiveness and initiative, the enthusiasm and inconsistencies, the moods and conflicts which are manifested during the period. In fact it was customary for several decades, as a result of the early studies of G. Stanley Hall, to describe adolescence as a period of "storm and stress," characterized by inner emotional conflicts and turbulence; these in turn were attributed to the biological changes which were taking place, and the increasingly complex social demands upon the adolescent. There is no doubt that during adolescence the emotions increase in range, quality, and intensity. However, there is considerable doubt that such development necessarily makes adolescence a period of emotional instability. The preponderance of research has failed to support the theory of "storm and stress." Most studies in the area have revealed that the emotions tend to unfold gradually during the earlier periods; and that during adolescence they become fuller and richer, react with greater intensity to a wider variety of stimuli, and exercise considerable influence upon thought and action. Moreover, other characteristics of development which occur during adolescence — increased perceptual ability, vivid imagination, improved capacity for reasoning, enlarged social consciousness, and interest in adult activities — enable the individual to attach deeper emotional significance to experiences, objects, events, and activities.

While the research evidence has indicated that adolescence is not necessarily a period of general "storm and stress" characterized by emotional upheaval and unpleasantness, neither is it an idyllic period free of all problems. In fact there are many typical situations which may be disturbing, may constitute important sources of anxiety and stress, and may exercise potent influence on attitudes and behavior during adolescence. Anxiety is most frequently caused by the individual's reaction to characteristics incidental to physical growth and development.

In fact, any physical characteristic which marks the individual as different from his peers may become a matter of serious concern. Clumsiness and awkwardness resulting from unevenness of growth may become embarrassing and increase self-consciousness, particularly among boys during the early stage of the period. Disproportionate growth of any organ or feature, such as unusual size of hands or feet, or shape of nose or ears, may cause uneasiness and worry concerning appearance and the impression made upon others. Unhealthy and unsightly complexion due to skin blemishes and eruptions may also be a cause for concern. Changes in circulation may likewise generate anxieties. Early or late maturation may lead to insecurity, particularly among small boys who have not attained average height and weight, and among large or tall girls who have developed early. Both early development of the secondary sex characteristics and also retarded development of these characteristics may provide possibilities for worry and disturbance.

Since many new situations requiring adjustments and decisions must be faced throughout the period of adolescence, the individual, because of lack of experience and social awkwardness, may develop feelings of inadequacy in meeting these situations. As a result he is likely to become embarrassed easily, to be oversensitive to criticism, reprimands, and slights. Feelings of inadequacy are often accentuated by ridicule, by thoughtless criticism, by sarcasm, by any event in which the adolescent is placed in a disadvantageous position or is subjected to the scorn of his peers. Likewise, feelings of inadequacy may have their origins in such situations as failure to measure up to ideals, to attain the approval of others, to achieve acceptance by the group. Reaction against these feelings of inadequacy may be evidenced in shyness, in unwillingness to undertake new tasks, in withdrawal, in daydreams. It may also be expressed in overly aggressive behavior, in defiance, in a show of apparent indifference, and in outward bravado in an attempt to bolster self-esteem.

Moodiness is quite common during the period of adolescence. The individual fluctuates from absorbing enthusiasm to indifference, from cheerfulness to depression, from self-confidence to timidity and insecurity. He may be alternately generous and selfish; many manifest, at times, surprising maturity and equally surprising returns to immaturity. He often seems torn between admiration and denial, between attraction and repulsion; he often finds himself in situations in which his emotions may be markedly ambivalent; that is, he may manifest antagonistic and positive tendencies toward the same object or event. Likewise spurts of energy and intense activity are often followed for no obvious reason by periods of listlessness, inertia, and apparent laziness.

The development of the sexual functions which marks the inception of adolescence also exercises an influence upon emotional development, and plays a fundamental role in the process of emotional adjustment. This involves new desires and longings, the effects of which are frequently not understood by the adolescent. The boy and the girl become aware of the charms and grace of each other, and desire in turn to be attractive to the opposite sex. Interest in and companionship between the sexes replace the antagonistic spirit of the preadolescent years, but they come at a time when the individual feels hampered by self-consciousness and lack of confidence. The sex attraction is a basic and permanent fact which is one of the significant aspects of adolescence. Under wholesome conditions and adequate supervision, association of the sexes with each other is part of the normal development of youth from which both the boy and the girl profit.

By the beginning of adolescence both boys and girls should have acquired a correct, dignified, and reverent attitude toward sex. This attitude should be founded upon solid religious and moral principles. The way in which the adolescent regards sex will be dependent upon the manner in which it was dealt with in childhood and preadolescence. The understanding of sex as a normal part of life should have been acquired from correct sources, primarily the parents, through a gradual and continuous process which was sufficiently personal to meet and to anticipate slightly the needs of the individual. If, however, sex is a matter of ignorance, fear, or shame then the adolescent years will be disturbed. Beyond doubt the sex aspect of emotional development has received considerable, perhaps too much, emphasis, and many if not all of the tensions and difficulties of the period have been attributed to the awakening of sex interest. This should be rejected as an unwarranted oversimplification.

Social Development. During the early part of the period, the adolescent develops not only a consciousness of self as a person, but likewise a social awareness more complex than any he has heretofore known. Although social development has been a gradual and continuous process taking place within the family, the home, and the neighborhood since infancy, and in the school since early childhood, the adolescent becomes increasingly aware that he is a member of a social environment which is much wider in scope than the home, the neighborhood, and the school. Throughout the early years of adolescence he manifests this social awareness through the expression of new interests and attitudes, as well as in the extension and improvement of relationships of a social nature. Social contacts become wider with respect both to number of persons and also to the diversity and complexity of situations within which these contacts occur. In turn this increasingly complex social environment involves considerable adjustment in terms of habits, values, ideals, manners, and social poise.

Although socializing with age-mates in play groups and in school has constituted a natural part of the individual's experience since earliest childhood, it is not until adolescence is reached that he becomes fully aware both of his relationship to the group, and the significance of belonging to and being accepted by a group of his peers. Then group membership becomes a prerequisite for complete social development. This very evident aspect of social development during early adolescence is expressed through participation in the activities and in sharing in the experiences of a group of age-mates. Social success is achieved through acceptance by and approval of peers whose good will and esteem are valued. These peer relationships are important for and significant to the adolescent. They are the expression of the need to belong and to be an integral part of a social group. The achievement of approval, recognition, and status within the group is evidence of successful social adjustment on the part of the adolescent, since he is not accepted automatically in the group but must achieve a place in it for himself.

Peer culture, that is, the modes of behavior and social pressures of his own age-mates, constitutes a highly influential factor in determining how the adolescent thinks and acts. Because the peer culture is more demanding than and frequently in direct opposition to family control, it may become a source of conflict within the home. Conformity to peer-group customs and behavior constitutes a compelling form of maturation. Adolescents react more readily to prestige within their own age group than to most forms of adult approval.[7]

The adolescent displays enthusiasm and pride in peer-group activities. He is keenly aware of and attaches great importance to the opinions and attitudes of the group. There is an acceptance of and loyalty to

[7] See F. L. Goodenough and L. E. Tyler, *op. cit.*, pp. 400–401.

group ideals, standards, and principles. Conformity to group standards is demonstrated even to the point of adopting bizarre fashions in dress, appearance, and speech. Fads and oddities of dress include not only garments but also the manner of wearing them. The adolescent wants the same kinds of clothes, uses the same slang expressions, does the same things in the same way, enjoys the same amusements as his or her peers. By conforming to modes of dress, speech, and manners the adolescent is manifesting, at least on the surface, peer adjustment. Membership in the peer group provides the means for achieving personal security and a feeling of personal worth. To be different from the group becomes for the adolescent an intolerable situation. Deviation from the standards and values of the group means nonacceptance, and the adolescent finds rejection by the group a very disturbing factor since he thereby loses many opportunities for social contact that are important to his development.

The common form of the peer group in early adolescence is the "crowd." This is a spontaneous social unit composed of individuals who tend to share similar socioeconomic backgrounds and interests, and who participate in the same social activities. Generally the members of the crowd live in the same neighborhood and attend the same school. The crowd is composed of both boys and girls, usually, but not necessarily, in equal numbers. Its reason for being is to make provision for the establishment of normal social contacts between adolescent boys and girls which involve participation by and are suitable to both sexes. While the activities of the crowd vary, usually they consist of a few definite social functions such as parties or dances, but for the most part are informal recreational activities which often seem to be aimless. These include such things as watching television, listening to radio and to records, general group conversation, and social dancing — a favorite recreational activity during early adolescence. These activities sometimes take place in the home of one of the members of the crowd; sometimes in community centers or in school or church facilities; sometimes at a meeting place or "hangout" such as a confectionary or drugstore. The crowd is important because it involves both social contacts and a place to work out social relationships within the group, and in addition affords the young adolescent opportunity to learn and to express social skills. In a favorable setting, and under adequate guidance, the crowd has real value. It provides the opportunities for experience in getting along with others, for acquiring competence in social skills, for promoting and practicing the qualities both of leadership and cooperation, and for stimulating a "sense of responsibility."

Within the peer groups there are also adolescent "cliques." These are small, selective, restricted groups of individuals who share a close-knit association, common interests, and similar social values. The members of the clique usually have similar family, social, and ethnic backgrounds. The clique itself is likely to be snobbish and exclusive. Intense loyalty to each other and intolerance of outsiders are characteristics of the members. The clique is likely to be unhealthy both socially and emotionally. Various cliques compete with one another in socially unacceptable ways and frequently may interfere seriously with the orderly conduct of school activities.

During the later part of adolescence, that is, from age sixteen to twenty, the nature of the crowd changes to some extent. It tends to be composed of couples, is smaller in number than during the early years of the period, and its members engage in activities which are planned in a more definite fashion. Both the boy and the girl are likely to pay more attention to grooming and personal appearance in order to improve their personal assets. Facial appearance, hair, fingernails, and choice of clothes are matters of concern, and among girls the use of cosmetics increases. As the end of the period is approached the standards and values of the peer group tend to exercise less influence on the individual.

Approach to maturity during the later years of adolescence is evident also in a growing interest in and concern with social problems. This interest and this concern are manifested in the frequent expression of very definite opinions regarding social issues and world affairs, and in the quest for sincerity and honesty. In fact, at this time the adolescent may express impatience with existing conditions, and great enthusiasm for bringing about radical changes in the world, particularly in political, economic, and social conditions. Many adolescents seek to render social service and find opportunities to do so. This is an important attribute of adolescent idealism, which is characterized by altruistic and supernatural motives rather than by self-interest and social approval. A significant function of education during adolescence is to direct this idealism to things and actions of real and permanent value.

Interests During Adolescence. Among the significant aspects of development during the period of adolescence is the maturing of interests, which involves an expansion of and changes in the interest patterns and leisure-time activities of youth. The expansion and changes are reflected particularly in the recreational, social, and intellectual activities in which adolescent boys and girls engage. An additional characteristic of the period is the emergence of definite vocational interests and consequent planning in order to select an occupation. A vast number of descriptive research studies have been conducted in order to determine what are the interests of adolescents and in what activities they engage. While these investigations have not resulted in general agreement concerning adolescent interests and activities, nevertheless they have indicated that interests usually become fewer and deeper as well as increasingly complex in nature during the years of adolescence. Also these interests and activities are influenced by such factors as age, sex, degree of physical and mental development, environment, and social status.

Among the leisure-time activities in which adolescents engage, reading ranks very high. Reading interests become broader, are individualized and specialized, and usually give evidence of being more discriminative and critical. Since adolescence is characterized by tendencies toward hero worship, adventure, and achievement, it is natural that the reading preferences of the boy during this period should run to biography, travel, historical and adventurous narratives, sports, and war stories in which the fundamental motives are heroic example, courage, and loyalty. During the later part of the period the boy manifests an increasing preference for nonfiction and informational books in technical and scientific subjects. When he reads fiction, the boy's taste is likely to be manifested in sport and science stories. Adolescent girls usually manifest decided maturity in types of reading materials preferred. They read a great deal more fiction than do boys. They also express preference for poetry and for books on nature study, as well as for historical novels and for stories of home and school life flavored with a dash of romance. It is noteworthy that the interest in comic books, which were so popular in the early periods of development, persists among both sexes during the early years of adolescence, but declines during the later part of the period, particularly among girls.

During the adolescent period there is a notable increase in the number of magazines which are read, probably because of their greater availability. Boys manifest a preference for magazines that deal with sports, mechanics, science, mystery; and during the later part of adolescence they add magazines that feature world events and the political and economic aspects of life. The adolescent girl is more likely to express interest in magazines which feature "true-life" stories, motion-picture stars, and adult fiction of a sentimental type. During later adolescence both the boys and the girls appreciate the subtleties of adult humor in both books and magazines.

Among adolescents the reading of newspapers is universal. Both boys and girls exhibit interests in selected sections. The comic section, sports, front page, and editorials are popular in that order with both sexes throughout adolescence. In addition, the adolescent girl manifests considerable interest in the social section, the women's page, and in the motion-picture and theatrical reviews. The sports section continues to rank high among boys throughout the period and on into adulthood. As maturity is approached both sexes manifest an increasing interest in local and world news as well as in editorials.

In general, during the period of adolescence girls read more than do boys. However, the boy spreads his interest out over more kinds of reading materials. Among both boys and girls reading is a more popular activity in early adolescence than during the later stage of the period. Probably by the age of seventeen or eighteen the reading interests of both sexes have so matured that little if any difference can be detected from those of adults. From this stage on, reading interests become more individualized and specialized. Reading interests during adolescence derive their importance from the role which the resulting reading habits may play both in the effective use of leisure and in the formation of character.

Play activities tend to decrease as the years increase, but are never entirely discontinued. During adolescence, play takes the form of contests in sports and games, and competition between schools, between teams and clubs as well as individuals. Play activities become more complex and better organized than in previous periods. Although emphasis on individual superiority is still a prominent factor, the adolescent evidences willingness to seek superiority for the team or group as well as for himself. Both boys and girls engage in team sports and participate in athletic activities. Among boys especially, competitive physical activities constitute an influential factor in determining peer status. During early adolescence boys are interested first in team sports, then in individual sports, and in such outdoor activities as hiking and camping, in that order. During early adolescence, while girls also express interest in and participate in games and sports, they prefer individual sports and outdoor activities. During later adolescence, except for a few who manifest superior achievements in athletics, the interests of both boys and girls shift from active participation to watching as spectators. Watching sports rather than participating in them increases with age; interests which require vigorous physical activity decline, and the decline is more abrupt and more marked among girls than boys. During later adolescence interests turn to other recreational activities such as dating, dancing, and parties which promote social contact with the opposite sex.

Additional changes in activities and interest of a recreational nature are evident also in the increasingly mature choices made in such universal leisure-time interests as motion pictures and radio and television programs. Interest in motion pictures and tastes in movie entertainment during early adolescence seem to develop somewhat in harmony with interests and tastes in reading. Boys prefer movies which feature adventure, historical incidents, war, sports, and comedy. Girls, while favoring primarily romantic dramas, also manifest interest in a variety of types of movies including comedy, musical, and sports pictures. During later adolescence attendance at movies becomes less frequent, and both boys and girls become more discriminating with respect to choice of motion pictures. It is to be noted that during later adolescence attendance at movies is preferred to many other types of leisure-time interests, because such attendance with a member of the opposite sex as part of the dating process affords opportunity to engage in a desirable social activity.

With regard to radio-listening activities, there has been considerable decline since the advent of television. However, studies concerning radio interests have indicated that adolescent boys have expressed preferences for programs which feature sports, news, comedy, and the most modern fads in music; girls during the adolescent period have expressed greater interest in musical, dramatic, and comedy programs. Throughout the period radio interests seem to be similar to interests in reading and motion pictures. To a great extent television has supplanted radio. The interests of adolescents in TV programs tend to be consistent with interests in reading, motion pictures, and radio programs, with the exception of an added interest in "western" programs, which is very strong in early adolescence and which persists to a lesser extent during later adolescence and perhaps also into maturity. Adolescents devote a considerable amount of time, approximately 12 to 15 hours per week, to television programs. This is less, however, than the time devoted to this activity during preadolescence.

The emergence of vocational interests during adolescence is due to the recognition of approaching maturity and the necessity for adjusting to adult life. As has previously been indicated, among the developmental tasks of adolescence are those of selecting and preparing for an occupation, in order to assure the economic independence for which the adolescent is striving. Thus, as the adolescent becomes more mature mentally and socially he begins to think of the years of adulthood, becomes interested in possible future vocations or occupations, and makes plans concerning his lifework. The aim is to ascertain the vocation or occupation in which one's abilities and talents can be utilized best, in which satisfaction may be found and service rendered, and in which a reasonable recognition of one's worth as a person may be attained. Making a vocational choice is among the most significant problems which confront the adolescent. In practically all investigations concerning the problems encountered during the period, that of choosing a vocation or occupation and the necessary preparation or training for entering it ranks very high among the problems enumerated.

Throughout the early periods of development, both the boy and the girl express vocational interests and aspirations which reflect the fantasies, wishful thinking, daydreaming, and play activities of childhood. Attracted by the spectacular within the environment, by television and by the comics, the child expresses interests in becoming a cowboy or policeman or spaceman or movie actress, and the like, because these occupations seem to represent what is adventurous and glamorous. Since these childhood interests are characterized by such variety and instability, they are not real vocational interests, and should not be interpreted as the bases for later occupational aspirations. During early adolescence, however, the consideration of vocational interests and preferences becomes more conventional and realistic.[8]

Vocational interests probably become well developed shortly after the individual enters high school, and well-organized patterns of vocational preference are apparent usually at about the sixteenth year. A vocational

[8] F. J. Crowley, "The Goals of Male High School Seniors," *Personnel and Guidance Journal,* 37:488–492, 1959.

choice involving definite and vital decisions is made late in the period of adolescence, probably toward the end of high school when the boy or girl is faced with the necessity for taking a next step, that is, either entering the world of work or planning additional education and training in order to prepare for a vocation.

Educators and psychologists have investigated many aspects of the complex problem of selecting and preparing for a vocation or occupation. The results of many of these investigations seem to indicate that with respect both to education and occupations the aspirations of adolescents, particularly boys, are likely to be relatively high. There seems to be a tendency on the part of many adolescents to overestimate both their own abilities and the existing opportunities to enter professions, with the result that hopes tend to exceed expectations. Social prestige and family pressures also are important elements in the choice of professions. Girls generally are more mature both in aspirations and career choices than are boys. Many of the recent investigations indicate that the increased prestige attached to scientific and technical fields is reflected in the widespread interests of adolescents in these areas.

Developmental Tasks of Adolescence. Havighurst has enumerated the developmental tasks of adolescence as follows:

1. Achieving new and more mature relations with age mates of both sexes. The goal: to learn to look upon girls as women and boys as men; to become an adult among adults; to learn to work with others for a common purpose, disregarding personal feelings; to learn to lead without dominating.
2. Achieving a masculine or feminine role. The goal: to accept and to learn a socially approved adult masculine or feminine social role.
3. Accepting one's physique and using the body effectively. The goal: to become proud or at least tolerant of one's body; to use and protect one's body effectively and with personal satisfaction.
4. Achieving emotional independence of parents and other adults. The goal: to become free from childish dependence on parents; to develop affection for parents without dependence upon them; to develop respect for other adults without dependence upon them.
5. Achieving assurance of economic independence. The goal: to feel able to make a living, if necessary. This is primarily a task for boys, in our society, but is of increasing importance to girls.
6. Selecting and preparing for an occupation. The goal: to choose an occupation for which one has the necessary ability, to prepare for this occupation.
7. Preparing for marriage and family life. The goal: to develop a positive attitude toward family life and having children; and (mainly for girls) to

get the knowledge necessary for home management and child rearing.

8. Developing intellectual skills and concepts necessary for civic competence. The goal: to develop concepts of law, government, economics, politics, geography, human nature and social institutions which fit the modern world; to develop language skills and reasoning ability necessary for dealing effectively with the problems of a modern democracy.

9. Desiring and achieving socially responsible behavior. The goal: to participate as a responsible adult in the life of the community, region and nation; to take account of the values of society in one's personal behavior.

10. Acquiring a set of values and an ethical system as a guide to behavior. The goal: to form a set of values that are possible of realization; to develop a conscious purpose of realizing these values: to define man's place in the physical world and in relation to other human beings; to keep one's world picture and one's values in harmony with each other.[9]

The achievement of the development tasks is by no means easy or simple for the adolescent. Yet each task represents a major personal accomplishment which will contribute to the ultimate goal of adolescence, namely the attainment of mature patterns of thought, decision, behavior, and action which are characteristic of the adult. In order to accomplish these tasks the adolescent must: (1) attain a fuller understanding of his environment; (2) establish self-confidence; (3) widen social relationships in order to take his place in peer and later in adult groups; (4) attain success according to his abilities, interests, and limitations; (5) become competent in self-management; (6) develop personal independence; (7) make important life decisions, particularly with respect to the selection and preparation for a future vocation; (8) attain emotional maturity; (9) achieve mature values and social responsibility.

Educational Provisions for the Adolescent. During the period of adolescence the capacity to learn reaches, or at least approximates, maximal development. Youth is as nearly capable as he will ever be of pursuing studies which require ability to deal with abstractions, to generalize, to form adequate judgments, to reason efficiently, to think logically and critically. In terms of grade placement within the school, the adolescent usually progresses during the period from Grades 7 or 8 through Grade 14, that is, from the junior high school level through the senior high school, and perhaps into the first or second year of college. At the inception of the period it is likely that most youth will have completed the elementary school grades in which the fundamentals and tools of learning, especially proficiency in reading skill, should have been acquired.

[9] R. J. Havighurst, *Human Development and Education* (New York: Longmans, Green and Co., 1953), pp. 111–158.

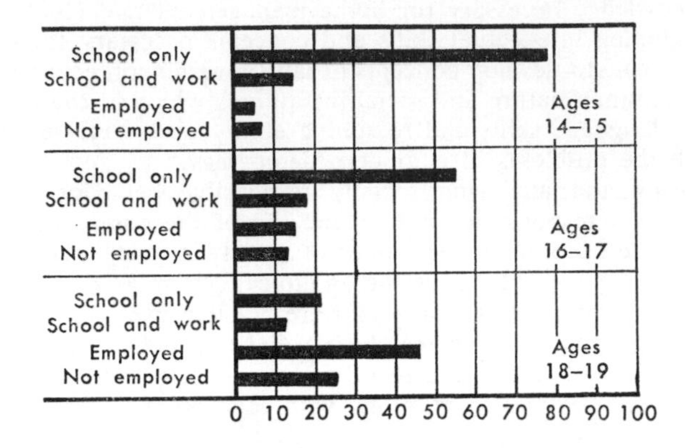

Fig. 4. School attendance during adolescence.[10]

During the early phase of adolescence, Grades 7 or 8 through 10 will be completed. During the later stage of the period Grades 10 through 12 on the secondary level and, if the individual enters college, at least the first and possibly even the second year will be completed. However, many adolescents leave school upon reaching the compulsory attendance age, which is usually sixteen years.

Universal secondary education for youth has been an ideal in the United States for several decades. At the present time all states require school attendance through the age of sixteen years, and in some states to the ages of seventeen or eighteen. Secondary education is considered essential for all youth for attaining self-realization as a person, for developing character, for establishing social relationships, for acquiring economic efficiency and as preparation for the responsibilities of citizenship. In short, secondary education constitutes the process through which the developmental tasks of the period of adolescence are achieved. While all normal adolescents enter and spend some time in the secondary school, many drop out before completion. In 1950 slightly more than 50 percent of the adolescents in the United States completed secondary school. Data presented in Figure 4 indicate the sharp decline in high

[10] From Fact Finding Committee, Midcentury White House Conference of Children and Youth, *A Graphic Presentation of Social and Economic Facts Important in the Lives of Children and Youth* (Washington, D. C.: National Publishing Co., 1951).

school attendance which occurred after the sixteenth year. A noteworthy factor is that a larger proportion of boys than of girls drop out before completion of high school. However, there seem to be indications that the realization of the ideal of universal secondary education is being approached. Investigations of "dropouts" and "early school leavers" indicate that the holding power of the secondary schools seems to be increasing steadily.

The primary purpose of secondary education is that of all education, the harmonious development of the whole person. To attain this purpose it is essential that secondary education should embody in its curriculum the fundamental principles, implemented by materials and techniques, which are essential for developing increasing competence for responsible living. A considerable body of ongoing research is devoted to the determination of learning experiences within the secondary school which will not only lead to continued self-improvement but will also be intellectually challenging to adolescents. The organization of these learning activities within the curriculum and the methods of presenting them have also constituted the subject of many investigations. There seems to be general agreement among many of the investigators that the basic concerns of the secondary school curriculum include the acquisition and expansion of knowledge, the establishment of the values inherent in the various subject-matter areas, the development of efficient work skills, and the improvement of study habits.

The secondary school must offer a varied program to meet the needs of all youth of high school age. A practical list of *ten imperative needs* of youth which the secondary school should meet has been formulated by the Educational Policies Commission of the National Education Association. These needs are as follows:

1. All youth need to develop salable skills.
2. All youth need to develop and maintain good health and physical fitness.
3. All youth need to understand the rights and duties of the citizen of a democratic society.
4. All youth need to understand the significance of the family for the individual and society.
5. All youth need to know how to purchase and use goods and services intelligently.
6. All youth need to understand the influence of science on human life.
7. All youth need an appreciation of literature, art, music, and nature.

8. All youth need to be able to use their leisure time well and to budget it wisely.
9. All youth need to develop respect for other persons.
10. All youth need to grow in ability to think rationally.[11]

In the endeavor to educate all youth at least to the age of sixteen or eighteen years the secondary school is confronted with the vast differences in capacity to learn, in interest in school work, in eagerness to attend school, and in home environment and background which exist among adolescents. Since the aim is to enrich the quality of secondary education for all youth, the task is to adjust and adapt the curricular content, activities, and experiences to the capacities and needs of each youth. Accordingly, various plans and techniques have been devised to provide programs for the academically talented which will challenge their abilities and aid in the development of creativity. These have included improved counseling with regard to the selection of curriculum and elective subjects, ability grouping, provision for adequate acceleration, and many types of enrichment involving more intensive and more comprehensive tasks in keeping with the individual's capacities and interests. For the average and also for the slow learning, many of whom will drop out of high school or for whom high school will be the terminal formal education, much of curriculum adjustment is designed to aid in the development of character and to emphasize marketable skills. Since all experience within the school setting influences the interests, attitudes, and values of youth much stress is placed upon counseling and guidance in the secondary school. The choices and decisions made during adolescence will limit or broaden definitely the social and vocational activities which will be open to the individual during adulthood. The cocurricular activities within the secondary school likewise offer opportunities for the cultivation of interests, for the development of leadership ability, and for the facilitation of social adjustment.

EXERCISES

1. Outline this chapter.
2. List and define the terms which you have learned from your study of this chapter.

[11] Reprinted by permission from *Planning for American Youth*, National Association of Secondary School Principals, 1951, p. 9. Copyright: Washington, D. C.

3. Distinguish between:
   a) Adolescence and puberty;
   b) Gang and crowd;
   c) Interest and attitude.
4. List the important changes which characterize the transition from childhood to adolescence. How do these differ for boys and for girls?
5. Discuss the following statements:
   a) "Adolescents of the present day are taller than their parents were at a comparable age."
   b) "Change of voice is more evident in the boy than in the girl."
   c) "Emotional development is the outstanding characteristic of adolescence."
   d) "Peer culture is a highly influential factor in determining the thoughts and actions of the adolescent."
6. Discuss the following topics:
   a) Leisure-time interests and activities of the adolescent;
   b) Vocational interests of the adolescent;
   c) Intellectual development during adolescence.
7. Discuss social development and emotional adjustment during the period of adolescence.
8. Explain why guidance is especially necessary during the period of adolescence. What personal and professional characteristics are essential in one who is to provide adequate guidance for adolescents?
9. Discuss the developmental tasks listed for the period of adolescence.
10. Describe the educational provisions made for the adolescent in the modern secondary school.

SELECTED REFERENCES FOR STUDY AND READING

Ausubel, D. P., *Theory and Problems of Adolescent Development* (New York: Grune & Stratton, 1954).
Bier, W. C., ed., *The Adolescent: His Search for Understanding* (New York: Fordham University Press, 1963).
Cole, L., *Psychology of Adolescence,* 5 ed. (New York: Holt, Rinehart and Winston, Inc., 1959).
Crow, L. D., and Crow, A. V., eds., *Readings in Child and Adolescent Psychology* (New York: Longmans, Green and Co., 1961).
Garrison, K. C., *Psychology of Adolescence* (Englewood Cliffs, N. J.: Prentice-Hall, Inc., 1956).
Geoghegan, Sister Barbara, Pollard, Sister Marie Baptista, and Kelly, W. A., *Developmental Psychology* (Milwaukee: The Bruce Publishing Co., 1963), Chap. 11.
Gesell, A., Ilg, F., and Ames, L. B., *Youth the Years From Ten to Sixteen* (New York: Harper and Row, 1956).
Grinder, R. E., *Studies in Adolescence* (New York: The Macmillan Co., 1963).
Hanna, G. R., and McAllister, M. K., *Books, Young People and Reading Guidance* (New York: Harper and Row, 1960).

Havighurst, R. J., *Human Development and Education* (New York: Longmans, Green and Co., 1953).

Horrocks, J. E., *The Psychology of Adolescence,* 2 ed. (Boston: Houghton-Mifflin Co., 1962).

Jersild, A. T., *Psychology of Adolescence* (New York: The Macmillan Co., 1957).

Muuss, R. E., *Theories of Adolescence* (New York: Random House, Inc., 1963).

Rogers, D., *The Psychology of Adolescence* (New York: Appleton-Century-Crofts, 1963).

Schneiders, A. A., *Personality Development and Adolescence* (Milwaukee: The Bruce Publishing Co., 1960).

Seidman, J. M., *The Adolescent: A Book of Readings,* rev. ed. (New York: Holt, Rinehart and Winston, Inc., 1960).

Strang, R., *The Adolescent Views Himself: A Psychology of Adolescence* (New York: McGraw-Hill Book Co., 1957).

Wattenberg, W. M., *Adolescent Years* (New York: Harcourt, Brace and World, 1955).

chapter 6

Individual Differences

Human Variations and Differences. From the time of Aristotle, psychology has been concerned with the common aspects of mental life and of behavior. To this general interest, educational psychology has made a special contribution, namely, the study of the human variations in these common aspects. These variations have been termed individual differences. Educational psychology recognizes that although all human beings, because of the fact that each is man, possess the same general mental capacities, nevertheless there are among individuals quantitative and qualitative differences in the development of these capacities. This fact of the existence of individual differences is most evident and obvious, particularly in the classroom. Teachers recognize that pupils differ greatly from one another in practically every respect, but they frequently fail to recognize the extent of the differences. Pupils differ in the amount and character of previous training, of physical health and vigor, of study habits, of zeal and interest, of ambition and persistence. Every pupil has distinctive characteristics and qualities which constitute his individuality. Some are tall, others, short; some are choleric, others, phlegmatic; some are frail, others, strong. They differ also in features, in dress, in behavior, as well as in race and in social position. They differ in color of hair and of eyes, in shape of nose and of teeth, in the size of hands and of feet, and in many other respects. While racial, physical, and social differences are significant, nevertheless for educational purposes greatest emphasis must be placed on differences in mental capabilities and in the capacity to learn. Each mental function and ability means the capacity to do something; that is, to perceive, to form images, to remember, to reason. Every normal child possesses these capacities. Yet, whatever feature of intellect, of character, of will is examined, variabilities among individuals are noticed. The children in a classroom differ in their reactions to schoolwork. Some will be conspicuous for their facility in learning; others, for their slowness. These are the extremes, and between these extremes are all the grades and shades of apparent difference and also innumerable variations which are not apparent. It is the function of educational psychology to note individual differences, the specific demands which school work makes upon certain capacities, and to endeavor to direct individuals according to their capacities, powers, and interests, so that they may develop to the maximum. Thus, individual differences exist, may be measured, and are of educational significance.

The diversity of capacities and abilities existing among children, particularly with regard to their mental capacity and performance, presents one of the most important and constant of school problems. However, the statement that individual differences exist must not be taken to mean that human beings differ profoundly from one another. It is very evident that all men are more alike than different; they possess more common traits than distinctive traits. Individuals differ from each other quantitatively; that is, they differ not in the kind of traits but in the degree. They differ qualitatively also, that is, in the ways in which the individual's capacities and abilities are organized or patterned or structured. All children in school have the same kinds of powers and capacities, but some children are more or less richly endowed than others. These pupils, then, differ in degree rather than in kind. They possess more or less capability in memory, in attention, in voluntary control, in judgment, in reasoning, and the like. All children possess the same basic mental equipment in virtue of their very nature, composed as they are of the substantial union of soul and body, endowed with mental capacities, a nervous system, and sense organs. However, they possess these in varying amounts of perfection, so that as a result their mental and scholastic achievements show the widest variations.

Since children come to school variously equipped, both physically and mentally, the pupils in school will differ in degree of ability and of achievement. Since the ability to learn is present in every child, differences between individual pupils may be attributed not to inability to learn but rather to differences in progress in learning. Some pupils can and do learn more rapidly than others. Some excel in dealing with abstract ideas and do well in mathematics, grammar, and the like. There are others whose best work is done in dealing with concrete situations. There are also some who excel in appreciation and enjoyment of art, literature, and music. There are, likewise, those who manifest strong tendencies to action and to leadership and who are especially capable of managing and controlling situations. Some pupils have superior ability in memory. There are others who form habits readily and well. Some solve problems more accurately and more rapidly than others. While most pupils are a composite mixture of all these types, it is noteworthy that there are many pupils who possess one or more of these types as dominant characteristics. It is also worthy of note in this connection that correlation, not compensation, is the law of nature, and abilities tend to be correlated. This means that the pupil who has more than average ability in one mental power will seldom have less than average ability in any other. Desirable mental abilities are usually found together and so, too, are deficiencies. The pupil who excels in one capacity will probably excel in many others, while deficiency in one capacity tends to be accompanied with deficiencies in others. Occasionally, however, it is possible to find what seems to be an exception to this principle. It is possible, but not usual, that a student who does superior work in mathematics or in language may be doing poor work in other subjects. This can probably be explained on the basis of interest rather than of mental ability.

Some of the individual differences which should be taken into consideration in teaching are those in:

a) Physical growth and development
b) Mental development, including maturation and readiness to learn
c) Social maturity, including interests, attitudes toward self and others, play, and leisure-time activities
d) Academic achievement and performance as well as previous learning experiences
e) Personality and character, including emotional maturity and volitional control
f) Home environment and socioeconomic status
g) Aptitude

The Causes of Individual Differences.[1] It is most important that the teacher possess a knowledge of the causes of individual differences. The

[1] F. T. Tyler, "Individual and Sex Differences," in C. W. Harris, ed., *Encyclopedia of Educational Research,* 3 ed. (New York: The Macmillan Co., 1960), pp. 680–688.

causes as listed generally are heredity, maturation, environment, and training, to which must be added also effort of will. Individual differences in capacity are due in part to heredity and in some degree to the influence of environment, and may be magnified by training and by voluntary effort to use and develop abilities. Just how important a factor each of these causes is and for what each is responsible has never been fully and accurately determined. In studying the problem of individual differences, it is impossible to investigate the role of heredity apart from environment. In fact, one of the most debatable and debated questions in educational psychology has to do with the relative importance of heredity and environment or "nature vs. nurture" as causes of individual differences. Furthermore, the difficulty of finding a solution to the problem is increased by the fact that both are essential factors in life and one does not exist without the other. However, so far as the school is concerned, the real problem is providing proper environment and training, and motivating the will to learn.

With reference to individual differences, heredity implies that native capacities worthy of cultivation must be discovered, stimulated, and directed. Likewise, it implies that native limitations must be compensated for, through the cultivation of desirable capacities. Heredity bestows the general native equipment, the bodily structure, the nervous system, and the native endowment of powers, and capabilities for the acquisition of knowledge and skill. Environment includes all the factors, surrounding conditions, influences, and forces which modify development. Heredity determines to a great extent what is possible for one to do and to become, while what one actually does and becomes is determined largely by his environment, his training, and his voluntary efforts. Heredity, then, provides the raw materials with which environment, training, and volition interact.

The factors of heredity and environment and the role which these factors play in the growth and development of the child have been described in the chapter "The Processes of Growth and Development." However, it is of interest and importance to indicate at this point that psychologists and biologists have endeavored to determine the relative influence of both heredity and environment upon individual differences. The endeavors to determine the effects of heredity have taken the form of studies of resemblances within the families of eminent men, studies of degenerate families, and studies of twins both fraternal and identical, particularly identical twins who had been reared apart. The endeavors to determine the effects of environment have taken the form of studies of environmental conditions of men of distinguished achievement, studies of canal boat and gypsy children, studies of the relationship existing between mental abilities and occupational groups, and studies of children in foster homes. It is impossible in a work of this type to present a description of these studies, but the student who is interested in pursuing this aspect will find adequate accounts of the findings in works on differential psychology.

Training is closely allied to environment and includes all of the social, educational, cultural, moral, and religious agencies with which the child comes into contact. In the schoolroom the same educational influences, guidance, and stimulation work upon all pupils. While some learn rapidly, and others slowly, nevertheless the important principle to be remembered is that each can learn something. Training in the proper environment can make individuals very different from what they otherwise would have been. However, while it cannot make all alike, while it cannot render all equally efficient, it can make each more efficient than he would have been otherwise. Differences among individuals due to training include differences in morality, in attitudes, in interests, in ideals, in habits.

By means of the will, inherited capacities are realized and intellectual opportunities are utilized. Will is man's capacity to direct and to restrain thought, action, emotion. Since its influence extends over all of the powers and capacities of man, it is thus a controlling factor in the causing of individual differences. The will realizes or neglects the capacities which heredity bestows; it improves or disregards the opportunities which environment and training present.

It is also frequently asserted that individual differences may be attributed in part at least to sex or race. However, variations due to sex[2] are neither as great nor as important as was once maintained. Many studies have been conducted, but usually the samplings have been small and unrepresentative. However, these investigations have revealed that, with

---

[2] L. Carmichael, ed., *Manual of Child Psychology,* 2 ed. (New York: John Wiley & Sons, Inc., 1954), pp. 1064–1075; also L. E. Tyler, *The Psychology of Human Differences,* 2 ed. (New York: Appleton-Century-Crofts, Inc., 1956), Chap. X; J. R. McCall, *Sex Differences in Intelligence: A Comparative Factor Study,* The Catholic University of America Studies in Psychology and Psychiatry, Vol. IX, No. 3, 1955.

regard to all psychological traits, a considerable amount of overlapping exists and also that there are no uniform and regularly appearing sex differences.[3] The results of these studies indicate that (*a*) boys tend to be more active and aggressive, less neat and exacting than girls; (*b*) boys seem to be superior in mathematical and scientific subjects, while girls excel in the language arts, art, spelling, and penmanship; (*c*) boys surpass girls in tests of a spatial nature, of mechanical aptitude, and of general information, while girls excel in tests of manual dexterity, speed, and precision; (*d*) a smaller percentage of girls than of boys tend to be mentally retarded; (*e*) reading disabilities and speech handicaps also seem to occur more frequently among boys than among girls. Naturally there are distinctive differences between the sexes, which extend alike to physical and mental constitution and likewise to interests as all true educators recognize. The Church's attitude on coeducation, as expressed by Pope Pius XI in his *Encyclical on Christian Education of Youth,* is based on sound educational as well as moral and religious principles.[4] For the rest, psychological research has indicated that the mental abilities of men and of women as measured by psychological tests approximate the same curve of distribution. Apparent differences between the sexes in ability to achieve success in certain areas of work or study are attributable to such circumstances as traditional attitudes, interests, and opportunities to succeed.

There do not exist any substantial differences among the various races with respect to mental abilities. The native equipment of human beings is universal. Every man, in virtue of the fact that he is a man, regardless of the place of birth or of color, possesses a body and soul, is endowed with the same kind of mental capacities, a nervous system, and sense organs. Any differences in mental capacities among the various races seem to be due to environmental conditions, cultural influences, and training rather than to be innate. There seems to be general agreement among investigators who have made studies of racial differences that variation within one race is far more significant than the differences among races.

The Range and Distribution of Individual Differences. Educational psychology is concerned with the extent, that is, the range and distribu-

---

[3] J. A. McGeoch and A. L. Irion, *The Psychology of Human Learning* 2 ed. (New York: Longmans, Green and Co., 1952), pp. 552–553.

[4] Pope Pius XI, *Encyclical on Christian Education of Youth* (New York: The America Press, 1936), pp. 22–23.

tion of individual differences in mental capacities among schoolchildren. The amount and the quality of the achievement of pupils in schoolwork demonstrate that there is a marked variation in these capacities. There is considerable variability in achievement within a single grade. In an ordinary classroom will be found pupils who can read in a given time from two to five times as much as some other pupils, who can solve in the same period of time from two to five times as many problems in arithmetic, or who can master their work from two to five times as well as other students. These differences between the best and the poorest pupils in a class are considerable. A testing program may reveal a range of achievement which involves a spread of several grades in arithmetic or reading ability among the pupils in a single grade. Thus in reading, for example, the best pupil in the fifth grade may read as well as the typical tenth grade student, while the poorest may be able to read only on the level of the typical third grade pupil. Because of the fact that such differences affect methods of instruction, numerous studies have been made in order to ascertain the extent and distribution of individual differences. How great a variation may a teacher expect among the pupils in a given class? In an ordinary class in the elementary school, and probably also in the secondary school, the majority of pupils will be found to be grouped about the average, with a few variants at either extreme. Those at the upper end are the unusually capable, while those at the lower end are the dull and the slow. Those at the top are described as intellectually superior, gifted, or academically talented, while those at the bottom are described as dull or borderline — some even as mentally retarded. Variations in the schoolroom will be less marked than among mankind in general. In mankind in general variations are very marked, ranging from idiot to genius with wide variations in ability between these extremes. However, the great bulk of people is much alike and is designated as normal. Psychologists have classified these individual differences in mental capacity as follows: genius, superior, bright, average, dull, borderline, feebleminded, including in the last the moron, the imbecile, and the idiot.

When sufficiently large numbers of individuals are measured in any ability or in any trait, for which relatively accurate measuring devices exist, the resulting distributions tend to be symmetrical and may be represented graphically by a bell-shaped curve. Whatever the physical traits or mental abilities measured, they approximate the form of this bell-shaped curve. This symmetrical or bell-shaped distribution is so nearly universal

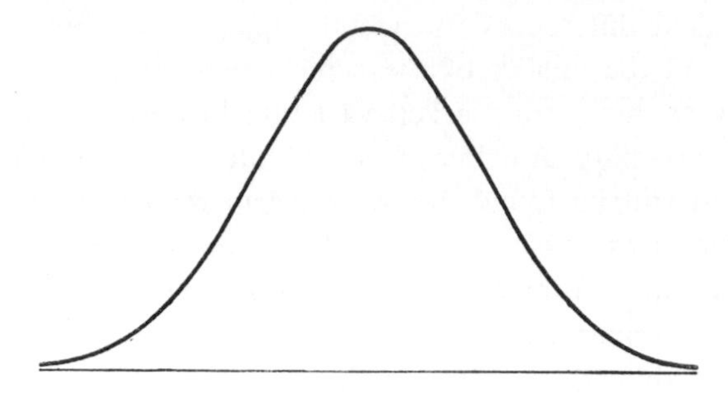

Fig. 5. The theoretical normal distribution curve.

that it has come to be known as the curve of normal distribution or the normal probability curve.[5]

This normal curve has become the common manner in which the amount of variation of any given ability or trait is represented. The greater the number of cases, the more closely will the distribution approximate the normal curve. The theoretically determined ideal normal distribution curve is illustrated in Figure 5.

This curve describes the manner in which achievements and abilities are distributed among individuals. It illustrates the concentration of individuals around the average or central tendency and demonstrates also the progressive and gradual diminution in numbers in the direction of both extremes. It should not be supposed that in every classroom such a distribution of mental capacities or scholastic achievements will be found. In fact, the smaller the number of pupils in the class, the less likely it is that the distribution will approximate closely that of the normal curve.

Differences in rate of mental development among pupils in a given grade may be shown by means of the *age-grade table*. The age-grade relationship reveals the amount of retardation of some pupils, the acceleration of others, and the fact that the majority are in the proper grade which normally corresponds to their age. This overlapping of pupils in various grades is an indication of the range and distribution of individual differences among pupils. Table 2 presents the distribution of pupils from Grades 3 to 12 in one city school system.

In addition Table 3 which indicates the distribution of mental ages by

[5] It should be noted that the tendency to normal distribution of a measured trait may be due to natural factors, or it could be due to methods of measurement used.

TABLE 2. Distribution of Ages in Grades 3 to 12

Age	GRADE										Totals
	3	4	5	6	7	8	9	10	11	12	
7	10										10
8	242	48	2								292
9	151	323	58	1							533
10	79	303	331	55							768
11	27	164	323	260	36	5					815
12	15	75	173	286	196	42	8	1			796
13	1	19	85	193	242	221	155	7			923
14	1	16	33	83	162	222	791	127	8		1443
15			12	30	83	133	1126	589	117	9	2099
16	1		4	6	16	57	527	689	538	87	1925
17				2	2	10	163	332	523	490	1522
18							31	69	204	404	708
19							12	19	63	147	241
20							2	10	11	50	73
21									3	17	20
22										3	3
Totals	527	948	1021	916	737	690	2815	1843	1467	1207	12,171
Accel.	10	48	60	56	36	47	163	135	125	96	776
At-age	393	626	654	546	438	443	1917	1278	1061	894	8,250
Retard.	124	274	307	314	263	200	735	430	281	217	3,145
% Accel.	2	5	6	6	5	7	6	7	8	8	6
% At-age	75	66	63	60	60	65	68	70	72	74	68
% Retard.	23	29	31	34	35	28	26	23	20	18	26

grades, illustrates both the wide variation occurring within any given grade and also the overlapping of mental age which occurs from grade to grade. In the sixth grade, for example, the mental age of pupils varies from 8 years and 6 months to 16 years and 6 months, a range of 8 years. The teacher's problems in adapting the work of this grade to pupils within such a wide range are bound to be manifold.

Adaptation of Instruction to Individual Differences. The extent of individual differences in capacity to learn, in aptitude, and in achievement has directed attention to the need for adjusting methods of instruction and school tasks to the learning capacity and aptitude of the individual pupil. Many methods and plans have been devised which have made possible, to a greater or less extent, the individualization of instruction within the general framework of mass education. Prominent among these were ability grouping and the laboratory plans characterized by the unit assignment,

TABLE 3. Distribution of Mental Ages by Grades

	GRADE						
Mental Age	1	2	3	4	5	6	Total
16–6	...	...	...	...	...	5	5
16–0	...	...	...	...	...	4	4
15–6	...	...	...	...	...	3	3
15–0	...	...	...	1	1	13	15
14–6	...	...	...	...	3	19	22
14–0	...	...	...	1	4	29	34
13–6	...	...	...	2	9	28	39
13–0	...	...	...	5	23	49	77
12–6	...	1	...	19	41	49	110
12–0	...	...	4	21	58	60	143
11–6	...	2	6	47	88	56	199
11–0	...	5	19	60	106	32	222
10–6	...	15	67	69	73	23	247
10–0	4	36	116	76	47	11	290
9–6	7	83	143	88	45	4	370
9–0	22	81	101	51	24	1	280
8–6	43	98	90	53	14	2	300
8–0	87	70	33	32	3	...	225
7–6	127	67	23	22	...	...	239
7–0	127	28	5	7	...	...	167
6–6	132	7	1	2	...	...	142
6–0	86	3	2	1	...	...	92
5–6	71	1	...	...	...	...	72
5–0	22	...	...	...	...	...	22
4–6	8	...	...	...	...	...	8
4–0	8	...	...	...	...	...	8
TOTAL	744	497	610	557	539	388	3335

which in the past constituted the major provisions for the adaptation of instruction to individual differences.

Ability Grouping. This is primarily an administrative device which is used to make provisions for individual differences among pupils within a grade level, but which does not involve a change in the ordinary classroom procedure. It is frequently termed *homogeneous grouping* and usually means the placing together of pupils with similar mental ability and academic aptitude for purposes of instruction. Strictly speaking, homogeneous grouping may involve other bases of grouping, such as sex, future plans, and the like. The success of this plan depends upon securing adequate means of determining homogeneity. Usually the means used are:

teacher's ratings, scores attained on tests of mental ability and achievement, past academic achievements, maturation, and special aptitudes. Ordinarily there are three groups: the superior, the average, and the slow which are designated as rapid, normal, and slow learning classes. There are also three differentiated curricula. Each group progresses at its own rate of speed. The slow group covers only the minimum essentials of the subject matter or of the course; curriculum and teaching procedures are adjusted to their limited abilities. The average group covers in addition to the minimum essentials, such additional materials as are commensurate with the abilities of the members of the group. For the superior group the curriculum is enriched and frequently honors classes are organized for this group. In this way instruction and materials fitting to the abilities of the different groups are offered. Likewise, all pupils are given instruction according to their individual needs insofar as this can be done under the group technique. The objective of the homogeneous grouping plan has been to establish classes for students of seemingly equal mental and educational status, upon the assumption that they will be consistent in rate of mental and educational development and so will be able to progress at a similar rate. However, it should be noted that, while homogeneous grouping emphasizes two types of maturation, namely, mental and educational, it fails to take into consideration the social development of the pupil as reflected in his interests and activities, and it neglects to take account of physical maturity. Thus grouping on the basis of mental ability tends to overemphasize the intellectual and tends also to ignore other aspects of development which are equally important.

A variation of ability grouping, *intraclass* grouping, may be carried out within the class, especially at the elementary school level. In such grouping classes may be subdivided for particular purposes, such as instruction in reading or in language or in arithmetic. In this type of grouping the constitution of the groups will probably vary from subject to subject and the makeup of the groups may change from time to time according to the progress attained by the pupils. While formal plans of ability grouping may seem to have waned somewhat, schools have by no means abandoned ability grouping. In fact, there are some recent indications of increased interest in the movement. However it is no longer expected to solve all aspects of the problem of adjustment of instruction to individual differences.

The Laboratory Method. This method was the outstanding feature of the Morrison Unit Mastery, the Dalton, and the Winnetka Plans, which were elaborately designed and organized to permit each pupil to master successive units of work at his own rate of speed. These plans have been superseded in recent years by other approaches and methods of individualizing instruction. No one of these plans is utilized in its original form at the present time. Nevertheless, something of each, particularly the unit organization of textbook materials, has found its way into accepted patterns of school procedures, and has become part of common practice.

In addition to the provisions of ability grouping and laboratory plans, procedures of a less comprehensive nature have been devised and utilized to aid in the adjustment of instruction to individual differences. These procedures, which may be employed either as aspects of the major provisions or as independent devices or in combinations, include such familiar techniques as supervised and directed study, remedial instruction, differentiated and supplementary assignments, and workbooks.

Likewise, the adjustment teacher and the opportunity class serve a function in the process of adjusting instruction to individual differences. The adjustment teacher works with slow learners, with those who cannot benefit from the regular class instruction, and with others who for various reasons are in need of specialized instruction, including children who have been absent due to illness, and transfer students. This work may be conducted on an individual or group basis. When conducted on a group basis it is commonly referred to as an "opportunity class."

No one of these procedures or devices for adapting instruction to individual differences has won general approval and acceptance. Each possesses some elements of value, and each has met with greater or less success in facilitating the work of the teacher in dealing with a wide range of individual differences. All of these plans and devices are based upon the recognition of individual differences existing among pupils. All attempt to provide for each individual pupil better opportunities in his schoolwork. They endeavor to make it possible for the slow child to progress at his own pace and to do his work thoroughly and completely. They also seek to enable the superior pupil to work up to his full capacity and offer him exceptional advantages, primarily through enrichment. However, the existence of these procedures and devices should not be understood to mean that group instruction is without value. Group instruction is an essential feature of schoolwork, through which are developed in the individual social qualities of importance. Group instruction subjects the individual to the stress of competition which is necessary for the full development of his capacities. Furthermore, group instruction is more economical, and is simpler in administration. The chief disadvantages of these procedures and devices for individual instruction are that they fail to provide the stimulus of classroom discussion and that they are difficult to adapt to all subject-matter areas.

Present-day concern with the adaptation of education to individual differences is evident in the vast amount of research reported in the area of curriculum adjustment. Likewise, such devices as activity programs, the experience curriculum, the core program, and the life adjustment program have commanded considerable attention. While careful appraisal and critical evaluation of the underlying principles and the implications of these devices are necessary, it is to be noted that they are based upon endeavors to ascertain the capacities, needs, and interests of pupils and the consequent organization and adaptation of curriculum content and methodology to meet these capacities, needs, and interests. A commendable trend in modern education has been the consideration devoted to maturation as the foundation upon which the adaptation of instruction to individual differences must rest. This has involved the determination of maturation levels, together with activities which are characteristic of each level, and the placement of many aspects of the school curriculum in terms of the maturational status of the pupils. Information concerning *readiness* has resulted in many changes in the school program, particularly with regard to the placement of learning materials.

The Nongraded School.[6] This is primarily an organizational device utilized at the elementary school level in an effort to modify the right graded structure. It is frequently designated as the *Continuous Progress Plan.* The underlying pattern involves the elimination of grades and provision for greater flexibility. Each pupil moves through school at his own best rate in each subject-matter area. Learning situations compatible with the maturity, ability, experience, and interest of the pupil are provided. Nonpromotion disappears in this plan. The slow learner is enabled to

[6] J. I. Goodlad and R. H. Anderson, *The Non-graded Elementary School* (New York: Harcourt, Brace & World, Inc., 1959). See also J. I. Goodlad, "Individual Differences and Vertical Organization of the School," in N.S.S.E. Sixty-First Yearbook, Part I, *Individualizing Instruction,* 1962, pp. 209–238.

move at a pace commensurate with his abilities and without the stigma of repeating a grade. So also are the bright, and the average pupils of high motivation, provided with opportunities to progress according to their abilities. As a result they may complete the requirements of the elementary level in a shorter span of time, or may within the usual time take enriched programs.

Team Teaching.[7] This involves a plan of organization and a technique for the efficient use of specialized talents among teachers. A team is composed of a group of several teachers, usually varying from three to six, who have joint responsibility for planning, executing, and evaluating an educational program for a specified number of pupils, usually twenty-five to thirty times the number of teachers on the team. Each team is led by an experienced and able senior teacher. The team technique may be applied at both the elementary and secondary levels. While no standard pattern has yet evolved, each teacher has special competency and interests in one subject-matter field or in a combination of fields within a curriculum area so that the teaching team is composed of specialists. Also, aspects of guidance and counseling, particularly educational guidance, are involved in the work of the team. Team teaching permits the school to make the most of the differences among teachers, capitalizing upon individual experience, subject specialization, and variations in personality and outlook. By relaxing the rigid classroom pattern to permit large groupings for certain lectures, tests, and the like, it makes teacher time available for small group classes and extensive individual work. It enables the team to undertake advanced and likewise remedial work with the small groups and individuals, as well as to guide the development of special interests and abilities.

Technological innovations which have served to facilitate mass instruction have also been utilized to some extent as devices for the adaptation of instruction to individual differences. These include: educational television and such audio-visual devices as tape recorders, video tape ma-

[7] R. H. Anderson, "Organizing Groups for Instruction," in *Individualizing Instruction,* N.S.S.E. 61st Yearbook, 1962, pp. 255–260; see also A. D. Morse, *Schools of Tomorrow — Today* (Garden City, N. Y.: Doubleday & Co., Inc., 1960), pp. 11–25. It is to be noted that a large share of the expanding literature on team teaching at the secondary school level reflects the influences of the work of the Commission on the Experimentation of the Utilization of Staff in the Secondary School, an agency of the National Association of Secondary School Principals. See also *Decade of Experiment* (New York: The Fund for the Advancement of Education, 1961), pp. 51–53.

chines, language laboratories, and overhead projectors. However another technological innovation, *the teaching machine,*[8] seems to offer the most effective approach to the adaptation of school tasks to individual differences.

The teaching machine is an autoinstructional device by which a program of subject matter is presented to the learner. It is obvious that the machine *per se* does not teach. The essential factor is the program which is inside the machine. Thus the term *teaching machine* is inappropriate and the designation *programed instruction* is preferable. A program[9] consists of subject-matter content organized in a carefully planned, logical series of sequential steps, referred to generally as *frames,* which are usually presented one item or step at a time. Provision is made for the student to record an overt response to each item; that is, the learner must be active. Immediate knowledge of results, that is, confirmation of success or failure (feedback) is provided. Thus, when the student has successfully mastered an item or step, he is "reinforced." Adaptivity to the specific needs of each student is considered to be an outstanding feature of programed instruction, since the student paces himself, that is, progresses at his own rate, advancing to more difficult material only when he has mastered previous stages. In addition programed instruction provides for the student to test himself.

---

[8] See J. E. Coulson, *Programmed Instruction: A Perspective* (Santa Monica, Calif.: System Development Corporation, 1962); E. J. Green, *The Learning Process and Programmed Instruction* (New York: Holt, Rinehart and Winston, Inc., 1962); C. I. Foltz, *The World of Teaching Machines* (Washington, D. C.: Electronic Teaching Laboratories, 1961); O. Milton and L. J. West, *Programmed Instruction — What It is and How It Works* (New York: Harcourt, Brace and World, Inc., 1961); *Decade of Experiment* (New York: The Fund for Advancement of Education, 1961); A. A. Lumsdaine and R. Glaser, eds., *Teaching Machines and Programmed Learning* (Washington, D. C.: National Educational Association, Department of Audio-visual Instruction, 1960); E. H. Galanter, *Automatic Teaching: The State of the Art* (New York: John Wiley & Sons, Inc., 1959); B. F. Skinner, "Teaching Machines," *Science,* 128:969–977, 1958; *Journal of Educational Research* "The Teacher and the Machine," 55:(9), 1962 complete issue; L. M. Stolurow, *Teaching by Machine* (Washington, D. C.: United States Department of Health, Education and Welfare, 1961); B. F. Skinner, "Why We Need Teaching Machines," *Harvard Educational Review,* 31:377–398, 1961; B. F. Skinner, *Cumulative Record* (New York: Appleton-Century-Crofts, Inc., 1959); Edward Fry, *Teaching Machines and Programming* (New York: McGraw-Hill Book Co., 1963); J. P. Lysaught and C. M. Williams, *A Guide to Programmed Instruction* (New York: John Wiley & Sons, Inc., 1963); "Mechanized Learning on Trial," *Childhood Education,* 39:155–186, 1962; F. J. Tyler, "Teaching Machines, Programs and Research on Learning," *School Review,* 71:123–150, 1963.

[9] It is to be noted that a program may be presented in various physical forms. It may be presented in the form of tapes or strips of paper, or a series of microfilmed slides, or a notebook. See E. J. Green, *op. cit.,* p. 117.

There are two basic types of programs, the *linear* and the *branching* or *intrinsic*. The linear or straight-line program has been developed by Skinner.[10] It is probably best suited for use in the simpler types of machines now available. It is composed of small steps leading through subject matter from unit to unit and from topic to topic. The increments which the student is expected to master are small, and it is important that the student make as few errors as possible. The second type, the branching or intrinsic program, was developed by Crowder.[11] This type is based upon the principle that student errors may have a meaning regarding students' needs. Several sequences of learning are built into one program. In this kind of program the student is presented with a problem and several alternative (multiple-choice type) answers, only one of which is correct. When the student selects an answer he is instructed to move to a specified frame which indicates whether his answer was correct or incorrect and, if it was incorrect, explains why. An incorrect answer may indicate that the student needs a review. Accordingly, the frame may return the student to the original item which was answered incorrectly, for another trial, or it may direct him through a "subprogram," further instructing him in the basic knowledge required; that is, the student is "branched" to a review sequence. A correct answer is presumed to indicate comprehension and understanding on the part of the student, and so he is "branched" to an advanced presentation or to a telescoped sequence of the subject-matter material. Thus those who favor the intrinsic program maintain that the presentation of larger logical units which explain some principal units entirely is more effective than the linear type which breaks down the program into minutiae. Programs run the gamut from simple factual presentations to complicated provisions for enrichment.

The effectiveness of programed instruction will depend upon how well the materials are organized for presentation. The construction of a good program, whether linear or intrinsic, requires specialized knowledge of the subject matter, application of the principles of curriculum construction, and the sequencing of skills within each subject-matter field, as

[10] B. F. Skinner, "Why We Need Teaching Machines," *Harvard Educational Review*, 31:377–398, 1961.

[11] C. I. Foltz, *op. cit.*, p. 16; also N. Crowder, "Automotive Tutoring by Means of Intrinsic Programming," in E. H. Galanter, ed., *Automatic Teaching: The State of the Art* (New York: John Wiley & Sons, Inc., 1959).

well as sound knowledge of the learning process, that is, of the ways in which pupils assimilate and gain understanding of materials.

An evaluation of both types of programs gives evidence that each possesses potentialities for meeting at least some of the needs of the individual since each type "starts where the pupil is" and permits him to advance at his own pace. Careful and logical analysis of subject matter into short steps in the linear program is an aid to the slow learning and also the average pupil, while the intrinsic program is helpful to the brighter student.

To evaluate further the potentialities of programed instruction the results of research investigations should be studied carefully. To date the research has been limited and many of the investigations have yielded conflicting results. However, some general trends[12] seem to be evident. These investigations indicate that the average pupil learns faster and more efficiently through programed instruction. Superior students also learn faster but do not seem to learn more or to achieve greater comprehension. The use of the features of small steps and repetition of subject matter seems to give promise of great usefulness in the teaching of the mentally retarded. Also it has been reported that programed instruction is quite effective with deaf children. Finally, research investigations have revealed that no one type of programing appears to be more successful than another in producing effective learning.

Exceptional Children and Youth. Consideration of the topic of individual differences has revealed that each child differs from his fellow beings to some degree, however minor. Included within this broad framework is a smaller population of children and youth who differ so markedly in either mental, physical, or emotional traits from the average that they have been termed "exceptional children." Meeting the educational, physical, socioemotional, and spiritual needs of these children frequently involves modified and diversified programs of treatment, care, and education; hence, within the educational structure of the school, provisions for exceptional children are classified under the heading of special education. While many children have exceptional traits that may be of medical or psychosocial importance such as a shortened leg or protruding teeth, a child is classified as exceptional for educational purposes only

---

[12] L. M. Stolurow, *op. cit.*, and *Journal of Educational Research,* "The Teacher and the Machine," 55:(9), 1962 entire issue.

TABLE 4. Estimated Incidence of School-Aged Exceptional Children and Youth in the United States[14]

Areas of Exceptionality	Percent of Incident	Estimated Number of School-Aged Children (in round numbers)
Visually handicapped (blind and partially seeing)	0.20	68,000
Crippled	1.50	510,000
Special health problems	1.50	510,000
Deaf and hard-of-hearing	1.50	510,000
Speech handicapped	2.00	680,000
Socially and emotionally maladjusted	2.00	680,000
Mentally retarded	2.00	680,000
Gifted	2.00	680,000
Total	12.7	4,318,000

when it is deemed necessary to alter the school program and provide specialized educational arrangements to meet his needs.[13]

Considered in relative terms, exceptional children constitute but a small proportion of all school-aged children. However, their numerical representation is large. The estimated incidence of exceptional children and youth in the United States, based on 1952 census data, is summarized in the following table.

Thus some four million children and youth, representing approximately 13 percent of the total school-aged population, can be classified as exceptional. By comparison, a survey of special education enrollments in public day schools in the United States reveals that less than one million children are actually receiving special education services in public school programs. Table 5 provides a summary of these data, based on statistics reported as of 1958. Comparison of Tables 4 and 5 reveals that only 20 to 25 percent of all exceptional children are enrolled in special education classes in public schools. The enrollments listed in Table 5 do not include exceptional children in public and private institutions and in private special day school programs. Nor do the data presented in this table take into account the exceptional children living at home and not receiving any type of

[13] S. A. Kirk, *Educating Exceptional Children* (Boston: Houghton Mifflin Company, 1962), p. 5.

[14] R. P. Mackie and L. M. Dunn, *College and University Programs for the Preparation of Teachers of Exceptional Children* (Washington, D. C.: U. S. Department of Health, Education, and Welfare, 1954), p. 3.

TABLE 5. Enrollment of Exceptional Children and Youth in Local Public School Systems in the United States[15]

Areas of Exceptionality	Number of Pupils
Visually handicapped	11,442
Crippled	29,311
Special health problems	23,077
Deaf and hard-of-hearing	19,537
Speech handicapped	486,944
Socially and emotionally maladjusted	28,260
Mentally retarded	218,185
Gifted	52,269
Other (mixed categories)	13,041
TOTAL	882,066

educational service. Moreover, if slow learners, constituting approximately 15 percent of the population, were to be included, the estimated incidence of exceptional children would be more than doubled. Kirk has estimated that in low socioeconomic communities, the number of slow learners may be 300 per 1000 school-aged children.[16]

These data also do not indicate the increase in special education enrollments over a period of decades. For example, in 1937–38, the figure for public school enrollments in special education programs[17] throughout the country was 18,150, exclusive of the socially and emotionally maladjusted who were not reported. As of 1958, the figure,[18] again exclusive of the socially and emotionally maladjusted for comparative purposes, was 853,806. Hence, while many exceptional children are still not receiving special education geared to meet their learning needs, the increase in programs for them over a twenty-five-year period has been considerable. The growth of special education within Catholic schools during the past ten

[15] R. P. Mackie and P. Robbins, *Exceptional Children and Youth: A Chart Book of Special Education Enrollments in Public Day Schools of the United States* (Washington, D. C.: U. S. Department of Health, Education, and Welfare, 1961), p. 3.

[16] S. A. Kirk, *op. cit.*, p. 92.

[17] M. C. Rice and A. S. Hill, *Statistics of Special Education for Exceptional Children*, 1952–53, *Biennial Survey of Education in the United States*, Chap. 5 (Washington, D. C.: U. S. Department of Health, Education, and Welfare, 1954), p. 13.

[18] R. P. Mackie and P. Robbins, *op. cit.*, p. 3.

years is particularly notable.[19] The Catholic Church has a long and distinguished history of identification with residential programs for exceptional children; the development of parochial day-school programs, however, has been a relatively recent one. Provision for mentally retarded children has been the major focus, and a number of dioceses throughout the country are now offering special classes for these children as part of the total parochial day-school program.

Programs at the college and university level[20] to prepare teachers to work with these children have been upgraded and expanded since World War II, and studies of the competencies needed by teachers of exceptional children have been carried out to assist those in higher education, as well as administrators and supervisors of special education, in providing better preparation and in-service training for such teachers.[21] The postwar period has also witnessed the development of parent organizations, legislation at local, state, and national levels, and improved research techniques, all of which have been concerned with the extension of knowledge regarding the exceptional, and improvement of services for these children.

The Mentally Superior Child. The mentally superior child is usually described as one who possesses general intellectual ability markedly above the average for children of the same chronological age. The terms *gifted* and *genius* or *extremely gifted* are also utilized frequently to designate these children. The best known and most intensively conducted studies of mentally superior children have employed scores attained on tests of mental ability or of scholastic aptitude as the primary means of identifying such children. Frequently an IQ of 130 attained on an individual mental examination has been accepted as the lower level of mental superiority. Terman,[22] however, considered an IQ of 140 as measured by the *Stanford Revision of the Binet Simon Scale* as the lower level of the group which he designated as gifted. A similar method of identifying gifted children has been proposed by a subcommittee of the Division of School

---

[19] W. F. Jenks, C.SS.R., ed., *Directory of Catholic Facilities for Exceptional Children in the United States,* 2 ed. (Washington, D. C.: National Catholic Educational Association, 1956).

[20] W. M. Cruickshank and G. O. Johnson, eds., *Education of Exceptional Children and Youth* (Englewood Cliffs, N. J.: Prentice-Hall, Inc., 1958), pp. 25–28.

[21] R. P. Mackie, L. M. Dunn, and L. F. Cain, *Professional Preparation for Teachers of Exceptional Children: An Overview* (Washington, D. C.: U. S. Department of Health, Education, and Welfare, 1960).

[22] L. M. Terman, *Mental and Physical Traits of a Thousand Gifted Children, Genetic Studies of Genius,* Vol. 1 (Stanford University, Calif.: The Stanford University Press, 1925).

Psychologists of the American Psychological Association which specified "a rate of mental growth of 1.4 or 1.5 mental years per calendar year or faster."[23] It has seemed advisable, however, to supplement tests of mental ability by other criteria in order to identify mentally superior children. These criteria include data from standardized achievement tests, the judgment of teachers, the quality of the child's daily schoolwork, and age-grade placement.

When measures of creativity are developed further, these should also be utilized as a criteria in determining superior mental ability. Creative thinking is considered by some to be the "highest" of the higher mental processes.[24] Investigators, however, are not in agreement concerning the exact nature of creativity. Guilford[25] has suggested that originality and flexibility which characterize creative thought are products of a discrete factor of intelligence which he has designated as "divergent thinking," that is, the tendency to respond to a problem with a variety of solutions. Creativity undoubtedly exercises the purely cognitive abilities. The uniquely appropriate solution achieved by a creative response results from a more efficient ordering of the elements of a problem. However, until a more thorough examination of the creative processes has been made, the *Stanford-Binet Scale* or similar devices will probably remain the most practical single indicator of giftedness.

Investigations of gifted children have revealed that such children are likely to be superior also in physical, social, and moral traits, and generally are well adjusted with respect to personality. With regard to physical characteristics, it has been found that mentally superior children tend to be slightly taller and heavier than unselected children of the same chronological age, that their general health conditions are likely to be as good as and possibly better than those existing among average children. Likewise investigations have demonstrated that intellectually superior children tend to reach puberty and to become adolescent earlier than those of average mental capacity. Decades of longitudinal studies prove that this superiority persists throughout adult life.

---

[23] American Psychological Association, Division of School Psychologists, Subcommittee on Needed Research on Gifted Children, "Needed Research on Gifted Children," *American Psychologist,* 9:77–78, 1954.

[24] D. H. Russell, "Higher Mental Processes," *Encyclopedia of Educational Research,* C. W. Harris, ed., 3 ed. (New York: The Macmillan Co., 1960), p. 652.

[25] J. P. Guilford, "Three Faces of Intellect," *American Psychologist,* 14:469–479, 1959. See also J. W. Getzels and P. W. Jackson, *Creativity and Intelligence* (New York: John Wiley & Sons, Inc., 1962).

With regard to the social characteristics which gifted children have revealed, particularly in play interests and activities, many investigations have reported that these children manifest tendencies to show:

a) Little interest in competitive games but considerable interest in play activities requiring thinking and involving complex rules and system;

b) Preference for quiet, sedentary, and solitary play;

c) Preference for companions older than themselves or of equal mental ability;

d) Ability to get along well with others and to display self-confidence;

e) Leadership ability.

As a group the gifted have better than average social adjustment and seem to be able to cope capably with social problems.

The distinguishing feature of the gifted is naturally superior mental ability. The following mental characteristics distinguish the gifted:

a) Superior ability in handling symbolic materials, forming generalizations, and solving problems quickly and logically;

b) Unusual powers of observation, concentration, and sustained attention;

c) An accurate and logical memory;

d) A lively yet controlled imagination;

e) Ability to perform complicated and lengthy work projects; readiness to initiate and to assume responsibility for such projects;

f) A wide range of interests evidenced in reading habits, conversation, and hobbies;

g) Prudence and sophistication of judgment that promotes a precocious degree of emotional control.

The formal education of the gifted presents many problems. Practically all educators agree, however, that the gifted are most neglected, that the programs designed for the average cannot meet their needs or challenge their abilities. In order to provide adequate opportunity for the gifted to make the most of their abilities several procedures have been suggested. These include: (*a*) acceleration or rapid advancement through the conventional pattern of the elementary and secondary school; (*b*) enrichment of the standard curriculum while the child remains at all times with his chronological age group; (*c*) ability grouping, including special classes and types of programs which usually combine enrichment procedures with a moderate degree of acceleration.

Acceleration is most commonly employed at the elementary school level. It has certain advantages in that it involves few administrative difficulties, and teachers do not need to have "split-level" classes. At the secondary and college levels, acceleration may take the form of increased course loads. Early admission to college is a recent variation of acceleration. Similar in nature is the Advanced Placement Program of the College Entrance Examination Board, through which high school students may take college-level courses while still in the secondary school. The credits received for these courses enable the student to complete his undergraduate work in less than the usual time. The primary objection to acceleration at the elementary school level consists in the recognition that the physical development and social maturity of the child may not keep pace with his mental growth with the result that physical and social maladjustment may be brought about by placement among older children. There is little if any opposition to this procedure at the secondary and college levels.

Enrichment of the standard curriculum through instruction and guidance is ordinarily considered to be the most effective procedure because it provides the child with situations most nearly like those which he will meet in life. This plan provides for the gifted child opportunities to observe and to respect the abilities of others whose endowments are different from his own, helps him to realize that individuals with abilities different from his own have a definite part to play in the world, and also that the completion of many worthwhile endeavors requires the use of many varied abilities, skills, and talents. Enrichment of the curriculum consists of the assignment of more intensive work and of more comprehensive academic tasks, which will both open areas of intellectual exploration to him as well as challenge his capacities and interests. In addition enrichment often imposes social responsibilities which encourage leadership and stimulate initiative. Creative activities in the fields of art or music or literature, hobbies and interests, wide contacts with the best books of all ages are considered to be aspects of enrichment. Such enrichment is more than merely the addition of new activities. It involves a modification of the curriculum in breadth and in depth to secure the opportunity for mentally superior children to do work on their intellectual level, to broaden their understanding of a specific area, and to attain thoroughness, mastery, and originality in order to deal with more difficult aspects of subject matter.

Ability grouping through special classes and programs for the gifted has several advantages. Since this procedure provides classes restricted to students of superior ability and achievement, it provides more than a speeded-up trip through the traditional curriculum. This procedure permits the gifted child to progress rapidly without omitting any essential portions of the subject matter. Furthermore it raises the level of competition, since the child is competing with equally capable pupils and thereby furnishes a more stimulating atmosphere. The gifted child needs to be rewarded for performing at his maximum rather than at his minimum level. Through moderate enrichment in the special class or program, provision is made for a variety of challenging tasks and for the encouragement of more efficient work habits.

Slow-Learning Children and Youth. Mentally slow children and youth constitute a sizable portion of the school population, and estimates of incidence of slow-learningness vary from 10 to 30 percent, depending on the IQ limits selected and the geographic area studied. The most frequently mentioned IQ range for slow-learningness is 76–89, although some school districts extend this to 71–89. In addition, slow learners, and mentally retarded children as well, are found more frequently among school populations in large urban areas where there are concentrations of low-income families.

Slow learners differ from children of average intellect primarily in their inability to achieve academic success at a rate commensurate with their chronological age. Their mental slowness is most evident in the areas of reading and reasoning. A more detailed description of mental characteristics would include the following:

a) Their rote memories are considerably better than their logical memories.

b) As their ability to abstract and to reason is limited, they learn more slowly than do average children.

c) They experience difficulty in forming associations; hence, word meanings and vocabulary are acquired slowly.

d) Their attention span is short.

e) They require more direction in their work; usually they are slow in detecting and correcting errors in their work.

In nonintellectual characteristics, slow learners do not differ markedly from average children, but are a little less well developed physically and have less well-adjusted personalities than do the average.[26] Slow learners are capable of mastering enough of the general academic curriculum of the schools, however, to insure, in adulthood, vocational independence, and adequate social adjustment.[27]

Methods recommended to identify slow learners include: (1) study of age-grade-progress status of pupils; (2) use of cumulative records for background information on health and home status; and (3) utilization of standardized intelligence tests.[28] A comprehensive study of junior and senior high schools revealed that the four most commonly used methods, of a list of twenty, utilized to identify slow learners, were teachers' marks, group intelligence tests, teachers' estimates of school achievement, and information on physical health. Results of standardized achievement tests, as well as appraisal of pupil interests, information on vocational plans and home environment, were also utilized, with individual intelligence tests well down the list of procedures employed.[29]

Accurate identification of these children as intellectually slow is often complicated by the fact that many of them come from homes and neighborhoods in which environmental influences are repressive, culturally deprived, and educationally restricted. Lack of positive intellectual and social experiences in the preschool years, as well as lags in the identification process during the early school years, often result in no educational adjustments for slow children until the upper elementary or junior high school years, when efforts in remediation and expanded cultural experiences may be less fruitful. Early identification of such children may salvage some from the ranks of both the slow learning and upper retarded range.[30]

Educational adjustments to meet the needs of slow-learning children and youth have included grouping within the regular grades and homogeneous grouping in special classes. The former method is more frequently

---

[26] W. B. Featherstone, *Teaching the Slow Learner,* revised and enlarged (New York: Bureau of Publications, Teachers College, Columbia University, 1951), pp. 4–7.

[27] S. A. Kirk, *op. cit.,* p. 86.

[28] W. B. Featherstone, *op. cit.,* chap. II.

[29] A. Jewett and J. D. Hull, coordinators, *Teaching Rapid and Slow Learners in High Schools* (Washington, D. C.: U. S. Department of Health, Education, and Welfare, 1954), p. 18.

[30] S. B. Sarason and T. Gladwin, "Psychological and Cultural Problems in Mental Subnormality," Part II of R. L. Masland, S. B. Sarason, and T. Gladwin, *Mental Subnormality* (New York: Basic Books, Inc., 1958), pp. 289–301.

employed[31] and, with some reservations, generally supported.[32] When children are grouped within the regular grades, some additional adjustments made in the teaching program include resource rooms for special activities and remediation, as well as special classes, particularly at the junior and senior high school levels, for instruction in practical applications of academic skills and guidance in vocational and social adjustment. It is essential that teachers selected for work with slow children and youth be individuals of strong professional qualifications, willing to accept the academic limitations of these children, and able to devise educational methods and approaches that are realistic and supportive.[33] Guidelines for teaching these children would include: (1) goals and objectives that are realistically adapted to meet the needs of slow learners in their life situations; (2) concrete activities including much firsthand and pictorial experience; (3) activities marked by simplicity of organization, generous use of demonstration and practical experiences, frequent drill and practice in skills and habits; (4) evaluation at frequent intervals to determine progress and needed adjustments or remedial procedures.[34]

The aim throughout the formal school careers of slow learning children must be to provide them with training suited to their capacities, to stimulate and direct their mental development as fully as possible, to make the utmost use of whatever resources and skills they possess. More important than either academic education or vocational training are the moral and social habits and attitudes which these children form as the result of their daily experiences in school. They must be prepared through school training for the responsibilities which will devolve upon them and must develop particularly the ability to get along with others.

Mentally Retarded Children and Youth. The term "mental retardation" is broadly used to describe children with subaverage general intellectual functioning originating during the developmental period and associated with impairment in one or more of the following aspects of adaptive behavior: (1) maturation; (2) learning; and (3) social adjustment.[35] Subaverage general intellectual functioning has been described by

---

[31] A. Jewett and J. D. Hull, *op. cit.*, p. 13.

[32] W. B. Featherstone, *op. cit.*, pp. 24–29; S. A. Kirk, *op. cit.*, p. 88.

[33] J. B. Conant, *Slums and Suburbs* (New York: McGraw-Hill Book Company, Inc., 1961), pp. 66–69.

[34] Adapted from W. B. Featherstone, *op. cit.*, p. 69.

[35] R. Heber, "A Manual on Terminology and Classification in Mental Retardation," Monograph Supplement to the *American Journal of Mental Deficiency*, 64: 2:3–4, September, 1959.

TABLE 6. Descriptive Terminology, Estimated Rate of Incidence, and School Achievement in Mental Retardation

TERMINOLOGY						
Social	Educational	Legal	IQ Range	M.A. Range at Maturity	Estimated Rate Per 1000 School-Age Children*	Estimated Maximum Educational Achievement by Grade at Maturity
Mild or High Grade	Educable	Moron	50–70/75	7-12	10–50**	Gr. 2–6
Moderate or Middle Grade	Trainable	Imbecile	25–50	3–7	4	Gr. K-2
Severe or Low Grade	. . .	Idiot	0–25	0–3	1	. . .

*** Adapted from S. A. Kirk, *op. cit.*, p. 92.**
**** Dependent upon socioeconomic level of community (low socioeconomic level: 50 children; middle socioeconomic level: 25 children; high socioeconomic level: 10 children).**

Heber as referring to performance which is greater than one standard deviation below the population mean, of the age group involved, on measures of general intellectual functioning.[36] This would include all children below, approximately, 88 IQ. However, in general educational practice, the IQ range 70 to 75 is designated as the upper level of functioning for placement in a class for retarded learners.

Moderately retarded children and youth with IQs between 50 and 70/75 are most frequently found in elementary and secondary day schools and have been termed the educable mentally retarded. Some schools also provide classes for children between 25 and 50 IQ, and these children have been termed the trainable retarded. Many children below 25 IQ are found in public and private residential institutions for the retarded where the emphasis is on protective care. The number of retardates at all intellectual levels living with their families and receiving no specialized training or treatment is not known but is believed to be quite high. The majority of retarded children and youth are found in the educable range, with the estimate of children below 50 IQ at less than 1 percent. In Table 6 are summarized terminologies used to describe these children, as well as the estimated rate of incidence and school achievement at each level.

Identifying retarded children below 50 IQ at an early age is generally less difficult than is the case with the mildly retarded, since in the more

[36] *Ibid.*, p. 3.

severely retarded the developmental lag is quite marked from an early age. Moderately, or educable, retarded children often do not vary significantly in their preschool development from nonretarded children and are physically quite normal in appearance. A large proportion of educable retarded children come from home environments similar to those of slow learners, and some of the same problems of early identification are encountered.[37] With this group of children, a major causative factor in their retardation is considered to be cultural and, in this respect, the line of demarcation between them and the slow-learning group is often difficult to determine. While heredity cannot be entirely ruled out as a causative factor in many slow-learning and educable retarded children, recent studies suggest that deprived home environments may be a major factor in setting intellectual limits at an early age.[38] In such children, it is not uncommon to find that one or more siblings as well as either or both parents have been identified as slow learners or educable retardates and, for this reason, they have been referred to as familial retardates.

Another category of causation includes some rather rare types of retardation, known to be the result of definitive genetic or hereditary factors. In a third group, acquired organic damage after conception seems to play a far more significant role in causality. In this last group, organic damage can occur prenatally, perinatally, or postnatally. An example of damage occurring during each of these temporal sequences would be, respectively, maternal infection resulting in damage to the foetus, injury to the child during the birth process, or infective disease, such as encephalitis, during the early years of life. Hence, cultural deprivation, genetic determinants, or organic damage may all be causes, either singly or in combination, of mental retardation.[39] The highest incidence of retardation is associated with the first category; however, a more severe degree of retardation is generally found in the second and third categories.

Educational provisions for retarded children are most frequently made for those in the educable range. These children are generally provided for in special classes located in regular elementary, junior high, and less frequently, senior high school buildings. Some do remain, as do most slow learners, in regular classes with or without modification of the curriculum to meet their needs. Unlike slow learners, educable mentally retarded

[37] S. B. Sarason and T. Gladwin, *op. cit.*, pp. 289–301.

[38] S. A. Kirk, *Early Education of the Mentally Retarded* (Urbana: University of Illinois Press, 1958).

[39] S. A. Kirk, *Educating Exceptional Children, op. cit.*, pp. 92–102.

children have been the subject of much less controversy regarding their educational placement in special classes. However, some questions as to the efficacy of special classes have been raised.[40] Other arrangements for these children include special segregated schools, modified special classes, and ungraded classes. Special segregated schools for educable children are not widespread and are utilized more frequently in the education of moderately retarded or trainable children. Modified special class programs are found more often in smaller communities with relatively few retarded children, and may take the form of placement in a wide-age-range special class for part of the day with placement in a regular class for the balance of the day. It may also involve placement in a regular class of reduced size with an itinerant teacher assigned to work with the retarded children on a part-time basis. Ungraded classes usually include in one room children from six to sixteen and are becoming less frequent as school districts merge and diversify their educational programs.

Special class programs for educable retarded children in large school districts usually include the following levels: Primary for children with C.A.'s between six and ten and M.A.'s of about three to six; intermediate, C.A. ten to thirteen and M.A. six to nine; secondary or junior high level, C.A. thirteen to sixteen and M.A. eight to twelve. A few school systems offer preschool programs as well as senior high and postschool classes. In most systems, the educable retarded terminate their education at age sixteen, leaving from a junior high school to find employment. Vocational provisions for retarded youth beyond sixteen years of age are growing, however, and combined schoolwork programs have been introduced into some senior high school systems to prepare the retarded adolescent more adequately for the world of work.

Curricula for the educable mentally retarded have been developed with social, vocational, and personal adjustment as major objectives. The academic program requires considerable modification because of the marked mental inability to comprehend and generalize. Rote memory is sometimes quite good, but logical memory and creative imagery, as well as verbal skills in reading, vocabulary, and writing, are generally much below average. Arithmetical concepts beyond the four basic computations are usually lacking. Many of these children can learn to read up to a

[40] B. Blatt, "Some Persistently Recurring Assumptions Concerning the Mentally Subnormal," in J. H. Rothstein, *Mental Retardation: Readings and Resources* (New York: Holt, Rinehart and Winston, Inc., 1961), pp. 118–121.

fourth- or fifth-grade level by the junior high school years, but teachers face the challenge of finding reading materials that combine high interest with low reading level. Programs are often developed around the unit plan[41] and include simple, practical experiences simulating the activities of daily living which the retarded face in their out-of-school lives. Programs at the primary and intermediate levels focus on readiness for and development of skills in the tool subjects to provide these children with academic skills which they may later need to live purposeful, economically self-sufficient, and useful lives. Programs at the secondary level are designed to prepare the retarded for life outside the school environment.[42]

The entire program of education for the educable mentally retarded should be designed to further the development of physical efficiency, adequate social relationships, wise use of leisure time, vocational independence and self-sufficiency, and acceptance within their capacities of home and community responsibilities.[43] In addition, the educational program should foster the development of moral habits, particularly integrity, honesty, and truthfulness. The Catholic retarded child should be given a sound program of religious instruction either in a special class within a parochial school or in a released-time program of religious education designed to help him understand and live by those truths and teachings of his faith which are within his understanding. The entire purpose of the educational program for the mentally retarded is to provide such children and youth with opportunities to develop those potentialities they may possess.

Emotionally Disturbed and Socially Maladjusted Children and Youth. Behavior and conduct disorders in children and youth are among the most serious problems confronting educators today, particularly in large urban school systems. Such children and youth are unable to adjust to the usual requirements of life within the home, school, and community. These disturbances vary in degree from the barely detectable, especially in the early school years, to pronounced antisocial and psychotic traits which may result in delinquency, crime, and ultimate institutionalization. These behavior disorders are not confined to any particular period of maturation, nor are they due primarily either to mental deviation or

---

[41] C. P. Ingram, *Education of the Slow-Learning Child,* 3 ed. (New York: The Ronald Press Company, 1960).

[42] S. A. Kirk and G. O. Johnson, *Educating the Retarded Child* (Boston: Houghton Mifflin Co., 1951), p. 130.

[43] E. H. Martens, *Curriculum Adjustments for the Mentally Retarded,* 2 ed. Washington, D. C.: U. S. Department of Health, Education, and Welfare, 1953), p. 12.

physical handicap. Older children and youth with conduct and behavior disorders do not usually have to be discovered, for they make themselves known by their deviant behavior. A needed area of continuing research is the identification of these children in the early years of their schooling in order to prevent and correct social and emotional maladjustments before they become irremediable.[44]

Kirk has defined a behavior deviation as "that behavior of a child which (1) has a detrimental effect on his development and adjustment and/or (2) interferes with the lives of other people."[45] Emotionally disturbed children, sometimes referred to as unsocial, have been described as withdrawn, irritable, peculiar, neurotic, or nervous. Socially maladjusted children, sometimes referred to as antisocial, are frequently described as incorrigible, destructive, quarrelsome, rebellious, and cruel, and are usually found to be socially immature as well as educationally retarded. The emotionally disturbed child has been termed a "truant from life"[46] while the socially maladjusted child is in reality often a truant from school. The distinction between the two is not always clear, however, with a combination of neurotic and aggressive behavior not infrequently present. The underlying causative factors, not always easily isolated and identified, are often the same for both types of behavior deviations.

The child marked by social maladjustment may ultimately enter the ranks of delinquency and criminality as he reaches adolescence and maturity; the emotionally unstable child may eventually manifest symptoms of severe mental illness and may need placement in a residential institution for the mentally ill.

It has already been noted that causative factors in emotional disturbance and social maladjustment may be similar. Chief among these is, undoubtedly, disruption in the home environment resulting in a disturbed parent-child relationship. Broken marriages; homes marked by quarreling, neglect, and indifference; by economic instability and deprivation; by alcoholism; by inconsistent discipline of the child, either too severe or too permissive, all contribute to behavior disorders. In the case of the socially maladjusted child, particularly, the home is often characterized by immoral behavior on the part of parents and older siblings, profanity, untruthfulness, and criminality. These patterns of behavior are

[44] E. Bower, *Early Identification of Emotionally Handicapped Children in School* (Springfield, Ill.: Charles C. Thomas, 1960).
[45] S. A Kirk, *Educating Exceptional Children, op. cit.*, p. 330.
[46] B. Bettelheim, *Truants from Life* (Glencoe, Ill.: The Free Press, 1955).

usually reinforced in the child by the neighborhood in which he lives, which may consist of substandard housing with overcrowding, undesirable companions, little or no adult control over the community and domination by destructive juvenile gangs.

It should be noted that poverty of economic and social environment, of themselves, do not cause socially maladjusted or delinquent behavior. Good home training and proper parental supervision enable the child to withstand considerable environmental pressure of an antisocial nature, while lack of these factors may make for social irresponsibility. Moreover, antisocial problem children have come from homes of every economic and social status. It should be remembered that the influence wielded by the home is not due to physical surroundings but rather to the degree of unity and harmony, and to the family spirit in the home.

While mental deviations and physical handicaps are by no means to be equated with behavior disorders, they may contribute to maladjustment and may predispose the child toward unsocial or antisocial behavior. The child may be placed in situations which he is not capable of meeting and may compensate for his inadequacies, depending on many complex factors, by withdrawal or by aggressive acts. For this reason, then, a first step in the detection and correction of behavior disorders should be careful assessment of the child's physical and mental capacities, and the provision of therapy and educational adjustments where needed as a means of modifying deviant emotional reactions.

Ideally, prevention rather than correction should be the focus in considering problems of emotional and social deviation. Prevention is primarily the task of the home and involves providing the child with security, stability, and opportunities to utilize his developing capacities for initiative, autonomy, and self-accomplishment. Sound moral and religious training, as well as a home environment which stresses self-control and wise discipline, are also essential. Realistically, the educator is faced with the fact that many homes do not provide such guidance and support for children and youth and, hence, the school must cope with the problem of correction or, at least, the reduction of behavior disorders. In this area of exceptionality, perhaps more than in others the teacher cannot work unaided; school social workers, attendance officers, visiting teachers, as well as child guidance and mental hygiene clinics, juvenile courts, and probation officers provide important supplementary services.

Educational programs within the schools have occasionally included special classes for socially and emotionally disturbed children, although where these are found it is usually on a segregated basis and for the more severely maladjusted. Some school systems have initiated pilot programs of a preventive nature within the regular school, which include special classes at the primary and intermediate levels for children who give evidence of presenting more severe difficulties at a later age. A number of large cities have inaugurated intensive programs for culturally deprived children as a positive approach to the problem of undermotivated youth and potential dropouts.[47] Not all such children and youth are by any means disturbed or maladjusted; but the relationship between disinterest in educational achievement and behavior disorders has been too frequently noted to be ignored, particularly in large urban communities.

Despite the growth of specialized educational programs for children and youth with behavior disorders, major responsibility for these children continues to fall to the teacher in the regular grades. Some of the distinguishing symptoms of emotionally disturbed, withdrawn children are as follows:

a) Habitual avoidance of group activity;
b) Frequent depression, suspiciousness, and resentfulness;
c) Fearfulness, extreme timidity, and shyness;
d) Boisterousness and/or oversubmissiveness;
e) Temper tantrums, overaggressiveness, obstinacy;
f) Speech disturbances;
g) Nail biting, persistence of infantile behavior;
h) Excessive daydreaming, withdrawal, self-consciousness.

Socially maladjusted children and youth may also exhibit many of these traits with more emphasis, however, on aggressive, disruptive behavior and expressed dislike of school rather than on withdrawing, submissive tendencies. The antisocial child in the classroom directs his frustrations and anxieties outward against the teacher and other children rather than in upon himself as in the case of the emotionally disturbed child.

It has already been noted that social maladjustment may take the form of truancy and, in the adolescent years, delinquency. Truancy is usually the first overt antisocial act of the child who later becomes seriously maladjusted and delinquent. Truancy has been called the "kindergarten of crime" because it involves and implies (*a*) unsupervised activity in an

[47] J. B. Conant, *op. cit.*, pp. 60–63.

unsatisfactory environment; (*b*) irregular and, hence, fragmented formal education; (*c*) the formation of attitudes of opposition to school control and authority which may result in consistent antagonism toward society and its laws. The conditions which breed truancy and delinquency are similar and have already been described. Characteristics associated with these children and youth which can often be identified by the classroom teacher include the following:

a) Dislike of school and consequent lack of desire to attend;
b) Limited ability to learn or failure to learn;
c) Expressions of boredom toward the school program and resentment of school routine and restriction;
d) Parental indifference to the school program;
e) Unkempt appearance and lack of suitable clothes;
f) Expressions of bitterness toward parents and other authority figures;
g) Destruction of school materials or property;
h) Cruel and bullying behavior on the playground.

Many of these traits have been listed by Kvaraceous in his *Delinquency Proneness Check List.*[48] The delinquent has been described by Kvaraceous and Miller as the nonadult who has come into conflict with the law with sufficient frequency and/or seriousness so as to provide a firm basis for legal action against him.[49] A broader definition would be that delinquency is a social and moral disorder involving antisocial conduct which is evidenced through offenses against morals, against property, against persons, and against the peace of the community. While many causes of delinquency have been detailed, basic to the problem is neglect of moral training and lack of proper religious instruction. Moral training involves reinforcement of the principles according to which life is to be lived. It involves a knowledge of the distinction between right and wrong, of the authority of moral law, of the sacredness of duty, of the inviolability of conscience, of respect for the rights and property of others. However, morality cannot be divorced from religion. There is no satisfactory substitute for religious sanction in morality. The child must be systematically instructed in religion if he is to function dynamically in his life and in all his activities.

Knowledge of the behavior characteristics of emotionally disturbed and

[48] W. C. Kvaraceous, "Juvenile Delinquency," *What Research Says to the Teacher*, No. 15 (Washington, D. C.: American Educational Research Association of the National Educational Association, August, 1958), p. 17.

[49] W. C. Kvaraceous and W. B. Miller, *Delinquent Behavior: Culture and the Individual* (Washington, D. C.: National Education Association, 1959), p. 54.

socially maladjusted children and youth should assist the school and the individual teacher to identify some of the factors which can reduce the problems of such children.[50]

a) Adjustment of broad curricula goals to meet the realistic vocational and social needs of children whose lives are characterized by failure, uncertainty, and limited academic interest;

b) Adaptation of instruction to individual abilities within the regular grades to develop confidence, efficiency, and academic success;

c) Provision of worthy teacher example, as a means of moral training and character formation, through self-control, just and consistent discipline, avoidance of extreme conditions of stimulation and inhibition;

d) The building of realistic habits and attitudes that result in wholesome behavior and the fostering of worthy ideals, presented in comprehensible form, that the child may strive to imitate;[51]

e) Provision of opportunities for pupils to assume responsibilities, to make clear-cut decisions, and to abide by them, thus encouraging the facing of reality;

f) Development of a classroom environment that is physically attractive, intellectually stimulating, and free of social and emotional tensions.

While the teacher and the school cannot accomplish single-handedly what should be the primary responsibility of the home, education's responsibility for the emotionally disturbed and socially maladjusted child is a considerable one. The school must strive, insofar as possible, to create an environment for learning that motivates the disturbed child to find satisfaction in realistic accomplishments, and assists the socially maladjusted child to divert his aggressions and hostilities into constructive channels.

Children and Youth With Physical Handicaps. Children and youth with physical handicaps may be considered broadly to include the following categories: the blind and partially sighted, the deaf and hard-of-hearing, the speech handicapped, children with crippling conditions and special health problems, and multiple handicapped children.

Identification of these children varies in difficulty and complexity, and those with marked sensory or physical handicaps, such as blindness, cerebral palsy, or stuttering, are usually recognized, although not necessarily

[50] Adapted from S. A. Kirk, *op. cit.*, pp. 352–354.

[51] In schools under religious auspices, a direct program of systematic training in religion as the core of the curriculum can facilitate the development of such goals.

treated, at an early age. Children with marginal handicaps, such as partial sight, heart conditions, or diabetes, are sometimes not identified as readily, to the detriment often of their physical well-being and their educational progress. Many physically handicapped children are educationally retarded, although not necessary mentally below average, because of lack of early identification, or as the result of hospitalization and prolonged programs of physical therapy.

Educational programs designed to meet the needs of these various types of children vary depending usually on the extent to which the handicap interferes with their ability to learn. Provisions for blind and deaf children generally take the form of segregated special schools, either residential or day, through the elementary and junior high schools levels. The intellectually bright and gifted among these children are often capable of integration into the regular grades in the later years of their schooling. Experimentation in integration of the deaf as early as the fourth grade has already been attempted with some success.[52] Partially sighted and hard-of-hearing children are usually educated in regular classes with special materials and equipment, as well as a resource or itinerant teacher available to aid both the regular teacher and the handicapped children in his class. The same approach is generally utilized with speech-handicapped children, who often leave the regular classroom for one or more periods a week for speech therapy with an itinerant speech teacher.

Children with crippling conditions, as well as special health problems, may also be integrated into regular classroom programs, usually with success. It is important that the teacher be provided with sufficient information on medications or restriction of physical activity insofar as these relate to the child's participation in the educational program. Architectural adjustments such as ramps, guard rails, and wide doors on elevators and rooms, rather than mental ability, may determine whether an orthopedically handicapped children can participate in the regular school program.

Children with more severe crippling conditions, particularly the cerebral-palsied who often represent a complex of handicaps, may need the less competitive environment of a special class with a teacher who is qualified by preparation and experience to work with such children. This

[52] J. Justman and S. Moskowitz, *The Integration of Deaf Children in a Hearing Class: the Second Year* (New York: Bureau of Educational Research, New York City Board of Education, 1957).

is also true of children with more than one minor handicap such as a combination of partial vision and speech defect, neither of which alone might cause him to be placed in a special class. In addition to these arrangements within the framework of the school program, some physically handicapped children are provided for by itinerant teachers who go directly to home or hospital to carry out the educational program. Closed-circuit television and special telephone arrangements between the classroom and the home bound or hospitalized child are supplementary features sometimes utilized in such programs. The educational adjustments and electronic devices that can be employed to meet the needs of handicapped children are constantly increasing, as education and technology widen their horizons to include within their scope all children who can be educated.

Studies of the personal and social adjustment of physically handicapped children reveal that there is no clear-cut relationship between degree of physical disability and adequacy of adjustment and, hence, that it is an oversimplification to assume that the more disabled the individual, the more difficult is the achievement of good adjustment.[53] The attitudes of parents, in particular, as well as of teachers toward the child would seem to be of far more importance in forming the child's self-concepts than the severity of the disability and concomitant handicap.

The home training and formal education of the physically handicapped child must emphasize the principle that such a child need not be a liability but rather that he is potentially a social asset. Many handicapped individuals, though burdened by seemingly insuperable physical defects, have accomplished noteworthy achievements in many fields of industry, art, and science. Others, less well known, have made excellent, or at least adequate, adjustments to their disabilities. The physically handicapped child must receive that type of training and education which will enable him to adjust to his handicap to the greatest possible extent and to realize his capacities to the fullest measure. Such training and education must aim at building stability of character, self-dependence, and responsibility, so that the child may live a useful and contented life.

The Educational Implication of Individual Differences. Individual differences in mental abilities, in academic aptitudes, and in school achievements constitute a basic factor in education. Therefore, one of the out-

[53] B. A. Wright, *Physical Disability — A Psychological Approach* (New York: Harper & Row, 1960), pp. 53–57.

standing problems in education is to devise methods of dealing with large numbers of pupils in such a way that each pupil will receive the direction, guidance, and special work which he requires in order to improve himself to the maximum of his capacities.

EXERCISES

1. Outline the chapter.
2. List and define the terms which you have learned from your study of this chapter.
3. Explain the nature of individual differences and the factors which influence individual differences.
4. Select one plan or device designed to adapt instruction to individual differences and then analyze the principal features of the plan or device, stating its advantages and its limitations.
5. Discuss the following statements:
   a) "Ability guarantees achievement."
   b) "Interest and diligence will enable the individual to surpass ability limits."
   c) "Correlation, not compensation, is the law of nature."
   d) "All men are more alike than they are different."
   e) "Differences among pupils are of degree rather than of kind."
   f) "The effect of homogeneous grouping is to breed conceit in the bright and feelings of inferiority in the dull."
6. It is frequently observed by teachers that the youngest child in the class is the most capable in learning while the oldest is usually the least capable. How can this situation be explained? What are its causes and its educational implications?
7. Discuss the effectiveness of each of the following:
   a) The nongraded school;
   b) Team teaching;
   c) Programed instruction.
8. What provisions have been made to adjust education to the capacities of the gifted? Which of these provisions is most satisfactory?
9. What provisions have been made to adapt instruction to the limitations of slow learners? of the mentally retarded?
10. What is the educational significance of individual differences?

SELECTED REFERENCES FOR STUDY AND READING

Anastasi, A., *Differential Psychology,* 3 ed. (New York: The Macmillan Co., 1958).

Baker, H. J., *Introduction to Exceptional Children,* 3 ed. (New York: The Macmillan Co., 1959).

Carmichael, L., ed., *Manual of Child Psychology,* 2 ed. (New York: John Wiley & Sons, Inc., 1954), Chaps. 16 and 17.

Cruickshank, W. M., ed., *Psychology of Exceptional Children and Youth* 2 ed. (Englewood Cliffs, N. J.: Prentice-Hall, Inc., 1963).
Cruickshank, W. M., and Johnson, G. O., eds., *Education of Exceptional Children and Youth* (Englewood Cliffs, N. J.: Prentice-Hall, Inc., 1958).
Cutts, N. E., and Moseley, N., eds., *Providing for Individual Differences in the Elementary School* (Englewood Cliffs, N. J.: Prentice-Hall, Inc., 1960).
Dunn, L. M., ed., *Exceptional Children in the Schools* (New York: Holt, Rinehart and Winston, Inc., 1963).
Everett, S., ed., *Programs for the Gifted* (New York: Harper and Row, 1961).
Faerber, L. J., *Provisions for Low-Ability Pupils in Catholic High Schools* (Washington, D. C.: The Catholic University of America Press, 1949).
Featherstone, W. B., *Teaching the Slow Learner,* rev. ed. (New York: Bureau of Publications, Teachers College, Columbia University, 1951).
French, J. L., ed., *Educating the Gifted: A Book of Readings* (New York: Holt, Rinehart and Winston, Inc., 1959).
Gallagher, J. J., *Teaching the Gifted Child* (Boston: Allyn and Bacon, Inc., 1964).
Garrett, H. E., *Great Experiments in Psychology,* 3 ed. (New York: Appleton-Century-Crofts, Inc., 1951), Chap. 13.
Haring, N. G., and Phillips, E. L., *Educating Emotionally Disturbed Children* (New York: McGraw-Hill Book Co., Inc., 1962).
Heber, R., *et. al., Bibliography of World Literature on Mental Retardation, January 1940–March 1963* (Washington, D. C.: U. S. Government Printing Office, 1963).
Ingram, C. P., *Education of the Slow-Learning Child,* 3 ed. (New York: The Ronald Press Co., 1960).
Jenkins, J. J., and Paterson, D. G., eds., *Studies in Individual Differences* (New York: Appleton-Century-Crofts, Inc., 1961).
Jenks, W. F., *Individual Differences in Elementary and Secondary School Children* (Washington, D. C.: The Catholic University of America Press, 1956).
Jordan, T., *The Exceptional Child* (Columbus, Ohio: Charles E. Merrill Books, Inc., 1962).
Kephart, N. C., *The Slow-Learner in the Classroom* (Columbus, Ohio: Charles E. Merrill Books, Inc., 1962).
Kirk, S. A., *Educating Exceptional Children* (Boston: Houghton Mifflin Co., 1962).
Magary, J. F., and Eichorn, J. R., *The Exceptional Child: A Book of Readings* (New York: Holt, Rinehart and Winston, Inc., 1960).
National Society for the Study of Education, Forty-Ninth Yearbook, Part II, *Education of Exceptional Children,* 1950.
——— Fifty-Second Yearbook, Part I, *Adapting the Secondary School Program to the Needs of Youth,* 1953.
——— Fifty-Seventh Yearbook, Part II, *Education for the Gifted,* 1958.
——— Sixty-First Yearbook, Part I, *Individualizing Instruction,* 1962.
Sarason, S. B., *Psychological Problems in Mental Deficiency,* 3 ed. (New York: Harper and Row, 1959).
Stevens, H. A., and Heber, R., *Mental Retardation: A Review of Research* (Chicago: The University of Chicago Press, 1964).

Sumption, M. R., and Luecking, E. M., *Education of the Gifted* (New York: The Ronald Press Co., 1960).

Terman, L. M., and Oden, M. H., *The Gifted Child Grows Up: Genetic Studies of Genius,* Vol. IV (Stanford, Calif.: Stanford University Press, 1947).

——— *The Gifted Group at Middle Life: Genetic Studies of Genius,* Vol. V (Stanford, Calif.: Stanford University Press, 1959).

Theodore, Sister Mary, *The Challenge of the Retarded Child* (Milwaukee: The Bruce Publishing Co., 1963).

Tyler, L. E., *The Psychology of Human Differences,* 2 ed. (New York: Appleton-Century-Crofts, Inc., 1956).

Wechsler, D., *The Range of Human Capacities,* 2 ed. (Baltimore: Williams and Wilkins Co., 1952).

part IV

LEARNING

chapter 7

The Learning Process

The Definition of Learning. Learning constitutes the central theme of Educational Psychology — an understanding of how pupils learn and of the conditions under which they learn best is the first and major contribution which psychology can make to educational practice. It is the purpose of this chapter to explain what learning is; how and under what conditions it takes place; the kinds of learning; the theories devised to account for it; and the factors, both physiological and psychological, which influence it. In the field of educational psychology, learning is the core or central topic to which more space and attention have been devoted than to any other aspect. This is as it should be, for the school is a special environment for the facilitation of learning. The major task of the school is to provide for the effective acquisition and utilization of knowledge and skill. Hence, in this chapter the discussion of learning has been restricted to the basic fundamental facts and principles of learning as it occurs in the school situation, which presupposes learners, teachers, a purpose for learning, subject matter, methods, and the necessary equipment.

Learning is the most universal and important occupation of man; it is the great task of childhood and of youth, and it is the only means of achieving progress at any period in life. The capacity to learn is the most significant native endowment of man, for it is the primary characteristic of his rational nature. It is the foundation of every human act and of all human achievement. Psychologists consider that the capacity to learn constitutes the best single measure of man's intelligence. Likewise, since it is obvious that education is possible only because man can learn, it is evident that learning is the basic phenomenon and the key aspect of the educative process. The major activities of the school consist in the motivation, guidance, direction, and evaluation of the process of learning in order to aid pupils to gain an appreciation of and control over the values of life.

Learning involves mental activity by means of which knowledge and skill are acquired, retained, and utilized. Learning always implies that a change or modification has been produced in the response, reaction, thought, conduct, or attitude of the learner. This change or modification may range from that which is comparatively simple in character to that which is extremely complex. Hence, learning may be described as the *mental activity by means of which knowledge and skill, habits, attitudes, and ideals are acquired, retained, and utilized, resulting in the progressive adaptation and modification of conduct and behavior.*[1] The learning process consists of the way in which learning takes place and involves primarily the capacities and activities by means of which knowledge is gained, skill is produced, habits, attitudes, and ideals are acquired. The study of the learning process involves an analysis of the functioning of the mental capacities by the activities of which the products of learning, that is, knowledge, skill, habits, attitudes, and ideals, are attained.

How Learning Takes Place. Actually how effectively and efficiently the pupil in school will learn depends upon how well the classroom teacher understands and applies what is known about the learning process. The most significant characteristic of learning is the activity of the learner. This means that learning cannot be merely a process of passive assimilation or absorption, but is rather a process of adaptation which necessitates purposeful effort on the part of the learner. Mere exposure to learning is not sufficient, since learning takes place in proportion to the activity of the learner. The pupil in school learns through participating in such activities as reading textbooks, writing themes, solving problems, listening attentively to explanations presented by the teacher, answering questions orally, writing examination papers, looking up reference materials, working in the industrial-arts shops, preparing experiments in the laboratory, and the like. His learning occurs progressively and is an activity of his mind. Learning, therefore, depends not merely on the materials which books contain and which teachers present, but rather more

---

[1] See B. R. Bugelski, *The Psychology of Learning* (New York: Holt, Rinehart and Winston, Inc., 1956), pp. 5–9, for a consideration of a variety of definitions of learning.

on the way in which the mind of the pupil reacts in response to such extrinsic agents as books and teachers. Learning is self-development through self-activity, involving the organization and integration of experiences by means of intellect and will. Learning involves the development of the individual's capacities and the gradual actualization of his potentialities.

The objectives of the learning process in the school situation are: the acquisition of knowledge; the development of skills and habits involving ability to perform tasks or to acquire patterns of behavior; the functioning of the power to think clearly, resourcefully, and independently. All of these are present in all school learning, but not to the same proportion or degree.

In order to understand how learning takes place, it is essential to know the nature of the learner and the nature of his mind. Learning takes place because man is a rational being endowed with an intellect. However, in this life there is an intimate dependence of mind on bodily functions, for the substantial union of soul and body forms the source of all activity. While the major factor in learning is the intellect, nevertheless the intellect by itself does not provide man with knowledge. The learning process includes the development and utilization of all of man's powers and capacities, both physical and mental. This means that learning cannot be accounted for wholly in terms of the mental or wholly in terms of the physical, for both are necessary. The physiological basis of learning is the plasticity of the nervous system, while the functioning of the cognitive powers constitutes the mental basis. These powers include perception, imagination, memory, attention, and the acts of the intellect, that is, the formation of concepts, judgment, and reasoning. In addition, the feelings and emotions constitute an important factor in the learning process. They aid in the facilitation of learning and are aspects of motivation. Likewise, habit is a basic factor in the learning process, since learning becomes a permanent acquisition through the formation of appropriate habits. Finally, all learning involves essentially an act of the will, which is evident in the decision made concerning the goal or purpose sought in learning as well as in the choice of the means to achieve that goal.

An adequate description of the nature of the learning process must take into consideration an important element which exercises an influence upon the successful functioning of that process, namely, the learner's stage of maturity.[2] Learning is dependent upon the level of development attained by the learner, which is usually designated as "readiness to learn." This involves a level of maturity, physical, mental, social, and emotional; an experiential and understanding level; and a background of interests which are indicative of a state of readiness, both physiological and psychological, to engage in learning activity. In order that learning may be both effective and economical, learning tasks, together with the materials and methods of instruction, must be adapted to the level of the child's development.

The Types of Learning. A better understanding of the nature of learning may be attained by classifying learning according to the psychological functions which are obviously involved in responding to situations, or according to the outcomes or products sought. There are four major types of learning which include the principal activities of the school. Such activities as gaining an understanding of a philosophical principle, or solving originals in geometry, or discovering the meaning and application of a scientific law, are clearly intellectual in nature and involve general concepts, judgment, reasoning, understanding of relationships, and reflective thinking. This type of learning is designated as *rational,* and the outcome sought is knowledge. Other activities such as typing, handwriting, industrial arts, playing a musical instrument involve sensation, perception, muscular responses, coordinated movements, and the elements of observation and practice. This type of learning is designated as *motor,* and the outcome sought is skill. In addition, there are school activities which are concerned chiefly with the acquisition of responses in a fixed sequence, such as spelling, committing a poem to memory, dates and events which involve the processes of memory and association. This is designated as *associative* learning, and the outcome sought is the fixing of verbal materials in the mind. Finally, there are activities within the areas of the fine arts, such as the enjoyment of music, creative work in art, development of taste for good literature. These involve feelings and emotions, attitudes, and ideals. This is designated as *appreciative* learning, and the outcome sought is an attitude of value and appreciation.

Rational Learning. The outcome sought in this type of learning is *knowledge* which may be described as the "mental assimilation of any

---

[2] G. L. Anderson and A. I. Gates, "The General Nature of Learning," National Society for Study of Education, Forty-Ninth Yearbook, Part I, *Learning and Instruction,* 1950, pp. 12–28.

object, fact, principle, or law within the natural or supernatural order."[3] Rational learning is clearly intellectual in nature and involves the process of abstraction by which concepts are formed. It implies the development of basic meanings of terms which constitute the specialized vocabularies of the various school subjects such as mathematics, science, and language, together with the understanding and utilization of these terms. It involves, likewise, the process of judgment, that is, the comparison, identification, discrimination, and discernment of ideas which are expressed in the form of rules, principles, laws. Finally, it involves the process of reasoning, particularly in the recognition of cause-and-effect relationships, in the drawing of inferences, in the formulation of generalizations, in the analysis of difficulties, and in the solution of problems. Moreover, it should be noted that rational learning is concerned not merely with the acquisition of new knowledge but likewise with the integration of the new with knowledge which has previously been acquired. In fact rational learning is fundamental in all types of learning since "all learning is to some extent cognitively controlled."[4]

Since the pupil in school acquires his knowledge by a gradual process involving experience and training, it is necessary that the teacher understand clearly the main elements in this process. Knowledge, which is the product of rational learning, begins with concrete experiences. The first element to be considered in rational learning, therefore, is the reception of impressions through the external senses. This involves sensation, which is the most fundamental form of conscious life and the elementary unit of mental experience. Sensation is the consciousness resulting from the stimulation of a sense organ, making known the existence and properties of the particular objects which stimulated the senses. The first source of knowledge is sensation, by means of which the individual becomes aware of the objective world which exists apart from and independent of the mind. The pupil comes into contact with the teacher, with books, and the materials, content, and subjects of study by means

[3] J. D. Redden and F. A. Ryan, *A Catholic Philosophy of Education,* rev. ed. (Milwaukee: The Bruce Publishing Co., 1956), pp. 157–158; see also T. W. Guzie, S.J., *The Analogy of Learning* (New York: Sheed and Ward, Inc., 1960), pp. 4–14.

[4] E. R. Hilgard, *Theories of Learning,* 2 ed. (New York: Appleton-Century-Crofts, Inc., 1956), p. 343. See also M. B. Arnold and J. A. Gasson, S.J., *The Human Person* (New York: The Ronald Press Co., 1954), p. 337, where Arnold has defined learning as "setting up a new goal of knowing and doing and finding rationally approved means to achieve it. This definition implies that human learning is rational, based upon recognition of means-ends relations and deliberate choice of means and ends."

of the sense organs. The child acquires his knowledge of the world about him through his sensory equipment. Through the organs of hearing he becomes accustomed to and identifies various kinds of sounds. Through the organs of vision he becomes aware of distances, form, color, size, and movement of objects. Through the organs of touch he acquires information concerning shape, texture, and temperature.

However, there is no sensation without perception, which is the means by which sensations are interpreted and given a meaning. If the pupil possesses normal sense organs, his progress in learning depends not only upon a clear and accurate reception of sense impressions but also upon a faithful interpretation of these impressions in terms of previous experiences. What is learned and how it is learned depends upon what is observed and perceived and how it is observed and perceived. Therefore, perception furnishes the groundwork of all knowledge.

The second element in rational learning is the formation and construction by the imagination of sensory representations of particular objects perceived. These representations are retained in the memory and may be recalled and recognized as past experiences when the objects are not present to the senses. Learning would be impossible without memory. To learn means to have acquired, to have retained, to have reproduced, and to have recognized experiences. To learn implies that one have memory, while to remember means that one must have learned. Memory in turn is dependent upon association, which is the mental process by which past ideas, perceptions, and experiences are brought into consciousness by their connection with others in it. Proper intellectual training consists in the establishment of a wide variety of logical associations according to the laws of similarity, contrast, and contiguity. Since association leads to the formation of systems of thought, all learning is dependent upon the formation and establishment of orderly associations. If in the process of learning new materials are related to what is already known, and if these relationships are revived regularly, the knowledge acquired can be used effectively as the occasion demands.

Since all learning takes place best under conditions of clear and undivided attention, it is evident that a primary factor in rational learning is attention. Without attention, clear thought and deliberate volitions are impossible. Attention is the concentration of consciousness upon a specific object, condition, or mental process. The primary effect of attention is the intensification of the mental state on which one concentrates. The importance of attention as a factor in learning has been described as follows:

> People who are good learners have what is commonly called a high power of concentration. . . . Poor learners are poor in attention. Their conscious processes are not clear-cut; the difference between the clear and the vague is not so marked. Good learners are able to stick to a task and maintain a continuously high level of attention. . . . Poor learners vacillate; they cannot stick to a task long at a time. . . . The poor learner does not work so long at the same task as does the good learner, nor does he work so effectively while he does work. Another difference between good and poor learners is that the former see what is significant. The important, meaningful aspects of their experience are apparent to them. The world in general is to them a more meaningful world. . . . Aspects and attributes of objects appear to the good learner that do not appear to the poor learner.[5]

The third element in rational learning is to make sensory experiences intelligible, since knowledge cannot be explained by sensory experiences alone. The active intellect abstracts from the image the conditions, characteristics, and distinctive qualities which individualize it, and pierces to the substantial nature or the *essence;* the potential intellect forms the abstract or general concept which represents only those features which are absolutely essential to the object and, therefore, common to all objects of the same kind. Thus, the intellect conceives as abstract the selfsame objects which the senses perceive as concrete. The concept is not knowledge in the strict sense but only the starting point of knowledge. By means of judgment the intellect makes use of concepts. Judgment involves the discernment of agreement or disagreement between two concepts. Thinking essentially takes the form of judgment. One knows when he has compared, identified, discriminated, discerned ideas. However, the crux of rational learning is the *reasoning process,* which involves comparison of judgments for the purpose of drawing conclusions. *Inductive reasoning* consists in forming judgments concerning a number of particular cases or instances and then deriving a rule or principle by ascertaining the common qualities presented by these cases or instances. *Deductive reasoning* consists in the application of a general rule or law or principle to a particular fact. The development of rules and principles is a process of induction and their application is a process of deduction.

Thus rational learning involves principally the operation of intellection, which is the capacity of the intellect to generalize experiences through the formation of concepts and judgments utilized in reasoning.

[5] W. H. Pyle, "A Theory of Learning," *Psychological Review,* 31:321–327, 1924.

By means of these acts of the intellect the most important single factor in the assimilation of knowledge is accomplished, namely, the *understanding* of the materials learned. To understand the materials of knowledge is a most important essential of learning, because only when these materials are understood can they be used effectively, and because the better they are understood, the more economically can they be learned. *Understanding means clear discernment by the intellect.* The pupil who understands is able to associate new ideas with previous knowledge and, moreover, is aware of the relationship. Because the pupil understands, he is able to concentrate more readily and to retain for a longer period of time.

Rational learning should culminate in the application of the knowledge acquired, for the effective use of knowledge is the real goal of living. As a result of rational learning the pupil should develop mastery of the intellectual tools, particularly language, number facility, and reading. Rational learning should provide the foundation for the mastery of principles, the application of generalizations, the determining of relationships, especially of cause and effect, and the development of additional knowledge through the reorganization of experiences. It should provide the bases of the ability to deal adequately with physical and social environment and to recognize values. The most significant manner of utilizing and applying rational learning is in problem solving, which is a primary and fundamental aim of all education.

The most effective technique for solving problems is reflective thinking,[6] which should be the outcome of rational learning. The purpose of rational learning is to train pupils to think analytically and constructively, leading to comprehension and understanding which will enable them to make applications of ideas and principles in the solution of problems. A problem involves a difficulty or question for which a solution or an answer may be found only by a process of thinking. A problem involves a challenge whether it has its source in a classroom procedure or in a life situation. To solve a problem it is necessary to utilize knowledge and experience constructively. This involves the following steps:

1. Recognition of the difficulty and an analysis of the situation and also the goal to be achieved;

[6] H. G. Hullfish and P. G. Smith, *Reflective Thinking* (New York: Dodd, Mead & Co., 1961).

2. Search for essential facts, for relationships, for similarities and differences with past experiences or facts previously known as well as for general rules and principles that may apply;
3. Organizing in orderly arrangement the data obtained;
4. Critical evaluation of possible solutions;
5. Testing and verification by application to other data;
6. Formulation of conclusions clearly and concisely.[7]

Motor Learning. The outcome sought in this type of learning is *skill,*[8] which may be described as the adaptation of movement to stimuli resulting in speed and precision of performance. Skill may vary from simple muscular reactions to complex motor processes. However, it always involves the development of patterns of neuromuscular coordination and adjustment to a perceptual situation. Thus, accuracy of perception is a basic factor in motor learning. In some aspects of motor learning the method of trial, error, and success is fundamental, usually because the learner does not have a clear percept of the skill. In this method the learner fixes his attention on the result which he wishes to produce and then attempts to repeat the movements which prove successful. The first step in the development of skill is characterized by a great amount of futile movement and by the expenditure of considerable useless energy. The second stage consists of the gradual elimination of unsuccessful trials and the selection and use of successful trials. In this stage each successful trial is a step toward perfection. The third stage involves the repetition and practice, with careful attention, of the movements found to be successful. The progress from the first to the final stage

[7] R. M. W. Travers, *Essentials of Learning* (New York: The Macmillan Co., 1963), pp. 316–341; R. L. Thorndike, "How Children Learn the Principles and Techniques of Problem Solving," in National Society for the Study of Education, Forty-Ninth Yearbook, Part I, *Learning and Instruction,* 1950, pp. 192–215; W. A. Brownell, "Problem Solving," in National Society for the Study of Education, Forty-First Yearbook, Part II, *The Psychology of Learning,* 1942, pp. 438–440; D. M. Johnson, "A Modern Account of Problem Solving," *Psychological Bulletin,* 41:201–229, 1944; K. Duncker, *On Problem Solving,* Psychological Monographs, Vol. 58, No. 5, 1945; Mother Margaret Guest, R.S.C.J., "Process and Product in Generalizing," *Catholic Educational Review,* 52:217–237, 1954; J. Deese, *Psychology of Learning,* 2 ed. (New York: McGraw-Hill Book Co., Inc., 1958), pp. 273–300.

[8] C. E. Skinner, *Educational Psychology,* 4 ed. (New York: Prentice-Hall, Inc., 1959), pp. 499–512; National Society for the Study of Education, Forty-Ninth Yearbook, Part I, *Learning and Instruction,* 1950, pp. 71–77, 81–89; D. Wolfe, "Training," in S. S. Stevens, ed., *Handbook of Experimental Psychology* (New York: John Wiley & Sons, Inc., 1951), pp. 1267–1286; N. L. Munn, "Learning in Children," in L. Carmichael, ed., *Manual of Child Psychology,* 2 ed. (New York: John Wiley & Sons, Inc., 1954), pp. 387–407.

in the development of any skill is effected through the elimination of useless movements from the total activity and the perfecting of appropriate and useful movements. The acquisition of skill is thus primarily a process of the selection of movements.

While very little formal school learning can be described strictly and wholly in terms of trial, error, and success, nevertheless motor learning is used in many aspects and activities of the school. In such forms of skill as drawing, writing, typing, industrial arts, gymnastic activities, and the playing of the various musical instruments, the goal sought is physical or muscular skill. The development of the proper touch, ease, freedom, and rapidity of movement in writing, typing, and playing musical instruments depends in some measure on the trial, error, and success method. However, the chief function in learning is not primarily to be able to make correctly the separate elementary movements, but rather in relating them together so that they follow readily in proper order. While trial, error, and success probably cannot be wholly eliminated from motor learning, the amount can be reduced by proper instruction and analysis. It is evident that the pupil will become much more efficient if he is able to substitute deliberate mental control for trial, error, and success. Hence, the teacher's task is to supplement the trial, error, and success method by guidance through the use of verbal direction, imitation, and demonstration of correct performances. This usually consists in furnishing to the learner an analysis which he is unable to make for himself. For example, the manner of holding the pen, the placing of the paper, the position at the desk, and numerous other elements contribute toward the success or failure of the pupil learning to write. The teacher of typing demonstrates that there are certain fingers which are best to use in pressing certain keys. The teacher of music rightly insists that the pupil achieve certain elementary practices in hand position. In every sensorimotor learning situation there is a definite technique which is best for the learner to use. This means that the achieving of this technique or form cannot be left to the trial, error, and success method, but must be taught by imitation and by verbal direction. Imitation is the starting point, while verbal direction and instruction are employed as measures of correction and as aids in developing efficiency. In addition, drill, which requires a vast amount of exact repetition, is necessary in sensorimotor learning.

Mere adoption of good form and repetition are not, however, the only prerequisites. Much better results will be achieved in motor learning if the pupil makes an intellectual analysis of the problem; if he centers his attention on the details to be mastered, if he understands clearly the act to be performed, since the role played by the understanding increases with the complexity of the skill involved; if he concentrates on points giving difficulty; and if he uses his will to secure a faithful application of effort during periods of practice. As practice continues, there should be a reasoning out of the best methods of adjustment to meet the demands of the task. This involves the application of knowledge to the development of skill. Actually then rational learning is basic in motor learning. Although the highest degree of expertness in any skill is not sought by the school, nevertheless some measure of skill is sought in many school activities. Since that is the case, the school must strive to direct the child so that he will apply his knowledge to shorten the sensorimotor process and its repetition and also to make further gains in the process of acquiring skill.

Associational Learning. The outcome sought in this type of learning is the acquisition and retention of facts and information. This type of learning involves the development of associative patterns by which ideas and experiences are retained, recalled, and recognized through the process of linking together or establishing relationships between and among these ideas and experiences so that one will serve as the stimulus for the revival and recall of the other or others previously experienced. Thus, this type of learning is manifested primarily in the functioning of the processes of association and memory. It has reference to the manner in which facts and materials are ordinarily acquired in many school subjects, that is, in a serial order. Examples of such facts and materials include: spelling; number combinations; dates and events, or persons and events in history; grammatical relationships; formulae in mathematics and science; vocabulary in foreign languages. The associational type of learning involves drill, frequent repetition, and review, but it is more than a mere repetition and accumulation of experiences. The facts and materials acquired by this method should have significance, that is, should be understood by and should be meaningful to the pupil. In order that they may, it is essential that the facts and materials be organized systematically, articulated and integrated with previous experiences and knowledge through the process of establishing meaningful relationships in terms of the laws of contiguity, contrast, and similarity.

Appreciational Learning. The outcome sought in this type of learning is *appreciation* or *aesthetic improvement,* which may be defined as follows:

> Appreciation which involves both intellectual and emotional elements, is a sensitive awareness to and perception of the importance or utility of information in its relation to other fields and in the development of attitudes and tastes.[9]

Appreciational learning[10] involves the process of acquiring attitudes, ideals, satisfactions, judgment, and knowledge concerning values as well as the recognition of worth and importance which the learner gains from participating in learning activities. It involves the acquisition of a taste for, the development of liking for, and the expression of enjoyment of certain aspects of life, such as literature, music, fine arts, and the like. This type of learning is determined in large measure by training and experiences, but involves also the constructive imagination, the processes of association and understanding which are necessary for the formation of appreciation. It connotes desirable emotional accompaniments or affective outcomes, as well as, and in addition to, knowledge and understanding. This type of learning is not well understood and constitutes a neglected area of education. However, the development of appreciation has considerable significance, particularly because of the influence it may exert on such leisure-time interests and activities as selection of reading materials, choice of radio and television programs, preference for kinds of music and type of movies, and hobbies of various sorts.

The Curve of Learning. The progress made in learning, particularly in the acquisition of skill, may be represented graphically by the use of a curve showing the levels of achievement and the increase in efficiency attained at the various stages of training or practice in terms of time or trials. There are two ways of constructing the curve, one of which indicates the amount of work accomplished in a given period of time, and the other, the units of time required to do a given amount of work. Usually the relation between the two variables of time and work is represented by a curve in which one function, ordinarily that of the time required, is represented along the base line and the other, usually the amount of work accomplished, is represented along the vertical axis.

---

[9] A. E. Nixon, "The Meaning of Appreciation," *Science Education,* 19:35–40, 1945.

[10] J. L. Mursell, "How Children Learn Aesthetic Responses," in National Society for the Study of Education, Forty-Ninth Yearbook, Part I, *Learning and Instruction,* 1950, pp. 183–191.

It is necessary that the teacher know how the curve of learning is constructed, how it may be interpreted, and what its values are.

While there is no typical learning curve, in the sense that all curves are alike in shape, practically all curves of learning have several common characteristics. The first is that no learning curve is ever absolutely smooth, for *fluctuations,* either slight or marked, are in evidence rather than steady improvement. These fluctuations may be explained as due to the presence of distractions or to lack of consistent application or may stem from numerous variables in the physical or emotional condition of the individual. The second characteristic is the usually rapid *initial rise or spurt* which many learning curves show. This is termed *negative acceleration;* that is, the rate of learning is greatest in the initial stage and is followed by a gradual diminution in rate as learning proceeds. Thus the shape of the learning curve indicates the rate of improvement. This characteristic is usually explained as being due to the element of novelty of a new task, an element which wears off with fuller acquaintance; to the previous knowledge of or skill in the activity involved; to the fact that in the early stages of practice rapid progress is more easily attained, because strong motivation is often present at the beginning of a learning task. The third characteristic is the *plateau* or place of long or short duration on the learning curve covering few or many trials where little or no apparent progress is being made. The plateau is a characteristic of all learning curves, and various explanations have been offered to account for its appearance. The plateau may be due to a decline in interest and attention, or to a lapse of effort after the novelty of the situation has worn off, or to lack of understanding, or to lack of motivation, or to fatigue, or to the adoption of improper methods of learning, or to particularly difficult material, or to interference by previously learned material, or to satisfaction with the present level of achievement, or to the pupil's having reached the limit of usefulness of a poor method of study or work.

Regardless of these explanations it is evident that the plateau represents a critical period in which the learner may become discouraged easily, if he is aware of his lack of progress. Therefore, the appearance of a plateau on the learning curve should cause both the pupil and the teacher to exert special effort to terminate the period, particularly if it is due to decline of motivation or to a lag of interest and attention or to a lapse of effort or to improper methods of learning. If the plateau is caused by any of these, it is evident that it does not represent a profitable period, and hence practice should cease for a time or a means must be found to renew attention and effort. If the plateau persists, it may be necessary to supply new motivation, to change the method of teaching, or to adopt a new method of learning.

However, another and perhaps better explanation of the plateau has been offered. Because the plateau period is usually succeeded by a marked rise in progress, it should be regarded as a sort of breathing space in which the learner prepares for a new outburst of energy. This would constitute the plateau a period of assimilation and organization in which the learner gathers together or consolidates all that he has acquired thus far, in which he eliminates the superfluous and confusing elements, in which he selects and gains control over the essential phases of the learning situation. According to this explanation the plateau is not a period during which the individual is acquiring nothing new. If this explanation is accepted, it is very encouraging for the pupil to know that continued effort at this stage will be rewarded by a later period of progress.

The fourth characteristic of the learning curve is the fact that, in general, the rate of progress becomes less as the pupil approaches the *limits of improvement.* These limits are both *physiological and mental.* The former involve the physical functions, while the latter involve the intellectual process.[11] It is evident that since this is true, relatively greater credit should be given for a unit of progress made in the more advanced stages than for a unit made in the earlier and easier stages.

In considering the limits of improvement it is possible to describe learning as vertical and horizontal in character. The former indicates the altitude or height, while the latter indicates the latitude or breadth or range or extent of applicability. Vertical learning refers to the addition of knowledge in an area in which learning has already taken place, the improvement of a skill previously acquired, and the intensifying of interests and attitudes already possessed. Horizontal learning refers to

[11] In all learning there are both *quantitative* and *qualitative* aspects. The first refers to the *amounts* of learning and the second to how these amounts are organized and reorganized. Plateaus may well represent nature's signal that amounts of learning have become too rapid, and hence nature "forces" the individual to stop increasing the quantity until such time that it may become organized effectively. Actually, therefore, during plateau periods learning definitely is still going on, but in its qualitative rather than quantitative aspect. It is obvious that the qualitative aspects of learning cannot be represented quantitatively.

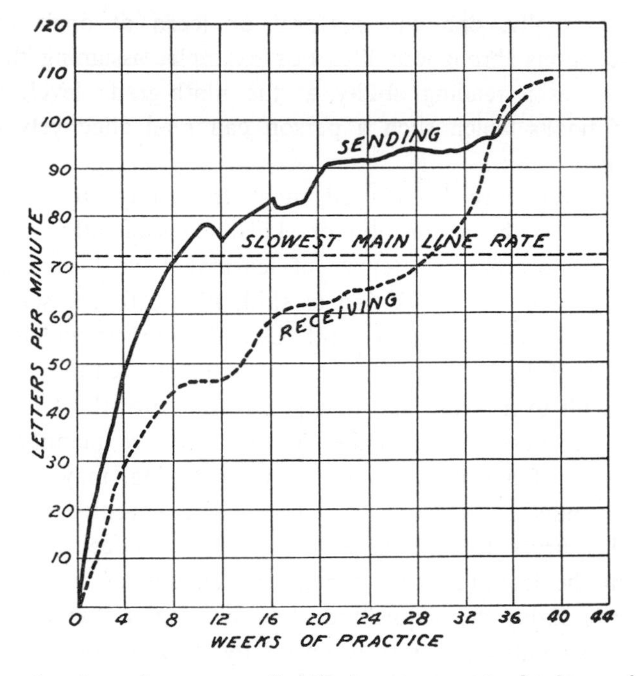

Fig. 6. Learning curve of skill. Improvement of telegraphy.
(After Bryan and Harter)

the enrichment of knowledge, the perfecting of skills, the expansion of interests. Vertically, there is a limit both physiologically and psychologically for the learning of each individual. For example, on the physiological level there is a limit to the facility with which the eyes can move in reading, or the fingers in typing. Accordingly, there is a physiological limit to the amount of skill or degree of speed which may be attained in reading or typing. Likewise, in the intellectual realm many lack the mental equipment to learn Sanskrit or astrophysics, or to understand adequately the theory of relativity. Although every individual has a vertical limit in learning power, few reach or approach it. Some by employing effective work habits and study skills, through the efficient organization of time and direction of effort, reach an "optimum" limit which is below the actual limit. Many pupils, however, seem content to achieve a "practical" limit, which involves routine preparation of work in order to "get by," and seem to be satisfied with this degree of proficiency. Horizontally, one can perform or learn at one's own level with few exceptions throughout life. For example, assuming that an individual possesses a reading ability at the ninth-grade level, there are thousands of books which such a person can read effectively and with understanding.

Learning curves have been used most frequently to represent the rate of progress in the acquisition of skills. Consequently, most of the generalizations concerning the curve of learning have been based upon curves that represent the acquisition of skill. Figure 6 represents a curve of learning for the acquisition of skill. Learning curves which represent the acquisition of knowledge are not as frequently employed, because it is very difficult to measure and to represent the growth of the practical usefulness or richness of knowledge in the objective manner in which the development of a skill, such as ability in typing, may be measured by testing the number of words typed during a specified unit of time. The available curves for the acquisition of knowledge differ in some respects from the learning curve for the acquisition of skill. The learning curve representing the acquisition of knowledge is characterized ordinarily by a slow initial progress followed by intervals of rapid learning interspersed with periods during which no apparent progress is made. This means that the shape of the learning curve for the acquisition of knowledge is most frequently *concave,* or positively accelerated, which is a marked contrast to the usually *convex* or negatively accelerated curve for the acquisition of skill. However, it should be noted that the learning curve for the acquisition of knowledge has also been classified as *convex-*

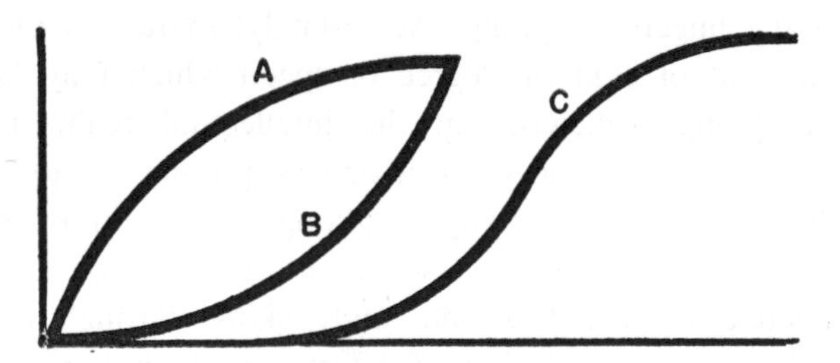

Fig. 7. Representative Curves of Learning:[12] Curve A represents negative acceleration; Curve B represents positive acceleration; Curve C represents positive followed by negative acceleration.

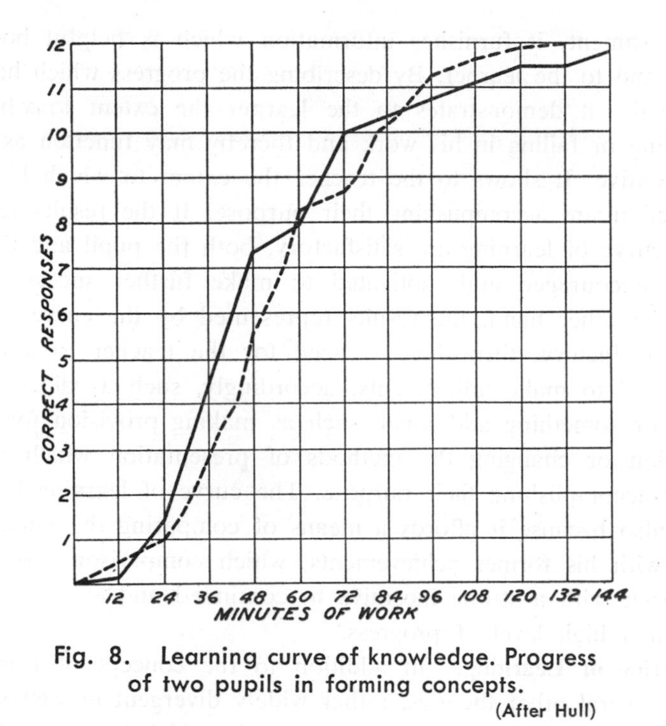

Fig. 8. Learning curve of knowledge. Progress of two pupils in forming concepts.
(After Hull)

concave, or S shape, beginning with positive acceleration and later becoming negatively accelerated and as variations of these forms. Figure 7 presents the representative curves of learning.[12] Because, horizontally considered, there is no physiological limit in the acquisition of knowledge and because the number of facts which may be learned is practically unlimited, the curve is ordinarily concave for a considerable distance. The plateau on the curve for the acquisition of knowledge probably represents a period during which the preliminary knowledge is assimilated and organized before the learner proceeds with the remainder of the process. Figure 8 represents a curve of learning for the acquisition of knowledge.

The curve of learning is a representation of the learner's progress which has already been made. The learning curve, however, is not predictive of progress to be expected. Employed as a means of visualizing

[12] J. A. McGeoch and A. L. Irion, *Psychology of Human Learning,* 2 ed. (New York: Longmans, Green and Co., 1952), p. 27.

accomplishment, it furnishes information which is helpful both to the teacher and to the learner. By describing the progress which has already been made, it demonstrates to the learner the extent to which he is succeeding or failing in his work and thereby may function as an effective incentive. It shows to the teacher the extent to which his methods of direction are accomplishing their purpose. If the results represented by the curve of learning are satisfactory, both the pupil and the teacher will be encouraged and motivated to make further successful efforts. If, on the other hand, the results represented by the curve of learning are unsatisfactory, then there is need for the teacher to look for the reason and to make adjustments, accordingly, such as diagnosing difficulties, or something additional, such as making provision for increased motivation or changing the methods of presentation which apparently are not accomplishing their purpose. The curve of learning is a helpful device also because it affords a means of comparing the pupil's present record with his former achievements, which comparison should furnish the learner with a strong incentive to continued and even greater effort to attain a high level of progress.

Theories of Learning. In addition to the concept of learning presented, several other theories, rather widely divergent in viewpoint, have been formulated to account for the ways in which learning takes place. A brief description of each of the most prominent of contemporary theories[13] is presented here. These theories have been designated by the terms *conditioning, connectionism,* and *field*. It should be noted that there are variations within each theory and that it is usually impossible to classify most educational psychologists strictly as adherents of one or the other of these theories. It is noteworthy also that, although each of these theories has sought to explain learning wholly on a materialistic basis, yet there are some aspects of each which are considered to be of value.

[13] For complete descriptions and evaluations of those theories consult the following: J. P. Chaplin and T. S. Krawiec, *Systems and Theories of Learning* (New York: Holt, Rinehart and Winston, 1960); E. R. Hilgard, *Theories of Learning,* 2 ed. (New York: Appleton-Century-Crofts, Inc., 1956); The National Society for the Study of Education, Forty-First Yearbook, Part I, *The Psychology of Learning,* 1942; L. P. Thorpe and A. M. Schmuller, *Contemporary Theories of Learning* (New York: The Ronald Press, 1954); B. B. Wolman, *Contemporary Theories and Systems in Psychology* (New York: Harper & Brothers, 1960); W. K. Estes, *et al., Modern Learning Theory* (New York: Appleton-Century-Crofts, Inc., 1954); M. H. Marx and W. A. Hillix, *Systems and Theories in Psychology* (New York: McGraw-Hill Book Co., Inc., 1963).

The Theory of Conditioning. The basic theory of conditioning is *Behaviorism.* The formulation of this system of psychology is usually attributed to John B. Watson who was undoubtedly the most vigorous of its early exponents. It should be noted that there were other early Behaviorists including such well-known psychologists as A. P. Weiss, E. B. Holt, W. S. Hunter, K. S. Lashley, and P. I. Franz. According to Watson, "Psychology as the Behaviorist views it is a purely objective experimental branch of natural science. Its theoretical goal is the prediction and control of behavior."[14] It was the contention of Watson and others among the early Behaviorists that, in order to be scientific, psychology must be based upon and deal exclusively with data derived through overt, objective observation and experimentation. It avoided any consideration of the factor of consciousness since conscious states are subjective experiences and not overt behavior. The data of psychology were considered to be specific neurological, muscular, and glandular responses made to physical stimuli and the resulting environmental products. The object of study and the central factor in learning was considered to be the behavior, that is, the overt responses of animals and man which are observable and measurable. All such behavior, including that which is customarily designated as mental, was explained in terms of physical responses to physical stimuli. This led to the denial of conscious experience and the development of a strictly mechanistic theory or system. When faced with the need to account for the process of thought Watson maintained that thinking was subvocal or implicit speech, that is, talking to one's self. According to Hilgard,[15] he believed that sensitive instruments would be able to detect tongue movements or other movements accompanying thinking.

Influenced by the experimental studies on the conditioning of animals which had been conducted by the Russian physiologist, Pavlov,[16] Watson

---

[14] J. B. Watson, "Psychology as the Behaviorist Views It," *Psychological Review,* 20:158–177, 1913.

[15] E. R. Hilgard, *op. cit.,* p. 49.

[16] Pavlov, who was a physiologist rather than a psychologist, conducted over a period of many years systematic laboratory studies of conditioned salivary responses in dogs. He noted that the sight of food constituted a stimulus (S_1) which brought about flow of saliva (R_1). In the conditioning process when the food was presented to the dogs, at the same time a bell was sounded or a light flashed (S_2). With repeated presentations of these stimuli, $S_1 + S_2$ together, the original response to food, that is, salivation, became associated with the neutral stimulus of the bell or the light. After a number of such simultaneous presentations the reaction of salivation (R_1) appeared in response to the neutral stimulus (S_2) in the absence

constructed his theory entirely on the concept of conditioning, that is, of inducing reactions to stimuli mechanically in the form of conditioned responses. Conditioning is a process by which a stimulus originally inadequate to produce a certain response is presented simultaneously with an adequate stimulus. After some practice the inadequate stimulus becomes so associated with the adequate stimulus, that it is capable of producing the response originally evoked only by the adequate stimulus.

$$S_1 \rightarrow R_1; \quad \begin{matrix} S_1 \\ S_2 \end{matrix} \rightarrow R_1; \quad S_2 \rightarrow R_1$$

Thus, since all conditioning is in essence mechanistic, learning is interpreted wholly on a physiological basis. The process of learning consists in the acquisition of new ways of reacting to stimuli developed through attaching new stimuli to established modes of behavior. Education then would consist wholly of one's organized conditioning. Such a mechanistic explanation of learning failed to account for thinking, understanding, and volitional activity.

Watson maintained that through the control of environmental factors, that is, the stimuli to which an individual would be exposed, and through the process of conditioning him to the stimuli to which he should react, the direction of development could be determined:

> Give me a dozen healthy infants, well formed and my own specified world to bring them up in and I will guarantee to take any one at random and train him to become any type of specialist I might select — regardless of his talents, penchants, tendencies, abilities, vocations and race of his ancestors.[17]

The Neo-Behaviorists. It has been recognized generally that the original theory of Behaviorism is too narrow to explain learning adequately. Adaptations of the theory of conditioning, however, have been made by psychologists who have been designated as *Neo-Behaviorists.* With regard to influence exercised in Educational Psychology, the principal Neo-Behaviorists are Hull, Guthrie, and Skinner. The Neo-Behaviorists are in agreement that all learning can be explained wholly on a physiological basis, and consequently they give no consideration to mental

---

of food (S_1). This reaction constituted the original response to the conditioned stimulus of bell or light. See I. P. Pavlov, *Conditioned Reflexes* (London: Oxford University Press, 1927).

[17] *Behaviorism,* by John B. Watson, Copyright 1924, 1925, by The People's Institute Publishing Co., Inc.; Copyright 1930, Rev. Ed., W. W. Norton and Co., Inc., p. 104 — Copyright 1952, 1953 by John B. Watson.

activity in the classical sense of that term. They reject consciousness and conscious states and recognize conditioning as the controlling factor in all learning. However, conditioning is *instrumental* as distinguished from the Pavlovian or classical conditioning. Instrumental conditioning is a higher form of conditioning in which the learned response is *instrumental* in securing reenforcement, that is, the learner is forced to do something in order to receive a reward, or to avoid a rebuke, or to escape from pain.

The Neo-Behaviorists consider the individual as active in the process of conditioning rather than as merely the passive recipient of stimuli. There is also the same tendency among the Neo-Behaviorists to derive data from and to define those data wholly in terms of overt, observable, objective behavior. The Neo-Behaviorists recognize the presence of some sort of motivating factor, that is, *need* or *drive,* but tend to account for needs and drives as caused only by physiological factors, generally glandular or neurological in nature. The theory presented by each of the Neo-Behaviorists has been derived almost wholly from animal experimentation. It is obvious that where such concepts as need and drive are introduced, conditioning no longer is a process of inevitably bringing about desired responses, since variables have been introduced which influence the degree of conditioning of responses. The Neo-Behaviorists have designated these variables by the term *intervening variables.* They insist that these intervening factors be those which are observable.

Systematic Behavior Theory. Clark L. Hull[18] (1884–1952) formulated an objective quantitative theory of Neo-Behaviorism which is designated as *Deductive Behaviorism.* It is based upon the results of animal experimentations. From these experiments, principles were derived which have been utilized to explain the behavior not only of animals but also of human beings, no matter how complex the behavior may become. In order to state the underlying principles of this theory, Hull developed a unique, elaborate system in which he utilized postulates, theorems, and correlates, expressed in terms of mathematical equations. According to Hull behavior involves an interaction between stimuli in the environment and the responses which the organism makes to these stimuli. This interaction, which constitutes learning, involves fundamentally the biological

---

[18] C. L. Hull, *Essentials of Behavior* (New Haven: Yale University Press, 1951); *A Behavior System* (New Haven: Yale University Press, 1952); *Principles of Behavior* (New York: Appleton-Century-Crofts, 1943).

adaptation of the organism to its environment. Influenced by Darwin's theory of survival, Hull maintained that it was "necessary to think of the organism in a setting of organic evolution in which certain optimal conditions were essential for survival." Biological adaptation facilitates survival. When, however, the conditions necessary for survival are less than optional, a *state of need* arises within the individual. The function of behavior is to satisfy needs. A state of need operates upon an event or state designated as *drive* which is a state of lack or privation in the organism that arouses activity and demands satisfaction or *reducing*. Under pressure of needs and drives the organism undertakes adaptive action in order to bring about a reduction of the need. Thus drive is the motivating factor which stimulates to activity and impells the individual to make a response. Without drives the organism does not behave. Since drives bring out responses, they constitute the dynamics of behavior and thus are the bases for all behavior. The resulting action is goal-directed, the goal being the reduction of the drive. This reduction of drive must occur in order that learning takes place.

The central principle in Hull's theory is *reinforcement,* which refers to "any set of conditions which when appropriately employed, favors learning." Many of his experiments were devoted to the study of reinforcement. It has the effect of reducing need; that is, it involves the strengthening of the process of interaction between stimuli and responses. Reinforcement is the key principle in learning since "learning takes place only when the action that is performed is reinforced or rewarded." Whether or not a response will be repeated depends upon whether or not it has been rewarded.

In Hull's theory a distinction has been made between *primary* and *secondary reinforcement*. Primary reinforcement refers to the reduction of the basic needs of the organism. Secondary reinforcement refers to stimuli originally neutral but which when closely and consistently associated with the reduction of a primary need or satisfaction of a drive tends to acquire reinforcing properties in its own right. Hull also considered that reinforcement constitutes the primary conditions for habit formation, acquisition, and development which is the central factor in learning. He employed the term *habit strength* to refer to "how firmly a particular stimulus-response relationship has been established." Habit is the result of the occurrence of stimulus, response, and reinforcement in close temporal conjunction. Reinforcement brings about an increase in habit strength, and learning occurs when habit grows. Habit strength is determined by the frequency with which a certain response has been rewarded or followed by a reward. Hull distinguished also between *positive* and *negative* reinforcers. "Stimuli which when added to a situation strengthen the possibility of responses are *positive reinforcers.*" However, stimuli which when removed strengthen the possibility of response are *negative reinforcers.*

The Contiguity Theory. Edwin R. Guthrie (1886–1959) has developed the theory of *contiguous conditioning.* Interested only in observable responses, and utilizing the S → R hypothesis that stimulus and response are the most observable factors in behavior, he has endeavored to develop a theory of learning which has no recourse to the principle of reinforcement. The framework of this theory is conditioning and the basis of learning is the principle of association of stimulus and response by contiguity in time. The associations are believed to be formed instantaneously, completely, and automatically without reinforcement or repetition. Since Guthrie sought to reduce all principles of learning to this one of conditioning through contiguity in time, it has frequently been designated as the lowest common denominator of the theory. This basic low has been expressed as follows:

> A stimulus pattern that is acting at the time of a response will, if it recurs, tend to produce that response.[19] A combination of stimuli which has accompanied a movement will on its recurrence tend to be followed by that response.[20]

Thus learning is considered to be an adaptation in behavior which results from the development of associations between and among stimuli and responses occurring simultaneously or at least closely together in time. Responses consist of two types: *movement* and *act. Movement* refers to specific glandular and motor patterns of action. An *act* is a class of movements defined in terms of its effects or the form of behavior which results, regardless of the pattern of motor or glandular activity involved. Classical conditioning is concerned with movements while instrumental conditioning is concerned with acts. Movement constitutes the raw

---

[19] E. R. Guthrie, "Conditioning: A Theory of Learning in Terms of Stimulus, Response, and Association," in National Society for Study of Education Forty-First Yearbook, *The Psychology of Learning,* 1943, p. 23.

[20] E. R. Guthrie, *The Psychology of Learning,* rev. ed. (New York: Harper & Brothers, 1952), p. 23. See also V. W. Voelks, "Formalization and Clarification of a Theory of Learning," *Journal of Psychology,* 30:341–362, 1950; and "Acquisition of S-R Connections: A Test of Hull's and Guthrie's Theories," *Journal of Experimental Psychology,* 47:137–147, 1954.

material and basic data in Guthrie's theory. Guthrie has maintained that the basic laws of learning apply directly to movements rather than to acts.

Unlike other Neo-Behaviorists, Guthrie does not consider reinforcement, as it has been employed to account for the strengthening of learned responses, to be an essential condition of learning. He has rejected the idea that reward for correct performance, or success, or favorable aftereffects, function to establish associations between stimuli and appropriate responses. Rewards, success, or favorable aftereffects may, however, function as auxiliary aids to learning. Thus, when a correct response is followed by a reward or by a favorable aftereffect, this changes the situation with the result that the response is the last to occur in a given situation. Since the response is the last to occur, it will remain associated with the situation and accordingly will recur whenever the situation arises again. Thus reinforcing serves the purpose of keeping or preserving it among the set of associations.

Repetition is considered to be unnecessary in Guthrie's theory, since association is established and "gains full strength" in a single trial. He has stated that:

> A stimulus pattern gains its full associative strength on the occasion of its first pairing with a response.[21]

This seems to be an apparent contradiction since typically conditioning develops gradually. However, repetition or practice is considered to function effectively in the formation of associations among the separate movements or activities which constitute a complex skill. This is explained as due to the "enlistment of increasing numbers of stimuli as conditioners and not the result of the strengthening of individual connections."[22] The more varied the stimuli are, the more repetition will be required.

In this theory forgetting has been explained as due to inhibition of old connections by new ones, rather than as a result of the weakening of old associations through disuse. Forgetting is considered to be a process of unlearning which results from the acquisition of new responses which are incompatible with the old responses.[23]

Wolman in evaluating Guthrie's theory has stated:

---

[21] E. R. Guthrie, N.S.S.E. Forty-First Yearbook, p. 30.

[22] E. R. Guthrie, "Conditioning as a Principle of Learning," *Psychological Review,* 37:412–418, 1930.

[23] J. P. Chaplin and T. S. Krawiec, *Systems and Theories of Psychology* (New York: Holt, Rinehart and Winston, 1960), p. 219.

Thus one may wonder whether Guthrie's theory explains anything at all. His system is a description of *how* events take place without tackling the question of *why* they happen. It is more a presentation than an explanation.[24]

Operant Conditioning. Burrhus F. Skinner has claimed that he has avoided theory, preferring to utilize the "fresh-start" approach.[25] This involved a comprehensive experimental program the purpose of which was to study the ways in which behavior may be predicted and controlled. Although the early data were derived from experiments on rats and pigeons, these were later supplemented by data derived from experiments with human subjects, both children and adults. His system has been designated as *Inductive Behaviorism*[26] as opposed to Hull's deductive approach. Skinner has presented a description rather than an explanation of behavior. This *descriptive behavior* is devoted entirely to the study of responses since learning is considered to be the acquisition of conditioned responses.

The framework around which Skinner *has organized* his experimental data is *conditioning.* However, he has made a sharp distinction between two types of conditioning: *respondent* and *operant.* Respondent conditioning is designated as Type S because the responses are *elicited* by known stimuli and the emphasis is upon the stimulus. This is the Pavlovian or classical conditioning. Operant or instrumental conditioning is designated as Type R because of the importance of the response in the process. In operant conditioning, the response is *emitted* rather than elicited as is the case in respondent conditioning. *Elicited* means that the response has been caused or produced by a specific stimulus. *Emitted* means that the response occurred "randomly"; that is, it is spontaneous behavior in response to no one specifiable stimulus or at least to a stimulus which cannot be identified easily. Skinner considers that most behavior is operant and accordingly Type R is more important than Type S. Thus the basic behavioral data in Skinner's system are operant responses. The term *operant* indicates that behavior "operates" upon environment in order to produce consequences.

In operant conditioning, once the response has been made, if it is followed as soon as possible by reinforcement (reward), then the strength

---

[24] B. B. Wolman, *Contemporary Theories and Systems in Psychology* (New York: Harper and Brothers, 1960), p. 104.

[25] B. F. Skinner, "Are Theories of Learning Necessary?" *Psychological Review,* 57:193–216, 1950.

[26] B. B. Wolman, *op. cit.,* pp. 125–126.

of the operant response is increased. Reinforcement must be presented immediately following the response if conditioning is to occur. Skinner has stated this as the *law of acquisition;* that is, "if the occurrence of an operant is followed by presentation of a reinforcing stimulus, strength is increased."[27] Reinforcement is contingent upon response. If the proper response is not emitted then reinforcement is not forthcoming. The whole process of operant conditioning depends upon the making of proper responses by the organism. Thus in operant conditioning the organism plays an active role in the learning process. The individual must "operate" on his environment in order to produce reinforcement. Through this operation in environment he is *instrumental* in producing reinforcement. By knowing the effects of reinforcement, behavior can be predicted and controlled. Thus in order that learning may occur these factors are essential: a stimulus, a response, and a reinforcement. Each time that these three factors occur together there is an increase in the tendency for that stimulus to evoke that response. After these three factors have been associated a number of times, the tendency for the stimulus to evoke the response becomes strong. Then the effect of reinforcement is to increase the probability of response.

Reinforcement is dependent upon *discrimination of stimuli* and also upon *differentiation of response.* Discrimination involves breaking down a complex situation in order to make reinforcement contingent upon response to one of two or more stimuli. Differentiation involves variability of response and appropriate adjustment in the form of the response to the situation. Skinner has made a distinction very similar to that made by Hull, between reinforcers which are *positive* and those which are *negative.*[28] The former term has been employed to indicate all those stimuli which when added to a situation strengthen the probability of an operant response. The latter term has been utilized to designate those stimuli which when removed from a situation strengthen the probability of an operant response.

Reinforcement has been classified as *primary* and *secondary. Primary reinforcement* indicates that some stimuli by nature act in a reinforcing manner either as positive or negative reinforcers. These constitute a very minor position of reinforcers. *Secondary reinforcement* indicates that

[27] B. F. Skinner, *The Behavior of Organisms* (New York: Appleton-Century-Crofts, Inc., 1938), p. 21.

[28] B. F. Skinner, *Science and Human Behavior* (New York: The Macmillan Co., 1953), p. 73; also E. R. Hilgard, *op. cit.*

responses are strengthened or weakened by events or activities which have acquired reinforcing properties, as approval, disapproval, praise, blame, and the like.

In operant conditioning the principles of *extinction* and *generalization* have been stated. *Extinction* involves the withholding of reinforcement in order to unlearn an already conditioned response. This is different from forgetting since extinction results from nonreinforcement whereas forgetting is due to disuse or to passage of time. *Generalization* involves the tendency of stimuli possessing common properties to be effective in arousing behavior. It is somewhat akin to transfer of learning by common elements (see pp. 306–308). Thus conditioned responses which initially were set up in relation to specific stimuli have a tendency to *generalize* to similar stimuli.

With regard to the timing of reinforcement, in general experimental evidence has indicated that reinforcement (rewards and punishments) should occur as closely as possible to the response if the consequences of making correct responses are to exercise a facilitating effect upon the acquisition of behavior.

Application of operant conditioning involving the skillful and economic use of reinforcement to human learning in the school situation is found in *programed learning* which utilizes *teaching-learning machines.* Such machines operate on a general principle, whether electronically controlled or less elaborately mechanized; a moving tape presents a series of well-organized tasks or problems or statements to each of which the student is to make a response. By means of these tasks, problems, or statements, learning is broken down into a series of minute steps which permit reinforcement at each stage of learning. If the response made by the student is correct, the machine immediately moves on to the next task or step. If the response is not correct the tape remains static and the student must try again. Thus the student has the satisfaction of knowing immediately and effectively that he has or has not made the correct response. Here success constitutes reinforcement of learning and helps to strengthen and confirm the learning acquired. Thus learning is reinforced by the learner's immediate awareness of the correctness of his response. Skinner has maintained that this type of learning is effective because the student's own response is instrumental in bringing about immediate reward or reinforcement, that is, the awareness of success in having completed correctly the given step in the learning sequence.

2. The Theory of Connectionism. This theory which is also designated as "trial, error and effect" was formulated by Edward Lee Thorndike (1874–1949).[29] For many years Thorndike exercised a very extensive, and in many ways unfavorable, influence upon educational practice. According to this theory learning consists in the formation of or in the strengthening of a *connection* or *bond* between a specific *situation* or *stimulus* and a specific *response*. This connection is usually referred to as an $S \rightarrow R$ bond. By *situation* or *stimulus* is meant "any state of affairs or event which influences a person." By *response* is meant "any state of affairs or condition within the organism." By *connection* is meant "the fact or probability that a given stimulus will evoke a certain response." In the formation of the $S \rightarrow R$ bonds emphasis has been placed upon the modifiability of the neural mechanism and excludes any element of consciousness. Castiello[30] has characterized this conception of learning, "if logically carried to its true conclusions," as "mechanistic, fatalist and determinist," not allowing for "any sort of spontaneous autonomous human activity" and "a practical denial of the most essential human functions: responsibility and autonomous intelligence." Connectionism denies the real acts of learning, that is, abstraction, judgment, and reasoning, by claiming that these are purely neural and mechanistic in nature.

The principles of Connectionism have been expressed by Thorndike in the form of laws of learning.[31] These laws include the following:

The *Law of Readiness,* which states that when a connection between a situation and a response is ready to function, for it to do so is satisfying. When, however, the connection is not in readiness to function, for it to be forced to do so is annoying. Likewise, when the bond is in a state of readiness to function and the response is blocked, it is annoying. The purpose of this law seems to be to account for the motivational aspects of learning.

---

[29] For his earlier description of Connectionism see E. L. Thorndike, *Educational Psychology,* Vol. II (New York: Teachers College, Columbia University, 1913). For later changes in the theory of Connectionism see the same author's *Human Learning* (New York: Appleton-Century-Crofts, Inc., 1931); *Fundamentals of Learning* (New York: Teachers College, Columbia University, 1932); *The Psychology of Wants, Interests and Attitudes* (New York: Appleton-Century-Crofts, Inc., 1935).

[30] J. Castiello, S.J., *Real Psychology in Education* (New York: The Fordham University Press, 1936), pp. 7, 8, and 9.

[31] E. L. Thorndike, *Educational Psychology,* Vol. II (New York: Teachers College, Columbia University, 1913).

The *Law of Exercise,* which involves strengthening of connections with practice, seems to be fundamental in the theory of Connectionism. In order to form a bond between the stimulus and response, the learner must make the response. The more frequently the connection is exercised, the more securely will it be fixed. There are two aspects to this law, termed *use* and *disuse. Use* strengthens the bond while *disuse* weakens it.

The *Law of Effect* supplements the law of exercise and aids in explaining how learning takes place. This law states that when a response is accompanied or followed by a satisfying state of affairs, the strength of the connection is increased. When, however, the response is accompanied or followed by an annoying state of affairs, the strength of the bond is decreased. Thus satisfyingness and annoyingness are effective in learning to the extent that they are connected with the response; that is, responses tend to be repeated and to be mastered more easily or to be avoided and not learned in proportion to the satisfaction or dissatisfaction which they give.

In addition to the three major laws of learning, Thorndike formulated five secondary characteristics for the purpose of amplifying the basic laws. These secondary characteristics were designated by the terms *multiple response, mind-set, partial activity, analogy,* and *associative shifting.* By *multiple response* was meant that in a situation where some elements are new, the learner will respond in one way, and if such response does not prove satisfactory, he will try one response after another until the appropriate response is attained, that is, trial-and-error learning. This response, being satisfying, will be selected and "stamped in." *Mind-set* or *attitude* meant that learning is guided by the attitude (mind-set) of the individual dependent upon or based upon previous experiences and dispositions. This attitude determines how the learner will react, and what will be satisfying and annoying to him. *Partial activity* designated the fact that an element or an aspect of a situation may be "prepotent" in causing a response. This involves selectivity in learning. The learner may select the important elements from a situation instead of responding in an unselected way or at random. *Analogy* indicated that when a situation involves a stimulus for which the learner has no native or acquired response, he may react by interpreting the situation in the light of similar experiences, and adjust himself as best as he can. *Associative shift* seems to be related to the conditioned reflex. When stimuli occur together fre-

- NEW ELEMENTS
- GUIDED
- ASPECT or ELEMENT
- NATIVE OR ACQUIRED RESPONSE

quently, the response elicited by each will tend to become attached to the others as well. When responses occur frequently together, the stimulus for each tends to suggest the others as well.

Concerning the importance of these secondary characteristics, Thorndike stated:

> No matter how subtle, complicated and advanced a form of learning one has to explain, these simple facts — the selection of connections by use and satisfaction, and their elimination by disuse and annoyance, multiple reaction, the mind's set as a condition, piecemeal activity of a situation, with potency of certain elements in determining the response, response by analogy, and shifting of bonds — will, as a matter of fact, still be the main, and perhaps the only facts needed to explain it.[32]

Thorndike later modified somewhat the original law of effect.[33] As a result of the findings of a number of experiments conducted to determine the influence of rewards and punishments, the fact was confirmed that satisfying consequences or rewards tend to strengthen the responses which they follow and thus lead to a continuation of given behavior. However, it was noted that annoying consequences do not necessarily exercise weakening effects. Thus annoying consequences or punishment were less effective than satisfying consequences, and the effects of reward and punishment were not equal.

An additional modification of the law of effect which resulted from the experimental study of reward is termed *spread of effect.* It was found that the influence of a reward acts not only to strengthen the S → R connection to which it belongs but also tends to strengthen other S → R relationships that occurred relatively close in time, both before and after the rewarded connection. Thus the spread of effect was bidirectional; that is, reward affected other responses which were temporarily adjacent, those preceding and those following the rewarded response.

In Thorndike's later works emphasis has been placed upon the concept of *"belongingness"* as a necessary element in learning and as a supplement to the laws of effect and exercise. He stated, "Repetition in the sense of mere sequence of two things in time has little power to cause learning. Belonging is necessary."[34] While *"belongingness"* has not been defined in

---

[32] E. L. Thorndike, *Educational Psychology, Briefer Course* (New York: Teachers College, Columbia University, 1914), p. 137.

[33] L. Postman, "The History and Present Status of the Law of Effect," *Psychological Bulletin,* 44:489–563, 1947.

[34] E. L. Thorndike, *Human Learning* (New York: Appleton-Century-Crofts, Inc., 1931), p. 46.

a formal way, it seems evident that by it is meant a relationship or an association existing between two situations which causes the individual "to feel that there is a certain fitness in connecting the two," and thus the connection between them is more easily formed. Thus belongingness seems to be one of the most important factors influencing the strength of the connections.

In later years, Thorndike also devised several additional explanatory terms as modifications of the original laws of learning.[35] These terms included *impressiveness, polarity, identifiability, availability,* and *mental systems. Impressiveness* was employed to indicate the strength or intensity of a stimulus; that is, one is more likely to respond to a strong impression than to a weak one. *Polarity* was used to indicate "the tendency for the stimulus-response sequences to function more readily in the order in which they were practiced than in the opposite order." Polarity involves a tendency to relate objects and experiences that have common associations. *Identifiability* was used to indicate that a connection which can be identified easily is likely to be learned readily. *Availability* was used to indicate that the more ready a response was to function, the more easily it can be called into play. *Mental systems* represented a vague attempt to explain something over and above ordinary connections or S → R bonds in order to account for the more difficult kinds of habit formation.

The best criticism of Connectionism from the Catholic point of view has been made by Pax.[36] His work contains a critical analysis of the philosophical assumptions underlying Connectionism, as well as of the laws of learning and their bases and applications.

3. The Field Theory. There are actually several major varieties of this theory including *organismic, Gestalt,* and *topological,* which differ "slightly in terminology, content, emphasis, and characteristic choice of problems to be investigated,"[37] but all stress the dominant role of the *field* or surroundings in which behavior occurs. The *Gestalt* theory is the most familiar to educational psychologists and is employed at least in part by many to explain the learning process. This theory was developed in Ger-

[35] L. P. Thorpe and A. M. Schmuller, *op. cit.,* pp. 57–59; also P. Sandiford, "Connectionism: Original Features" in N.S.S.E. Forty-First Yearbook, Part II, *The Psychology of Learning,* 1942, pp. 126–128.

[36] W. T. Pax, *A Critical Study of Thorndike's Theory and Laws of Learning,* The Catholic University of America Educational Research Monographs, Vol. XI, No. I, 1938.

[37] G. W. Hartmann, "Field Theory: Educational Consequences" in N.S.S.E. Forty-First Yearbook, Part II, *The Psychology of Learning,* 1942, p. 173.

many and was introduced into the United States during the 1920's. Psychologists who are representative of the classical[38] Gestalt point of view include Wertheimer, Kohler, and Koffka; representative of the organismic[39] point of view are Wheeler and Hartmann, while Lewin[40] represents the topological point of view.

The Gestalt theory of learning stresses *wholes,* that is, the whole field or the situation in its entire setting and the whole person of the learner. Learning is a process involving both the whole being of the child and the total situation. It is usually defined as the organization and reorganization of behavior which arises from the *dynamic* interaction of a maturing organism and its environment, involving the activities of *differentiation* and *integration,* that is, the recognition of significant relationships and similarities and likewise of significant differences between and among experiences and the understanding of the situation or problem in all its relations. Learning involves a process of forming proper *gestalts.* The original German term *gestalt* is very difficult to translate satisfactorily. The terms *whole, configuration, pattern, form* are used ordinarily to connote the idea implied in *gestalt.* The term signifies that actually there is no particular stimulus or object to which a response may be directly attached, but that each situation or object has its own setting and thereby possesses certain relationships within a meaningful whole. The individual reacts to this meaningful whole, for a stimulus when removed from its setting may become something quite different from what it was in that setting. Consequently, the individual does not react merely to the stimulus itself but rather to the stimulus in relation to its background and setting. Thus the situation or object in relation to its setting, "a *figure* embodied in a *ground,*" is considered to be the *gestalt* or *pattern* or *configuration.* Learning is accounted for in this theory through *insight* rather than through trial, error, and success processes or experiences, or practice, or association, or conditioning. *Insight* means a grasping or understanding of the situation or object or materials in such a way that significant rela-

---

[38] M. Wertheimer, *Productive Thinking* (New York: Harper & Row, 1945); W. Kohler, *Gestalt Psychology* (New York: Liveright Publishing Co., 1947); K. Koffka, *Principles of Gestalt Psychology* (New York: Harcourt, Brace and World, 1935).

[39] R. H. Wheeler and F. T. Perkins, *Principles of Mental Development* (New York: Thomas Y. Crowell Co., 1932); G. W. Hartmann, *Educational Psychology* (New York: American Book Co., 1941).

[40] K. Lewin, *Principles of Topological Psychology* (New York: McGraw-Hill Book Co., 1936).

tions are apparent. It is the form of gestalt or pattern in which the relevant factors fall into place with respect to the whole. It involves total organization and implies a mental integration by which a situation or problem is understood in all its relations. The measure of progress in learning is the degree of insight attained in a situation. *Maturation* is an essential basic condition in learning. This term is used to indicate that the neural and mental growth of the learner is sufficiently advanced, functioning efficiently to enable him to comprehend a given stimulus or object, that is, physiological and psychological readiness for learning. Learning also involves *goal seeking* or *motivation,* since it is a response to a need and is guided by the purpose or intention of the learner. The goal sought may be a concrete object, an abstract idea, an ideal toward which the learner purposefully strives. The goal is the motivating force involving the "will to learn" and consists in the purposeful direction of activity toward a definite end.[41]

Although the Gestaltists are "less mechanical in their conceptions than either the Behaviorists or the Connectionists, nevertheless they are fundamentally materialistic monists"[42] and as a result they are unable to offer satisfactory explanation for many of their observations. However, in the practical order the Gestalt theory of learning has made valuable contributions to education. The influence of the Gestalt theory seems to be evident in such trends as the offering of orientation or survey courses in broad areas of knowledge, the presentation of fields of learning in organized patterns such as the integrated curriculum, the emphasis upon general rather than on highly specialized education, the *recognition* of the significance of problem-solving experiences with discovery as the essence of learning, the stress on "readiness" for learning, level of aspiration, and emphasis upon the integrated personality.

Purposive Behavior. Edward C. Tolman has constructed a theory of learning which seeks to combine the best features of Behaviorism and of the Gestalt System, and to include as well many aspects of functional psychology. While this may seem to be something of a paradox, neverthe-

---

[41] Since this brief treatment of the Gestalt theory of learning has been limited to a few important aspects of the theory, students interested in broader knowledge should consult the descriptive accounts presented in the following: L. P. Thorpe and A. M. Schmuller, *op. cit.;* E. R. Hilgard, *op. cit.;* B. B. Wolman, *op. cit;* A. A. Roback, *History of American Psychology* (New York: Library Publishers, 1952); J. P. Chaplin and T. S. Krawiec, *op. cit.;* M. H. Marx and W. A. Hillix, *op. cit.*

[42] J. D. Redden and F. A. Ryan, *op. cit.*, p. 79.

less in the field of modern psychology serious consideration has been devoted to this theory, which has been designated as *Purposive Behavior* or *Sign Gestalt theory*.[43] It is Behavioristic since it has rejected introspection and its data have been derived from objective, observable behavior. From Gestalt theory, Tolman has borrowed the concept of *insight*. The theory is purposive since it maintains that behavior is organized in terms of purposeful activity, that is, of striving toward a goal. The basic research upon which the theory rests consists of experiments with animals. It should be noted also that the concept of *intervening variables* was introduced by Tolman.

In Tolman's theory learning is not considered to be a matter of conditioned response. In this theory, the core of learning consists of *sign gestalts,* that is, in "cognitive" processes which are acquired relationships between environmental stimuli and responses. Behavior is determined by the perception of a stimulus. This perception constitutes the *sign gestalt;* that is, the learner has recognized the significance of a stimulus and its various features. By following a series of recognizable signs toward a specific goal, learning becomes purposeful. The term *cognitive maps* has been applied to the pattern of sign gestalts which are built up through practice. Learning is explained in terms of cognitive maps which organize the relationships between stimuli and responses. The term *reward expectancies* has been utilized to indicate that the learner comes to anticipate the presence of a reward. If reward expectancy is confirmed, then the sign gestalt is strengthened. However, if reward is absent or changed, behavior is disrupted. According to Tolman's theory, what is learned is a cognitive map which is reinforced when reward expectancy is confirmed. Practice plays a role providing opportunities for the acquisition of sign gestalts but, in and of itself, is not effective in producing learning. Reward is concerned with the regulation of performance but is not considered to serve as a reinforcement of *correct* responses. Reward, however, seems to emphasize the direction of that behavior which seems to be the most promising route to the good sought. The term *latent learning* has been employed to designate learning which is "hidden," that is, which goes on unobserved but which under certain conditions may be revealed in performance.

---

[43] E. C. Tolman, *Purposive Behavior in Animals and Men* (New York: Appleton-Century-Crofts, Inc., 1932); *Behavior and Psychological Man: Essays in Motivation and Learning* (Berkeley: University of California Press, 1958).

Theories of Learning and Classroom Learning. The various theories of learning discussed in this chapter seek to provide information concerning how learning takes place, what can be learned, and the specific ways in which definite types of materials can be learned. Accordingly, these theories of learning should be expected to exercise considerable influence upon the aims set for, the objectives sought by, and the methodology employed in the educative process. However the practical value of the various theories of learning in educational practice is very doubtful and their influence on educational procedure has been very limited.[44] This may be accounted for by the fact that while each of the various theories has endeavored to explain some segment or part of the total learning process, each has tended to draw from such explanation of a segment, general conclusions concerning the total learning process.[45] In addition, the explanations offered by each theory have been derived from experimentation conducted in psychological laboratories, generally with animals as the subjects of the experiments. The findings of such experimentation are likely to have very limited applicability in the classroom and cannot be transferred directly and immediately into classroom practices, not only because of the nature and type of both subjects and materials but also because the conditions in the laboratory are not the same as those prevailing in the classroom. While not denying the need for laboratory research, it should be recognized that experimental findings are useful only insofar as they relate to actual conditions and purposes within the school. Caution must be exercised regarding attempts to make hasty translation of the experimental findings of any theory to the classroom since learning in the clasroom has a much broader denotation than in the laboratory. The situations in school learnings are much more complex, involve the interaction of many factors, and consequently do not follow the simple model of the experimental laboratory.

A serious limitation is that so much of the current theories of learning has been elaborated from evidence furnished almost exclusively by studies of animal behavior. Granted that animal studies offer certain advantages in the way of simplification and control, nevertheless experiments with rats or pigeons or other animals which lack symbolic and verbal capabilities cannot provide adequate information concerning how children learn

---

[44] K. W. Spence, "The Relation of Learning Theory to the Technology of Education," *Harvard Educational Review*, 29:84–93, 1959.

[45] M. B. Arnold and J. A. Gasson, *The Human Person* (New York: The Ronald Press Co.. 1954), pp. 324–325.

the meaning of fractions or grasp the significance of the printed word. Results of animal studies, no matter how sophisticated and adequate for animals, cannot be used by analogy to direct learning practices with children in school.

Any theory of learning which is meaningful and comprehensive must be based upon an adequate and correct understanding of the nature of man and of his mind. It is necessary to know what man is before it is possible to study effectively what man does. The current theories of learning consider man as a "physicalistic machine"[46] and maintain that "learning occurs in a child chiefly as a result of something that is done to him from the outside."[47] However, the nature of man as a being in whom reasoning is dominant indicates that human learning is *rational* and accordingly the aspect which must be stressed is the *cognitive factor.* "It is in the intellectualization of his behavior that man shows his great superiority over brute animals."[48] That education is concerned with concept formation, with problem-solving, with critical and reflective thinking, with discovering and expanding meaning, with deepening understanding points the direction for the formulation of a theory of learning that is applicable in the classroom.[49]

The Guiding Principles of the Learning Process. It is the task of the teacher to know not only what skills the child must acquire but also the process by which they are acquired. The first principle in directing the acquisition of skill is *to understand the characteristics of sensorimotor learning as used in the school.* The second principle consists of the *choice of superior methods of direction and guidance toward worthy performance.* The third principle consists of the *careful selection of good models, pictures,* and other *graphic* and *mechanical aids for imitation.* The fourth principle is *to give,* by means of verbal direction, *clear and adequate instructions about what is to be done and how it is to be done.* The fifth principle is the *motivation and stimulation of interest, effort, and attention.* The final principle is never to forget that *skill can be acquired only through the activity of the pupil.*

[46] E. A. Haggard, "The Proper Concern of Educational Psychologists," *American Psychologist,* 9:539–543, 1954.

[47] D. A. Prescott, *Factors That Influence Learning* (Pittsburgh: University of Pittsburgh Press, 1958), p. 7.

[48] W. D. Commins and B. Fagin, *Principles of Educational Psychology,* 2 ed. (New York: The Ronald Press Co., 1954), p. 59.

[49] J. F. Travers, "Learning Theory — Animal or Human," *Catholic Educational Review,* 59:227–238, 1961.

Of much greater importance, however, is the duty of the teacher to understand the process by which the child acquires knowledge. The first principle in the directing of the acquisition of knowledge is the realization that *no teacher can induce knowledge.* This means that the basis of knowledge is to be found in the abilities, the capacities, and the potentialities of the pupil. It means that the teacher must understand thoroughly the nature of the child. This principle has been described adequately as follows:

> I am profoundly convinced that, whatever else the teacher must do, he is never called upon to get inside the mind and do any burnishing or repair work there. We use a figure of speech when we talk of the gardener causing the plant to grow, and surely we use a figure of speech, and a very misleading one, when we speak of education as the process of molding, sharpening, forming, or perfecting minds. Much as it may contribute to our pride to think of ourselves as performing such a service, the thing is inconceivable. We have no such creative power. In the Harvard Club in Boston there is one room set apart for the use of the graduates of the Medical School, and over the fireplace in that room there is an inscription, a motto, which states in a sentence the philosophy of the medical profession. It reads, "We dress the wound, God heals it." If a devoted student of education should attempt to construct a similar motto which would in like manner set forth the object of his profession, what form ought it to take? This, I think: "We feed the mind. God makes it."[50]

The second principle defines the *teacher's function as that of guide and director,* who proposes materials, stimulates and motivates the mind, but who understands that it is the pupil himself who must perform the final act of acquiring knowledge. The third principle consists in the *development of meanings or concepts* which are the fundamental and most important resources of knowledge. The fourth principle may be stated as the *guidance in the concentration of attention* on these abstract elements and their use in the reasoning process. The fifth principle consists in *setting up definite attainable goals* in order that the pupil who has his facts, who has a motive for thinking, may assimilate and organize and apply his knowledge. The final principle is the *realization that the process and technique of learning must be worked out in detail for each particular school subject upon an understanding of broad, general principles of the learning process.*

The Educational Significance of the Learning-Teaching Process. While learning is a process of mental development, it requires guidance, direc-

[50] E. C. Moore, *What is Education?* (Boston: Ginn and Co., 1915), pp. 16, 17.

tion, motivation, and control. The problem of education is to direct and to guide the child's mental development by means of proper motivation and effective control. It is the function of the school to make it possible for all types of desirable learning to take place in an efficient way. It is likewise the task of the school to make it possible that the knowledge of the various school subjects may be acquired in a manner which will enable every pupil to achieve, in addition to the special knowledge, information, and skill obtained in the mastery of these subjects, the ability to use the highest type of learning of which he is capable. It is the purpose of the school to make it possible that the most valuable things are learned in the most economical way by actually practicing the most efficient methods of learning. The chief goal of education is to have the pupil *learn how to learn,* how to acquire knowledge and skill which may be used successfully in further learning, in controlling his conduct, and in making better adjustments to his environment.

The efficient instrumental cause of learning is teaching, which is the stimulation, guidance, direction, and encouragement of learning. Teaching includes all the activities performed in directing the progress of learning. The teacher's function is to stimulate learning activity. Therefore, it is of utmost importance that the teacher have an accurate knowledge of the nature of the learning process, a complete understanding of how and when learning takes place, of how it may be directed in order that all the desirable skills and knowledge may be acquired efficiently, effectively, and economically.

Hence, the relationship of the teacher to the learner is one of greatest importance, for it is the teacher's task to help pupils surmount difficulties in learning; to help pupils discover the best methods of study and of work; to help pupils develop useful habits of learning; to help pupils assimilate and organize knowledge in a natural way; to motivate and stimulate effort on the part of the pupil; to make the surrounding conditions, both physical and mental, favorable to learning; to develop in pupils an attitude of permanent interest in knowledge; to help pupils understand the purpose and the nature of learning.

EXERCISES

1. Outline this chapter.
2. List and define the terms which you have learned from your study of this chapter.

3. *a*) Explain the nature of the learning process.
   b) Why is it essential to have an adequate and true understanding of the nature of man and the nature of the mind in order to explain learning properly?
4. *a*) What are the characteristics of curves of learning?
   b) What are the values and uses of these curves?
5. *a*) Describe the types of learning.
   b) Discuss the steps involved in problem-solving. Justify each step.
6. Describe and evaluate:
   a) The basic theory of conditioning (Watsonian Behaviorism);
   b) The theory of Hull (Systematic Behavior Theory);
   c) The theory of Guthrie (Contiguity Theory);
   d) The theory of Skinner (Operant Conditioning).
7. Describe and evaluate the theory of Connectionism and the Gestalt theory. Then compare these theories with respect to completeness of system and contribution to education.
8. Are there basic similarities in all learning theories? What are these similarities? Explain.
9. Discuss the following statements:
   a) "All educational practices have psychological foundations."
   b) "Learning takes place in proportion to the activity of the learner."
   c) "Connectionism if logically carried to its true conclusions is mechanistic, fatalistic, and deterministic."
   d) "Repetition in the sense of mere sequence of two things in time has little power to cause learning."
   e) "There is no typical learning curve."
   f) "The ability to learn is the most significant native capacity of man."
   g) "The most effective technique for solving problems is reflective thinking."
   h) "In all learning there are both quantitative and qualitative aspects."
10. *a*) What is the teacher's function in the learning process?
    b) What is the educational significance of learning?

SELECTED REFERENCES FOR STUDY AND READING

Arnold, M. B., and Gasson, J. A., *The Human Person* (New York: The Ronald Press Co., 1954).

Braun, J. R., *Contemporary Research in Learning* (Princeton, N. J.: D. Van Nostrand Co., Inc., 1963).

Bugelski, B. R., *The Psychology of Learning* (New York: Holt, Rinehart & Winston, Inc., 1956).

Chaplin, J. P., and Krawiec, T. S., *Systems and Theories of Psychology* (New York: Holt, Rinehart, and Winston, Inc., 1960).

Deese, J., *The Psychology of learning,* 2 ed. (New York: McGraw-Hill Book Co., Inc., 1958).

Estes, W. K., *et al., Modern Learning Theory* (New York: Appleton-Century-Crofts, Inc., 1951).

Garrett, H. E., *Great Experiments in Psychology,* 3 ed. (New York: Appleton-Century-Crofts, Inc., 1951).

Guzie, T. W., *The Analogy of Learning* (New York: Sheed and Ward, 1960).

Harris, T. L., and Schwahn, W. E., *Selected Readings on the Learning Process* (New York: Oxford University Press, 1961).

Hilgard, E. R., *Theories of Learning,* 2 ed. (New York: Appleton-Century-Crofts, Inc., 1956).

Hilgard, E. R., and Marquis, D. G., *Conditioning and Learning,* 2 ed., rev. by G. A. Kimble (New York: Appleton-Century-Crofts, Inc., 1961).

Hill, W. F., *Learning: A Survey of Psychological Interpretations* (San Francisco: Chandler Publishing Co., 1963).

Hullfish, H. G., and Smith, P. G., *Reflective Thinking: The Method of Education* (New York: Dodd, Mead and Co., 1961).

Lawson, R., *Learning and Behavior* (New York: The Macmillan Co., 1960).

Marx, M. H., and Hillix, W. A., *Systems and Theories in Psychology* (New York: McGraw-Hill Book Co., 1963).

McGeoch, J. A., and Irion, A. L., *The Psychology of Human Learning,* 2 ed. (New York: Longmans, Green and Co., 1952).

Mowrer, O. H., *Learning Theory and Behavior* (New York: John Wiley & Sons, Inc., 1960).

National Society for the Study of Education, Forty-First Yearbook, Part II, *The Psychology of Learning,* 1942.

——— Forty-Ninth Yearbook, Part I, *Learning and Instruction,* 1950.

Pax, W. T., *A Critical Study of Thorndike's Theory and Laws of Learning,* The Catholic University of America Educational Research Monograph, Vol. XI, No. 1, 1938.

Seagoe, M. V., *A Teacher's Guide to the Learning Process* (Dubuque, Iowa: Wm. C. Brown Company, 1956).

Thorndike, E. L., *Educational Psychology,* Vol. II (New York: Teachers College, Columbia University, 1913).

——— *Human Learning* (New York: Appleton-Century-Crofts, Inc., 1931).

——— *The Fundamentals of Learning* (New York: Teachers College, Columbia University, 1932).

——— *The Psychology of Wants, Interests, and Attitudes* (New York: Appleton-Century-Crofts, Inc., 1935).

——— *Selected Writings From a Connectionist's Psychology* (New York: Appleton-Century-Crofts, Inc., 1949).

Thorpe, L. P., and Schmuller, A. M., *Contemporary Theories of Learning* (New York: The Ronald Press Co., 1954).

Wolman, B. B., *Contemporary Theories and Systems in Psychology* (New York: Harper & Row, 1960).

chapter 8

Efficiency in Learning

RETENTION AND FORGETTING

The efficiency with which learning takes place is influenced by many factors and conditions. It is well recognized that the background of previous learning experiences, the learner's level of mental ability and stage of maturation attained, the types of motivation utilized, the study skills employed, the interests, attitudes, and values of the learner, as well as the proper functioning of the senses, freedom from physical defects, and lack of fatigue, all constitute important factors in determining the efficiency of learning. In addition, the nature of the material to be learned, the methods employed in learning, the extent to which material is mastered, the organization and use to be made of material also influence the effectiveness of learning. However, the major factor in efficiency of learning is *retention.* Unless knowledge and skills possess some degree of permanence, further learning cannot take place. To have learned means to have retained; hence all learning involves retention. The usual test of learning is how well the material has been retained. Accordingly, whatever improves retention makes for effectiveness and efficiency in learning.

Retention. By *retention* is meant the persistence of learning, that is, the extent to which material originally learned is preserved so that it may subsequently be recalled and recognized. Successful learning is dependent upon the individual's ability to retain what is essential and to forget the nonessential. All teaching is based upon the assumption that retention will occur. The first requisite for good retention is thorough learning.

Measurement of Retention. There are various ways of measuring retention. However, three of these are considered to be classical methods, namely the *recall,* the *recognition,* and the *savings* methods. The method most familiar to the teacher is *recall* which requires the pupil to reproduce whatever he can of the materials which have been acquired. Examples of this type are the classroom recitation and the essay examination. The *recognition* method involves the ability to select from a list of items those which have been learned previously. An example of this method is the multiple-choice test. The *savings* or *relearning method* is considered to be a more sensitive measure than either recall or recognition. In this method the subject is required to learn the material, for example, a list of words to a certain standard of proficiency such as to the point of one perfect repetition. Then after the lapse of a definite period of time in which no review takes place, the individual relearns the original materials under the original conditions. The difference between the amount of effort in terms of time, or the number of trials or number of errors required in the original learning and that needed for relearning is the savings score. Thus if twenty repetitions were required in the original learning situation to attain the point of perfect recall and only five repetitions were required in relearning the material, then there was a savings of fifteen repetitions or 75 percent. The "savings score" is often presented as a percentage referred to the original learning.

Forgetting. Retention and forgetting stand in inverse relationship to each other. Forgetting which is a normal, everyday event denotes the gradual or rapid loss of material. It involves the failure of learning to persist. It is obvious that a great deal of what is learned in school is soon forgotten. In early discussions of forgetting the most common explanation offered to account for it was decrease in recall due to lack of use of material and to the passage of time. Undoubtedly disuse of material and the passage of time constitute minor factors in the process of forgetting. Some forgetting is the result of failure to use learning, or the lessening of a need for the material, or lack of practice. However, disuse and the passage of time are not sufficient in and of themselves to explain forgetting. This is evident from the fact that when several things are learned at the same time one or more may be forgotten much more rapidly than the others. Moreover, forgetting is a selective process. There is a tendency to forget that which does not seem important or essential; that to which no personal interest is attached and also that which is unpleasant. Forgetting may also be the means of solving some internal conflicts and likewise of satisfying important emotional needs.

The more recent view to account for forgetting is that it takes place as a result of an active process of interference with what is learned by subsequent learnings. Psychologists agree generally that most, if not all, forgetting is due to interference from subsequent experiences or later learning — what has been learned is forgotten because other things learned block recall. This inhibition can come from two directions. Earlier learning may interfere with the retention of later material or later learning may interfere with the recall of material acquired earlier. Interference is greater between some types of materials and for some methods of learning than it is for others. Usually the greater the similarity between two types of material the greater the possibility of decreased retention. When materials are learned thoroughly they are less subject to interference. The same is true for materials which are meaningful and interesting.

The interference which later learning exerts upon the retention of prior learning has been designated as *retroactive inhibition.* This has been described by McGeoch as "a decrement in retention resulting from activity, usually a learning activity, interpolated between an original learning and a later measurement of retention."[1] Thus one fails to recall something already learned because it is inhibited by new learning. It has frequently been demonstrated that the greater the similarity between the learning task and the interpolated activity, the greater is the possibility for interference. Thus, when the learning task is Latin and the interpolated activity is French, the interference with retention will be greater than when the learning task is Latin and the interpolated activity is geometry.

The interference which prior learning exercises upon later learning is designated as *proactive inhibition.* This type works forward from the past to the present, disrupting later or subsequent learning. Frequently when new materials are learned, they compete with older learnings with the result that the new learning is disturbed. In order to reduce this type of inhibition it is necessary that teachers point out elements in new and older learnings which may be confused and also ascertain that the concepts of pupils are based upon meaningful experiences.[2] Care should be exercised in the planning of curricula to minimize such sources of inefficiency in the process of retention.[3]

---

[1] J. A. McGeoch and A. L. Irion, *The Psychology of Human Learning,* 2 ed. (New York: Longmans, Green & Co., Inc., 1952), p. 404.

[2] J. Deese, *The Psychology of Learning,* 2 ed. (New York: McGraw-Hill Book Co., Inc., 1958), pp. 256–261.

[3] R. M. W. Travers, *Essentials of Learning* (New York: The Macmillan Co., 1963), p. 302.

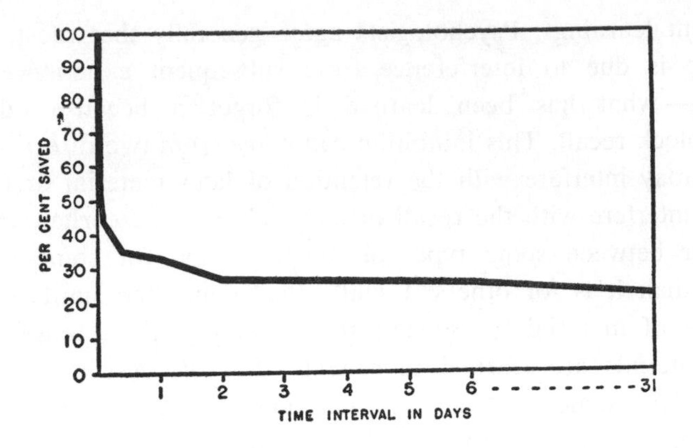

Fig. 9. Ebbinghaus' curve of retention.

The Rate of Forgetting. The rate of forgetting was first investigated in 1885 by Ebbinghaus,[4] in what was probably the first experiment in educational psychology. He was concerned with the degree of retention of what was originally learned after certain intervals of time had elapsed. Ebbinghaus developed experimental techniques and materials, notably *nonsense syllables,* which are still used extensively. He was his own subject and employed the learning of a series of meaningless nonsense syllables in order to determine how the process of forgetting would proceed when left merely to the influence of time. He made use of the savings or relearning method. The series of nonsense syllables was learned to the point of one perfect repetition. Then after the lapse of definite periods of time the materials were relearned. The retention was determined by the time saved in relearning the series after periods of twenty minutes, one hour, eight hours, one day, six days, and thirty days. He found that 41.8 percent of the material had been forgotten in twenty minutes, 55.8 percent at the end of one hour, 66.3 percent at the end of one day, 75 percent at the end of six days, and 78.9 percent at the end of one month. He plotted the first curve of retention which is presented in Figure 9. This curve indicates that forgetting takes place very rapidly immediately after learning and then becomes slower as time passes. Thus the importance of Ebbinghaus' work lies in the demonstra-

[4] Ebbinghaus, *Memory,* 1885, translated by H. A. Ruger and C. E. Bussenius (New York: Teachers College, Columbia University, 1913).

Table 7. The Percent Retained From Nonsense Syllables and Poetry[5]

(From Ebbinghaus and Radosavljevich)

	EBBINGHAUS	RADOSAVLJEVICH	
PERIOD AFTER LEARNING	Nonsense Syllables	Nonsense Syllables	Poetry
5 minutes	..	98	100
20 minutes	59	89	96
1 hour	44	71	78
8 hours	36	47	58
24 hours	34	68	79
2 days	28	61	67
6 days	25	49	42
14 days	..	41	30
30 days	21	20	24
120 days	..	3	7

tion that the initial stage of forgetting is more rapid than the rate at later stages.

In 1907 Radosavljevich[6] conducted an experiment in which several subjects participated and both nonsense syllables and meaningful material, that is, poetry, were used. He reported results which were not markedly different from those of Ebbinghaus. A comparison of the results of the experiments of Ebbinghaus and Radosavljevich are presented in Table 7. It will be noted that in the Radosavljevich study, forgetting was more gradual in the beginning and that in general the retention of meaningful material was similar to that of nonsense syllables but the level of retention was higher throughout.

Many similar studies in retention and forgetting have been conducted. Although some of these studies have shown variations from the results of Ebbinghaus, in general, the curve of retention still conforms to that of Ebbinghaus. After an extensive review of many experimental studies McGeoch stated: "It may be concluded that, over a wide range of conditions, the cause of retention may be represented by a curve which has its most rapid fall during the time immediately after the cessation of practice and which declines more and more slowly with increasing interval."[7]

---

[5] J. A. McGeoch and A. L. Irion, *op. cit.*, pp. 356–357.

[6] H. E. Garrett, *Great Experiments in Psychology,* 3 ed. (New York: Appleton-Century-Crofts, Inc., 1951), p. 107.

[7] McGeoch and Irion, *op. cit.*, pp. 111 and 112.

FACTORS AFFECTING EFFICIENCY IN LEARNING

Among the factors which influence directly the efficiency of learning are the following: overlearning, review, recitation, the length and distribution of practice, whole and part learning, the nature of the material to be learned, and lapse of time, particularly the summer vacation.

Overlearning. Since a direct relationship exists between retention and the degree of learning, whatever improves retention makes for effectiveness in learning. Retention depends upon the extent to which material has been learned originally. Whatever is well learned is well retained. *Overlearning* improves retention and is the fundamental technique for counteracting forgetting. Overlearning is any learning over and above that necessary to attain a criterion, usually one or several complete reproductions. It involves additional practice beyond the point of simple recall. The amount retained is proportional to the amount of overlearning. Repetition, association, organization, and application of materials are all involved in overlearning. A great deal of overlearning takes place in school as a natural consequence of instructional procedures. Much overlearning is achieved through drill which utilizes repetition for the purpose of strengthening the retention of subject matter. However, this repetition must not be merely mechanical and rote but meaningful which makes for greater understanding. This is especially true where facts and principles are utilized in daily life, such as addition and multiplication combinations, spelling, language usage, and speech habits. Likewise, some overlearning takes place when the pupil actually makes use of previous learning in new situations. Accordingly, materials should be so organized that they may be utilized in further learning; for example, in learning a foreign language, speaking and written exercises should be so organized that the pupil continuously employs in these exercises the vocabulary which has already been learned. It should be noted also that many skills are overlearned to the extent that they are never forgotten. Such skills include swimming, riding a bicycle, skating, and the like. Verbal materials which have been practiced a great deal may also be retained indefinitely. Research on overlearning has been concerned with the effects of various amounts of practice in preventing forgetting and the results have indicated very clearly that overlearning enhances retention.[8]

---

[8] W. C. F. Krueger, "The Effect of Overlearning on Retention," *Journal of Experimental Psychology,* 12:171–178, 1929; "Further Studies in Overlearning," *Journal of Experimental Psychology,* 13:152–163, 1930.

Review. Retention is facilitated by *review,* the purpose of which — through repetition and critical reexamination — is to attain a more complete understanding of relationships and a better organization of materials previously learned. Review involves critical thinking about these materials for the purpose of systematization and reorganization. Review should also serve the purpose of providing new insights into and of attaining useful generalizations concerning the materials previously learned. Since the rate of forgetting is most rapid during the period immediately following learning, review should serve the purpose of reducing this rapid rate of forgetting.[9] The first review should come soon after initial learning, probably in the form of a summary at the end of the class period. Each day there should be a review of the materials learned during the previous day. Each week there should be a review of the materials learned during that week. Review practices and activities include summaries, classroom discussions, repeated testing, examinations, and all other provisions made in instructional procedures for the use of previously learned materials in new situations and problems. In fact, the most effective kind of review is that which results from putting materials previously learned to some actual use in school and life situations.

Recitation. The term *recitation* is used here to indicate the attempt of the pupil to recall and to restate to himself, or to another person, material which he has studied. Recitation constitutes a valuable means of inducing recall of material. After the pupil has read the material several times he should attempt to recall it by self-testing or self-recitation, verifying the accuracy of his recitation or testing by reference to the material. This affords the individual a means of giving expression to his impressions of the material and also provides a way for checking on his progress in learning. It also aids in ascertaining difficult sections or portions of the material to which effort must be applied. It encourages pupil initiative and resourcefulness. It has motivational possibilities also since the learner becomes aware immediately of success or of error in his achievement. In self-recitation the individual is practicing active recall and is learning the material in the way in which it will be used later in the classroom or in a testing situation. Experimental

[9] H. F. Spitzer, "Studies in Retention," *Journal of Educational Psychology,* 30: 641–656; A. M. Sones and J. B. Stroud, "Review, with 1939 Special Reference to Temporal Position," *Journal of Educational Psychology,* 31:665–675, 1940; H. R. Tiedman, "A Study of Retention in Classroom Learning," *Journal of Educational Research,* 41:516–531, 1947–1948.

investigations[10] have demonstrated that recitation is both economical of time and also much more effective than devoting the same amount of time to rereading of material.

Length and Distribution of Practice. Practice as a condition affecting the rate and progress of learning involves two important factors: namely, the length of the period of specific practice; and the frequency of practice necessary in order that the pupil make the maximum progress in the skill to be attained and in the knowledge to be acquired. While each type of learning probably has an optimum length and frequency of practice periods, it is generally agreed that

1. Distributed practice or spacing of repetitions produces more effective results than concentrated or massed practice; that is, periods of practice or study distributed over a longer period of time will be more effective and result in greater retention of material, both meaningful and meaningless, than the same amount of time massed together in one period.
2. Periods of practice should consist of parts of hours followed by intervals of rest.

In general a summary of the data presented in research studies[11] in this field seems to justify the conclusion that several short periods are more effective than fewer longer periods. This conclusion concerning the distribution of specific practice periods should influence several elements of schoolwork. First, the course of study should provide for an adequate distribution of reviews of content to be mastered. Second, the textbooks should include systematic reviews of material to be learned. Third, the teacher's organization of content and methods should be based upon this conclusion concerning the distribution of practice periods. Fourth, the pupil's habits of study should likewise be based upon this principle.

While much more experimentation concerning the distribution of practice periods under a wide variety of conditions is necessary, it is now possible to draw several conclusions. The minimum length of the practice period depends upon the nature of the material to be learned. For drill work in school subjects and for mechanical learning in the case of young

[10] A. I. Gates, "Recitation as a Factor in Memory," *Archives of Psychology*, No. 40, 1917; G. Forlano, *School Learning with Various Methods of Practice and Rewards* (New York: Teachers College Contributions to Education, No. 688, Teachers College, Columbia University, 1936); H. A. Peterson, "Recitation or Recall as a Factor in the Learning of Long Prose Selections," *Journal of Educational Psychology*, 35:220–228, 1944.

[11] J. Deese, *op. cit.*, pp. 187–197; R. M. W. Travers, *op. cit.*, pp. 306–309.

children, very short periods of practice appear to be favorable. However, for older pupils and for tasks involving rational learning, longer periods seem to be necessary, provided they are not long enough to lead to fatigue. Thus, the age, level of maturation, abilities, and interests of the learners must be taken into consideration in the arrangement of practice periods.

Whole and Part Learning. A very practical problem in the efficiency of learning is "Will material be learned more efficiently and effectively by the *whole* or by the *parts* methods?" The *whole method* of learning involves securing an idea of the material in its entirety, together with its chief divisions and subdivisions, and then developing it as a unit or a whole. The *parts method* of learning involves the division of the material into sections or parts, each of which is studied separately until mastered; and then the various parts are combined into a whole. There has been a great deal of experimental investigation into this problem. The early experimental results were usually in favor of the whole method as the more effective. However, recent investigations have not substantiated the findings of the earlier studies, but seem to indicate that the two methods are equally effective.[12] Consequently, no generalization concerning the superior effectiveness or significant advantage of either method seems warranted. However, there appear to be situations and conditions in which the whole method is relatively more effective than the parts method. Among these situations and conditions to be considered are the type, the length, and the difficulty of the material to be learned and the intelligence of the learner. With meaningful material,[13] the whole method seems more effective. The same seems to be the case where the material to be learned is short and not difficult.[14] Likewise, in the case of mentally superior children[15] or those whose IQ is 140 or better, the whole method is more effective, probably because superior intellectual

[12] See G. O. McGeoch, "The Whole-Part Problem," *Psychological Bulletin,* 28: 713–739, 1931. This report has pointed out that an analysis of 30 experiments has revealed only six in which statistically reliable results were secured; see also J. A. McGeoch and A. L. Irion, *op. cit.,* pp. 499–510.

[13] M. V. Seagoe, "Influence of the Degree of Wholeness on Whole-Part Learning," *Journal of Experimental Psychology,* 19:763–768, 1936.

[14] M. L. Northway, "The Nature of the Difficulty With Reference to a Study of Whole-Part Learning," *British Journal of Psychology,* 27:399–403, 1937; also M. B. Jensen and A. Lemaire, "The Experiments on Whole and Part Learning," *Journal of Educational Psychology,* 28:37–54, 1937.

[15] G. O. McGeoch, "The Intelligence Quotient as a Factor in the Whole-Part Problem," *Journal of Experimental Psychology,* 14:333–358, 1931.

capacity means the use of the ability to comprehend and to respond to relationships. It is generally agreed that whatever superiority the *whole* method may possess depends upon opportunity for the meaningful organization of materials and the practice of the function in the way in which it is subsequently to be used.[16]

It may be stated, however, that the whole method of learning possesses considerable value as an aid in the developing of meaning, in outlining, in organizing, and in establishing associations. Where the material is of such a character that it makes possible the employment of the whole method, it should be used. When the subject-matter material to be learned is read through as a whole, associations between the parts and their place in the whole may be readily observed. Then, when the material has been learned sufficiently well for the difficult sections to stand out, these points may be mastered by the parts method. Finally, a return should be made to the whole method in order to organize and to complete the learning. In situations where the entire material to be learned is too lengthy to be learned as a whole, it is best to separate the material into several large natural divisions or units, each of which has meaning, each of which is a logical and unified section, capable of standing by itself, each of which can be learned within a reasonable period of time.

The Nature of the Material to Be Learned. The relationship between type of material to be learned and retention has been demonstrated in many studies. Learning, as has been indicated, depends upon comprehension and understanding. In order to comprehend and to understand material, the significance of its *meaning* must be clearly grasped. *Meaningfulness* of material is the key to efficient and effective learning. Meaningful material involves a wealth of associations, good organization, and emphasis on the uses of what is learned. Common sense would indicate that meaningful material is learned and retained with more facility and thus more economically than material which is meaningless. In fact McGeoch[17] has stated that "the rate of learning is a direct function of the meaningfulness of the material." Also Ebbinghaus pointed out that he could learn a given number of poetic syllables in their natural setting in one tenth as

---

[16] See S. S. Stevens, ed., *Handbook of Experimental Psychology* (New York: John Wiley & Sons, Inc., 1951), pp. 640–642; also, P. M. Symonds, *What Education Has To Learn From Psychology* (New York: Bureau of Publications, Teachers College, Columbia University, 1958), pp. 49–59.

[17] J. A. McGeoch, "Learning," in E. G. Boring, H. S. Langfeld, and H. P. Weld, *Introduction to Psychology* (New York: John Wiley & Sons, Inc., 1939), p. 323.

many trials as were required to learn an equal number of nonsense syllables. Experimental evidence[18] seems to justify the general conclusion that meaningful materials are learned more readily, and likewise, that material learned in logical arrangement is retained more fully and for a longer period than material learned in rote fashion.[19] Also concepts and content organized around principles are retained much better. Consequently, in order that learning be effective and economical, the teacher has the task of making the subject matter, content, and material meaningful through the establishment of connections and relationships between the materials being learned and the student's background of experience as well as through the logical organization of materials.

Lapse of Time. Many experimental investigations have been conducted to determine the effect of lapse of time upon the retention of materials learned. These studies have been chiefly concerned with the amount of material in various subjects and at different academic levels forgotten or lost over a specified period of time, as, for example, over the summer vacation. The studies, although by no means consistent in their findings, have significance for the classroom teacher. Insofar as it is possible to generalize the findings of these studies, the following conclusions seem to be justified. With respect to reading, there was to be a slight loss during the summer vacation in the primary grades[20] and a slight gain in the intermediate and junior high school grades.[21] Spelling

---

[18] H. B. English, E. L. Welborn, and C. D. Killian, "Studies in Substance Memorization," *Journal of General Psychology,* 2:233–260, 1934; also E. B. Greene, "The Retention of Information Learned in College Courses," *Journal of Educational Research,* 24:262–273, 1931.

[19] H. B. Reed, "Meaning as a Factor in Learning," *Journal of Educational Psychology,* 29:419–430, 1938; W. A. Brownell, *Meaningful vs. Mechanical Learning* (Durham, N. C.: Duke University Press, 1948); R. E. Michaels, "Relative Effectiveness of Two Methods of Teaching Certain Topics in Ninth Grade Algebra," *Mathematics Teacher,* 42:83–87, 1949; J. Deese, *op. cit.,* pp. 166–167, 237–238; J. F. Sharpe, *The Retention of Meaningful Material,* The Catholic University of America Educational Research Monographs, Vol. XVI, No. 8, 1952; G. A. Miller and J. A. Selfridge, "Verbal Context and the Recall of Meaningful Material," *American Journal of Psychology,* 63:176–185, 1952; B. J. Underwood and R. W. Schulz, *Meaningfulness and Verbal Learning* (Philadelphia: J. B. Lippincott Co., 1960).

[20] Sister M. Irmina, *The Effects of Summer Vacation Upon the Retention of the Elementary School Subjects,* The Catholic University of American Educational Research Bulletins, Vol. III, Nos. 3 and 4, 1928.

[21] E. Bruene, "Effect of Summer Vacation on the Achievement of Pupils in the Fourth, Fifth, and Sixth Grades," *Journal of Educational Research,* 18:309–314, 1928; L. D. Morgan, "How Effective Is Special Training in Preventing Loss Due to Summer Vacation?" *Journal of Educational Psychology,* 20:466–471, 1929; M. Schrepel and H. R. Laslett, "On the Loss of Knowledge by Junior High School

ability invariably showed a loss during the summer vacation, the lower grades losing more and requiring a longer time to regain the loss after the resumption of school.[22] Likewise, computational skill in arithmetic and in algebra showed a greater loss than problem-solving ability in these subjects.[23] In the content subjects a gain in history and literature[24] was found at the intermediate school level. However, at the junior high school level a loss of one fifth of the material in history was found.[25]

At the high school level, a very comprehensive investigation of retention over the period of the summer vacation was conducted by Sister Barbara Geoghegan.[26] The participating subjects were 2250 pupils enrolled in Grades 9, 10, and 11 of four parochial high schools located in Midwestern cities. Some loss occurred in every subject-matter field. In elementary algebra there was a comparatively high degree of retention. Computational skills were least well retained, while problem-solving showed a small gain. In intermediate algebra, large losses occurred in computational skills, chiefly those most recently learned, while there was a significant improvement in problem-solving ability. In plane geometry there was a significant loss, the greatest decrease occurring in knowledge of geometric facts and principles. In general science, however, there was almost complete retention. In both biology and chemistry significant losses were found. In Latin, at both the ninth- and tenth-grade levels, losses occurred chiefly in knowledge of grammatical construction, while there was a high degree of retention of vocabulary.[27] In world history

---

Pupils Over the Summer Vacation," *Journal of Educational Psychology,* 27:299–303, 1936; H. E. Elder, "The Effect of Summer Vacation on Silent Reading Ability in the Intermediate Grades," *Elementary School Journal,* 27:541–546, 1927.

[22] E. Bruene, *op. cit.;* Sister M. Irmina, *op. cit.;* M. J. Nelson, "How Much Time Is Required in the Fall for Pupils in the Elementary School to Reach Again the Spring Level of Achievement?" *Journal of Educational Research,* 18:305–308, 1928.

[23] M. Schrepel and H. R. Laslett, *op. cit.;* E. Bruene, *op. cit.;* Sister M. Irmina, *op. cit.;* M. D. Challman, "The Retention of Arithmetic and Algebra in Relation to Achievement in Plane Geometry," *Mathematics Teacher,* 39:77–79, 1946. R. A. Davis and E. J. Rood, "Remembering and Forgetting Arithmetical Abilities," *Journal of Educational Psychology,* 38:216–222, 1947.

[24] Sister M. Irmina, *op. cit.;* O. W. Kolberg, "A Study of Summer Time Forgetting," *Elementary School Journal,* 35:281–287, 1935.

[25] F. D. Brooks and S. J. Bassett, "The Retention of American History in the Junior High School," *Journal of Educational Research,* 18:195–202, 1928.

[26] Sister Barbara Geoghegan, "The Retention of Certain Secondary-School Subject Matter over the Period of the Summer Vacation," unpublished Ph.D. dissertation, Fordham University, New York, 1950.

[27] See also L. R. Kennedy, "The Retention of Certain Latin Syntactical Principles of First and Second Year Latin Students after Various Time Intervals,"

there was a significant loss and a lesser decrease in American history. This investigation revealed that the participating pupils who possessed the greatest amount of knowledge at the close of the school year sustained the greatest losses over the vacation interval; likewise, the more intelligent sustained larger losses than the less intelligent. There were no appreciable differences between the retention of boys and that of girls. However, there was apparent a definite tendency toward retention of materials involving reasoning and understanding. The greatest losses occurred where there was evidence that initial acquisition had involved rote learning. In general, the materials which were best understood were best retained and those which had been overlearned were well retained.

On the college level, studies indicated a loss of two fifths of the material in botany,[28] and losses varying from one third to one half of the materials in zoology, psychology, chemistry, and physics.[29] In general, students at the college level retained best the ability to apply principles and scientific facts and failed to retain specific information and such technical skills as ability to balance equations and to employ scientific terminology.

It seems logical to conclude from these studies that meaningful material will be retained, that retention is better in the case of ideas and principles than in factual material,[30] that organization aids retention,[31] that subject-matter materials which are used and applied are retained better than those which are not.[32]

It is to be noted that other factors including praise and reproof, reward and punishment, and knowledge of results may also be important conditions affecting the efficiency of learning. These factors and the re-

---

Journal of Educational Psychology, 23:132–146, 1932; Sister Miriam de Lourdes McMahon, "The Effects of Summer Vacation on the Retention of Latin Vocabulary," unpublished M.A. thesis, Fordham University, New York, 1946.

[28] P. O. Johnson, "The Permanence of Learning in Elementary Biology," *Journal of Educational Psychology,* 21:37–47, 1930.

[29] E. B. Greene, "The Retention of Information Learned in College Courses," *Journal of Educational Research,* 24:262–273, 1931.

[30] L. J. Briggs and H. B. Reed, "The Curve of Retention for Substance Material," *Journal of Experimental Psychology,* 32:513–517, 1943.

[31] A. R. Gilliland, "The Rate of Forgetting," *Journal of Educational Psychology,* 39:19–26, 1948.

[32] A. H. Word and R. A. Davis, "Individual Differences in Retention of General Science in the Case of Three Measurable Objectives," *Journal of Experimental Education,* 7:24–30, 1938; "Acquisition and Retention of Factual Information in Seventh Grade General Science During a Semester of Eighteen Weeks," *Journal of Educational Psychology,* 30:116–125, 1939.

search studies conducted to demonstrate the effectiveness of each have been discussed in the chapter on motivation under the heading of "The Effectiveness of Various Types of Incentives."

PHYSIOLOGICAL FACTORS WHICH INFLUENCE EFFICIENCY IN LEARNING

These factors relate to the effect of the physical condition of the learner upon the efficiency and effectiveness of learning. They include sensory defects and general physical conditions resulting from such causes as diseased tonsils and adenoids, defective teeth, malnutrition, glandular maladjustments, fatigue, loss of sleep, and the like. While these physical factors affect the efficiency and accuracy, as well as the amount and kind of improvement that will be made in learning, nevertheless the exact influence which they exert upon the efficiency and effectiveness of learning has yet to be determined adequately. Many research investigations[33] have been conducted in an endeavor to ascertain the effects of these physiological factors upon learning. It is generally recognized that imperfections of the senses impair the effectiveness of learning, for the sense organs, especially those of sight and hearing, play a vitally significant role in learning. Defects in these organs affect in various ways and degrees the character and range of sensations and will result in a partial or distorted view of the environment, and consequently of the ideas derived from them, since there is "nothing in the intellect which was not first in some manner in the senses." Both defective vision and defective hearing are prevalent among school children. It has been stated frequently that defects in these sense organs are considered to be causal factors in the retardation of children in school. While this seems to be the case, however, it should be noted that the extent to which these deficiencies operate as causal factors has yet to be determined. Since sensory experiences are basic in the learning process, the first principle in directing the learning of the child is to make certain that the sense organs are in condition to function properly. Detection and correction of physical defects is of primary importance in any program designed to increase the efficiency of learning.

---

[33] W. M. Cruickshank and G. O. Johnson, eds., *Education of Exceptional Children and Youth* (Englewood Cliffs, N. J.: Prentice-Hall, Inc., 1958), pp. 265–385; L. M. Dunn, ed., *Exceptional Children in the Schools* (New York: Holt, Rinehart and Winston, Inc., 1963), pp. 339–462.

Likewise, such common physical defects as diseased tonsils and adenoids, defective teeth, and malnutrition are considered to have a retarding effect upon learning and to decrease learning efficiency. However, again the exact influence of these defects has not been ascertained. The point for the teacher to realize is that these physical defects are discoverable, can be corrected and cured. Since it is never wise to rely on the child outgrowing these defects, early discovery and early correction must be stressed in order to *prevent* these physical defects from exercising a retarding influence upon learning.

Fatigue is considered to be a factor which is detrimental to learning efficiency. Fatigue is the term used to indicate the temporary decrease in mental functions due to continuous and prolonged exercise. Many studies have been conducted to determine the effects of fatigue,[34] the classic study having been made by Arai.[35] Her study revealed that fatigue lessens efficiency, and other experimental investigations seem to confirm that conclusion. It is the teacher's task to proportion the work of attaining skill and acquiring knowledge in such a way that pupils will be most efficient. Fatigue is an important factor in efficiency and is, therefore, a condition to be avoided in schoolwork. Although psychologists do not agree either on the manner in which fatigue is to be defined or upon the causes of it, nevertheless they are in general agreement that as a result of fatigue there is a detrimental reaction which frequently shows itself in a pronounced temporary dislike for the activity which produced it. The physical effects of fatigue are well known. The mental effects of this factor include loss of interest, the prevalence of distraction, the slackening of mental process, the lessening of power of will, and reduction of general efficiency. The teacher's duty is to correct as far as possible the conditions causing fatigue and to make the schoolwork more vital to the interests of the child. It is of utmost importance that the child should acquire gradually the capacity to work persistently in spite of the inconveniences which appear as a result of prolonged work.

Closely related to fatigue is the question of the effect of loss of sleep upon learning.[36] It is generally acknowledged that the tired child is not

[34] S. H. Bartley and E. Chute, *Fatigue and Impairment in Man* (New York: McGraw-Hill Book Co., Inc., 1947); S. S. Stevens, *op. cit.*, pp. 1357–1359.

[35] T. Arai, *Mental Fatigue,* Contributions to Education, No. 54 (New York: Teachers College, Columbia University, 1912); T. L. Huxtable *et al., A Re-performance and Re-interpretation of the Arai Experiment in Mental Fatigue,* Psychological Monographs V 59, No. 5, 1946.

[36] See the following studies concerning loss of sleep: L. M. Terman and A.

capable of learning in an efficient manner. Loss of sleep seems to affect especially the attention, the interest, and the initiative of the child. These are essential factors in the efficient and effective functioning of the learning process.

EXERCISES

1. Outline this chapter.
2. List and define the terms which you have learned from your study of this chapter.
3. In what ways may retention be measured? Which is the method used most frequently in research investigations?
4. Explain this statement: "Psychologists agree generally that most forgetting is due to interference from subsequent experiences or later learning."
5. Distinguish between retroactive and proactive inhibition.
6. What is the significance of Ebbinghaus' studies in the rate of forgetting? Explain the curve of retention.
7. Discuss the influence of each of the following upon efficiency in learning:
   a) Overlearning;
   b) Review;
   c) Recitation.
8. What have research investigations demonstrated concerning each of the following:
   a) Length and distribution of practice;
   b) Whole vs. part method;
   c) The nature of the material to be learned;
   d) The effects of summer vacation.
9. Discuss the following statements:
   a) "Learning is most efficient when one first grasps the meaning and organization of the whole, and then proceeds to give attention to the parts and the relation of each part to other parts and the whole."
   b) "Learning is more efficient when the material to be learned is meaningful and rich in associations."
   c) "To have learned means to have retained."
   d) "Retention is likely to be better in the case of ideas and principles than in factual material."
10. Report on a recent experimental study in the field of retention and forgetting: state the problem; describe the subjects, the materials, the procedures; present the findings and conclusions; give an evaluation of the investigation.

Hacking, "The Sleep of School Children," *Journal of Educational Psychology,* 4:138–147; 198–208; 269–282, 1913; H. R. Laslett, "Experiments on the Effects of Loss of Sleep," *Journal of Experimental Psychology,* 11:370–396, 1928; T. F. Weiskotten and J. E. Ferguson, "A Further Study of the Effects of Loss of Sleep," *Journal of Experimental Psychology,* 13:247–266, 1930; also J. B. Stroud, *Psychology in Education* (New York: Longmans, Green and Co., 1946), pp. 434–441.

SELECTED REFERENCES FOR STUDY AND READING

Bartlett, F. C., *Thinking* (New York: Basic Books, Inc., 1958).
Bugelski, B. R., *The Psychology of Learning* (New York: Holt, Rinehart and Winston, Inc., 1956).
Burton, W. H., *The Guidance of Learning Activities,* 3 ed. (New York: Appleton-Century-Crofts, Inc., 1962).
Cofer, C. N., and Musgrave, B. S., eds. *Verbal Behavior and Learning* (New York: McGraw-Hill Book Co., Inc., 1963).
Crafts, L. W., Schnierla, T. C., Robinson, E. E., and Gilbert, R. S., *Recent Experiments in Psychology,* 2 ed. (New York: McGraw-Hill Book Co., Inc., 1950).
Deese, J., *The Psychology of Learning,* 2 ed. (New York: McGraw-Hill Book Co., Inc., 1958).
Kingsley, H. L., and Garry, R., *The Nature and Conditions of Learning,* 2 ed. (Englewood Cliffs, N. J.: Prentice-Hall Inc., 1957).
Lawson, R., *Learning and Behavior* (New York: The Macmillan Co., 1960).
McGeoch, J. A., and Irion, A. L., *The Psychology of Human Learning,* 2 ed. (New York: Longmans, Green & Co., Inc., 1952).
Seagoe, M. V., *A Teacher's Guide to the Learning Process* (Dubuque, Iowa: Wm. C. Brown Co., 1956).
Symonds, P. M., *What Education Has to Learn From Psychology* (New York: Bureau of Publications, Teachers College, Columbia University, 1958).
Travers, R. M. W., *Essentials of Learning* (New York: The Macmillan Co., 1963).

chapter 9

Motivation in School Learning

The Meaning and Nature of Motivation. Motivation is recognized as an essential condition upon which learning is dependent. However, motivation is a very broad term which has been employed to designate a wide range of concepts which seek to explain the *why* of behavior. The purpose of this chapter is to present some of the essential facts and principles which the teacher should bear in mind in his endeavor to understand, to direct, and to control the learning and the conduct of pupils. Motivation, it should be noted, is not only a significant factor in learning; it is also basic in methodology and school management, for the purpose which method and management serve is to provide incentives, activities, and surroundings which will be conducive to learning.

The terms *motivation, motive,* and *motivating schoolwork* are frequently employed in educational writings. Since there is no general agreement concerning the fundamental meanings of these terms, they carry various connotations in the works of different authors. They are all derived from the Latin verb *movere,* which means "to move" or "to set in motion" or "to prompt to action." The term *motive* in its broadest meaning is anything which "energizes" behavior, that is, initiates, sustains, and directs activity. In the present chapter this term is employed to indicate any thing which induces an individual to learn. Motive has been defined as:

> . . . an object or cause of action intellectually judged to be *good,* that is, suitable, desirable, useful, effective, etc., or *evil,* that is, unsuitable, undesirable, dangerous, etc.[1]

> . . . any specific goal or object which, on a conscious level, directs conduct whether it is sensory or rational.[2]

[1] M. B. Arnold and J. A. Gasson, S.J., *The Human Person* (New York: The Ronald Press Company, 1954), p. 39.

[2] J. E. Royce, S.J., *Man and His Nature* (New York: McGraw-Hill Book Company, Inc., 1961), p. 160. Used by permission.

Motive involves a choice of certain responses rather than others.

Motivation, in the broadest sense, is the process by which behavior is initiated and accelerated and which involves the stimulation of action toward a particular object or goal. Educationally, *motivation* means providing with motive, that is *stimulating the intention or "will to learn."* In its educational significance the term *motivation* connotes anything that impels or moves the pupil to activity. As used in this chapter the term *motivation* means the purposeful presentation to the pupil of adequate and fitting incentives together with the necessary guidance and direction for utilizing these incentives. It is a *process* of inducing motives which will "energize" learning and behavior. It involves the stimulation of pupils to apply themselves willingly to the tasks of the classroom by making school tasks significant and purposeful. Ideally, pupil-learning and conduct should be stimulated adequately by the enjoyment derived from the learning activity, by the intrinsic interest in the work, by the realization of its usefulness, by recognition of the need for its mastery,[3] rather than by such extrinsic goals as grades or later competitive advantage.

In keeping with the findings of animal experimentation and the Neo-Behavioristic theories which are generally employed to interpret these findings, the tendency in psychology at the present time is to describe motivation within the framework of *needs, drives,* and *goals*. Thus motivation is used to describe "need satisfying and goal seeking behavior"[4] and includes all of the factors which contribute to the initiation of behavior and the direction of that behavior toward a goal. It involves the complex interaction between conditions within the individual and the total environment. Behavioral activities are considered to be directed by the fundamental or basic needs, which are physiological conditions common to all human beings. A *need* is usually defined as a lack of something which is necessary or suitable for self-realization. Need exists when an individual lacks something which is either necessary for survival or which through past learning has become important to him and serves to direct behavior toward certain goals. Need satisfaction is considered to be an im-

---

[3] Such motivation is sometimes designated as intrinsic and distinguished from extrinsic motivation, which is not "an orginal function of the material to be learned or of the learner's attitude toward it," but consists of "an incentive or goal artificially introduced into the situation." See D. G. Ryans, "Motivation in Learning," N.S.S.E. Forty-First Yearbook, Part II, *The Psychology of Learning,* 1942, pp. 296–297.

[4] E. R. Hilgard and D. H. Russell, "Motivation in School Learning," in N.S.S.E. Forty-Ninth Yearbook, Part I, *Learning and Instruction,* 1950, p. 38.

portant factor in motivation. Need creates a *drive* which activates the organism and makes it perform. Thus behavior is considered to be influenced by a host of needs which operate as driving forces in life activities. Accordingly *drive* refers to the internal tensions which act as stimuli to particular kinds of behavior and initiate activity in connection with a particular goal. In turn, *goals* are ends or objects toward which behavior is directed and which tend to satisfy the particular needs of the individual.

Psychologists have classified needs in various ways, usually in accord with their assumptions concerning personality. However, while the various classifications may vary with respect to nonessentials, they generally agree upon the basic human needs. While there is no generally accepted classification most psychologists have sought to utilize a threefold classification into the following categories: (*a*) the basic physical or organic needs; (*b*) the psychosocial or the emotional and social needs; (*c*) the ego-integrative needs.

a) The basic physical or organic needs are concerned with the well-being of the individual and include need for air, water, food, sleep, rest, and the like.

b) The psychosocial or emotional and social needs include the necessity for safety, for emotional security, for belonging to a group, for being loved and for loving, for acceptance by others, for a sense of personal worth, for self-esteem, for achievement and success.

c) The ego-integrative needs include values and purposes for the life one leads, the acceptance of self, and the ability to cope with the realities of life.

These needs are both mutually complimentary and also highly interrelated.

Learning is considered by modern theorists to be based upon need satisfaction. Accordingly these theorists maintain that, since motivation should stem from fundamental needs, knowledge of these needs constitutes a significant factor in determining both educational objectives and also teaching goals, in planning learning experiences, and in developing in an effective manner the organization of these experiences.[5]

Motivation or stimulating the "will to learn" is a central factor influ-

[5] Current theory and research on motivation are presented in the annual series, *Nebraska Symposium on Motivation* (Lincoln: University of Nebraska Press). The first volume in this series appeared in 1953.

encing the learning process. Since learning is not a process of passive absorption, learning cannot take place in the absence of intention or "will to learn." Some type of motivation must be present in all learning and in all conduct. The individual learns only when he is motivated to learn; that is, learning cannot take place without motivation and the effectiveness of learning is in direct proportion to the motivation of the individual. Motivation is then the primary condition of learning around which all problems of learning, teaching, and discipline center.

The purpose of motivation may be considered to be threefold: (1) *to arouse interest;* (2) *to stimulate a desire to learn* which leads to effort; and (3) *to direct these interests and efforts toward the accomplishment of suitable purposes and toward the attainment of definite goals.* Motivation is, then, not a teaching procedure, but rather an aspect of all teaching procedures. It is not something external to learning, but is an aspect of every learning situation. It involves *interest* and *effort on the part of pupil, direction and guidance* of the pupil's interest, and effort *on the part of the teacher.* It is worthy of note that motivation involves comprehension of the relationship between the school task and the purpose for which it is performed and the goal or end sought by its performance. The more definite is the pupil's appreciation and understanding of this relationship, the more compelling are the motives for learning and for behavior.

Motivation or the stimulating of pupils in a natural and interesting manner to more effective schoolwork is the underlying problem of all methods of teaching. The problem involves two factors. The first is to find motives that will stimulate interest and effort on the part of the pupil; the second is to guide and direct the pupil's interests and efforts in such a way that he will permanently cultivate worthy, lofty, uplifting motives. It is noteworthy that, frequently, when a child of average or superior intellectual capacities, with adequate social and educational background, fails to accomplish his school tasks successfully, the problem is one of motivation. This involves the finding of adequate motives and sufficient guidance and direction for those interests and efforts that are aroused.

Incentives and Motivation. Incentives represent some type of goal for the attainment of which learning is a necessary means in a given situation. They are those elements of school situations which are purposely set up by the teacher to stimulate the motives of pupils for school tasks. They are external devices and procedures, factors and influences introduced to stimulate and arouse motives which modify the pupil's action along desirable lines. If the pupil is indifferent, if the subject matter itself stimulates no interest, then this indifference must be overcome, and interest must be derived from other sources. The teacher sets the stage, as it were, provides stimuli, arranges certain conditions and situations, that is, provides *incentives* or what is sometimes termed *extrinsic motivation* in the form of directions, suggestions, problems, commendations, and the like, which are intended to stimulate interest and lead to effort. The teacher's task is to furnish the pupil with adequate incentives for doing his work rapidly, accurately, and efficiently by setting up situations in which pupils will learn because knowledge is useful and meaningful. The teacher should direct at the beginning of each task an initial attack which includes a proper introduction to subject materials; he should provide sufficient time to organize and assimilate what has been learned in such a way that the entire process produces a feeling of satisfaction. Incentives should have a real and permanent value.

Incentives are external, while motives are fundamental and vital. Motives tend to be internal to the person and to constitute an inherent part of the learning activity. Motivation goes beyond incentive, supplying larger and more worthy ends for attainment. Incentives are devices and procedures, usually rewarding objects, situations, and events, used to arouse interest and participation in school tasks where little interest and participation might otherwise have been developed. Incentives are a means to an end. The purpose of incentives is to initiate interest and action, while motive not merely initiates but also sustains interest and action. Motivation is a long-range affair. It is self-directive in action. Accordingly, the ideally motivated class would require few or no incentives.

Interest and Motivation. Interest is a primary and fundamental source of motivation. It has been defined as *the pleasurable or painful feeling produced by an idea or object with the power of attracting and sustaining attention.* It involves selective attention and the attitude or feeling that an object or event is of concern to the individual. It is the feeling which accompanies special attention to some content, an attitude characterized by focusing attention on cognitive data. It is the means by which the mind is attracted to an object and is an important factor in the acquisition of knowledge. Interest secures economy in learning and efficiency in response, since it implies not only a favorable disposition toward an object but also a tendency toward making further responses to that object. The awakening and sustaining of interest must always be the primary aim of the teacher. The teacher, because of his superior knowledge and in virtue of his understanding of child nature, must be able to secure and to maintain the interest of his pupils. He must inspire an urge to know and to use knowledge effectively.

Interest connotes ordinarily the pleasurable feelings resulting from and accompanying attention to objects. Interest may vary from mild to intense. It is either *native* or *acquired. Native interest* is the value which an object possesses in and of itself to attract attention. *Acquired interest* is derived from the association of an object with others in which interest already exists. Interest generates *effort.* However, where a subject or task makes no appeal to the pupil, genuine effort involving voluntary attention will usually develop and maintain interest. In fact, learning to work effectively and under varying circumstances involves knowing how to work up interest in accomplishing partially distasteful, but nevertheless necessary activities. Interest does not reduce the amount of work necessary to perform a task, but it makes the effort pleasant, thus accelerating learning. The pleasure that comes from the work makes it satisfying. Furthermore, interesting is not the same as easy, and developing interest in schoolwork through motivation does not mean making subjects easy. Developing interest through motivation does not mean mere entertainment, but it implies sustained voluntary *attention* and "vitalized" effort.

The means of developing interest of the type that inspires to wholehearted endeavor are:

1. Place the pupil in contact with a wide range of desirable activities.
2. These activities must be proportionate to his capacities, and the method of presenting them must be adapted to his mental ability.
3. Conditions which insure satisfaction must be present since interests grow out of satisfying experiences.

The Sources of Motivation. Every response made in the classroom has some motive as its source. These motives which influence the progress and improvement of learning and conduct may vary greatly. Their sources range from the most fundamental sensory objects to the most lofty ideals, from what is merely momentary to the great permanent forces of life. In general the sources upon which motivation depends may be said to be *intellectual, emotional,* and *social* in nature.

Examples of such sources of motivation include the following:

1. Appreciation of the value and worth of the subject matter itself;
2. Recognition of a value inhering in the subject matter either as a foundation for other schoolwork or as preparation for a vocation or occupation;
3. Curiosity which stimulates a desire to acquire information or to achieve understanding;
4. The influence and personal inspiration resulting from example set by a teacher;
5. Social approval involving commendation of teachers, parents, fellow students;
6. Competition of various types;
7. Praise, approval, encouragement of others (reproof and disapproval also);
8. Desire for distinction, which includes grades, prizes, rewards, honor roll, and the like.
9. Economic necessity;
10. Desire to meet standards of accomplishment and to avoid the consequences of failure.

The Basic Factors in Motivation. The basic factors in motivation are three. The first factor is *the pupil* whose development, learning, and conduct are the objects of motivation. The second factor is *the teacher* whose task it is to guide and direct the interests and efforts of the pupil toward the accomplishment of suitable purposes and toward the attainment of definite goals. The third factor consists of *the techniques and devices* of which the teacher makes use in order to stimulate, to guide, and to direct the intention or "will to learn."

In order to guide and direct the interest and efforts of the pupil toward the accomplishment of suitable purposes and toward the attainment of definite goals, the teacher must be possessed of three qualifications. The first qualification is a *thorough understanding of the process of growth and development* and of the changes which take place in the individual as he progresses from infancy to maturity. Effective motivation is dependent upon the "readiness," the interests, and the activities of the learner. Since the child during school age is passing through a series of changes in interests and in capabilities, it is the teacher's task both to know the characteristic of the different periods of childhood and to use methods of guiding and directing the child which will keep pace with these changes in interests and capabilities. To stimulate successfully the "will to learn," the teacher must have an insight into the needs of the individual pupil, must know his special abilities and disabilities. This means that adequate recognition must be given to the part played by individual differences, environment, and home background. Since the child's interests form a very important source of motivation, it is essential that the teacher know and utilize interests in reading, movies, television, radio, play, and the like. It means also that the teacher must have some knowledge of the pupil's vocational hopes and ambitions. The second qualification is a *clear understanding of the function of teaching.* This means that the teacher must direct the activities stimulated — physical, mental, and emotional activities — in such a way that they will find worthwhile expression not only in carrying out present school tasks but in building permanent interests, attitudes, ideals, habits, and skills. Hence, it is of utmost importance that the teacher have an accurate knowledge of the learning process, a complete understanding of how and when learning takes place, of how it may be directed in order that desirable skills and knowledge may be acquired efficiently, effectively, and economically. The teacher must have an intelligent appreciation of the relation of adequate motivation to economy in learning. The third qualification is a *clear understanding of the chief goal of the educative process.* No one is a teacher merely of one subject; all are builders of character. The aim of all education is the development of character. The purpose of motivation is to aid in fulfilling this function of education by directing the "will to learn" in such a way that the pupil becomes a self-reliant, self-controlled, self-disciplined individual.

Level of Aspiration.[6] This term is employed to designate the standard or goal which a pupil sets for himself and which he expects to attain in a particular learning situation. Level of aspiration is not a technique of motivation. It is indicative, however, of what the pupil expects to achieve or accomplish and is determined largely by his conception of his own abilities and by his previous experiences and achievements. It involves also

[6] See L. Carmichael, ed., *Manual of Child Psychology,* 2 ed. (New York: John Wiley & Sons, Inc., 1954), pp. 957–959; P. S. Sears, "Levels of Aspiration in Academically Successful and Unsuccessful School Children," *Journal of Abnormal and Social Psychology,* 35:498–536, 1940; J. D. Frank, "Recent Studies of the Level of Aspiration," *Psychological Bulletin,* 38:218–226, 1941; A. L. Baldwin, *Behavior and Development in Childhood* (New York: The Dryden Press, 1955), pp. 148–151.

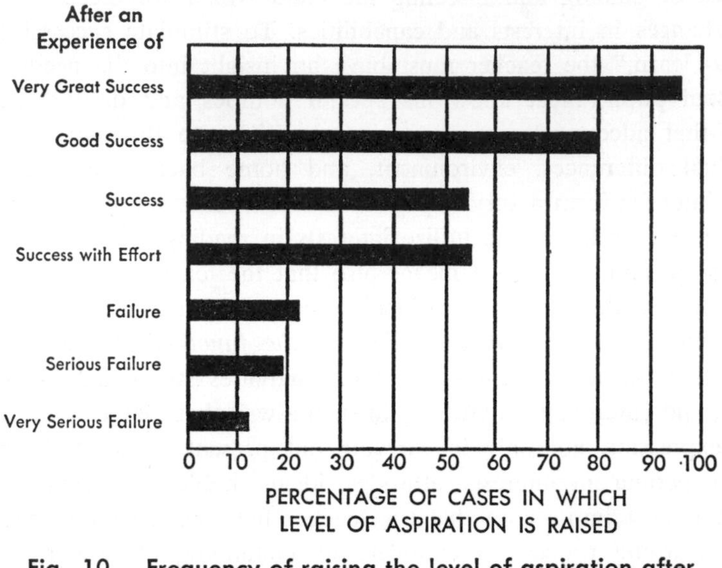

Fig. 10. Frequency of raising the level of aspiration after various degrees of success and failure.[7]

the pupil's evaluation of himself, that is, his self-concept. It is significant in motivation because upon the level of aspiration depends the source of success and failure. In the case of one student the level of aspiration may be to achieve a place on the honor roll, while a second pupil may aspire to make the football team and a third, to attain a passing grade to avoid the consequences of failure. The extent to which each attains his aspiration becomes his own evaluation of success or failure.

Experimental investigations conducted in the area of level of aspiration have revealed that pupils who experience continued success tend to be realistic and to set goals which can be realized. However, some pupils set goals below their level of ability and so fail to develop their best potentialities. Likewise, other pupils whose level of ability is low set goals which are too high. Success requires that goals be in proportion to ability. These investigations have also indicated that in general, if a pupil reaches or exceeds his level of aspiration, he is likely to increase it, that is, to set new goals at a higher level. However, when a pupil fails seriously to reach

[7] A. L. Baldwin, *op. cit.*, p. 149. Data derived from K. Lewin, *et al.*, "Level of Aspiration," in *Personality and Behavior Disorders*, J. M. V. Hunt, ed. (New York: The Ronald Press Co., 1944), pp. 333–378.

his goal, then the tendency usually is to lower the level of aspiration. The teacher's function is to aid individual pupils to set levels of aspiration which will enable them to achieve as much success as possible in proportion to their abilities, and which at the same time will stimulate effort and increase learning.

The Effectiveness of Various Types of Incentives. The selection of subject matter, the direction of learning, and the mechanics of classroom management necessarily involve the effectiveness of various types of incentives. A considerable number of experimental investigations have been conducted in the attempt to determine the effectiveness of various types of incentives. The types of incentives, the effectiveness of which has been studied, include: *praise and reproof; reward and punishment; knowledge of results; competition and rivalry*. The findings of some of the better known of these investigations are presented briefly here. However, detailed descriptions of the conditions under which these investigations were conducted as well as descriptions of the experimental techniques employed have not been presented, since such descriptions have not been considered essential in an introductory text of this type. Consequently, merely the outcomes of the investigations are cited.

a) *Praise and Reproof*. The investigations made to determine the effectiveness of *praise* and *reproof* as incentives are of two types. In addition to the experimental studies, several questionnaire studies have been made. Accordingly representative studies of both types are included. Questionnaire studies conducted by Laird[8] and by Briggs,[9] although sharing the deficiencies and limitations of the questionnaire method, are of significance because they indicate that students considered that "reprimands before others, ridicule, and sarcasm" were generally productive of unfavorable results in learning, while "public commendation" was considered to be most effective in producing improvement in learning. However, private reprimand was recognized as an effective incentive in a considerable number of cases. Probably the most widely quoted experimental study dealing with this aspect of motivation was made by Hurlock.[10] She endeavored

[8] D. A. Laird, "How the College Student Responds to Different Incentives to Work," *Pedagogical Seminary*, 30:366–370, 1923; also D. A. Laird, "How the High School Student Responds to Different Incentives to Work," *Pedagogical Seminary*, 30:358–365, 1923.

[9] T. H. Briggs, "Praise and Censure as Incentives," *School and Society*, 26:596–598, 1927.

[10] E. B. Hurlock, "An Evaluation of Certain Incentives Used in School Work," *Journal of Educational Psychology*, 16:145–159, 1925.

to determine the value of praise as compared with reproof in learning. As subjects she used four groups of elementary school children, which were designated as the *Praised,* the *Reproved,* the *Ignored,* and the *Control* groups. The first group was publicly praised for excellence in accomplishment. The second group was reprimanded for its poor work. The third group was neither praised nor reproved. The fourth group was given no motivation beyond that which was normal in its work. The first three groups worked together in the same classroom, while the fourth group worked in another room. The outcome of this study was that the Praised group showed most improvement. The Reproved group also showed improvement, but less than that of the Praised group. The Ignored group showed the least improvement, while the Control group showed a slight loss. In addition, Hurlock found that girls were influenced more by praise than by reproof. The reverse was true of boys. However, even among boys reproof was not as effective as praise. Likewise, it was discovered that children of inferior mental capacity responded well to praise. Among the early experimental investigations in the effectiveness of praise and reproof as incentives were those made by Gilchrist[11] and by Gates and Risland.[12] Gilchrist, using college students as subjects, found that praise was a more effective incentive than was reproof. Likewise, Gates and Risland, who also used college students as subjects of their study, found that greater improvement in learning resulted from praise than from reproof.

It is worthy of note, however, that later investigations have demonstrated that there is relatively little difference between praise and reproof as incentives. Both constitute effective incentives, but a slight advantage seems to exist in favor of praise. Brenner[13] found little difference between praise and reproof, but noted that praise given immediately was more effective than praise delayed a day after work had been accomplished. Schmidt[14] found no significant difference in the effectiveness of praise and reproof, but called attention to the fact that the personality of the teacher

---

[11] E. P. Gilchrist, "The Extent to which Praise and Reproof Affect a Pupil's Work," *School and Society,* 4:872–874, 1916.

[12] G. S. Gates and L. Q. Risland, "The Effect of Encouragement and Discouragement Upon Performance," *Journal of Educational Psychology,* 14:21–26, 1923.

[13] B. Brenner, *Effect of Immediate and Delayed Praise and Blame Upon Learning and Recall,* Contributions to Education, No. 620 (New York: Teachers College, Columbia University, 1944.

[14] H. O. Schmidt, "The Effects of Praise and Blame as Incentives to Learning," *Psychological Monographs,* Vol. 53, No. 3, 1941.

administering praise or reproof constituted a decisive factor in the effectiveness of either incentive. Wood,[15] using three groups of college students as subjects, found a slight advantage in favor of the praised group. However, the reproved group made almost as much gain while a control group improved little, if any. Thompson and Hunnicutt[16] reported that a group of introverted children and another composed of extraverted pupils were subjected to praise at certain times and to blame at others. The extraverted pupils made greater improvement in achievement when they received blame than when they were praised. With the introverted group the results were the opposite. Likewise, both praise and blame were more effective than no external incentive. It should be noted that in the use of reproof the personality of the teacher and also that of the child as well as the circumstances under which reproof is given make a great deal of difference in the effects.

b) Reward and Punishment. Akin to and perhaps a concrete expression of praise and reproof are *reward* and *punishment* as types of incentives. Several investigations of the effectiveness of *reward* reveal that those of a material nature, including "candy" and "money"[17] for young children and "financial aid"[18] for college students constitute effective incentives to learning. With regard to the effectiveness of *punishment,* it has been demonstrated that it is possible for punishment to exercise a favorable effect[19] in producing improvement in learning, particularly when the learner understands the purpose of the punishment. However, investigations on the effectiveness of this type of incentive have not been satisfactory.

Worthy of mention in a discussion of the effectiveness of reward and

---

[15] T. W. Wood, "The Effect of Approbation and Reproof on the Mastery of Nonsense Syllables," *Journal of Applied Psychology,* 18:657–664, 1934.

[16] G. G. Thompson and C. W. Hunnicutt, "The Effect of Repeated Praise or Blame on the Work Achievements of Introverts and Extroverts," *Journal of Educational Psychology,* 35:257–266, 1944.

[17] C. Meier, "Effects of Prizes in Increasing the Word Learning of Subnormal Children," *Training School Bulletin,* 32:146–157, 1935; also C. J. Leuba, "A Preliminary Experiment to Quantify an Incentive and Its Effects," *Journal of Abnormal and Social Psychology,* 25:275–288, 1930; also E. L. Thorndike, *The Psychology of Wants, Interests and Attitudes* (New York: D. Appleton-Century Co., 1935).

[18] A. B. Crawford, "Effects of Scholarship: A Study in Motivation," *Journal of Personnel Research,* 4:391–404, 1926.

[19] M. E. Bunch, "Certain Effects of Electric Shock in Learning a Stylus Maze," *Journal of Comparative Psychology,* 20:211–242, 1935; also E. L. Thorndike, *op. cit.;* also J. M. Stephens, "The Influence of Punishment on Learning," *Journal of Experimental Psychology,* 17:536–555, 1934.

punishment as incentives is a questionnaire investigation conducted by Kirkendall.[20] Although subject to the usual limitations of this type of study, the investigation presented several interesting conclusions. The subjects answering the questionnaire were elementary school children. The conclusions from their answers included the following: A larger proportion of pupils felt they would work harder after a scolding; boys have a tendency to react more antagonistically to scolding and ridicule when used as incentives than do girls; marks were considered effective incentives; compositions displayed in the classroom were considered to constitute a more effective incentive than rewards received from parents because of the excellence of the composition.

c) *Knowledge of Results.* Among the earliest studies on the effectiveness of knowledge of progress in learning, and perhaps the best known, is that made by Book and Norvell.[21] The subjects of the investigation were two groups of college students. One group was informed of progress, received records of scores, and was encouraged to improve, while the other group was not informed of progress. An interesting feature of this study was that when two thirds of the time allotted to the experiment had elapsed the conditions were reversed. From that point to the end of the experiment the previously uninformed group was given information of its progress, while such information was withheld from the group which had previously received it. The outcome in each instance favored the group which had been informed of progress made. Up to the time of the reversal of conditions, the group informed of progress improved more rapidly than the uninformed group. However, when the incentive, "knowledge of progress," was removed, learning decreased. Likewise, when the incentive was provided for the group which previously had not been informed of progress, learning for that group increased.

Ross,[22] using college students as subjects, substantiated this finding. Likewise, Deputy,[23] also using college students as subjects, demonstrated that in a classroom situation the group informed of progress made greater

[20] L. A. Kirkendall, "The Influence of Certain Incentives in the Motivation of Children," *Elementary School Journal,* 38:417–424, 1938. See also, P. M. Symonds, *What Education Has to Learn From Psychology* (New York: Bureau of Publications, Teachers College, Columbia University, 1958), pp. 11–36.

[21] W. F. Book and L. Norvell, "The Will to Learn," *Pedagogical Seminary,* 29: 305–362, 1922.

[22] C. C. Ross, "An Experiment in Motivation," *Journal of Educational Psychology,* 18:337–346, 1927.

[23] E. C. Deputy, "Knowledge of Success as a Motivating Factor in College Work," *Journal of Educational Research,* 20:327–334, 1929.

improvement than a group not informed. Brown,[24] using elementary school children as subjects in a classroom situation, also demonstrated that knowledge of progress is an effective incentive, that is, that children informed of progress made both higher scores and more consistent gains than did uninformed pupils. Panlasigui and Knight[25] in a study using elementary school pupils as subjects also found that children informed of progress by means of class and individual progress charts made significant gains over those not so informed. Similar results were revealed in studies by Arps,[26] by Symonds and Chase,[27] and by Forlano.[28] Likewise, Mother Gervase Lapadula[29] found that the achievement of eighth-grade pupils was increased significantly by knowledge of the results attained on unit-type tests.

d) *Competition and Rivalry.* Of the incentives discussed thus far, *praise and reproof, reward and punishment* are considered to be emotional in nature, while *knowledge of progress* is considered to be intellectual in nature. *Competition* and *rivalry* are considered to be social incentives. The investigations on the effectiveness of competition and rivalry as incentives to learning have been concerned with two aspects, namely, *group* and *individual* competition and rivalry.

Hurlock[30] studied the effectiveness of group rivalry as an incentive. She used two equivalent groups of elementary school children as subjects. One of these served as a control group, in which the pupils worked in a separate room and the type of motivation consisted merely of urging them to do their best work. In the other group, the experimental, the subjects were divided into two matched groups. Each of these matched

---

[24] F. J. Brown, "Knowledge of Results as an Incentive in School Room Practice," *Journal of Educational Psychology,* 25:532–552, 1932.

[25] I. Panlasigui and F. B. Knight, "The Effect of Awareness of Success or Failure," in Twenty-Ninth Yearbook, N.S.S.E., Part II, *Research in Arithmetic,* pp. 611–619, 1930.

[26] G. E. Arps, "Work With Knowledge of Results vs. Work Without Knowledge of Results," *Psychological Monographs,* Vol. 28, No. 3, 1920.

[27] P. M. Symonds and D. H. Chase, "Practice vs. Motivation," *Journal of Educational Psychology,* 20:19–35, 1929.

[28] G. Forlano, *School Learning With Various Methods of Practice and Rewards,* Contributions to Education, No. 688 (New York: Teachers College, Columbia University, 1936).

[29] Mother M. Gervase Lapadula, "The Effectiveness of Two Methods of Using Informal Objective Type Unit Tests Upon the Motivation of Learning and Upon the Retention of Factual Materials," unpublished Ph.D. dissertation, Fordham University, New York, 1951.

[30] E. B. Hurlock, "The Use of Group Rivalry as an Incentive," *Journal of Abnormal and Social Psychology,* 22:278–290, 1927.

groups competed against the other. The subjects in the matched competitive groups improved decidedly in their work, while those in the control group did not. Hurlock concluded that group rivalry constituted an effective incentive in creating both speed and accuracy of work. Leuba,[31] also using elementary school pupils as subjects, likewise found that group rivalry as an incentive was effective in improving performance.

Sims[32] studied the effectiveness of both group and individual competition, making use of three groups of college students as subjects. One of these groups was subdivided into two sections which competed against each other. In the second group, the subjects were paired, each competing against the individual with whom he was paired. The third group served as a control, and for the students in this group no competitive incentive was provided. The results of this investigation revealed that a gain was made by all three groups. However, in the case of the control group, the gain was very slight. A larger gain was made by the students competing in groups. However, the largest gain was made by the individuals competing against each other. This gain was almost six times that made by the students competing in groups. This investigation demonstrated that, while group rivalry is an effective incentive, nevertheless, individual competition is more effective. Maller,[33] likewise, studied the effectiveness of both group and individual rivalry, using elementary school pupils as subjects. It was found that competition for an individual prize constituted a more effective incentive than competition for a group prize. When given a choice whether to compete for one's self or for the group, three fourths of the subjects chose to compete for themselves. Both the Sims and the Maller studies indicate that competing for one's self constitutes a more effective incentive than competing for the group. Thus, for elementary school pupils, individual competition seems to be a stronger incentive than group competition. Zubin,[34] likewise, conducted an experimental investigation on individual competition using elementary school children as subjects and

---

[31] C. J. Leuba, "A Preliminary Experiment to Quantify an Incentive and Its Effects," *Journal of Abnormal and Social Psychology,* 25:275–288, 1930.

[32] V. M. Sims, "The Relative Influence of Two Types of Motivation on Improvement," *Journal of Educational Psychology,* 19:480–484, 1928.

[33] J. B. Maller, *Cooperation and Competition,* Contributions to Education, No. 384 (New York: Teachers College, Columbia University, 1929).

[34] J. Zubin, *Some Effects of Incentives: A Study of Individual Differences in Rivalry,* Contributions to Education, No. 532 (New York: Teachers College, Columbia University, 1932).

demonstrated that this form of rivalry constituted a significantly effective type of incentive. However, Sister M. Gertrude Maleszka[35] studied the relative effectiveness of group, individual, and self-competition at the elementary school level and found that group competition resulted in greater interest in work and produced more effective results on tests. Klugman[36] also reported that children of average mental ability attained more correct answers in group problem solving than when working alone.

After a consideration of the studies on the effectiveness of the various types of incentives the following conclusions and recommendations seem to be justified:

1. Among the strongest incentives for effective learning is success in the pursuit of schoolwork. Successful accomplishment results in satisfaction.
2. The most satisfactory type of motivation is a desire on the part of the pupil to do his task without outside pressure.
3. Improvement is rapid when the learner comprehends his task and recognizes that it fits in with his immediate interests, that it is relevant to his purpose, that it meets a felt need.
4. Knowledge of results increases speed and accuracy, improves achievement, and helps to maintain vigor in pursuit of goals.
5. A definite objective results in more work and less fatigue.
6. Commendation, praise, and encouragement are effective types of incentives which are universally recognized.
7. As a general rule the presence of a group improves performance, but this is not equally the case with all types of work.
8. Competition is an effective type of incentive with school children for stimulating achievement. Self-competition is especially desirable.
9. Individual motivation is superior to group motivation.
10. Positive incentives are better than negative incentives.

Whatever type of incentive used, it should always make provision for individual differences. It should take into consideration the nature of the child and should adapt the incentive to his mental ability. For

---

[35] Sister M. Gertrude Maleszka, "A Study to Determine the Relative Influence of Three Types of Competition on Achievement in Arithmetic," unpublished M.A. thesis, Fordham University, New York, 1946.

[36] S. F. Klugman, "Cooperative vs. Individual Efficiency in Problem Solving," *Journal of Educational Psychology,* 35:91–100, 1944.

the younger child motives should be selected the influence of which can be felt quickly. As the child grows older, dependence upon extraneous incentives should be displaced by self-reliance. Extremes in types of motivation should be avoided. The type of incentive used should appeal to the highest motive which the child can appreciate.

In connection with the discussion of the effectiveness of the types of incentives, it is worthy of note that one of the best types is to encourage the pupils to keep a graphic record of progress from day to day, week to week, month to month. Careful systematic habits of work are encouraged when the pupil knows his status, the direction, and rate of his progress. These graphic records are termed *motivation charts* or *progress charts* and take the form of curves, scales, bar diagrams, profiles, and the like.

The Educational Implications of Motivation. The child must be supplied with motives sufficiently strong to induce him to work, to think, and to be virtuous. The teacher's function is to help the child to understand these motives, to make them stimuli for action. The complete education must establish ideals, form habits, develop interest, provide rational and ethical motives, to guide and direct the child in performing the daily tasks of the school and the daily acts of life. The child must be guided, directed, and stimulated to apply himself to tasks regardless of whether or not these tasks come within the range of his individual interests. The school which fails to provide for the development of will and of concentrated attention through the frequent setting of tasks which are not in themselves interesting is failing in its purpose. Motivating schoolwork does not mean that the aim of the school is to entertain, to make work easy. Motivation of the right type must lead to increased voluntary control, to greater effectiveness, and to a higher level of mental and spiritual development. The teacher's problem in motivation is twofold. The first problem is one of practical procedures, of finding adequate motives to stimulate activity of the right type; the second is concerned with the subsequent effects of the use of motivation, for motivation exerts both a directing effect and also a re-enforcing effect upon learning.[37] Motivation is something far more fundamental than the mere application of devices by the teacher to bring about temporary results. It is the direction and development of the child's interests and efforts by tasks

---

[37] D. G. Ryans, *op. cit.*, p. 298.

adapted to his level of maturity and experience to realize desirable and lasting results. Devices may be and are used to good advantage, but their true significance must be comprehended by the teacher in their relation to the purposes of education. The teacher's task in motivation is to develop cooperative attitudes, to direct sustained attention to tasks, and to encourage initiative.

EXERCISES

1. Outline this chapter.
2. List and define the terms which you have learned from your study of this chapter.
3. Explain the nature of motivation and its significance in learning.
4. Distinguish between:
   a) Incentive and motive;
   b) Interest and motive.
5. Explain the significance of each of the three basic factors in motivation.
6. What is the relationship of motivation to each of the following:
   a) The learning process;
   b) The formation of character;
   c) Constructive discipline;
   d) The acquisition of effective methods of study.
7. Explain the effectiveness of each of the following types of incentives:
   a) Praise and reproof;
   b) Reward and punishment.
   Substantiate your explanation by reference to experimental studies.
8. What conclusions and recommendations seemed to be justified from an analysis of the studies on the effectiveness of the various types of incentives?
9. Discuss the following statements:
   a) "The more closely the mark, reward, or punishment used as a motive as a natural outcome of the learning process, the better effect it has."
   b) "In intrinsic motivation the drive is desire for the activity in question; the incentive is an immediate goal, participation in the activity."
   c) "Motivation has both a directing effect and a reinforcing effect upon learning."
   d) "The type of incentive employed in classroom learning should appeal to the highest motive which the child can appreciate."
   e) "Motivation does not mean that the aim of the school is to entertain or to make work easy."
   f) "A most important factor in the choice of goals and expected level of performance is the child's self-concept."
10. How are an individual's aspirations related to motivation? What have research investigations revealed concerning the nature of aspirations?

SELECTED REFERENCES FOR STUDY AND READING

Brown, J. S., *The Motivation of Behavior* (New York: McGraw-Hill Book Co., Inc., 1961).

Burton, W. H., *The Guidance of Learning Activities,* 3 ed. (New York: Appleton-Century-Crofts, Inc., 1962).

Combs, A. W., and Snygg, D., *Individual Behavior* (New York: Harper and Row, 1959).

Deese, J., *The Psychology of Learning,* 2 ed. (New York: McGraw-Hill Book Co., 1958).

Fuller, J. L., *Motivation* (New York: Random House, Inc., 1962).

Hall, J. F., *Psychology of Motivation* (Philadelphia: J. B. Lippincott Co., 1961).

Hilgard, E. R., and Russell, D. H., "Motivation in School Learning," National Society for the Study of Education, Forty-Ninth Yearbook, Part I, *Learning and Instruction,* 1950, pp. 36–69.

Kingsley, H. L., and Garry, R., *The Nature and Conditions of Learning,* 2 ed. (Englewood Cliffs, N. J.: Prentice-Hall, Inc., 1957).

Lawson, R., *Learning and Behavior* (New York: The Macmillan Co., 1960).

Lindzey, T., ed., *Assessment of Human Motives* (New York: Holt, Rinehart and Winston, Inc., 1959).

Madsen, K. B., *Theories of Motivation* (Cleveland: Howard Allen, Inc., Publishers, 1963).

Marx, M. H., "Motivation," in *Encyclopedia of Educational Research,* C. W. Harris, ed., 3 ed. (New York: The Macmillan Co., 1960), pp. 888–901.

McClelland, D. C., ed., *Studies in Motivation* (New York: Appleton-Century-Crofts, Inc., 1955).

McGeoch, J. A., and Irion, A. L., *The Psychology of Human Learning,* 2 ed. (New York: Longmans, Green and Co., 1952).

Ryans, D. G., "Motivation in Learning," National Society for the Study of Education, Forty-First Yearbook, Part II, *The Psychology of Learning,* 1942, pp. 289–331.

Stacey, C., and DeMartino, M., eds., *Understanding Human Motivation* (Cleveland: Howard Allen, Inc., Publishers, 1963).

Symonds, P. M., *What Education Has to Learn From Psychology* (New York: Bureau of Publications, Teachers College, Columbia University, 1958).

Young, P. T., *Motivation and Emotion* (New York: John Wiley and Sons, Inc., 1961).

chapter 10

The Process of Effective Study

What Effective Study Means. Having determined how progress in learning takes place, there remains the task of determining how pupils acquire the art of effective study. To *study* means to apply one's mental capacities purposefully to the acquisition, understanding, and organization of knowledge. Study is a phase of formal learning by means of which the individual seeks to gain new facts, to establish new habits, to acquire new attitudes, and to perfect new skills in an efficient and economical way. It consists of all the mental efforts to acquire and organize knowledge. In the general use of the term as it is related to school work, to *study* means to learn subject matter through the use of books and other appliances with the intent of mastering the subject matter. The purpose of study is to acquire facts and information, systems of thought, mastery of skills, and techniques by means of which knowledge may be organized, expressed, and utilized in problem-solving. The purpose of study is also to master important foundational and immutable principles of life and of conduct. Learning and studying are mutually related. Hence, training in the art of effective study must mean efficient guidance in learning.

Qualities of Effective Study. The process of effective study does not consist merely in storing up facts and information. The process of effective study does not consist merely in reading. By its very nature, the process of effective study constitutes a disciplinary training. This means that the pupil studies in order to learn, in order to fit himself for the intellectual encounters of life. The process of effective study must conform to certain physiological and psychological laws and principles. Since the process of effective study involves the exercise of the mental activities by which knowledge is acquired, it embraces all of the activities of both mind and body which are included in the process of learning. Since bodily conditions affect mental activity, the primary prerequisite for effective study is a sound mind in a healthy body. The physical conditions for effective study include proper amounts of food, rest, exercise, recreation, and sleep, as well as suitable posture, sufficient light, heat, and ventilation. The psychological laws and principles involved in the process of effective study include those governing attention, interest, will, habit, and the affective states. Furthermore, study requires such qualities and factors as precision, promptness, thoroughness, decision, voluntary attention, moral control. Since learning is the goal of study and since motivation is essential for all learning, the kind of studying done will depend upon the motive or purpose, and the amount of studying accomplished will be determined by the strength of that motive.

The most natural and the most successful way to attain a thorough development of the process of effective study is to have stored up from many sources a supply of images, experiences, facts, associations, and memories, in order that some point of contact may be found, readily and easily, between new material and that which has been acquired previously. However, effective study must involve a great deal more than an endeavor to retain and to recall. Effective study means that there must be on the part of the pupil a recognition of what has been retained and recalled: an understanding of its relation to and significance for the present subject matter. Effective study involves the evaluation of facts, the forming of judgments, reasoning, and utilizing what has been obtained through the process of study. The process of effective study always implies thinking and includes an organization, classification, and arrangement of facts in relation to a central or core thought.

While the way to achieve success in effective study is through arousing interest in every school subject, nevertheless it is worthy of note that not every step in education can be interesting and that it is frequently necessary to appeal to an effort of will. The purpose of effective study is to encourage and to promote advantageous methods of learning and to discourage and overcome disadvantageous ways. The process of effective study may reach its fullest development in those pupils who have sufficient native ability to profit from the proper means of instruction, who have adequate motives, and who practice assiduously the correct principles of effective study.

The Factors in the Process of Effective Study. In order that teachers may help pupils to develop proper habits of effective study, it is necessary that they know the principal factors influencing the process of effective study. The first principal factor is *purposefulness;* that is, the individual who studies with a specific purpose studies effectively. The second principal factor consists of the assimilation and application of facts, information, ideas, and knowledge acquired in the process of study. The third factor consists of organization of knowledge and the distinguishing of salient features from minor points. The fourth principal factor involves the development of soundness of judgment and thoroughness of reasoning. The fifth important factor is the exercise of memory. The sixth important factor consists of the provisions for opportunities for the exercise of initiative, self-activity, self-reliance, and self-control on the part of the pupils.

The Teacher's Function in the Process of Effective Study. Educational psychology deals with the mental processes and with the methods and procedure for guiding intellectual growth and development. The teacher by means of his knowledge of the principles of educational psychology is able to analyze the requirements of the various school subjects and to adapt his teaching procedure accordingly so that each individual in the class may be able to learn in an efficient and economic way. The teacher's task is to encourage and to help pupils to study effectively, to aid them in securing confidence and faith in themselves, to provide a strong motive, to provide a definite time for study. The most important function of the teacher is to direct the pupils in such a way that they acquire right methods of study. It is unlikely that the pupils will achieve good habits of reading, of thinking, and of studying merely by the method of trial, error, and success. Hence, the pupil should be trained directly in the proper use of the mental processes that underlie effective thinking and studying.

Pupils fail to do their schoolwork successfully for one or more of several reasons: they may have physiological difficulties such as poor sight or hearing; they may lack the intellectual ability to do the work required; they may lack the foundation and background of knowledge required; they may not be exerting sufficient effort of will to achieve results; their surrounding environment may not be suitable for study; or they may lack a knowledge of the proper methods of study.

It is the teacher's task to cultivate worthwhile mental habits, to direct the voluntary attention of the pupil to his work, to assist him in analyzing his study activities, to aid him in comprehending the materials studied. To do these things the teacher must first emphasize the fact that the pupil, while working at school tasks, is forming his mind and that, therefore, the pupil must be aware of what he is doing and why he is doing it. It is also necessary for the teacher to emphasize the fact that the pupil must study ideas and their meanings, must make them his own possessions, must apply them to the solution of his own problems. The teacher must realize also that not only the pupils who have scholastic difficulties but also the ordinary and the bright pupils require thorough and constant instruction in the methods of effective study in order that they may become increasingly efficient in their work.

The teacher's function in laying the foundations for the acquisition of methods of effective study is to instruct the pupils in the following respects:

a) How to use the textbook;
b) How to take and to keep notes on schoolwork;
c) How to use the library;
d) How to gather materials from sources;
e) How to use source and reference materials;
f) How to organize and classify facts and information;
g) How to evaluate facts and data;
h) How to control attention;
i) How to utilize memory economically.

The Pupil's Function in the Process of Effective Study. The pupil must realize the necessity for acquiring, through his schoolwork, methods of effective study. He must realize the need for developing an interest in his work. He must realize the importance of voluntary attention. He must realize the necessity for an abundance of clear ideas. His daily aim as he becomes more efficient in the process of effective study should be to prepare his schoolwork in less time or to achieve a greater degree of mastery in the same time.

There are certain conditions prerequisite for the achievement of methods of effective study by the pupil. In the first place, the pupil must be intellectually capable of studying effectively. Secondly, the pupil must have the opportunity to do the necessary studying under favorable conditions. Thirdly, the pupil must have a motive which is sufficiently strong to cause him to take advantage of his opportunities and to study effectively within the limits of his capacities.

With these prerequisites as a basis, helpful rules for study should be taught. However, the mere giving of such rules carries no guarantee that the pupil will study more effectively. These rules will have to be modified considerably to meet the individual differences existing among the pupils. The following factors must be taken into consideration: In the first place, pupils differ because of heredity as to the amount they are capable of learning. Second, they differ because of environment, training, and will power as to the amount which they will learn. Therefore, for the slow and the dull pupils there must be prescribed specific study procedures which are in harmony with the general principles for effective study. Then sufficient practice in these procedures must be provided in order to reduce them to functioning habits.

The Principles of Effective Study. The habits of study which are formed in school are perhaps of greater significance than are the subjects which the student strives to master. Effective study involves the following essential principles. If these principles are adhered to carefully, they will guide the student in the acquisition of desirable mental habits.

1. BUDGET TIME. The student should make out a daily study program, arranging a definite time to be devoted to the study of each subject.

2. DISTRIBUTE STUDY TIME EFFECTIVELY. The student should realize that, ordinarily, distributed practice produces better results in learning than unspaced practice; that is, short work periods are more effective than long periods. Thus, if three hours were to be devoted to the study of a particular subject, then a half-hour period during each of six days would result in greater learning than one continuous three-hour period.

3. ARRANGE TASKS ECONOMICALLY. This involves establishing a routine. The pupil should have a determined order in which the various subjects are studied and adhere to it. He should study first those subjects which require fresh attention and later those in which concentration is easier.

4. STUDY ACTIVELY WITH VIGOR AND DETERMINATION. This principle means that the pupil should not lose time in getting ready for study. He should sit down and begin work at once. He should concentrate on his work. He should cultivate the will to learn. The pupil

should develop a proper attitude toward his work. A definite purpose in every task is a great aid.

5. UNDERSTAND THE ASSIGNMENT. The pupil should be able to answer the following questions:

a) What readings, problems, experiments, topics, or units were assigned?

b) What part of the preparation requires written work?

c) What important points and what difficulties were emphasized by the teacher in making the assignment?

d) Which principle of effective study did the teacher advise the class to follow?

e) What is the scope, the content, the form of the assignment?

6. SYSTEMATIZE THE MATERIALS IN THE LESSON. This principle means that the pupil should learn to take notes on the directions and suggestions given by the teacher in order to understand the assignment.

7. HAVE PROPER STUDY CONDITIONS AND NECESSARY MATERIALS. The pupil should work in a quiet room which is conducive to study, which is not too warm, and in which there is sufficient light. The pupil should sit in a straight but comfortable chair at a desk or table. He must also provide himself with the materials and equipment required to do his work. These materials include notebooks, maps, dictionary, textbook, and any other special equipment which is necessary.

8. LEARN TO USE THE TEXTBOOK PROPERLY. This principle means that the pupil should understand the purposes of such devices as the index, appendix, footnotes, maps, illustrations, and vocabulary, and should use them frequently.

9. DEVELOP EFFECTIVE METHODS OF READING. Since poor reading habits are usually basic in study difficulties, the pupil should learn to do two kinds of reading. He should read rapidly when seeking to find the major points or to make a survey of the lesson. He should read deliberately and critically such material as problems, directions, explanations, and any material which must be mastered or interpreted; that is, he should read for ideas. The pupil should analyze any confusing statements. He should keep the main idea in mind while reading and should notice how the various divisions are related to one another. Making brief notes in the margin will also help, as will marking important passages for later review. Every effort should be made to coordinate what is read with what is learned in the classroom.

10. INCREASE WORD POWER (VOCABULARY). The fundamental requisite in understanding any subject is a knowledge of the vocabulary of that subject, that is, a comprehension of the meanings of the concepts and terms employed. This understanding will be promoted by a knowledge of formal grammar. Language is the medium of thought, and grammar is the skeleton of language. There is a relationship between thought processes and linguistic organization. Until the pupil can express clearly the materials which he has studied, he does not understand those materials. He should, therefore, strive to make the ideas in the assignment his own possession, and then he should endeavor to express those ideas in good idiomatic English. Such expression denotes definiteness and exactness of meaning.

11. DEVELOP AND USE HABITS OF CRITICAL THINKING. This means a clear recognition and adequate understanding of terms employed; the exercise of precise judgment; the detection of similarities and differences; a careful examination of all materials in order to draw inferences and to recognize assumptions; logical and constructive use of the reasoning process.

12. USE ALL THE MATERIAL AIDS AVAILABLE. The pupil should make use of such aids as the index, appendix, notes, vocabulary, illustrations in his text, and of such references and source materials as books, journals, encyclopedias, dictionaries, and the like.

13. CONNECT EACH DAY'S LESSON WITH THE LESSON OF THE PREVIOUS DAY. The pupil should begin his study by recalling the main points of the lesson of the previous day. Then he should get clearly in mind the assignment which he is about to study, endeavoring to recognize important points and their relationship with one another.

14. UTILIZE THE WHOLE METHOD OF LEARNING. The pupil should learn in large units rather than in piecemeal fashion. The size of the unit or lesson to be learned will be the determining factor. It is well to begin with an overview of the whole unit or lesson. Then the parts can be considered and logical connections established between and among these parts. When this has been done there should be a return to the whole, and a weaving of the parts into this whole.

15. MAKE AN OUTLINE OF THE LESSON. The pupil should analyze the important points and topics; note how the minor parts are related to these. He should arrange ideas in a synopsis in which relationships between and among them are evident. This will help considerably to

make materials meaningful. Outlining involves organization of materials.

16. EVERY LESSON IS A TASK FOR ONESELF. This principle means that the pupil should consider the assignment as a task for himself and not as a piece of work to be done for the teacher.

17. WORK INDEPENDENTLY. The pupil should learn to form his own judgments, to solve his own problems. This means that the student should cultivate self-reliance, determination, and independence in his work. He should seek help only after he has exhausted his own resources.

18. PREPARE EACH LESSON EVERY DAY. This principle is particularly important because adherence to it develops habits of regularity and of punctuality.

19. TEST THE PREPARATION. The pupil should express the ideas in the text in his own words; write out a brief summary of each paragraph or other unit; frame questions to measure the success of his preparation. At the end of the lesson the pupil should summarize in writing the most important points in the lesson.

20. APPLY THE KNOWLEDGE ACQUIRED. This principle means that the pupil should endeavor to put into practical use the facts and information which he has acquired. This he should do as soon as possible and as much as possible by thinking, talking, and writing about the subjects and materials which he has learned. He should apply them to present-day conditions and illustrate them in familiar terms since opportunities for transfer assist learning.

21. REVIEW SYSTEMATICALLY AND PERIODICALLY AND AVOID CRAMMING. Review, which involves reflecting, recalling, and evaluating of ideas in order of importance, leads to successful mastery, and increases the permanency of learning. Well-conducted plans of teaching suggest that each class period begin with a brief review of the work of the preceding day. Each period should close with a brief summary of the work just completed. At the end of each week the matter covered in that time should be reviewed and a selective review or overview should take place just before the examination.

22. DEVELOP AN INTEREST IN SCHOOL SUBJECTS. This principle is indicative of a most important factor in the process of effective study, namely, that the pupil should consider his task of value and worth doing, because it is related to things already known or liked and because it is now or will be useful. Good learners develop an interest in their work while the contrary is true of many poor learners.

23. STRIVE TO EXCEL. This means that the pupil must not be contented merely to "get by." He must convince himself of the genuine value of doing well in all his schoolwork. He must have faith in himself and be able to perform his work with confidence and satisfaction.

Formulas for Study. In order to help students both to acquire and to practice efficient study techniques, several formulas have been devised, each of which has endeavored to provide a simple framework upon which to build adequate and correct study-skills. These formulas include the following:

Robinson[1] has devised the *SQ3R* method of study which is based upon two central factors: techniques of selecting and comprehending what is important; ways to retard forgetting. This method involves five steps:

1. SURVEY. In this step the student makes a rapid survey of the headings in the assignment in order to determine both the major ideas presented and also the sequence in which these have been presented.

2. QUESTION. In this second step chapter and paragraph headings are converted into questions in order to focus attention on what to look for in each section.

3. READ. In the third step the student reads the section under each heading in order to answer the questions. The purpose of the second and third steps is to aid the student in organizing his thinking on the topic about which he has been reading.

4. RECITE. In the fourth step, having read each section through with understanding, the student tests himself to determine whether he can answer each question. If not it will be necessary to reread. A recommended way of self-testing is to jot down phrases in brief outline forms. The purpose of self-recitation is to fix the material in meaning.

5. REVIEW. In this last step, there should be a brief review immediately after reading. The total outline should be looked over in order to obtain an overall easily visualized picture of the material and also to refresh the memory on major points. Memory should be checked by covering notes and endeavoring to recall the major points in the chapter.

Farquhar, Krumboltz, and Wrenn[2] have also presented a basic formula to enable students to get the most from study, particularly from reading assignments. It is designated as the *Triple S Technique* which consists of the following three steps:

[1] F. P. Robinson, *Effective Study,* rev. ed. (New York: Harper & Bros., 1961).

[2] W. W. Farquhar, J. D. Krumboltz, and C. J. Wrenn, *Learning to Study* (New York: The Ronald Press Co., 1960), pp. 30–48.

1. SCAN. This step involves becoming familiar with the organization of materials. The main advantage of scanning is that details gain more meaning as they relate to the whole organization and comprehension is increased.

2. SEARCH. The second step is concerned with finding and keeping the meaning of the materials studied. It involves such activities as raising questions, reading to find the answers to these questions, and self-recitation.

3. SUMMARIZE. The third step involves looking carefully for interrelationships and integrating materials by asking and answering broad organizational questions in order that relationships and ideas may be organized logically, understood, and retained.

Garrison and Gray[3] also have presented a formula for study which they have designated by the letters *P-I-R.* In this formula *P* indicates that the student should *preview* what is to be studied; *I* indicates that study should involve the *identification of what is important in the materials; R* represents *review* of the important aspects until these are learned thoroughly. Proficiency in all three is essential to the acquisition of good study skills.

Investigations on Study Habits and How-to-Study Courses. Undoubtedly there has existed, since the beginnings of formal education, a general recognition of the importance of effective methods of study. Likewise, there seems to have existed always a general realization that the instruction, guidance, and training of pupils in order that they may establish effective habits of study constitutes one of the major problems of teaching. By the term *study habit* is meant the student's accustomed method of approach to units of learning, his consistency in ignoring distractions, his attentiveness to the specific material being studied, and the efforts which he exerts throughout the process. Pupils who study effectively and efficiently demonstrate that they have developed methods of learning which aid in the acquisition, the retention, and the application of knowledge, of facts, and of information derived from textbooks, from class discussions, from lectures, from source materials. Through practice and use in the performance of school tasks, these methods become habitual.

Within the past several decades there has developed among educators

[3] K. C. Garrison and J. S. Gray, *Educational Psychology* (New York: Appleton, Century, Crofts, Inc., 1955), p. 435.

at all scholastic levels a widespread interest in determining how students should be guided and directed so that they may acquire as habits methods of study which will function effectively both in school and in life. From this interest there have resulted a large number of research investigations dealing with various aspects of the how-to-study problem. In particular, two aspects of this problem have been subjected to extensive investigation. The first of these aspects has involved attempts to discover the actual study skills which students possess and practice. The second aspect of this problem has involved endeavors to devise ways of training pupils in the application and use of what are considered to be effective methods of study. One of the major weaknesses of much of this research has been that it emphasizes the student's knowledge of good study procedures rather than his habitual use of them.

Investigations of Study Skills Possessed by Students. The purpose of these investigations has been to determine the study skills actually employed by students in their schoolwork. Such investigations usually make use of questionnaires or check lists as the means of discovering study skills possessed and practiced by students. The results of these inquiries indicate wide variations in the study habits of pupils. Two of the early investigators, using college students as subjects, reported that inferior study techniques were used by these students. Charters[4] found that of 258 college women less than half use active, efficient methods of preparing assignments. Butterweck[5] reported that less than 25 percent of a group of college freshmen practiced methods necessary for intelligent study.

More recent investigations seem to indicate that the study skills which students possess have been acquired haphazardly and incidentally through the process of trial and error, early in the scholastic career of the individual. Cuff,[6] using a questionnaire of 75 items, investigated the study activities of 1250 pupils in Grades 4 to 12. He concluded that "the median scores from Grades 4 to 12 show neither progressive nor reliable differences. This suggests that study habits are formed early as a result of trial and error or other selective and fixative factors and that there-

[4] Jessie Charters, "How 258 Junior College Women Study," *Journal of Educational Research,* 11:41–48, 1925.

[5] J. S. Butterweck, "The How to Study Problem," *Journal of Educational Research,* 18:66–76, 1928.

[6] N. B. Cuff, "Study Habits in Grades Four to Twelve," *Journal of Educational Psychology,* 28:295–301, 1937. See also W. E. Rosenstengel and F. B. Dixon, "General Study Habits of High School Pupils," *School Review,* 44:127–131, 1936.

after the vectors tend to remain constant unless effective remedial programs planned by alert teachers result in changes." Previously Wilson[7] had conducted an investigation in which junior and senior high school pupils were tested on knowledge of study techniques. He, too, reported that in general the pupils improve but little in knowledge of study techniques as they progress through the junior and senior high school grades. In a study conducted on the senior high school level, Sister St. Mary Esther Camden[8] has reported slight but statistically insignificant progress in the acquisition of study skills as the subjects participating in her investigation advanced from Grades 10 to 12.

Investigations have also been made to determine what differences exist between superior and poor students with respect to study techniques employed. Strangely enough, some of these studies have found that successful and failing students use the same study methods in their schoolwork. Eurich[9] used a self-rating scale of 100 items to ascertain whether the ratings of good students were markedly superior to those of inferior students at both the high school and college level. His findings revealed a striking similarity between the two groups. A detailed evaluation of the items constituting the rating scale revealed that there were only four items out of the 100 which clearly differentiated between the two groups. Likewise, Ross and Kleise[10] in an investigation in which college students were the subjects found that "the intelligent and unintelligent seem to be employing the same methods of study." They concluded that the abler group succeeded because they used skillfully a good method, while the same method used clumsily or indifferently gave no assurance of success. Johnson[11] also endeavored to discover to what extent good and poor students on the college level utilized the same

[7] C. B. Wilson, "Pupils' Knowledge of Study Techniques," *Education,* 52:362–363, 1932. See also W. J. Howell, "Work Study Skills of Children in Grades 4 to 8," *Elementary School Journal,* 50:384–389, 1950.

[8] Sister St. Mary Esther Camden, "An Analysis of the Study Habits of the Students in a Catholic High School," unpublished M.A. thesis, Fordham University, New York, 1943; also "An Analysis of the Study Habits of Catholic High School Students," *Catholic Educational Review,* 43:542–549, 1945.

[9] A. C. Eurich, "An Analysis of Self-Ratings on Studiousness Traits," *Journal of Applied Psychology,* 14:577–591, 1930.

[10] C. Ross and N. Kleise, "Study Methods of College Students in Relation to Intelligence and Achievement," *Educational Administration and Supervision,* 13:551–562, 1927.

[11] R. I. Johnson, "The Problem of How to Study," *School Review,* 45:577–584, 1937.

recommended methods of study. He presented a checklist of 50 items dealing with concentration and distraction of attention when studying, with textbook assignments, with notetaking, and with time schedule to two groups of students, the 30 who ranked highest in total achievement in scholastic work and the 30 who ranked lowest. He found that out of the 50 items there were only seven which differentiated most clearly between the good and poor students and that when these seven items were eliminated from consideration no significant variations could be discovered with respect to the remaining items. He concluded that the question of study habits among good and poor students is largely one of attitude. Brown[12] in a similar study on the college level found that in general the failing students reported using correct study habits as frequently as did the successful students and both neglected to make use of many efficient study techniques. Douglass and Bauer[13] analyzed the study habits of high school students, using a checklist to gather the data. Replies were tabulated on the basis of intelligence ratings. They stated:

> An analysis of the data disclosed the startling fact that within any given small range of intelligence, with few exceptions, there were no material differences in average high school marks between those who had different practices with respect to the study techniques involved.

These investigations, which seem to infer that study methods are of little importance in academic achievement, may prove disconcerting to teachers who have expended time and effort on the task of instructing students in efficient methods of attaining knowledge and of solving problems. However, other investigators have found opposite results, namely, that students of superior mental ability do employ better study techniques. Cuff's[14] data indicated that students who ranked high in academic achievement had better study habits than did failing students. Mills[15] reported that in the opinion of high school teachers and adminis-

---

[12] C. W. Brown, "Study Habits of Failing and Successful Students in the First Two Years of College," *Journal of Experimental Education,* 9:205–208, 1941.

[13] H. R. Douglass and H. C. Bauer, "The Study Practices of Three Hundred and Ninety-Five High School Pupils," *Journal of Educational Psychology,* 29:36–43, 1938.

[14] N. B. Cuff, *op. cit.*

[15] H. C. Mills, "Teachers' Attitudes Towards the Study Habits of High School Students," *Educational Administration and Supervision,* 20:619–624, 1934.

trators there were definite and real differences in the study habits and needs of superior and average students. In another investigation Mills, Eckert, and Williams[16] found that scholastically superior high school students possessed different, and presumably better, study habits than students of low achievement, notably with respect to techniques involving a higher type of study morale, including "effort, curiosity, perseverance, and common sense." Locke,[17] in an investigation conducted on the college level, using a study skills inventory of 56 items, obtained significant differences in the mean scores of students with high grades and students with low grades. Sister St. Mary Esther Camden also found significant differences between the study habit inventory scores obtained by bright and by slow students as well as by academically successful and non-successful.

She found that the items on the study habits inventory which tended to differentiate the most successful from the least successful students were the following:

1. Ignores distractions.
2. Has a definite time for studying a specific lesson.
3. Begins work promptly.
4. Reads rapidly.
5. Anticipates questions which may be asked in class or on an examination.
6. Sets a goal for the study period.
7. Works alone.
8. Follows directions exactly.
9. Has a clear notion of the task before beginning to study.
10. Overlearns to assure retention.[18]

In addition Sexton[19] reported that students who achieved high scores on

---

[16] H. C. Mills, R. E. Eckert, and M. W. Williams, "Study Habits of High School Pupils," *School Review,* 42:755–761, 1934. See also C. G. Wrenn and W. J. Humber, "Study Habits Associated With High and Low Scholarship," *Journal of Educational Psychology,* 32:611–616, 1941.

[17] N. M. Locke, "The Students' Skills Inventory: A Study Habits Test," *Journal of Applied Psychology,* 24:493–504, 1940.

[18] Sister St. Mary Esther Camden, *op. cit.*

[19] M. L. Sexton, "A Study of Success and Failure Among Ninth Grade Pupils," unpublished Ph.D. dissertation, Fordham University, New York, 1953. See also C. P. Duncan, "How the Poorer Student Studies," *Journal of Educational Research,* 45:287–292, 1951; H. D. Carter, "Methods of Learning as Factors in the Prediction of School Success," *Journal of Psychology,* 26:249–258, 1948; W. J. Howell, "Work-Study Skills of Adolescents in Grades VII through XIV," *School Review,* 61:277–282, 1953; P. D. Cristantiello and J. J. Cribbin, "The Study Skills Problem," *Journal of Higher Education,* 27:35–38, 1956.

a study habits' inventory were more successful in schoolwork than pupils who achieved low scores on the inventory.

Investigations on how-to-study courses. In the how-to-study course the purpose is to guide the pupil so that he may acquire a knowledge of the techniques of study and become efficient in the use of these techniques. This is accomplished through instruction which is designed to impart knowledge of those study techniques which are common to many subject-matter fields. While the content of such courses is not standardized, the topics generally considered include: *Aids to concentration; planning a time schedule; need for adequate preparation; efficient reading methods; problem solving; outlining; development of vocabulary; note-taking; preparation of themes; reports and term papers; memorization; reviewing and studying for examinations; use of library.* Usually, in addition to instruction in these techniques, provision is made for training in the use of effective study skills under guidance. This may involve laboratory periods and the use of remedial measures in individual cases. Thus, the specific aim of such courses is not only to instruct students how to study but also to develop through practice actual habits of using study techniques.[20]

Many of the investigations on the effectiveness of how-to-study courses have been conducted at the college level, usually in the freshman or sophomore year. The studies of the early investigators indicated that how-to-study courses have proved beneficial and have contributed to the successful adjustment of college students. Several noteworthy investigations of the effectiveness of the how-to-study course at the high school level have also been made. Gatchel measured the effectiveness of a how-to-study course upon scholastic achievement. The group trained in the how-to-study course demonstrated superiority in nearly all subjects over the group which had not received such instruction. Achievement in English, science, junior business practice, and history benefited especially from the course. Moreover, both the teachers and students participating in the experiment expressed opinions favoring the inclusion of a how-to-study course in the high school curriculum. Gatchel concluded from this experiment, "It seems evident from this investigation that it is

[20] M. E. Tresselt, "How to Study Courses," *Journal of Psychology,* 34:31–35, 1952; also G. F. Wooster, "How to Teach How-To-Study Methods," *Educational Research Bulletin,* 33:66–68, 1954; also G. H. DeLong, "Reading and Study for the Average Student," *Educational Research Bulletin,* 27:121–124, 1948; also P. Shaw, "The Brooklyn College Program," *School and Society,* 71:151–153, 1950.

possible to train pupils in methods of study and that such training carries over into a variety of subjects."[21]

Wagner and Strobel[22] also conducted an extensive controlled investigation on the effectiveness of a how-to-study course in the third and fourth years of high school. On the basis of average marks received in academic subjects, the group instructed in how-to-study was reliably and significantly superior to the control group which did not receive instruction in study techniques. It is noteworthy that the authors concluded that "superior high school juniors seem to benefit from a course in study techniques as much as if not more than those of lesser accomplishment." However, Mills,[23] employing the same syllabus, obtained very dissimilar results. He found no noticeable improvement in scholastic achievement among the students instructed in study techniques.

In this regard, Schlesser and Young have maintained that:

> . . . if one wishes to improve a student's work, it is less important to coach him in techniques of study than to inculcate in him the motives for and habits of vigorous persistent effort. Probably if such habits are obtained, the student will of his own accord learn the techniques that are compatible with his level of ability. If he does develop persistence but does not learn the techniques, he can then profitably be taught the techniques. On the other hand, emphasis on techniques might even encourage some students in the belief that good results can be achieved without strong effort.[24]

This would seem to indicate that the student will learn his own techniques, since acquiring study habits is a matter of attitude and character.

An interesting experiment was conducted by Butterweck,[25] who compared a group of high school students who were given actual practice in good study habits in geometry with a group of students who were given instruction in good study habits in that subject. He found that in solving originals, in reviewing and taking a test, and in reading for the purpose of study, the practice group generally made better scores.

[21] D. F. Gatchel, "Results of a How-to-Study Course Given in High School," *School Review,* 39:123–129, 1931.

[22] M. E. Wagner and E. Strobel, "Teaching High School Pupils How to Study," *School Review,* 43:577–589, 1935.

[23] H. C. Mills, "How to Study Courses and Academic Achievement," *Educational Administration and Supervision,* 21:145–151, 1935.

[24] G. E. Schlesser and C. W. Young, "Study and Work Habits," *School Review,* 53:85–89, 1945.

[25] J. S. Butterweck, *The Problem of Teaching High School Pupils How to Study,* Contributions to Education, No. 237 (New York: Teachers College, Columbia University, 1926).

He concluded that "the effectiveness of the practice method over the nonpractice method increases with a decrease in the intelligence of the pupils and is, therefore, far superior for pupils in the lowest quarter or lower half in intelligence."[26] Likewise, Butterweck found instruction in good study methods to be equal or superior to practice only for pupils in the highest quarter in intelligence. However, since the number of students within each quarter of intelligence was very small, it was impossible to justify broad generalizations in this study.

DiMichael[27] conducted an experimental investigation to determine the effectiveness of a how-to-study course given at the ninth grade level in a parochial high school. The object of the experiment was to determine the direct and transfer effects of a how-to-study course upon pupils of various levels of intelligence. The investigator devised a *Knowledge of Study Skills Test* in order to determine the information concerning efficient study techniques which students entering high school possessed. He found that generally ninth-grade students were deficient in such information. However, he discovered that students of superior mental ability possessed more information than did students of lower intellectual capacity. The experiment demonstrated that the how-to-study course had increased significantly the knowledge of study techniques among students of all levels. In an analysis of the transfer effects[28] of instruction in how-to-study upon achievement in history, Latin, and algebra it was found that the transfer effects of such instruction were most evident among students in the middle level of mental ability, that is, between the twenty-fifth and the seventy-fifth percentiles. In addition, investigations conducted by McKinnon and Burton,[29] by Simpson,[30] Wittenborn,[31] and Shaw[32] have

---

[26] *Ibid.*, pp. 72–73.

[27] S. G. DiMichael, "Increase in Knowledge of How-to-Study Resulting from a How-to-Study Course," *School Review*, 51:353–359, 1943.

[28] S. G. DiMichael, "The Transfer Effects of a How-to-Study Course Upon Different I.Q. Levels and Various Academic Subjects," *Journal of Educational Psychology*, 34:166–175, 1943.

[29] N. J. McKinnon and W. H. Burton, "An Evaluation of Certain Study Procedures in History," *Elementary School Journal*, 40:371–379, 1940.

[30] R. H. Simpson, "Students Help Set Up Criteria to Aid in Deciding What to Study," *Journal of Educational Research*, 36:192–199, 1942.

[31] J. R. Wittenborn, "Classes in Remedial Reading and Study Habits," *Journal of Educational Research*, 37:571–586, 1944.

[32] J. G. Shaw, "An Evaluation of a Study-Skills Course," *Personnel and Guidance Journal*, 33:464–468, 1955.

also presented evidence that courses designed to improve study practices have produced favorable results.

Sister St. Mary Esther Camden[33] also conducted an investigation to compare the effectiveness of two types of training in how to study upon the knowledge of study procedures and upon scholastic achievement in algebra, English, Latin, and general science at the ninth-grade level. One type, designated as the Training Method, consisted of instruction presented in the form of an organized how-to-study course. The second type, designated as the Practice Method, consisted of the same instruction implemented by specific practice in the application of the rules and principles presented in the how-to-study course. She found that the Practice Method was more effective both with regard to knowledge of study procedures and likewise with respect to progress in achievement in the four subject-matter fields. In general, investigations have indicated that a how-to-study course which provides practice is more effective than one in which only instruction in how-to-study is given.

Entwisle[34] made an evaluative investigation of twenty-two study skills courses conducted at the secondary and college levels. She presented the following conclusions:

1. A study-skills course will usually be followed by improvement.
2. A course will be most beneficial for students desiring to take it.
3. Students wishing to take a study-skills course but prevented from doing so, and therefore presumably of comparable motivation to those enrolled, fail to show significant improvement.

Devices for Appraising and Measuring Study Habits. Endeavors to appraise and measure study habits have been made by several of the investigators who previously have been mentioned. These include Eurich,[35] Douglass and Bauer,[36] Mills,[37] Cuff,[38] and DiMichael.[39] The techniques employed to measure study habits in these endeavors have included questionnaires, checklists, rating scales, inventories, and diagnostic devices.

---

[33] Sister St. Mary Esther Camden, "A Comparative Study of the Relative Effectiveness of Two Types of Training in How-to-Study Knowledge of Study Skills and Upon Achievement in Four Subject Matter Fields at the Ninth Grade level," unpublished Ph.D. dissertation, Fordham University, New York, 1946.

[34] D. R. Entwisle, "Evaluation of Study-Skills Courses: A Review," *Journal of Educational Research,* 53:243–251, 1960.

[35] Eurich, *op. cit.*

[36] Douglass and Bauer, *op. cit.*

[37] Mills, Eckert, and Williams, *op. cit.*

[38] Cuff, *op. cit.*

[39] DiMichael, *op. cit.*

However, these instruments were devised for use in the particular investigations and have not been made available for general use. Additional instruments of this type, which have not been published separately for testing purposes, include Kelley and Greene's *Check Chart of Study Habits*[40] and a test which Kenneally[41] devised for use in the intermediate grades as a diagnostic measure to ascertain the study skills in which specific training was required.

There are available many published instruments for the appraisal and measurement of study habits. Among the early devices, is the *Wrenn Study Habits Inventory* (revised edition, Grades 12 to 16). This is a checklist composed of 28 statements of habits and attitudes that may affect the use of study time and as a result influence success or failure. These statements are grouped into four sections. The first section, designated as "Reading and Note-taking Techniques," consists of 5 items; the second, "Habits of Concentration," contains 4 items; the third, "Distribution of Time and Social Relationships in Study," is composed of 8 items; the fourth, "General Habits and Attitudes of Work" contains 11 items. The student checks his response to each item under the headings of *rarely or never, sometimes,* and *often or always.* Weights have been assigned to the responses upon the basis of research conducted by Wrenn.[42] A total score may be obtained, but the author of the *Inventory* has recommended that attention be devoted to the scores attained on the individual items.

The Tyler-Kimber Study Skills Test, which is also one of the early instruments, was devised for the high school and college levels, Grades 9 to 16. This test has been designed to provide "eight separate measures of skills and fundamental understandings of study techniques employed in practically all fields of academic work, together with a highly accurate measure of general study skill mastery."[43] It is composed of 175 items. The separate measures have been designated as:

---

[40] V. H. Kelley and H. A. Greene, *Better Reading and Study Habits* (Yonkers, N. Y.: World Book Co., 1947), pp. 48–49.

[41] K. G. Kenneally, *The Construction and Evaluation of a Diagnostic Test of Study Skills for Grades 4, 5 and 6,* Catholic University of America Studies in Psychology and Psychiatry, Vol. VI, No. 8, 1947.

[42] C. G. Wrenn, *Manual of Directions of the Study Habits Inventory* (Stanford University, Calif.: Standford University Press, 1941).

[43] H. T. Tyler and G. C. Kimber, *Manual for Tyler-Kimber Study Skills Test* (Stanford University, Calif.: Stanford University Press, 1937), p. 2.

I.	Finding What You Want in a Book	(10 items)
II.	Using an Index	(10 items)
III.	Using General Reference Books	(30 items)
IV.	Recognizing Common Abbreviations	(20 items)
V.	Using the Library Card Catalog	(20 items)
VI.	Interpreting Maps	(20 items)
VII.	Knowing Current Periodical Literature	(30 items)
VIII.	Interpreting Graphs	(35 items)

This test is self-administering and is a power test. While no specified time limit has been set, ordinarily 60 to 90 minutes will be required for students to complete it. The score on each part is the number of right answers, while the total score is the sum of the part scores.

The Brown-Holtzman Survey of Study Habits and Attitudes has been devised primarily for use with college freshmen. It is composed of 75 items, the responses to which are made in terms of a five-point scale: *rarely, sometimes, frequently, generally, almost always.* The 75 items concern study methods, motivation for studying, and attitudes toward scholastic activities important in the classroom. The purposes of this test are

(a) to identify students whose study habits and attitudes are different from from those of students who earn high grades;
(b) to aid in understanding students with academic difficulties;
(c) to provide a basis for helping such students to improve their study habits and attitudes and thus more fully realize their best potentialities.[44]

This test is recommended for use as

(a) a screening device, to identify among freshmen entering college those most likely to need early preventive help;
(b) a diagnostic instrument and counseling aid;
(c) a teaching aid, not only in remedial or how-to-study classes but also in elementary psychology and education courses;
(d) a research tool, in investigations of the learning or the counseling processes.

An inventory entitled *Survey of Study Habits* for use in Grades 8 to 14, which was devised by Traxler, was published in an experimental edition and was used in 1944 testing program sponsored by the Educational Records Bureau. This inventory contains 85 items grouped under seventeen headings as follows:

[44] W. F. Brown and W. H. Holtzman, *Manual of the Brown-Holtzman Survey of Study Habits and Attitudes,* rev. ed. (New York: The Psychological Corporation, 1956), p. 3. See also W. F. Brown and W. H. Holtzman, "Use of the Survey of Study Habits and Attitudes for Counseling Students," *Personnel and Guidance Journal,* 35:214–218, 1956.

1. Keeping in Physical Condition for Study.
2. Understanding the Assignment.
3. Planning a study schedule.
4. Finding the Necessary Study Materials Skillfully and Quickly.
5. Applying One's Self Consistently.
6. Fixing Material in Mind.
7. Reflecting.
8. Working Independently.
9. Completing Work Promptly.
10. Persisting in Overcoming Difficulties.
11. Paying Attention in Class.
12. Participating in Class Activities.
13. Reviewing.
14. Memorizing.
15. Increasing Vocabulary.
16. Improving Reading Rate.
17. Maintaining a Study Attitude.

The student response involves checking for each item whether the study technique is *seldom or never, sometimes, usually or always* employed. A weight of zero is assigned to the responses checked as *seldom or never,* one to those checked as *sometimes,* and two to those which are checked as *usually or always* employed. The author[45] has stated that this inventory is intended to be used mainly as a counseling instrument on the basis of responses made to the individual items.

The Spitzer Study Skills Test has been developed to measure the mastery of several basic skills which contribute to effective learning in many areas of the high school and college curriculum, particularly language arts, social studies, and science. Designed for use with high school students and college freshmen, it is available in two comparable forms, each consisting of 160 items. It is composed of five subtests designated as:

1. Using the Dictionary.	(26 items)
2. Using the Index.	(26 items)
3. Understanding Graphs, Tables, and Maps.	(42 items)
4. Knowledge of Sources of Information.	(24 items)
5. Organization of Facts in Note-Taking.	(optional)

The fifth subtest may be used as an optional measure to supplement information attained from other parts of the test. This subtest has been

[45] A. E. Traxler, *Manual of Directions, Survey of Study Habits* (New York: Educational Records Bureau, 1945), p. 4; also *The Improvement of Study Habits and Skills,* Educational Records Bulletin, No. 41, rev. ed. (New York: Educational Records Bureau, 1954), pp. 6, 34–39.

designed to measure ability to select the important facts from among those given in a series of paragraphs and to organize them in relation to the main problem and to one another. The results of this test[46] may be used for evaluation of individual and group performance, for improving instruction, and for guidance purposes.

The California Study Method Survey[47] is a self-inventory designed to reveal the nature of study skills and attitudes of students. It is composed of 150 items, standardized questions which reflect the consistent differences in study methods and attitudes between high and low achieving students. It yields scores on attitudes toward school, mechanics of study, planning and system, and verification. The results of this test may be utilized for educational counseling, for comparison of group data, for prediction.

The S.R.A. Achievement Series.[48] *Work Study Skills,* Grades 4–6 and 6–9, is part of a battery. The test for Grades 4–6 consists of 82 multiple-choice items and is administered in two periods. These items are divided into four sections as follows:

1. Use of Table of Contents (19 items)
2. Use of Index (17 items)
3. Use of Reference Materials (20 items)
4. Reading Graphs and Table (26 items)

The test for Grades 6–9 is composed of 94 items of four alternate multiple-choice types. These items are presented in four sections as follows:

1. Use of References (20 items)
2. Use of Table of Contents (10 items)
3. Use of Index (15 items)
4. Reading Graphs, Tables and Maps (49 items)

How-to-Study Manuals. In an endeavor to present in condensed and vivid form the general principles governing study and to provide guidance in the application of effective techniques of study, *How-to-Study Manuals* have been devised.[49] The purpose of these manuals is to provide practical

[46] H. F. Spitzer, *Manual of Directions, Spitzer Study Skills Test* (Yonkers: Harcourt, Brace and World, 1954), pp. 7–9.

[47] H. D. Carter, *Manual of Directions, California Study Methods Survey,* Grades 7–13 (Los Angeles: California Test Bureau, 1958).

[48] L. P. Thorpe, D. W. Lefever, R. A. Naslund, *S.R.A. Achievement Series, Manual for the School Administrator* (Chicago: Science Research Associates, 1958).

[49] Listed below are some the manuals which have been devised for high school and college use:
Armstrong, W. A., *Study Is Hard Work* (New York: Harper and Brothers, 1956).
Brown, H. E., *This Is the Way to Study* (Philadelphia: J. B. Lippincott Company, 1958).

rules and suggestions which apply generally to learning situations and to stimulate the interest of pupils in the acquisition of proper study habits

---

Centi, Paul, *Basic College Skills* (New York: Holt, Rinehart and Winston, Inc.).

——— *How to Study More Effectively* (New York: Fordham University Press, 1955).

Cole, Luella, *Students' Guide to Efficient Study,* 4 ed. (New York: Holt, Rinehart and Winston, Inc., 1960).

Coleman, J. C., and Libaw, F. B., *Successful Study* (Chicago: Scot, Foresman and Company, 1960).

Dudycha, G. J., *Learn More with Less Effort* (New York: Harper and Brothers, 1957).

Ehrlich, Eugene, *How to Study Better and Get Higher Marks* (New York: Crowell Company, 1961).

Farquhar, W. W., Krumboltz, J. D., and Wrenn, C. G., *Learning to Study* (New York: The Ronald Press Company, 1960).

Flesch, R. F., and others, *How You Can Be a Better Student* (New York: Sterling Publishing Company, 1957).

Froe, O. D., and Lee, M. A., *How to Become a Successful Student* (New York: Arco Publishing Company, 1959).

Gerken, C. d'A., and Kemp, A., *Make Your Study Hours Count* (Chicago: Science Research Associates, 1956).

Gunthorp, G. L., *Practical Guide to Efficient Study* (New York: Exposition Press, 1957).

Handen, W. J., *Little Learning* (Westminister, Md.: Newman Press, 1956).

Hardy, L. L., *How to Study in High School* (Palo Alto, Calif.: Pacific Books, 1955).

Morgan, C. T., and Deese, J. E., *How to Study* (New York: McGraw-Hill Book Company, 1957).

Pauk, W., *How to Study in College* (New York: Houghton Mifflin Co., 1962).

Preston, R. C., *Teaching Study Habits and Skills* (New York: Rinehart and Company, 1959).

Reed, P. A., S.J., *Do It Right* (New York: Jesuit Educational Association, New York Province, Secondary School Division, 1951).

Robbins, P. A., *How to Make Better Grades* (Los Angeles: Par Publishing Company, 1957).

Robinson, F. P., *Effective Study,* rev. ed. (New York: Harper and Row, 1961).

Shaw, P. B., *Effective Reading and Learning* (New York: Thomas Y. Crowell Company, 1955).

Shefter, Harry, *How to Get Higher Marks in School* (New York: Washington Square Press, 1961).

Smith, S., *Best Methods of Study,* 3 ed. (New York: Barnes and Noble, Inc., 1958).

Spaney, E., and Jennings, L. A., *Art of Studying* (Philadelphia: J. B. Lippincott Company, 1958).

Strang, Ruth M., *Guided Study and Homework,* "What Research Says to the Teacher," No. 8 (Washington, D. C.: National Education Association of the United States, 1955).

Tussing, Lyle, *Study and Succeed* (New York: John Wiley & Sons, 1962).

Wheeler, P. M., *Learn and Like It* (Hingham, Mass.: Palmer Company, 1955).

Wilcox, G. W., *Basic Study Skills* (Boston: Allyn and Bacon, Inc., 1958).

Wrenn, C. G., *Study Effectively, a Manual of Answers to Two Major Questions Which Confront Every Student* (Stanford, Calif.: Stanford University Press, 1955).

Wrightstone, J. W., *How to Be a Better Student* (Chicago: Science Research Associates, 1956).

through exercises in the application of study techniques. These study manuals have been designed not only to help the failing and unsuccessful students but also to enable the bright and successful students to become more efficient in the use of study skills. A large number of these how-to-study manuals are available for use at both the high school and the college levels. Laycock and Russell[50] have analyzed the contents of 38 how-to-study manuals which were published in the United States between the years 1926 and 1939. These manuals had been designed for use at the high school and college levels. The analysis revealed that a total of 517 study habits and skills was listed as exercises, examples, and sources of discussion in the 38 manuals. Furthermore, many of these 517 study habits and skills were broken up into more specific techniques. Of the 517 study habits and skills, 313 appeared four or more times, while 35 were mentioned 20 or more times. The analysis revealed further a tendency to place emphasis upon the following topics:

1. Reading habits and skills;
2. Preparing for and taking examinations;
3. General habits of learning;
4. Outlining and note-taking;
5. Classroom activities;
6. Memorizing;
7. Using the library;
8. The physical and psychological conditions for studying.

Likewise it was noted that in the manuals analyzed "there was a lack of research references on specific problems of study and much disagreement regarding the most effective study habits and skills."

The Educational Implications of the Process of Effective Study. The process of effective study is the foundation of all progress in education. Effective study techniques constitute a most important part of the equipment of the learner. There exists an altogether too prevalent idea that merely reading schoolwork constitutes study. While study involves reading, nevertheless the mere act of reading does not imply effective study. This process of effective study means mastery and command of the tools of knowledge. Therefore, methods of effective study should be taught throughout the entire educative process as an approach to learning beginning with the early grades. Now it is realized that the mere giving of

[50] H. R. Laycock and D. H. Russell, "An Analysis of Thirty-eight How-to-Study Manuals," *School Review*, 49:370–379, 1941.

rules for study, although these are valuable aids, offers no guarantee that the pupil will be enabled to study more effectively. Since every teacher has responsibility for helping pupils to develop efficient study habits and techniques, methods of study must be taught consistently and thoroughly throughout the entire school career of the child. It is just as essential to teach pupils how to study as it is to teach them what to study. It should never be taken for granted that pupils know how to study. It should be an essential function of teaching to ascertain whether or not pupils know how to study. There should be daily direction and supervision of the process from the primary grades right through the secondary school and perhaps even in the early years of college as well. There should be regular periodic diagnoses of the study habits of individual pupils in order to remedy their deficiencies in this matter and to aid them in substituting desirable habits and skills for those which are undesirable.

There is still need for a great deal of research to be done by teachers on this problem of how to study. This research should involve the investigation of actual study practices used by pupils, by those who are bright, by those who are average, by those who are slow, by those who are successful in their work, and by those whose accomplishments are poor. These investigations should cover all levels of the educative process, the primary grades, the elementary school, the junior and senior high school, and perhaps even the junior college. Necessarily such investigations should be carried on in the classroom itself and be reflections of conditions which actually exist among pupils. The purpose of these investigations should be to determine what study habits and skills used by pupils are advantageous and what are disadvantageous. Then remedial and follow-up work to improve the use of advantageous habits and skills, to reenforce and strengthen these habits and skills, in order to eliminate the disadvantageous, should become an essential part of the teaching process. There is further need for individual diagnoses and case studies to determine the effectiveness of various kinds of remedial work with individual students.

How to study is significant and important in the educative process. It is one of the finest fruits of education and one of the important factors in the integrated development of the child. The results of education in the form of specific knowledge pass early from man. Most of the contents of the school texts vanish with the years. This implies that education really imparts to the mind not so much a possession to be stored away, but rather a more effective way of acting in a present situation. Education not only affords mental content but also, and perhaps more important, it imparts mental method. The practicable thing is not to remember all facts, but to know when and how to observe them, the books that treat of them, and the authorities to consult about them. Therefore, guidance, direction, and instruction in how to study should aim at familiarity with the world's best knowledge, at an efficient method of attaining it, and at stimulating continuous advancement throughout life.

EXERCISES

1. Outline this chapter.
2. List and define the terms which you have learned from your study of this chapter.
3. *a*) What is the nature of effective study?
   b) What role does motivation play in the process?
4. What is the function of the teacher in the process of effective study? of the pupil?
5. What proportion of the principles of effective study is concerned with the mental aspects of study? What mental activities are involved in the acquisition of effective study habits?
6. Of what value are such formulas for study as the SQ3R and the Triple S techniques? Do these apply in all subject-matter areas? Why or why not? Where and how does motivation enter into these formulas?
7. The formation of the general habit of effective study involves many specific skills and techniques. Explain these and demonstrate their importance. Wherever possible, substantiate your explanation by reference to the findings of experimental investigations.
8. What have research investigations revealed with regard to:
   a) Study skills possessed by pupils?
   b) How-to-study courses?
   c) Measurement and appraisal of study skills?
   d) The use of how-to-study manuals?
9. Report one experimental investigation on how-to-study courses. State the problem, the subjects, the materials, the procedures, and the findings. Then give your evaluation of the investigation.
10. Discuss the following statements:
    a) "Study does not occur by itself; it must be motivated."
    b) "Cramming is a risky method of study."
    c) "Study is an individual and not a social activity."
    d) "Effective study requires consistent motivation and clear directions which will result in purposefulness, interest, and attention."
    e) "Learning and studying are mutually related."

SELECTED REFERENCES FOR STUDY AND READING

Bird, C., and Bird, D. M., *Learning More by Effective Study* (New York: Appleton-Century-Crofts, Inc., 1945).

Broom, L. S., and Sheldon, W. D., *Developing Efficient Reading* (New York: Oxford University Press, 1959).

Brueckner, L. J., and Bond, G. L., *Diagnosis and Treatment of Learning Difficulties* (New York: Appleton-Century-Crofts, Inc., 1955).

Burton, W. H., Kimball,, R. B., and Wing, R. L., *Education for Effective Thinking* (New York: Appleton-Century-Crofts, Inc., 1960).

——— *The Guidance of Learning Activities,* 3 ed. (New York: Appleton-Century-Crofts, Inc., 1962).

DiMichael, S. G., *Improving Personality and Study Skills in College* (Milwaukee: The Bruce Publishing Co., 1951).

Harris, A. J., *How to Increase Reading Ability* (New York: Longmans, Green and Co., 1961).

Kitson, H. D., *How to Use Your Mind,* 4 ed. (Philadelphia: J. B. Lippincott Co., 1961).

Meenes, M., *Studying and Learning* (New York: Random House, Inc., 1954).

Miller, L. F., *Increasing Reading Efficiency* (New York: Holt, Rinehart and Winston, Inc., 1956).

Mursell, J. L., *Using Your Mind Effectively* (New York: McGraw-Hill Book Co., Inc., 1951).

Robinson, F., *Effective Study,* rev. ed. (New York: Harper and Row, 1961).

Voeks, V., *On Becoming an Educated Person* (Philadelphia: W. B. Saunders Co., 1957).

chapter 11

The Transfer of Learning

The Meaning of Transfer of Learning. Education not only involves training by means of instruction and exercise but also implies an end or purpose which this training is to fulfill. It is a fundamental principle of education that the systematic development of knowledge and skill, the methodical formation of habits of thought and of action, can have no significance unless they are directed toward the achievement of human excellence. Education involves the development, naturally and harmoniously, of all the powers and capabilities of the individual. It consists of building in the individual an organization of knowledge and skills, of habits and attitudes, of values and ideals which will aid in fulfilling life's purposes. The chief aim of education is to help each individual to make of himself all that it is possible for him to become. The real purpose of education is not merely to prepare the child to make his living but likewise to train him to live his life. However, the school cannot prepare a pupil specifically for all the activities which will constitute his life. Hence, training in the school must consist of the developing and strengthening — by instruction, direction, and guidance — of the pupil's powers, abilities, and capacities of perceiving, feeling, imagining, remembering, thinking, judging, reasoning, and willing. The efficacy of the school in developing worthwhile knowledge, skills, habits, attitudes, ideals, and values which will enable the individual to meet effectively the demands of life depends upon the extent to which this training may be transferred from the classroom situations to other situations, in and out of school. The degree to which the individual's powers, capacities, and abilities function in life situations is, then, the measure of transfer of learning.

The term *transfer of learning* is used to indicate the outcomes or effects of learning that may be used advantageously in further learning and in the performance of life tasks. It involves the application of concepts, principles, values, attitudes, and skills learned previously to new learning tasks and problems both within the school and also in life situations. It implies a process of carrying over and applying to one situation the knowledge and skill acquired in another. It refers to the application of *methods, ideals, values, habits,* and *attitudes* learned in one field to other fields and to life situations. The term *formal discipline* has also been used to indicate the carry-over or transfer from one field to another which results from the increase in efficiency or from the improvement in the method of using the mental power or capacity to generalize which has resulted from orderly thinking and training. It implies that the efficiency gained in dealing with one situation should be applicable in other situations which call for the functioning of the same capacity or power. Formal discipline has been defined here because it is one way, the traditional way, of explaining transfer of learning. Most present-day educational psychologists have asserted a belief in transfer, although they have rejected the theory of formal discipline as the method of explaining transfer of training or of learning. Kolesnik has described formal discipline as follows:

> According to formal discipline, education consists in strengthening or developing the powers of mind by exercising them, preferably on difficult, abstract material such as Latin, Greek and mathematics. For disciplinary purposes, the content of school subjects is held to be of secondary importance. It is the form which is thought to be especially efficacious in the creation of minds able to operate well in any field of endeavor.[1]

He has also made a distinction between mental discipline and formal discipline. The former is the broader term and signifies "the psychological view that man's mental capacities can somehow be trained to operate more efficiently in general and the philosophical conviction that such training constitutes one of the chief purposes of schooling."[2]

Transfer may be *positive, negative,* or *zero. Positive transfer* means that training in one subject, task, or situation improves or facilitates performance in the second subject or situation. Transfer is *negative* when training in one subject, task, or situation interferes with, retards, or is detrimental to performance in the second subject, task, or situation. *Zero transfer*

---

[1] Reprinted with permission of the copyright owners, The Regents of the University of Wisconsin, from W. B. Kalesnik, *Mental Discipline in Modern Education,* 1958, p. 4, The University of Wisconsin Press.

[2] *Ibid.,* p. 3.

indicates that training in one subject, task, or situation produces no observable influence or change in efficiency in the second subject or situation. This is sometimes designated by the term *indeterminate.*

The basic problem in transfer of learning concerns the disciplinary values of education. This problem, which is as old as education itself, may be expressed in the form of the questions: (1) Will the training and development which the child gains through his education in school, that is, through the knowledge and the skill acquired in the various school subjects, function in such a way that the child will be able to adapt himself more efficiently to new situations not only in his schoolwork but also throughout his life? (2) To what extent does the training which the pupil has received in mathematics or Latin or any other school subject carry over into later life and become useful either directly or indirectly through the fact that the individual who has been trained by means of these subjects is better able to adjust himself to the world about him, to solve his problems, to live his life? (3) Since all education seeks to achieve learning which can be transferred to new situations both within the curriculum and ultimately in life, then what learning and experience will be most profitable — training in specific skills or a background of general materials and content?

It is very important that the teacher be able to answer satisfactorily these questions, for upon his answer will be based practically his entire philosophy of education. The extent to which transfer of learning is considered to take place will be a determining factor in the selection of the subject-matter content to be included in the curriculum, especially at the secondary-school level. If the knowledge and skill acquired in the various school subjects are generalized and thus function in such a way that the child is enabled better to adjust to new situations both within and outside of school, if the training in one field of study carries over into others, then the course of study will of necessity consist of the general materials and content contained in the traditional or conservative curriculum. If, however, the presumption prevails that transfer is insignificant or nonexistent, then the course of study will be composed of subject-matter content and material designed to develop specialized skills, specific habits, and individual attitudes.

All education has been influenced to a considerable extent by transfer. It has been stated: "That which does not transfer is educationally worthless, if indeed not a positive encumbrance. Except for past learning one could not learn anything in school; the simplest sentence, spoken or written, would be utterly incomprehensible. If a school subject does not transfer in profitable amounts, it is that subject, not transfer, which is invalidated."[3] Thus, the problem of transfer of learning is significant not only in the area of educational psychology but also in the entire educational process. The materials which constitute the curriculum and the methods of teaching are both determined to a large extent by the point of view held concerning the *nature* and *extent* of transfer and the *conditions* under which it takes place.

The Nature of the Transfer of Learning. The traditional doctrine of *formal discipline* was based upon the theory that certain school subjects, especially those of an abstract nature, and notably the classics and mathematics, when studied properly and intelligently, are better suited for mind training than others. This theory maintains that the most important function of education is its discipline, or training of the mental and moral powers and capacities so that the individual will think, express ideas clearly, analyze problems, and make intelligent decisions. The child in school by means of instruction, study, and exercise in these subjects develops his powers and capacities for perceiving, feeling, imagining, remembering, thinking, and willing. Through his study of these subjects the pupil has so disciplined his mind that it is an efficient instrument ready to be turned to whatever task is set before him. The capability thus acquired is applicable to other fields of endeavor both in school and throughout life which require the functioning of these powers and capacities, not, however, irrespective of the mental ability or purposes of the learner. The basis for this consists in the fact that education not only affords mental content but also imparts mental method. The object of formal discipline is to prepare the pupil's powers and capacities by thorough and proper exercise so that the individual may subsequently be able to deal with any situations or materials which involve these powers and capacities.

---

[3] J. B. Stroud, "Experiments on Learning in School Situations," *Psychological Bulletin,* 37:777–807, 1940. Quotation from p. 787. See also E. R. Hilgard, *Theories of Learning,* 2 ed. (New York: Appleton-Century-Crofts, Inc., 1956), pp. 7 and 8. "Some transfer of training must occur or there would be no use in developing a foundation for later learning. Nobody denies that it is easier to build a vocabulary in a language after you have a start in it, or that higher mathematics profits from mastery of basic concepts. The question is really one of how much transfer takes place and what its nature is."

The theory of formal discipline supposes the existence of a mind and the possibility of training that mind.[4] Herein is the difficulty which underlies any discussion of the subject of transfer of learning. Most modern educational psychologists are *monists;* that is, they recognize no distinction between bodily and spiritual capacities. Therefore, since they consider the mental merely as a phase of bodily organism, theirs is a psychology without a soul. Consequently, most moderns begin their argument against transfer of learning by denying that there is a mind or soul which can be trained. Hence, it is the opinion of many modern educational psychologists that the disciplinary value of education cannot be justified.

The explanation and interpretation of the nature of transfer of learning require a proper understanding of the nature of man, of his mind, and of the learning process. This is necessary because the diversity and the opposition of many of the views concerning transfer are due fundamentally to the difference in the conception of the nature of man, of his mind, and of the learning process.

Learning is the development of the individual's capacities. It is the actualization of his potentialities. Learning is the mental activity by means of which knowledge, skill, habits, attitudes, values, and ideals are acquired, resulting in the modification of behavior and conduct, and culminating in the acquisition of an appreciation of the values of life, as well as the gaining of control over one's attitudes toward them. Learning takes place because man is a rational being endowed with an intellect. The intellect is the spiritual cognitive power of the mind by which human knowledge is acquired. Mind and soul are one and the same reality. The Scholastics defined mind as the ultimate internal principle considered as the subject of conscious life. This mind or soul does not act directly by itself but through the medium of these powers, capacities, capabilities which the Scholastics termed faculties. A faculty denotes the capability of the mind for performing a particular function. It is a special mode of mental activity, an instrument through which the mind acts. It is not self-existent nor does it produce an energy of its own. These faculties are not parts of the soul or mind, for the soul is simple and indivisible. The mind is a unit, but it is an active unit. The various activities it carries on are distinguished in kind and designated as faculties or potentialities or capabilities or powers. Learning is facilitated not because any increase

[4] See W. J. McGucken, S.J., *The Catholic Way in Education,* rev. ed. (Milwaukee: The Bruce Publishing Company, 1937), pp. 120 and 121.

takes place in the faculties, but rather because better and more comprehensive methods, values, or ideals have been acquired.

The proper understanding of the nature of man, of the mind and of the learning process, has been stressed because the extreme reaction against the theory of formal discipline has been based upon the fact that it is considered to be an outgrowth of the so-called "faculty psychology." This "faculty psychology" has been described as maintaining that the mind is an intricate machine[5] composed of various separate and distinct parts or faculties, each of which could be improved by exercise in appropriate tasks much as could the muscles of the body. It is worthy of note also that the values of these tasks were considered to consist chiefly in their difficulty and disagreeableness.

Many modern writers in the fields of psychology and education have misinterpreted Scholastic Psychology and have assumed that it and this so-called "faculty psychology" are the same. They have ascribed to Scholastics a theory or concept of faculty which no Scholastic ever held. There is a vast difference between the teachings of Scholasticism and this so-called "faculty psychology." This faculty psychology which interprets the mind as something analogous to an intricate machine, the various parts of which correspond to the faculties, is a monistic and materialistic theory based upon the work of Christian Wolff (1679–1754). In 1734 Wolff published a book entitled *Rational Psychology* which embodied this faculty theory. Scholasticism considers that the true notion of human personality is the composite of *body and soul.* By soul is meant the ultimate internal principle by which man thinks, feels, and wills. It is true that the Scholastics also have made use of the term *faculty,* but they defined faculties as the instruments by means of which the powers of the soul are manifested. One soul, the principle of all conscious states, possesses a multitude of capabilities for engaging in particular kinds of activities. The Scholastics have never regarded the faculties as independent realities or as separate agents, but rather as special modes through which the soul itself acts.

The History of the Problem of Transfer of Learning. The theory of formal discipline has held for centuries a dignified and influential status in educational history, doctrine, and practice. The theory of formal dis-

---

[5] H. E. Garrett, *Great Experiments in Psychology,* 3 ed. (New York: Appleton-Century-Crofts, Inc., 1951), pp. 83–87. See also C. A. Hart, *The Thomistic Concept of Mental Faculty* (Washington, D. C.: The Catholic University of America, 1930).

cipline probably originated among the Greeks. At any rate, the first written record[6] of the theory is contained in the seventh book of Plato's *Republic.* The doctrine of formal discipline was implied in the educational practices of the Greeks and the Romans. Both of these ancient peoples made use of gymnastics, music, mathematics, and oratory to develop physical and mental discipline. The doctrine of formal discipline was also implied in the teachings of Scholasticism. The *trivium* and *quadrivium* of the medieval schools were based upon formal discipline. Likewise, the Renaissance with its stress upon the cultural values of the classics did much to promote the doctrine of formal discipline.

John Locke (1632–1704) expressed one form of the disciplinary concept of education[7] as follows:

> Would you have a man reason well, you must use him to it betimes, exercise his mind in observing the connection of ideas and following them in train.
>
> Nothing does this better than mathematics, which therefore, I think should be taught all those who have the time and opportunity, not so much to make them mathematicians, as to make them reasonable creatures; for though we call ourselves so, because we are born to it if we please, yet we may truly say nature gives us but the seeds of it. We are born to be, if we please, rational creatures, but it is use and exercise that makes us so, and we are indeed so not further than industry and application has carried us. I have mentioned mathematics as a way to settle in the mind the habit of reasoning closely and in train; not that I think it necessary that all men should be deep mathematicians, but that having got the way of reasoning, which that study necessarily brings the mind to, *they might be able to transfer it to other parts of knowledge as they have occasion.*[8]

Although Locke did not use the terms *formal discipline* or *mental discipline* as such, it might be noted that he seems to have been the first to have employed the term *transfer* in this sense.

In modern times European schools generally have based their curricula upon the doctrine of formal discipline. In American education the doctrine of formal discipline has exercised considerable influence upon the curricula and teaching practices of the high school and college. In fact, the theory

---

[6] See Paul Monroe, *Source Book in the History of Education* (New York: The Macmillan Co., 1921), pp. 204, 205.

[7] W. T. Kane, S.J., and J. J. O'Brien, *History of Education,* rev. ed. (Chicago: Loyola University Press, 1954), pp. 195–198; also P. J. McCormick and F. P. Cassidy, *History of Education,* 3 ed. (Washington, D. C.: The Catholic Education Press, 1953), pp. 475–481.

[8] John Locke, *Of the Conduct of Understanding* (Oxford: Clarendon Press, 1894), pp. 19, 23.

of formal discipline is still adhered to quite widely and influences much of the school's work.[9]

It was not until the last half of the nineteenth century that the validity of this theory was seriously questioned. Then the works of Herbart (1776–1841) and of Spencer (1820–1903) aroused some criticism regarding formal discipline. It was not until 1890 that the first attempt was made to attack the doctrine experimentally. The first experiment was performed by William James[10] (1842–1910) at Harvard University. He attempted to measure the improvement in memorizing due to training. Present-day psychologists recognize that James's experiment, using himself as the subject, was inadequate and even crude, that his investigation ended without proving anything. Historically, however, it is important because it aroused a deep and widespread interest in the topic and furnished the suggestion for the many other experiments which have followed. It seems that James's work exercised no immediate effects, for in 1892 The Committee of Ten on Secondary School Studies published its report based upon the traditional disciplinary theory of education.

This report exercised a strong influence upon American secondary education for a period of three decades. The turning point in the controversy seems to have been an experiment in the field of perception performed in 1901 by Thorndike and Woodworth.[11] The purpose of the experiment, using the single group technique, was to determine the amount of transfer due to practice in estimating areas of rectangles, in judging length of lines, in the discrimination of weights, in the observation of words containing certain combinations of letters. The result of the experiment was that some transfer was found to take place. The investigators explained the transfer effects obtained as due to the presence of "identical elements." At the time this experiment was considered to have disproved formal discipline as an explanation of transfer of learning. Since that time several hundred experiments have been carried on in an endeavor to remove from the realm of controversy the question of transfer of learning. Improvements have been made in the methods of conducting transfer experiments, and a variety of materials utilized.

---

[9] W. J. McGucken, S.J., *op. cit.*, p. 121.

[10] William James, *Principles of Psychology,* Vol. I (New York: Henry Holt and Co., 1890), pp. 666–668.

[11] E. L. Thorndike and R. S. Woodworth, "The Influence of Improvement in One Mental Function Upon the Efficiency of Other Functions," *Psychological Review,* 8:247–261; 384–395; 553–564, 1901.

As a result of these early experiments, which seemed to indicate that if transfer occurred it was very limited, for several decades emphasis was placed upon the negative aspect of transfer. As a result many educators rejected the possibility of any transfer of learning. As a consequence, education went to extremes in attempting to revise curricula upon the basis of these experimental findings. Naturally, such a radical change affected profoundly the content of the curricula of the school, leading to a persistent demand that subject matter be practical and that methods of instruction be socialized.

Bagley described some of the results of this rejection of the disciplinary theory as follows:

> In sharp contrast to education in most of the civilized countries, an outstanding characteristic of education in the United States is its virtually complete rejection of the disciplinary ideal in the fields of both mind and of morals. The rejection of mental discipline as an ideal was not entirely — nor even chiefly — due to the teachings of educational theory. Nor is the rejection of the disciplinary ideal in the field of morals to be charged entirely against the theorists. In both cases, and in a quite real sense, theory has served to rationalize and justify a certain — although a somewhat inarticulate — popular demand. . . .
>
> Symptomatic of the present situation in American education is the wide vogue and increasing popularity of the so-called "Progressive" school of educational theory. . . .
>
> The extreme left wing of the Progressive school not only rejects the ideal of discipline; it would abandon prearranged programs, assigned tasks, and learning activities of all kinds that are imposed from without. . . .
>
> In spite of the fact that no less widely recognized an authority than John Dewey has both disclaimed and denounced so absurd and perilous a limitation of the teacher's function, the notion that all learning activities must take their cue from the spontaneous purposes of the learner is accepted as both law and gospel by thousands of American teachers, and is reflected in such popular slogans as the "play way," the "creative impulse," the "free school," the "child-centered school," and the like.[12]

However, about 1910 a counterreaction had set in, and the pendulum started to swing back to the belief that training does transfer. In 1915, Judd published his *Psychology of High School Subjects* in which he attacked vigorously the critics of transfer of learning. In 1917, the Conference on Classical Studies in Liberal Education was held at Princeton University. At this conference West defended the disciplinary value of the classics in the following words:

---

[12] W. C. Bagley, *Education, Crime, and Social Progress* (New York: The Macmillan Co., 1931), Preface, pp. vii to x.

> Men sometimes say that they have forgotten their Latin and Greek and conclude that they were therefore poorly taught and that the time spent on them was wasted. Do they remember more than the scraps of other studies unless they have kept them up? Do they hold in active view many items of physics or chemistry or philosophy? Can they state accurately the law of gravitation or recall much of anything outside the studies of description and narration? Even there, how many can repeat from memory the list of our Presidents or recite The Star-Spangled Banner? Try it. What we can remember is worth much, but what we had to nourish our minds in school and college counts for far more. It is like food. Who, unless he was on fixed diet, remembers what he ate a week ago last Thursday? or can recall his menu for each day of the past month? Yet the effects continue. And it is the nature of our diet in youth, as all know, which does much to determine our health in manhood.[13]

In 1923, the Report of the National Committee on Mathematical Requirements, under the auspices of the Mathematical Association of America, was published under the title *The Reorganization of Mathematics in the Secondary Schools.* The report of this committee summed up very well the status of transfer of training at that time as follows:

> 1. The two extreme views for and against disciplinary values practically no longer exist. As the question now stands, as transfer of training, the psychologists quoted here almost unanimously agree that transfer does exist.
>
> 2. A large majority agree that there is a possibility of negative transfer, and of zero transfer, caused by interference effects. Professor Thorndike is of the opinion that negative transfer is comparatively rare and can be avoided by proper methods of training.
>
> 3. Very few if any experiments have shown the full amount of transfer between the fields chosen for investigation. The reason for this is to be found in the imperfections of the experimental setting. . . .
>
> 4. The amount of transfer in any case where transfer is admitted at all, is very largely dependent upon methods of teaching. This is probably the strongest note struck by the psychologists in their comments. Twelve of them out of twenty-four make some explicit reference to the matter.
>
> 5. A majority of the psychologists, judging from their remarks . . . seem to believe that, with certain restrictions, transfer of training is a valid aim in teaching.
>
> 6. Transfer is most evident with respect to general elements — ideas, attitudes, and ideals. These act in many instances as the carriers of transfer. . . .[14]

---

[13] A. F. West, *Value of the Classics* (Princeton: Princeton University Press, 1917), p. 10.

[14] "The Present Status of Disciplinary Values in Education," *The Reorganization of Mathematics in Secondary Education.* National Committee on Mathematical Requirements, Mathematical Association of America, Part II, 1923, pp. 89–104.

In 1924, the General Report of the Classical Investigation, conducted by the Advisory Committee of the American Classical League, was published. In this report the opinion was also expressed by psychologists that mental functions are subject to transfer, and they described the manner in which this transfer was secured as follows:

> . . . the development of certain desirable habits and ideals which are subject to spread, such as habits of sustained attention, orderly procedure, overcoming obstacles, perseverance; ideals of achievement, accuracy and thoroughness; and cultivation of certain general attitudes such as dissatisfaction with failure or with partial success.[15]

In 1924 Thorndike returned to the problem of transfer. He conducted an investigation of the effect upon intellectual achievement of a year's work in the various high school subjects.[16] In 1927 Thorndike elaborated upon this study.[17] In 1928 Orata[18] made his study on the *Theory of Identical Elements* in which he described the results of the experiments which were conducted between 1890 and 1927. In 1928, likewise, Whipple[19] described the status of transfer of learning with emphasis upon the methods and materials employed in experimental investigations. He summarized several typical research studies and presented the theories by which the results of these investigations had been explained. In 1933, Norem's[20] critique of some of the experimental studies in the field of transfer appeared. Norem in this work evaluated forty-eight studies in the field of transfer and concluded that thirty-eight were probably invalid. In 1934, Castiello[21] summarized in his study, entitled *Geistesformung,* the findings of experimental investigations conducted between 1890 and 1932. He presented the results of the various investigations classified according to the mental function involved. The objectivity and clarity of his report

[15] *The Classical Investigation, General Report,* Part I (Princeton: Princeton University Press, 1924), p. 55.

[16] E. L. Thorndike, "Mental Discipline in High School Studies," *Journal of Educational Psychology,* 15:1–22; 83–89, 1924.

[17] C. R. Broyler, E. L. Thorndike, and E. Woodyard, "A Second Study of Mental Discipline in High School Studies," *Journal of Educational Psychology,* 18:377–404, 1927.

[18] P. T. Orata, *The Theory of Identical Elements* (Columbus: Ohio State University Press, 1928).

[19] N.S.S.E. Twenty-Seventh Yearbook, Part II, *Nature and Nurture,* 1928, pp. 179–209.

[20] G. M. Norem, *Transfer of Training Experiments Revalued,* University of Iowa Studies in Education, Vol. VIII, No. 6, 1933.

[21] J. Castiello, S.J., *Geistesformung* (Berlin: Ferd. Dümmlers Verlag, 1934).

makes for a balanced interpretation and estimation of the experimental work in the field of transfer. In addition Father Castiello added to the research studies two investigations of his own and also presented an excellent résumé of the formulae for explaining transfer. In 1935 Orata[22] made his second survey and constructive interpretation of the experimental evidence in the field of transfer of training which had been reported between 1927 and 1935. Again in 1941, Orata[23] summarized and interpreted the experimental investigations conducted in transfer between 1935 and 1940. The increasingly large number of experimental investigations reported within recent years indicates that the problem of transfer is still among the most important and fundamental in the entire educational process.

In 1958 Kolesnik[24] presented a comprehensive overview of mental discipline in American education during the first half of the twentieth century in order to ascertain what problems were involved and to evaluate some of the solutions proposed.

Experimentation in the area of transfer has passed from endeavors to establish the fact or the possibility of transfer to the determination of the conditions under which transfer occurs and to the discovery of effective methods for promoting, increasing, and controlling transfer. In 1961 Bruner stated the modern view on transfer of learning as follows:

> Virtually all of the evidence of the past two decades on the nature of learning and transfer has indicated that, while the original theory of formal discipline was poorly stated in terms of the training of faculties, it is indeed a fact that massive general transfer can be achieved by appropriate learning, even to the degree that learning properly under optimum conditions leads one to learn "how to learn." These studies have stimulated a renewed interest in complex learning — designed to produce general understanding of the structure of a subject matter.[25]

Experimental Techniques Used to Investigate Transfer of Learning.[26] Various techniques have been devised by psychologists to establish experi-

---

[22] P. T. Orata, "Transfer of Training and Educational Pseudo-Science," *Mathematics Teacher,* 28:265–288, 1935.

[23] P. T. Orata, "Recent Research Studies in Transfer of Training With Implications for the Curriculum, Guidance, and Personnel Work," *Journal of Educational Research,* 35:81–101, 1941.

[24] W. B. Kolesnik, *op. cit.*

[25] J. S. Bruner, *The Process of Education* (Cambridge: Harvard University Press, 1961), p. 6, see also p. 17.

[26] See also R. M. Gagné, H. Foster, and M. E. Crowley, "The Measurement of Transfer of Training," *Psychological Bulletin,* 45:97–124, 1948.

mentally the effect of training, to discover to what extent transfer occurs, and to determine how transfer takes place. Among these techniques are the older devices, designated as the *individual method* and the *single group method,* both of which have proved to be inadequate. Consequently, these techniques were discarded as methods of investigation in favor of newer techniques, including the *equivalent group method* and the *three group method.*

a) *The Individual Method.* In this technique the person conducting the investigation was both the experimenter and the subject. This method is not considered to possess scientific validity, and the results obtained through the use of this technique have little or no value beyond their historical significance. The individual method was used by William James and several other early experimenters.

b) *The Single Group Method.* This technique consisted in testing a group of subjects in one function or activity, after which followed training in a second function or activity for a definite period of time. Then at the completion of the training period the group was retested in order to determine the effect, if any, of the training in the second function. This method was used by Thorndike and Woodworth in their 1901 experiment and also was used by many of the early investigators in the field.

While the single group method was without doubt an improvement over the individual method, nevertheless it was defective in that, if a gain were made by the group, improvement made in the first function could not be assigned definitely and wholly to the exercise of the second function. This was true because the repetition of the test of the first function also constituted an exercise of that function. Consequently, it was essential that a method of experimentation be devised by which the effect of the exercise of the second function upon the first function could be isolated.

c) *The Equivalent or Parallel Group Method.* By this technique two groups of subjects as nearly equivalent as possible with respect to age, sex, mental capacity, grade in school, ability in the function tested and other relevant factors are compared. The two groups are usually designated *experimental* and *control* groups. The procedure involves testing both groups in the first function at the beginning of the experiment. Then the experimental group is given special training or practice in a second function for a specified period of time. The control group, however, is not given this special training or practice. Then both the experimental and control groups are tested on the first function. The gain made by the experimental group is compared with that made by the control group, if any. The difference in gain made represents the influence of training or the transfer effect. Among the early investigators making use of this type of procedure were Winch, Sleight, Rugg, Judd, and Hewins. This technique has likewise been used in most of the recent investigations.

d) *The Three Group Method.* This technique represents a refinement of the equivalent group method. It involves the use of three equivalent groups, designated usually as the *control,* the *practice,* and the *training* groups. All three groups take the initial and final test on the first function. The training group receives both practice and instruction in the second function. The practice group receives an equal amount of practice, but no instruction in the function. The control group receives neither practice nor instruction. This technique seems to have been devised by Woodrow.[27] It was used also by Meredith and other investigators.

Experimental Evidence Concerning Transfer of Learning. Since the first experimental study of transfer, made in 1890 by William James, several hundred investigations have been reported in this field. These investigations are of two types, the *laboratory study* and the *classroom experiment.* Of 211 investigations on transfer analyzed by Orata, 91 were laboratory studies, while 120 were classroom experiments. The *laboratory studies* generally dealt with artificial and very limited tasks, such as canceling letters, tossing balls, estimating the size of objects, memorizing lists, learning codes, and the like. They offer little material of a practical nature to the teacher. The *classroom experiments* carried out in the school situation have sought to determine the effects of training and instruction in one subject upon learning in another subject or in other subjects. When properly interpreted many of these classroom experiments are of significance and of interest to the teacher. However, it should be noted that many of the earlier investigations, both laboratory and classroom, are open to criticism because of lack of thoroughness, inadequate planning, and erroneous interpretation of results.

Transfer studies have been made in the fields of perception, memory, judgment, reasoning, and attention. The school subjects, the transfer effects of which have been studied, include arithmetic, geometry, grammar, spelling, sciences, languages, both modern and Latin, and the manual

---

[27] H. Woodrow, "The Effect of Type of Training Upon Transference," *Journal of Educational Psychology,* 18:159–172, 1927.

arts. In addition one ambitious study[28] was conducted to determine the transfer effects of the various subjects in the high school curriculum. In addition studies have been conducted to determine the transfer effects of generalized ideals and attitudes.

It is not intended, in fact it would be impossible within the scope of a single chapter, to review or even to list the investigations made in the field of transfer. A rather complete list of classroom experiments on transfer conducted previous to 1940 has been made by Stroud.[29] It is recommended that the student consult regularly the *Education Index* and *Psychological Abstracts* in order to keep in touch with current studies in the field of transfer.

Orata has reported in three comprehensive surveys and summaries the experimental investigations made in the field of transfer from 1890 to 1940. His first report[30] analyzed the 100 studies made between 1890 and 1927. The second survey[31] analyzed the sixty-eight studies made between 1927 and 1935. The third report[32] analyzed the forty-three studies made between 1935 and 1940. The results of these three surveys are presented in the following tables:

TABLE 8. Statistical Results of Transfer Experiments From 1890 to 1940[33]

Amount of Transfer	1890–1927		1927–1935		1935–1940		Total	
Claimed	No.	%	No.	%	No.	%	No.	%
Considerable	32	32	15	22	6	14	53	25
Appreciable	49	49	31	44	15	35	95	45
Varies with conditions of learning	..	..	4	7	12	28	16	8
Very little	8	8	7	10	5	12	20	9
No transfer	2	2	5	8	2	5	9	4
Others (duplications excluded)	9	9	6	9	3	6	18	9
Total	100	100	68	100	43	100	211	100

[28] C. R. Broyler, E. L. Thorndike, and E. Woodyard, *op. cit.*

[29] J. B. Stroud, *op. cit.*, pp. 787–791.

[30] P. T. Orata, *The Theory of Identical Elements* (Columbus: Ohio State University Press, 1928).

[31] P. T. Orata, "Transfer of Training and Educational Pseudo-Science," *The Mathematics Teacher,* 28:265–289, 1935.

[32] P. T. Orata, "Recent Studies on Transfer of Training with Implications for the Curriculum, Guidance and Personnel Work," *Journal of Educational Research,* 35:81–101, 1941.

[33] *Ibid.*, p. 82.

TABLE 9. **Summary of Results**[34]

Amount of Transfer Claimed	1890–1927 No.	%	1927–1935 No.	%	1935–1940 No.	%	Total No.	%
Clear evidence of transfer	81	81	50	73	33	77	164	78
Very little, no transfer, ambiguous evidence, interference, etc.	19	19	18	27	10	23	47	22

From these three surveys of the transfer investigations, Orata has drawn these conclusions:

> 1. Transfer is a fact, as revealed by nearly eighty per cent of the studies;
> 2. Transfer is not an automatic process that can be taken for granted, but it is to be worked for;
> 3. The amount of transfer is conditioned by many factors, among which are: age; mental ability; (possibly) time interval between learning and transfer; degree of stability attained by the learned pattern; "knowledge of directions, favorable attitude toward the learning situation, and the efficient use of past experience"; accuracy of learning; "conscious acceptance by the learner of methods, procedures, principles, sentiments and ideals"; meaningfulness of the learning situation; the personality of the subject — greater transfer in extroverts than in introverts; method of study; suitable organization of subject matter presentation; the provision for continuous reconstruction of experience.[35]

The extensive research carried on over a period of more than six decades has demonstrated adequately that transfer does take place. The interest of investigators now seems to center upon two problems: (1) How can transfer be accounted for and explained? (2) What factors influence transfer?

Theories to Explain Transfer. Nowhere in the reports of the investigations of transfer can there be found a concise, clear formula which defines exactly the nature of transfer. Yet the teacher must know not only whether or not transfer is possible, but also he must know how it takes place. Two theories to explain the nature of transfer and how it takes place have been proposed to interpret the experimental investigations in this field and also to replace the theory of formal discipline. The *theory of identical components,* originally designated as *identical elements,* which is considered to include identity of content, of aims, and of procedure, has

---

[34] *Ibid.,* p. 83.
[35] *Ibid.,* pp. 81–82.

been advanced by Thorndike. The *theory of generalization,* which is considered to include generalization in methods, aims, procedures, ideals, attitudes, habits, and reasoning, was proposed by Judd. Both of these theories have considerable practical significance, yet as Webb[36] has pointed out, while each attempts to describe how and where transfer takes place, neither is able to explain the *cause of transfer.*

1. THE THEORY OF IDENTICAL COMPONENTS. This theory, which is consistent with Thorndike's concept and laws of learning, is based upon specific habit psychology which maintains that mental functions are specific to such an extent that training in one function will not result in the improvement of another. Advocates of this theory hold that when improvement in the learning of a given activity is reported to have occurred as a result of training and practice in another activity, it is because of identical elements or components which exist in the two. Thorndike described this theory as follows:

> The answer which I shall try to defend is that a change in one function alters any other only in so far as the two functions have as factors identical elements. The change in the second function is in amount that due to the change in the elements common to it and the first. The change is simply the necessary result upon the second function of the alteration of those of its factors which were elements of the first function and so were altered by its training.
>
> Chief among such identical elements of practical importance in education are associations including ideas about aims and ideas about methods and general principles, and associations involving elementary facts of experience such as length, color, number, which are repeated again and again in differing combinations.
>
> By identical elements are meant mental processes which have the same cell action in the brain as their physical correlate. It is of course often not possible to tell just what features of two mental abilities are thus identical. But, as we shall see, there is rarely much trouble in reaching an approximate decision in those cases where training is of practical importance.[37]
>
> One mental function or activity improves others in so far as and because they are in part identical with it, because it contains elements common to them. Addition improves multiplication because multiplication is largely addition; knowledge of Latin gives increased ability to learn French because many of the facts learned in the one case are needed in the other. The study of geometry may lead a pupil to be more logical in all respects, for one element of being logical in all respects is to realize that facts can be

[36] L. W. Webb, "The Transfer of Training," in *Educational Psychology,* C. E. Skinner, ed., 4 ed. (Englewood Cliffs, N. J.: Prentice-Hall, Inc., 1959), p. 489.

[37] E. L. Thorndike, *Educational Psychology,* Vol. II (New York: Teachers College, Columbia University, 1913), pp. 358, 359.

absolutely proven and to admire and desire this certain and unquestionable sort of demonstration.

These identical elements may be in the stuff, the data concerned in the training, or in the attitude, the method taken with it. The former kind may be called "identities of substance" and the latter "identities of procedure."[38]

This theory is based upon the hypothesis that learning consists of the establishment of specific bonds or associations between various specific elements; consequently one form of learning influences another whenever bonds established in the former may be utilized by the latter. This really is an elaborate way of saying that there is no such thing as transfer of learning. It means simply that one repeats without change what he has learned to do previously. The educational significance of this theory of identical components is that the school would have to discover the specific items of information and the specific reactions which the child will use in life outside of school and then to make certain that the child possesses these and only these.

Thorndike has explained the theory further in the following manner:

. . . the intellectual values of studies should be determined largely by the special information, habits, interests, attitudes, and ideals which they demonstrably produce. The expectation of any large differences in general improvement of the mind from one study rather than another seems doomed to disappointment. The chief reason why good thinkers seem superficially to have been made such by having taken certain school studies, is that good thinkers have taken such studies, becoming better by the inherent tendency of the good to gain more than the poor from any study. When the good thinkers studied Greek and Latin, these studies seemed to make good thinking. Now that the good thinkers study Physics and Trigonometry, these seem to make good thinkers. If the abler pupils should all study Physical Education and Dramatic Art, these subjects would seem to make good thinkers. These were, indeed, a large fraction of the program of studies for the best thinkers the world has produced, the Athenian Greeks. After positive correlation of gain with initial ability is allowed for, the balance in favor of any study is certainly not large. Disciplinary values may be real and deserve weight in the curriculum, but the weights should be reasonable.[39]

The theory of identical components has been criticized adversely by many educational psychologists. Perhaps the most systematic criticism as well as the best refutation is Orata's thorough study of it, in which he drew the following conclusions:

---

[38] E. L. Thorndike, *Educational Psychology,* Briefer Course (New York: Teachers College, Columbia, 1914), pp. 276–277.

[39] E. L. Thorndike, "Mental Discipline in High School Studies," *Journal of Educational Psychology,* 15:98, 1924.

On the surface, the theory of identical elements seems to be plausible, since it is claimed to be supported by experimental evidence; and besides, observation tells us that general education is far from fulfilling expectations. Reflection, however, makes us hesitate to subscribe to this point of view, for two reasons. First of all, it really leaves the problem of transfer where it was, since as will be shown later, it simply provides for smaller faculties under the guise of specific abilities. Secondly, it advocates a type of education and opens an apprenticeship system, which is incompatible with our ideal of democracy. Education according to this doctrine is specific preparation for a more or less predetermined set of activities, thus leaving the child little freedom in determining his future life career. Furthermore, too much emphasis upon the practical does not leave room for logical organization of knowledge which makes for maximum social insight and intellectual interest.[40]

Thorndike's theory of identical elements either has to explain transfer of training as formal discipline does, or else it explains it away. If by specific ability Thorndike means a subdivision of a faculty, he is back to where he started, namely, faculty psychology and formal discipline all over again. A small faculty is still a faculty whether we call it a specific ability or by some other name. Consequently and logically, transfer takes place through the training of faculties.

On the other hand, if by specific Thorndike means a specific ability for each specific act, the problem of transfer is impossible and unnecessary. But, the existence of transfer is undoubted in the sense that we use old experience in our dealing with new situations. This fact must be explained in some way but to account for this by saying "identical elements" is to name the problem, not to explain it. For, as we said before, transfer is essentially that process of identifying the new and the old, and consequently an hypothesis that does not explain how this process of identification comes about is inadequate. The theory of identical elements not only fails to give an explanation of how identification takes place, but it also assumes that which is to be achieved, namely, making the new and the old identical.[41]

The Neo-Behaviorists, particularly Hull, Guthrie, and Skinner, have interpreted transfer of learning in practically the same way as Thorndike. Hull maintained that the greater the similarity between and among stimuli, the greater the magnitude of the generalized response. Guthrie's explanation was virtually identical with Thorndike's — namely that learning transfers to new situations because of common elements within the new and the old. Skinner used the term *induction* as equivalent to *transfer*. He employed that term to indicate the tendency for stimuli possessing common properties to be effective in arousing behavior.

[40] P. T. Orata, *The Theory of Identical Elements* (Columbus: Ohio State University Press, 1928), p. 8.
[41] *Ibid.*, p. 22.

2. The Theory of Generalization. One of the most strenuous opponents of the contention that training is wholly specific was Judd, who maintained that valuable education results are lost unless there is taken into consideration the necessity of cultivating attitudes that function generally. This is known as the *theory of generalization.* It explains transfer of learning in terms of a conscious recognition of the fact that experience obtained in one connection is applicable to other situations. Thus, habits of sustained attention, orderly procedure, and perseverance, ideals of accuracy, neatness, and thoroughness, methods of attacking problems, of organizing materials, and such general attitudes as annoyance at failure and satisfaction with success experienced in one situation are applicable to other situations.

The following quotations describe this theory:

> The important psychological fact . . . is that the extent to which the student generalizes his training is itself a measure of the degree to which he has secured from any course the highest form of training. One of the major characteristics of human intelligence is to be defined by calling attention . . . to the fact that a human being is able to generalize his experience.[42]
>
> Trained intelligence is particular in its contents but general in its methods. It is characteristic of human thinking that wherever one encounters any phenomenon one tends to interpret it in terms of general categories. If one comes in contact with a single object, such as a chair or a table, one thinks of this single object in terms of a general classification which is represented by the word "chair" or "table." The reason why the same word can be applied to many different objects is that all have the same general use whatever their individual peculiarities. The recognition of general uses is what gives words their meaningful character. Human language and human thought exhibit a tendency toward what we call "generalization." By this statement we indicate the fact that no experience remains in the human mind in isolated form. One never thinks of an item which is presented to one's senses without relating it to the other experiences which make up the content of one's thinking. If the relations in which ideas are brought together in one's mind are purely accidental, as they are when a training of ideas passes through the mind in periods of idle fancy, then the individual gains little for his present training or future adaptation. If, on the other hand, the relations established by attentive thinking are carefully guarded and critically perfected, it is possible to prepare in a most productive way for action and for later constructive thinking.[43]
>
> . . . the highest powers of the mind are general not particular, . . . mental

[42] C. H. Judd, *The Psychology of High School Subjects* (Boston: Ginn and Co., 1915), p. 413.

[43] *Ibid.*, p. 417. See also C. H. Judd, *Educational Psychology* (Boston: Houghton Mifflin Co., 1939), pp. 514–515.

development consists not in storing the mind with items of knowledge nor in training the nervous system to perform with readiness particular habitual acts, but rather in equipping the individual with the power to think abstractly and to form general ideas.[44]

Bagley, who also proposed a theory which resembled that of Judd, expressed his theory as follows:

> . . . functions may be improved by the application of "ideas" or procedure and method gained in other fields: or, inasmuch as the effective employment of any "idea" as a goal or aim of adjustment depends, as has been suggested in previous sections, upon the emotional coloring of the idea, it is better to use the term "ideal" to designate the agency that usually accomplishes the transfer. For example, the close thinking that is trained in mathematics may come to function in other fields, — in political economy or in psychology or even in the work of practical, everyday life, — provided that one has gained from the study of mathematics a certain respect or perhaps even reverence for the rigid, clear-cut mathematical method. If mathematics is taught, however, in a purely mechanical fashion, with no attempt to make its methods conscious to pupils or to give them an *appreciation* of the virtues of the method, the "spread" will manifestly be an uncertain quantity. Indeed, one may very easily be prejudiced against a method by poor teaching, and so resist any temptation to apply it to other situations.[45]

The Gestaltists have developed a theory to account for transfer which is also similar to that of generalization. They account for transfer in terms of "the development of meanings and the flexibility of habits." The term *transposition* is employed instead of transfer. By this term is indicated that a pattern of relationships discovered or understood through insight in one situation may become applicable in another, provided that the learner recognizes in the new situation the pattern of relationship which was familiar in the original. Since meaning consists in the perception of relations, then the more meaningful the materials and the deeper the understanding — that is, insight into meaning and relations — the greater will be the possibility that transfer will take place.

Lest it be assumed that the theories of *identical components* and *generalization* are mutually exclusive, it should be noted that transfer is a very complex process and includes not only *identical components* and *generalization* but also several additional elements to which insufficient attention has been devoted in the experimental investigations. These in-

[44] C. H. Judd, *Psychology of Secondary Education* (Boston: Ginn and Company, 1927), p. 441.

[45] W. C. Bagley, *Educational Values* (New York: The Macmillan Co., 1911), pp. 190, 191.

clude the *effort* exerted by the student, the *interest* in the subject matter, and the *attitude* of the learner.[46] Accordingly, both the theory of identical components and that of generalization are of practical significance. It is interesting to note that, while each theory attempts to describe *how* and *where* transfer takes place, neither explains *why* it takes place. These theories have failed to offer an explanation of the nature and cause of transfer. To some extent, Thorndike's theory of identical components is correct. However, because of his materialistic psychology, he was unable to explain how things perceived through the senses can be generalized. His inability to do so was due to an erroneous interpretation of the mind as "the sum of mechanical responses or habits." Likewise, the theories of generalization have failed to offer an explanation for a power or capacity which would account for the process of generalizing. In order to explain transfer as a process of generalization of experience, man must possess a power or capacity which makes such generalization possible.

What then constitutes an adequate explanation of transfer? Castiello has described it as the "spiritualization of learning."[47] By this he meant that transfer takes place through the medium of abstract ideas. The link which binds common elements together so that their similarities and differences no matter how slight are recognized, the link between and among specific experiences which enables the individual to generalize is his intellectual power of abstraction. It is this power which carries the mind to the heart of any problem, be it industrial, commercial, scientific, philosophical, or social. New problems are best solved by comparing them with old problems which have already been solved, but before the individual can perceive an analogy which will suggest a solution, he must reduce both the old and the new problems to their most abstract and general forms.

This, man can do because he possesses an intellect, the power to think, that is, to abstract the essence of objects and to form concepts; to judge, that is, to compare, identify, and discriminate these concepts; and finally, to reason, that is, to compare judgments, to formulate conclusions which become principles broadly applicable. It is because the soul is a spiritual entity that a human being can form universal ideas, and it is because he can form universals that transfer can take place.

Because man has this power of abstraction, he is able to learn; that is,

---

[46] T. V. Moore, *Cognitive Psychology* (Philadelphia: J. B. Lippincott Co., 1939), p. 475.

[47] J. Castiello, S.J., *Geistesformung*, p. 136.

he has the power to discern the essence of objects, to note similarities and differences, to classify objects and ideas, that is, to arrange them in a logical organization according to the differences which they manifest, and then to generalize, that is, to reason out conclusions or general methods of meeting problems and situations whether in classroom or in life. In a word, transfer depends upon man's abstract reasoning power by which he consciously adapts means to ends. All of education must then be a process of building concepts, of training in accurate judgment, and of guidance of the reasoning process. School subjects are valuable for transfer in proportion as they impart an interest and facility in abstract thinking. In this way alone can transfer be facilitated, for through his intellectual process man assimilates the methods, the ideals, the principles which he will employ in meeting all of the situations, both simple and complex, in his life. Education of necessity consists of training in thinking, in judging, in reasoning, in logical organization, and not merely in habit formation and drill. While habits are utilized in all of life's activities, it is well to remember that they are under the control of the intellect and of the will. Accordingly, there is no warrant for the notion that education should be satisfied merely to equip the individual with specific items of information and with specific skills. It is of interest to note the following paragraph with which McGeoch has closed his chapter on transfer:

> The learning of complex, abstract, meaningful materials, and the solution of problems by means of ideas (reasoning) are to a great extent functions of transfer. Where the subject "sees into" the fundamental relations of a problem or has "insight," transfer seems to be a major contributing condition. It is, likewise, a basic factor in originality, the original and creative person having, among other things, unusual sensitivity to the applicability of the already known to new problem situations. Perceiving, at whatever level, is probably never free of the influence of transfer. In a word, there is no complex psychological function or event which is not in some way a function of training.[48]

The essential test of learning is its transfer value and such transfer can be achieved only by promoting understanding, by generalizing insights, by making relationships meaningful in order that learning may be applied to a wide range of situations both within the classroom and also in life.

Factors Influencing Transfer of Learning. In considering the experi-

[48] J. A. McGeoch and A. L. Irion, *The Psychology of Human Learning,* 2 ed. (New York: Longmans, Green and Co., 1952), p. 347.

mental evidence of transfer of learning, the findings of Orata's 1941 summary of the research in the field were quoted. The third of these findings was to the effect that the experimental evidence indicated that the amount of transfer is influenced by many factors. It is the purpose of the present section to indicate briefly several factors which both influence the amount of transfer and also have a significant bearing upon the work of the teacher. From among the many influential factors the following three have been selected for consideration in this section as having the greatest significance for the teacher: (1) *mental ability of the learner;* (2) *method of teaching;* (3) *attitude of the learner.*

MENTAL ABILITY OF THE LEARNER. Among the statements made by Whipple in his summary of transfer investigations was one to the effect that the amount of transfer depends upon native ability, that teachers may expect bright children to surpass dull children in amount of transfer. This fact has been substantiated experimentally in investigations which have demonstrated that a positive correlation exists between amount of transfer and degree of intelligence. Among the investigations demonstrating that amount of transfer is positively related to mental ability were those made by Brooks,[49] by Thorndike,[50] by Carroll,[51] by Ryans,[52] by Pratt.[53] Overman,[54] likewise, in his story of factors affecting transfer noted that the procedures of "generalization" and "rationalization" were most effective with students who ranked in the upper third of the group with respect to mental age.

METHOD OF TEACHING. Method signifies a definite way of performing a task. It involves, particularly, careful selection of materials, the

[49] F. D. Brooks, "The Transfer of Training in Relation to Intelligence," *Journal of Educational Psychology,* 15:413–422, 1924.

[50] E. L. Thorndike, "Mental Discipline in High School Studies," *Journal of Educational Psychology,* 15:1–22; 83–98, 1924; also C. R. Broyler, E. L. Thorndike, and E. Woodyard, "A Second Study of Mental Discipline in High School Studies," *Journal of Educational Psychology,* 18:377–404, 1927.

[51] H. A. Carroll, "Generalization of Bright and Dull Children, a Comparative Study with Reference to Spelling," *Journal of Educational Psychology,* 21:489–499, 1930.

[52] D. G. Ryans, "An Experimental Study of Transfer of Training with Special Attention to the Relation of Intelligence Test Performance," *Journal of Educational Psychology,* 27:492–500, 1936.

[53] K. C. Pratt, "Intelligence as a Determinant of the 'Functional' Value of Curricular Content," *Journal of Educational Psychology,* 29:44–49, 1938.

[54] J. R. Overman, *An Experimental Study of Certain Factors Affecting Transfer in Arithmetic* (Baltimore: Warwick and York, Inc., 1931). See also S. G. DiMichael, "The Transfer Effects of a How-to-Study Course Upon Different I.Q. Levels and Various Academic Subjects," *Journal of Educational Psychology,* 34:166–175, 1943.

adaptation of these materials to the abilities of the students, the organization and presentation of materials in logical sequence. It implies choice of a means in order to accomplish an end. It involves both understanding of the means and direction and application of the means to the accomplishment of the desired end. In the school situation where the *understanding* of the means includes a process of generalizing facts, ideas, values, and procedures and where the *direction* has included a clear cut indication of where and how the facts, ideas, values, and procedures apply both in other subjects and in life, then transfer is facilitated. Many experimental investigations conducted in classroom situations have demonstrated that methods of teaching which sought for interrelationships among ideas and experiences, and which provided opportunities to apply principles appropriately in varied situations, constituted a more significant factor in facilitating transfer than did the subject-matter materials studied.

The first of these experimental investigations is among the best known and most frequently referred to in the literature of transfer. Overman,[55] using elementary school children as subjects and arithmetic as the material studied, demonstrated that various types of instruction in the process of generalizing and reasoning facilitated transfer. Not only was transfer greater in amount when the subjects were instructed in the process of generalizing procedure from practice with specific problems, but also the amount of transfer increased significantly when the subjects were taught both to generalize on procedure and also to "rationalize," that is, to note reasons and principles involved in solving problems.

Woodrow,[56] making use of the three group technique with college students as subjects, demonstrated that practice in memorizing plus instruction in and discussion of methods of memorizing led to significant improvement. Salisbury,[57] using junior and senior high school pupils as subjects and measuring the effect of instruction in methods of outlining and summarizing upon test scores in intelligence, in reading, and in several subject-matter fields, further corroborated the fact that methods of teaching constitute an important factor in transfer. Meredith,[58] using

[55] J. R. Overman, *op. cit.*

[56] H. Woodrow, "The Effect of the Type of Training Upon Transference," *Journal of Educational Psychology,* 18:159–172, 1927.

[57] R. Salisbury, "A Study of the Transfer Effects of Training in Logical Organization," *Journal of Educational Research,* 28:241–254, 1935.

[58] G. Meredith, "Consciousness of Method as a Means of Transfer of Training," *Forum of Education,* 5:37–45, 1927.

the three group technique in an endeavor to determine the effectiveness of instruction in the method of defining words together with instruction concerning the fundamental principles involved in the process of defining, found that such instruction was a significant factor in increasing the amount of transfer. Barlow[59] reported that considerable transfer resulted when training was given in methods of analyzing, abstracting, and generalizing.

Stephens has given five general rules for increasing transfer by the method of teaching used:

1. Bring out the feature to be transferred.
2. Develop meaningful generalizations.
3. Provide a variety of experiences.
4. Practice application to other fields.
5. Practice in transfer — just as students can learn to learn, so they may have some success in learning to transfer.[60]

Castiello stressed the importance of method of teaching as a factor in transfer as follows:

> Teachers who desire to obtain transfer should explicitly point out the *values* and *methods* which can be acquired in the learning of any subject, and should clearly indicate the possibility of transferring those *values* and *methods* to other fields.[61]

Likewise, in another work Castiello has made the following comment regarding the influence exercised by the two factors considered thus far in this section:

> The amount of transfer is in direct proportion to the degree of intelligence possessed and the method of teaching. A powerful intellect is capable of seeing many relations, unifying his knowledge more and, therefore, making much more transfer. That has been shown in an experiment by Overman. What Overman did not know is that he was restating St. Thomas' thesis on the synthetical power of "genius." The very intimate connection between method of teaching and transfer has also been proved by numerous experiments. In fact, it has been shown that the amount of transfer can be multiplied by five or six if the method is changed. That is what one would

[59] M. C. Barlow, "Transfer of Training in Reasoning," *Journal of Educational Psychology,* 28:122–129, 1937. See also R. C. Craig, *The Transfer Value of Guided Learning* (New York: Bureau of Publications, Teachers College, Columbia University, 1953); G. Katona, *Organizing and Memorizing* (New York: Columbia University Press, 1940); M. M. Kosteck, "A Study of Transfer: Sex Differences in the Reasoning Process," *Journal of Educational Psychology,* 44:449–458, 1954.

[60] J. M. Stephens, "Transfer of Learning," in *Encyclopedia of Educational Research,* C. W. Harris, ed., 3 ed. (New York: The Macmillan Co., 1960), p. 1542.

[61] J. Castiello, S.J., *Geistesformung,* p. 137.

expect. Narrow views and sheer mechanical drill coop up the mind. Breadth of intelligence and a capacity for linking up and unifying all knowledge must effect much more transfer from one field to another.[62]

ATTITUDE OF THE LEARNER. Undoubtedly, teachers have always recognized that the attitude of the learner necessarily plays a significant role in transfer. In spite of this general recognition, however, the experimental evidence for the significance of attitude as a factor influencing the amount of transfer is distinctly limited. Perhaps, the best known investigation on the effectiveness of the learner's attitude was made by Dorsey and Hopkins.[63] Using the equivalent group method and college students as subjects, the investigators sought to determine whether suggestions made to subjects concerning the performance of a task build attitudes on the part of the learner which result in transfer. Three situations were employed. In the first the suggestion was to use methods of study already acquired. In the second situation the suggestion was to use previous knowledge of Latin to determine the meanings of words in a test. In the third situation the suggestion was to use recently acquired knowledge of descriptive geometry in answering test questions. These suggestions that previous training was related to present tasks were made to the experimental group, but not to the control group. Both groups performed the same tasks. However, in every instance the experimental group accomplished better results and showed a significantly greater amount of transfer. The investigators maintained that the attitude of readiness produced by the suggestions was a very influential factor in producing transfer.

The Educational Implications of Transfer of Learning. Every course of study in both the elementary and secondary school is a testimony to the belief of educators in transfer of learning. The subjects taught in school are the means of education and not ends in themselves. They are means for the developing and the sustaining of desirable knowledge, skills, habits, ideals, values, and attitudes. They are the means for developing correct methods of reasoning and increased ability to make logical analyses. The amount of transfer which results from studying school sub-

---

[62] J. Castiello, S.J., *A Humane Psychology of Education* (New York: Sheed & Ward, 1936), p. 172.

[63] M. F. Dorsey and L. T. Hopkins, "The Influence of Attitude Upon Transfer," *Journal of Educational Psychology,* 21:410–417, 1930.

jects depends not merely upon the content of these subjects, but rather more upon the organization and method of presenting the subject matter. Transfer will not be automatic. The teacher and the pupil both must work to achieve it. The teacher is naturally and necessarily concerned with deriving the greatest value from the classroom experiences of his students. This involves primarily training in methods of abstracting, analyzing, organizing, and generalizing, in order to aid pupils in understanding and applying as many useful relationships and principles as possible. The teacher's purpose is to seek transfer to many activities and functions and to render each subject broadly productive in other fields. The teacher through his methods of instruction and guidance must endeavor to make the pupil aware of the principles, values, methods which are to transfer, must stimulate the pupils to make as wide as possible an application of what they have acquired in the study of each subject both to other subjects and to life situations.

Education is training applied to the whole personality. Regardless of the existence of individual differences, each pupil's concern is to make the most of himself and of all his mental powers. The method by which this is accomplished is persistent determination in the task of increasing his equipment of knowledge, of ideals, and of worthwhile habits in the best possible way, through the best methods of study and of work. Deliberate application of these methods in whatever tasks are undertaken and widespread utilization of all of these principles makes transfer most natural and most nearly automatic.

The purpose of all education is the achievement of human excellence. Education should transform the individual by training him to deal masterfully with existing conditions, and by training him to adjust himself effectively to his environment. A system of psychology, like specific-habit psychology, which reduces learning to mere efficiency, makes of education something other than personal development, something other than a training in the ways of approaching life tasks and of evaluating life experiences. Genuine education implies general training and transfer, for it is an interest which never becomes exhausted but which grows always broader and wider, improving everything one does. It is not mere possession of knowledge but ability to reflect on one's knowledge, to grow in wisdom, to develop oneself, to translate life's values into concrete acts.

EXERCISES

1. Outline this chapter.
2. List and define the terms which you have learned from your study of this chapter.
3. Distinguish between:
   a) Formal discipline and transfer;
   b) The theory of "identical components" and "generalization";
   c) Positive and negative transfer.
4. How is transfer best explained? What can be transferred? What means should be employed to obtain the maximum of transfer?
5. Why does the explanation and interpretation of transfer require a thorough understanding of the nature of man? of the nature of the mind? of the nature of the learning process?
6. In order to maximize transfer of learning, what changes in curricula and instruction should be made at one of the following levels:
   a) Elementary school?
   b) Secondary school?
   c) College?
7. How is transfer influenced by:
   a) Mental ability of the learner?
   b) Methods of teaching?
   c) Attitude of the learner?
8. Evaluate:
   a) Orata's studies of the experimental evidence in the field of transfer;
   b) Father Castiello's *Geistesformung;*
   c) Kolesnik's *Mental Discipline in Modern Education.*
9. Discuss the following statements:
   a) "Transfer takes place only where there is some conscious effort on the part of the learner."
   b) "All subjects possess potentialities for present and future transfer."
   c) "School subjects are valuable for mental training in proportion as they impart an interest and facility in abstract thinking."
   d) "A keenly analytic mind is one that can detect very minute similarities between things that look different."
   e) "The extent to which transfer of training is believed to take place will be a determining factor in the selection of the subject matter to be included in the curriculum."
   f) "Assimilation, organization, synthesis, evaluation, and application of materials studied will increase substantially transfer potential."
10. *a*) Explain the experimental techniques which have been used to determine transfer.
    b) Report on an experimental study in the field of transfer: state the problem; describe the subjects, the materials, the procedures; present the findings and the conclusions; give an evaluation of the experiment.

SELECTED REFERENCES FOR STUDY AND READING

Castiello, J., *A Humane Psychology of Education* (New York: Sheed & Ward, 1936), pp. 170–194 (reissued by Loyola University Press, Chicago, 1962).

Craig, R. C., *The Transfer Value of Guided Learning* (New York: Bureau of Publications, Teachers College, Columbia University, 1953).

Deese, J., *The Psychology of Learning,* 2 ed. (New York: McGraw-Hill Book Co., Inc., 1958).

Garrett, H. E., *Great Experiments in Psychology,* 3 ed. (New York: Appleton-Century-Crofts, Inc., 1951), Chap. V.

Grose, R. F., and Birney, R. C., *Transfer of Learning* (Princeton, N. J.: D. Van Nostrand Co., Inc., 1963).

Kolesnik, W. B., *Mental Discipline in Modern Education* (Madison, Wis.: University of Wisconsin Press, 1958).

McGeoch, J. A., and Irion, A. L., *The Psychology of Human Learning,* 2 ed. (New York: Longmans, Green and Co., 1952).

National Society for the Study of Education, Forty-Fifth Yearbook, Part I, *The Measurement of Understanding,* 1946.

——— Forty-Ninth Yearbook, Part I, *Learning and Instruction,* 1950.

Orata, P. T., *The Theory of Identical Elements* (Columbus: Ohio State University Press, 1928).

Stephens, J. M., "Transfer of Learning" in *Encyclopedia of Educational Research,* C. W. Harris, ed., 3 ed. (New York: The Macmillan Co., 1960), pp. 1535–1542.

Travers, R. M. W., *Essentials of Learning* (New York: The Macmillan Co., 1963).

Wesman, A. G., *A Study of Transfer of Training from High School Subjects to Intelligence,* "Contributions to Education," No. 909 (New York: Teachers College, Columbia University, 1945).

part V

MEASUREMENT AND EVALUATION

chapter 12

Measurement and Evaluation: An Overview

The Meaning of Evaluation. The effectiveness of the teaching-learning process is determined by means of evaluation. To evaluate means to ascertain the value of something. This something may be a total school program, a curricular procedure, an individual, or group of individuals. By means of evaluation the progress of the learner's attainment of his educational goals is ascertained, and the future direction toward these educational goals is determined. Moreover, evaluation is always qualitative and in terms of the educational maturity of the learner. Educationally, then, evaluation is that phase of the educative process which results in a practical judgment or assessment of the progress of, attainment of, or direction toward acceptable, suitable, and desirable educational goals, purposes, attributes, values, or objectives. The purposes of evaluation are threefold, namely, the adaptation of instruction in accordance with the differing and individual needs of students, the educational and personal guidance of the learner, and the appraisal of the total school program.

This process of evaluation involves four distinct operations: (1) the identification of the educational goals,[1] attributes, objectives, or purposes judged to be of value or worth in the specimen to be evaluated; (2) the development and employment of means to assess the educational goals or attributes validly and reliably; (3) the synthesis of the evidence yielded by these procedures into a final judgment of attainability and goodness of the desired change in behavior; and (4) the redefining

[1] For a classification of educational goals, see B. S. Bloom, ed., *Taxonomy of Educational Objectives* (New York: Longmans, Green and Co., 1956), pp. 62–200.

of these educational goals and purposes in terms of new and desired changes or directions necessitated by these practical judgments of the evidence.

The evaluation of the learner's readiness, progress, and attainment of educational goals should not be final, but should be a continuous assessment from the day he enters school until he leaves this educational setting. The evidence upon which the evaluative decisions are made should be valid, accurate, and comprehensive. Moreover, these value decisions should be arrived at by the cooperative effort of all the educational personnel involved in the process, including teachers and the learners themselves.

The physical, psychological, educational, and environmental factors are the areas to be evaluated continuously in an interrelated fashion. Specifically, the teacher should be concerned with student status and change in:

1. Subject-matter knowledge and skills;
2. Mental ability;
3. Work and study habits;
4. Attitudes;
5. Personal adjustment . . . ;
6. Individual and group relationships;
7. Interests and special talents;
8. Reading ability;
9. Health;
10. Physical condition;
11. Language usage;
12. Personal appearance . . . ;
13. Disposition;
14. Acceptance of responsibility.[2]

Measurement and Testing. Before it is possible to make a practical judgment regarding some aspect of status or change in pupil behavior, this change of behavior must be measured. Measurement means to quantify something. It implies some constancy of units. The methods of scaling, arranged in ascending level, are: (1) either/or procedure as, for example, Johnny can or cannot perform certain arithmetic problems; (2) qualitative description, Johnny solves arithmetic problems faster than Mary; (3) ranking, Johnny ranked third in a class of thirty in achieving

[2] A. Schwartz and S. C. Tiedeman, *Evaluating Student Progress in the Secondary School* (New York: Longmans, Green and Co., 1957), p. 22.

these math problems; and (4) the quantitative measurement, Johnny solved six complex problems in ten minutes.

Some of the means or measures employed in evaluating this student status or change are the interview, the questionnaire method, paper and pencil tests, performance tests, observation of behavior in lifelike and testing situations which employ rating sheets, checklists, and inventories.

Tests. One of the measures of evaluating student status or change is the psychological test. Such tests are objective, standardized instruments designed to measure some ability, aptitude, achievement, interest, or aspect of personality. Only a sample of the behavior in question is measured. The stimuli which will elicit the desired responses usually comprise a set or series of test items which may be blocks, designs, work-pairs, incomplete sentences, listing of various experiences, activities, or occupations, and the like.

Division of Tests. Most psychological tests may be classified according to:

1. ABILITIES MEASURED. There are three kinds of tests, namely, aptitude, achievement, and personality. Aptitude tests measure one's capacity for learning, i.e., what one can learn with further training. They measure the potential ability to acquire proficiency in an area with training. The three types of aptitude tests are: (1) general intellectual tests, from which is derived an overall estimate of intellectual functioning; (2) the multiple aptitude batteries which differentiate among an individual's special mental assets and liabilities; and (3) the special aptitude tests which measure capacity to acquire proficiency in specific areas of learning, such as music, art, or mechanics.

Achievement or educational tests are measures of the results of education, i.e., what one has actually learned as a result of study in a course, subject-matter area, or series of subject fields at a certain grade or level of education. The three types of achievement tests are survey, diagnostic, and prognostic. There are several types of personality tests, namely, interest inventories, attitude scales, tests of emotional adjustment, social traits, character, motivation, and study habits and skills.

2. ADMINISTRATION. There are tests which must be given individually such as the *Stanford-Binet* and the *Rorschach Test;* others may be administered either individually or in groups such as the *Stanford Achievement Tests* and the *Differential Aptitude Tests.*

3. MEDIUM OF MEASUREMENT. There are three ways of administering psychological tests, namely, orally, by means of paper and pencil tests, and by manipulating objects, mechanical appartus, pictures, or blocks; these last are called performance tests. The paper and pencil tests include the use of phonograph records, tape recordings, motion-picture film, television, printed test forms, and/or separate answer sheets.

4. LANGUAGES. Tests wherein written and/or spoken language is required either in the instructions to the examinees or in the test items or in both are designated as language tests. Most of the published psychological tests are of this type. Nonlanguage tests are those wherein no written or spoken language is employed either in the instructions, the test items, or both. The instructions for these tests are usually administered by gesture, pantomime, and demonstration. These nonlanguage tests are usually used with foreign-speaking, deaf, and illiterate persons. The *Pinter Non-Language Test,* the *Army Examination Beta,* the *Progressive Matrices, IPAT Culture Free Intelligence Test* are examples of nonlanguage tests.

5. RATE AND POWER. A pure rate or speed test such as the *Minnesota Clerical Test* is one which is concerned only with the number of easy questions or problems which a testee can perform in a specific period of time. A pure power test such as the *Stanford-Binet Scale of Intelligence* is concerned only with what one actually can do. However, most of the published psychological tests are combinations of rate and power tests wherein minimal emphasis has been placed on time limits.

Essential Characteristics of Psychological Tests. The characteristics which a worthwhile psychological test should have are five, namely:

1. Standardization;
2. Objectivity;
3. Validity;
4. Reliability;
5. Practicality.

The first characteristic of psychological tests is *standardization.* This is the process of establishing uniform objectives, goals, and aims, which are suitable; uniform materials to be employed; uniform procedure in administering and scoring the test; uniform method of recording responses; uniform methods of interpreting and using test results. Moreover, the circumstances surrounding the administration of the test and the condition of the subject are presumed to be uniform. Thus every detail of the test and the test situation is as uniform as possible for all the testees.

When a test is standardized, norms are established. Norms describe the typical test performance of reference groups of students of various ages or grades on whom the test was standardized. This reference group is called the standardization sample, which is a large, representative group of the type of individual for whom the test has been designed. Without norms, the test scores or results would be meaningless.

There are two kind of norms, namely, national and local. National norms are established to compare any testee's results with the typical test performance of individuals in the nation for whom the test is constructed. These national norms are those which are most frequently published in test manuals. Local norms are those established for a more localized population, such as those for a region, state, particular school system, or specific school. Local norms are always more important and meaningful for many users than are published norms.

There are two types of norms most frequently employed in schools, namely, age and grade norms, or the combined age and grade norms. Age or grade norms are scores or values which represent average or typical performance for persons classified according to age or grade, respectively. The two most commonly employed means or forms of expressing norms are percentiles and standard scores. A percentile is an individual's rank in a standard group of 100 persons which represents the total range of the standardization sample. This means that if a student obtains a percentile rank of 84 or achieves at the 84th percentile on a particular test, his standing is considered to surpass 84 percent of the standardization sample for this test. It also indicates that 16 percent of the standardization sample excel this individual's test performance. Standard scores are derived scores obtained by transforming raw or original scores so that they have a normal distribution with a fixed mean and standard deviation.[3]

The second characteristic of standardized psychological tests is *objectivity,* which refers to the extent to which the opinions of the scorer have been eliminated in the scoring of the test. The conditions under

[3] See Chapter 15 for an explanation of normal distribution, mean and standard deviation.

which the test is given and scored must be so explicit that different persons giving and scoring the same test will arrive at the same test scores. This means that there is no chance for subjective estimate or judgment on the part of the scorer. Objectivity means greater accuracy in scoring. This objectivity has been obtained by the form in which the test items are stated; that is, the fact that in well-constructed tests only one answer or one series of answers, determined at the time of construction of the test, satisfies the requirements of the test item. Objectivity has been secured also by the use of mechanical methods of scoring the exercises of the test.

The third and most important single characteristic of psychological tests is its *validity* which is the truthfulness of the test. It refers to the degree to which the test actually measures that which it claims to measure. Validity should indicate the degree to which the test is capable of achieving its specified aims.

There are four types of validity, namely, content, predictive, concurrent, and construct validity. These four types of validity are not all discrete and a test may involve information about all types of validity. *Content* validity refers to an analysis of the extent to which the content of the test samples the subject matter or behavior domain about which inferences are to be drawn. The sampling of the test content must be representative or adequate. This type of validity is essential in achievement and proficiency measures. *Predictive* validity refers to the effectiveness of a test in predicting some future outcome. The usual means of ascertaining this type of validity is to find the relationship between test scores and a subsequent criterion measure. The statistical technique which is most frequently employed in discovering this relationship is the coefficient of correlation, which is simply the relationship between any two sets of scores. The criterion measures most frequently cited in test manuals are general academic achievement, on-the-job performance, and performance in specialized training. School grades, promotion and graduation records, educational test scores, and special distinction or awards are some of the specific indices employed as criterion measures of achievement. Predictive validity is most relevant in the selection and classification of personnel. The third type of validity is *concurrent* validity. It is a statistical relationship between test scores and measures of criterion performance or status obtained at approximately the same time. An example of this type of validity would be to compare test scores of college students with their cumulative grade-point averages which were obtained at approximately the same time. The only difference between concurrent and predictive validity is the time element. However, concurrent validity may not have predictive validity. This type of validity is frequently used in differentiation of vocational groups and in the classification of patients. *Construct* validity refers to the logical and empirical analysis of the psychological qualities which a test measures. It demonstrates that certain theoretical constructs or traits account to some extent for performance on the test. In intelligence tests, construct validity is determined by means such as age differentiation, correlation with other tests, and factor analysis.

The fourth characteristic of psychological tests is *reliability* which denotes the accuracy, consistency, and stability of test scores. Reliability means the degree to which a test accurately or consistently measures the abilities, achievements, interests, or personality factors which it attempts to measure. The reliability of a test is expressed in terms of a reliability coefficient. There are three types of reliability coefficients, namely, the coefficients of stability, equivalence, and internal consistency. The coefficient of stability refers to the correlation between a test and its retest with an intervening period of time. This difference in score variance between the first and second administration of the test is due to the random daily fluctuations in the condition of the subject, in the testing environment, or both. The coefficient of equivalence is determined by correlating scores from two forms of a test obtained at essentially the same time. The error variance in this instance is due to the adequacy of test item sampling. The coefficient of internal consistency is based on an internal analysis of data obtained on a single trial of a test. The two most common methods of determining internal consistency are the split-half method and the Kuder-Richardson Formula 20 Method. The difference in the total scores between the one half and the other half of the test is due to two factors, namely, the adequacy of the test item sampling and the consistency of performance on all the test items. Other reliability coefficients are combinations of the above three.

An alternative means of expressing test reliability is the statistical technique termed the standard error of measurement, which is employed in interpreting individual scores. This standard error of a score estimates how adequately the individual's obtained score represents his true score.

The fifth characteristic of standardized psychological tests is *practicability* which refers to the test's economy in administration, scoring, interpretation, and recording, and to its facility in evaluating and using the test results. This means that the directions for giving and scoring the test, and for interpreting and recording the test results must be simple, clear, and easily understood, but at the same time complete and adequate. The provisions and directions for scoring, interpreting, and recording should be of such a type as to simplify the procedure and economize both time and effort as much as possible. Moreover, the test should be economical in the financial sense for any industrial or educational enterprise. Also, the tests developers must make available to the test user adequate norms for the groups or individuals to be tested by means of the specific measuring instrument. Furthermore, a guide indicating the test's unique value and utility, be it for purposes of survey, selection, diagnosis, or classification, must be provided.

Ethics. The American Psychological Association[4] has published a code of ethical standards for the control of use of psychological tests and diagnostic techniques. Three principles from the APA code are especially significant for test users. The first principle is concerned with the need for secrecy of test content. Test results are invalidated if the test content becomes too familiar to the testees. This may happen when exactly the same test items found in psychological tests are published in popular magazines, books, newspapers either for self-analysis or for descriptive purposes. Likewise, a well-intentioned but misinformed teacher may have her students practice on problems closely resembling those found in standardized intelligence or achievement tests. The second principle is concerned with restricting the use of psychological tests. This means that these tests should be sold and distributed only to qualified personnel who possess the qualifications, training, and supervised experience necessary to administer the tests and interpret the test results. With a minimum of training and experience, teachers, counselors, and school administrators may become qualified in the administration and interpretation of educational, vocational proficiency, and group intelligence tests. However, a longer period of training and supervised experience is necessary for administration and interpretation of individual intelligence tests and

[4] American Psychological Association, *Ethical Standards of Psychologists* (Washington, D. C.: American Psychological Association, 1953) and American Psychological Association, *Technical Recommendations for Psychological Tests and Diagnostic Techniques* (Washington, D. C.: American Psychological Association, 1954).

personality measures. The third principle is concerned with release of test results. This means that test scores and results should be released only to persons, including parents, who are qualified to interpret them. Likewise, in this regard, the privacy of the individual must be respected at all times. Before the testee reveals personal information about himself, he must be aware of the purposes of the test and also of the manner in which the divulged information will be used.

The Educational Significance of Measurement and Evaluation. Evaluation is considered one of the most important phases of the teaching-learning process. There are two types of evaluation, namely, the evaluation of each institution's total school program and the evaluation of each student's progress within the school. Every teacher should be intimately involved in both types of evaluation.

The concept of educational evaluation originated as a protest against the overemphasis placed upon specific knowledge and skills tests in the measurement field during the 1930's.[5] There was a need, at that time, for an assessment of the "whole child" and "the total school program" which would include the appraisal of such intangibles as character, attitude, and student personality. Then there followed a period of research concerned with the different techniques employed in the evaluation process. Today the institutional evaluation[6] is "action-research oriented" with the school's own personnel involved in the evaluation. In this way, school personnel are able to ascertain the values and defects within their own school programs and to remedy the situation if need be.

Each student's readiness for, progress toward, and attainment of desired goals must be continually evaluated. The teacher, the student, the parents, the school administrators, and counselors must share in this responsibility for evaluation. Moreover, this evaluation must be comprehensive in scope so that every facet of the student's educational progress is examined and his educational goals redefined in terms of his current status. The school personnel should employ as many media as

[5] For a summary of fifty years of objective measurement, see D. E. Scates, "Fifty Years of Objective Measurement and Research in Education," *Journal of Educational Research,* 41:241–64, December, 1947.

[6] For a sample of evaluative criteria, see National Study of Secondary School Evaluation, *Evaluative Criteria* (Washington, D. C.: National Study of Secondary School Evaluation, 1960). For samples of major evaluation projects, see P. L. Dressel, ed., *Evaluation in General Education* (Dubuque, Iowa: W. C. Brown Co., 1954); E. R. Smith, et al., *Appraising and Recording Student Progress* (New York: Harper and Row, 1942); and H. M. Bell, *Youth Tell Their Story* (Washington, D. C.: American Council on Education, 1938).

are necessary to evaluate the student's educational progress. These media may include the interview technique, standardized and teacher-made tests, observations, anecdotal records, checklists, the questionnaire method, and the cumulative record.

EXERCISES

1. Outline this chapter.
2. List and define the terms which you have learned from your study of this chapter.
3. Distinguish between:
   a) Evaluation and measurement;
   b) Measurement and testing;
   c) Language and nonlanguage tests;
   d) Rate and power tests;
   e) Content and construct validity;
   f) Predictive and concurrent validity;
   g) Reliability coefficients of stability, equivalence, and internal consistency.
4. List and discuss the classification of psychological tests.
5. Describe the different kinds, types, and means of expressing norms employed in schools.
6. List and discuss:
   a) The purposes, the process, the areas of educational evaluation;
   b) The essential characteristics of psychological tests;
   c) Ethical considerations with regard to psychological tests.
7. Discuss four types of validity and indicate what distinguishes each type.
8. Ascertain the extent of training and experience that teachers should have in order to interpret the results of: (*a*) group tests; (*b*) individual tests.
9. Discuss the following statements:
   a) "The effectiveness of the learning-teaching process is determined by means of evaluation."
   b) "Evaluation involves the illumination of the strengths and weaknesses of the child."
   c) "If a student is to get the most out of evaluation, he must help to evaluate."
   d) "All evaluative techniques should be directed toward determining the quality of the learning which takes place."
10. What is the educational significance of educational evaluation?

SELECTED REFERENCES FOR STUDY AND READING

Ahmann, J. S., and Glock, M. D., *Evaluating Pupil Growth,* 2 ed. (Boston: Allyn and Bacon, Inc., 1963).

Anastasi, A., *Psychological Testing,* 2 ed. (New York: The Macmillan Co., 1961), Chaps. 1 to 7.

Angoff, W. H., "Measurements," in *Encyclopedia of Educational Research,* C. W. Harris, ed., 3 ed. (New York: The Macmillan Co., 1960), pp. 807–817.
Baron, D., and Bernard, H. W., *Evaluation Techniques for Classroom Teachers* (New York: McGraw-Hill Book Co., Inc., 1958), Chaps. 1 to 4, 13, and 14.
Buros, O. K., *Tests in Print: A Comprehensive Bibliography of Tests for Use in Education, Psychology, and Industry* (Highland Park, N. J.: The Gryphon Press, 1961).
——— *The Third Mental Measurements Yearbook* (New Brunswick, N. J.: Rutgers University Press, 1949).
——— *The Fourth Mental Measurements Yearbook* (Highland Park, N. J.: The Gryphon Press, 1953).
——— *The Fifth Mental Measurements Yearbook* (Highland Park, N. J.: The Gryphon Press, 1959).
Cronbach, L. J., *Essentials of Psychological Testing,* 2 ed. (New York: Harper and Row, 1960), Chaps. 1 to 6.
Downie, N. M., *Fundamentals of Measurement: Techniques and Practices* (New York: Oxford University Press, 1958), Chaps. 1 to 5.
Furst, E. J., *Constructing Evaluation Instruments* (New York: Longmans, Green and Co., Inc., 1958), Chaps. 1 to 6.
Gerberich, J. R., Greene, H. A., and Jorgensen, A. N., *Measurement and Evaluation in the Modern School* (New York: David McKay Co., Inc., 1962), Chaps. 1 to 3.
Hagen, E., and Thorndike, R. L., "Evaluation," in *Encyclopedia of Educational Research,* C. W. Harris, ed., 3 ed. (New York: The Macmillan Co., 1960), pp. 482–485.
Lindvall, C. M., *Testing and Evaluation: An Introduction* (New York: Harcourt, Brace and World, Inc., 1961), Chaps. 1 to 3.
Nunnally, J. C., *Tests and Measurements: Assessment and Prediction* (New York: McGraw-Hill Book Co., Inc., 1959), Chaps. 1, 3 to 7, 18.
Remmers, H. H., Gage, N. L., and Rummel, J. F., *A Practical Introduction to Measurement and Evaluation* (New York: Harper and Row, 1960), Chaps. 1 to 6.
Rothney, J. W., *Evaluating and Reporting Pupil Progress* (Washington, D. C.: American Educational Research Association, 1955).
Schwartz, A., and Tiedeman, S. C., *Evaluating Student Progress in the Secondary School* (New York: Longmans, Green and Co., 1957).
Thorndike, R. L., and Hagen, E., *Measurement and Evaluation in Psychology and Education* (New York: John Wiley & Sons, Inc., 1961), Chaps. 1 and 2, 5 to 8.
Torgerson, T. L., and Adams, C. S., *Measurement and Evaluation for the Secondary School Teacher* (New York: Dryden Press, 1956), Chaps. 1 to 3, 24 to 27.
Wandt, E., and Brown, G. W., *Essentials of Educational Evaluation* (New York: Holt, Rinehart and Winston, Inc., 1957), Chaps. 1, 10.
Wrightstone, J. W., Justman, J., and Robbins, I., *Evaluation in Modern Education* (New York: American Book Co., 1956), Chaps. 1 to 4.

chapter 13

The Measurement of Intelligence

What the Measurement of Intelligence Involves. To measure means to describe quantitatively. However, there is no general agreement among psychologists at present concerning the meaning of intelligence. In fact, considerable confusion exists concerning the meaning of this term.[1] Yet it is desirable that a rigid definition of intelligence should precede all attempts at measurement. Intelligence is obviously akin to intellect. Both terms are derived from the Latin word *intelligere* which is composed of *intus* and *legere,* meaning to read within a thing the very reason for its being. *Intellect* is derived from the perfect passive participle of *intelligere,* while *intelligence* is derived from the present active participle. As these sources indicate, the intellect means man's cognitive capacity or power,

[1] Symposium, "Intelligence, Its Measurement," *Journal of Educational Psychology,* 12:123–147; 195–216, 1921. Among the many definitions of *intelligence* presented in the above article are included the following, which demonstrate the divergence of opinion among psychologists:

"The ability to do abstract thinking" (Terman).

"The ability to learn to adjust to one's environment" (Colvin).

"The power of good responses from the point of view of truth or fact" (Thorndike).

"The capacity to profit by experience" (Dearborn).

"Intellect plus knowledge" (Henmon).

"A biological mechanism by which the effects of a complexity of stimuli are brought together and given a somewhat unified effect in behavior" (Peterson).

"An acquiring capacity" (Woodrow).

"The ability to learn" (Buckingham).

"Quickness of learning, quickness of apprehension" (Freeman).

See also L. J. Bischoff, *Intelligence, Statistical Concepts of Its Nature* (Garden City, N. Y.: Doubleday and Co., Inc., 1954), pp. 5–18; F. S. Freeman, *Theory and Practice of Psychological Testing,* 3 ed. (New York: Holt, Rinehart and Winston, Inc., 1962), pp. 149–156.

while intelligence means the actual operation of the intellect. Hence, intelligence must be defined in terms of essential intellectual activities, particularly comprehension, judgment, and reasoning. Since intelligence means the exercise of cognitive capacity, then to measure the intelligence of an individual means to determine quantitatively the extent to which he is able to grasp, to understand, to judge, and to reason about realities that fall either directly or indirectly within his environment.

One of the great difficulties in defining intelligence is the fact that the word has acquired two meanings. Popularly, it means keenness or quickness or braininess; psychologically and educationally, it refers to mental age or brightness. From the educator's point of view the distinguishing feature of intelligence is the ability to make use of intellectual capacity to learn. The outcome of learning is knowledge, which begins with sensory experiences and implies perceptual capacity, reproductive and constructive imagination, attention, abstraction, judgment, and ability to reason. Likewise, there is implied memory, which preserves for further use the material presented by sensory experiences, and recalls it for further elaboration. It is important to test these mental activities which are accessory to cognitive functions; but, since they vary in the proportions in which they participate in man's intellectual activities, it is not advisable to test each separately. Therefore, they are included in the tests of general intelligence. Hence, for test purposes, intelligence is considered to be the active cognitive capacity together with such accessory mental capacities as perception, imagination, attention, and memory.

The measures of intelligence are examinations of general intelligence; that is, they are tests of operations of the intellect, of capacity to learn, rather than of information. These tests do not measure mechanical ability, character, physical stamina, social qualities, volition, or moral qualities. So far as education is concerned, they measure best the ability to succeed in school or in academic work or scholastic aptitude. This ability is considered innate. However, the intelligence tests do not measure innate intellectual capacity directly. What they measure is the manifestation of intellectual capacity in action or in behavior. They measure actualized potentialities. It is assumed in the intelligence tests that the behavior of the individual expresses or represents the maximum of which he is capable. From this behavior or action of the individual his general intellectual capacity is inferred. Intellect is native in virtue of the fact that man possesses a soul; but, for its proper functioning, environment and training are necessary. Therefore, at the moment of being tested, the native capacity of the individual is combined with the results of his training. Since training is thus always involved as a factor in determining present ability, it is necessary to determine how it is possible to distinguish native capacity from the results of training. It is important, likewise, to explain how it is possible to determine what differences among individuals are due to native capacity rather than to the types of training which they have received. Intelligence tests are designed to meet this difficulty, so far as possible, by the manner in which the activities, in which the individuals are to be tested, are selected from among those which are common to the experiences of all persons.

Intelligence tests are based upon certain assumptions. These are:

1. What has been learned is an index of what can be learned.
2. The training factor is constant; that is, the training or experiences in the activities which constitute the test have been equal or as nearly so as possible for all.
3. A typical functioning of a given ability can be secured for the purpose of testing.
4. Testing conditions can be controlled not only throughout a single testing period but also on subsequent occasions and by different examiners. These conditions include the explanation of the test, the time element, the attitude of the pupil, the effort which the pupil makes, and all factors which affect the performance of the child.

History of the Intelligence-Testing Movement.[2] The now familiar term *mental test* was used probably for the first time in 1890 by James McKeen Cattell, of Columbia University, in an article[3] describing tests which he administered to freshman classes. However, the first intelligence test, as that term is now understood, was devised in 1905 by Alfred Binet (1857–1911) and Theophile Simon. In 1904, the French Minister of Public Instruction appointed a commission of psychologists, physicians, and educators to formulate methods and to make recommendations for the instruction of the feebleminded children in the public schools of Paris. Binet and Simon were among that group. Binet at the time was director of the Laboratory of Physiological Psychology at the Sorbonne and editor of *L'année Psychologique,* which he had founded ten years previously.

[2] H. E. Garrett, *Great Experiments in Psychology,* 3 ed. (New York: Appleton-Century-Crofts, Inc., 1951), Chapters 1 and 2.

[3] J. M. Cattell, "Mental Tests and Measurements," *Mind,* 15:373–380, 1890.

As a direct outgrowth of the work of the commission, Binet and his collaborator, the physician Simon, published, in 1905, the first rough scale for measuring intelligence. By applying these tests to children of various ages, Binet found what was the average attainment of normal children of various ages in the various tests. He enlarged and revised the scale in 1908, arranging the tests into age groups. This scale is of particular historic interest because here for the first time Binet used the term *mental age*.[4] In 1911, shortly before his death, Binet made his final revision, arranging fifty-four tests in age groups from three years to the adult level.

Translations and revisions of the Binet-Simon test soon appeared in other countries. In Germany, William Stern adapted the test to the conditions of his country and for the first time made use of the term *mental quotient* as a measure of brightness. In England, the most authentic revision was made by Cyril Burt. In America, the first adaptation of the scale was made by H. H. Goddard in 1911. He translated the 1908 revision of the scale into English, made some changes in the terminology and in the position of certain tests, in order to adapt it to the experiences of American children. He used the scale at the Training School for the Feeble-Minded at Vineland, New Jersey, where he was chief psychologist. There he applied the test to four hundred feebleminded children. He also administered it to two thousand normal children attending the public schools of Vineland. Since that time, several other revisions have been formulated. In 1912, Kuhlmann, of the University of Minnesota, revised the scale; and, in 1922, hc modified it by extending it at both ends, beginning his tests at the three months' age level. In 1915, Robert M. Yerkes, of Harvard University, assisted by Bridges and Hardwick, revised the Binet scale and substituted the point scale for mental age as the unit of measurement. In 1916, Lewis M. Terman, of Leland Stanford University, and his colleagues devised the *Stanford Revision* of the *Binet-Simon Scale.* To the original scale Terman added the interpretation of fables, the vocabulary test, and the ball-and-field test. Terman made several other significant changes in the scale. The *Stanford Revision* contained ninety tests instead of the fifty-four originally devised by Binet.

---

[4] See F. L. Goodenough, "An Early Intelligence Test," *Child Development,* 5:13–18, 1934, for an account of an American physician, S. E. Chaille, who in 1887 developed tests for judging the mental level of young children. Chaille, although not using the explicit term *mental age,* seems to have implied the concept in his work. See also F. L. Goodenough, *Mental Testing, Its History, Principles and Applications* (New York: Holt, Rinehart and Winston, Inc., 1949), pp. 50–51.

Many of Binet's tests were moved up or down the scale. The tests were also evenly distributed at each age, carefully adapted to American children and conditions, and standardized. In 1922, John Herring, Director of the Bureau of Research, New Jersey Department of Institutions and Agencies, also revised the Binet scale. The *Herring Revision* contains thirty-eight tests.

In 1937 Terman,[5] in collaboration with Merrill, presented a new revision and a thoroughgoing refinement of the original *Stanford-Binet Scale.* This new revision was designed to remedy the major defects and limitations which had been recognized in the original revision. The improvements in the new revision included the following:

1. *Two equivalent forms (L and M) were provided.* These two forms, although differing in content, were equivalent in difficulty, range, reliability, and validity. Each form contained 129 test items. These two equivalent forms permitted retesting through the use of the parallel form.

2. *Extension was made at both upper and lower age levels.* The 1937 revision began at year two, whereas the lower limit of the original revision was year three. Between years two and five tests were provided at half-year intervals. Between years five and fourteen tests were provided for at year intervals. In order to provide an adequate measure for adolescent and adult years, one test was included for the Average Adult Level and three for the Superior Adult Level. This represented an addition of two tests at the Superior Adult Level.

3. *Standardization of the new revision was based upon large and representative populations of American born white children and youths between two and eighteen years af age.* Both urban and rural populations were sampled in tests given in seventeen communities, representing eastern, western, northern, and southern sections of the United States. Occupational groups were represented in proportions closely approximating those of the population at large.

4. *Instructions for giving and scoring the tests were defined precisely* in order to secure greater objectivity in administration and scoring.

In 1939 Kuhlmann[6] made a third revision of his original work on the

---

[5] L. M. Terman and M. A. Merrill, *Measuring Intelligence* (Boston: Houghton Mifflin Co., 1937), pp. 3–5.

[6] F. Kuhlmann, *Tests of Mental Development* (Minneapolis: Educational Publishers, 1939).

Binet Scale. This revision has been designated as *Tests of Mental Development.* It is an extension of the 1922 revision, containing eighty-nine tests and nineteen supplementary tests and making provision for determining mental age from four months to sixteen years.

In 1947 Cattell constructed the *Cattell Infant Intelligence Scale* which was an attempt to extend downward Form L of the *Stanford-Binet Scale.* It provides for a determination of mental age from two to thirty months.

In 1960 Terman and Merrill[7] made a third revision of the *Binet Scale* which is basically the same as the 1937 scale. This revision improved the general structure of the test and eliminated out-of-date content. The changes in the 1960 revision included the following:

1. *Only one form designated as L-M was provided.* The best subtests from the 1937 revision were selected and incorporated into a single scale. The basis of selection of the subtests was their difficulty level which was determined by comparing the percent of individuals passing single tests in the 1950's with the percent passing in the 1930's.

2. *The deviation intelligence quotient was introduced* to overcome the inadequacies of conventional ratio IQs. The deviation IQ means that the relative mental ability at different chronological ages remains the same. This deviation IQ is a standard score with an assured mean of 100 and a standard deviation of 16 and is based on the degree of deviation of an individual's score from that which is normal for his chronological age.

3. *Extension had been made at the upper age level.* The 1960 Pinneau revised IQ tables include the determination of the deviation IQ for individuals of seventeen and eighteen years of age. This extension was made because mental development seems to continue to at least age eighteen according to retest findings.

4. *Ambiguities of scoring principles and test administration were clarified to a greater extent.*

5. *At each age level, an extra or alternate subtest is provided* which may be substituted when a test has been spoiled during administration.

6. *An abbreviated scale is suggested* when time does not permit the administration of the entire test.

---

[7] L. M. Terman, and M. A. Merrill, *Stanford-Binet Intelligence Scale* (Boston: Houghton Mifflin Co., 1960), pp. 12–40.

In addition to the various revisions and extensions of the *Binet-Simon Scale* listed above, there have been devised other individual mental tests not based upon Binet's work. These individual tests include among others the *Merrill Palmer Scale* and the *Minnesota Preschool Scales.* Both of these individual tests have been designed for children of preschool age. Others include many of the nonverbal tests of intelligence or performance tests such as the *Arthur Performance Scale,* the *Pinter-Paterson Performance Scale,* and tests of a similar nature.

However, the administration of any of the various revisions of the Binet test requires from an hour to an hour and a half for each individual tested. Furthermore, the services of a skilled clinician are required to administer and to interpret adequately the individual tests. To overcome such a laborious and expensive process, Otis formulated the first tests which could be given to large groups at one time. In April, 1917, when America entered World War I, this test had not yet been published, so it was used by the committee appointed by the American Psychological Association to prepare a test for measuring adequately the varying degrees of intelligence of, and classifying, training recruits. This committee, under the direction of Yerkes, formulated two group tests. The first group test was the *Army Alpha* for literates, and the second group test was the *Army Beta* for illiterates. Each test required fifty minutes for examining a group of from 75 to 400 men. Between September, 1917, and January, 1919, these tests were administered to 1,727,000 men. The Army tests were the starting point for a host of group tests designed to measure general intelligence. Group tests are used most widely at present in schools and colleges, chiefly for classifying and guiding students.

The Individual Intelligence Test. The first successful individual intelligence test was devised by Binet and Simon. In order to understand this individual test, it is necessary first to know something of Binet's concept of intelligence upon which the method of testing and the scale were based. The *Binet Scale* was designed to measure general intelligence, which, according to Binet, is characterized by the mind's tendency to take and to maintain a definite direction, its capacity to make adaptations for the purpose of attaining a desired goal, and the power of self-criticism. In attention, in reasoning, in judgment, in constructive imagination the differences in intellectual ability are most likely to manifest themselves.

Hence, according to Binet, it is possible to sum up the notion of general intelligence in four words, namely, "comprehension, invention, direction, and censorship." De La Vaissiere[8] analyzed these four fundamental operations which were proposed by Binet to define general intelligence and demonstrated that they are in full accord with traditional and sound philosophy.

Having defined general intelligence, Binet had to devise a method by which the degree of intelligence possessed by individuals could be indicated. So he constructed a series of 54 tests involving complex tasks in time orientation, in comprehension of language, in knowledge about common objects, in free association, in number mastery, in induction, in the apprehension of contradictions, in the combination of fragmentary parts into a unit, in the understanding of abstractions, in memory span, in meeting new and unforeseen situations, in discrimination and comparison, in the interpretation of pictures and proverbs. These tests were based upon facts that all children would have ample opportunity to encounter under reasonably normal conditions, but that none or at least very few would have been trained to solve. Hence, in order to measure native intellectual ability, it was necessary that Binet in his scale avoid testing the materials commonly taught in the classroom. The basic assumption underlying the *Binet Scale* is that the more the child has learned, as compared with a group of individuals of the same age who have had approximately the same opportunities for acquiring the items measured, the greater is his intelligence as compared with the rest of the group. By means of these tests, it is possible to note the relative progress of intellectual expression with the age of the child, that is, whether he is intellectually advanced, or retarded, or average.

Throughout the history of the development of mental testing in America, the *Stanford Revisions,* 1916, 1937, and 1960, have been both the best known and the most widely used tests of intelligence employed in schools, clinics, and courts. Samples[9] of test items at the three different age levels contained in *Form L-M of the 1960 Revision of the Stanford-Binet* are presented here in order to give the student an idea of the nature of the test.

---

[8] See J. De La Vaissiere, S.J., *Educational Psychology* (St. Louis: B. Herder Book Co., 1930), p. 186.

[9] See L. M. Terman and M. A. Merrill, *Stanford-Binet Intelligence Scale, op. cit.,* pp. 71–73, 86–88, 99–102.

YEAR III

1. Stringing beads which involves complex motor coordination.
2. Picture vocabulary which involves recognition and recall of appropriate names for common objects in a picture.
3. Building a block bridge in imitation of the examiner's model.
4. Picture memories using four cards with animal pictures.
5. Copying a circle printed in record booklet.
6. Drawing a vertical line.

YEAR VII

1. Detecting absurdities in pictures.
2. Recognition of the similarity or likeness of two objects, such as "iron and silver."
3. Drawing a diamond from model in the record booklet.
4. Comprehension involving an understanding of what should be done in a definite situation as, for example, "What's the thing for you to do when you have broken something that belongs to someone else?"
5. Opposite analogies which is really a type of controlled association, as for example, "Snow is white; coal is ——."
6. Repeating in correct order without error, after a single reading, a series of five digits.

YEAR XII

1. Vocabulary. Definition of at least 17 words out of a list of 45 words arranged in order of difficulty.
2. Detection of verbal absurdities in brief narrative statements.
3. Response to picture by explaining what absurdity is represented therein.
4. Repetition of five digits in reverse order after a single reading.
5. Definition of abstract terms, such as "curiosity" and "grief."
6. Completion of sentences by filling in blanks where words are missing.

The *Wechsler-Bellevue Intelligence Scale*[10] was devised in order to meet the need for an instrument by means of which the mental ability of adults could be measured. This test, which is a point scale, has been designed for use at all age levels from adolescence (age 10 years) to 70 years. It is available in two parallel forms, I and II. Each form is composed of eleven subtests, five of which constitute the verbal scale and five of which make up the nonverbal or performance scale, while the eleventh subtest consists of a vocabulary test of 42 items which was originally used as an alternate, but is now usually included in the verbal scale. The

[10] This test was originally published in 1939 and revised in 1944. See D. Wechsler, *The Measurement of Adult Intelligence,* 3 ed. (Baltimore: Williams & Wilkins Co., 1944). Also for a discussion and an evaluation of this test see A. Anastasi, *Psychological Testing,* 2 ed. (New York: The Macmillan Co., 1961), pp. 303–334.

types of subtests which constitute the verbal scale are: general information, general comprehension, arithmetical reasoning, digits forward and backward, similarities. The performance scale consists of the following subtests: picture completion, picture arrangement, object assembly, block design, digit symbol. Scores on each test are transmuted into standard scores and the total of these scores is converted into IQ equivalents by means of a table which takes into account the age of adults. The *Wechsler-Bellevue* yields three quotients: a Verbal IQ; a Performance IQ; and a Full Scale IQ. This test has been widely used in clinics and is considered to be a very satisfactory and useful instrument for the measurement of the mental ability of adults.

In 1949 the *Wechsler Intelligence Scale for Children* (WISC) appeared. It is a downward extension of the *Wechsler-Bellevue* and has been standardized for ages 5 through 15 years. This test is composed of twelve subtests, two of which are alternates. In form it is very much like the *Wechsler-Bellevue,* consisting of a verbal scale and a performance scale. Each of these is made up of five subtests together with an alternate. It also yields an IQ based upon scaled scores for each age level, and a separate IQ can be derived from either the verbal or the performance scale.

In 1955 Form I of the *Wechsler-Bellevue Intelligence Scale* was revised, extended, and restandardized. It has been entitled the *Wechsler Adult Intelligence Scale* (WAIS).[11] It has been designed for use with adolescents and adults from age 16 to over 75. In organization it is composed of eleven subtests, six of which comprise the verbal scale and five of which constitute the performance scale. All eleven subtests, that is, both the verbal and the performance, are combined to make up the full scale. The verbal scale consists of the following subtests in order of administration: information, comprehension, arithmetic, similarities, digit span, and vocabulary. The performance scale consists of the following subtests in order of administration: digit symbol, picture completion, block design, picture arrangement, and object assembly. The six verbal and five performance tests yield scores which are converted into scaled scores. The verbal score is the sum of the scaled scores of the six verbal tests; the performance score is obtained by adding the scaled scores of the five performance tests; the full scale score is the sum of the verbal score and

[11] D. Wechsler, *Manual for the Wechsler Adult Intelligence Scale* (New York: The Psychological Corporation, 1955).

performance score. The verbal, performance, and full scale scores are converted into IQ's by reference to tables which take into account the age of the examinee. The WAIS yields three quotients: a Verbal IQ, a Performance IQ, and a Full Scale IQ.

The Group Intelligence Test. The first group test of intelligence was the *Army Alpha Intelligence Examination* which was used to classify men in the armed services during World War I. This test was formulated by the National Committee for the Psychological Examination of Recruits. Committee members were Yerkes, Bingham, Goddard, Haines, Terman, Wells, Whipple, and Otis. Five alternative forms of the *Army Alpha Test* were developed. Each form contained eight subtests, each with a definite time limit. Each subtest was sufficiently easy for every literate person to do some of it, and difficult enough so that no one, or at least very few, could do all of it in the allotted time. The eight subtests were composed of two hundred and twelve separate items including questions, exercises, and problems as follows:

1. Ability to understand oral directions
2. Arithmetical reasoning
3. Practical judgments
4. Synonym — antonym
5. Disarranged sentences
6. Number series completion
7. Analogies
8. General information

The *Army Alpha Test* was the basis for a large number of group tests designed to measure general intelligence. These group examinations have made use of other types of test materials in addition to the eight employed in the *Army Alpha.* These types include symbol substitution, verbal reasoning, facility in comprehending relationships, the interpretation of proverbs, facility in the use of numbers, vocabulary, memory span, speed of perception, constructive imagination, completion of sentences and of number series. Among the well known and widely used of these group tests are the following:

A. KINDERGARTEN AND PRIMARY SCHOOL LEVELS

1. *California Test of Mental Maturity*
2. *Kuhlmann-Anderson Intelligence Tests*
3. *Otis Quick-Scoring Mental Ability Tests*
4. *Pintner General Ability Tests: Verbal Series*
5. *Science Research Associates (S.R.A.) Primary Mental Abilities*
6. *The Lorge-Thorndike Intelligence Tests*

B. ELEMENTARY AND JUNIOR HIGH SCHOOL LEVELS

1. *Academic Promise Tests*
2. *California Test of Mental Maturity*
3. *Cooperative School and College Ability Tests*
4. *Henmon-Nelson Tests of Mental Ability*
5. *Kuhlmann-Anderson Intelligence Tests*
6. *Otis Quick-Scoring Mental Ability Tests*
7. *Pintner General Ability Tests: Verbal Series*
8. *S.R.A. Tests of Educational Ability*
9. *The Lorge-Thorndike Intelligence Tests*

C. SENIOR HIGH SCHOOL AND COLLEGE LEVELS

1. *Army General Classification Test (A.G.C.T.)*
2. *California Test of Mental Maturity*
3. *College Entrance Examination Board Scholastic Aptitude Tests* (college entrants)
4. *College Placement Test* (college entrants)
5. *Concept Mastery Test*
6. *Cooperative School and College Ability Tests (SCAT)**
7. *Differential Aptitude Tests* — verbal reasoning, numerical ability, and abstract reasoning tests
8. *Henmon-Nelson Tests of Mental Ability*
9. *Kuhlmann-Anderson Intelligence Tests* (Grades 9 to 12)
10. *Otis Quick-Scoring Mental Ability Tests*
11. *Pintner General Ability Tests:* verbal series
12. *S.R.A. Tests of Educational Ability*
13. *Terman-McNemar Test of Mental Ability*
14. *The Lorge-Thorndike Intelligence Tests*

Differential Factor Test Batteries.[12] Most of the intelligence tests discussed thus far are considered to be "global" in nature. This means that they yield one score which describes the overall intellectual functioning of an individual. Since about 1945 psychologists have been interested in the intraindividual differences on subtests of intelligence tests. Through factor-analysis "pure" or independent factors of intelligence are discovered which differentiate significantly among abilities essential for prediction of success in different curricula, courses of study, and occupations. Each of the tests in these intelligence test batteries measures a relatively inde-

* These tests have been designed to replace the *American Council on Education Psychological Examination.*

[12] For a discussion of the pioneer research works on differential factor test batteries, see T. L. Kelley, *Crossroads in the Mind of Man* (Stanford, Calif.: Stanford University Press, 1928), and L. L. Thurstone, *The Vectors of the Mind* (Chicago: University of Chicago Press, 1935).

pendent factor of mental functioning and for each of these tests in the battery separate norms are provided. Moreover, each of these tests is separately validated for different occupations, courses of study, and curricula.

Examples of these differential factor test batteries, which are also called differential-aptitude tests, multiple-aptitude batteries, multifactor tests, and multiple-factor tests, are the *S.R.A. Primary Mental Abilities,* the *Differential Aptitude Tests,* and the *Holzinger Crowder Uni Factor Tests.* The *S.R.A. Primary Mental Abilities* measures the following kinds of mental operations: verbal meaning, spatial perception, reasoning, number, and word fluency. At the lower levels it measures three other factors, namely, perceptual speed, quantitative and motor abilities. The *Differential Aptitude Tests* measure the following eight independent but not "factorially pure" abilities: verbal reasoning; numerical ability; abstract reasoning; space relations; mechanical reasoning; clerical speed and accuracy; language usage, Part I, which is a spelling test; and language usage, part II, which is a grammar, punctuation, and word usage test. These batteries, which yield a profile of an individual's score, were constructed primarily for educational selection and guidance.

The Performance Test. Children who have language disabilities, are deaf, illiterate, or have reading or speech difficulties could make but a poor showing on either the individual or the group intelligence tests, since these involve verbal ability. For this reason the performance and nonlanguage tests have been devised. These tests consist of the performance of various manipulative tests, do not make use of oral responses, do not require a knowledge of reading, and ordinarily may be administered without making use of the spoken word. Essentially these tests consist of concrete problems which the child can solve without the use of language. For this reason such tests are ordinarily designated as nonverbal. While there are various types of these tests, the underlying principles are the same in all. They involve the measurement of speed and accuracy of manipulative and perceptual abilities together with discrimination, judgment, and logical selection.

The individual performance tests usually make use of the form board which was first introduced by Seguin in his work with the mentally retarded. In this technique figures of various sizes and shapes are to be fitted into corresponding recesses of a board. Norms for the time required to fit the insets into the recesses have been established for various age levels. Likewise, these tests include variations of the picture puzzle technique including the feature profile, the manikin, the ship, and the mare and foal tests. The individual performance test is employed frequently in clinical practice to supplement the *Stanford-Binet* and similar types of largely verbal tests. Among the widely used individual performance tests are the *Arthur Point Scale of Performance Tests, Cornell Coxe Performance Ability Scale, Pintner-Paterson Scale of Performance Tests.*

The nonlanguage group tests originated with the *Army Beta Intelligence Examination,* which was devised and used in World War I for testing illiterates and non-English-speaking members of the armed forces. It was a nonverbal scale composed of a series of seven subtests. Each subtest consisted of a series of pictures or drawings which could be understood without the aid of language, since directions were administered by means of gestures and pantomime. A widely used group nonlanguage test is the *Pintner General Ability Tests — Non-Language Series,* for use in Grades 4 to 9, as is the *Goodenough Draw-a-Man Test.*[13] Another test which may be considered to be of this type is the *Davis-Eells Test of General Intelligence or Problem Solving* (Davis-Eells, Games) for use in Grades 1 to 6. This test is entirely pictorial in nature; and, while free of reading requirements, it requires that the child understand and respond to a variety of verbal materials since instructions are given orally by the examiner.

A third type of performance and nonlanguage test is that which has been devised to meet the needs of physically handicapped children. Tests of this type include the *Nebraska Learning Aptitude Test for Young Deaf Children* for use with deaf and hard-of-hearing children from 4 to 10 years of age, and the *Columbia Mental Maturity Scale* devised for cerebral-palsy children and others with impaired physical or verbal functioning. The age range on this test extends from 3 to 12 years. Both of these tests are administered individually.

A fourth type of performance and nonlanguage intelligence test is that which had been devised to test different cultural groups. These tests are designated as cross-cultural or culture-free tests wherein items common to many cultures are included and where test results are validated against multilocal criteria in varied cultures. In this type of test an attempt is made to eliminate or at least minimize the specific influences due to differences

[13] This test is suitable for use either as a group or as an individual test; see F. L. Goodenough, *op. cit.,* pp. 314–316.

in educational opportunities, training, social class, environment, etc., among cultural groups. Tests of this type include the *Cattell Culture Fair Intelligence Tests* with an age range extending from 4 years to superior and unselected adults and the *Progressive Matrices* which were developed in England by Raven and whose age range extends from 8 to 65 years.

Validity and Reliability of Intelligence Tests. *Test validity* means that the test truly measures what it claims to measure. The *Stanford-Binet* seems to have much content validity. Also, abilities seem to increase with age. The validity of intelligence tests when correlated with other individual or group intelligence tests ranges from moderate to high. The relationship between IQ and academic achievement such as school grades, teachers' ratings, and achievement test scores ranges from substantial to high with a median about .55. *Reliability* refers to the consistency of the test scores. The reliability coefficient of stability for the Stanford-Binet ranges from .46 to .85. This reliability coefficient seems to decrease with successive ages. The reliability coefficients for group intelligence tests seems to be high.

Mental Age. One of the most commonly used terms in connection with intelligence testing is *mental age,* the meaning of which should be understood clearly and its use known thoroughly. In order to make an individual's score on an intelligence test meaningful, measures of general intelligence have been standardized in terms of mental age. The term *mental age* expresses the individual's general ability as measured by the test at the time it was given, in comparison with average children of different ages. Hence, mental age is really a statement of the child's mental maturity or mental level at the time the test was given. Thus, a particular child whose achievement on the test is equivalent to that of the average ten-year-old has the general mental ability of a ten-year-old regardless of what the actual chronological age of the particular child may be. The average ability of children at each age is taken as the standard. This mental age may have little relation to the child's chronological age. *Mental age* means the degree of mental development of an individual as compared with the average person of a particular chronological age. This is determined by the scores made on the intelligence test. Therefore, a certain mental age means that the individual can attain about the same score in a test that the average person of that age does. Since mental age differs according to the test used, the name and form of the test as well as the date of administration should always be recorded. For example,

1. Oct. 3, 1962: *Stanford-Binet,* L-M form, MA 10 years 6 months.
2. Sept. 8, 1960: *Terman-McNemar,* Form D, MA 14 years 2 months.
3. Jan. 20, 1961: *Otis Self-Administering Examination,* Form C, MA 12 years 10 months.

The Intelligence Quotient. For practical purposes, it is both desirable and necessary to know more than the amount of general mental ability in terms of mental age. For this reason, the *intelligence quotient,* usually expressed as IQ, was devised. The intelligence quotient is a device by means of which is expressed the ratio which is secured by dividing the mental age by the chronological or life age of the child at the time of taking the test. This ratio is expressed as follows: $IQ = \frac{MA \times 100}{CA}$.
The mental age and the chronological age are both expressed in terms of months. Early in the history of intelligence testing, the German psychologist, Stern, noted that the ratio of the mental age to the chronological age was fairly constant. He proposed a measure for expressing this ratio which measure he termed mental quotient. Terman in revising the Binet Scale adopted this measure, but designated it the *intelligence quotient.*[14]

The pupil who has an MA of 10 years or 120 months and a CA of 10 years or 120 months has an IQ of 100. The pupil who has an MA of 12 years or 144 months and a CA of 10 years or 120 months will have an IQ of 120. The pupil who has an MA of 8 years or 96 months and a CA of 10 years or 120 months will have an IQ of 80. The IQ is usually considered to be a measure of capability and an indication of general ability to meet new experiences. If a child's IQ is close to 100, it is assumed that his mental development is equal to the mental development of the average child of his age. If the child's IQ is appreciably more than 100, it is assumed that he is brighter than the average child of his age. If the child's IQ is considerably less than 100, it is presumed that he is duller than the average child of his age. The classifications of IQ formulated by Terman, and later by Terman and Merrill, have been generally accepted in the field of educational psychology.

These classifications are presented in Tables 10 and 11 and in Figure 11.

[14] Several substitutes for IQ or alternative methods for indicating intelligence have been proposed. Among these are: *Index of Brightness* (IB); *Personal Constant* (PC); *Percentile Scores,* and *Standard Scores.* See F. L. Goodenough, *op. cit.,* pp. 189–212; J. L. Mursell, *Psychological Testing,* 2 ed. (New York: Longmans, Green and Co., 1949), pp. 395–396.

TABLE 10. Distribution of the 1937 Standardization Group[15]

IQ	Percent	Classification
160–169	0.03	
150–159	0.2	Very superior
140–149	1.1	
130–139	3.1	
120–129	8.2	Superior
110–119	18.1	High average
100–109	23.5	Normal or average
90–99	23.0	
80–89	14.5	Low average
70–79	5.6	Borderline defective
60–69	2.0	
50–59	0.4	Mentally defective
40–49	0.2	
30–39	0.03	

TABLE 11. Distribution of Intelligence Quotients in a Normal Population[16]

Classsification	IQ	Percentages of All Persons
Near genius or genius	140 and above	1
Very superior	130–139	2.5
Superior	120–129	8
Above average	110–119	16
Normal or average	90–109	45
Below average	80–89	16
Dull or borderline	70–79	8
Feeble-minded: moron	60–69	2.5
imbecile, idiot	59 and below	1

It is worthy of note that in using the term IQ the significance depends upon the test employed in determining the mental age. Therefore, since the IQs obtained from the various tests vary, the test should be reported with the IQ as, for example, *Stanford-Binet, Form L-M,* IQ, 95; *California Mental Maturity Test,* IQ, 110; *Kuhlmann-Anderson,* IQ, 90; *Pintner Non-Language,* IQ, 88.

---

[15] L. M. Terman and M. A. Merrill, *Stanford-Binet Intelligence Scale, op. cit.,* p. 18.

[16] Adapted from L. M. Terman, and M. A. Merrill, *Measuring Intelligence, op. cit.,* pp. 38–41; J. R. Gerberich, H. A. Greene, and A. N. Jorgensen, *Measurement and Evaluation in the Modern School* (New York: David McKay Co., Inc., 1962), p. 118.

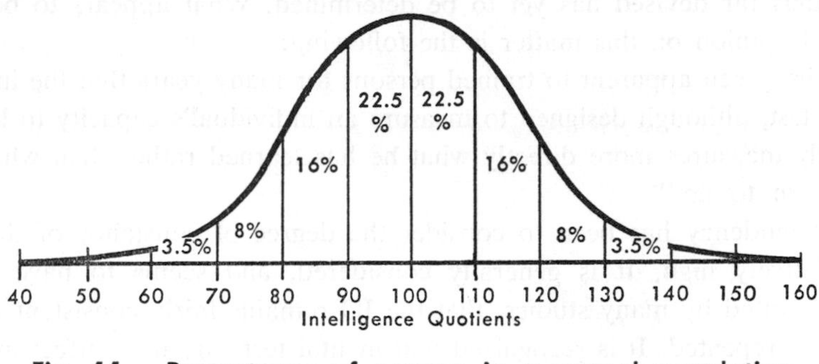

Fig. 11. Percentages of persons in a normal population at different levels of intelligence.

The Constancy of the Intelligence Quotient.[17] The usefulness of the intelligence quotient depends to no small extent upon the assumption that it will remain fairly *constant* or *stable* throughout the process of growth and development under ordinary or typical conditions of home and school life. The constancy of the intelligence quotient connotes that the ratio of mental age to chronological age remains approximately the same or at least does not vary greatly as the child grows older. If the child's intelligence quotient does remain constant or nearly so, i.e., if the fluctuations are relatively small, then the IQ possesses high predictive value as a means for indicating the probable rate of the future mental growth of the child. Thus an IQ of 100 will mean that the child probably has grown, is growing, and will continue to grow at an average rate in mental ability. An IQ of 120 will mean that the child probably has grown, is growing, and will continue to grow in mental ability more rapidly than the average. An IQ of 80 will mean that the child probably has grown, is growing, and will continue to grow less rapidly than the average.

The constancy of the IQ has been considered to be an aspect of the comprehensive problem of the influence of heredity and environment. Presumably, if intelligence tests could measure innate intellectual capacity directly, then it should be expected that environmental influences would be ineffective in modifying intellectual capacity. However, the extent to which native intellectual capacity is measured by means of the intelligence

[17] See N. Bayley, "On the Growth of Intelligence," *American Psychologist,* 10: 805–818, 1955; S. R. Pinneau, *Changes in Intelligence Quotient: Infancy to Maturity* (Boston: Houghton Mifflin Co., 1961); J. McV. Hunt, *Intelligence and Experience* (New York: The Ronald Press Co., 1961).

tests thus far devised has yet to be determined. What appears to be the general opinion on this matter is the following:

"It has been apparent to trained persons for many years that the intelligence test, although designed to measure an individual's capacity to learn, actually measures more directly what he has learned rather than what he can learn to do."[18]

The tendency has been to consider the degree of constancy of the IQ as relatively high. It is generally considered, and seems to have been demonstrated by many studies, that the IQ remains fairly consistent when tests are repeated. It is recognized that mental tests are not perfect instruments and consequently that moderate variations may sometimes occur. However, the literature on the topic also contains studies in which radical changes in IQ, increases in particular, have been reported. While very large changes in IQ are not to be expected generally and are not the usual rule, yet, when such sizable variations do occur, they have been accounted for in various ways. Among the explanations offered are included the following: inadequacies of tests; major changes in environment involving radical improvement of surroundings and opportunities; improvement in the cooperation of the child with the tester; removal of emotional blockings or other interferences with maximum performance in the test; changes in physical organism involving the functioning of the endocrines and the nervous system.

The constancy of the IQ has been the subject of controversy since the very beginnings of the mental test movement. Binet, the founder of the movement, appears to have been aware of the problem, for he wrote:

> Some recent philosophers appear to have given their moral support to the deplorable verdict that the intelligence of an individual is a fixed quantity, a quantity which cannot be augmented. We must protest and act against this brutal pessimism. We shall endeavor to show that it has no foundation whatsoever.[19]
>
> A child's mind is like a field for which an expert farmer has advised a change in the method of cultivating, with the result that in place of desert land, we now have a harvest. It is in this particular sense, the only one which is significant, that we say that the intelligence of children may be increased.

[18] L. G. Humphreys and P. L. Boynton, "Intelligence and Intelligence Testing," in *Encyclopedia of Educational Research,* W. S. Monroe, ed., rev. ed. (New York: The Macmillan Co., 1950), p. 602.

[19] Alfred Binet, *Les Idées Modernes Sur Les Enfants* (Paris: Ernest Flammarian, 1909), p. 141.

One increases that which constitutes the intelligence of a school child; namely, the capacity to learn, to improve with instruction.[20]

Early in the history of intelligence testing in America, Terman and Bagley engaged in a controversy regarding the constancy of the IQ. Terman[21] maintained that intelligence is essentially a native function which is relatively unaffected by school training or other environmental factors and that, therefore, given a child's IQ, the limits of his educability can be predicted accurately. Bagley,[22] however, characterized this belief as *educational determinism* and insisted that intelligence is influenced by schooling and other environmental factors including experiences, activities, guidance, and the like. Bagley maintained that education, far from being merely an expression or concomitant of intelligence, plays a positive and indispensable role in the development of intelligence and that, perhaps, in a limited but very real sense, education operates as an equalizing force among individuals of varying degrees of native intelligence.

The controversy concerning the constancy of the IQ became heated again during the late 1930's when a series of studies made at the University of Iowa, particularly the investigations made by Wellman,[23] Skeels,[24] and Skodak,[25] reported evidence of very large improvements in the IQ. The Iowa studies proposed to demonstrate the possibility that the IQ is influenced in a significant manner by favorable environment including nursery school training and placement in carefully selected foster homes. Stoddard[26] has presented analyses and interpretations of these studies.

---

[20] *Ibid.*, p. 146. The citations quoted above were translated by G. D. Stoddard and used by him in an article. "The I.Q.: Its Ups and Downs," *Educational Record,* 20:44–57, 1939, Supplement No. 12.

[21] See L. M. Terman, *The Intelligence of School Children* (Boston: Houghton Mifflin Co., 1919), pp. 268–269; also L. M. Terman, "The Psychological Determinist or Democracy and the I.Q.," *Journal of Educational Research,* 6:57–62, 1922.

[22] See W. C. Bagley, *Determinism in Education* (Baltimore: Warwick and York, Inc., 1925), pp. 11–46. Also W. C. Bagley, "Educational Determinism or Democracy and the I.Q.," *School and Society,* 15:373–384, 1922. W. C. Bagley, "Professor Terman's Determinism: A Rejoinder," *Journal of Educational Research,* 6:371–385, 1922.

[23] B. L. Wellman, "The Effect of Preschool Attendance on the I.Q.," *Journal of Experimental Education,* 1:48–69, 1932.

[24] H. M. Skeels, "Mental Development of Children in Foster Homes," *Journal of Consulting Psychology,* 2:33–43, 1938. Also H. M. Skeels, R. Updegraff, B. L. Wellman, and H. M. Williams, *A Study of Environmental Stimulation,* University of Iowa Studies in Child Welfare, Vol. XV, No. 4, 1938.

[25] M. Skodak, *Children in Foster Homes: A Study of Mental Development,* University of Iowa, "Studies in Child Welfare," Vol. XVI, No. 1, 1939.

[26] G. D. Stoddard, *The Meaning of Intelligence* (New York: The Macmillan Co., 1942), especially pp. 343–352; 382–392; "The I.Q.'s: Its Ups and Downs," *Educational Record,* 20:44–57, 1939, Supplement No. 12; also National Society for the

However, other subsequent investigations have not succeeded in producing results uniformly similar to those obtained in the Iowa Studies, although some studies have indicated the possibility of a change in IQ as a result of improved environment. A great deal of criticism was directed toward these studies, especially by Simpson,[27] Goodenough,[28] and McNemar[29] who attacked the Iowa Studies chiefly upon the basis of inadequacy of sampling and the use of questionable statistical procedures.

The problem of the constancy of the IQ remains unsettled at the present time. In spite of the large number of studies made to determine the constancy, the results still seem to be inconclusive. However, the general conclusion seems to be that data concerning the intelligence quotient indicate a considerable, but by no means absolute, constancy.

Whether or not the answer to the question of the constancy of the IQ is ever known with certainty, the teacher should be aware of the controversial nature of the problem and of the implications arising from it.

Educational Uses of Intelligence Tests. The functions and uses of tests of mental ability which have become a recognized feature in educational procedure are many. Among them are the following:

1. To aid in determining readiness to do schoolwork;
2. To classify pupils in accordance with their ability to learn so that their tasks may be sufficiently difficult but still within their ability;
3. To aid in selecting for special instruction and treatment the slow learning, and the retarded;
4. To aid in identifying pupils of superior mental ability;
5. To aid in the diagnosis of the causes of learning difficulties and failures;
6. To aid in the process of educational, occupational, and vocational counseling;

Study of Education, Thirty-Seventh Yearbook, Part II, *The Scientific Movement in Education,* 1938, 421–434; and National Society for the Study of Education, Thirty-Ninth Yearbook, Parts I and II, *Intelligence, Its Nature and Nurture,* 1940.

[27] B. R. Simpson, "The Wandering I.Q.: Is it Time for It to Settle Down?," *Journal of Psychology,* 7:351–367, 1939; 9:31–48, 1940.

[28] F. L. Goodenough and K. M. Maurer, "The Relative Potency of the Nursery School and the Statistical Laboratory in Boosting the I.Q.," *Journal of Educational Psychology,* 31:541–549, 1940. See also National Society for the Study of Education, Thirty-Ninth Yearbook, Part II, 1940, pp. 161–178; 361–384.

[29] Q. McNemar, "A Critical Examination of the University of Iowa Studies of Environmental Influences Upon the I.Q.," *Psychological Bulletin,* 37:63–92, 1940.

7. To help in dealing with the problems of emotionally and socially maladjusted children, particularly in a clinical situation;
8. To aid in the selection of students seeking admission to colleges and professional schools;
9. For research purposes such as in studies of overachievement and underachievement, longitudinal studies, and studies of variations in pupil performances resulting from other factors with intelligence being held constant.

It is well to note, however, that the usefulness of tests of mental ability depends upon the proper selection of the test in terms of the situation in which and the purpose for which it is to be used. In addition, the usefulness of test results is dependent upon the accuracy with which the test is administered and scored and, likewise, upon the carefulness with which the results are interpreted.

Limitations of the Intelligence Tests. Some enthusiastic educators have claimed for the intelligence tests values which cannot be substantiated. There are limitations in these tests which are recognized and understood by those familiar with their nature, their use, and their interpretation. There are certain things which these tests do not and cannot discover. Hence, caution must be exercised in the use and interpretation of these tests.

1. Intelligence tests must not be considered to constitute the final gauge of an individual's intellectual capacity. The fallibility of these tests should be recognized. However, it is well to note that many of the limitations are not of the tests, but are limitations of the tester's ability to make scientific observations and interpretations. It is particularly unwise to estimate intelligence on the basis of a single test.

2. Intelligence tests are not designed to discover distinctive qualities, mental habits, or special talents, but are intended to be measures of general intellectual capacity. Therefore, the intelligence tests cannot measure school accomplishments, but only the probable rate at which the child could learn under favorable conditions, and if he worked up to his full capacity.

3. Intelligence tests should not be considered the sole criteria to be used in classifying children in school, because such important factors as industry, interest, social adaptability, perseverance, dependability, and emotional stability are not measured by intelligence tests.

4. Intelligence tests suffer their greatest limitation perhaps in the fact

that their use has caused attention to be centered upon intelligence to the detriment of other capacities. Intellectual capacity, while of utmost importance for educational development, should not take precedence over character formation.

Educational Significance of Measurement of Intelligence. A very significant contribution which could be made by psychology to education would be the means for complete and accurate measurement of intellectual capacity. The present-day intelligence tests are definite steps toward the accomplishment of this goal. These tests, which are now an accepted educational necessity, will have more important bearing on the educational practices of the future, particularly in the sphere of diagnosis and prognosis. In fact, at the present time, the IQ is considered to be probably the most important and meaningful information[30] that may be had about a pupil's intellectual ability. To the teacher, the IQ is evidence of the innate possibilities of the pupil whom he must guide, direct, and instruct. At the present time, because of the fact that many research studies have revealed that there exists a high correlation between the results of intelligence tests and success in school, curricula have been modified to accommodate differences in intellectual ability. Likewise, at the present time, admission to college is determined in part by intelligence tests. Perhaps the greatest significance of the intelligence tests is the fact that they are based upon the concept of a general intelligence which can be affected to a significant degree by special training and which can be influenced in a substantial measure by specific learning activities. This should influence the trend toward mental discipline in education.

EXERCISES

1. Outline this chapter.
2. List and define the terms which you have learned from your study of this chapter.
3. How do you account for the lack of agreement among psychologists concerning the meaning of intelligence? Which definition presented in the symposium referred to in footnote 1 is most acceptable?
4. Present a brief history of mental testing.

---

[30] "The I.Q. itself is under attack and may in time be replaced by a more satisfactory measure," J. R. Gerberich, H. A. Greene, and A. N. Jorgensen, *op. cit.*, p. 119.

5. Distinguish between:
   a) Intellect and intelligence;
   b) Global and multifactor intelligence tests;
   c) Verbal and culture-free intelligence tests;
   d) Quotient-type and deviation-type intelligence quotients.
6. Explain the validity and reliability of mental tests.
7. List and discuss:
   a) The assumptions upon which mental tests are based;
   b) The functions and uses of mental tests;
   c) The limitations of mental tests;
   d) The purposes for which performance tests are used.
8. What is the present status of the controversy on the constancy of the IQ? What are the implications for the classroom teacher?
9. Explain how the IQ is derived. Discuss the classification and distribution of intelligence quotients. How is intelligence distributed among the population as a whole?
10. Discuss the following statements:
    a) "The intelligence quotient is far from a perfect measure of brightness."
    b) "The intelligence test, when administered to an entire group, frequently uncovers a bright child who has been content to go on with the group without revealing his real ability, or a dull child who has made excellent use of his limited abilities."
    c) "Pupils who have visual, language or physical handicaps that preclude reliable testing of their abilities by group intelligence tests should be tested by individual scales or by performance tests."
    d) "The I.Q. is subject to improvement under desirable conditions of stimulation."
    e) "If schools are to let every student progress to the limit of his potential, they must be seeking continuously to identify their potential."

SELECTED REFERENCES FOR STUDY AND READING

Anastasi, A., *Psychological Testing,* 2 ed. (New York: The Macmillan Co., 1961).

Bayley, N., "Mental Development," in *Encyclopedia of Educational Research,* C. W. Harris, ed., 3 ed. (New York: The Macmillan Co., 1960), pp. 817–822.

Bischof, L. J., *Intelligence: Statistical Concepts of Its Nature* (Garden City, N. Y.: Doubleday and Co., Inc., 1954).

Buros, O. K., *The Fifth Mental Measurements Yearbook* (Highland Park, N. J.: Gryphon Press, 1959).

Cronbach, L. J., *Essentials of Psychological Testing,* 2 ed. (New York: Harper & Row, 1960).

Freeman, F. S., *Theory and Practice of Psychological Testing,* 3 ed. (New York: Holt, Rinehart and Winston, Inc., 1962).

Gerberich, J. R., Greene, H. A., and Jorgensen, A. N., *Measurement and Evaluation in the Modern School* (New York: David McKay Co., Inc., 1962), Chap. 6.

Guilford, J. P., "Three Faces of Intellect," *American Psychologist*, 14:469–479, 1959.

Harris, C. W., "Intelligence," in *Encyclopedia of Educational Research,* C. W. Harris, ed., 3 ed. (New York: The Macmillan Co., 1960), pp. 715–717.

Humphreys, L. G., and Boynton, P. L., "Intelligence and Intelligence Tests," in *Encyclopedia of Educational Research,* W. S. Monroe, ed., rev. ed. (New York: The Macmillan Co., 1950), pp. 600–612.

Hunt, J. McV., *Intelligence and Experience* (New York: The Ronald Press Co., 1961).

Lindvall, C. M., *Testing and Evaluation* (New York: Harcourt, Brace & World, Inc., 1961), Chap. 12.

Michael, W. B., "Aptitude," in *Encyclopedia of Educational Research,* C. W. Harris, ed., 3 ed. (New York: The Macmillan Co., 1960), pp. 59–61.

Noll, V. H., *Introduction to Educational Measurement* (Boston: Houghton Mifflin Co., 1957), Chap. 10.

Nunnally, J. C., *Tests and Measurements: Assessment and Prediction* (New York: McGraw-Hill Book Co., 1959), Chaps. 2, 9, and 10.

Pinneau, S. R., *Changes in Intelligence Quotient: Infancy to Maturity* (Boston: Houghton Mifflin Co., 1961).

Richardson, C. R., *Introduction to Mental Measurement and Its Applications* (New York: Longmans, Green and Co., 1955).

Terman, L. M., and Merrill, M. A., *Stanford-Binet Intelligence Scale: Manual for the Third Revision* (Boston: Houghton Mifflin Co., 1960).

Thorndike, R. L., and Hagen, E., *Measurement and Evaluation in Psychology and Education,* 2 ed. (New York: John Wiley and Sons, Inc., 1961).

Vernon, P. E., *Intelligence and Achievement Tests* (New York: Philosophical Library, 1961).

Wechsler, D., *The Measurement and Appraisal of Adult Intelligence,* 4 ed. (Baltimore: The Williams & Wilkins Co., 1958).

chapter 14

The Measurement of Educational Achievement

What the Measurement of Achievement Involves. Closely related to the measurement of intelligence is the measurement of achievement. Again, to *measure* means to describe quantitatively, while *achievement* signifies the ability to accomplish. The method used to measure achievement is the subject-matter examination. The term *examination* has been derived from the Latin word which means a weighing or a consideration. In its present usage, the term *examination* denotes a systematic test of knowledge or of skill to determine how much of a given subject a student has learned. The examination is among the oldest and most important of educational practices.[1] As early as 2200 B.C. the Chinese had an elaborate national system of examinations for the purpose of selecting public officials. The examination was a familiar process to both Grecian and Roman teachers. From 500 B.C. both the Athenians and the Spartans held periodic examinations for testing the skill and capacities of their youth. Socrates used the oral quiz when he submitted his pupils to an exhaustive and searching process of questioning. The catechetical method used by the early Christians was a form of oral test. From time immemorial the examination has been part of the classroom routine. It has been related directly, intimately, and necessarily with the work of the teacher. The medieval universities, particularly Bologna and Paris, had a rigid examination system in the thirteenth century. In 1702, Cambridge University introduced the written examination into England. It was soon adopted by

[1] See J. R. Gerberich, H. A. Greene, and A. N. Jorgensen, *Measurement and Evaluation in the Modern School* (New York: David McKay Co., Inc., 1962), pp. 19–29, for a brief, comprehensive history of the development of tests.

Oxford and was incorporated as a feature in the schools established in America by English Colonists.

In 1845, the city of Boston, through its school committee, administered a thoroughly prepared written examination to the pupils attending all of the schools of that city. Horace Mann, then secretary of the Massachusetts State Board of Education, was greatly interested, and he formulated the points of superiority of the written examination over the oral quiz as follows:

1. It is impartial.
2. It is just to the pupils.
3. It is more thorough than the older forms of examination.
4. It prevents "officious interference" by the teacher.
5. It determines beyond appeal or gainsaying whether pupils have been faithfully and competently taught.
6. It removes "all possibility of favoritism."
7. It makes the information obtained available to all.
8. It enables all to appraise the ease or difficulty of the questions.[2]

However, in 1864 an English schoolmaster, George Fisher, made the first known attempt at standardized objective testing. He prepared a scale book in which he included tests of the various subjects. He also provided numerical values for different degrees of efficiency. These numerical values ranged in order of merit from *one,* which was the lowest, to *five,* which was the highest, with intermediate fourths between each value. However, Fisher's work in this direction seems to have produced no lasting effects on educational practice.

The first event which seems to have had any direct connection with modern educational measurement was the work of J. M. Rice.[3] In 1894, he devised a standardized spelling scale, and in 1903 he prepared similar tests in arithmetic and language. His techniques were not adopted generally, but he seems to have focused the attention of educators upon the possibilities of objective measurement.

What may be termed the initial stages of scientific measurement in education began in 1909, when Thorndike developed his *Handwriting Scale.*[4] During the next few years several standardized tests and scales

[2] See O. W. Caldwell and S. A. Courtis, *Then and Now in Education 1845–1923* (Yonkers, N. Y.: The World Book Co., 1923), pp. 37–41.

[3] L. P. Ayres, "History and Present Status of Educational Measurements," National Society for the Study of Education, Seventeenth Yearbook, Part II, *The Measurement of Educational Products,* 1918, pp. 11 and 12.

[4] E. L. Thorndike, "Handwriting," *Teachers College Record,* 11:83–175, 1910.

appeared, particularly in the field of elementary education. These included the *Courtis Arithmetic Tests,* the *Hillegas Composition Scale,* the *Buckingham Spelling Scale,* the *Ayres Spelling and Handwriting Scales,* the *Stone Arithmetic Reasoning Test.* Since 1913 the number of standardized measuring instruments in school subjects has increased to more than a thousand, and includes tests for all fields of education. In addition, scores of books describing and evaluating the testing movement have been published.

These developments in the measurement of achievement which have taken place within the past fifty years have been in part an outgrowth of the interest in the process of growth and development; in part, also, an outgrowth of the emphasis placed on the teaching of the child rather than the teaching of the subject matter; in part, likewise, an outgrowth of the more recent adaptation of statistical procedures to the study of educational problems. The factors which have speeded the progress of the measurement of achievement include:

1. The studies of the reliability and accuracy of teachers' marks;
2. The survey movement, which led to intensive investigations of the educational conditions existing in many school systems;
3. Research, particularly that done by research bureaus in school systems and universities and by graduate students in the form of dissertations.
4. State and regional testing programs.

The measurement of achievement involves the testing of the pupil's accomplishments and attainments in school subjects which are outcomes of instruction in the school situation. The achievement test consists of a series of items carefully selected to measure a cross section of instruction in a subject-matter area. The purpose of the measurement of achievement is to help the teacher and the pupil to evaluate and to appraise the degree of success attained in various school subjects, as well as to provide incentives for further progress in learning. Hence, this measurement of pupil achievement in school subjects is as necessary in education as accounting is in business or as evidence is in the law court. The measurement of achievement involves the functioning of knowledge, of habits, and of conduct. The measurement of achievement has for its aims to discover whether or not the pupil has learned, to diagnose pupil difficulties and to redirect teaching, to supply data for administrative purposes. The measurement of achievement has great value to the teacher as an instrument for the comparison, instruction, and guidance of pupils.

Achievement may be measured in various ways. However, the most universally recognized way of measuring achievement is by means of the examination or test. Teachers have always endeavored to measure the progress of the pupil toward the achievement of learning, and have endeavored also to diagnose his defects in achievement by means of tests. The test has always been considered an indispensable aid to teaching. Since the early years of the present century, however, there has taken place an extension and an improvement in this old but significant educational devise of testing. As a result, the *standardized achievement tests* have been developed and have come into general use. These tests are definite, scaled, objective, standardized instruments for measuring achievement in school subjects. The fact that these tests are *scaled* means that they are made up of specific units of measurement or series of exercises arranged in a definite order or position, usually in ascending order of difficulty or value. The fact that they are *objective* means that the personal element or subjective judgment has been eliminated in the scoring of the test. The fact that these tests are *standardized* means that the test has been tried out, revised, tried out again, and demonstrated to be a valid and accurate measure of achievement in the particular subject. The fact that they are standardized means also that *norms* or standards of comparison are provided which indicate what an average individual may be expected to achieve under normal circumstances. These norms have been developed for different ages and for different grades. These tests measure the *range,* the *quality,* the *speed,* the *accuracy* of accomplishment.

Kinds of Achievement Tests. There are two kinds of achievement tests, namely, the formal or standardized educational tests and the informal or teacher-made accomplishment tests. The standardized achievement test is employed for comparison of learnings between schools, classes, cities with different types of courses of study and for this reason these standardized educational tests must be general in nature. Teacher-made tests are employed to measure the amount and extent of learnings within a particular course given by a specific instructor. Since teachers of the same course devote varying amounts of time to course topics and vary the emphasis on learnings within the subject, standardized educational tests are inappropriate in the evaluation of specific learnings taught by individual instructors during the school year. Moreover, the results of standardized achievement tests are seldom if ever used for class grades.

There are three generally recognized types of standardized tests according to the function served: the *survey* test, the *diagnostic* test, the *prognostic* test.

The *survey* test is one which yields a general or all-round measure of pupil achievement in one or in several school subjects. Ordinarily the survey test includes several or more exercises on each of the chief divisions or phases of the subject or subjects under consideration. Usually the survey test tends to emphasize the minimum essentials of the subject or subjects. There are three types of survey tests. The first type is designed for use in a single subject-matter field and yields independent measures of a number of specific achievements within a given subject. For example, such a test in the modern language field would probably include several exercises dealing with each of the following phases: vocabulary, declension, conjugation, grammatical rules, translation. Such tests are used extensively in both the elementary and the secondary school. Examples of this type of survey test are the:

1960 Cooperative English Tests;
Crary American History Test;
Cooperative World History Test;
Madden-Peak Arithmetic Computation Test;
Chicago Plane Geometry Test;
Cooperative Science Tests;
Peltier-Durst Civics and Citizenship Test;
Lankton First-Year Algebra Test;
Cooperative French Listening Comprehension Test;
Cooperative Latin Tests;
Barrett-Ryan-Schrammel English Test, New Edition.

The second type of survey test is designed to measure general achievement in several school subjects. Examples of this type of survey test are the:

Stanford Achievement Tests;
Metropolitan Achievement Tests;
Iowa Tests of Basic Skills;
Essential High School Content Battery;
California Achievement Test Batteries.

All of these consist of batteries of achievement tests in the various school subjects including arithmetic or mathematics, reading, science, history, language. The third type of survey test is usually termed a classification test. This type is a specialized battery and includes in addition to achievement tests an intelligence test for the purpose of classifying pupils by means of a single test on the bases of mental development and classroom achievement. An example of this type of survey test is the *Otis Classification Test,* which consists of achievement tests in reading, spelling, language, grammar, arithmetic, geography, history, civics, hygiene, vocabulary, music, and art, together with one devoted to the measurement of intelligence.

The *diagnostic* test has been devised in order to analyze in detail the pupil's capacity and performance, to identify specific strengths and weaknesses which may be used as a basis for guidance, to determine, particularly, the elements in a subject in which there are specific learning difficulties, to provide a means of discovering the causes of difficulties. The diagnostic test must yield detailed information concerning the capacity and accomplishment of the child in order to discover the specific learning difficulty of the pupil in the phase of the subject test or in the subject itself. It must provide the teacher with sufficient specific information regarding pupil achievement that may be used for diagnostic purposes. This means that diagnostic testing is one of the most complicated and extensive processes in the field of education. The location of the difficulties of both individuals and classes in any given subject matter is one of the most important and most helpful procedures in teaching. In order that a test be genuinely diagnostic, it must test all of the separate units or phases of knowledge and skill which are most important and which are to receive most emphasis in the teaching of the subject matter. In addition, each separate unit or phase of knowledge and skill must be measured accurately. Furthermore, the diagnostic test must indicate the extent of specific remedial and corrective instruction which will be needed. This means that not only must the diagnostic test possess real analytical power but also it must be followed by remedial practices. Some tests which are diagnostic in character are the:

Diagnostic Tests and Self-Helps in Arithmetic;
Gates Reading Diagnostic Tests;
Diagnostic Reading Tests;
Durrell Analysis of Reading Difficulty, New Edition;

Iowa Silent Reading Tests;
Diagnostic Test in Basic Algebra;
Power's Diagnostic Latin Test;
The Greene-Stapp Language Abilities Test;
Essentials of English Test, Revised.

The *prognostic* test is used to measure potential ability or academic aptitude in a subject, and for this reason it is frequently termed an *aptitude test.* Its purpose is not to measure the accomplishment of the pupil in a particular subject matter, but rather to predict what the probable achievement or success of the pupil will be in that particular school subject. The prognostic test has been designed to measure underlying capacity which is essential for success in a particular subject. It measures the capacity of the pupil to engage with success in a particular line of activity or phase of schoolwork. Some of the more commonly used prognostic or aptitude tests in specific academic subjects[5] are the following:

Modern Language Aptitude Test;
Lee-Clark Reading Readiness Test;
California Algebra Aptitude Test;
Lee Test of Geometric Aptitude;
Iowa Plane Geometry Aptitude Tests;
Orleans Algebra Prognosis Test;
Lee Test of Algebra Ability;
Monroe Reading Aptitude Test;
Gates Reading Readiness Tests;
Lauria-Orleans Modern Language Prognosis Tests;
Symonds Foreign Language Prognosis Test;
Metropolitan Reading Readiness Test.

Innovations in the area of achievement tests include four batteries, namely, the *Iowa Tests of Educational Development* (ITED), the *U S A F I Tests of General Educational Development,* the *Sequential Tests of Educational Progress,* and the *Project Talent Test Battery.* The ITED battery consists of nine tests designed to provide a comprehensive description of the general educational development of the individual high school pupil. These tests are designed to measure ability to understand

[5] Tests of vocational aptitudes will be discussed in the chapter on "Guidance Aspects of Education."

and interpret materials in the social studies, natural sciences, and literature. Essentially they have been developed to measure the pupil's ability to do critical thinking in broad areas. They are concerned not so much with what specific information the pupil has learned, but rather with how well he can use what he has learned in acquiring, interpreting, and evaluating new ideas, in relating new ideas to old, and in applying broad concepts and generalizations to new situations and in the solution of problems.[6] The U S A F I battery was devised to provide an adequate basis for educational and vocational guidance, and for granting credits to returned servicemen after World War II. This battery was developed for the high school and college levels. The high school battery derived from the *Iowa Tests of Educational Development* was composed of five examinations in the fields of English composition, the social studies, the natural sciences, literature, and mathematics. The college-level battery omitted the mathematics test.[7] Both batteries have been used extensively. The *Sequential Tests of Educational Progress*[8] (STEP) were undertaken by committees of teachers to measure student development of increasing skill in solving new problems based on past achievement. They were designed to measure general outcomes of education rather than specific course content. The reading, writing, listening, and essay tests probe the critical communication skills, while the mathematics, science, and social studies tests evaluate a student's application of knowledge in these subject areas. A continuous system of measurement from the fourth grade through the sophomore year in college is provided by the four levels of tests in each of the learning fields. The *1960 Project Talent Test Battery*[9] was the first scientifically planned national inventory of human aptitudes which might predict vocational and educational success. The twenty-three aptitude and achievement tests, the three information, activity, and interest inventories, the themes section, and the Preference Test which comprise the battery were administered in 1960 to 440,000 high school students who will be followed up for the next twenty years. This study should provide an inventory of human resources, a set of standards for

[6] *The Nature and Purposes of the Iowa Tests of Educational Development* (Chicago: Science Research Associates, 1948).

[7] P. L. Dressel and J. Schmid, *An Evaluation of the Tests of General Educational Development* (Washington, D. C.: American Council on Education, 1951).

[8] *Cooperative Sequential Tests of Educational Progress* (Princeton, N. J.: Educational Testing Service, 1958).

[9] John C. Flanagan, *et al., Design For A Study of American Youth* (Boston: Houghton Mifflin Co., 1962).

educational and psychological measurement, a comprehensive counseling guide which will indicate the patterns of aptitude and ability predictive of success in different careers, a better understanding of how young people choose their lifework, and a better understanding of the educational experiences which prepare young people for their lifework.

Additional innovations in the area of achievement tests include the *Wrightstone Test of Critical Thinking in the Social Studies* and the *Watson-Glaser Critical Thinking Appraisal.* These are noninformational tests designed to measure more complex educational objectives.[10]

The Form of Achievement Tests.[11] In the development of achievement tests two general forms of items have become standard. These two forms are known as the essay which is usually employed today in teacher-made tests and objective test items which are employed in both kinds of tests, namely, standardized achievement tests and teacher-made tests. The essay[12] is a form of test question and response by means of which the examinee is required to compose in his own words an answer to a question for which no single answer may be considered as perfect, correct, or complete, and whose answer is graded on the basis of relative quality of worth. The three types[13] of essay test items are: the *simple recall* which requires a short response to questions such as who, when, where, what, and how many and which may be accurately scored; the *short answer* which requires a phrase or sentence to answer questions

---

[10] R. M. Travers, *Educational Measurement* (New York: The Macmillan Co., 1955), pp. 96–104.

[11] For samples of the various forms of items used in achievement tests, see: W. J. Michaels and M. R. Karnes, *Measuring Educational Achievement* (New York: McGraw-Hill Book Co., Inc., 1950), pp. 160–295; R. M. Travers, *How to Make Achievement Tests* (New York: The Odyssey Press, 1950); E. F. Lindquist, ed., *Educational Measurement* (Washington, D. C.: American Council on Education, 1951), pp. 185–249; R. L. Thorndike and E. Hagen, *Measurement and Evaluation in Psychology and Education,* 2 ed. (New York: John Wiley & Sons, Inc., 1961), Chaps. 16–17; E. J. Furst, *Constructing Evaluation Instruments* (New York: Longmans, Green and Co., 1958), pp. 203–274; B. S. Bloom, *et al., Taxonomy of Educational Objectives, Handbook I: Cognitive Domain* (New York: Longmans, Green and Co., 1956); K. L. Bean, *Construction of Educational and Personnel Tests* (New York: McGraw-Hill Book Co., Inc., 1953), pp. 37–87 and 107–127; J. R. Gerberich, *Specimen Objective Test Items: A Guide to Achievement Test Construction* (New York: Longmans, Green and Co., 1957); *Making the Classroom Test: A Guide for Teachers,* Evaluation and Advisory Service Series, No. 4 (Princeton, N. J.: Educational Testing Service, 1959), pp. 17–21; J. A. Green, *Teacher Made Tests* (New York: Harper & Row, 1963).

[12] J. M. Stalnaker, "The Essay Type of Examination," in *Educational Measurement,* E. F. Lindquist, ed. (Washington, D. C.: American Council on Education, 1951), Chap. 13.

[13] J. R. Gerberich, H. A. Green, and A. N. Jorgensen, *op. cit.,* pp. 204–213.

such as list, define, identify, and which may be accurately scored; and the *extended answer* which requires at least several sentences for a correct response to questions such as describe, explain, discuss, interpret, outline, compare, and contrast, and which cannot be easily and objectively scored. The latter type of the essay form is traditional and properly so called "essay." This "extended-answer" essay form is qualitative in nature and can measure the higher faculties of man including original thinking and reasoning. This type of essay form does not efficiently measure purely factual information. Moreover, it is more likely to reveal individuality on the part of the examinees. However, this extended-answer type of essay form possesses low validity because of limited sampling of content and low reliability because of subjectivity in scoring.

The objective form of test item demands that the testee either selects the correct response from given options or supplies the answer in a word or phrase. This objective form of test item consists of two types, namely, recall and recognition. The recall type consists of (*a*) the single-answer form and (*b*) the completion form. The recognition type consists of:

1. The alternate-response form which includes the following varieties:
   a) True-false;
   b) Yes-no;
   c) Right-wrong;
   d) Synonym-antonym.
2. The multiple-response form which includes the best-answer form.
3. The matching or association form.
4. Other forms which are not so commonly used, including:
   a) Identification;
   b) Analogies;
   c) Rearrangement;
   d) Correction-of-errors;
   e) Cross-out;
   f) Construction.

The objective form of test item efficiently measures knowledge and understanding of facts, decreases verbalism, and usually possesses high validity and reliability. Moreover, it should be noted that the objective form can measure the higher levels of reasoning.

Steps in the Construction of an Achievement Test. In the relatively new science of test construction, definite steps must be followed in order

TABLE 12. Sample Table of Specifications

Course: Psychological Measurement and Evaluation

Objective \ Content	History of Psychological Testing	Characteristics of Psychological Testing	Uses of Psychological Testing	Norms	Validity	Reliability Etc.
Classtime in Each Area (Hours)	4	½	½	1	2	2
A. Knowledge and understanding of						
1. Facts and terminology	10	2	2			
2. Ways and means of dealing with specifics		1				
3. Principles, generalizations, theories	3		1			
B. Application			2			
C. Analysis and synthesis			2			
D. Evaluation	2					

that an adequate, valid, and reliable instrument may be formulated. The first step in the construction of an achievement test is its planning stage. This planning stage involves three phases, namely, the development and expression of a general statement of purposes; the preparation of a table of specifications; and the determination of technique. In the first phase, the purposes for the construction of the evaluative instrument are clarified. For instance, if the aim of the test is to evaluate overall performance, then data for a total score based on adequate sampling of content are needed. However, if the purpose of the test is to ascertain the pattern of student strengths and weaknesses with a definite content, then part scores for each type of outcome are necessary. The second phase involves the construction of a table of specifications. This table consists of a chart on which there is a horizontal heading with a breakdown of content areas and a vertical heading with a breakdown of major types of objectives. Within the body of the chart is presented an apportionment of test items by objective and content area.

The third phase consists of decisions concerning technique. These decisions include length of the test, level and range of difficulty, and discrimination of test items, form of test, manner of recording responses, time limits, scoring system, directions for guessing, and the physical structure of the test. The second step involves the construction of test items in accordance with the table of specifications. The third step in the construction of an educational test is to review, assemble, and reproduce the test items. The fourth step is concerned with the administration of the test, the scoring and grading of the test responses, and interpretation of the test results. The last step involves test analysis and revision. In this stage, a logical and statistical analysis of the test is performed. Moreover, an item analysis is made to ascertain the difficulty and discriminating index of the test items. Then the reliability of the test is determined and changes are made within the instrument to improve its reliability.

The Functions of Achievement Tests. The general function which all tests of achievement should serve is to establish standards for the comparison, classification, guidance, and instruction of pupils. The specific functions of tests of achievement include the following:

Teacher Uses

1. Insight into class and individual status and progress with regard to achievement;
2. Adaptation of class instruction to level of student accomplishment;
3. Diagnosis of learning difficulties or deficiencies of individual pupils and class;
4. A means of instruction and learning;
5. Identification of underachievers and overachievers;
6. Organization of group for class activities;
7. Evaluation of the accomplishment of the pupil and the class;
8. Motivation of review;
9. Incentive to daily preparation;
10. Determination of the success of learning procedures of the pupil;
11. Enabling the individual pupil to know his progress;
12. Determination of the extent to which emphasis is being placed on a phase of a subject or on the entire subject;
13. Determination of the efficiency of instruction;
14. Improvement of instruction;
15. Promotion of pupils;
16. Determination of school marks;
17. Reporting student progress to parents.

Counselor Uses

1. Determination of student's and class's anticipated achievement in specific courses, curricula, and within educational levels;
2. Educational and vocational guidance and counseling;
3. Modification of the curriculum to meet the needs of students;
4. Placement of new pupils entering school system;
5. Provision of data for case studies.

Administrative Uses

1. Comparison of pupils, class with class, school with school;
2. Comparison of various methods and materials of instruction and supervision;
3. Horizontal and vertical grade gradation and placement of students;
4. Grouping into special classes;
5. Planning of curricular revision;
6. Assist in initiating instructional and remedial programs;
7. Setting and maintaining standards of student performance;
8. Conducting research;
9. Certification of students;
10. Interpretation of the school program to the community.

Of these special functions which the achievement tests serve, several are of particular interest to the teacher. These are classification, motivation, and guidance. There is at present an increasing use of achievement tests as devices for classifying pupils into advanced, average, and slow groups within grades or within subjects. While the intelligence tests are used extensively as bases for such classification, nevertheless any such classification to be adequate must take into consideration the accomplishment of the pupils in subject-matter areas. The child may have a high intelligence quotient and still have failed to master his schoolwork. For purposes of classification and promotion, the child's accomplishment in the various school subjects must be taken into account.

The proper purpose of all testing is the improvement of instruction. Achievement tests are very useful in motivating both the teacher and the pupil to accomplish better results. The chief motivation comes in the use of tests in which the pupil compares his own achievement either with that of other pupils of his class or with the norm for his age and grade. Furthermore, good teaching requires an intimate knowledge of each pupil's potentialities and limitations. The use of diagnostic and survey tests to obtain an understanding of learning difficulties and shortcomings motivates the teacher to adjust instruction to the needs and abilities of his pupils. Likewise, the teacher may be guided thereby in the selection of methods and procedures.

The achievement tests used in guidance, both educational and vocational, usually include all types, but with particular emphasis upon the prognostic or aptitude tests both in academic and vocational areas. These tests are used to supplement mental ability tests. By means of these tests, pupils interests in school subjects are discovered and ability to master these subjects is determined. Educational guidance requires that the child be placed in classes and in subjects suited to his intellectual and accomplishment level. Vocational guidance so far as tests are concerned has progressed considerably, and the possibilities in this area are increasing with the development of instruments designed to measure vocational interests and aptitudes.

Validity and Reliability of Achievement Tests. The most important single characteristic of the achievement test is its *validity*. This means the worthwhileness or general merit or truthfulness of the test. Validity means the degree to which a test measures the capabilities, the capacities, the skills, the knowledge which it is designed and intended to measure. Usually an achievement test is sufficiently valid if it is in agreement with the course of study; with the materials set forth in the basic textbooks on the subject; with the minimum essentials for the subject which have been established by qualified authorities. It is also possible to determine the validity of a test statistically by means of the coefficient of correlation. If there exists a high degree of correlation between the test and some other known measuring device for that function, the usefulness of which has been established previously, then the test is a valid one. Moreover, achievement test scores seem to predict quite well subsequent scholastic success as determined by school grades in specific subjects and by grade-point averages.

Reliability as a characteristic of achievement tests denotes the accuracy and consistency of a test. Reliability means the degree to which a test measures accurately and consistently the capabilities, capacities, skills, and knowledge which it attempts to measure. In order that a test be reliable, it should be composed of a large number of independent items. These should be selected carefully and extensively from the field which the test is designed to measure. The range of difficulty should be sufficiently wide to give full scope to the range of ability and accomplishment within the class. A test is reliable to the extent to which the pupil's scores on repeated trials of the same test or on duplicate forms of the test do not have large fluctuations from one form to the next. For practically all standardized tests the reliability coefficient is stated in the manual of directions accompanying such tests. Authorities in the field of testing seem to be agreed that, if a test is to be used for individual diagnosis, then a reliability coefficient of .90 or higher is required. However, for group work a coefficient of .80 or more may be considered satisfactory. The reliability coefficients of most standardized achievement tests seems to be high.

Educational Quotient and Accomplishment Quotient. The educational quotient or EQ is obtained by dividing the educational age or EA by the chronological age or CA. The formula for finding the educational quotient is $EQ = \frac{EA \times 100}{CA}$. The educational age is a single score in terms of months, which combines the different subject ages, like arithmetic age, spelling age, reading age, and the like. These subject ages are determined from tables of achievement-age scores accompanying the various standardized subject-matter tests. The score which the pupil makes on the achievement test is noted, and the age for which this score is the norm or standard is located. The EQ is a means of showing what an individual pupil's educational ability is compared with the average achievement of pupils of the same age. Thus, a pupil whose EA is 120 months and whose CA is 144 months would have an EQ of 83.3. A pupil whose EA is 144 months and whose CA is 144 months would have an EQ of 100. A pupil whose EA is 180 months and whose CA is 144 months would have an EQ of 125. An EQ of 80 would mean that the pupil's achievement is 80 percent of that of the average attainment for pupils of his age. Therefore he is 20 percent below the average. The pupil who has an EQ of 100 is exactly average. An EQ of 125 means that the pupil's achievement is 25 percent above the average.

However, the important matter for the teacher is the amount which the pupil accomplishes in proportion not merely to his CA but also to his mental capacity or MA. Hence, the use of both the intelligence and achievement tests in the school has led to a comparison of the scores made by pupils in the two kinds of tests. The interpretation of achievement in terms of intelligence is stated in the accomplishment quotient or AQ, which expresses the ratio of what the child does, that is, his accomplishment, to what he could do, that is, his capacity. It is a measure of effort and motivation. The AQ is determined by dividing the EA by the MA and is expressed in the formula, $AQ = \frac{EA \times 100}{MA}$. For example, a pupil with an EA of 132 months and an MA of 156 months would have an AQ of approximately 85. A pupil whose EA is 120 months and whose MA is 120 months would have an AQ of 100. A pupil whose EA is 144 months and whose MA is 120 months would have an AQ of 120. Thus, an AQ of 85 would mean that the pupil's achievement is only 85 percent of his ability. An AQ of 100 would mean that the pupil's achievement is exactly what it should be for one of his mental capacity. Likewise, an AQ of 120 would mean that the pupil is putting forth more than the ordinary amount of effort.[14] It is worthy of note that an AQ which is well below 100 notifies the teacher that the accomplishment of the pupil is not in proportion to his capacity. Such a situation calls for a diagnosis to discover the causes of inefficiency, which causes usually are either negligence on the part of the pupil or faulty instruction on the part of the teacher. While the AQ gives a partial measure of how well the school is enabling the pupil to realize his mental capacity, nevertheless it is important to note that in measuring achievement two very significant factors, those of emotion and volition, are not easily evaluated.

The educational quotient and the accomplishment quotient are not as well known and as widely used as the intelligence quotient. The significance of the EQ is not as fully understood as that of the IQ. However, theoretically, if the tests upon which the subject ages are determined have been as carefully developed as the intelligence tests, then the EQ should be as accurate as the IQ. The utilization of the EQ in educational testing is growing and, with the improvement of the achievement tests,

[14] Theoretically an AQ of more than 100 should not occur. It does occur occasionally, probably because the norms of the subject-matter tests are too low. Likewise, it should be noted that achievement does not depend upon ability alone, but also upon other factors including interest, motivation, and the like. See J. R. Gerberich, H. A. Greene, and A. N. Jorgensen, *op. cit.*, pp. 182–183.

should take its place in importance with the IQ. The AQ is psychologically sound in principle and is useful in practice. However, authorities have pointed out limitations and dangers in the use of the AQ.[15] For this reason it should be used very cautiously where the individual pupil is concerned, but may be used to determine general tendencies. However, its use even with groups is not recommended.

In 1957 Shanner[16] introduced the concept of *anticipated achievement* and *anticipated achievement grade-placement* norms. The anticipated achievement of a student is ascertained from the anticipated achievement grade-placement norms which are developed for an achievement test of the classification type. By means of this classification test typical proficiency performance is determined for particular groups homogeneous with respect to mental-age, chronological-age, and school-grade classification. Horn introduced the concept of the *expected grade placement* which is a "computed score representing the achievement test performance of an individual based on a regression technique which is a function of both mental age and chronological age and expressed in grade placement units."[17]

Values and Limitations of the Achievement Tests. Standardized tests of the achievement of pupils constitute one of the important factors in teaching. They help to indicate whether or not an individual's accomplishments in school are commensurate with his ability. They aid in analyzing deficiencies and in providing a basis for more effective teaching. They cover a wide range of detail within subjects. They are useful in predicting future achievement. They help to render the teacher's judgment of the pupil more trustworthy. However, there are certain limitations and disadvantages involved in these standard tests of achieve-

[15] It has been pointed out generally by authorities in the field of measurement that the AQ is a ratio resulting from two quantities, EA and MA, which are subject to errors of measurement. These unreliabilities produce relatively greater unreliability in the AQ. For further discussion on the AQ see J. R. Gerberich, H. A. Greene, and A. N. Jorgensen, *loc. cit.;* T. L. Kelley, *The Interpretation of Educational Measurements* (Yonkers: The World Book Co., 1927), p. 22; H. B. Greene, *Measurements of Human Behavior,* rev. ed. (New York: The Odyssey Press, 1952), pp. 213–214; F. L. Goodenough, *Mental Testing, Its History, Principles and Applications* (New York: Holt, Rinehart and Winston, Inc., 1949), pp. 333–336; J. L. Mursell, *Psychological Testing,* 2 ed. (New York: Longmans, Green and Co., 1949), pp. 398–399.

[16] *A Glossary of Measurement Terms* (Del Monte Research Park, Monterey, Calif.: California Test Bureau), p. 2.

[17] *Loc. cit.,* p. 6.

ment. Since the relative merits of the standard achievement tests have not yet been judged finally, their limitations should be recognized. Ordinarily these limitations are as follows:

1. The standard achievement tests tend to stress factual knowledge and to measure information chiefly.

2. Certain limitations of standard achievement tests are inherent in the test themselves, such as inadequate samplings, ambiguous exercises, improper emphases upon content areas, and inadequate working time limits.

3. The standard achievement tests do not improve instruction *per se.*

4. The standard achievement tests neglect to indicate exactly where and how the individual achieved the information.

5. The standard achievement tests tend to measure memory rather than ability to think logically and to express oneself clearly and coherently.

6. The guessing element enters into standard achievement tests.

7. The standard achievement tests neglect language training.

8. The standard achievement tests make essential the formal learning of isolated facts rather than the assimilation and appreciation of relationships and meanings.

Educational Significance of Measurement of Achievement. The examination has always been considered as an extremely important part of the educative process. It has been considered that the examination tends to develop mental powers which are of use in everyday life. These mental powers include attention, judgment, volition, reasoning, self-reliance, verification, and other intellectual powers.

To measure the efficiency with which pupils apply their mental capacities to the assimilation of learning, there have been developed within the past score of years devices for measuring achievement in all school subjects. More refined as well as more adequate instruments for measuring achievement have been devised. These tests and measures of achievement, because of their definiteness and objectivity, reveal to the teacher the status of the achievement of his class and the extent to which the objectives of instruction have been attained. They point out individual differences in capacity and in accomplishment; they make it possible to set up specific goals for attainment; they reveal the results of special types of emphasis and of special methods of instruction; they are useful in providing for the pupil proper guidance, both educational and vocational. Moreover, they often reveal the specific learning difficulties of individual pupils so definitely that the teacher is in a position to apply effective remedial instruction.

Furthermore, another phase of the measurement of achievement has been the application of the methods and procedures employed in standardized tests to the improvement of the examinations constructed by the teacher.

Concerning the relative merits of various tests both of mental ability and of achievement and as an aid in the selection of tests, the student should consult such sources as the *Mental Measurements Yearbooks,*[18] edited by Buros, and the periodic evaluations which appear in the *Review of Educational Research.* Approximately every three years, an issue of this journal is devoted to educational and psychological tests. A section on educational measurement is included under the heading of "Educational Psychology" in each issue of *Psychological Abstracts* which is published bimonthly by the American Psychological Association.

EXERCISES

1. Outline this chapter.
2. List and define the terms which you have learned from your study of this chapter.
3. Distinguish between:
   a) Formal and informal tests;
   b) Survey and diagnostic tests;
   c) Diagnostic and prognostic tests;
   d) EQ and AQ.
4. List and discuss:
   a) The functions of achievement tests;
   b) The limitations of achievement tests;
   c) The relative merits of each of the forms of achievement tests.
5. What is the value of the accomplishment quotient? Discuss its defects and also its possible uses.
6. List and discuss:
   a) The functions of batteries of achievement tests;
   b) The advantages of such batteries;
   c) The limitations of such batteries.
7. List and discuss the steps in the construction of an achievement test.

[18] O. K. Buros, ed., *The Third Mental Measurements Yearbook* (New Brunswick, N. J.: Rutgers University Press, 1948), which covers the period of 1940 to 1947; *The Fourth Mental Measurements Yearbook* (Highland Park, N. J.: The Gryphon Press, 1953), which covers the period of 1948 to 1951; *The Fifth Mental Measurements Yearbook* (Highland Park, N. J.: The Gryphon Press, 1959), which covers the period of 1952 to 1958.

8. How may various aspects of the school program be evaluated by the use of achievement tests?
9. How may the application of the methods of test construction to the improvement of teacher-made examinations be of value in improving the work of the teacher?
10. Discuss the following statements:
    a) "Tests when properly used can be one of the most effective tools available to the teacher."
    b) "The comparison between educational growth and mental growth represented by the AQ could also be shown in terms of underachievement and overachievement."
    c) "Some people fear that the constant use of objective-type tests will lead to inability to use effective expression."
    d) "The essay test is notoriously low in reliability."
    e) "In a very real sense, the test maker determines the curriculum of the school."

SELECTED REFERENCES FOR STUDY AND READING

Ahmann, J. S., and Glock, M. D., *Evaluating Pupil Growth,* 2 ed. (Boston: Allyn and Bacon, Inc., 1963).

Anastasi, A., *Psychological Testing,* 2 ed. (New York: The Macmillan Co., 1961), Chaps. 6 and 7.

Baron, D., and Bernard, H. W., *Evaluation Techniques for Classroom Teachers* (New York: McGraw-Hill Book Co., 1958), Chaps. 6, 7, 11, and 12.

Bauernfeind, R. H., *Building a School Testing Program* (Boston: Houghton Mifflin Co., 1963).

Bradfield, J. M., and Moredock, H. S., *Measurement and Evaluation* (New York: The Macmillan Co., 1957).

Brueckner, L. J., and Bond, G. L., *Diagnosis and Treatment of Learning Difficulties* (New York: Appleton-Century-Crofts, Inc., 1955).

Downie, N. M., *Fundamentals of Measurement: Techniques and Practices* (New York: Oxford University Press, 1958), Chaps. 6 to 11.

Durost, W. N., and Prescott, G. A., *Essentials of Measurement for Teachers* (New York: Harcourt, Brace and World, Inc., 1962).

Ebel, R. T., and Damrin, D. E., "Tests and Examinations," in *Encyclopedia of Educational Research,* C. W. Harris, ed., 3 ed. (New York: The Macmillan Co., 1960), pp. 1502–1516.

Furst, E. J., *Constructing Evaluation Instruments* (New York: Longmans, Green and Co., Inc., 1958), Chaps. 7 to 13.

Garrett, H. E., *Testing for Teachers* (New York: American Book Co., 1959).

Gerberich, J. R., *Specimen Objective Test Items: A Guide to Achievement Test Construction* (New York: Longmans, Green and Co., Inc., 1956).

Gerberich, J. R., Greene, H. A., and Jorgensen, A. N., *Measurement and Evaluation in the Modern School* (New York: David McKay Co., 1962).

Goslin, D. A., *The Search for Ability* (New York: Russell Sage Foundation, 1963).

Green, J. A., *Teacher Made Tests* (New York: Harper and Row, 1963).
Lindvall, C. M., *Testing and Evaluation: An Introduction* (New York: Harcourt, Brace and World, Inc., 1961), Chaps. 4 to 10.
National Society for the Study of Education, Sixty-Second Yearbook, Part II, *The Impact and Improvement of School Testing Programs,* 1963.
Noll, V. H., *Introduction to Educational Measurement* (Boston: Houghton Mifflin Co., 1957).
Nunnally, J. C., *Tests and Measurements: Assessment and Prediction* (New York: McGraw-Hill Book Co., Inc., 1959), Chaps. 8 and 12.
Remmers, H. H., and Rummel, J. F., *A Practical Introduction to Measurement and Evaluation* (New York: Harper and Row, 1960), Chaps. 7 to 9.
Thomas, R. M., *Judging Student Progress,* 2 ed. (New York: Longmans, Green and Co., 1960).
Thorndike, R. L., and Hagen, E., *Measurement and Evaluation in Psychology and Education,* 2 ed. (New York: John Wiley & Sons, Inc., 1961), Chaps. 3, 4, 11, 16, and 17.
Wood, D. A., *Test Construction* (Columbus, Ohio: C. E. Merrill Books, 1960).
Wrightstone, J. W., Justman, J., and Robbins, I., *Evaluation in Modern Education* (New York: American Book Co., 1956), Chaps. 5, 6, 14, and 15.

chapter 15

Statistical Methods in Education

The Definition of Statistics. The term *statistics* is employed to designate that branch of applied mathematics which deals with the collection, study, and analysis of numerical data. Statistical processes have assumed an important role in psychology. This is true not only of psychology in general but also of educational psychology. As the study of man's mind advanced to its present state, it became apparent that general-descriptive methods of research and causal inference were inadequate. As the body of knowledge in psychology increased in volume and precision, the need for a corresponding improvement in descriptive and inferential methods became evident. In the physical sciences new problems create a demand for new measurement and research techniques. Similarly, in psychology and educational psychology the development of more advanced research procedures has been a natural accompaniment of the specialized advance in human knowledge. It also seems that as the research tools and methods in any science become more complex they become less a "tool" and more an integral part of the science. At the present time statistics and statistical methods have developed as tools in aiding the expansion of the body of psychological truth and also in their own right have made significant contributions to human learning.

Originally statistics were used to study important governmental affairs, such as the number of men available for military service, the allotment of taxes, and the collection of census material. As such, statistics were used by the Greeks and the Romans. However, statistics have become much more comprehensive, and at present they are used in the study of all forms of social life. This general social application of statistics dates back to the middle of the eighteenth century, when the beginnings of modern vital statistics and insurance statistics were introduced. The use of statistics in education began when Wundt, in 1879, established the first psychological laboratory at the University of Leipzig. The use of statistics in psychology was promoted by Sir Francis Galton, who, in 1884, established a psychological laboratory in London and made extensive studies in individual differences. One of the most valuable statistical techniques, that of correlation, was formulated by Galton and extended in scope by Karl Pearson at the University of London. During the latter part of the nineteenth century many American educators studied in Europe especially under the guidance of Wundt and Galton. One of these students, James McKeen Cattell, studied under both and became so enthusiastic over their methods that he introduced statistical methods into American education, when he later became professor of psychology at Columbia University. Two other Americans, Titchener, of Cornell University, and Judd, of the University of Chicago, also studied under the direction of Wundt. The influence of these men was widespread, and they developed, in America, the use of statistical techniques in education. Edward Lee Thorndike, of Columbia University, who was a student under Cattell, adapted these statistical procedures to educational psychology and applied them to the first educational test, which was published in 1910.

In recent years the following trends have been notable in the application of statistical methods in educational psychology:

1. The extensive and fruitful use of analysis of variance and covariance in the design and conduct of experiments has encouraged more studies conducted in real situations. The classical single variable experiment has been superseded by more true-to-life multivariable investigation.

2. There has been an increase in the availability and use of methods for treating imprecise data or data which are nominally or qualitatively classified. The increase has enabled firm conclusions to be drawn concerning data which were not formerly considered amenable to statistical tests of significance.

3. The development of factor analysis has made major contributions toward the improvement of certain types of tests and to the understanding of complex interrelationships of a variety of psychological data.

The Need for Statistical Methods in Education. The study of educational psychology involves the consideration of collections of data. The analysis and interpretation of these data are based upon a knowledge of statistical methods. Teaching seeks to produce changes in pupils and this calls for measurement of pupil ability. Marks and grades occupy an important and permanent place in the work of the teacher. Hence, it is an advantage to the teacher to be able to classify pupils according to their standing in various abilities and traits. Since a knowledge of statistical techniques is useful in the daily routine of the teacher, some of the basic methods of analyzing educational data should be known.

Furthermore, a considerable body of educational literature has been published in recent years, and much of it has been of a statistical nature. The growing number of new books and the professional educational magazines take for granted a knowledge of statistics, since they are replete with statistical terms and techniques. Current educational literature in the form of surveys, financial reports, theses, monographs, and pamphlets issued by the federal and state governments and by private institutions has created a need for statistical training. Since such a vast amount of educational literature makes use of statistical methods, teachers will be able to read professional literature intelligently and to understand it in proportion to their knowledge of statistical methods. Another field in which knowledge of statistical techniques is essential is that of standardized tests which have widespread application to such problems as pupil classification, diagnosis of special abilities, evaluation of instructional methods, counseling, and vocational guidance.

Accordingly, the very utility and practical value of statistics constitute the most vital reason for studying it. The elementary concepts of statistical methods form a part of the common culture which integrates the teaching profession. Therefore, to understand, to participate, and to contribute to the teaching profession in an intelligent and effective manner the teacher must be familiar with the essential elements of statistical methods. These essential elements which may be used so frequently in the classroom are:

1. The classification, tabulation, and graphical presentation of data;
2. The measures of central tendency — mean, median, mode;
3. The measures of dispersion or variability — range, interquartile deviation, standard deviation;
4. The measures of position — standard scores, percentiles, percentile ranks, ranks;
5. The measures of relationship and prediction — correlations and regression equations.

In addition to these practical measures which can be readily employed in the classroom, the teacher should have some familiarity with the application and conclusions of the more complex statistics, namely:

6. Measures of sampling variability or reliability — standard error of the mean, standard error of a difference;

7. Measures for testing hypotheses — critical ratio, t-ratio, F-ratio, chi-square.

The Classification and Tabulation of Data. Statistics exist only where there are data. However, data consist of facts, some of which are *descriptive* or *qualitative* while others are *measurable* or *quantitative.* The descriptive or qualitative facts are characteristics which cannot be expressed in numerical terms. These facts are termed *attributes.* Statistics deals with attributes insofar as they can be classified into nominal or ordinal categories. The numerical frequencies in the attribute categories can be analyzed and compared. Among the attributes are sex, health, parental occupation, national origin, instructional method, and school type. The measurable or quantitative facts are usually expressed in numerical terms. These are designated *variables.* Statistics deals directly with these variables because they are expressed in numerical terms. Among the variables in educational data are school grades in the various subjects which are expressed in per cent values, the scores of standardized achievement and intelligence tests, which are expressed in points or mental ages or quotients, height and weight measurement, and the like.

Data may be either *discrete* or *continuous.* Data are discrete when each object is a unit by itself and does not merge into that which follows; that is, a real gap exists between one object and the next. For example, a family can have two children or three children, but not two and one-half or three and one-sixth children. Discrete data are exact and are usually obtained by counting. Data are continuous when they assume any value in some interval of values. Continuous data are approximate and are usually obtained by measuring. All measurements are approximate, for instance, measures of height and weight and the like are continuous since they offer the possibility of infinite subdivision between one measure and the next longer one. The accuracy of the approximation of any measurement depends upon the precision of the measuring instrument. All measurements are approximate and are continuous data. For example, a test is the measuring instrument most frequently used by the teacher and usually yields scores which are in whole-number units. A score of 78 means that the individual's ability has been measured to be between 77.5 and 78.5, and this is best indicated by a mark of 78. A more precise test might give scores in stages of .5 which would make the real limits of a score of 78 from 77.75 to 78.25. The real limits of any test score are halfway between that score and the next higher and lower scores. This principle of continuity will be important in the treatment of data in later sections of this chapter.

The first and in many ways the most important topic that arises in connection with the handling of data is that of tabulation and classification. The inductive process in human learning seeks to arrive at a principle, generalization, or class concept from numerous specific events. In the effort to find order in external reality, man finds it helpful to classify into categories the large number of specific events with which he is concerned. In statistics, this is exemplified at the most elementary level where a large amount of raw data are grouped into convenient orderly classes for inspectional or computational purposes. This orderly grouping system is called a *frequency distribution.* Data which have been so classified are termed *grouped data.* Efficient short-cut methods have developed to compute statistics form these data.

The value of the frequency distribution in helping the teacher organize and interpret data may be illustrated by the following example. Fifty students in the twelfth grade took an objective history test composed of 100 items and made the following scores: 65, 84, 60, 62, 43, 77, 79, 69, 59, 56, 80, 53, 74, 64, 71, 66, 82, 48, 72, 70, 59, 59, 60, 75, 95, 83, 84, 78, 83, 69, 81, 74, 90, 82, 86, 67, 69, 81, 83, 75, 81, 83, 81, 77, 90, 42, 84, 59, 75, 76.

It is difficult to comprehend the information contained in the individual scores. If the scores are put in order of size, it will be somewhat easier to interpret them. If the scores are grouped into convenient intervals a more comprehensive picture of the group can be obtained. This group picture is obtained with some loss of precision since the scores lose their individuality. The usual practice is to have more than ten but less than twenty groups in a frequency distribution depending on the number of scores. It will be noted that the range of scores on the history test extended from 42 to 95, or a range of 53 points. If this range were to be divided into intervals of five points, there would be eleven intervals or groups. For the sake of convenience in tabulation and ease in computing, the class interval to contain the lowest scores is chosen as 40 to 44, even though the

TABLE 13. Frequency of Distribution Scores on a History Test With Class Intervals of Five

Class Interval	Midpoint	Tally	Frequencies
95–99	97	/	1
90–94	92	//	2
85–89	87	/	1
80–84	82	~~////~~ ~~////~~ ////	14
75–79	77	~~////~~ ///	8
70–74	72	~~////~~	5
65–69	67	~~////~~ /	6
60–64	62	////	4
55–59	57	~~////~~	5
50–54	52	/	1
45–49	47	/	1
40–44	42	//	2
			N 50

lowest score is 42. This increases the number of intervals to twelve. Then, after tallying the scores in the proper intervals, the tallies are totaled to obtain the frequency in each class interval. Table 13 represents the frequency distribution with intervals of five.

There are certain assumptions inherent in the use of a frequency distribution. The distribution is assumed to be continuous; that is, in the lowest class interval of 40 to 44 the real limits are 39.5 to 44.5 which gives a true width of five units. The next class interval of 45 to 49 begins at 44.5 and extends to 49.5. Each class interval contains five units and begins where the previous class interval ends. It is also assumed that the scores tallied within a class interval are spread evenly throughout the interval and that their average is the midpoint of the interval. These assumptions may not be met exactly but are necessary for mathematical treatment of the data, and the error is not serious. When it becomes necessary to compute the median, mean, and other measures, the exact beginning of the interval must be known, or some score must be selected to represent the entire interval. The preceding assumptions permit the designation of the lower limit and the midpoint of the interval to fill these needs. The lower real limit is always one-half unit below the lowest score in the interval. The midpoint is found by adding half the number of points in the class interval to the lower limit of the interval. Thus, in the interval 40 to 44, the lower real limit is 39.5. There are five units in the interval and half of five is 2.5. Accordingly 2.5 is added to 39.5 and the midpoint of the interval is 42.

Presenting Materials Graphically. Large numbers of scores are more readily comprehended when presented graphically. There are several graphic methods which are very commonly used to represent the distribution of scores. These methods include the histogram, or column diagram, and the frequency polygon, which is also called the surface of frequency.

The Histogram. Of these graphic methods the histogram is recommended as preferable, because it is a very simple and very accurate method of graphic presentation and therefore easily understood and interpreted. The histogram is composed of a series of rectangles, each of which has as its base one class interval and as its height the number of cases in the particular interval which it represents. Figure 12 is an illustration of the histogram of frequency.

It will be noted that the horizontal scale is measured off in terms of class intervals, from low at the left to high at the right, and that on the vertical scale the frequencies are indicated. The distribution of scores graphed represents the scores of 162 high school students on an intelligence test. The frequency for each interval is noted, and a column for this interval is erected to the height of this frequency as determined by the vertical scale. Thus in the first interval the frequency is 6, the second is 8, and so on.

The Frequency Polygon. The second method of representing a dis-

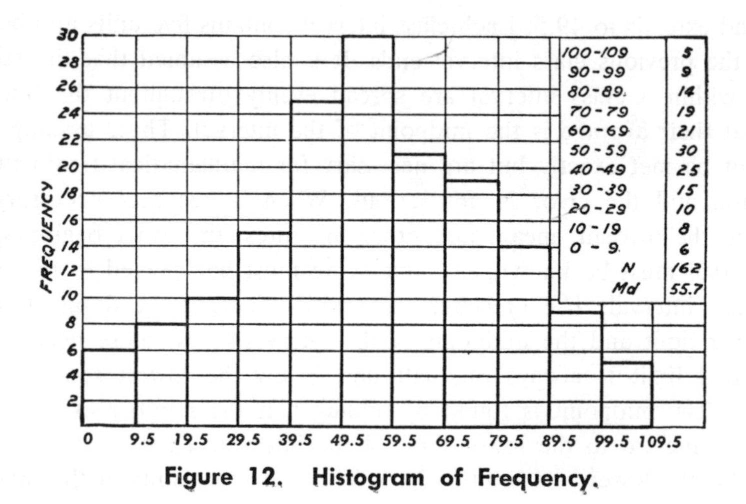

Figure 12. Histogram of Frequency.

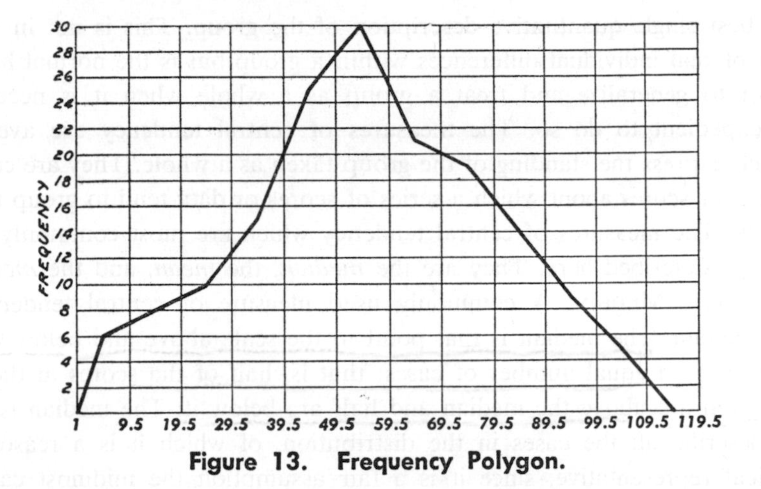

Figure 13. Frequency Polygon.

tribution graphically is by use of a frequency polygon. The simplest method of constructing the frequency polygon is to connect by straight line segments what would be the midpoints of the top horizontal lines of the histogram if it were drawn. Figure 13 illustrates a frequency polygon using the same data represented by the histogram plotted at the midpoints of the intervals.

The frequency polygon may be converted into a smooth curve by averaging the frequencies in successive sets of three and adding two zero frequency intervals at each end of the distribution. This tends to flatten and spread out the polygon and should not be done without good reason.

Other graphic methods employed in representing the distribution of scores include the scatter diagram, the block diagram, the bar chart, the pictogram, and the percentile curve. A discussion of these graphic methods seems to be beyond the scope of this elementary chapter.

The Measures of Central Tendency. In addition to arranging and grouping scores so that the whole series may be easily comprehended, it is helpful in understanding and describing these scores to determine the particular score which tends to be representative of the group as a whole. The development of a class concept or characteristic with which to describe a group is one of the basic inductive processes of the human being. The measures of central tendency represent the quantitative aspect of the process. If the group or class must be described or treated as a single entity with one common characteristic, a measure of central tendency is the best single quantitative description of the group. This is not in violation of real individual differences within a group but is the normal human effort to generalize and treat a group as a whole when it is necessary or expedient to do so. The measures of central tendency are averages which express the standing of the group taken as a whole. They are central points or scores about which a series of scores or data tend to group themselves. The measures of central tendency which are most commonly used will be described here. They are the *median,* the *mean,* and the *mode.*

a) THE MEDIAN. A commonly used measure of central tendency is the median. The median is that point in the scale above and below which there are an equal number of cases; that is, half of the scores in the distribution are above the median and half are below it. The median is used to describe all the cases in the distribution, of which it is a reasonable typical representative, since it is a fair assumption the midmost case or score is typical of the group. The abbreviation for the median is Md. Table 14 illustrates how the median is computed from grouped data.

TABLE 14. Group Method of Finding the Median

Class Intervals	Frequencies
95–99	1
90–94	2
85–89	1
80–84	14
75–79	8
70–74	5
65–69	6
60–64	4
55–59	5
50–54	1
45–49	1
40–44	2
	N 50

Reading up

$N = 50$

$\frac{N}{2} = 25$

Cumulating frequencies upward

$2 + 1 + 1 + 5 + 4 + 6 + 5 = 24$

Number needed to reach $\frac{N}{2} = 25 - 24 = 1$

Part of next class interval needed = ⅛

Number of score units needed from interval 75–79 = ⅛ × 5 = .625

Lower limit of 75–79 = 74.5

Median = 74.5 + .625 = 75.125 or 75.13

Reading down (check)

Cumulating frequencies downward

1 + 2 + 1 + 14 = 18

Number needed to reach $\frac{N}{2} = 25 - 18 = 7$

Part of next class interval = ⅞

Number of score units from interval 75–79 = ⅞ × 5 = 4.375

Upper limit of interval 75–79 = 79.5

Median = 79.5 − 4.375 = 75.125 or 75.13

Since the median represents that point on the scale above and below which there are exactly equal numbers of cases, the first step is to determine what number constitutes half the cases. Since N is 50 in Table 13, there should be one half of 50 or $\frac{N}{2}$ cases or 25 cases on each side of the median. The next step consists in starting at the bottom and adding up the frequencies until it is found that the twenty-fifth case falls in the interval 75–79. This indicates that the median is somewhere between a score of 74.5, the beginning of the interval, and a score of 79.5, the end of the interval.

Counting the number of cases up to the lower limit of the interval, 74.5–79.5, it is found that there is a total of 24 cases. If counting were to be continued to the upper level of the interval, 8 cases more would be added and that would be beyond the median. Since only 1 more case is needed to reach the required 25, it is necessary to include only 1 to find the exact median, or one eighth of the interval to find the exact median. Since the interval covers a range of five scores and it is necessary to secure one eighth of that distance, the next step is to find ⅛ of 5 which equals .625. This number is then added to the beginning of the interval or to 74.5, and the median, 75.125 or 75.13, is found. This is the upper limit of the twenty-fifth score and there are 25 scores on each side of that point.

Where there are only a few scores and a frequency table is not desirable, the median may be computed from ungrouped data. The first step is to rank the scores according to size. For example, the following eleven scores are ranked according to size: 40, 39, 38, 37, 35, 34, 30, 28, 24, 22, 21. The second step is to find the middle score. There are eleven scores and the middle score is 34, for above it there are 5 scores, and below it there are 5 scores. If, however, the number of scores is even, the median will be halfway between the two midmost scores.

b) THE MEAN. The best known, most important, and generally most reliable measure of central tendency is the mean. The mean is the arithmetic average and where the number of cases is small may be found by totaling the individual scores and dividing this sum by the number of cases.[1] If, for example, there are 20 scores to be averaged and their total adds up to 1640, then the mean is the result of 1640 divided by 20, that is, 82. However, the mean may be defined more exactly and specifically as that point on the score scale above and below which the score deviations are equal. The mean may be thought of as the fulcrum on which the scale rests so that the measures above and below acting as weights maintain a perfect balance. The abbreviation for the mean is **M** or $\mathbf{\bar{X}}$.

P. 519

$$AM = 77$$

$$\frac{\Sigma fx'}{N} = \frac{-48}{50}$$

$$\frac{\Sigma fx'}{N} \cdot i = \frac{-48}{50} \times 5 = -4.8$$

$$M = 77 - 4.8 = 72.2$$

The arithmetic method of finding the mean becomes rather laborious for larger numbers of cases; and furthermore, in the case of a frequency distribution, the situation becomes more complicated. However, statisticians have worked out a short method of computing the mean from grouped data. Table 15 illustrates this short method of computing the mean from grouped data.

In computing the mean by the short method the first step is to assume a mean, that is, an arbitrary or guessed mean. In Table 15, the assumed mean selected is the midpoint of the class interval 75–79 or 77. The devi-

[1] This is the method of computing the mean from ungrouped data.

TABLE 15. Short Method of Computing the Mean[2]

Class Interval	Midpoint	f	x′	fx′	
95–99	97	1	4	4	
90–94	92	2	3	6	
85–89	87	1	2	2	
80–84	82	14	1	14	+ 26
75–79	77	8	0	0	
70–74	72	5	— 1	— 5	
65–69	67	6	— 2	— 12	
60–64	62	4	— 3	— 12	
55–59	57	5	— 4	— 20	
50–54	52	1	— 5	— 5	
45–49	47	1	— 6	— 6	
40–44	42	2	— 7	— 14	— 74
		N 50		Σfx′ = —48	

ations in terms of intervals from this assumed mean are listed in the fourth column under the heading *x′*. There are four intervals above and seven below the assumed mean. Those above are the positive and those below are the negative deviations. The next step is to multiply the deviations by the frequencies and place the products in the fifth column under the heading *fx′*. Then add up the *fx′*s above the assumed mean and the sum is found to be +26. Add up the *fx′*s below the assumed mean and the sum is found to be —74. Then +26 and —74 are added algebraically and the result or sum of the *fx′s* is found to be —48. This is the total deviation from the assumed mean in terms of class intervals. If the assumed mean had been the real one the sum of the positive *fx′s* would have been equaled by the sum of the negative *fx′s*. The average of this total deviation (—48 divided by 50), is the class interval distance between the assumed mean and the real mean. However, since there are five steps in the interval, this must be multiplied by five which gives as the result —4.8. The actual mean then equals the midpoint of the interval 75–79 algebraically added to the average deviation from the midpoint or 77 — 4.8. The actual mean then is 72.2. However, if the average deviation from the midpoint had been positive, then the actual mean would have been larger than the assumed mean.

c) THE MODE. The mode is defined as the most frequent score, or the

[2] In Table 15 the following symbols are used: *N*, Σ, *x′*, *and fx′*. *N* indicates the *number* of cases; Σ, the *sum* of; *x′*, the *distance from the assumed mean; fx′*, the *frequency times the deviation.*

midpoint of the interval in which the greatest frequency occurs. In some distributions there is more than one mode. Thus the expressions *bimodal, trimodal,* etc. Thus, in Table 13 (page 385), the modal interval or the interval in which there are the greatest number of cases is the interval 80–84. The midpoint of this interval, or 82, is considered as the mode. The modal frequency or the actual number of cases is 14.

The Uses of Measures of Central Tendency. The median is the counting average and considers only the number of cases above and below itself. The mean is the arithmetic average and takes into consideration the amount of deviation of each score from the central tendency. The mode is the inspection average and is merely the actual unit occurring most frequently. The median is used when a quick and easily computed measure of central tendency is necessary and when there are extremely high or low scores which would affect the average unduly. The mean is used when it is desirable that each measure should have equal weight in determining the central tendency and when the highest reliability is sought. It is also used when the coefficient of correlation is to be computed by the product-moment method. The mode is used when a quick approximate measure of concentration is desired and when only the most frequently occurring score is sought.

Measures of Variability or Dispersion. Human experience has shown the dangers of relying only on generalizations and has shown the impropriety of applying the "best group measure" to each member of the group. Statistics reflects the need of a more adequate group description by providing for some indication of how the members of the group deviate from the average or central measure. The measures of central tendency of a group do not tell the whole story. It is necessary also to know how nearly alike or how far apart the scores of the individuals in a group are. It may happen that two groups have the same median or mean and yet differ widely in the way in which the individual cases cluster around this average. One group will be homogeneous with a comparatively small spread of scores above and below this average, while the other group might have a number of very high and very low scores. The latter group would have a larger variability. Hence, it is useful to know how closely the scores cluster around the central tendency, to know whether they are packed closely, or scattered widely. Measures of variability or dispersion help to express these differences numerically.

There are several measures of variability, namely, the *range, the quartile deviation, the standard deviation, the average deviation,* and *the median deviation.* Only the quartile deviation and standard deviation will be considered here. Obviously the range, the highest score minus the lowest score, is a very inaccurate measure of variability.

a) THE QUARTILE DEVIATION. One of the commonest and most easily computed measures of deviation is the quartile deviation, which is also designated as the semi-interquartile range. As the second expression indicates, it is half the distance from the first quartile up to the third quartile. Since there is one fourth or 25 percent of all the cases between each quartile and the median, the quartile deviation is the average distance from the median to the score limits of the middle 50 percent of the group. The symbol for the quartile deviation is Q, and the formula for finding the quartile deviation is $Q = \frac{Q_3 - Q_1}{2}$. The procedure for finding the quartile points Q_3 and Q_1 is basically the same as that used in finding the median.

Thus, in Table 14 (page 388), the quartile deviation of the scores made on a history test by fifty pupils of the twelfth grade is found as follows:

Q_3
$N = 50$
75 percent of 50 $= 50 \times .75 = 37.5$

Cumulating upward $2 + 1 + 1 + 5 + 4 + 6 + 5 + 8 = 32$
$37.5 - 32 = 5.5$
$\frac{5.5}{14} \times 5 = 1.96$
$Q_3 = 79.5 + 1.96 = 81.46$

Q_1
$N = 50$
25 percent of 50 $= 12.5$

Cumulating upward $2 + 1 + 1 + 5 = 9$
$12.5 - 9 = 3.5$
$\frac{3.5}{4} \times 5 = 4.37$
$Q_1 = 59.5 + 4.37 = 63.87.$

$$Q = \frac{Q_3 - Q_1}{2} = \frac{81.46 - 63.87}{2} = \frac{17.59}{2} = 8.795 \text{ or } 8.80$$

b) STANDARD DEVIATION. The standard deviation is a measure of dispersion which depends upon the distances from the mean to each of the scores in a distribution. The standard deviation is a measure of variability about the mean and is used in connection with that measure. It is represented by the symbol *SD* or by the Greek letter sigma or σ. The definition of the standard deviation is $SD = \sqrt{\frac{\Sigma x^2}{N}}$ where x is the distance of a score from the mean. The formula is cumbersome to employ and more efficient computing methods are normally utilized.

The formula for computing the standard deviation from grouped scores is $SD = i\sqrt{\frac{\Sigma fx'^2}{N} - \left(\frac{\Sigma fx'}{N}\right)^2}$. Table 16 illustrates the method of computing the standard deviation.

TABLE 16. Method of Computing the Standard Deviation

Class Interval	f	x′	fx′	fx′²
95–99	1	4	4	16
90–94	2	3	6	18
85–89	1	2	2	4
80–84	14	1	14 + 26	14
75–79	8	0	0	0
70–74	5	—1	—5	5
65–69	6	—2	—12	24
60–64	4	—3	—12	36
55–59	5	—4	—20	80
50–54	1	—5	—5	25
45–49	1	—6	—6	36
40–44	2	—7	—14 —74	98
	N 50		Σfx′ —48	Σfx′² 356

$$
\begin{aligned}
SD &= i\sqrt{\frac{\Sigma fx'^2}{N} - \left(\frac{\Sigma fx'}{N}\right)^2} \\
&= 5\sqrt{\frac{356}{50} - \left(\frac{-48}{50}\right)^2} \\
&= 5\sqrt{7.12 - (-.96)^2} \\
&= 5\sqrt{7.12 - .9216} \\
&= 5\sqrt{6.1984} \\
&= 5 \times 2.49 \\
&= 12.45
\end{aligned}
$$

It will be noted that the procedure in obtaining the standard deviation is similar to that of computing the mean. The first step is to assume arbitrarily a mean, which in Table 16 was the interval 75–79, the midpoint of which, 77, represents the assumed mean. Then, as in the computation of the mean, the deviations above and below the assumed mean are entered in the x' column, and the fx' values are obtained by multiplying. The next step is to multiply the fx' values by the corresponding x' value and place the product in the fx'^2 column. Then the sum of all the deviations squared times the frequencies is obtained and the formula applied.

Use of the Measures of Deviation. Quartile deviation is used when the median has been used to describe the central tendency, and standard deviation is used when the mean has been employed as the measure of central tendency. The quartile deviation does not possess the statistical refinements and advantages to be found in the standard deviation, but it is sufficiently accurate for many practical purposes for which educational data are used by the teacher. The standard deviation, since it is mathematically defined, cannot be explained verbally with any clarity. However, the extensive use of this measure in most higher level statistical procedures makes it an especially important statistic. The normal curve, standard scores, reliability, and tests of hypotheses all depend upon this fundamental measure of variability.

Measures of Position. In interpreting an event or experience man necessarily depends on his previous experience and also on the total context in which the event occurs. Quantitative descriptions of performance or of persons in terms of the group in which they occur are measures of position. These measures of position are employed frequently in educational psychology, namely, ranks, percentile ranks, and standard scores. When persons or measures of performance are placed in order they can be assigned ranks which are direct measures of position. The conventional proceeding is to assign the highest score or best performance a rank of one, and to assign a higher numbered rank to each score in turn. If there are equal scores or tied performances, each of the tied scores is assigned the average of the ranks involved. For example, if the seventh, eighth, ninth, and tenth scores in the series were all equal they would all be assigned a rank of 8.5 (the average of 7, 8, 9, and 10).

It is evident that a rank of 20 would be meaningless unless the size of the group were known. If there were only twenty cases, this rank would be the lowest, but if there were eighty cases it would be near the top.

Therefore a more meaningful measure of position is often employed to indicate the position in the group. This is percentile rank, which indicates position in the group without regard to the actual size of the group. A percentile rank of 80 means that for the measures under consideration the pupil assigned that rank has obtained a score which exceeds 80 percent of the individuals in his group. The computation of percentile ranks is basically the problem of determining how many scores in a distribution are below a given score. This is an uncomplicated process similar to the reverse procedure of finding a median or percentile.

The third and more precise method of comparing scores within a single distribution is through the computation of *sigma* or *standard scores.* This method requires that the mean and standard deviation of the distribution be computed first. Then each score is converted to a standard score by dividing its deviation from the mean (x) by the standard deviation (SD). This $\frac{x}{SD}$ score is very descriptive of an individual score within a group, since it tells how many standard deviations the score is above or below the mean. For example, if the mean of a distribution is 37 and the standard deviation is 4.5, then a score of 42 would have a deviation from the mean equal to 42 — 37, or 5. The deviation 5 divided by the standard deviation 4.5 is equal to 1.11. This means that a score of 45 is 1.11 standard deviations above the mean. A score of 32 would have a sigma score of —1.11 or 1.11 standard deviations below the mean. When this method is used each score is described in terms of the characteristics of the distribution from which it comes. As a rough estimate, scores which lie within one half a standard deviation of the mean are considered to be more or less average; scores which are between one-half and one and one-half standard deviations above or below the mean are considered to be definitely above or below average respectively, while scores which are more than one and a half standard deviations above or below the mean are considered to be definitely superior or inferior respectively. This method of standardizing scores is commonly used to equate tests of unequal difficulty, to scale raw scores on standardized tests, and to equate measurements made in different units such as weight and height.

Measures of Relationship. In his efforts to attain greater control over his environment man has sought to discern and employ relationships between observed events. The accumulation of experience has yielded not only class concepts and generalizations of a descriptive nature but also relationships which have some useful predictive value. In statistics there are the parallel quantitative processes of correlation and regression. The various correlation coefficients are measures of the degree of relationship between observed events.

These coefficients give a quantitative expression to the amount of one measure which is related to or explainable by another measure. The correlation coefficient indicates the extent to which knowledge of one variable or condition will aid in predicting the related variable or condition. The regression equation is the actual prediction formula. The regression equation includes all of the information on a particular sample of data. The assumption is made that any new data or subjects obtained in a similar fashion will possess the same characteristics as the original sample. This assumption is identical with man's natural tendency to judge new data on the basis of what he has previously learned or experienced. Insofar as the previously learned relationship is true, the predictions based on it will be true. If the relationship is not strong, or not accurately determined, the actions based on it will contain error. The most frequently employed measure of relationship is the Pearson product-moment correlation. There are other useful correlation coefficients which are really special cases of the product-moment correlation. The characteristics and limitations of the data or of the variables determine which coefficient is most suitable. For the purposes of this chapter a simplified discussion and computation of the product-moment coefficient and the corresponding regression equation will be presented.

The coefficient of correlation is a measure of how closely persons' positions or scores on one measure correspond to their positions or scores on another measure. For example, if the heights and weights of a group of children were measured it would not be surprising to find that the taller children tended to be heavier and the shorter children tended to be lighter. The correlation coefficient would not be high but would indicate that the position of each child on the height measure would be some indication of his position on the weight measure.

The magnitude of the coefficient of correlation is always between 0 and 1.00. The direction of the relationship may be either positive or negative. If a higher score in one variable is accompanied by a higher score in the other variable (a child's age and his height) the correlation is positive. If a higher score on one variable is accompanied by a lower score on the other variable (intelligence test score and time needed to solve a reasoning problem) the correlation is negative. If there is no tendency for the size of the score on one variable to be accompanied by a particular size score in the other variable (number of pages in a book and the frequency of use of the book) the correlation is zero.

The definitional formula for the coefficient of correlation is

$$r = \frac{\Sigma xy}{\sqrt{\Sigma x^2} \cdot \sqrt{\Sigma y^2}}.$$

Table 17 illustrates the computation of the coefficient of correlation by the Product-Moment Method.

The first step in computing the coefficient of correlation by the Product-Moment Method is to find the mean of each series of scores. The mean

TABLE 17. Computation of the Coefficient of Correlation by the Product-Moment Method

(Data represent scores made on two history tests)

Pupil No.	Test A(x)	Test B(y)	Deviations x	y	x^2	y^2	xy +	—
1	93	89	8	1	64	1	8	
2	89	86	4	−2	16	4		8
3	98	114	13	26	169	676	338	
4	96	104	11	16	121	256	176	
5	100	117	15	29	225	841	435	
6	59	58	−26	−30	676	900	780	
7	91	114	6	26	36	676	156	
8	94	105	9	17	81	289	153	
9	73	82	−12	−6	144	36	72	
10	85	76	0	−12	0	144	0	
11	88	92	3	4	9	16	12	
12	83	65	−2	−23	4	529	46	
13	87	78	2	−10	4	100		20
14	82	103	−3	15	9	225		45
15	78	62	−7	−26	49	676	182	
16	64	76	−21	−12	441	144	252	
17	68	72	−17	−16	289	256	272	
18	94	109	9	21	81	441	189	
19	93	95	8	7	64	49	56	
20	85	69	0	−19	0	361	0	
	1700	1756			2482	6620	3127	73
M	85	88					3054	

$$r = \frac{\Sigma xy}{\sqrt{\Sigma x^2} \times \sqrt{\Sigma y^2}} \qquad SDx = \sqrt{\frac{2482}{20}} = 11.14$$

$$r = \frac{3054}{\sqrt{2482} \times \sqrt{6620}} = \frac{3054}{49.9 \times 81.3} \qquad SDy = \sqrt{\frac{6620}{20}} = 18.19$$

$$r = \frac{3054}{4056.87} = .75$$

of Test A is found to be 85, and that of Test B is 88. The second step is to find the deviation of each score in Test A from the mean of the series and to record that deviation in the x column, keeping the plus and minus signs. The same is done for Test B and placed in the y column. The third step is to square the x deviations and the y deviations. These computations are placed in the x^2 and y^2 columns, respectively. The fourth step is to compute the products of the pairs of deviations which are recorded in the x and y columns and to enter these in the xy column, retaining the signs resulting from the multiplication. Finding the algebraic sum of the xy column is the fifth step, and this is divided by the product of the square root of the sum of the x^2 column times the square root of the sum of the y^2 column.

This illustrative example has been designed to show the application of the method without undue complications with decimals and large numbers. If the means had not been whole numbers, the deviations would have been decimals, and their squares and products would have been very laborious to compute. However, there is a short method similar to that which was used to compute the mean and the standard deviation.

The Uses of the Coefficient of Correlation. The coefficient of correlation is one of the most widely used statistical techniques. It has been very helpful in expressing the relationships between physical and psychological measurements. It has also been of great value in expressing the statistical aspects of test validity and reliability. Coefficients of correlation constitute the basic data which factor analysis techniques seek to explain. Prediction and selection techniques employ regression equations which include correlation coefficients and the fundamental concept of quantitative relationship. The interpretation and significance of a coefficient of correlation is dependent upon several factors. With respect to magnitude Garrett[3] has presented a broad tentative classification to

[3] H. E. Garrett, *Elementary Statistics,* 2 ed. (New York: David McKay Company, Inc., 1962), p. 100.

be accepted with reservations as a general guide to the interpretation of the coefficient.

.00 to +.20 denotes indifferent or negligible relationship
+.20 to +.40 denotes low correlation present but slight
+.40 to +.70 denotes substantial marked relationship
+.70 to +1.00 denotes high to very high relationship

However, the true significance of a coefficient of correlation depends on more than mere size. It is also necessary to consider other correlations in the same field which may differ enough from any given correlation to make that correlation or the experiment suspect. There is need also for care in the selection of the group so that only those variables investigated affect the correlation.

The Regression Equation. For simple prediction from one variable, the formula for the regression equation is:

$$Y' = r \frac{SD_y}{SD_x} (X - M_x) + M_y$$

Employing the data from the problem in Table 15 (p. 390) the formula becomes:

$$Y' = .75 \frac{18.19}{11.14} (X - 85) + 88$$
$$Y' = 1.22X - 103.70 + 88$$
$$Y' = 1.22X - 15.70$$

The regression equation is assumed to be generally applicable to scores of individuals like those in the original problem. If a person obtained an X score 92, the prediction procedure for his most probable Y score would be:

$$Y' = 1.22(92) - 15.70$$
$$Y' = 96.54$$

The prediction will not be perfect since the relationship (r) is not perfect. For a large group of individuals, all with X scores of 92, some would score well above or well below the Y' prediction of 96.54. However, the average attained Y' score would be 96.54 as long as the basic assumptions are met. The new group must be like the old group and the relationship must be linear.

The Normal Distribution. The distributions of many psychological

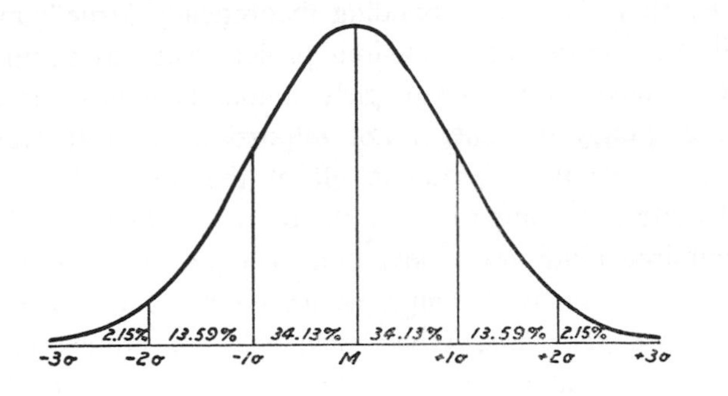

Fig. 14. Curve areas and standard deviation.

measurements tend to follow the *normal curve.* This normal frequency distribution is a mathematically defined or derived distribution which is convenient to employ because of its completely known properties. Although in reality very few measurement distributions are exactly normal, the approximation to normality is so close that the error involved is negligible. The areas or number of cases under any selected portion of the normal curve have been derived and are available in tables. These tables are usually presented in terms of standard scores, or sigma units. A diagram of the percent of the total area which is included under certain selected portions of the curve is presented in Figure 14. The normal distribution is employed in many statistical decisions concerning the size of differences. The decisions are based on the area of frequency of such differences in a normal distribution.

Measures of Sampling Variability or Reliability. Man is seldom able to examine all of the members of the group of objects about which he seeks to learn. He is restricted usually to studying samples from the total group. Generally man must infer the characteristics of the total group from his limited experience with some members of the group. This is true whether he is studying human behavior or the tensile strength of steel. These inferences are based on the assumption that the sample, if properly selected, is representative of the group. However, the dangers of such generalizations are well known. Measures of sample reliability or sampling error are needed to safeguard the process of arriving at truth through inference. For every sample there is a larger population of which the sample constitutes a part. For every "obtained" statistical measure there is a corresponding theoretically "true"[4] measure. For example, if the purpose of a research project were to compare the IQs of ninth-grade boys with those of girls at the same level, it would obviously be exceedingly difficult, if not impossible, to test every boy and girl enrolled in the ninth grade in all of the high schools throughout the United States. A comparison could be made, however, between IQs of a few hundred ninth-grade boys and an equal number of ninth-grade girls selected as a random[5] sample or as a representative[6] sample of all ninth-grade boys and girls. When such selected groups are made the bases for a generalization there will be differences due to chance variation in the cases selected. Interpretation of the obtained difference must be in terms of the usual or normally expected difference. The generic term for the variability or reliability of statistical measures is *standard error*. Generally each statistic has a standard error which is the standard deviation of these values computed from samples. However, some of these standard errors are useful only under very restricted conditions. Since the major concern has been the comparison of groups and since sample means are sensitive reflectors of group characteristics, the standard error of the mean has been found to be very useful.

Standard Error of the Mean. The standard error of the mean is one of the most frequently employed measures of sampling variability. The standard error of the mean is the standard deviation of the means of many samples of a given size which have been randomly drawn from a large population. The mathematical expression of this variability has been derived from a few basic assumptions and may be estimated from the data of a single sample. The formula is $SE_m = \frac{SD}{\sqrt{N - 1}}$ where SD equals standard deviation of the sample, and N equals the size of the sample. It may be noted that the means of larger samples are more

---

[4] The *true* measure is the value which would be obtained if, instead of using a sample, a very large (theoretically an infinite) number of cases or all the cases in the category under investigation were used.

[5] A *random* sample means that the subjects were selected in some arbitrary manner which is used to obtain an unbiased cross section of the population and which is considered to be free from the influence of any of the variables under investigation.

[6] A *representative* sample means that the distribution of scores in the sample closely parallels that of the population and contains approximately the same proportion of subjects from each geographical area, age group, racial group, and occupational group as the entire population from which the sample is drawn.

homogeneous; that is, they do not vary from sample to sample as much as the means of smaller samples. Since the means of large samples are normally distributed above and below the mean of the population, certain probability statements can be made about the population mean. For example, with relatively large samples, N equaling 100 or more, the interval of about two (1.96) standard errors above and below the sample mean is called the 95 percent confidence interval. This is a brief way of stating that if many samples had been drawn and similar intervals (mean $\pm$ 1.96 SE) were computed for each sample, that 95 percent of such intervals would include the population mean. This is not the same as stating that "the population mean is between those limits." The statement is that 95 out of 100 such intervals do include the mean and since this is one of those intervals we are 95 percent sure that the population mean is included.

With smaller samples (N less than 100) the shape of the distribution of means departs from normality. The means of smaller samples are more widely dispersed and the 95 percent confidence interval is somewhat larger. The t distribution is employed for smaller-sized samples rather than the normal distribution. The difference in the confidence limits is not greater than the normal distribution by more than 10 percent when the sample size is above 40. Applying this procedure to the data presented in Tables 15 and 16 where the mean was 72.2 and the standard deviation was 12.45 and the sample size was 50, the following result is obtained:

$$SE_{\text{m}} = \frac{12.45}{\sqrt{50 - 1}} = \frac{12.45}{7} = 1.78$$

Sixty-eight percent of the intervals like 72.2 $\pm$ 1.78 include the true mean. One can be 68 percent confident that the true mean is included between 70.42 and 73.98. One can be 95 percent confident that the true mean is included between 72.2 $\pm$ 1.96 (1.78) and 72.2 — 1.96 (1.78).

Significance of the Difference Between Two Means. In order to make a decision concerning the difference between the mean IQs of the ninth-grade boys and girls, mentioned earlier, it is necessary to know the sampling variability or usual size of such mean differences. This standard error of the difference between means (SE_{diff}) is the standard deviation of a large number of sample differences. The obtained difference is compared to this normal variability or fluctuation by means of a critical ratio or *t*-ratio: $CR = \frac{diff}{SE_{diff}}$. If the obtained difference between the means is much larger than the expected average mean difference of zero, then the critical ratio will be large and the difference will be considered unusual or significant. The term *significant* is encountered very frequently in research literature and it is synonomous with "unusual" or "not ordinary."

All statistical tests of hypotheses are basically comparisons of what has been observed with what would be the usual expectation. If the occurrence is easily attributed to chance sampling variations it is called nonsignificant. If, however, the observed condition is not easily attributed to chance variation, it is called significant. In this sense, whether it is a mean difference, a correlation, a variance ratio or a *chi* square, when the value is significant it means that it is more reasonable to ascribe the observation to some factor other than chance sampling variation.

The classical tests of significance of differences between two means have been critical ratios which are actually standard scores. The critical ratios are measures of how many standard deviations the observed difference is above or below the mean.

The formula for the standard error of the difference between the means of independent (*independent* means that selection of an individual in one sample has no effect on who may be selected for the second sample) random samples is:

$$SE_{diff} = \sqrt{SE_{m1}^2 + SE_{m2}^2}$$

The following illustrates an application of the critical ratio test of a mean difference. A vocabulary test consisting of 200 items was administered to all the eighth-grade pupils in the schools of a small city. The following summary data were obtained prior to testing the significance of the difference between the means of the boys and the girls.

	Boys	*Girls*
Mean	139.84	153.20
SD	30.26	27.74
N	100	130

The standard error of the mean for the boys is $\frac{30.26}{\sqrt{99}} = 3.04$;

the standard error of the mean for the girls is $\frac{27.74}{\sqrt{129}} = 2.44$. The standard error of the difference is:

$$SE_{diff} = \sqrt{3.04^2 + 2.44^2} = \sqrt{9.24 + 5.95} = \sqrt{15.19} = 3.90$$

$$CR = \frac{153.20 - 139.84}{3.90} = \frac{13.36}{3.90}$$

$$CR = 3.43$$

The critical ratio is referred to the normal distribution table where it is found that a score which is 3.43 standard deviations away from the mean occurs less than once in one hundred times in a normal distribution. The difference is significant; that is, a difference as large as this or larger occurs very infrequently due to chance sampling fluctuations. It is not reasonable to attribute such a rare event to chance factors. It is more reasonable to ascribe the obtained difference to a real difference between the two groups and, by inference, to the population from which the samples were drawn.

Other Statistical Tests. There are two statistical tests which are worthy of mention, because of their increased frequency of use in research and in the literature of educational psychology. These are analysis of variance and chi-square.

Analysis of variance is a generalized test of differences between means when it is possible to compare many means at one time with data which have been classified according to several variables. This enables independent testing of several pertinent, interrelated hypotheses with only one set of data with the consequent increase in the efficiency of use of available information.

Chi-square is a test of conformity of a set of observed frequencies to a set of hypothesized frequencies. Chi-square permits an hypothesis or theory to predict an outcome in terms of an expected distribution of responses or events. The actual obtained distribution is compared with the predicted distribution and the magnitude of the chi-square indicates the degree of discrepancy. If the discrepancy is large, then it is unlikely that it is due to chance variations, and the disagreement between theory and observation is considered significant. Chi-square is very useful in treating qualitative classifications such as questionnaire responses, occupational categories, and broad measurement groupings due to imprecise data.

The Educational Significance of Statistics. In presenting this elementary and fundamental account of statistical methods and devices, the purpose has been to apply these to educational situations. The classroom teacher needs to be familiar with statistical methods and devices in order to perform intelligently the necessary professional and clerical tasks of his occupation. While computational efficiency is helpful in these tasks, understanding is vital. A fundamental understanding of statistics must be attained by every teacher in a society which relies so greatly upon an extensive numerical record and evaluation system. In order to comprehend and employ efficiently and effectively the extensive data concerning each student and concerning each class group, the teacher must resort to some systematic interpretative process, or else not employ the data or employ it incorrectly. Moreover, the active teacher continues to grow in the profession and some of this growth is acquired through the reading of professional literature. The importance of statistics in educational, psychological, and other scientific and learned publications has increased considerably in recent years. The same situation holds in the case of guidance personnel, who must be especially knowledgeable concerning the statistical bases of psychological tests and other measurement procedures. The validity, reliability, and norms of standardized tests are either defined or demonstrated statistically. The intelligent use of test results requires familiarity with statistical methods and devices. The educational administrator requires a sophisticated understanding of statistical processes. As the individual who is responsible for major decisions in directing the educational process, the administrator must understand the more complex statistical decision procedures and the valid application of such procedures in research and decision-making.

EXERCISES

1. Outline this chapter.
2. List and define the terms which you have learned from your study of this chapter.
3. How were statistical methods introduced into the field of education? What is the need for statistics in education?

4. Distinguish between:
   a) Discrete and continuous data;
   b) Attributes and variables;
   c) Mean and median;
   d) Standard deviation and standard error;
   e) Random and representative sample;
   f) Obtained and true statistical measure.
5. Compute the mean, median, standard deviation, and quartile deviation of the following data:

Scores	*f*	*Answer*
39–41	3	Mean = 31.375
36–38	5	Median = 31.68
33–35	9	$\sigma =$ 5.01
30–32	11	Q = 3.165
27–29	6	
24–26	2	
21–23	3	
18–20	1	
	N = 40	

6. Compute the mean, median, quartile deviation, standard deviation, and thirtieth percentile for the following data:

Scores	*f*	*Answer*
80–84	2	Mean = 55.75
75–79	3	Median = 56.17
70–74	8	Q = 6.765
65–69	10	$\sigma =$ 11.45
60–64	17	$P_{30} =$ 50.9
55–59	24	
50–54	20	
45–49	12	
40–44	5	
35–39	6	
30–34	3	
25–29	1	
20–24	1	
	N = 112	

7. Construct a frequency polygon and a histogram for each of the above distributions.
8. Explain the uses of:
   a) Measures of central tendency;
   b) Measures of deviation;
   c) The coefficient of correlation.
9. Explain the uses and the value of each of the following:
   a) Standard scores;
   b) Ranking;
   c) Critical ratio.
10. What is the educational significance of statistical methods?

SELECTED REFERENCES FOR STUDY AND READING

Blommers, P., and Lindquist, E. F., *Elementary Statistical Methods in Psychology and Education* (Boston: Houghton Mifflin Co., 1960).

Cornell, F. G., *Essentials of Educational Statistics* (New York: John Wiley & Sons, Inc., 1956).

Crowley, F. J., and Cohen, M., *Basic Facts of Statistics* (New York: Collier Books, 1963).

Garrett, H. E., *Statistics in Psychology and Education,* 5 ed. (New York: David McKay Co., Inc., 1958).

——— *Elementary Statistics,* 2 ed. (New York: David McKay Co., Inc., 1962).

Guilford, J. P., *Fundamental Statistics in Psychology and Education,* 3 ed. (New York: McGraw-Hill Book Co., 1956).

Hammond, K. R., and Householder, J. E., *Introduction to the Statistical Method* (New York: Random House, Inc., 1962).

Hoel, P. G., *Elementary Statistics* (New York: John Wiley and Sons, Inc., 1960).

Manuel, H. T., *Elementary Statistics for Teachers* (New York: American Book Co., 1962).

Peatman, J. G., *Introduction to Applied Statistics* (New York: Harper and Row, 1963).

Smith, G. M., *A Simplified Guide to Statistics,* 3 ed. (New York: Holt, Rinehart & Winston, Inc., 1962).

Tate, M. W., *Statistics in Education* (New York: The Macmillan Co., 1955).

Townsend, E. A., and Burke, P. J., *Statistics for the Classroom Teacher* (New York: The Macmillan Co., 1963).

part VI

GUIDANCE AND ADJUSTMENT

chapter 16

Guidance and Counseling in the School

Historical Perspectives. Since the early years of the twentieth century there has been a slow but steady growth in the recognition accorded to *guidance* and *counseling* as essential aspects of the school program. During the first quarter of the century very few schools had organized or planned programs of guidance services. In fact it is only since the end of World War II that such programs have attained widespread acceptance at the secondary school level. Very recently there has become evident a slowly developing trend toward the recognition of the value of guidance services at the elementary school level. The trend has extended also to the colleges and universities, many of which now provide for guidance and counseling as a function of student personnel services.

While the movement toward organized guidance services is a relatively recent development, it is to be noted that traditionally and philosophically education has always been concerned with the guidance of youth. In particular, educational institutions under the sponsorship and direction of various religious organizations have stressed moral and spiritual guidance and have provided specific programs to meet these needs. This has been the core of Catholic education. In public and private schools, dedicated teachers, both lay and religious, have always assisted individual students to understand themselves and to develop their potentialities toward realistic goals. Thus it is evident that guidance in the schools is not new. What is of recent origin, however, is the recognition that the traditional approaches toward the discharge of this responsibility are no longer effective and the realization that the guidance function within the school involves a special responsibility which demands specific competencies and preparation differing in many respects from those of the classroom teacher and the administrator. Guidance and counseling in the modern school constitute a distinct aspect of education.

The terms *guidance* and *counseling* were seldom employed in early educational literature. Jesse Davis in Detroit and Grand Rapids, Eli Weaver in New York City, and Frank Parsons in Boston are the persons most frequently associated with the earliest use of the terms with reference to programs in schools. Davis as principal of a high school in Detroit from 1898 to 1907 counseled eleventh-grade boys and girls regarding their educational and career problems, and later, when he moved to Grand Rapids, instituted a weekly period in English composition devoted to the topics of vocational and moral guidance for all students. He made use of these terms in an address[1] at the meeting of the National Education Association in 1912, and two years later published a book entitled *Vocational and Moral Guidance.*[2] In 1908, the Vocational Guidance Association of Brooklyn was founded and Eli Weaver, a teacher at Boys High School, became its first president. Weaver was concerned with improving the placement possibilities of his students through guidance while they were still in school. Frank Parsons, who is often called "the father of the vocational guidance movement," used the term in a report published in 1908. Parsons was the founder and director of the Breadwinners Institute, which involved an educational program presented on evenings and Saturdays at Civic Service House which was a social settlement. He was greatly concerned with unemployed young men who had no occupational goals. In 1908 he became the director of the Vocation Bureau of Boston, with the title "vocational counselor," and in 1909 his book entitled *Choosing a Vocation*[3] was published posthumously. His ideas set the guidelines which influenced the practice of vocational guidance for almost fifty years. He stressed knowledge of self, knowledge of the possibilities and limitations in the work world, and realistic reasoning on the relation between self and work, as basic to wise vocation choice. These beginnings quickly stimulated similar movements in other cities and conferences on vocational guidance were held, the first in Boston in 1910,

---

[1] J. B. Davis, "Vocational and Moral Guidance through English Composition," *Proceedings and Addresses, National Education Association,* 50:713–718, 1912.

[2] J. B. Davis, *Vocational and Moral Guidance* (Boston: Ginn and Co., 1914).

[3] Frank Parsons, *Choosing a Vocation* (Boston: Houghton Mifflin Co., 1909). See also J. M. Brewer, *History of Vocational Guidance* (New York: Harper and Row, 1942), for a complete account of the pioneer work of Parsons and others.

and the National Vocational Guidance Association was founded in 1913.

The emphasis in these early days was on vocational planning for the purpose of assisting young people to select, prepare for, and enter upon suitable occupations. Truman Kelley,[4] in 1914, used the term *educational guidance* as the title of his doctoral dissertation in which he attempted to develop a more scientific method of classifying students in order to aid them in the selection of high school subjects. Other terms, *recreational, social, personal,* and *health,* were soon coupled with guidance. These, however, grew out of the initial efforts with vocational guidance.

The guidance movement has been subjected to many influences as knowledge in this and allied fields has increased. Concepts and practices have changed over the years. An illustration of the direction of such change is found by comparing the definition of vocational guidance adopted by the National Vocational Guidance Association in 1924: "Vocational Guidance is the giving of information, experience and advice in regard to choosing an occupation, preparing for it, and progressing in it," to that adopted by the same organization in 1937: "Vocational guidance is the process of assisting an individual to choose an occupation, prepare for it, enter upon and progress in it," with the current thinking that the school counselor's responsibility is to help students to become purposeful in their actions. These changing concepts in regard to the practice of school guidance and counseling have evolved as the result of many developments.

In the first decade of this century secondary schools were attended by a comparatively small percentage of the population, and a still smaller percentage continued on to college. School programs ordinarily were prescribed and there was little opportunity for choice or election of subject matter. Teachers, in general, knew their students and likewise the neighborhoods from which they came; family ties were closer; job opportunities were less varied. Technological change, rising immigration, and rapidly increasing populations in cities, however, made it virtually impossible for teachers to keep abreast of employment needs and job possibilities for their students. Hence, the early emphasis was placed on vocational guidance, which marked the beginning of a specialty. Occupations were fairly stable, job and training opportunities were relatively few, and so it was feasible for the school counselor to help the individual to understand his aptitudes, abilities, interests, strong points, and limita-

[4] T. L. Kelley, *Educational Guidance,* Contributions to Education, No. 71 (New York: Teachers College, Columbia University, 1914).

tions, to study the requirements, advantages, and opportunities in different lines of work, and then to select a suitable occupation and plan for the training necessary to enter the occupation. This essentially was the content of the school guidance program for many years. Relatively little was known about the psychology of individuals, of occupations, and about personality and motivation. It was possible to learn a great deal about some occupations, and this information was relatively static. Jobs did not change a great deal from year to year. In 1932 Brewer[5] was able to state: " . . . the literature of occupational life is much nearer to adequacy than it was in 1908." At the present time no idea could be more outdated. The occupational world changes so rapidly that the skilled worker and the technician is quite likely to experience several occupational shifts during his working life. Industries and processes become obsolete. Automation replaces workers but demands greater skill of those who remain. Workers will not have a generation in which to adjust to a declining occupational field. The responsibility of the school counselor is no longer "to help an individual choose an occupation, prepare for it, enter upon and progress in it." Among the responsibilities in this rapidly changing era is the essential one of helping young people to prepare for change, which involves aiding them to learn how to make decisions, in order to be purposeful in their behavior.

In the early stages of the guidance movement there were no psychological tests. As these developed, psychologists and school counselors looked to such tests for solutions to all of the mysteries of the human individual with the result that guidance passed through the era of the "square peg in the square hole." Tests were administered, and test profiles were drawn, and were matched with occupational profiles. Much of vocational guidance consisted of a process of matching tested aptitudes and abilities with the requirements of occupations. Thoughtful counselors, however, found this statistical matching left much to be desired since there were many variables which were not taken into account. In turn they emphasized, as the most significant aspect of counseling, concern for the person who was involved in making the occupational decision.

As compulsory education laws required more children to remain in school for longer periods and as more research results concerning individual differences became available, schools broadened their educa-

[5] J. M. Brewer, *Education as Guidance* (New York: The Macmillan Co., 1932), p. 369.

tional programs at the secondary level and a greater variety of choices were provided in order to meet the needs and abilities of the school population. Students needed help in electing their training programs, and so school counseling emphasized primarily the educational aspects of guidance. Counselors, who now were increasingly and almost exclusively drawn from the ranks of classroom teachers, rarely had previous broad job experiences and consequently were more secure in the educational rather than the occupational areas.

School enrollments mounted rapidly while the number of counseling positions in school failed to increase proportionately. Counselors, in short supply, were devoting more and more of their time to the troubled and disturbing student with the result that school guidance programs in many schools became, in large measure, problem-centered. In others, because of rising college enrollments and increasing difficulties experienced in relation to college admission, some guidance programs were concentrated almost exclusively on the college-bound students.

The tremendous population growth following World War II, and the need for school systems to get ready for the "population explosion," stimulated many studies of school programs during the 1950's. During the same period, the cold war focused attention upon the manpower needs of the country. Since the development of trained manpower is a problem with which American education is intensely involved, studies under the auspices of the National Manpower Council[6] and the National Education Association presented suggestions for educational policy in the light of the manpower situation. One of the most forceful and influential recommendations is that made by the Educational Policies Commission:

> Guidance services, uniquely characteristic of American education, should be further improved, and so increased in scope as to involve all who teach and to reach all who learn. Guidance programs should be soundly rooted in an understanding of the manpower situation.[7]

This and similar recommendations of other studies influenced the Congress to pass the National Defense Education Act of 1958, which provided federal support of guidance activities in two ways: (1) The granting of funds in aid of training for secondary school counselors

---

[6] David Henry, *Education and Man Power* (New York: Columbia University Press, 1960).

[7] *Man Power and Education* (Washington, D. C.: The Educational Policies Commission of the National Education Association, 1956), p. 126.

who had no previous training and for those who required upgrading of their professional competencies in order to be better prepared to identify and counsel able youth. This provision of the Act not only vastly increased the quantity and quality of the professional preparation of counselors on a national scale, but it has also been responsible in large measure for a change in approach to counselor education and for the upgrading of counselor education standards. (2) The granting of funds to states, to be used in the school systems for the guidance, counseling, and testing of able students. These funds have been used to broaden testing programs; to increase counseling staffs in schools by underwriting salary costs; to provide for in-service training and upgrading of counseling programs. This provision of the Act has helped to increase guidance services in schools so that the normal, the gifted, and the "problem child" can all receive needed guidance services.

These developments focused the attention of school counselors and of counselor educators on the need for strategic analysis of the directions in which guidance is going. Consequently, a five-year study of counselor education standards[8] was launched in April, 1960. This study was sponsored by the Association for Counselor Education and Supervision and the American School Counselor Association, both of which are divisions of the American Personnel and Guidance Association.

The original professional association of guidance workers had been the National Vocational Guidance Association. As guidance developed, other organizations, representing special interest groups, were established. The National Association of Deans of Women, the American College Personnel Association, the Alliance for Guidance of Rural Youth joined with the National Vocational Guidance Association to become the American Council of Guidance and Personnel Associations. In 1954, this Council became the American Personnel and Guidance Association. This organization now (1964) has six divisions: National Vocational Guidance Association, Association for Counselor Education and Supervision, American College Personnel Association, Student Personnel Association for Teacher Education, American School Counselor Association, and American Rehabilitation Counseling Association. The official journal of the National Vocational Guidance Association, *Occupations, the Voca-*

[8] *Counselor Education: A Progress Report on Standards,* American Personnel and Guidance Association, Washington, D. C.: 1962. See also "A Report of the Committee on Professional Preparation and Standards," *Personnel and Guidance Journal,* 42:535–541, Jan., 1964.

tional Guidance Magazine, has become *The Personnel and Guidance Journal,* the organ of the American Personnel and Guidance Association. Each of the divisions also publishes a newsletter or a journal, of which the most important for teachers and counselors are *The Vocational Guidance Quarterly* and *The School Counselor.*

Since the early years of the present century, Catholic educators have not only been interested in but also have been active participants in the guidance movement. Catholic education, however, was somewhat slower to initiate guidance programs on a broad scale and this was due principally to two sets of facts: (1) the traditional close relationship between teacher and student in Catholic schools which made it possible, so long as schools and class size remained small, to provide guidance and direction, and (2) the fact that the guidance movement in the early stages had been linked to progressive education and therefore needed to prove itself. However, there were organized guidance programs functioning in Catholic schools and those which existed before 1936 were surveyed by Sister M. Theresa Gertrude Murray, O.S.B.[9] Cribbin[10] reported on the materials and programs which appeared between 1936 and 1950, while Sister Marion[11] presented an evaluation of studies made between 1950 and 1961. Books, articles, and research studies related to guidance have appeared in Catholic educational literature for many years. Catholic universities have long had degree programs at the master's and doctoral levels for the preparation of school counselors. The quality of such programs is evident in the fact that a number of Catholic universities, including Marquette, Loyola of Chicago, Boston College, and Fordham, have conducted guidance institutes under the National Defense Education Act.

There existed a long-felt need among Catholic school counselors for some means to exchange information concerning problems and practices, but there was available no formal organization to provide media for accomplishing this. The National Catholic Education Association had sponsored a few program meetings but did not provide a separate sec-

[9] Sister Teresa Gertrude Murray, O.S.B., *Vocational Guidance in Catholic Secondary Schools,* Contributions to Education, No. 754 (New York: Teachers College Columbia University, 1938).

[10] J. J. Cribbin, "An Analysis of the Theological, Philosophical, Psychological and Sociological Principles of Guidance Presented in Textbooks Published Since 1935," unpublished Ph.D. dissertation, Fordham University, New York, 1951.

[11] Sister Marion, S.S.M., "Counseling in Catholic Education: A Perspective," *The Catholic Counselor,* 5:129–137, 1961.

tion for counselors. In 1951 Catholic school counselors formed the Catholic High School Guidance Council of the Archdiocese of New York. This was the first well-established organization of Catholic counselors. In addition, Catholic counselors had been meeting informally during the annual conventions of the American Personnel and Guidance Association and the 1955 convention program of that organization listed for the first time a meeting for "Catholics in APGA." Since that time annual meetings have been held just preceding the opening of the annual convention of the American Personnel and Guidance Association. The New York Guidance Council and the Catholics in APGA initiated publication of a journal, *The Catholic Counselor,* in the fall of 1956, in order to foster the professional growth of Catholic counselors, and to serve as a forum for the discussion of matters of mutual interest and of problems peculiar to Catholic high school guidance.[12] In 1964, the name of *The Catholic Counselor* was changed to *The National Catholic Guidance Conference Journal.* The pattern of guidance councils under diocesan auspices spread rapidly.[13] Coordination and integration of the various efforts of Catholics in guidance accomplished the forming of the National Catholic Guidance Conference in 1962 with the purpose of supplementing the functions of APGA by concentrating on the guidance problems of American Catholic schools. Catholic education should have an especial interest in organized programs of guidance and counseling, staffed by professionally competent individuals, since the aim of Catholic education is the training and direction of the whole individual according to his true nature for the purpose of rendering more effective the formation of Christian character, citizenship, and leadership.

The Need for Guidance. Fundamentally the boy and the girl in school, particularly at the secondary level, need guidance and counseling not only because they are immature but also because they are faced with the task of making decisions concerning the future, some of which may well be irreversible. They are passing through the process of growth and development which involves the unfolding and expansion of powers and capacities, changes, both structural and functional, and adjustments of a mental, moral, social, and emotional nature. This expansion of powers, these changes and adjustments find expression in new thoughts,

[12] Editorial staff, "Catholic Guidance: A Brief History," *The Catholic Counselor,* 7:45–50, 1963.

[13] Brother J. M. Egan, F.S.C.H., "Guidance Councils on the Diocesan Level," *The Catholic Educator,* 1:3–6, 1956.

new experiences, new interests, and new strength as the individual progresses through the stages of childhood and adolescence to complete maturity. Throughout the process of growth and development the child needs guidance and direction in order that he may better understand himself and his problems, may learn problem-solving methods, and thus make progress toward the attainment of effective *self-direction.*

Basically, children and youth need guidance and counsel in order that they may know the meaning and purpose of life, and the goals which must be sought to attain that purpose. Moreover, guidance is essential in order that the individual may profit from his educational experiences and may develop fully all his powers, capacities, and capabilities. Likewise, guidance is necessary in aiding the individual to choose and prepare intelligently, either wholly or in part, for a work life in which he will find satisfaction, the means of self-support, a place in which to render service, and to achieve a reasonable recognition of his worth by his fellowmen. Consequently, the fundamental and basic reasons why guidance is essential are three. First, guidance is necessary in order that the individual may be aided to *live* a worthy, upright, useful, and happy life according to his nature, and to adjust himself adequately to the world and to his fellow men. Second, guidance is needed to assist the individual in acquiring the knowledge, skills, and attitudes which will enable him to enter an occupation and *to make his living.* Third, guidance is necessary to help the individual to attain the maturity of judgment, stability of emotions, and volitional control which are characteristic of true self-direction. Guidance is necessary because the individual needs and wants help in choosing the right objectives to fulfill the purpose of life and to aid him in every way as he strives to attain these objectives.

Moreover, certain factors and conditions existing in and characterizing modern life and education constitute additional evidence of the necessity for making adequate provision within the school for an organized program of guidance in its various aspects. Among the factors and conditions[14] frequently listed are the following:

---

[14] R. H. Mathewson, *Guidance Policy and Practice* (New York: Harper & Row, 1962), pp. 42–70; C. G. Wrenn, *The Counselor in a Changing World,* The Commission on Guidance in American Schools, American Personnel and Guidance Association (Washington, D. C.: 1961), pp. 1–51; C. H. Miller, *Foundations of Guidance* (New York: Harper & Row, 1961), pp. 18–33; P. W. Hutson, *The Guidance Function in Education* (New York: Appleton-Century-Crofts, Inc., 1958), pp. 110–150.

1. The increased complexity of modern life, particularly in its social, industrial, and economic aspects, which has led to specialization of occupations; the replacement of much unskilled labor by machines; a labor market which is unable to absorb the numbers of untrained young people entering the work world each year; the opening of many occupations to women; a demand that workers possess more education; urbanization of population; and greatly increased leisure time.

2. An increase in the amount of general education due to the larger number of youth remaining in school at the secondary level. In an attempt to meet as adequately as possible the needs of individuals, the great majority of whom are not planning or preparing to enter college, and in the attempt to prevent as far as possible "dropouts" and elimination for failure, the curriculum offerings and materials at the secondary school level have been both expanded and enriched, and in addition supplemented by a varied program of extracurricular activities.

3. Trends in education notable among which are: the emphasis upon the identification and development of academically talented youth; the introduction of new course work in science and stress upon the learning of languages; the concern for high school students whose level of aspiration is not in keeping with their scholastic potential; the rapid extension of community college facilities.

4. The growing emphasis placed upon the necessity for discovering and developing qualities of effective leadership among youth.

5. The unwholesome tendency for many of the responsibilities once considered as belonging entirely to the home to be shifted to the school due to changing patterns of family life.

6. A vital concern for an adequate solution for the problems of adjustment which have grown out of the uncertainty of world conditions.

7. The recognition of the great complexity and variation of the aptitudinal, mental, physical, interest, and personality differences with the consequent emphasis upon individual differences for the resulting expansion of the whole school program to provide for these differences.

It should be noted that the need for guidance is universal. Consequently, the need for guidance is not confined to the maladjusted, to the problem cases, to the failures, to those pupils whose economic and social backgrounds are considered inadequate. All children and youth need counsel and direction. Furthermore, the need for guidance is not confined to any one stage or period of growth and development or to any one level of education. Guidance is the concern of the entire educational process from the primary grades through the university. Yet, if any one period of growth and development were to be chosen as the stage at which effective guidance were most needed, that period would undoubtedly be *adolescence.* At that stage, youth is faced with the necessity of making strenuous efforts to adjust to many and complex phases of life. These efforts give rise to numerous problems and difficulties. At no other time in life is there greater need for providing thoughtful counsel, understanding guidance, and prudent direction in order that youth may achieve that self-control and self-sufficiency which will enable him to take his place in the adult world, which will help him to adjust to that world, which will aid him in performing the tasks necessary both to live his life and to making his living.

Definition of Guidance. Broadly conceived, guidance is that assistance given to the individual to help him be purposeful and effective in his behavior. In order to be purposeful, the individual needs to have knowledge of himself and also of the world in which he functions currently; to have some idea of the possibilities in his future; and to develop such attitudes about himself and his situation as will enable him to maximize his potential with benefit to himself and to society, always mindful of his eternal destiny.

In this complex world individuals need help in securing and utilizing information. Such information involves knowledge of themselves, particularly about their abilities, potentialities, interests, motivation, and emotional reactions. It also concerns the relative values of these characteristics both within themselves and in comparison with others as well as knowledge regarding the effect of their behavior on others. Such information must include facts about opportunities — educational, occupational, and social which are available not only in their own communities, but generally; not only currently, but with attention especially to trends and foreseeable future developments. However, the dissemination of information, by itself, rarely aids the individual to internalize and make use of it. Facts alone are insufficient. Individuals need help in utilizing facts in order to clarify their attitudes and to motivate their behavior. These accomplishments must be self-directed. Therefore, guidance aims to develop and to increase in the individual the ability for *self-direction.* Information is used to help the individual to understand the need to plan rather than to drift, to broaden his outlook, and to increase his appreciation of alternatives and their consequences, so that he may choose wisely, make sound decisions, and consciously control his behavior.

Too often it is assumed that the student's problem is solved by the counselor, that the counselor decides what is best for the student and tells him what to do. On the contrary, guidance services are directed toward the growth and development of the individual, as well as toward the solution of immediate problems, and, therefore, they must be directed toward the development of independence in the student where the responsibility for decisions must remain with the student; however, the counselor has the obligation of assisting the student to make adequate and correct decisions.

Guidance, then, may be defined as *the process of aiding the development of each individual by assisting him to make his own plans and decisions, consonant with his own unique potentialities as they relate to the requirements and opportunities of the society in which he lives and in accordance with moral, social, and spiritual values.*[15]

There are *nine essential elements* in this definition which may be discussed further:

1. *The process:* this denotes not an act or a number of discrete actions, but rather a long-term articulated series of guidance activities taking place over a period of years extending throughout school life during which the individual develops a more mature and self-sufficient outlook.

2. *The developmental aspects:* individuals develop progressively in their ability to understand themselves and to control their behavior; therefore guidance must be a continuous process the chief concern of which is the development of the *whole* individual.

3. *Guidance is not restricted to the disturbed, the gifted, the "problems,"* but rather that each may become increasingly *self-directive.*

4. The *focus is upon the individual,* even though some of the approaches in the process might be in a group setting.

5. The *assistance* given may involve counsel to the student, interpretation to the classroom teachers or parents, referral to other services, or a host of other procedures which may perform an enabling function for the individual.

6. *The individual has the right and the obligation of free choice:*

[15] This definition of guidance was formulated by Dr. Genevieve Hunter Loughran, formerly Associate Professor of Education, Division of Educational Psychology, Measurements and Guidance, School of Education, Fordham University, now of Hunter College.

guidance aims to increase the *self-direction,* and also the problem-solving and decision-making abilities of the individual.

7. A wise decision depends on *knowledge,* not just of the here and now, but of the possibility for the future. Guidance aims to help individuals understand, accept, and develop their true potentialities.

8. *Self-understanding, alone, is insufficient:* a realistic *appraisal* of the opportunities in the world in which he will live and work is important for the individual if he is to attain self-fulfillment and contribute to society.

9. *Values* are not just things desired, they are desirable according to some norm. Guidance helps the individual to understand himself in relation to the unchanging eternal values: his responsibility to himself, to his fellowman, to God. It helps him to become a valuing person.

Thus as a process designed to aid individuals in making *present adjustments* and in *planning for the future,* guidance cannot be an independent agency in education. Rather it is a function inherent in all education. As such a function it consists in instructing, counseling, and assisting pupils in the process of formulating, of choosing, and of attaining objectives which are meaningful, desirable, and worthy morally, educationally, and socially. These objectives must of necessity be attainable and within the range of the individual's abilities, interest, and development. Since guidance involves purposeful planning of life, it must be functional. It must be essentially a process by which the individual understands better and more fully his capacities, by which he focuses his interests, by which he develops his capacities in terms of his interests, and by which he relates both to worthwhile purposes and objectives. The aim of this process and the measure of its success is the achievement of *complete self-direction.* Thus, guidance consists of the methods and the means by which education emphasizes the goal of helping every pupil to achieve his fullest development, particularly through utilizing intelligently the experiences afforded by the school.

Guidance, as the definition implies, includes assistance in relation to varied problem areas. At one time this assistance was designated by the titles that related to the problem area. For example, *educational guidance* was the term applied to that help to pupils which was designed to aid them in adjusting themselves to the demands and environment of the school; *social-civic guidance* was the term applied to assistance designed to help pupils in making satisfactory social adjustments. However, guidance cannot be fragmented. The educational problem is often basically a problem of vocational choice, or lack of goal direction; the health problem is often one of social adjustment. Thus it is that current thinking reflects the interrelationship of problems and the integrated approach that is necessary to their solution. Guidance is concerned with the all-around development of the individual, his physical, mental, moral, social, and spiritual self. Guidance focuses on the individual and his problems in their totality. However, for convenience of discussion, problems may be classified into major areas as follows:

Problems in the *area of education* call for assistance and counsel in order to aid pupils in adjusting themselves to the demands and environment of the school; to aid them in choosing wisely, in planning intelligently, and in pursuing purposefully an educational program suited to their abilities and needs. Students need help in developing desirable work and study habits in order that they may strive to attain maximum results in accord with their abilities and capacities. Assistance with problems in this area requires on the part of the counselor a knowledge of the past achievements, interests, abilities, and difficulties of pupils.

Problems in the *area of health* require that pupils be helped in order to enable them to utilize to the utmost advantage all of the knowledge, equipment, and facilities of education designed for the promotion of the well-being of both body and mind. Such help involves the need to impart information and to apply corrective measures which will assure the retention and improvement of physical health. Likewise, it includes the need to acquire a knowledge of the sound principles and practices of mental hygiene which will be of assistance in the attainment, retention, and improvement of mental health, in the formation of correct attitudes, and in the adjustment to the difficulties arising out of the experiences of daily living.

Problems in the *vocational area* necessitate aid, assistance, and counsel to the individual pupil in his consideration of a future occupation, career, or state in life which is in accord with his abilities, interests, and potentialities, and to help prevent wrong choices. It implies the need to assist the individual in making informed choices by enabling him to know his own qualifications and capacities; to define success; to enable him to estimate the possibility of personal success in the field chosen; to enable him to understand that much depends upon his general abilities, upon his specific interests, upon his attitudes, and upon the effectiveness of his character. Guidance in the area of vocational problems includes the imparting of systematic information concerning the nature of occupations, the qualifications required, the means and methods for training, the opportunities offered in the field, and is concerned with predictable future developments. It focuses on the necessity to plan for change. Frequently this aspect of guidance involves, in addition to imparting information, such services as testing, placement in employment, and follow-up in order to determine how effectively the individual adjusts himself in his chosen field.

Problems in the *moral and religious areas*[16] involve the process of directing, assisting, and counseling the individual in order that he may acquire the necessary knowledge and understanding of the principles governing right conduct and by living in accord with that knowledge and understanding may put the principles of right conduct into practice in all aspects of life. Guidance in this area seeks the formation of character through the presentation of moral and religious ideals, through the formation of adequate habits, and through the attainment of self-control and self-reliance.

Problems in the *social-civic areas* require that help, assistance, and counsel be given to the individual to enable him to adjust himself to his social environment in order that he may become a worthy and interested participant in and function effectively as a member of society. It includes the need to expand and enrich interests and suitable recreational and leisure-time activities together with motivation to participate in these activities. Likewise, it includes the need to impart information and the formation of correct attitudes to enable the individual to assume worthily in adult life the rights, duties, and responsibilities of citizenship.

Pupil Personnel Services and Guidance. The operations of the school can be classified conveniently into three major areas: administration, instruction, personnel. The pupil personnel services have been defined as:

> . . . those professional services, other than classroom instruction, which are offered by the school to help pupils attain their maximum personal development, and further, to facilitate the efforts of parents and teachers in the guiding and teaching-learning process.[17]

[16] See C. A. Curran, *Counseling in Catholic Life and Education* (New York: The Macmillan Co., 1952); C. T. Hagmaier, C.S.P., and R. W. Gleason, S.J., *Counseling the Catholic* (New York: Sheed & Ward, Inc., 1960).

[17] R. Lowe, *A Rationale and Models for Organizing and Administering Programs of Pupil Personnel Services,* Bureau of Educational Research, School of Education, University of Oregon, Eugene, Oregon, 1962.

Wrenn[18] has included on the team of pupil personnel specialists the school counselor, school psychologist, school social worker, school health officer, and school attendance worker.

Guidance is one of the components of the pupil personnel services program. This program involves professional educational services functioning as an integral part of the school program with the common objective of facilitating the maximum development of individual potentialities through education. While these services are distinct from classroom instruction, they are supportive of it. These services have many concepts in common, namely: concern for the individual student; interest in all students, not just the atypical; an educational rather than a clinical orientation; emphasis upon the developmental process concerned with growth in self-direction; recognition of the key role of the teacher and the responsibility of the parent in child development. Likewise, there are many elements and activities which are common to all of the services including: understanding of the individual; providing information about pupils and about the environment; counseling; using other resources available both within and out of the school; feedback to teachers and administrators; research and evaluation. Despite these common elements, there is a high degree of specialization of function:

1. School attendance services are responsible for insuring regular attendance of all school-age children who should be in school, for providing leadership in promoting positive pupil and parent attitudes toward regular school attendance, for identifying and arranging for children with handicaps to enter educational programs outside the regular school program which are appropriate to their needs, for issuing employment certificates, and for providing liaison with law-enforcement agencies.

2. School health services are responsible for arranging and supervising physical examinations, for interpretation of health information to teachers, parents, and administrators, making referrals to community health agencies, and day-to-day health service and counseling.

3. School social work services are responsible for providing case work and consultative services for pupils, parents, teachers, and administrators; for referrals to community agencies concerned with child guidance and family welfare.

4. School psychological services are responsible for providing diagnostic

[18] C. G. Wrenn, *op. cit.;* see also W. F. Johnson, B. Stefflre, and R. Edelfelt, *Pupil Personnel and Guidance Services* (New York: McGraw-Hill Book Co., Inc., 1961).

and case-study information as a basis for remedial programs, for organizing and administrating the basic program of group testing, for interpreting special psychological needs of pupils to teachers and parents.

5. School guidance services are responsible for the early identification of pupils' abilities and needs, assistance to students and parents in terms of understanding of self and movement toward realistic educational and vocational goals, assistance to administrators and teachers in relation to improved understanding of students as basis for program planning.

In terms of structure, then, guidance is one of the pupil personnel services supporting and facilitating the instructional program of the school.

Guidance in the Elementary School.[19] The guidance program may have varying functions and may utilize different activities in the elementary school, in the high school, and in the college. However, the broad purposes are the same at all levels.

The expansion of guidance services at the secondary level, together with the research and evaluation which accompanied that expansion, has pointed up a number of facts that have been responsible, in large measure, for the recent rapid growth of guidance services at the elementary level:

1. The number of problems discovered and treated in the secondary school, the origins or causes of which might well have been identified years sooner, and remedial or preventive action undertaken before behavior and learning patterns had been firmly established:

2. The need for early identification and development of talent; underachievement can be detected very early;

3. The formulation of a philosophy of guidance which is developmental, continuous, preventive, which suggests that guidance must begin in the elementary school;

---

[19] See J. A. Barr, *The Elementary Teacher and Guidance* (New York: Holt, Rinehart and Winston, Inc., 1958); R. H. Knapp, *Guidance in the Elementary School* (Boston: Allyn and Bacon, Inc., 1959); E. Lloyd-Jones, R. Barry, and B. Wolff, eds., *Guidance in Elementary Education: A Case Book* (New York: Bureau of Publications, Teachers College, Columbia University, 1958); R. A. Martinson and H. Smallenburgh, *Guidance in Elementary Schools* (Englewood Cliffs, N. J.: Prentice-Hall, Inc., 1958); R. D. Willey, *Guidance in Elementary Education,* rev. ed. (New York: Harper & Row, 1960); H. Peters, A. Riccio, and S. Quaranta, *Guidance in the Elementary School* (New York: The Macmillan Co., 1963); E. W. Detjen and M. F. Detjen, *Elementary School Guidance,* 2 ed. (New York: McGraw-Hill Book Co., 1963); I. J. Gordon, *The Teacher as a Guidance Worker* (New York: Harper & Row, 1956); A. J. Jones, *op. cit.,* pp. 127–146; E. C. Johnston, M. Peters, and W. Evraiff, *The Role of the Teacher in Guidance* (Englewood Cliffs, N. J.: Prentice-Hall, Inc., 1959); G. T. Kowitz and N. G. Kowitz, *Guidance in the Elementary School* (New York: McGraw-Hill Book Co., Inc., 1959).

4. Research which suggests that the self-concept of the child is formed early and that his understanding and acceptance of self facilitates or impedes his learning and adjustment; teachers need help in understanding individual children and their needs in order to provide a learning climate which assists each individual in developing and accepting a realistic picture of self;

5. The increasing use of tests has made the work of studying children a more technical task;

6. Parents may be helped more positively when the child is in the elementary school than later.

Traditionally the elementary school teacher endeavored to meet the unique needs of each child. However, this has become an exceedingly difficult, if not impossible, task with such widely diverse groups of children attending the complex modern elementary school. The teacher's responsibility has increased tremendously as knowledge of individuals and of their behavior has increased, as the curriculum has been expanded and modified, as new educational media have been utilized in the instructional process. Many teachers have sought assistance from supporting services and they should have access to the skills of specialists in helping them to perform their instructional functions more effectively.

The organization of the guidance programs at the elementary level varies considerably from school to school. In some school systems the services of a full-time specialist are available, while in others several schools share the services of a counselor. The functions of the counselor vary also. However, in general, the school counselor at the elementary level provides direct services to children in individual and in group situations. The counselor also administers standardized psychological tests to individual pupils, counsels with them to aid in the attainment of better self-understanding, works with those who need special help in remedial or in emotional situations, and aids in the process of orientating new pupils who enter school during the year. Elementary school guidance centers around three major areas: namely, assisting students to understand and accept themselves, to develop satisfactory social relations with others, and to achieve successful experiences in academic areas.

With regard to assistance to teachers, the elementary school counselor consults with individual teachers in order to improve their understanding of the needs of individual pupils; helps teachers to identify pupils who need assistance; interprets test results and data from cumulative records to individual teachers and to groups of teachers in case conferences or in in-service training; assists teachers in conducting parent conferences; and makes direct contact with and provides consultation services for parents at the request of the teacher or of the principal.

With regard to assistance to the administration, the elementary school counselor serves in a resource capacity to teachers and administrators concerning guidance matters, assists with the in-service training of teachers for the guidance function, makes referrals to other specialists both within the system and in the local community, maintains an adequate supply of guidance literature for teachers and parents, organizes and maintains guidance records, conducts follow-up and research activities, and makes evaluation studies.

In addition, counselors at elementary school level frequently conduct group-guidance programs involving orientation to the work world, the establishment of effective study habits, and the adjustment problems of pupils. The elementary school counselor is responsible for the orderly transfer of students to the junior high school, and in K–8 systems, is responsible for the orientation of the pupil to senior high school, as well as for the selection of a suitable high school program.

The Guidance Program in the Secondary School.* The counselor at the secondary school level assists all students in educational and vocational planning and in personal and social development. He has responsibilities to individual students, to the teaching staff, to the parents, to the school administrators, and to the community. In order to discharge these responsibilities he utilizes a variety of activities and may work with individuals or with groups. The activities of the counselor at the secondary school level may be classified into those that are concerned with:

1. Information about students;
2. Information about opportunities;
3. Counseling;
4. Consultative services to the administrative and teaching staff, to parents, and to community;
5. Evaluation and research.

1. Information About Students. Assistance to students must be based on facts; therefore, an important responsibility of the counselor is to

* See the *Statement of Policy for Secondary School Counselors* and *Guidelines for Implementation of the A.S.C.A. Statement of Policy for Secondary School Counselors* (Washington, D. C.: The American Personnel and Guidance Association, 1964).

acquire the essential facts about the individual student. Zeran and Riccio have divided this information into five categories:

> 1) the identifying data gained from school entrance interview; 2) the information provided by previous school performance; 3) the information gained from standardized instruments; 4) the information gained from the students themselves; 5) the information gained from . . . others in the school situation.[20]

School counselors coordinate the collection and interpretation of information for the *cumulative record system.* The well-planned and carefully kept cumulative personnel or development record is indispensable in guidance and counseling. The purpose of the cumulative record is to present a composite picture of the individual pupil. Recognizing that sufficient information concerning the abilities, interests, and needs of pupils cannot be gathered in a brief period of time, through a process of conducting one or several interviews and through administering tests of various types, counselors and administrators have devoted considerable time to the development of cumulative record forms. The primary purpose of such forms is to assemble and organize in systematic fashion the pertinent data concerning the individual pupil. These data are then recorded on a permanent card or folder suitable for filing. The form employed varies with the requirements of the guidance program functioning within the school. Since only accurate information can produce the knowledge essential for giving effective guidance, for meeting needs, and for aiding in the formation of the plans of the individual, it is necessary that the data recorded be basic and significant. Jones[21] has listed several fundamental principles which are of value in determining the facts recorded on the cumulative record form: (1) record facts about the student; (2) record only facts; (3) record only facts that will be used; (4) record facts in such a way that the maximum of data can be recorded in a minimum of space; (5) record facts in such a way that the significance of the data can be seen quickly; (6) keep together all facts regarding the individual.

The basic data pertaining to the individual included on the cumulative record form should include information concerning:

1. History of previous school experiences and progress;

---

[20] F. R. Zeran and A. C. Riccio, *Organization and Administration of Guidance Services* (Chicago: Rand McNally & Co., 1962), p. 7 .

[21] A. J. Jones, *op. cit.,* pp. 107–108; see also A. E. Traxler, *Techniques of Guidance,* rev. ed. (New York: Harper & Row, 1957), pp. 191–232.

2. Home background, socioeconomic status, and community environment;
3. Health status;
4. Scores attained on tests of mental ability or scholastic aptitude, with separate scores for specialized capacities such as language, verbal, numerical, spatial;
5. Scores achieved on tests of scholastic achievement, school grades, teacher ratings;
6. Results of tests of scholastic and vocational interests;
7. Test ratings of social and personal development and adjustment;
8. Participation in school activities including extracurricular activities;
9. Participation in activities outside of school including work experiences;
10. Previous counseling.

The school counselor participates in developing group testing programs to appraise the abilities, aptitudes, achievement, and interests of the students and supervises the administration of standardized group tests. In the guidance process these *tests*[22] play an important role. These instruments are employed to determine the abilities, achievements, and interests of pupils. The resulting data are extremely important in guidance and counseling, when they are adequately interpreted and carefully evaluated. The types of tests employed in the guidance process include those of mental ability or scholastic aptitude; scholastic achievement in the various academic subject-matter and skill fields; special aptitudes; interests, both educational and vocational; and aspects of personality. Extensive treatment has already been given in previous chapters to tests of mental ability, scholastic achievement, and study skills. The results of tests of mental ability and scholastic achievement constitute a basis for effective guidance. The results of the tests of mental ability indicate

[22] See D. E. Super and J. O. Crites, *Appraising Vocational Fitness* (New York: Harper & Row, 1962); L. Goldman, *Using Tests in Counseling* (New York: Appleton-Century-Crofts, Inc., 1961); C. P. Froehlich and K. B. Hoyt, *Guidance Testing* (Chicago: Science Research Associates, Inc., 1959); J. W. Rothney, P. J. Danielson, and R. A. Heimman, *Measurement for Guidance* (New York: Harper & Row, 1959); R. F. Berdie, W. L. Layton, E. O. Swanson, and T. Hagenah, *Testing in Guidance and Counseling* (New York: McGraw-Hill Book Co., 1963); E. E. Ghiselli, *Measurement of Occupational Aptitude* (Berkeley: University of California Press, 1955); L. J. Cronback, *Essentials of Psychological Testing,* 2 ed. (New York: Harper & Row, 1960); R. L. Thorndike and E. Hagen, *Measurement and Evaluation in Psychology and Education,* 2 ed. (New York: John Wiley & Sons, Inc., 1961); A. J. Jones, *op. cit.,* pp. 65–82.

the level of maturation or readiness for learning attained by the pupil; identify the exceptional pupils, that is, the gifted and slow learning; aid in diagnosis of learning difficulties; determine reasonable expectation in achievement and the extent to which the pupil is working up to his capacity; indicate the need for effective motivation; and serve as a basis for the prediction of educational and vocational success. The results of the tests of scholastic achievement, particularly of the diagnostic type, provide data for judging the causes of pupil difficulties; are indicative of specific strengths and, likewise, of difficulties, problems, and needs in particular subject-matter areas, both of each pupil and of the entire class; reveal the status; appraise the progress in terms of age and grade placement of each pupil and of the entire class. The results of scholastic achievement tests are valuable also in aiding the student to plan a course of study, to select a major field of study, to think in terms of a career. In addition, the results of scholastic achievement tests, when considered together with those of tests of scholastic or learning aptitude, are helpful in locating pupils who are not achieving according to the level of their abilities. The various measures of study skills have value as counseling aids, since they are diagnostic measures the results of which may serve as the basis for remedial work and differential emphasis in teaching methods and motivation.

Tests of *special aptitudes* have been devised to supplement tests of mental ability and of academic achievement in attaining an adequate understanding of the abilities and potentialities of pupils and, likewise, to aid in predicting the probable success of pupils in specific educational and vocational fields. *Aptitude* has been defined as:

> A condition or set of characteristics regarded as symptomatic of an individual's ability to acquire with training some (usually specified) knowledge, skill, or set of responses such as the ability to speak a language, to produce music. . . .[23]

> The capacity to acquire proficiency with a given amount of training, formal or informal.[24]

An aptitude test then involves the assessment of knowledge, skill, and other characteristics which serve to predict some type of learning. There are several types of aptitude tests, including academic-aptitude or prog-

[23] H. C. Warren, *Dictionary of Psychology* (Boston: Houghton Mifflin Co., 1934).
[24] H. B. English and A. C. English, *A Comprehensive Dictionary of Psychological and Psychoanalytical Terms* (New York: Longmans, Green & Co., 1958).

nostic tests in special subjects which have been discussed previously, vocational-aptitude tests, and professional-aptitude tests.

Among the vocational-aptitude tests[25] frequently employed in the guidance process, the following are representative:

Meier Art Judgment Test;
Graves Design Judgment Test;
Seashore Measures of Musical Talent;
The General Clerical Test;
Minnesota Rate of Manipulation Test;
Minnesota Spatial Relations Test;
Revised Minnesota Paper Form Board Test;
S.R.A. Test of Clerical Competence;
Bennett Mechanical Comprehension Test;
Wrightstone-O'Toole Prognostic Test of Mechanical Abilities;
Turse Clerical Aptitude Test;
Johnson-O'Connor Finger Dexterity and Tweezer Dexterity Tests.

Professional aptitude tests are available in the fields of medicine, law, engineering, teaching, nursing, dentistry, pharmacy, and accounting. These tests are used primarily as selective instruments in determining the admission of students to professional schools. They are also employed for the purpose of counseling students concerning the appropriateness of professional choices. The *Graduate Record Examination* and the *Miller Analogies Test* have also been developed to test the aptitudes of students in various fields of graduate study.

In addition to the tests of special aptitudes, there have been devised integrated batteries of aptitude tests especially for use in educational and vocational counseling at the junior and senior high school levels. Representative of these aptitude batteries are the *Differential Aptitude Tests,* the *Multiple Aptitude Tests,* the *Flanagan Aptitude Classification Tests,* the *General Aptitude Test Battery,* the *Guilford-Zimmerman Aptitude Survey,* the *Holzinger-Crowder Uni-Factor Tests, Factored Aptitude Series of Business and Industrial Tests.* The *Differential Aptitude Tests* are composed of eight sections, namely, verbal reasoning, numerical ability, abstract reasoning, space relations, mechanical reasoning, clerical

[25] It is well to note that "Aptitude tests do not directly measure future accomplishments. They make no such pretense. They measure present performances. Then, in so far as behavior, past and present, is known to be symptomatic of future potentialities, the estimate is necessarily in terms of probabilities only." See W. V. Bingham, *Aptitudes and Aptitude Testing* (New York: Harper & Row, 1937), p. 22.

speed and accuracy, language usage (spelling and sentences). The *Multiple Aptitude Tests* consist of nine tests, namely, word meaning, paragraph meaning, language usage, routine clerical facility, arithmetic reasoning, arithmetic computation, applied science and mechanics, spatial relations two dimensions, and spatial relations three dimensions. The *Flanagan Aptitude Classification Test Battery* consists of twenty-one tests which have been designed to provide measures of an individual's aptitude for each of twenty-one job elements, namely, inspection, coding, memory, precision, assembly, scales, coordination, judgment and comprehension, arithmetic, patterns, components, tables, mechanics, and expression, vocabulary, reasoning, planning, ingenuity, alertness, tapping, and carving. *The General Aptitude Test Battery* consists of twelve tests which yield nine aptitude scores as follows: intelligence, verbal aptitude, numerical aptitude, spatial aptitude, form perception, clerical perception, motor coordination, finger dexterity, and manual dexterity. *The Guilford-Zimmerman Aptitude Survey* consists of seven parts and provides seven scores: verbal comprehension, general reasoning, numerical operations, perceptual speed, spatial orientation, spatial visualization, and mechanical knowledge. *The Holzinger-Crowder Uni-Factor Tests* have been designed to measure four types of mental ability which are considered to be significant in the prediction of academic success. These are: verbal ability, spatial ability, numerical ability, and reasoning ability. *The Factored Aptitude Series of Business and Industrial Tests* is composed of fourteen tests designed to measure eight factors as follows: comprehension, reasoning, systems, perception, fluency, memory, space relations, and coordination.[26]

Interests, because they are indicative directly of pupils' likes and dislikes and thus indirectly of their goals and purposes, are also given adequate consideration in the guidance process. However, it should be noted that interests in themselves do not constitute a sufficient basis upon which to select a vocation, because ability is a more significant factor. Accordingly, interests would not be a focal point in counseling. Likewise, it should be noted that during adolescence, interests, particularly in vocations, are likely to fluctuate, to lack permanency, to be impractical, and to be out of harmony with abilities. Nevertheless, interests should not be ignored in counseling. Accordingly, the best available measures

[26] See J. Samler, ed., *The Use of Multifactor Tests in Guidance* (Washington, D. C.: American Personnel and Guidance Association, 1958), for a complete description and evaluation of the above-listed aptitude batteries.

which have been devised to discover and to obtain information concerning interests should be employed in connection with the case study and the interview techniques, and the results recorded upon the cumulative record. Among the devices which counselors have found of value for the purpose of discovering and obtaining information concerning interests the following are representative:

Strong Vocational Interest Blank;
Kuder Preference Record;
Lee-Thorpe Occupational Interest Inventory and Vocational Interest Analyses;
Thurstone Vocational Interest Schedule;
Brainard Occupational Preference Inventory;
Edwards Personal Preference Schedule;
Allport-Vernon-Lindzey Study of Values.

These inventories have been designed to serve as aids in identifying the basic occupational interests of the pupil in order that he may be guided in exploring the possibilities of an occupation. Interest inventories do not measure abilities or potentialities; they are indicators rather than predictors. For this reason they should be used with caution and restraint.[27] However, in spite of their limitations there is evidence available which indicates that interest inventories and preference records are among the widely used tools of counseling.

Educators have long recognized that the "personality" of pupils constitutes a factor in the process of adjustment both in school and in life which is fully as significant as scholastic aptitude and achievement. However, the measurement of personality has presented many more difficulties than the measurement of mental ability and scholastic achievement, because the components of personality are considered by many psychologists to be intangibles. However, tests have been devised for the purpose of measuring these intangibles, namely, the emotional, social, and motivational aspects of adjustment. These tests have usually been designated as *personality inventories.* While the personality inventories thus far available lack a high degree of validity, nevertheless they sometimes have a value in the process of guidance. Designed as tools for discovering causes of maladjustment through the early identification of problems and as indicators of attitudes, they yield a quantitative statement of personal-

[27] E. C. Craven, *The Use of Interest Inventories in Counseling* (Chicago: Science Research Associates, Inc., 1961).

ity in the form of a score or profile. Examination of the profile of each student's personality inventory in order to determine areas of relative strength and weakness among the characteristics measured will enable the counselor to recognize those students whose personality patterns may lead them into academic, social, or vocational difficulties and to determine the areas in which guidance is most needed.

Among the personality inventories frequently employed in the counseling process are:

The California Psychological Inventory;
The Minnesota Counseling Inventory;
Bell Adjustment Inventory;
Bernreuter Personality Inventory;
California Test of Personality;
Heston Personal Adjustment Inventory;
Gordon Personal Profile;
Minnesota Multiphasic Personality Inventory;
Pintner Aspects of Personality;
Washburne Social Adjustment Inventory;
K-D Proneness Scale and Check List.

In addition to the various types of measuring instruments already described, the *problem checklist* is also frequently employed in the guidance process. The purpose of this device is to locate problem areas which affect a significant number of pupils within a school. The use of the problem checklist may reveal in addition needs for guidance in specific problem areas either in the form of group guidance in the homeroom or conference period or in counseling with individual pupils. Among the representative problem checklists are the *S.R.A. Youth Inventory* and the *Mooney Problem Check List.*

The school counselor employs the *interview technique*[28] for the purpose of obtaining information concerning the abilities, interests, personal characteristics, attitudes, and motivation of the pupil. He uses the *autobiography* and other *self-report techniques* as instruments of self-appraisal and also utilizes anecdotal records as means of enlarging his knowledge of the pupil. He encourages, arranges, and participates in *case conferences* for the study of students' growth and development. This may be done in the interest of better understanding of an individual student, or

[28] W. V. Bingham, B. V. Moore, and J. W. Gustad, *How to Interview* (New York: Harper & Row, 1959).

it may constitute a method of helping the school staff to develop greater understanding of all students. The counselor prepares case material for appropriate persons both within and outside of the school. The *case study*[29] and evaluation process may be described as a comprehensive factual account of all of the factors in an individual's life history which may lead to fruitful hypotheses regarding the nature and causes of difficulties or which may shed light upon specific behavior or personality development. It constitutes "the heart of the guidance and counseling process."[30] It involves the obtaining of information concerning the developmental background of the individual; the environmental conditions amid which he lives and which are significant because they help or hinder adequate adjustment. It includes also a record of the strong and weak points of character, of emotional reactions, of habits and attitudes, of the adequacy with which the individual customarily meets situations. It includes, likewise, relevant data concerning the interests, the plans, and the problems of the individual, his hobbies and work experience. The purpose of the case history is to present a complete picture of the pupil and all phases of his development in order to enable the counselor to attain a thorough understanding of the individual. Its object also is to aid in tracing maladjustments to their sources and to help in remedying undesirable behavior.

Among the many factors which might be presented in the case history, the following seem of most significance to the counselor: *family backgrounds, developmental history, health record, environment both at home and neighborhood, educational history including previous school experiences and progress, social development and adaptability, plans* (educational and vocational), *interests* (educational, vocational, and avocational), *test data* (intelligence, achievement aptitude, and personality), *significant episodes observed by teachers, and summaries of interests.* The case study utilizes the materials presented in the case history in order to enable the counselor to interpret and to evaluate these facts for the purpose of making recommendations for treatment. For this reason the trends and patterns of behavior described in the case history are of special significance.

---

[29] A. E. Traxler, *op. cit.*, pp. 266–281.

[30] R. H. Mathewson, *Guidance Policy and Practice* (New York: Harper & Row, 1962), pp. 263–264. See also L. Goldman, *op. cit.;* D. A. Prescott, *The Child in the Educative Process* (New York: McGraw-Hill Book Co., Inc., 1957), for the various techniques of case evaluation.

2. Information About Opportunities. The school counselor shares in the development and maintenance of informational resources which will assist students in their personal, social, and occupational planning and adjustment. Such materials include school and college catalogues, information concerning scholarships and loans, vocational training, jobs and careers, summer school, summer and part-time employment, community resources for employment, welfare, and other services. The counselor encourages and arranges field visits to educational institutions, businesses and industry and maintains up-to-date information on military obligations. The accumulation of information, however, is insufficient; the counselor must assure its use by students, parents, and teachers. He needs to be creative in motivating individuals to utilize the informational resources available.

3. Counseling.[31] The aim of the guidance program is to help the individual to increase his self-understanding and to achieve reasonable responsibility and self-direction. The goal of counseling is purposive self-direction. This involves learning activity on the part of the students, which is faciliated through the counseling process. The student is a unique individual who reacts to situations in his own way. The counselor seeks to understand the student in order to determine what is the best way to help this unique individual to recognize and to achieve his potential. The counseling process represents a direct service by the counselor to the student. It is an integral part of the guidance program but does not constitute the total program of guidance. "It should be the pivotal experience which serves to enlighten, consolidate, and relate other experiences to essential self-development."[32]

In the literature within the field of guidance little agreement has been expressed concerning the exact meaning and interpretation of the term *counseling*. At one time or another, advisement, the dispensing of in-

---

[31] J. F. McGowan and L. D. Schmidt, *Counseling: Readings in Theory and Practice* (New York: Holt, Rinehart and Winston, Inc., 1962); R. H. Mathewson, *op. cit.*, pp. 308–332; L. Tyler, *The Work of the Counselor,* 2 ed. (New York: Appleton-Century-Crofts, Inc., 1961); C. H. Patterson, *Counseling and Guidance in Schools* (New York: Harper & Row, 1962); D. Brady, *An Analytical Study of Counseling Theory and Practice With Recommendations for the Philosophy of Counseling* (Washington, D. C.: The Catholic University of America Press, 1952); W. C. Cottle and N. M. Downie, *Procedures and Preparation for Counseling* (Englewood Cliffs, N. J.: Prentice-Hall, Inc., 1960); J. W. Loughary, *Counseling in Secondary Schools* (New York: Harper & Row, 1960); D. S. Arbuckle, *Guidance and Counseling in the Classroom* (Boston: Allyn and Bacon, Inc., 1961).

[32] R. H. Mathewson, *op. cit.*, p. 321.

formation, and depth psychology have all been advanced as the keynote factor in the counseling process. The following definitions and interpretations of the term *counseling* are descriptive of the process involved:

> . . . a definite relationship where, through the counselor's sensitive understanding and skillful responses, a person objectively surveys the past and present factors which enter into his person confusions and conflicts and, at the same time, reorganizes his emotional reactions so that he not only chooses better ways to reach his reasonable goals, but has sufficient confidence, courage, and moderation to act on these choices.[33]
>
> . . . a face to face procedure in which by reason of training, skill or confidence vested in him by the other, one person helps the second person to face, perceive, clarify, solve and resolve adjustment problems.[34]
>
> . . . the heart and center of an organized *guidance program,* in which the counselor attempts to aid the student through personal interview to a better insight into his problems, decisions, and possible actions by providing him with an opportunity for more objective and adequate consideration of these factors.[35]

Zeran and Riccio have indicated that the characteristics shared by many definitions of the counseling process are the following:

1. Counseling is a learning process, developmental in nature.
2. Counseling involves two people, one of whom is by reason of training and experience in a position to assist the other in gaining new insights.
3. The counseling relationship is a warm and permissive relationship.
4. The counselor must have a genuine and abiding faith in the dignity and worth of his client.
5. Counseling must lead to self-insight on the part of the client which leads to action.
6. The counselor must be capable of viewing the client and his problem empathically.[36]

Counseling involves purposive personal conferences and interviews with individual pupils in order to ascertain their needs, interests, and abilities; to aid in the solution of individual problems; and to help the pupil to formulate specific plans for achieving his goals and purposes. It is a purposeful process by which the counselor through his understanding and skillful assistance, helps the student to:

a) Identify and understand the problem about which he is concerned;
b) Focus the problem in proper perspective;

---

[33] C. A. Curran, *op. cit.,* p. 1.
[34] E. G. Williamson and J. D. Foley, *Counseling and Discipline* (New York: McGraw-Hill Book Co., Inc., 1949). Used by permission.
[35] D. Brady, *op. cit.,* p. 14.
[36] F. R. Zeran and A. C. Riccio, *op. cit.,* p. 103.

c) Interpret available facts which have a bearing upon the problem;

d) Gain insight into and formulate constructive attitudes toward the problem;

e) Think for himself in order to make decisions, plans, and adjustments which will lead to the solution of the problem.

Counseling, which is directed toward meeting the needs of a particular boy or girl, is considered to be the task of the *counselor,* who should be a trained and qualified person, possessing technical preparation, educational experience, as well as an adequate philosophy of education and of life. In addition, the counselor should be friendly and sympathetic in his relationship with the student, should stimulate the pupil to think for himself and to develop his own plans. It is not, however, the province of the counselor to make decisions or to tell the student what to do, since the most important result sought through counseling is the development of the student's ability to guide himself effectively, which means making his own decisions intelligently.

It has been customary to classify the methods of counseling as *directive* or *clinical, nondirective* or *client-centered,* and *eclectic.* The first two methods have been very clearly described as follows:

> *Directive counseling* can be distinguished by the following identifying factors:
>
> 1. A formal plan for the discovery of meaningful elements in the counselee's make-up which will lead to a decision of the shortest route.
> 2. A presupposition that, until such time when the counselee can become self-directive, he is in need of a certain amount of regulation and that, unless the counselor supplies it, such direction will come from a less informed, less trained, and not infrequently unreliable source.
> 3. A recognition of the high goal of self-direction which it merely postpones until the counselee has acquired the insight and self-competence to make his own choices.
>
> The elements in *nondirective counseling* may be identified as follows:
>
> 1. The creation of a permissive and acceptant counseling climate by the counselor.
> 2. The free expression of opinions, feelings, attitudes, by the counselee.
> 3. Lack of criticism, censure, or direction on the part of the counselor whatever may be the attitudes expressed by the client.
> 4. The presupposition that the counselee is capable of making his own decisions if he is given the opportunity of expressing his most subjective and negative feeling to someone who will act as an objectifying agency.
> 5. A minimum of talking on the part of the counselor and perhaps sometimes an almost total absence of comment.[37]

---

[37] L. N. Recktenwald, *Guidance and Counseling* (Washington, D. C.: The Catholic

The *eclectic type* of counseling is the middle-of-the-road or *selective* approach and employs the techniques of both the directive and nondirective types in accordance with the demands of the particular counseling situation. Current differences of opinion concerning the amount of responsibility to be assumed by the counselor for the direction of the counseling interview have become less extensive and have been more clearly defined than was the case formerly. At the present time counselors agree generally that the eclectic approach offers the most effective method of counseling.

4. Consultative Services. The tasks of the counselor are by no means limited to the assistance rendered to students in order to aid them in solving problems, making choices, and achieving effective adjustment. The counselor also has the responsibility of rendering advisory and informational services to the school staff, both administrators and teachers, to parents and to the community. These advisory and informational services play an important role in the effective functioning of the guidance program within the school. The services to the school staff involve primarily assistance in understanding individual students; in enabling teachers to recognize and to meet the needs of students; in identifying talented pupils, potential "dropouts," and students with adjustment problems. These services include stimulating teachers to provide materials for the cumulative record, and likewise to utilize and to interpret in a professional manner the information contained in the cumulative record, which will encourage the growth of good teacher and learner relationships. The counselor can render valuable assistance to teachers in the development of guidance units within particular subject-matter areas as well as by providing and helping to obtain guidance aids and materials, especially educational and occupational information. The consultative functions of the counselor may also involve serving on school committees concerned with guidance and curriculum problems; aid in the development and conduct of in-service training programs, particularly concerning guidance and testing functions. The consultative tasks may likewise include recommendations to administrators concerning areas which merit research and further study and recommendations concerning long-range problems and practices.

University of America Press, 1953), pp. 112–113; see also D. Brady, *op. cit.,* pp. 62–66; F. W. Miller, *Guidance Principles and Services* (Columbus, Ohio: Charles E. Merrill Books, Inc., 1961), pp. 174–183.

The consultative services which the counselor most frequently renders to parents include imparting information concerning opportunities — both educational and occupational — particularly information regarding admission to college; interpreting and explaining information concerning the pupil's capacities in relation to his plans; arranging conferences, both individually and in groups, in order to discuss the developmental needs of pupils. Likewise the counselor has the responsibility of explaining and justifying the need for referrals to community resources when these become necessary for special problems which the school is not equipped to handle adequately.

The advisory and informational services rendered by the counselor to the community consist in participation in conferences concerning educational problems of general concern in which he interprets the guidance program to the community. The counselor likewise provides information to the community concerning whether the changing needs are being met. Fully acquainted with the occupational and educational opportunities available in the community, the counselor arranges cooperative relationships with business, industry, post-high school educational institutions, and the armed forces. Finally the counselor has the responsibility of keeping the community well informed regarding the guidance and counseling services rendered to the students. This will frequently involve participation in P.T.A. and similar public meetings, in club programs, in radio broadcasts, and the providing of accurate information to newspapers.

5. Evaluation and Research. *Evaluation* involves a process of appraising guidance services and activities in order to determine their value and worth in the educational process. The purpose of evaluation is to ascertain the extent to which guidance and counseling contribute to the development of the students and to the realization of the objectives of education. It should be a continuous appraisal of all guidance activities, designed to attain insight into the effectiveness of these activities in order to improve the quality of the guidance program. The nature of the evaluative procedures employed will depend upon the scope and comprehensiveness of the guidance services and activities. An efficacious method of accomplishing such evaluation consists of periodic follow-up studies through which contact is maintained with students who have graduated, and likewise with those who have dropped out of high school before graduation. Those students who have entered and are attending college should be contacted in order to determine how well the high school has prepared them for the particular college programs which they are pursuing, and also the degree of services and satisfaction which these students have attained at the college level. Students who have withdrawn from college should also be contacted in order to ascertain whether further assistance is needed, and whether and to what extent failure or change of plans might have been anticipated or avoided. Moreover, students who have graduated from high school but have not entered college should be contacted in order to determine how well the school has prepared them to take their places in the work world, as well as to offer assistance regarding post-high school education or training on a part-time basis. Likewise, the follow-up study of "dropouts" or "early school-leavers" will be valuable as a means of ascertaining whether the "dropouts" follow a definite pattern, and also of identifying as far as possible the causes of "dropouts." The follow-up study of the early school-leavers should likewise provide opportunity for assisting these individuals, particularly by encouraging them to obtain further education and training. The results of follow-up studies should lead to any necessary revision and in some instance to an enlargement of guidance services and practices. In addition, the findings of the follow-up studies should be presented to the administrative and teaching staffs of the school in order that they may be in a position to evaluate the effectiveness of the total school effort.

Research in the guidance program should be extended beyond the follow-up studies conducted for purposes of evaluation. This additional research should be designed to determine the effectiveness of the program in operation as well as the extent and quality of the services offered, and should lead to the improvement of these services. Among the areas in which research may be undertaken are the following: the identification of and provisions for the guidance of talented pupils; the identification of and provisions for the guidance of the handicapped, the underachievers, and the "reluctant learners." Likewise, experimentation should be undertaken to determine the efficiency of the techniques and the merits of the devices utilized in the guidance process. Moreover, valid research is necessary to determine the effectiveness of the counseling relationship. Other research studies could well deal with work experience programs; with the measurement of the persistence of educational and vocational choices in post-high school endeavors; with the devising of techniques to aid in meeting the needs of early school-leavers; with the problem of determining the extent to which the guidance program reflects awareness of both local and national needs.

Group Procedures in Guidance. The guidance program is concerned primarily with aid, assistance, and counsel to the individual pupil. However, the group approach is also utilized for the purpose of organized group discussions and projects, chiefly as a means for considering and imparting information concerning problems of common interest.[38] Usually the *homeroom* provides the place and the opportunity for group guidance. Primarily, the problems considered in group guidance include: (*a*) orientation of pupils to the program of the school; (*b*) adjustment of pupils educationally and socially; (*c*) information concerning educational opportunities; (*d*) consideration of vocational opportunities; (*e*) helping pupils to discover interests and capacities. Additional devices and procedures for providing group guidance which are in widespread use include: (*a*) core curriculum experiences; (*b*) extracurricular activities, including assemblies, athletics, clubs of various kinds, convocations, student government; (*c*) direct guidance, including pre-entrance contacts, avocational days, freshman week, homeroom and conference periods, group guidance courses, how-to-study courses, field trips, discussion of pertinent printed materials such as career pamphlets, college catalogs, bulletins, brochures, radio talks, television programs, motion pictures, vocational guidance journals, vocation day. To this list might also be added the *human relations class* as a device for the discussion of group problems and for the presentation of information concerning, particularly, the social and moral aspects of guidance.

The group approach is considered to have many merits and advantages. Representative of these merits are the following:

1. It provides a background of information that makes for effective individual counseling.
2. It assures every student of some attention, thus preventing the troublemaker from monopolizing services intended for all.
3. It enables students to discuss freely problems they might find difficult to broach in private interviews.

[38] M. Miles, *Learning to Work in Groups* (New York: Bureau of Publications, Teachers College, Columbia University, 1959); M. E. Bennett, *Guidance and Counseling in Groups,* 2 ed. (New York: McGraw-Hill Book Co., 1963); W. W. Lifton, *Working with Groups: Group Processes and Individual Growth* (New York: John Wiley & Sons, Inc., 1961); J. Warters, *Group Guidance Principles and Practices* (New York: McGraw-Hill Book Co., Inc., 1960); E. C. Glanz, *Groups in Guidance* (Boston: Allyn and Bacon, Inc., 1962).

4. It allows for a catharsis of hostile feelings, "gripes," and anxieties without fear of retaliation.

5. It provides for the solution of problems on the basis of group participation and allows for collective judgment of problems.

6. It is sound psychologically, since often students will accept from their peers suggestions which they reject from adults.

7. It allows for economy of time in handling many problems and points of information which are common to all in such areas as orientation, educational and vocational information, social attitudes, and personality development.

8. The give-and-take of group discussion is a good learning situation for both students and teachers.

9. Belonging to the group is a fundamental urge of the adolescent. The process of "rubbing shoulders" with others helps the student to secure those experiences that will help him to live acceptably with adults. These include the ability to get along with people, to respect the opinions that differ from his own, to handle himself in a social situation without embarrassment, and to learn a technique of co-operative action.

While it is true that group guidance has many merits, it must always supplement, never supplant, individual guidance. Its sole purpose is to increase the aid given each student by improving the total program. Furthermore, group procedures must be employed in such a manner that each member will remain conscious of his responsibility and rights as an individual, rather than be carried along with the crowd.

Teacher Competencies in Guidance. It is maintained generally that the most desirable arrangement for providing guidance at the secondary school level consists of a comprehensive balanced program of specialized services, professional leadership, and effective teacher participation, functioning within the framework of the complete resources of the school. In this arrangement guidance is not considered to be wholly the prerogative either of a special department or of the counselor. The teacher also has basic guidance responsibilities. These are evident in the functions of understanding, motivating, and directing the learning of the student, in diagnosing difficulties encountered in this process, in handling disciplinary problems, in providing pertinent information concerning the relationship of subject matter to educational and vocational plans, in stimulating interests, in fostering techniques of study, in providing leadership within the homeroom, in sponsoring extracurricular activities, and through many other opportunities which arise in the teaching-learning situation. Recognition of the indispensable role of the teacher in guidance has been adequately stated as follows:

> In most schools the classroom teacher is the only school officer who sees the pupils under normal conditions each day and knows their particular interests, ambitions, abilities, personality, weaknesses, and needs. No program of counseling and guidance can be well integrated, continuous, and consistent in its effects upon the pupil without the full cooperation of his teacher. No specialist in educational, emotional, physical, occupational, social or recreational guidance can safely neglect the information a child's teacher acquires about him by daily contacts in the classroom. No plans developed by the student on the basis of expert diagnosis and counseling can be carried out with maximum efficiency, without the full understanding of his teachers.[39]

Teacher participation in guidance functions and activities involves more than general information and good will. It requires also the development of certain competencies. The most fundamental of these competencies is a thorough understanding of the nature and the development of the *individual,* since the vital element in guidance is always the individual pupil, his needs, capacities, potentialities, and interests. This understanding of the individual must be supplemented by another competency, namely, a systematic knowledge of the principles, the aims, and the objectives of guidance. In addition, a third competency is essential, familiarity with the techniques employed in the guidance process, with the methods and devices by which guidance theory is translated into practice. The value of guidance as an educational service is determined by the teacher's understanding and appreciation of its nature and its purposes.

The Educational Significance of Guidance. That guidance is an integral part of the educational scheme, that it is fundamental in the educational process, is universally recognized. A functional relationship exists between guidance and every aspect of education. Particularly is this true at the secondary level where the growing complexity of present-day life has intensified the already crucial character of adolescent adjustments with the result that the task and responsibility of educators represent a greater challenge than they did just a few decades ago. The task involves helping youth to adjust to the demands resulting from economic, social, and cultural changes, while yet imparting the intellectual heritage of the ages. The responsibility involves helping youth to adjust emotionally and morally in a world which itself is visibly unadjusted. Guidance, in its various aspects, has come to be recognized as the

---

[39] M. R. Trabue, "Pupil Personnel Work: Counseling Service," *Encyclopedia of Educational Research,* W. S. Monroe, ed., rev. ed. (New York: The Macmillan Co., 1950), p. 932.

most adequate means of facilitating the accomplishment of this task and this responsibility. If guidance is to function as such a wholesome means, it must be a continuous process throughout the entire educational career of the child, concerned with every phase of life and not limited merely to the vocational aspect. However, guidance must be a function of and not a substitute for education. This point is made here because not infrequently the notion of guidance is confused with the broader notion of education. Some educators have enlarged the concept of guidance so that it engulfs the entire process of education. Guidance is not an entity distinct from education. It is rather a specific function within the complete process, seeking the harmonious development of all the powers, capacities, and capabilities of the individual. Education connotes instruction, training, and development, while guidance connotes appraisal, adjustment, and counsel. One demands the other, and a mutual interrelationship exists between them. Education without guidance would be as aimless as guidance without education.

EXERCISES

1. Outline this chapter.
2. List and define the terms which you have learned from your study of this chapter.
3. Explain the nature of counseling in the secondary school.
4. Explain the need for guidance and counseling in modern education.
5. Discuss the historical background and development of guidance.
6. Describe the guidance program as it functions in:
   a) The modern elementary school;
   b) The modern secondary school.
7. Discuss the following topics:
   a) The role of tests in guidance;
   b) The case-study technique;
   c) The interview;
   d) Group procedures in guidance;
   e) Teachers' competencies in guidance.
8. Discuss the following statements:
   a) "Modern guidance is merely an extension in the light of the findings of modern psychology and adapted to the needs of the modern world, of the age-old Catholic interest in moral and spiritual guidance."
   b) "It is impossible to teach without guiding or to guide without teaching."
   c) "Whatever techniques and methods are employed in the guidance process they must be directed toward the ultimate self-guidance which characterizes the person who has attained emotional, social, moral, economic, and intellectual maturity."
   d) "Counseling with inadequate data can result in dangerous decisions."

e) "Guidance in the Catholic school seeks the successful adjustment of the whole man — morally, personally, educationally, and vocationally — to the challenge and problems of living as citizens of two worlds, earth and heaven."
f) "Guidance is to serve not merely problem children but all children, particularly the ablest persons. Its aim is to strengthen the individual most at the points where he is already strongest."
g) "As a point of view, guidance is as old as education. It is modern, however, with reference to the areas of the student's life which are considered to be the responsibility of the school, the services which it offers to the students, the techniques employed to attain its ends."
h) "Guidance has come to be not only indispensable in education but is, in fact, one of the central bearings on which the effectiveness of the educational system now rests."
i) "Guidance is oriented about cooperation rather than coercion."

9. Discuss the following topics:
   a) Theories of counseling;
   b) Techniques of counseling;
   c) The qualifications of the counselor;
   d) Guidance services for the academically talented;
   e) Guidance services for the slow learner;
   f) The preparation of the teacher for guidance responsibilities.
10. What is the educational significance of guidance and counseling?

SELECTED REFERENCES FOR STUDY AND READING

Adams, J. F., *Problems in Counseling: A Case Study Approach* (New York: The Macmillan Co., 1962).

Andrews, D. C., and Willey, R. D., *Administration and Organization of the Guidance Program* (New York: Harper & Row, 1958).

Arbuckle, D. S., *Guidance and Counseling in the Classroom* (Boston: Allyn and Bacon, Inc., 1957).

——— *Counseling: An Introduction* (Boston: Allyn and Bacon, Inc., 1961).

Beck, C. E., *Philosophical Foundations of Guidance* (Englewood Cliffs, N. J.: Prentice-Hall, 1963).

Bennett, M. E., *Guidance and Counseling in Groups,* 2 ed. (New York: McGraw-Hill Book Co., Inc., 1963).

Byrne, R. H., *The School Counselor* (Boston: Houghton Mifflin Co., 1963).

Caldwell, C. E., *Group Techniques for the Classroom Teacher* (Chicago: Science Research Associates, Inc., 1960).

Cottle, W. C., and Downie, N. M., *Procedures and Preparation for Counseling* (Englewood Cliffs, N. J.: Prentice-Hall, Inc., 1960).

Crow, L. D., and Crow, A., *An Introduction to Guidance Principles and Practices,* 2 ed. (New York: American Book Co., 1960).

Dugan, W., *Counseling Points of View* (Minneapolis: University of Minnesota Press, 1959).

Foundations and Principles of Guidance (Boston: Allyn and Bacon, 1964).

Froehlich, C. P., *Guidance Services in the Schools,* 2 ed. (New York: McGraw-Hill Book Co., Inc., 1958).

Glanz, E. C., *Groups in Guidance* (Boston: Allyn and Bacon, Inc., 1962).

Guidance for the Academically Talented Student (Washington, D. C.: National Education Association and American Personnel and Guidance Association, 1961).

Humphreys, J. A., Traxler, A. E., and North, R. D., *Guidance Services* (Chicago: Science Research Associates, Inc., 1960).

Hutson, P. W., *The Guidance Function in Education* (New York: Appleton-Century-Crofts, Inc., 1958).

Johnson, M., Busacker, W. E., and Bouman, F. Q., *Junior High School Guidance* (New York: Harper & Row, 1961).

Johnson, W. F., Stefflre, B., and Edelfeet, R., *Pupil Personnel and Guidance Services* (New York: McGraw-Hill Book Co., Inc., 1961).

Jones, A. J., *Principles of Guidance,* 5 ed. (New York: McGraw-Hill Book, Co., Inc., 1963).

Lofquist, L. L., and England, G. W., *Problems in Vocational Counseling* (Dubuque, Iowa: Wm. C. Brown Co., 1961).

Mathewson, R. H., *Guidance Policy and Practice,* 3 ed. (New York: Harper & Row, 1962).

McDaniel, H. B., Lallas, J. F., Saum, J. A., and Gilmore, J. L., eds., *Readings in Guidance* (New York: Holt, Rinehart and Winston, Inc., 1959).

McGowan, J. F., and Schmidt, L. D., *Counseling: Readings in Theory and Practice* (New York: Holt, Rinehart and Winston, Inc., 1962).

Miller, C. H., *Foundations of Guidance* (New York: Harper & Row, 1961).

Miller, F. W., *Guidance: Principles and Services* (Columbus, Ohio: Charles E. Merrill Books, Inc., 1961).

Mortensen, D. G., and Schmuller, A. M., *Guidance in Today's Schools* (New York: John Wiley & Sons, Inc., 1959).

Moser, L. E., and Moser, R. E., *Counseling and Guidance: An Exploration* (Englewood Cliffs, N. J.: Prentice-Hall, Inc., 1963).

National Society for the Study of Education, Fifty-Eighth Yearbook, Part II, *Personnel Services in Education* (Chicago: University of Chicago Press, 1959).

Norris, W., Zeran, F. R., Hatch, R. N., *The Information Service in Guidance* (Chicago: Rand McNally & Co., 1960).

——— *Occupational Information in the Elementary School* (Chicago: Science Research Associates, Inc., 1963).

Patterson, C. H., *Counseling and Guidance in Schools* (New York: Harper & Row, 1962).

Peters, H. J., and Farwell, G. F., *Guidance: A Developmental Approach* (Chicago: Rand McNally & Co., 1959).

Peters, H. J., and Farwell, G. F., Shertzer, B., Heck, J. B., Stevic, R. R., and Van Atta, R. E., eds., *Counseling, Selected Readings* (Columbus, Ohio: Charles E. Merrill Books, Inc., 1962).

Peters, H. J., and Shertzer, B., *Guidance: Program Development and Management* (Columbus, Ohio: Charles E. Merrill Books, Inc., 1963).

Roe, Anne, *The Psychology of Occupations* (New York: John Wiley & Sons, Inc., 1956).
Rogers, C. R., *On Becoming a Person* (Boston: Houghton Mifflin Co., 1961).
Rosecrance, F. C., and Hayden, V. D., *School Guidance and Personnel Services* (Boston: Allyn and Bacon, 1960).
Stoops, E., and Wahlquist, G. L., *Principles and Practices in Guidance* (New York: McGraw-Hill Book Co., Inc., 1958).
——— ed., *Guidance Services: Organization and Administration* (New York: McGraw-Hill Book Co., Inc., 1959).
Super, D. E., *The Psychology of Careers: An Introduction to Vocational Development* (New York: Harper & Row, 1957).
——— *Vocational Development: A Framework for Research* (New York: Bureau of Publications, Teachers College, Columbia University, 1957).
Tolbert, E. L., *Introduction to Counseling* (New York: McGraw-Hill Book Co., Inc., 1959).
Tyler, L. E., *The Work of the Counselor,* 2 ed. (New York: Appleton-Century-Crofts, Inc., 1961).
Warters, J., *Group Guidance: Principles and Practices* (New York: McGraw-Hill Book Co., Inc., 1961).
Williamson, E. G., *Student Personnel Services in Colleges and Universities* (New York: McGraw-Hill Book Co., Inc., 1961).
——— *Counseling Adolescents* (New York: McGraw-Hill Book Co., Inc., 1950).
Wrenn, E. G., *The Counselor in a Changing World* (Washington, D. C.: The Commission on Guidance in American Personnel and Guidance Association, 1962).
Zeran, F. R., and Riccio, A. C., *Organization and Administration of Guidance Services* (Chicago: Rand McNally & Co., 1962).

chapter 17

Principles of Mental Hygiene in Education

The Meaning and Nature of Mental Hygiene. Since the early years of the twentieth century a potentially great movement has been assuming an ever increasing significance within the field of psychology. This movement, designated by the term *mental hygiene,* cannot, however, be considered either as a wholly new or even as a recently developed phase of psychology. Actually scattered tenets of what is now termed mental hygiene have been recorded, largely in the form of "common-sense" axioms, in the histories and traditions of practically all races and nations. Modern mental hygiene represents an organized endeavor to formulate this body of common sense knowledge, which mankind has long understood and perhaps frequently applied, into a definite set of principles and goals, based upon scientific data derived through clinical observation and experimental research in various areas concerned with the understanding of human behavior. In this way, mental hygiene has really become the legatee of all the accumulated knowledge of mankind concerning the understanding of human problems, conduct, and adjustment.

The basic purposes of mental hygiene are to spread knowledge of these principles, and to foster their application in the situations and conditions of life, primarily through a positive, constructive, comprehensive program of education. While the principles of mental hygiene apply to all people, the value and use of mental hygiene within the fields of education, medicine, and social service cannot be stressed too highly. Among the basic tasks of the teacher, the physician, the psychiatrist, the psychologist, the nurse, the clergy, and the social worker, all of whom have made themselves responsible in part at least for the welfare of others, are an understanding of human problems, practical guidance in the achievement of personal and social adjustment, and dissemination of information in order to stimulate interest in the importance of achieving, retaining, and increasing mental health.

Hygiene is that aspect of science which has for its purpose the conservation and promotion of health. In modern usage the term *health,* whether physical or mental, has a much more significant meaning and connotes broader aspects than merely freedom from disease. It is a positive achievement and implies functioning at the highest level of efficiency and attaining maximum self-realization. *Mental hygiene* is that phase of psychology which seeks to conserve and to promote the health of the mind, particularly in children and youth. It consists of the means, that is, the principles, methods, and techniques, by which mental health is realized. It involves the maintenance of mental health, the prevention of mental disorders, and the improvement of psychological adjustments in order to assure, as far as is possible, the maximum realization of potentialities and harmonious relationships with self and others. It is frequently designated by such terms as *the psychology of adjustment* and as *preventive psychology.* Mental hygiene endeavors to achieve a twofold objective. The first objective is the development of wholesome habits, attitudes, and interests which will aid in the achievement of *integrated personality* capable of meeting life's problems with courage and confidence. The second objective is the prevention of mental illness and of every type of mental maladjustment, whether serious or slight.

Physical hygiene, which modern man has grasped rather adequately in scope and adopted widely in practice, has for its purpose the development of "a better tabernacle for the soul of man to inhabit." Mankind has recognized the importance of physical well-being and has learned how to apply the discoveries of scientific medicine not only against conditions destructive of health but also to the eradication and prevention of physical disease, to the improvement of physical health, and to the prolongation of the span of life. Yet a perfectly developed body is useless unless directed by a well-balanced and capable mind. Physical well-being is of little use unless man is able to live better. So mankind is obligated to become equally and significantly interested in the problems of mental well-being in order to attain equal success in the field of mental health. As physical hygiene strives to save and to prolong life, so mental hygiene seeks to prevent *wasted lives* and to take *precautionary measures against mental, emotional, and moral maladjustments.* Thus, while physical hygiene seeks to increase the quantity of life, mental hygiene endeavors to improve the quality of life. Based upon the principle of "a sound mind in a healthy body,"[1] mental hygiene necessarily is concerned with social purposes and moral values as well as with physical development and mental adjustment. Hence, mental hygiene involves an organization, an evaluation, and a management of the social, moral, physical, and mental assets and liabilities of men. Mental hygiene seeks the functional unity and wholesome integration on the intellectual, volitional, and moral capacities, of the physical, social, and emotional characteristics of man. Its purpose is to guide the process of forming the complete person through the proper development of an effective and well-adjusted character.

Since the primary function of mental hygiene is the development and preservation of *integrated personality* (actually *integrating* personality would seem to be more appropriate and perhaps more accurate), then the principles and practices, the content and the methods of mental hygiene must be based upon a true understanding of *personality,* its nature and the factors which contribute to its development. By this term is expressed all the characteristic qualities of man which form his total constitution as a human being. These characteristic qualities include man's physical endowment, his intellectual capacity, his moral purpose, his volitional control, his aesthetic capabilities. The Christian view of human personality[2] is that body and soul by their union form one nature, one self, one person which is subject to all the states, aims, and activities of complete life. Physically, the person is subject to all the laws of growth and development which govern life processes in general. Spiritually, the person is capable of thought, judgment, reasoning, and is also capable of controlling and governing his entire life through the volitional process. Body and soul cooperate in the performance of every act. This means that human behavior involves an interrelation and interdependence of physical and spiritual factors.

---

[1] Juvenal, *Satires X:* 356, "Orandum est ut sit mens sana in corpore sano."

[2] See pp. 520–522 for additional consideration of the meaning of human personality. See also M. B. Arnold and J. A. Gasson, S.J., *The Human Person* (New York: The Ronald Press Co., 1954), p. 219. "Psychologically, personality is the patterned totality of human powers, activities and habits, uniquely organized by the person in the active pursuit of his self-ideal and revealed in his behavior."

Pope Pius XII defined personality as follows:

> We define personality as "the psychosomatic unity of man in so far as it is determined and governed by the soul."
>
> This definition refers first of all to the personality as a "unity" because it is considered as a whole, of which the parts, though preserving their specific characteristics, are not separated but are organically linked between themselves. This is why psychology can take equally into consideration the psychic faculties and their functions separately from the point of view of their individual structure and their immanent laws, as well as from the point of view of their organic whole.
>
> The definition then describes that unity as "psychosomatic." The opinions of the theologian and of the psychologist meet here on many points. In fact the technical works on psychology examine in detail the influence of the body over the mind to which it brings continued energies through its vital processes. A study is also made of the influence of the mind over the body. These studies endeavor to determine scientifically the modalities of the control of psychic tendencies by the spiritual soul and to draw from them practical applications.
>
> The definition then asserts that the psychosomatic unity of man is "determined and governed by the soul." The individual, in so far as he is a unity and indivisible totality, constitutes a unique and universal center of being and of action, an "I" which has self-control and is the master of itself. This "I" is the same in all psychic functions and remains the same despite the passage of time.
>
> The universality of the "I" in extent and duration applies particularly to the casual bond which links it to its spiritual activities. This universal and permanent "I," under the influence of internal or external causes consciously perceived or implicitly accepted, but always by free choice, acquires a definite attitude, and a permanent character, both in its interior being and in its external behavior.
>
> Since this specific character of the personality is ultimately derived from the spiritual soul, one describes it as being "determined by the soul." Since it is not the case of an occasional process but of a continuous process, one adds "governed by the soul."[3]

The proper development of human personality involves learning how to live a life in such a way that every type of abnormality and maladjustment, major or mild, may be prevented. Since the inability of the individual to adapt himself to life situations is due to some imperfection either in the organization or in the functioning of his capacities, mental hygiene endeavors to cultivate in the individual the following factors of mental health:

1. *The ability to adjust adequately to situations and conditions within*

[3] Pope Pius XII, "Morality and Applied Psychology," *Catholic Mind,* 53:354–55, 1958.

his environment. Every individual from birth faces the problem of making adaptations continuously to the complex situations which surround him. Adjustment connotes more than merely a passive adaptation to or a fitting into the conditions and situations which constitute environment. It implies in addition that the individual is oriented to and perceives his relationship to those conditions and situations and in addition has the ability to modify them through the use of intellect and will.

2. *The ability to live with others peacably, happily, and justly, to respect them and to work with them for common ends.* Since man is by nature a social being, mental health involves the ability to maintain personal relationships with others which are satisfying and lasting. These personal relationships involve the development of friendships and the participation in group social activities with the feeling that one is an accepted member of the group. These personal relationships involve also respect for the innate dignity of, consideration for the rights of, and contribution to the welfare of others.

3. *The ability to engage in effective activity which he considers satisfying both personally and socially.* This involves the pursuit of reasonable and purposeful, realistic goals, the recognition of assets and limitations without overestimating or underestimating abilities, the utilization of potentialities in order to realize success which is commensurate with capacities.

4. *The achievement of self-mastery.* This involves fundamentally *self-control,* which includes the evaluation of conduct and the control of emotions, thought, imagery, desires, and behavior. It includes also maintenance of balance and poise in the face of difficulties, trials, and disappointments. It involves self-reliance and the acceptance of responsibilities. Self-mastery implies an expanding *self-knowledge,* that is, insight into conduct, motives, ambitions, and interests, and the direction of thoughts, actions, and emotional responses in a way which is conducive to efficiency, health, and happiness. It implies the formation of worthy character.

5. *The formulation of a plan of life.* This involves the organization of values and ideals in keeping with the nature and dignity of the human person, in order that these may serve as a goal and a purpose in attaining an effective way of life.

Everyone is familiar with the concept of *integration.* It is common practice to speak of an individual "going to pieces," "breaking down," "cracking up," and of "pulling one's self together." Integration signifies the proper development and fitting coordination of the powers of intellect, will, and emotions into a functioning unit. Integration signifies a state of unity, of oneness, of wholeness whereby the powers of thought, of volition, and of feeling work together harmoniously toward the development of a complete and self-controlled personality. A well-integrated person possesses the ability to think, to act, to feel appropriately in the various situations and conditions of life. It is worthy of note that the chief characteristic of an integrated personality is *self-control.*

Mental Health. While the terms *mental hygiene* and *mental health* have frequently been used interchangeably, the concept of mental health[4] refers to a state or condition which must be achieved by the individual. It is to be noted that mental health is not something static or automatic but involves continuous adjusting and maintenance of human relationships. Mental health implies a degree of maturity of mind and also emotional development proportional to the individual's chronological age. It signifies judgment freed from distortions due to emotional pressure and consciousness freed from obsession with self. It involves good interpersonal relations with oneself, with others, with God. It involves ability to meet adequately the problems and demands of life as well as the acceptance of life's responsibilities.

Mental health has been described as follows:

> Mental health involves (1) continuous adjusting rather than a static condition and is therefore a progressive goal. It is an ability to cope with the present and in all likelihood to adjust satisfactorily in the future. It involves (2) physical, mental, and emotional phases of adjustive behavior as well as habits of work and attitudes toward situations and obstacles. Hence, mental health is (3) a point of view one takes of *all* phases of living. The concept includes (4) a social phase — referred to in the definitions by such words as "socially considerate behavior," "satisfaction with the social order," and "contributions to society." Mental health is not simply the absence of disease but is (5) a process of optimum functioning and maximum self-realization. For those who are ill it is a matter of getting well, for those who are "getting along" it is a matter of improvement, and for those who are robust it is a matter of maintaining and continuing achievement.[5]

[4] E. F. O'Doherty, "Religion and Mental Health," *Catholic Mind,* 55:413–421, 1957; M. Jahoda, *Current Concepts of Positive Mental Health* (New York: Basic Books, Inc., 1958).

[5] H. W. Bernard, *Mental Hygiene for Classroom Teachers,* 2 ed. (New York: McGraw-Hill Book Co., Inc., 1961), p. 14. Used by permission.

The History of the Mental Hygiene Movement. The mental hygiene movement had a dramatic beginning. Its founder, Clifford W. Beers (1876–1943), had been a patient for three years (1900–1903) in several public and private mental hospitals. While the actual mental breakdown occurred in 1900, the circumstances leading to it had been developing for six years previous to that time. During these years Beers had acquired an obsession that he would become an epilectic, since an older brother had been seized with, and later died of, what had been diagnosed as epilepsy. This obsession had developed insidiously to the point that it finally dominated his mind so completely that he reached the state where he preferred death to epilepsy. Acting on the obsession he attempted suicide, but fortunately escaped with minor physical injuries. That attempt to end his life seems to have transformed his mental processes. The obsession of epilepsy disappeared only to be replaced by delusions of persecution and later of grandeur. The period of the duration of these delusions extended over three years, during which time Beers was a patient in three institutions both public and private. In all of these institutions he was subjected to cruel, harsh, and stupid treatment, due to ignorance of the nature of his disorder and to the common lack of therapeutics. He progressed and regressed several times; but toward the end of the period the delusions disappeared, and he passed from a state of profound depression into one of extreme elation. At the end of three years he emerged from these hospitals, well on the road to full recovery, though he did suffer a minor relapse a year later.

Upon regaining his mental health, the keen recollection of his personal suffering while a patient in these institutions stimulated a zeal and a determination to devote his life to the task of arousing public interest in raising the standards for the care and treatment of the insane. His first effort was an autobiographical account of his experience in these institutions. This was submitted in manuscript form to a number of psychiatrists, psychologists, and educators for criticism and comment. Finally, in 1908 this book, entitled *A Mind That Found Itself,*[6] was published with an eloquent introduction by William James. Its publication marked the beginning of a remarkable crusade against mental illness and the inception of a new era of social service. Both in the United States and abroad a pro-

[6] C. W. Beers, *A Mind That Found Itself,* 7 ed. (Garden City, N. Y.: Doubleday and Co., Inc., 1948); N. Ridenour, *Mental Health in the United States: A Fifty Year History* (Cambridge, Mass.: Harvard University Press, 1961), pp. 1–26.

found impression was made by the book. Subsequently, it has passed through several editions.

Beers's second effort was to interest in his cause a group of prominent people who could provide the essential professional direction and obtain the necessary financial support for his plan. This plan involved inaugurating and furthering a program of reform in the care and treatment of the mentally ill, as well as an endeavor to convince the public that mental disorders were curable and also to improve mental health by devising methods and means of preventing mental illness. It received prompt and effective support. In 1908 he organized in Connecticut the first state mental hygiene society. In 1909 the movement was formally launched with the organization of the National Committee for Mental Hygiene. The movement received encouraging support from an extensive array of notable persons among whom was Cardinal Gibbons. The National Committee interested groups in other states in its plans, and zeal for the work spread rapidly. Thus encouraged by the National Committee, state societies have been organized in all states. These are supplemented as well by an increasing number of medical, educational, social, and religious organizations throughout the country which are working on programs to help meet the ever increasing need of preventing disorders of mental origin. Both national and state organizations have been active in promoting clinics and other facilities for the prevention and treatment of mental disorders. Committees for mental hygiene have also been organized in many countries throughout the world. Thus within two decades the mental hygiene movement had become worldwide in scope. In 1929 the International Committee for Mental Hygiene was established, and in May, 1930, the first international Congress on Mental Hygiene was held in Washington, D. C. At this meeting 53 nations were represented. Since that time several international meetings have been held.

The educational activities of the National Committee for Mental Hygiene have included the publication of a quarterly journal entitled *Mental Hygiene*. This journal presents authoritative information concerning mental health problems, reports of surveys, investigations, and methods of prevention and treatment. Likewise, the National Committee sponsored the publication of books and pamphlets dealing with the various phases of mental hygiene as well as a series of mental health films. Among the functions of the National Committee have been participation in extensive surveys and studies of mental hygiene services. The National Committee through its many activities has also served as a clearinghouse for information concerning mental disorders.

Although the driving force of Clifford Beers was the most potent factor in the development of the mental hygiene movement, progressive leaders in psychology, psychiatry, and education had already begun to think in terms of mental hygiene before Beers's first book was published. William James had spoken of it, and Burnham had written an article on it. However, it was Adolph Meyer who suggested to Beers that the term *mental hygiene* epitomized the ideas expressed in his book and the purposes behind his plan. Research has revealed that this term was not exactly new, for it had been used in America as early as 1843 by William Sweetser as the title of a book, *Mental Hygiene or an Examination of the Intellect and Passions.* Also in 1863, Dr. Isaac Ray, superintendent of Butler Hospital in Providence, Rhode Island, had used the term as the title of a book. In 1903, Forel of the University of Zurich had written a book which he entitled *Hygiene of the Nerves and Mind in Health and Disease.* Likewise, in 1906, Dr. T. S. Clouston published a book in England entitled *The Hygiene of the Mind,* in which the term *mental hygiene* was frequently used. Thus, the term *mental hygiene* even in its present specific application is not new. Moreover, the contents of these books were strikingly similar to recent publications in mental hygiene.

Originally the chief concern of the National Committee for Mental Hygiene was to humanize the care of the mentally ill, to eradicate the abuses and in many instances the brutalities inflicted upon them, to focus public attention on the real existing need for reform, to expand facilities for treatment, to raise the standards of care, to secure for the mentally ill treatment comparable with that accorded the physically ill in the modern hospital. However, the mental hygiene movement has passed on to a second stage. Unlike the initial purpose wherein the emphasis was placed upon the treatment and care of the mind diseased, this second stage has for its aim the prevention of all types of mental disorders, the promotion of sane healthy behavior, the enrichment of life. The second stage goes beyond the present problem of mental illness and emphasizes the cultivation of forces that will contribute to better mental health and work for happier and more efficient methods of living.

In 1950, the National Committee for Mental Hygiene merged with two other voluntary agencies in this field, the National Mental Health Foundation and the Psychiatric Foundation, for the purpose of strengthening the attack on the mental health problems of the nation. This new organization adopted the name The National Association for Mental Health.[7]

Likewise, in 1946, the National Mental Health Act was passed. By enacting this legislation the federal government began a nationwide drive to combat mental illness as a public health problem of first importance. The purpose of the Act was to provide a method for financing research and training programs and to assist the states in establishing mental health services. The National Institute of Mental Health, of the Public Health Service, Federal Security Agency,[8] has been given the responsibility for the administration of the program. The Joint Commission on Mental Illness and Health created by Congress under the Mental Health Act of 1955 to assess mental health conditions and resources throughout the United States for the purpose of making recommendations for a national mental health program has published a ten-volume series of reports on its findings.[9] The World Health Organization and the International World Federation for Mental Health have extended mental hygiene services, particularly the preventive aspect, throughout the world.

The chief purposes of mental hygiene as an organized social-educational movement have been:

1. To stimulate interest in the importance of mental health, in the tremendous economic waste due to mental illness, in the relationship between poor mental health and certain troublesome social and moral problems, particularly delinquency and criminality;

2. To present correct conceptions of the nature and causes of mental disorders as well as to demonstrate that such disorders are practically always preventable and, likewise, to a large extent, curable;

3. To endeavor to teach people to recognize early the warning symptoms of mental disorder and to educate in ways of healthy mental habits;

4. To promote programs for the reconstruction of those maladjusted, with a view to recovery and return to social usefulness;

5. To support measures for the prevention and remedial treatment of juvenile delinquency and other "behavior" disorders;

---

[7] The National Association for Mental Health, 10 Columbus Circle, New York City.

[8] The National Institute of Mental Health, Public Health Service, Bethesda, Maryland.

[9] N. Ridenour, *op. cit.,* p. 142; see also *Action for Mental Health,* "The Final Report of the Joint Commission on Mental Illness and Health" (New York: Basic Books, Inc., 1961).

6. To encourage psychiatric social work; to establish child guidance and other mental hygiene clinics; to develop trained personnel;
7. To stimulate research into the nature and causes of mental disorders;
8. To provide active support of legislation for general, medical, and scientific education as well as for the establishment of mental health research centers;
9. To stimulate the interest of youth in mental health work as a career.

The Importance of Mental Hygiene. Despite the fact that an adequate census of mental illness has never been conducted, there are available sufficient data concerning its extent that mental illness has been designated by the United States Public Health Service as America's number one public health problem. The incidence of mental illness has reached such proportions that at the present time one of every twelve children born each year will become at sometime during his life a patient in a mental hospital. Mental illness occurs in one out of every four families. More people are hospitalized for mental illness than for cancer, poliomyelitis, and tuberculosis combined, and each year approximately half a million new cases are admitted to mental hospitals. Such statistics concerning the extent of mental illness have been emphasized frequently in order to demonstrate the need for a sound national program of mental health. While these statistics reveal something of the extent and seriousness of mental illness, they fail to indicate the tragic story of the suffering, disability, and economic losses resulting from mental illness.

Mental illness has long been shrouded in superstition. It has been regarded as a disgrace, and, frequently, stigma have been attached to those requiring treatment in mental hospitals. Yet mental illness is no more blameworthy than physical disorders. Such misconceptions concerning mental illness have prevented many from seeking needed care and have made it difficult for recovered patients to adjust to community life.

Mental hygiene, however, has exercised considerable influence upon the interpretations of the nature of mental illness. It has directed attention toward the study of personality development and adjustment by maintaining that mental illness is the result of "a continuing series of stresses for which adequate methods of adjustment could not be found, originating in childhood and gradually increasing in intensity."[10] The development of

---

[10] L. Kaplan and D. Baron, *Mental Hygiene and Life* (New York: Harper & Row, 1952), p. 31.

mental illness is, therefore, gradual. With this knowledge as its basis, mental hygiene has been concerned with the possibility of preventing mental ill-health through an understanding of premonitory signs indicative of a threat to mental health and the recognition of these as danger signals. This aspect of mental hygiene involves the early recognition of inadequate adjustment and the identification of maladjustment. However, there is a more positive aspect which involves the development of effective personality and character as the means of preventing mental illness. The first aspect is ordinarily designated as the *preventive* phase while the second aspect is usually termed the *constructive* phase of mental hygiene. Each aspect is significant. The *preventive* phase involves activities by which assistance is provided to enable the individual to cope with problems, by which an environment is provided which facilitates the process of adjustment. The *constructive* phase involves a positive program of personality development and character formation by discovering and utilizing potentialities, by making life increasingly more worthwhile through inculcating habits, attitudes, and values which will strive to promote the perfection of personality. Actually, the *constructive* approach is the best way to *prevention.*

The Basic Consideration in Mental Hygiene. As the application of the principles of psychology and related sciences to the maintenance of mental health, to the prevention of mental disorders, and to the development of effective personality, the purpose of mental hygiene is to formulate ways and means by which mental health may be *achieved, retained,* and *increased.* This involves the prevention of all types of maladjustments as well as the promotion of healthy behavior and the endeavor to enable every individual to attain the highest degree of mental health and efficiency, by inculcating and cultivating attitudes and habits which will promote a sane healthy outlook on life and the perfection of personality.

The training of the teacher in the field of mental hygiene should enable him to detect deviations in behavior, in personality, and in character. This, moreover, is to be done while these deviations are incipient and even unsuspected, long before they have reached the stage where they will seriously affect the future life of the individual. The realization that seemingly insignificant peculiarities may be the warning signals of grave mental disturbance makes early recognition and treatment of utmost importance to save not only the individual and his family, but likewise, society from unnecessary suffering. In the field of physical hygiene, it is not considered safe to wait until the individual, particularly the child, becomes ill, but rather effort is made to prevent illness and disease. The same procedure is equally important in the field of mental health. In order to meet adequately the professional demands made upon the teacher, he should be familiar with the basic fact that mental hygiene is concerned with factors which produce *emotional stability,* thereby facilitating the functioning of mental abilities. This in turn involves successful *self-mastery.*

It is universally recognized that the emotions exercise a widespread influence upon personality. Because they are intrinsic in every experience and a factor in all action, conduct, and behavior, they constitute a valuable source of motivation. By imparting to life its tone they play an important role in the happiness and success of the individual. They are, likewise, significant factors in determining attitudes, and they exercise considerable influence upon the relationships of the individual with others. A large share of the value and meaning of life, therefore, centers in proper emotional responses. However, lack of emotional control constitutes a basic causal factor in practically all forms of maladjustment. Accordingly, the most basic problem in mental hygiene, in both its preventive and constructive aspects, is the establishment of *emotional stability.* This involves not merely the control of emotions to prevent maladjustments but also the mature expression of emotions at the times and in the ways which are appropriate, in order that effective personality may be developed. The remedy is neither the eradication of emotions nor yet enslavement to them, but rather the constructive utilization of them. The function of mental hygiene is to provide the guidance, the motivation, and the techniques which will lead to the establishment both of healthy control and of adequate expression in consistent behavior. Such control and expression of the emotions consists in learning to use them temperately under the direction of the intellect and will. This in turn involves the power of self-discipline and self-control. Mental hygiene in both the constructive and preventive phases must recognize the role of the will as the source of achievement and as the unifying factor in man's life. The will determines the manner and degree in which thoughts and actions, as well as emotions, are initiated, guided, and controlled. The basic consideration in mental hygiene is the establishment of *emotional stability* by means of self-control. Successful living in all its phases depends primarily upon *self-mastery.*

The Influence of Basic Psychological Needs. In order to apply the principles of mental hygiene, it is essential that teachers, and parents also, have an adequate understanding of the *influence of basic psychological needs* as determinants of emotional development and their relationship to the process of adjustment. Just as the child has basic physical and organic needs which must be met in order that he may live, so there are fundamental psychological needs which must be satisfied properly in order that the mind and emotions may function adequately. Need implies something which is required for the individual to attain an end or objective commensurate with his nature, origin, and destiny as a human person. No general agreement exists regarding the identification, enumeration, or classification of these needs.[11] However, they involve psychological satisfactions which can be attained largely through contacts with other people. Their significance rests in the fact that when fulfilled they become sources of satisfaction and when unsatisfied they become sources of increased tension and of conflict or frustration and are so manifest in behavior. Many of the maladjustments designated as "behavior problems" grow out of failure to satisfy fundamental psychological needs of the child. Among the individual's most important needs are *security, self-esteem, belonging, achievement, self-reliance.*

From the developmental viewpoint, the primary psychological need is for *security,* which involves love, care, understanding, affection, approval, and continual affirmation of personal worth and value. Love and warmth within the family and the home constitute the basis of security. The need for *self-esteem* is sometimes designated as a sense of inner security. It involves a feeling of adequacy, of personal worth, of wholesome self-regard and self-respect, including an awareness and a value of the dignity and uniqueness of the self as a human being. The need for *belonging* or being accepted by others is evident from the fact that man is by nature social. This involves having a place first within the family and then in social groups of friends and acquaintances as well as close companionship with others, especially age-mates or peers. This need is satisfied by participating in group activities and by receiving recognition, approval, respect, confidence, and companionship from the group. The need for *achievement,* which is also termed self-actualization, involves suitable opportunities to exercise initiative within the range of capabilities, the use and development of abilities, knowledge of progress,

[11] H. W. Bernard, *op. cit.*, pp. 25–56.

encouragement. The need for *self-reliance* is often designated as the need to be independent. In each stage of growth and development, as the individual gains an awareness of his capacities and potentialities, there arise a compelling urge to test and to use these capabilities. This is true from the infant learning to walk to the adolescent who considers himself to be grown up and so wants freedom from parental restrictions. Self-reliance involves the development of responsibility, the power to make decisions, and the development of a set of values.

The satisfaction of these basic psychological needs provides the child with feelings of worth and of confidence which help him to become well adjusted. When these fundamental needs are not met, it is natural for the child to feel insecure, inadequate, rejected, and perhaps also frustrated, tense, and angry. Such a child, though seriously disturbed, often does not realize why. However, he does recognize that he is unhappy and tense. Then he seeks in some substitute way to find satisfactions for these needs. Some children find their satisfaction dangerously in day-dreams and in withdrawing from reality into the world of fantasy. Others turn to overt action, to delinquent behavior in order to secure satisfaction. Out of the continued failure to satisfy these basic psychological needs emerge the various *defense* or *escape mechanisms* which also influence the course of emotional development. Thus a healthy satisfaction of the basic psychological needs constitutes an essential condition for wholesome emotional adjustment.

Mental Hygiene in Childhood and Youth. The effectiveness of mental hygiene depends upon the application of its principles in guiding the child's growth and development from birth through adolescence, especially in establishing self-control. Modern psychological research has revealed that disintegration is characterized by lack of self-control. Furthermore, it is well known that numerous mental disorders have their sources in childhood. Many unwholesome tendencies, maladjustments, and serious deviations are traceable to unsuitable environment, to lack of understanding of the child's nature, to inadequate guidance.

The profound significance of childhood experiences in determining patterns of behavior and adjustment which may persist throughout life is generally recognized. Yet, there are some who mistakenly assume that the years of childhood are characterized by an almost total lack of difficulties and problems, with the result that the child experiences a continuous and unusual happiness. This is incorrect, for childhood has its difficulties, its problems, its conflicts, its obstacles, many of which the child can neither understand nor overcome. Because children grow up in families, the most important of the child's early experiences concern his relationships with other persons within the home, particularly the parents. While parents cannot give the child mental health, they can provide the environment and atmosphere of love, affection, and security in which it will flourish. The infant is truly as helpless and appealing as he appears. His chances for present health and for future development depend largely upon the habits which he acquires during the period of his infancy. His physical needs are often so pressing that parents are inclined to forget that infancy marks the beginning also of social and mental development. Many unwholesome tendencies, problems, and difficulties seem clearly to be traceable to adjustments in the early years of life. The influence of childhood on later life, the importance of the home, the responsibilities and possibilities of parenthood are revealed anew by the principles of mental hygiene.

The mental hygiene of childhood begins with the parents. The child passes through a long period of physical, mental, social, and emotional adjustment during which he requires careful guidance and adequate direction and supervision. His adjustments to his surroundings begin at birth and become more and more complex as he grows and develops. The early discipline and training of the child have vitally determining effects on later habits and conduct. Properly guided and directed, amid suitable environmental surroundings, the child's personality will develop in a wholesome manner. Neglected and unguided, placed in unsuitable surroundings, the child's personality will be maladjusted. As the child grows and develops, he must be guarded in his associations to prevent exposure to unwholesome influences. It is essential that he be provided with rich opportunities for the development of security and affection.

The child is "father to the man," for childhood's potentialities become fulfilled in adulthood. To parents belong the responsibility of guiding and directing the child's early experiences which contribute so much to his later success or failure, happiness or misery. It is the duty of the parents to supply and implant values, meanings, and motives that will stimulate the finer capabilities of the child so that, as he grows and develops, the ideals set before him will be an inspiration to him, will guide him in forming correct attitudes toward life, will direct his conduct and life so that he may adjust himself to and take his part creditably, happily, and effectively in life's activities. The mental hygiene of early childhood is essentially a problem of efficient parenthood. To accomplish their tasks efficiently, it is essential that parents be self-controlled, alert to the implications of, and helps afforded by, mental hygiene. The home must assume primary responsibility for the mental health of the child, recognizing it as one of the most influential forces for molding superior character. Parents must recognize that they can both aid in preventing the problems of mental illness, of emotional disturbances, and also lay foundations for effective development of personality. Maladjustments very frequently have their roots in childhood experiences. In fact, the more deeply psychoanalysts, psychologists, and psychiatrists have probed into the sources of the influences which shape personality, the clearer has it become that the childhood experiences are supremely significant. It is then that the mental twists, the emotional maladjustments, the moral deviations, which may warp and distort the whole personality and character in later life are initiated and in part developed. Hence, it is essential that parents learn what to do and what to avoid in the training of the child; how to recognize warning signals and to detect early manifestations of maladjustments. It is to be remembered, however, that *mental hygiene is not a matter merely of guiding the individual safely in moments of confusion or uncertainty, but rather is it a program for building sound character.*

The many aids which mental hygiene has provided to parents for the guidance and direction of the emotional and social development of the child during the preschool years constitute a basic and valuable contribution. However, mental hygiene has equally basic and valuable aid to offer at two critical stages in the process of growth and development, when problems of adjustment are most likely to occur. The first of these stages is the time when the child enters school; the second is the period of adolescence.

Entering school is a critical factor in child life, as it involves the process of initiating the child into a new and larger world. The transition of the child from the home to the school involves an expansion of his environment, an increase in his activities, a change in his interests. It involves learning to make emotional and social as well as mental adjustments. It marks the beginning of a new pattern of living. The success of this transition from the home to the school will depend largely upon the experiences of the first six years spent in the home. When the child enters school, he must learn to accept the authority of the teacher, must enter into competition with other children, must find satisfaction in assuming the responsibility for doing things for himself. In the primary grades he acquires the fundamental skills and tools of learning upon which all later education will be based. There also he must learn interpersonal relationships with others of his age. He must learn the fundamental principle of self-control. During this time his judgment has developed sufficiently to enable him to establish connections between his actions and their consequences. It is significant that whatever the child learns during this time is rarely forgotten. If during these early school years the child finds satisfaction in the activities involved in his broadening experience and environment, he will develop healthy attitudes toward learning, toward getting along with others, toward himself; in a word, he will learn to adjust adequately.

However, it has been recognized generally that the time during which the wholesomeness of the child's previous development is tested severely is the period of *adolescence*.[12] It is then that the youth must learn to adjust himself to the adult level of behavior. It is then, likewise, that he develops so many new interests, social, educational, and vocational. It is then that the characteristics of the child are exchanged for those of the adult. Consequently, because he is called upon to adjust himself to so many new interests and circumstances, the youth will exhibit any unwholesome tendencies, any emotional disturbances, any lack of self-control and self-mastery, any deficiencies in previous training, guidance, and direction.

Mental Hygiene in the School.[13] The fundamental environments which contribute most to the development of the child's personality are the home and the school. Each has a share not only in the development of personality but also in molding character and laying the foundations for the future. They provide the main influence which determines adjustment and maladjustment. The home is the basic unit. It plays its major role during the preschool years. To be effective the home must provide the surroundings and atmosphere which will meet the fundamental needs of the child, not only the basic physical but also the psychological needs. In a good home atmosphere children experience

[12] See Chapter 5, "The Adolescent," for a complete account of the period; also H. W., Bernard, *op. cit.*, pp. 57–86.

[13] See W. Allinsmith and G. W. Goethals, *The Role of the School in Mental Health* (New York: Basic Books, Inc., 1962).

security and affection, self-esteem and achievement, realize happiness, and develop confidence which will carry over into their attitudes toward others, toward school, toward a vocation, toward life itself. The school is an extension of and supplements the home. The task of the school, like that of the home, is to guide and direct the effective development of the child's personality by inculcating habits, attitudes, and values which will promote the well-being and adequate adjustment of the individual. The basic function of the school is the guidance and direction of mental growth and development of the child in order that he may be prepared to live in, meet the problems arising in, and assume his responsibilities as a member of society. This involves also the guidance and direction of the social and emotional aspects of growth and development. Actually, the school is concerned with the development of the total personality of the child. Educators generally have expressed the view that, because their responsibility entails the development of the complete personality, mental hygiene, which plays such a significant role in that development, is likewise their concern. In fact, some educators have insisted that the aims and principles of mental hygiene are the same as those of education, as the following quotation indicates:

> The aim of mental hygiene, to help individuals develop integrated personalities so that they may adapt to the usual exigencies of life with feelings of competence and satisfaction, coincides with the view that education should provide experiences promoting growth in the direction of self-confidence, social adaptation, self-expression, and the facing of reality. Thus from the point of view of schools the phase of mental hygiene dealing with personality development is identical with some of the aims of education; both are directed toward the development of individuals capable of satisfactory living.[14]

The significance of mental hygiene functions of the teacher both in preventing maladjustments and in the development of the child's personality has been indicated as follows:

> For continuing health care and mental hygiene for children the schools are the chief agencies . . . not the clinics and the many specialists who can diagnose and treat the various ills, defects and handicaps, but the school personnel, especially the classroom teacher. What she does to and for

[14] American Association of School Administrators, Twentieth Yearbook, *Health In Schools* (Washington, D. C.: American Association of School Administrators, 1942), pp. 133 and 134; see also C. E. Winslow, *The School Health Program* (New York: The Regents Inquiry, 1938), pp. 22–23, for a statement to the effect that the "principles of modern education are identical with the principles of mental hygiene."

> children, as one personality acting, reacting, and interacting with members of the class, is the active daily process of mental hygiene. . . .
> The teacher in the classroom is the strategic person for mental health because she is the only one in the position to do what must be done to help children and youth grow up and achieve maturity with some degree of sanity and adequacy of social living.[15]

The ways in which the school applies the principles of mental hygiene in both its preventive and constructive phases include the utilization of such procedures, devices, and techniques as:

1. Provision for deviate children, that is, the identification of children who may experience serious difficulties and maladjustments. These children include the physically handicapped, the slow learning, the retarded, and, on occasion, the gifted. The provisions for these children involve primarily remedial and adjustment programs in order that they may utilize their potentialities.
2. Adaptation of instruction to individual differences, adjustment of school tasks to maturity levels, and curriculum expansion and adaptations at the various levels to meet interests and needs of pupils.
3. Special help for students who are underachieving academically, that is, who are accomplishing less than their intellectual potential.
4. Provision for guidance and counseling in all phases.
5. Adequate classroom management with stress on avoidance of tension and emotional problems through a constructive, consistent, and sensible program of discipline.
6. Development of effective methods of work and study.
7. Development of a system of appraisal and reporting progress that will give a clear picture of the child's achievement in relation to his capacity.
8. Provision for adequate psychological services through the work of the school psychologist and the school social worker.
9. A program of extra classroom activities which provides a means of aiding pupils to discover interests and aptitudes.

The teacher's task in applying the principles of mental hygiene involves:

1. *An understanding of pupils.* The greater the understanding the better will the teacher be equipped to aid the child in achieving wholesome development and the more effective he will be in preventing maladjustments. Such understanding includes the recognition of the child's

[15] L. K. Frank, "Mental Health in Schools," *Education,* 66:546, 555, 1946.

need to experience emotional security, self-realization, and recognition of achievement in relation to his peers.

2. *Adequate preparation with regard to the subject matter taught.* While it is true that "children, not subjects, are taught," nevertheless children are taught by means of subject matter. It is impossible to teach children without helping them to acquire knowledge and skills. While the emphasis and attention must center upon the child, the subject matter constitutes the medium by which the child is taught. Every subject in the curriculum offers possibilities of promoting the wholesome development of the child.

3. *A thorough understanding and appreciation of the aims of education.*

4. *A knowledge of the symptoms of maladjustment and the application of the principles of prevention.* The reeducation of an individual who is maladjusted is an uncertain, difficult, and complicated process, whereas prevention through understanding and effective guidance is a relatively simple matter and as satisfying as any known human undertaking.

In summary, the significant principles underlying both the adequate development of wholesome personality and the prevention of maladjustments may be stated as follows:

1. Recognize the importance of moral and spiritual values as fundamental in the motivation of conduct.

2. Provide for character training in all of the child's activities; that is, for the building of ideals, of habits, of attitudes that result in wholesome behavior. Character training will make for efficiency in the manner in which the individual will be able to meet all the experiences of life, in all of its complex relationships.

3. Train the child in self-mastery.

4. Guide the child in the establishment of hygienic physical habits which will be conducive to the development and maintenance of health.

5. Provide suitable environment, physical, mental, social, moral.

6. Help the child to recognize and to face reality.

7. Strive to prevent morbid fears and realize that the avoidance of worry is a requisite of mental health.

8. Direct the activities of every child so that he may acquire habits of attention and of orderly association.

9. Aid the child in the development of wholesome interests.

10. Establish self-confidence; give encouragement and assistance; exhibit an attitude of confidence.

11. Criticize constructively; avoid ridicule, sarcasm, and humiliation.

12. Train the child to make clear-cut decisions and to abide by them.

The Self-Concept.[16] An adequate and wholesome concept of self is essential for effective adjustment, and constitutes one of the most fundamental factors in mental health. The manner in which an individual regards himself exercises an important motivational influence on all behavior. The term *self-concept* is employed to designate the attitudes and feelings which a person has regarding himself and around which his values are organized. It is the individual's personal impression of himself. It is the complex picture which he has built up of the person he is and is becoming. It connotes the characteristics, good and bad, strong and weak, which the individual associates with himself together with the inferences he makes concerning his personal worth. It involves the person's appraisal of his physique, his capabilities and his potentialities, his assets and his limitations. It includes as a necessary condition an evaluation of his own adequacy and competence as a person. When this appraisal is objective and realistic it implies insight or knowledge of self, which should result in healthful self-respect, self-esteem, and self-acceptance. The greater the insight, the more probable it is that adjustment will be adequate and wholesome. Lack of insight is characteristic of disturbed and inadequate or maladjusted personalities.

The concept of self is formulated gradually and continuously throughout the entire process of growth and development. It undergoes continuous reorganization as experiences of many kinds accrue in the life of the child and result in increased awareness of personal attributes and resources. To a large extent it is a reflection of the reactions of others to the child's behavior. This expanding concept of self is influenced particularly by experiences within the home and the school as well as in peer groups, especially experiences which are indicative of approval and disapproval, of acceptance and rejection of the child. It is noteworthy that attitudes concerning self which are acquired within the child's first environment, the home, as a result of parental care, example, discipline, and guidance, not only constitute the most fundamental factors

[16] See M. E. Bonney, *op. cit.*, pp. 126–147; H. C. Smith, *Personality Adjustment* (New York: McGraw-Hill Book Co., Inc., 1961); A. W. Coombs and D. Syngg, *Individual Behavior,* 2 ed. (New York: Harper & Row, 1959); R. C. Wylie, *The Self-Concept* (Lincoln, Neb.: University of Nebraska Press, 1961).

in the formulation of the child's self-concept but also are very likely to persist throughout life. The school ranks second only to the home as an influence on the acquisition of the child's self-concept. This is particularly true in the areas of motivation and adjustment, which are the bases upon which success and failure rest. Accordingly, the school must utilize its resources to guide and assist pupils in the development of realistic self-understanding. In addition, the formulation of the self-concept of the child is dependent to some degree upon the evaluations and expectations, the respect and approval of the peer group.

It is evident then that the formulation of the child's self-concept is closely related to the needs for security, for self-esteem, for belonging, for achievement, and for self-reliance. The child who feels secure, loved, wanted, and adequate within the groups of which he is a member, that is, the family, the school, and the peer group, will be confident in his self-esteem and will adjust in a wholesome manner. The child who considers himself to be inadequate, unwanted and rejected by parents, teachers, and peers, whether or not this situation is objectively true, may develop a self-concept characterized by feelings of inferiority. He is likely to act accordingly and to endeavor in one way or another to compensate. He may project his inadequacies on others; he may cover up by extreme withdrawal; he may become overly assertive and aggressive in order to demonstrate that he really is adequate; he may assume an attitude of superiority; he may resort to temper tantrums, to feigned illness, to stealing, or to other types of antisocial behavior.

An adequate and wholesome concept of self involves the development of essentially positive attitudes and feelings which permeate all behavior. The individual who has attained an adequate and wholesome concept of himself is usually characterized by the following:

1. He is aware of his inherent dignity as a person.

2. He recognizes his weaknesses and limitations but does not seek either to minimize or to exaggerate them. He endeavors to set goals for himself which are realistically perceived and within his ability to attain.

3. He is cognizant of his potentialities, abilities, and good qualities and utilizes these to attain his goals.

4. He is self-reliant and has confidence in himself and his abilities. He considers himself to be capable and adequate in meeting and dealing with his problems. He makes choices and decisions for which he assumes and acknowledges responsibility.

5. He has achieved self-acceptance, that is, not mere complacency, but rather the ability to evaluate himself as he actually is and to utilize his abilities and qualities as bases for self-improvement.

6. He has developed and manifests, in his conduct, self-control.

7. He has established a set of values and principles as standards for directing his actions and behavior and adheres consistently to these values and principles.

The Process of Adjustment. Life involves a continuous process of adjustment to surroundings in the physical order, to situations in the social phase, and to problems in the mental, emotional, and vocational aspects. Every child in the process of growth and development from birth to maturity acquires habits of adjustment. As has previously been indicated, *adjustment* involves more than merely adapting to or fitting into surrounding conditions and environmental situations. It implies also that the individual understands his relationship to those conditions and situations, and in addition that, with increasing maturity, he acquires the ability to meet these situations adequately, that is, with "a minimum of stress and a maximum of efficiency." It implies, moreover, the ability to modify these conditions through the effective use of intellect and will. *Maladjustment,* on the other hand, is indicative of an inability to adapt to and to modify conditions and situations within the environment. The extent of maladjustment is determined by the number and kinds of situations and conditions in which the individual manifests inadequate behavior. Thus it is not the problems, adversities, and conflicts which determine mental health, but rather the way in which the individual reacts to these. The causes of maladjustment are many and varied. There is no single cause to which it may be attributed; that is, the principle of multiple causation applies.

There exist a variety of possibilities for reacting or responding to any situation. However, when an individual is confronted with a difficulty or a problem or a conflict, ordinarily he will react in one of these ways:

1. He may face reality squarely. He may meet the difficulty successfully, or, failing in his endeavors, become stimulated by failure to bring forth better efforts. Such an individual is well adjusted.

2. He may avoid meeting the difficulty by withdrawing or shrinking away from it entirely. Such an individual is maladjusted.

3. He may compromise with reality in order to escape punishment or to avoid unpleasant circumstances or to gain some advantage.

The wholesome method of reacting is the first, that is, to face reality squarely. One who reacts in that way is mentally healthy. He is adjusted because he is in touch with reality. He reacts to the conditions of life as they actually are. Such methods of reacting should be cultivated for the purpose of attaining mental health and for achieving a wholesome integrated personality.

The individual who reacts in the second way, that is, who avoids difficulties by withdrawing, is maladjusted. Such a reaction constitutes a menace to the happiness, efficiency, and mental health of the individual. Evasion is unwholesome. It is a step toward abnormality, since the individual is out of touch with reality. He substitutes in fantasy for the experiences and satisfactions of which he is deprived through his failure to meet reality. Such reactions breed anxiety, moodiness, dissatisfaction, and diffidence. Children should be protected against acquiring this attitude. Such protection consists essentially in meeting the basic psychological needs, that is, in providing opportunity for achievement, in developing self-confidence, in acquiring a feeling of success, in encouraging the child to take part in group activities.

The third way of reacting involves compromise with reality. It involves a failure on the part of the individual to adjust to conditions as they actually are. The individual who compromises seeks to evade responsibility and to set up a defense for his actions. Methods of compromise are called *adjustive mechanisms, personality dynamisms, defense mechanisms, defense reactions,* and *escape mechanisms.* The purpose is to safeguard reputation, to protect self-respect, to preserve pride. Such reactions are deadly to the spirit of initiative. There is lack of agreement concerning the way in which these defense mechanisms should be classified but there is common agreement that they are learned responses and acquired habits. However, several types of defense mechanisms are considered important in the study of maladjustment. These include: *projection, rationalization, compensation, daydreaming, regression, identification,* and *negativism.* A brief description of each of these types is presented.

Projection. Essentially *projection* involves an endeavor to "save face" and to avoid the unpleasant consequences of behavior by transferring the blame for personal failures, shortcomings, and inadequacies to other persons by maintaining that they have failed to cooperate, or have acted in an undesirable manner, or have demonstrated evidence of ill will. The failing student often attributes his lack of success to the unfairness of the examination questions. Likewise projection may take the form of blaming uncontrollable factors or circumstances for personal shortcomings and ineptness. The inadequate workman may seek to avoid responsibility by placing the blame on his tools. Projection may also be manifested in disparaging comparisons with others who are less competent or less fortunate. It may take the form of calling attention to the failures, shortcomings, and undesirable traits of others in order to divert attention from one's own weaknesses, through the implication that others are just as bad or perhaps even worse. No difficulties are ever solved by utilizing the mechanism of projection. In fact, projection usually diminishes the probability that problems will be met, or difficulties overcome, or inadequacies realized. It should be noted that projection may readily become habitual, and in extreme form may lead to hallucinations. Teachers can help pupils avoid the use of projection by demonstrating frequently the need for personal responsibility for one's actions, and likewise by refusing to accept projection as a valid excuse for not performing satisfactorily.

Rationalization. The most commonly employed defense mechanism is *rationalization.* This is a form of self-justification by which the individual seeks to justify his behavior, not only to others but also to himself, on the basis of reasonable motives. The individual who rationalizes endeavors to justify his behavior by presenting plausible reasons for that behavior. However, these plausible reasons did not actually motivate the behavior, and probably had little or no part in determining it, but are considered to be more acceptable than the true reasons. Rationalization, therefore, involves the assigning of false but logical appearing reasons as justification for behavior. It is based upon the desire to protect one's feeling of personal worth, to build up esteem, and to maintain prestige. There are two very common forms of rationalization. The first form is the "sour-grapes" mechanism which derives its name from Aesop's fable of the Fox and the Grapes. This involves an attempt to build up self-esteem by belittling that which one cannot achieve or does not possess by endeavoring to convince others that the things strived for were not really desired or worth possessing. Thus by belittling the importance of a goal, the failure to achieve it ceases to be a sign of failure or inadequacy. The second form is the "sweet-lemon" or Pollyanna mechanism which involves "saintly acceptance of unpleasant things" by endeavoring to convince oneself and others that failure to achieve a desired goal is in itself desirable. Rationalization, because it involves false reasoning, constitutes a serious impediment to clear thinking. Its primary danger lies in its seeming plausibility, which removes the necessity for facing reality and its problems.

Compensation. This type of defense mechanism involves an effort to make up for or to offset, through the development of other qualities, some deficiency or weakness or lack of a specific ability, either real or imaginary, physical or mental, which may interfere with achievement or prevent the individual from obtaining social recognition. It involves the substitution of attainable goals for those which are or seem to be unattainable because of some limitation or because of surrounding circumstances. The fundamental factor in the mechanism is a feeling of inferiority. Some forms of compensation may in certain instances be helpful in overcoming personal limitations and may even lead to superior accomplishments as well as to the development of qualities which might otherwise be neglected. Thus the pupil who is not accomplishing very well in academic work may bolster his self-esteem by making a success of his efforts in athletics or in some extra class activity; the frail boy who is unable to achieve in athletics may compensate by attaining the honor roll or excelling in debate. Compensation when deliberate and realistic may be especially worthwhile to the physically handicapped as a means of overcoming to a great extent this particular handicap. The blind, for example, frequently compensate for their handicap by developing unusual activity in the senses of touch and hearing. Many satisfactory adjustments can be made through compensation. The danger, however, lies in *overcompensation* in which the compensatory behavior may be so satisfactory to the individual that he may avoid attacking his problems directly.

Daydreaming. This is a type of defense mechanism in which the individual who is unable to meet the situations of life successfully solves his difficulties in fantasy. He gains satisfaction from imaginary achievement of success and approval. It is a form of escape from unpleasant reality. It is more frequently indulged in during adolescence, probably because of the increase in problems of emotional adjustment which is characteristic of the period. Daydreaming is a pleasant, inviting luxury in which it is easy to indulge. It is personally satisfying and centers around the individual himself. It leads to substitution of wishing and hoping, instead of doing. The tendency to repetition, to elaboration, and to systematization gives daydreaming its importance. Usually there is present a wish for approbation and success, so the dreamer becomes "a conquering hero" and pictures himself performing marvelous feats. However, if he feels misunderstood, he may picture himself as a "suffering martyr" who is the object of pity and sympathy. Daydreaming becomes serious when indulged in excessively and when it becomes a substitute for real accomplishment. It is dangerous because it renders the individual unfit for practical living. It makes for extreme sentimentalism. The best preventives are active work, the arousing and fostering of wholesome interests, providing opportunities for exercise of initiative, and activities which are satisfying and wholesome and which hold the attention of the individual.

Regression. This mechanism is also termed *retrogression.* It is essentially a retreat from reality. It consists in a form of withdrawal in which the individual reverts to behavior patterns that brought satisfaction and were effective during an earlier stage of development or adjustment when he is unable to meet a present difficulty satisfactorily. During adolescence, for example, the individual may manifest regression by reverting to temper tantrums, sulkiness, pouting, and feigning illness, all of which are infantile reactions for obtaining his own way. "Living in the past" is also a form of regression expressed by individuals who claim that "in the good old days, everything was much better." This aspect of regression is often termed "Old Oaken Bucket Delusion." It is to be noted that regression when carried to extremes may be symptomatic of future mental disorder, particularly schizophrenia.

Identification. This is an escape mechanism which involves the process of obtaining satisfaction vicariously through picturing one's self in fantasy as achieving the success and prestige attained by another or by others in situations in which the individual has found it very difficult or impossible to achieve success. Children and adolescents frequently endeavor to secure satisfaction and security by identifying themselves with the heroes and heroines of motion pictures, television, fiction, drama, sports, and perhaps on occasion even the "comics." Identification may be helpful when it is socially acceptable, in that it may increase the individual's feeling of personal worth. However, it may also prove to be a detrimental factor to adjustment when it is used as a substitute for action, when it causes the individual indulging in it to be satisfied with imagery instead of achievement, when it leads to excessive daydreaming and withdrawal from reality.

Negativism. This is a type of defense mechanism which involves a tendency to resist what is suggested or to refuse to comply with requests in order to escape unpleasant tasks and duties. It involves conduct which is stubborn, contrary, and noncooperative, and may vary from surliness to complete lack of response. It involves behavior which is the opposite of what is considered to be the normal and expected response. It is an attention-getting device which is a defense against insecurity. The individual who engages in this type of behavior has discovered, perhaps early in childhood, that he can secure more attention by antagonism or rebellion than by obeying and complying with requests. Such behavior which was effective in childhood may persist into adolescence and even into adulthood, and may be utilized as a technique for dealing with others. Individuals in whom such is the case habitually resist suggestions and advice, and likewise have difficulty in accepting the authority of other persons.

These defense reactions and escape mechanisms have their origins in childhood. They can be avoided through proper guidance and direction. Mental health is not achieved by avoiding or by compromising difficulties, but by learning how to meet them. McCarthy has stated that the chief safeguard of mental health is a well-formed character which can never be formed by avoiding difficulties, but only by meeting and overcoming them. An important function of mental hygiene in childhood and in adolescence is to provide the necessary guidance and direction so that the child will realize early in life that defense mechanisms are both unwholesome and undesirable.

Aids in Ascertaining Adjustment. There exists a very definite need in the field of mental hygiene for the development of diagnostic techniques which would enable teachers to ascertain which children are likely to become maladjusted. There exists a need also for the development of techniques for the accurate diagnosis of children who have already demonstrated tendencies toward maladjustment. At the present time some indications may be obtained through *observation* which will reveal such characteristics as inattention, withdrawal, shyness, aggressive behavior, and daydreaming. The *interview* will also provide some evidence, as will *anecdotal records.* However, in ascertaining the adjustment status of pupils, the teacher will probably receive the most effective aid from the various testing devices now available and used in the school situation. *Tests of mental ability* provide evidence of mental maturity and capacity to learn. In some cases this capacity may not be sufficiently adequate to enable the child to achieve in accordance with his desires, or to provide security, or to enable him to gain acceptance in his group. *Tests of achievement* provide the basis for an evaluation of skill and accomplishments in school subjects and make possible the comparison of the achievement of the child with the norms for his grade placement and age, as well as with the accomplishments of the group within which he is classified. However, tests of mental ability and of scholastic achievement fail to provide direct information concerning the personal phases of behavior. Accordingly, as a means of ascertaining as adequately as possible the emotional, social, and other motivational aspects of adjustment, the teacher will find the *personality inventories* of value. These have been devised as tools for determining the causes of maladjustment through the early identification of problems, and as indicators of attitudes. The personality inventory[17] is of help particularly in ascertaining specific areas of maladjustment. Among those employed frequently in the school situation are the *Bell Adjustment Inventory, The Bernreuter Personality Inventory, The Minnesota Multiphasic Personality Inventory, The California Test of Personality, The Rogers Test of Personality Adjustment, The S.R.A. Youth Inventory, Thurstone Temperament Schedule, The Brown Personality Inventory for Children, The Guilford-Zimmerman Temperament Survey, IPAT Personality Questionnaire.* Also useful in ascertaining areas in which the individual may display symptoms of maladjustment are the *Mooney Problem Check List* and devices of a similar nature, which reveal from the items underlined or circled some areas and symptoms of maladjustment. In addition, there has been devised the *Mental Health Analysis* for the purpose of ascertaining the extent to which a child possesses certain assets and liabilities in the area of mental health. The assets include close personal relationships, getting along with people, participating in group activities, satisfying work and recreation, philosophy of life. The liabilities include immature behavior, emotional instability, feelings of inadequacy, effects of physical defects on morale and "nervous" manifestations. Other devices for obtaining information concerning personality structure include projective techniques, the best known of which are the *Rorschach* and the *Thematic Apperception Test.* These should be administered and interpreted by a trained clinical psychologist. Also the

[17] For a comprehensive listing of personality inventories and a critical evaluation of these inventories, see O. K. Buros, ed., *The Fifth Mental Measurements Yearbook* (Highland Park, N. J.: The Gryphon Press, 1959); J. P. Guilford, *Personality* (New York: McGraw-Hill Book Co., Inc., 1959).

teacher may employ *sociometric measurement*[18] as a means of studying the social structure and ascertaining the emotional climate of the classroom. By this device, it is possible for the teacher to determine the nature of the interpersonal relationships existing among the children in the class.

Types of Mental Disorders. In order to establish an adequate program of prevention it seems essential that the teacher, whose task it is to put that program into effective operation, should understand at least the basic facts concerning the nature, causes, and effects of mental disorders. It is an accepted principle that inadequate adjustments may lead to disintegration of personality and that most mental disorders have their origin in inadequate adjustments during childhood. While diagnosis is not the teacher's task, nevertheless the teacher should be sufficiently acquainted with symptoms in order to realize the grave dangers indicated. Accordingly, in the interests of completeness and thoroughness, brief descriptions of the various types of mental disorder are presented.

In general, mental disorders have been classified as *organic or physiogenic* and *functional or psychogenic.* Organic disorders have a physical basis, and result from injury or damage to the central nervous system. Functional disorders on the other hand are considered to be the result of disturbing psychological factors and so far as can be ascertained have no observable organic or neurological basis. Mental hygiene is concerned with the *functional* disorders which are the results of maladjustments and emotional stress of psychological origin. The functional mental disorders result in disintegration of personality and cause disturbances in the functioning of the various mental powers. Chief among these are disturbances of perception, of thought, of volition, of feelings and emotions, of attention, of memory, of association. Those of *perception* include illusions, hallucinations, and disorientation; those of *thought* include delusions, morbid suspicions, obsessions, and ideas of persecution; of *volition,* impulsion, negativism, and suggestibility; those of the *affective states* include excessive elation, profound depression, morbid anger, and phobias; of *attention,* lack of ability to concentrate for any length of time upon a particular situation; of *memory,* amnesia, pathological forgetting, and retrospective falsification; of *association,* aphasia, incoherence, and flight of ideas.

The types of mental disorders described are the psychoses, the psycho-

---

[18] See M. E. Bonny, *Mental Health in Education* (Boston: Allyn and Bacon, Inc., 1960), pp. 258–275.

neuroses, and psychopathic personality. For a complete discussion of these the student is referred to standard works in psychiatry and abnormal psychology.

1. The Psychoses. The psychotic or demented person is an individual who has lost control of his mental powers after having attained mental development. This loss of mental powers may be temporary or periodic or permanent. *Psychosis* is a severe type of mental disorder in which there is an extensive disorganization of personality and consequent loss of contact with reality. The individual's mental functions are so profoundly disturbed that he is incapacitated for participating in everyday activities. The common types of psychoses which are considered to be the outcomes of emotional factors are *paranoia, manic-depressive psychosis, involutional melancholia,* and *schizophrenia* or *dementia praecox.* While any of these forms of psychosis may be characterized by delusions, paranoia is distinctively characterized by delusions and suspicion. The manic-depressive type is characterized by flight of ideas, by hallucinations, by periods of depression and elation. Involutional melancholia is characterized by feelings of dejection and hopelessness. Schizophrenia is characterized by delusions, by hallucinations, by disorders of attention and of memory, by confusion of thought. All of these psychoses involve disintegration of personality.

Schizophrenia, meaning literally *split personality,* is both the most prevalent and the most interesting form of mental illness. It has been termed also praecox or precocious dementia to indicate premature mental deterioration. It occurs most frequently among youth during the adolescent period, frequently in individuals of intellectual promise. The majority of the cases appear before the age of twenty-five. There are four common types, the *simple,* the *hebephrenic,* the *catatonic,* and the *paranoid.* The *simple* type is characterized by emotional indifference, intellectual deterioration, and gradual personality disintegration. When the onset of schizophrenia occurs during adolescence, it usually takes the form of *hebephrenia,* which means the mind of youth. The individual not only fails to put aside childish characteristics, but shows acute mental excitement without adequate cause. He becomes quarrelsome, irritable, suspicious, and profane. The most common type is the *catatonic,* which is characterized by psychomotor abnormalities, manifested in the form of stupor and passiveness or extreme excitability. The *paranoid* form, which is named because of its general resemblance to paranoia, also occurs frequently during the latter part of adolescence. Unsystematized or illogical and loosely organized delusions of grandeur and of persecution are characteristic of this form, as are auditory and visual hallucinations.

The causes of schizophrenia have not been determined with certainty. In all probability there is no single cause. Heredity probably plays some part. However, shocks, frights, emotional disturbances seem to constitute precipitating factors. The earliest symptoms are found in such emotional states as an aversion to things practical and an excess of fantastic daydreaming, which gradually weaken effective volition so that the individual is content to substitute the imagined for reality. While some cases of schizophrenia recover, most could be prevented if early symptoms were recognized, and all cases respond to treatment if detected in the early stages. There is a hope for restoration of many such individuals to a normal life if symptoms are detected and treatment begun early enough.

This disorder is functional; that is, it seems to be due to mental and emotional disturbances. It involves changes and deterioration of personality without any demonstrable disturbance of the brain or nervous system which could account for these changes and for the deterioration. Particularly susceptible to it are the shy, seclusive, lonely, sensitive, extremely introspective, peculiar youths who are not socially inclined. It originates in childhood maladjustments which served as a means for withdrawing from unpleasant situations. Particularly should the shy, "shut-in," withdrawing children be recognized, because these are the children in whom this disorder may develop at adolescence. It does not develop in socially and emotionally well-adjusted individuals. Likewise, it does not develop spontaneously, and rarely ever suddenly. It develops gradually for the most part from emotional maladjustments resulting from the inability of the child and the youth to meet successfully and solve satisfactorily the problems presented in daily living.

2. The Psychoneuroses. This term is derived from two Greek words which mean a nervous condition of the mind. Psychoneurosis is, then, a minor functional disorder due chiefly to unresolved emotional tensions resulting from conflicts, frustrations, and marked insecurity. However, this condition, while indicating emotional maladjustment, does not constitute one psychotic. While the condition lasts, the individual is peculiar in some respects, is aware of his peculiarities, but apparently is unable to control them. The important element of the psychoneuroses is that, although accompanied by physical symptoms, the disorders result from mental causes. Therefore, the main factor in the treatment of them is the psychological and mental-hygiene appeal. The principal psychoneuroses are *neurasthenia, psychasthenia,* and *hysteria.* These conditions usually begin in childhood and in many cases are considered to be the product of unfortunate childhood experiences, training, and environment. In popular terminology the psychoneurotic child is usually designated by such terms as nervous, peculiar, queer, erratic, emotionally unstable, and the like. In general, such a child, for reasons other than intelligence, does not get along in groups which are of his own intellectual development. It has been estimated that about 5 percent of the schoolchildren are psychoneurotic; that is, they are sufficiently unstable to be susceptible to emotional reactions which are easily aroused, controlled with difficulty, and which interfere with their adjustment. Such a condition is unfavorable to the healthy and coordinated functioning of the intellect, emotions, and will. Since any added stress, physical, mental, or social, may develop into serious mental disorder, such children require specific and hygienic treatment. Early diagnosis is desirable and every effort should be made to deal with such difficulties as they appear.

NEURASTHENIA. This term is derived from two Greek words which mean a weakness of the nerves. It is very commonly referred to as a "nervous breakdown," yet there is no indication that the "nerves" are damaged. It is characterized primarily by physical debility and the symptoms appear to be essentially physical. It is caused for the most part by mental and emotional conflicts and becomes manifest in emotional stress. It may be the accompaniment of an improper amount or kind of work, lack of proper rest, overwork, unfavorable environmental conditions of various sorts. It is a functional disorder manifested in emotional stress and characterized by such mental and physical symptoms as abnormal irritability, inability to concentrate attention, vague aches and pains, insomnia, lack of physical energy, states of discouragement, dissatisfaction, and hopelessness.

PSYCHASTHENIA. This term is derived from two Greek words which mean weakness of the mind. It is mental in origin, due chiefly to poor mental habits. It is less common than neurasthenia. Psychasthenia is characterized by *phobias, obsessions,* and *compulsions. Phobias* are persistent, abnormal, exaggerated, and unrealistic fears of an object or situation, the intensity of which is out of proportion to an external situation.

The phobias include such peculiar and extreme fears as agoraphobia or fear of open spaces, acrophobia or fear of high places, pathophobia or fear of disease, claustrophobia or fear of closed spaces, and an unlimited number of others. These are usually explained in terms of early experiences with the object or situation feared. *Obsessions* are persistently recurring, unwanted ideas or series of ideas which interfere with normal orderly thinking and which persist even when their irrational nature is recognized. Some common obsessions are self-accusatory thoughts, doubts concerning ability to make decisions even regarding simple matters, and thoughts about "losing one's mind." *Compulsions* are irresistible urges or impulses to perform some act which is recognized as unreasonable, absurd, or meaningless and which is contrary to one's better judgment. An example is the hand-washing compulsion which is due apparently to feelings of guilt or shame. Other compulsions include klyptomania or the impulse to steal, pyromania or the impulse to set fire to things, arithmomania or the impulse to count everything. Frequently phobias, obsessions, and compulsions are produced in the child either wholly or partly by association with and imitation of other persons in the environment.

HYSTERIA. This involves the conversion of psychological conflicts into physical symptoms. These physical symptoms are many and include fainting, a kind of convulsive seizure, spells of dizziness, contractures or paralyses of various kinds, peculiar areas of loss of sensation, tics which cannot be accounted for by any organic causes. Hysteria is an unconscious adaptation of a physical symptom or mental disturbance in order to escape a difficulty, to evade some responsibility, to avoid an intolerable situation, to excuse failure. It is characterized also by mental and emotional symptoms. The individual suffering from hysteria is likely to be peculiarly childish, self-centered, and fond of attention, moody, irritable, and desirous of sympathy. Likewise, the individual is likely to be overextravagant in the expression of his emotions. The cause of hysteria is mental; that is, an idea becomes a disease. Hysteria is really a *character defect* which is associated with lack of proper training and the failure to establish adequate habits in childhood. It is worthy of note that the hysterical temperament usually appears at an early age. Therefore, the teacher should become familiar with the symptoms as displayed among schoolchildren in order that such cases may be recognized early and given the guidance of which they are particularly in need.

In addition to the principal psychoneuroses which have been described, it is customary to list two additional types, *hypochondria* and *anxiety neurosis*. *Hypochondria* involves an abnormal preoccupation with and anxiety about one's state of health with a tendency to ascribe diseases and disorders to one's self. It serves as a way of avoiding the assumption of responsibilities and also as a means of gaining sympathy. Many children recognize very early in life that illness will arouse sympathy and release them from the performance of usual school and home tasks. They may learn to establish a pattern of developing symptoms of illness for the purpose of avoiding responsibility. *Anxiety neurosis* is characterized by an almost constant intense apprehension and fearfulness in situations which do not involve real problems or difficulties, or if the situation does involve some problem or difficulty, the apprehension and fearfulness are out of all proportion. In some cases psychosomatic symptoms such as headache, excessive sweating, nausea, rapid heartbeat may be manifested. Sometimes the individual who suffers from anxiety neurosis may endeavor to escape from his worries by overeating, overworking, or resorting to alcohol or narcotics.

3. The Psychopathic Personality. This term has been devised in order to classify those individuals who are severely maladjusted and yet are not considered by generally accepted standards to be either neurotic or psychotic. The *psychopath,* also designated frequently as the *sociopath,* is a chronically antisocial individual who exhibits marked emotional immaturity. Such individuals are characterized by a disregard for the rules and conventions of society, by the absence of reactions of guilt, and by lack of self-control. Because of the fact that the conduct disorders which characterize the psychopath seem to be due to defective control of the will, the trend at the present time is to account for the psychopathic personality in terms of defective character organization. The behavior of psychopathic individuals is impulsive and irresponsible. They are lacking in emotional control, have little perspective, manifest marked defects in judgment, and are unhampered by ethical considerations. They are eccentric, arrogant, extremely self-centered, and unstable in their emotional, social, and vocational adjustments. It is usually claimed that such individuals lack insight, that is, do not see themselves as others do and seem incapable of learning from or profiting by experience. For a long time it was believed that psychopathic personality was inherited. However, sound evidence to substantiate this belief is lacking. In addition no observable physical causes have been discerned to account for the condition. It is, therefore, considered to be psychogenic in origin. Treatment of the condition is difficult and usually unrewarding.

Psychological Services Which Implement Mental Hygiene. There are three services which have been developed and employed in modern education for the purpose of implementing the principles and techniques of mental hygiene. These are the *child-guidance clinic,* the *school social work program,* and the *school psychologist.*

a) THE CHILD-GUIDANCE CLINIC. The most important of the psychological services designed to implement mental hygiene is the child-guidance clinic. These clinics, which are also designated by such terms as mental health clinics or psychiatric clinics or habit clinics or psychological clinics, have been established in an effort to study the identification and treatment of emotionally disturbed children. The purpose of the child-guidance clinic is to assist in the diagnosis and training of maladjusted children. It is also the function of the child-guidance clinic to study the causes and effects of conduct disorders and to aid in the treatment of children who present problems of behavior and maladjustments of personality, such as disordered habits, emotional abnormalities, unacceptable social behavior, troublesome personality traits as indicated by shyness, worries, fears, retardation in intellectual development, shortcomings in mentally superior children who are not making full use of their endowment, psychoneurotic disorders, and disability in reading. Such maladjustments are serious, not only because of the immediate disturbance they create but also because they represent very often the early stages of mental illness. Therefore, the aim and purpose of the child-guidance clinic is to correct these conditions and tendencies which, if permitted to continue unchecked, would influence unfavorably the entire development of the individual.

The work of the child-guidance clinic is based upon an understanding of the *motives* which stimulate the behavior of the child. Thus motives constitute the fundamental matter rather than the conduct. The child does not misbehave, does not become disturbed and maladjusted without reason. The child who is a problem exhibits symptoms for which the motive or underlying cause must be found. The misconduct of the problem child, the difficult child, or the maladjusted child is a symptom arising from and associated with many conditions, social and intellectual, emotional and moral. The function of the clinic is to discover the underlying causes, and treatment consists of the removal of these underlying causes, together with the control of conduct in the light of the knowledge thus acquired. Such treatment must be concrete, constructive, and continuous, with the emphasis placed always on prevention.

To accomplish its purpose effectively the clinic must establish relations with such agencies as the home, the Church, the schools, case-working societies, courts, and other institutions which deal with children. Treatment necessarily means working out with parents methods of child training; with schools, the modification of teaching practices; with social agencies, techniques that will seek out the core of the difficulty. However, the clinic works no miracles, possesses no magic formulae, is in no position to supplant parents, teachers, judges, and other directors of the child. The proper time for clinical treatment is childhood, when the individual is still plastic enough to yield to the educational measures which may be provided to overcome his difficulties. It is noteworthy that the scientific studies of mental illnesses and their beginnings have revealed that childhood is the period of prevention. The one very fruitful path to prevention lies in correcting mental deviations in their incipiency, in establishing a mentally healthy environment for the child, in creating among adults an understanding of the needs of the child for healthful mental development. These are the functions which the clinic serves.

The basic staff of the child-guidance clinic is composed of a team consisting of a psychiatrist, a clinical psychologist, and a social worker. Occasionally child-guidance clinics have other specialists on the staff, including pediatricians, endocrinologists, neurologists, vocational counselors, and remedial teachers. The general plan of procedure is fairly well standardized. The first step is a statement of the problem and of the conditions which require correction. This involves a case study and social examination which is made by the social worker, implying a very careful study of the personal and social backgrounds of the child, determining relevant facts concerning the family background, upbringing, socioeconomic status, and relationships with others. The second step consists of a thorough physical examination. The third step is the psychological examination, involving the administration and interpretation of tests of mental ability, of aptitude, of educational achievement, of interests, and of personality. These tests are administered and interpreted by the psychologist for the purpose of ascertaining the child's intellectual capacity and to discover any special abilities or disabilities which he may possess. The fourth step consists of the neurological and psychiatric examination. This is made by the psychiatrist who is acquainted with the findings obtained in the previous three steps by the other members of the clinical staff. This fourth step involves an analysis and diagnosis of the problem. The fifth and final step in the clinical procedure involves a case conference or meeting of the staff at which the information concerning the child acquired by each specialist is pooled and a prognosis made. Then the members of the staff present their findings and collaborate in the formulation of comprehensive recommendations for psychotherapy.

The clinic brings to the consideration of each case the diagnoses and recommendations of the psychiatrist, the psychologist, and the social worker based upon a study of the child's family and social backgrounds, his mental ability, and his personality makeup. Children are referred to the child-guidance clinic principally by school authorities, welfare agencies, juvenile court judges, physicians, and parents. Very frequently the trouble is found to lie within the home. Even the wisest parents often meet problems in the growth and development of their children which they are unable to understand without outside expert assistance. To function as a preventive agency the educational work of the clinic must reach parents and must have their full and willing cooperation. The contribution of the clinic must take the form of a collection of information regarding children which will be of assistance to all parents, and to all teachers, and not only to those in need of expert assistance. The child-guidance clinic does not attempt to cure the child's disorders and maladjustments. Such cure can be accomplished only within the child's own environment in which the difficulties arose. The clinic endeavors to point out to parents and to teachers *the sources of the child's difficulties, and the means for remedying them.*

The first mental clinic seems to have been established in 1868 by the Out-Patient Department of the Orthopedic Hospital and Infirmary for Mental Diseases in Philadelphia. Perhaps the first of the child-guidance clinic was the Psychological Clinic of the University of Pennsylvania, which began its work in 1896 under the direction of Dr. Lightner Witmer. In 1909, The Institute for Juvenile Research in Chicago, conducted under the direction of Dr. William Healy, was established in connection with the juvenile court. This clinic was the first to employ the services of a psychiatrist, a psychologist, and a social worker functioning as a unit. In 1911, the Yale University Psycho-Clinic was established under the auspices of Dr. Arnold Gesell. In 1914, a clinic was established under the direction of Goddard in connection with the Department of Abnormal and Clinical Psychology at Ohio State University. The Judge Baker Foundation began its work in Boston in 1917 with a clinic directed by Healy and Bronner. In 1921, the first habit clinic for preschool children was established in Boston by Dr. Douglas A. Thom. Between 1925 and 1929, the National Committee for Mental Hygiene organized and operated with funds provided by the Commonwealth Fund five experimental child-guidance clinics. Since 1930 there has been a considerable increase in the number of child-guidance clinics. Many of these are sponsored by school systems, universities, courts, hospitals, as well as by community and public welfare agencies.

b) THE SCHOOL SOCIAL WORK PROGRAM. The second of the psychological services designed to implement mental hygiene in education is the *school social work program,* which is also known by such titles as the visiting teacher service, the visiting counselor service. This program provides a specialized form of case work and should constitute an integral part of the total school program. It is supplementary to the work of the teacher and must be coordinated with other school services. The school social work program is concerned with the preventive aspects of mental hygiene. It differs from the work of the child-guidance clinic in the respect that the school social worker deals with a type of problem less serious than that which leads the child to the guidance clinic. The school social worker is a specialist who is a trained social worker, with a background of teacher training and teaching experience, who is attached to a school, and whose task is to deal with conduct disorders which interfere with the child's efficiency in school. This service meets a need that has been felt by both social workers and educators. It is based upon the purpose of preventing, through the work of the school, many of the problems of juvenile delinquency, of mental, moral, and social maladjustment. The purpose of the program is twofold; the first is to have the school assume the responsibility for the adjustment of children who display minor types of maladjustments; the second is to bring about a better type of cooperation and of understanding between the home and the school.

The strategic factors in the development — mental, moral, emotional, physical, and social — of the child are the home and the school. Particularly in the school is there the opportunity to detect symptoms of minor maladjustments as they appear in the child. These maladjustments include failure and behavior for which the school is unable to account. These maladjustments are present also in the pupil who is retarded; in the restive child; in the irritable, the hostilely aggressive, the worried, the repressed, the violent-tempered child; in the neglected, the overworked child; in the truant; and in children who show tendencies toward delinquency. The school social worker will help parents to understand the child's problem at school, the responsibility of the school in relation to the child, and the manner in which the parents share this responsibility.

The results of the school social work program cannot be measured entirely or even adequately by means of statistical studies and graphic representations. However, the research studies which have been made demonstrate that a very large percentage of the children who have been under the care and guidance of the school social worker have improved in attendance, in scholarship, and in conduct.

c) THE SCHOOL PSYCHOLOGIST.[19] The third type of the psychological services designed to implement the principles and techniques of mental hygiene consists of services provided by the *school psychologist.* In many school systems which do not maintain a child-guidance clinic, there has developed since the 1920's a tendency to make a provision for psychological services through the employment of a school psychologist. He may function as the director of a limited psychological unit or he may be a staff member of a unit of special services which involves provision for a variety of educational services. The school psychologist is in a strategic position to apply the principles of mental hygiene. As a member of the school staff who deals with children in a school setting, he has many opportunities to carry on preventive and constructive as well as remedial phases of mental hygiene. Professionally prepared in the areas of clinical and educational psychology, he must foster the application of these areas within the school in order to facilitate and render more effective the activities of learning and teaching. The service functions of the school psychologist involve a wide range of responsibilities. The essential activities of the school psychologist are administering and interpreting individual psychological examinations and preparing diagnostic case reports. Other activities include:

---

[19] See M. A. White and M. W. Harris, *The School Psychologist* (New York: Harper and Row, 1961); S. W. Gray, *The Psychologist in the Schools* (New York: Holt, Rinehart and Winston, Inc., 1963); N. E. Cutts, ed., *School Psychologists at Mid-Century* (Washington: American Psychological Association, 1955); M. G. Gottsegen and G. B. Gottsegen, eds., *Professional School Psychology* (New York: Grune & Stratton, 1960); *The Psychologist on the School Staff,* report on the Committee on Reconsideration of the Functions of the School Psychologist, Division 16, American Psychological Association, 1958.

individual interviews; use of personality and adjustment inventories; conferences with teachers, principals, and other school personnel for the purpose of working out recommendations for adjustment of pupils; conferences with parents for the same reasons; contacts with community agencies for the purposes of referral; planning programs of remedial instruction and reeducation; supervision of the general testing program within the school; aiding in the classification of pupils; identification of exceptional children, including the gifted, mentally retarded, academically handicapped, socially maladjusted, and emotionally disturbed; and helping to plan appropriate educational and social experiences to meet their specific needs. Frequently also the school psychologist has the duty of interpreting the principles of mental hygiene to the school personnel through such devices as in-service courses, lectures, and suggestions for professional reading. He is a consultant, a diagnostician, an educator whose possibilities and contributions in the field of mental hygiene are almost without limits.

Educational Implications of Mental Hygiene. There is no other factor in education which concerns the school more intimately than the causes of, remedies for, and the prevention of, maladjustments, behavior disorders, and mental difficulties of children. From the point of view of mental hygiene, the teacher's task is to aid the child in achieving stability of character. This involves an understanding guidance which will enable the pupil to meet the stress and strain of life with a normal, healthy mind. This means that no teacher is merely an instructor of mathematics, of history, of languages, or of any subject, but that all teachers are builders of character. The possibilities of the school for service in this respect cannot rise above the capacities and limitations of its teaching personnel. While the teacher may be informed thoroughly about the principles of psychology, which have been presented in the previous chapters of this book, nevertheless the same teacher may be still relatively unsuccessful because he has overlooked some of the very important abnormal aspects of the child's mentality. Education is beginning to realize that many of the serious abnormalities of adult life can be prevented if detected in the early stages. Education is beginning to realize also that the teacher occupies a very favorable position for accomplishing the earliest work both in the detection of mental disorders and in the prevention of mental disturbances. Hence, attention is being centered on the school as a means of stemming the tide of the constantly increasing cases of mental abnormalities and behavior problems. The teacher's part in the program is vital and interesting. An understanding of the attitudes, emotions, and countless other forces which lead to maladjustments among children, fortunately may lead also to better adjustments in the lives of adults. The schools with a vastly improved attitude toward, and understanding of, mental hygiene have accepted the lead in this undertaking. Since the school deals with all the children, it must set an ideal and an example of enlightenment in its understanding and treatment of mental disorders and behavior problems. Therefore, the school must form the most effective agency of mental hygiene. Since mental health depends largely upon the development of proper mental habits, it naturally becomes a school problem. Every teacher in the school must study the problem of developing an adequately integrated personality in every pupil under his guidance. His task is to aid in the development of self-sustaining, self-controlling, adjusted, balanced, disciplined individuals.

EXERCISES

1. Outline this chapter.
2. List and define the terms which you have learned in your study of this chapter.
3. Why is an adequate understanding of the nature of man so important in mental hygiene?
4. What is the mental hygiene movement? What are its aims? What are the educational implications of mental hygiene? What is the present need for mental hygiene?
5. What are the nature, the purpose, and the value of the child-guidance clinic? Describe the functions of the staff of the clinic.
6. Distinguish between:
   a) Physiogenic and psychogenic;
   b) Neurasthenia and psychasthenia;
   c) Psychosis and psychoneurosis;
   d) Preventive and constructive aspects of mental hygiene;
   e) Mental hygiene and mental health.
7. Discuss the following:
   a) The principle of multiple causation in mental hygiene;
   b) The age levels at which problems of adjustment are likely to be particularly acute;
   c) Self-concept and its significance in mental hygiene;
   d) The significance of parent-child relationships;
   e) The basic psychological needs;
   f) The process of adjustment;
   g) Emotional stability;

h) The services provided by the school psychologist;
i) The relationship between mental hygiene and guidance;
j) The constructive and preventive aspects of mental hygiene.

8. What is the responsibility of the school in the area of mental hygiene? In what ways can the school fulfill this responsibility with respect both to teacher-pupil relationships and also to subject matter and administration aspects?
9. Why should the teacher know something of the symptoms of the functional mental disorders, of the psychoneuroses, and of defense mechanisms? What are the characteristics of mental health which mental hygiene endeavors to cultivate in the individual?
10. Discuss the following statements:
    a) "Emotional maturity is not achieved automatically, nor is it the gift of time; it must be striven for intelligently, and sometimes painfully."
    b) "All persons fall into one of two groups; the adjusted or the maladjusted."
    c) "A mental hygiene emphasis upon the identification of a few needy cases and upon therapeutic measures in these cases is much too negative. It must give way in education to a more positive program. Edution is not therapy."
    d) "There are surprisingly few neurotics among people who are genuinely humble."
    e) "In its fullest meaning mental hygiene is directed to developing personality to its greatest possibilities, so that every individual gives his best to the world and knows the deep satisfaction of a life nobly and fully lived."
    f) "It is the teacher's task to see to it that every child at some time, in some way, in some subject, achieves a success that will give him a decent respect for himself."

SELECTED REFERENCES FOR STUDY AND READING

Allinsmith, W., and Goethals, G. W., *The Role of Schools in Mental Health* (New York: Basic Books, Inc., 1962).

Allport, G. W., *Pattern and Growth in Personality* (New York: Holt, Rinehart and Winston, Inc., 1961).

Association for Supervision and Curriculum Development, Yearbook, 1950, *Fostering Mental Health in Our Schools* (Washington, D. C.: National Education Association, 1950).

Bernard, H. W., *Mental Hygiene for Classroom Teachers,* 2 ed. (New York: McGraw-Hill Book Co., Inc., 1961).

Bier, W. C., ed., *Personality: Development and Deviations* (New York: Fordham University Press, 1963).

Bonney, M. E., *Mental Health in Education* (Boston: Allyn and Bacon, Inc., 1960).

Caplan, G., ed., *Prevention of Mental Disorders in Children* (New York: Basic Books, Inc., 1961).

Cavanagh, J., and McGoldrick, J. B., S.J., *Fundamental Psychiatry,* 2 ed. (Milwaukee: The Bruce Publishing Co., 1958).

Crow, L. D., and Crow, A., eds., *Mental Hygiene for Teachers: A Book of Readings* (New York: The Macmillan Co., 1963).

Curran, C. A., *Counseling in Catholic Life and Education* (New York: The Macmillan Co., 1952).

D'Evelyn, K. E., *Meeting Children's Emotional Needs* (Englewood Cliffs, N. J.: Prentice-Hall, Inc., 1957).

Haring, N. G., and Phillips, E. L., *Educating Emotionally Disturbed Children* (New York: McGraw-Hill Book Co., Inc., 1962).

Heyns, R. W., *The Psychology of Personal Adjustment* (New York: The Dryden Press, Inc., 1958).

Jahoda, M., *Current Concepts in Positive Mental Health* (New York: Basic Books, Inc., 1958).

Jenkins, G. G., *Helping Children Reach Their Potential* (Chicago: Scott, Foresman and Co., 1961).

Kaplan, L., *Mental Health and Human Relations* (New York: Harper & Row, 1959).

Laycock, S. R., *Mental Hygiene in the School* (Toronto: Copp, Clark Co., Ltd., 1960).

Lippman, H. S., *Treatment of the Child in Emotional Conflict,* 2 ed. (New York: McGraw-Hill Book Co., Inc., 1962).

McCarthy, R. C., *Safeguarding Mental Health* (Milwaukee: The Bruce Publishing Co., 1937).

McKinney, F., *Psychology of Personal Adjustment,* 3 ed. (New York: John Wiley & Sons, Inc., 1960).

McKown, R., *Pioneers in Mental Health* (New York: Dodd, Mead & Co., 1961).

National Society for the Study of Education, Fifty-Fourth Yearbook, Part II, *Mental Health in Modern Education,* 1955.

Nunnally, J. C., *Popular Conceptions of Mental Health* (New York: Holt, Rinehart and Winston, Inc., 1961).

Prescott, D. A., *The Child in the Educative Process* (New York: McGraw-Hill Book Co., Inc., 1957).

Redl, F., and Wattenberg, W. W., *Mental Hygiene in Teaching,* 2 ed. (New York: Harcourt, Brace and World, Inc., 1959).

Ridenour, N., *Mental Health in the United States: A Fifty Year History* (Cambridge, Mass.: Harvard University Press, 1960).

Rogers, D., *Mental Hygiene in Elementary Education* (Boston: Houghton Mifflin Co., 1957).

Royce, J. E., *Personality and Mental Health* (Milwaukee: The Bruce Publishing Co., 1955).

Sawrey, J. M., and Telford, C. W., *Dynamics of Mental Health: The Psychology of Adjustment* (Boston: Allyn and Bacon, Inc., 1963).

Schneiders, A. A., *Personal Adjustment and Mental Health* (New York: Holt, Rinehart and Winston, Inc., 1955).

Seidman, J. M., ed., *Educating for Mental Health: A Book of Readings* (New York: Thomas Y. Crowell Co., 1963).

Shaffer, L. F., and Shoben, E. J., *The Psychology of Adjustment,* 2 ed. (Boston: Houghton Mifflin Co., 1956).
Smith, H. C., *Personality Adjustment* (New York: McGraw-Hill Book Co., Inc., 1961).
Stagner, R., *Psychology of Personality* (New York: McGraw-Hill Book Co., Inc., 1961).
Thorpe, L. P., *The Psychology of Mental Health,* 2 ed. (New York: The Ronald Press Co., 1960).
Vander Veldt, J. H., and Odenwald, R. P., *Psychiatry and Catholicism,* 2 ed. (New York: McGraw-Hill Book Co., Inc., 1957).

chapter 18

Constructive Discipline in the Classroom

The Meaning of Discipline. Among the foremost problems of teachers is that of discipline which involves the management, motivation, and direction of pupils in the classroom. The success or failure of an instructional program depends in no small way upon the ability of the teacher to control, to motivate, and to direct the activities of growing children and youth. The techniques involved in such control constitute a factor of vital importance in the educative process. Classroom discipline is a central aspect of the teaching-learning situation. How well pupils learn as well as what attitudes are acquired toward the school, the teacher, and fellow-pupils are influenced by the disciplinary techniques employed by the teacher. The term *discipline* in its educational applications has many facets and so has been assigned a variety of meanings. Originally the term was derived from the Latin word for instruction and teaching. In its broadest meaning, the term *discipline* has been used in education to connote the systematic training of the physical, mental, and moral capacities of the child, through exercise and instruction. Thus defined, discipline is as comprehensive as education; insofar as it includes mental, physical, and moral training, it involves the entire development of the individual. Discipline, in this broad sense, is also a factor in the development of character, since it includes the control, the regulation, and the guidance of all the forces that contribute to the acquisition of character. As such, discipline must be inherent in all the work of the school. As such, discipline is not for the few, but it is for all; not for the slow or retarded only, but for the bright as well; not for the unruly alone, but also for the well behaved. As such, discipline must be considered one of the principal aims of education.

In its narrowest significance, the term *discipline* has more rigorous implications, since it is usually employed to connote punishment or chastisement, the aim of which is to deter pupils from misbehavior. This, unfortunately, is the meaning which has been attached most frequently to the term. In modern education, however, disciplinary procedures are no longer basically *punitive*. They have become increasingly educative in nature and are based upon sound principles of mental hygiene. In its ordinary present-day educational usage, it is employed to indicate *all of the teaching procedures adopted for the better conduct of the school, particularly with reference to the orderly behavior of the pupils*. In this sense it denotes more than mere influence exercised by the teacher over the pupils; it denotes a great deal more than mere external conformity to the rules of good order. It implies training, instruction, and guidance which mold, improve, strengthen, and correct conduct and aid the pupil to become increasingly self-directed. Thus discipline indicates the development of orderliness in conduct and behavior through self-control, an orderliness which stems from attention to purposeful activity. In its present usage, this term *discipline* implies two essential elements. The first element is to secure on the part of the pupils the type of conduct and behavior that will be conducive to good, orderly working conditions within the learning environment, since neither desirable learning nor wholesome personality development can be expected to occur in an atmosphere of chaotic confusion. The second and more important element is to secure this conduct and behavior in such a way that it continually enriches the life of each individual mentally, morally, and emotionally, and in such a way that it contributes to the formation of character. The first element endeavors to achieve immediate results and involves attention to the outward aspects of school and classroom management. The second element implies the acquisition of habits and of skills, of ideals and of attitudes which make for social efficiency, for emotional stability, and for moral growth and development. This second element, likewise, implies on the part of the teacher an insight into and an understanding of the nature and the interests, attitudes, and needs of the individual pupils. Discipline involves both the maintenance of order so that learning may proceed effectively and the establishment of sound behavioral patterns.

The Functions of Discipline. Discipline involves a learning process which must lead to right behavior, to the exercise of ethical judgment, to the development of a sense of responsibility, to sustained application to tasks, to the formation of proper attitudes in keeping with the level of maturity attained by the pupil. It is likewise the purpose of discipline to equip the child to meet the realities of life. Therefore, it must consist of direct and insistent supervision of the child's conduct and behavior throughout his life in school. The beginning of all real discipline is obedience. Discipline must include training in cooperation. It involves learning to do cheerfully and skillfully things which do not come easily. It necessitates learning to do things which at times are disagreeable. It involves particularly the training of attention, of intellect, and of will, the direction of the emotions and of habit formation. From the teacher's viewpoint, discipline is essentially a process of motivating and guiding conduct which will lead to self-control. This is not something discrete and separate from teaching. It is an important aspect of all teaching, an integral part of the educative process, and a means of achieving fundamental educational goals.

The Basic Principles of Discipline. The specific purposes and aims of all discipline must be set forth clearly and understood thoroughly by the teacher and by the student. Discipline is not an end in itself, but it is regarded both as a means and as an end of the educational process. That aspect of school discipline which comprises the rules and regulations made for the purpose of fostering successful class management and instruction constitutes a means. However, that phase of discipline which is concerned with the mental and moral characteristics of the pupils is an end. Discipline, as a means, is important because it makes possible the orderly functioning of the school. Discipline, as an end, is significant because it leads to behavior which is moral, desirable, and necessary in itself.

The principles underlying effective and constructive discipline are:

1. It is the teacher's task to maintain adequate and orderly conditions within the classroom in order to provide a wholesome atmosphere and an environment conducive to learning.

2. Constructive discipline must develop ideals, attitudes, values, and habits which are desirable both in school and in mature life, to the end that the individual may become self-controlled and self-directed. This principle includes also the stimulation of worthy motives and of cultural appreciations.

3. Discipline must conform to the nature of the child and must be built upon a recognition of his inherent dignity as a person, of his needs, of his duties, of his responsibilities.

4. Discipline in order to be effective must be vital and meaningful, sympathetic and humane.

5. The standards of discipline imposed by the teacher for the guidance and direction of the pupils must constitute the basis of self-discipline.

6. Constructive discipline must be an outstanding objective of the entire educative process.

These principles are stressed here because unfortunately at one time there was manifested a widespread adherence to an extreme type of permissiveness which in the name of "progressive education" seemingly exalted the personal choice of the child over the sensible requirements of the school. There is no justification for such an extreme theory that the child should be unrestrained and so permitted to follow his impulses and tendencies, and that thus unguided he will grow and develop into an intelligent, civilized, moral human being. Restrictions are part of living and some are obviously necessary in the classroom. Discipline must be imposed upon the child for his own protection. There is a definite place for imposed discipline in the modern school. The child needs routines and rules in order to foster his sense of security. There is, furthermore, no justification for labeling such views "progressive," particularly since that particular theory not only regarded character and citizenship as the outstanding aims stressed in the curriculum but also as the ideals to which all activities of the school were supposed to contribute. Constructive discipline, however, is the chief means to good citizenship and the most effective means of developing character.

The Factors in Discipline. The factors in discipline are three. The first factor is *the teacher,* whose task it is to guide and to direct the pupil in his development in order that he may make right adjustments. The second factor is *the pupil,* whose development, behavior, and attitudes are to be guided and directed. The third factor consists of *the methods and techniques* which the teacher employs in order to secure orderliness and effective control of classroom conditions; it further embraces *the methods* of developing in the pupil habits, ideals, and attitudes of self-control and of right living.

a) THE TEACHER AS A FACTOR IN DISCIPLINE. There are two principal aspects of the teacher as a factor in discipline which must be considered here. The first aspect is *the teacher's scholastic and professional qualifications.* The second aspect consists of the teacher's *personal characteristics.* The teacher's scholastic and professional qualifications include his command of the subject matter taught, his cultural background, and his professional training. The teacher's personal qualifications include his physical, mental, and moral characteristics. The teacher's physical characteristics must include good health, a pleasing voice and manner of expression, dignity, and poise. The teacher's mental characteristics must include insight into the abilities, needs, and interests of pupils, tact, a zeal for accuracy, orderliness, system, industry, and a sympathetic understanding of human nature. The teacher's moral characteristics must include integrity, justice, and strength of will. These qualifications are essential, for the teacher sets the standard of discipline in the school. When a teacher possesses these qualities, he will have few disciplinary problems, for with these qualities, he is capable of inspiring, managing, controlling, and guiding the pupils under his direction.

The teacher in order to maintain suitable disciplinary conditions must possess qualities of personality and of character together with an adequate knowledge of subject matter which will command the respect and confidence of his pupils. However, it is not amiss here to point out some facts about the personality of the teacher. Personality as used here designates the character and the influence of the teacher. The teacher's personality should impart conviction to, should inspire, should vitalize his teaching. It should stimulate attention, arouse enthusiasm, encourage and produce effort. It should enable the teacher to exercise an influence over his class. However, the difficulty is that too much emphasis, faith, and reliance are likely to be placed upon the personality of the teacher. Too much reliance on the teacher's personality as an instrument of influence will not develop the character of the pupil. The teacher must use his personality as a means of setting up ideals of good conduct. This accomplished, his next task is to guide the pupils in such a way that they will share these ideals and work for the realization of them. This means that the intellect must know these ideals, that the will must be motivated by them, and that the pupils must achieve satisfaction in living up to them.

The teacher must realize that an important source of satisfactory disciplinary conditions is his authority and the use which he makes of it, for authority has a very definite place in good discipline. The very nature of the child makes authority necessary. Authority wisely used inspires confidence in the child and cultivates a spirit of respect which should be evident in every classroom. Intelligent respect for authority is necessarily a part of the equipment for living in an organized society. The chief use of authority is as the basis for obedience in the school. Obedience does not destroy the freedom and independence of the child, but rather it lays the only true foundation for independence. In fact, only one who has learned to obey can know how to be a good citizen, a leader of others, and a man of upright character. The best type of obedience is a reasoning, cooperative acceptance.

b) THE PUPIL AS A FACTOR IN DISCIPLINE. The second factor in discipline is the pupil, whose development, behavior, and attitudes are to be guided and directed. The maladjustments, the behavior problems, the poor attitudes of the child are effects for which causes exist. The pupil who is habitually disorderly in the classroom and who defies standard measures of correction is one in whom unsolved personal problems exist. It is necessary, therefore, that the teacher understand child nature in order to discover these causes and motives for nonconformity. Many teachers are still far from understanding the various means which pupils employ in their efforts to adjust themselves to their problems.[1] The usual outwardly evident reactions, and the only reactions, so far as some teachers are aware, are the troublesome ones, involving either an actively negativistic attitude toward the teacher and the work of the school or open rebellion against authority. Disturbing as these are, however, they do not constitute the only reactions, or even the most important. The teacher must understand and appreciate not only what is taking place in the classroom but also in the mind of the child. He must realize that the child does not become a disciplinary problem all at once, that the child does not suddenly break away from reasonable behavior, that changes in conduct occur gradually. He must be prompt to recognize symptoms, successful in diagnosing and inferring causes. The causes of disciplinary problems are *subjective* and *objective*.

The *subjective* causes of disciplinary problems include:

1. Obstinacy, stubbornness, perversity;
2. Ill health, including nervous irritability;
3. Immaturity and irresponsibility;
4. Unwholesome fears;

[1] It is recognized that there are situations in which the teacher cannot ascertain or is not in a position to determine the causes of the maladjustment, the attitude, or the misconduct which constitutes a particular disciplinary problem. In this event it will be necessary for the teacher to have recourse to whatever mental hygiene services are available, that is, the school psychologist, the counselor, the child-guidance clinic.

5. Lack of sufficient mental ability to keep up with the class;
6. Desire for the approval of their fellows;
7. Poor habits of study and work;
8. Lack of respect.

The *objective* causes of disciplinary problems include:

1. Difficulty of material;
2. Lack of interest which results in boredom;
3. Home environment;
4. Lack of stimulating activity;
5. Inadequate teaching;
6. Lack of poise or self-control on the part of the teacher.

c) METHODS AS A DISCIPLINARY FACTOR.[2] The third factor in constructive discipline consists of the procedures used to secure and maintain orderly conditions and to train in self-discipline. There are two types of procedure, namely, the positive methods of discipline and the corrective methods of discipline. In any scheme of constructive discipline the corrective methods will play a subordinate part.

The positive methods of discipline endeavor to establish and to maintain situations in which proper conduct and behavior become natural and in which disorder and misbehavior will not occur. The positive methods of discipline are frequently termed indirect methods of control. They are based upon the theory that the best way of eliminating the undesirable is to nurture the desirable. The positive methods for securing and maintaining good order in the classroom and in the school which will aid in achieving self-discipline on the part of the pupils include:

1. Maintaining proper physical conditions in the classroom;
2. The removal of distracting factors in order that learning may take place in an economical fashion;
3. Specific explanation of what is to be accomplished and a clear exposition of the purposes of the rules which must be obeyed;
4. Promptness in starting and vigor in carrying on purposeful activities within the classroom;

[2] It is not possible to provide a series of procedures or methods which could be applied to specific types of misconduct. The management of children is a complex problem which cannot be expressed in terms of simple techniques. There are no procedures which apply uniformly in all situations. Each situation involves a variety of personal and environmental factors which must taken into consideration. See N. E. Cutts and N. Moseley, *Teaching the Disorderly Pupil in Elementary and Secondary School* (New York: Longmans, Green & Co., 1957.

5. Provision of incentives for self-improvement;

6. Stimulation and fostering of pride in being considered trustworthy and responsible;

7. Expecting mature conduct and developing this attitude in the students;

8. Provision of worthy example which pupils may imitate and by which they may be influenced;

9. Providing proper emotional tone for classwork;

10. Affording opportunities for initiative and for assuming responsibility.

The corrective methods of discipline are used chiefly in cases which do not conform to the requirements which are set up as reasonable for all pupils in the class and in the school. Ordinarily to use corrective methods means to deal with offenders when the failure of positive methods makes this action necessary. No matter how skillful the teacher may be, there will be some cases of misconduct which will require the use of corrective methods. Among the types of corrective methods of discipline, authorities on this subject include the following:

1. The use of group judgment, that is, social disapproval;

2. Reproof, first in private and then, if necessary, in the presence of the group;

3. Temporary isolation under supervision;

4. Detention for a specific purpose which is clearly stated and achieved during detention;

5. Withdrawal of specified privileges for a stated period of time but not to interfere with learning;

6. Utilization of reports to and conferences with parents, since unsatisfactory home relationships are frequently basic in many disciplinary problems;

7. Individual work with the pupil;

8. Referral of pupil to the principal or other school officer after the teacher has exhausted all his possibilities;

9. Expulsion in extreme cases — this method should be used discriminatively and rarely.

Corrective methods of discipline should be based upon the principle that the means of correction employed should:

1. Be associated in the pupil's mind with the undesirable act.
2. Be uniform and consistent.
3. Act as a deterrent to the repetition of that act by the individual and

also indirectly prevent the occurrence of the misconduct on the part of other pupils.

4. Be chosen with regard to the circumstances connected with the act and the qualities of the pupil concerned.

5. Be proportionate to the offense and should be just.

6. Be selected according to the motive for and not the act of misconduct.

7. Avoid imposition of school tasks for punitive reasons.

8. Be economical of the teacher's time and effort.

9. Never cause the child to think that having offended once he has offended for all time and hence that there is no use of his trying again.

10. Never be administered in anger or involve sarcasm, personal affront, or indignity.

11. Never be based upon vengeance or vindictiveness, but should have for their purposes the reformation of the individual, the stimulation to better conduct by the adoption of proper motives, and the development of sound attitudes toward wrongdoing.

The Functions of Constructive Discipline. In keeping with modern mental hygiene, the fundamental function of all constructive discipline should be the prevention of every type of misconduct and of all behavior problems. To achieve such a purpose, constructive discipline must consist of the direction of the child's activities throughout the entire school. This means that in order to achieve its aim, constructive discipline must be a function of the whole teaching process and of every school subject. As such, it must afford training in healthful, normal, mental, moral, social, and emotional development. The best preventive measure is excellent teaching which leads to superior classroom organization and control. Effective teaching and good discipline are highly correlated; good teaching procedures are effective in developing good discipline. Good teaching procedures include the use of attractive teaching aids, enthusiastic presentation of materials, and the use of mechanical routines for certain classroom procedures. The best indication of excellent teaching is clearness of instruction. In order to accomplish this, the teacher must have an excellent command of his subject matter. Such a teacher is able to devote his attention to his real task which is not teaching subject matter, but teaching pupils by means of subject matter. However, the teacher not only must know his subject but also must believe profoundly in its significance for the enrichment of life. He must have confidence in the good intentions of the pupils, but at the same time he must be able to recognize any attempt to impose upon him. Pupils always respect a teacher who knows what to do under any circumstance which may arise. The teacher who would prevent disciplinary problems must be thoroughly prepared for every class. His attitude toward his pupils must be cheerful and courteous, but always businesslike.

The best method for achieving excellent teaching is the stimulation and motivation of interest. The teacher, because of his superior knowledge and in virtue of his understanding of child nature, must be able to secure and to maintain the interest of his pupils. He must inspire an urge to know and to use in the most effective manner the knowledge thus acquired. Frequently, lack of interest is due to a presentation of material which is lacking in vividness. It may be due to a slavish adherence to the use of one textbook, to assignments which are not problematic, to poor equipment, to lack of correlation with other work. Interest does not mean mere entertainment, but implies sustained voluntary attention. Interest in schoolwork is an especially valuable preventive means because it leaves no opportunities for misdirected energy and cleverness to exhibit themselves. Therefore, it is essential to make all studies interesting in order that constructive discipline inhere in all schoolwork.

The role of the teacher in constructive discipline is to function as guide and director of learning experiences which will provide opportunities for the development of self-discipline. Sheviakov and Redl have listed the following as the principles which guide discipline:

1. Teachers use positive ways of guidance which communicate this belief in the value of each personality, rather than negative ways which undermine self-confidence and self-esteem.
2. Teachers consider each incident when discipline or order has broken down in relation to the particular persons involved, their needs and their life histories.
3. Schools provide a climate in which mutual respect and trust are possible.
4. Teachers build understanding and communication between individuals and groups.
5. Teachers help children to understand the reasons for standards and rules, and to foresee the consequences of their own behavior.
6. Schools provide for children's growth in self-government, through which they share increasingly in planning their own activities.
7. Teachers study children's behavior scientifically, searching for causes and formulating hunches and hypotheses about how changes may be made.

8. Teachers help young people to understand the reasons for their own and others' behavior and to develop more effective ways of meeting common conflicts.[3]

The Educational Significance of Constructive Discipline. Disciplinary problems have always played an important part in the work of the teacher. In fact, lack of ability to maintain discipline is the most frequent cause of teacher failure. Therefore, a knowledge of disciplinary procedures is an essential part of the teacher's preparation. The principles which have been set forth in this chapter are the general basic principles of discipline. They serve only as guiding factors. They mark out the broad lines within which the proper procedures in any given case must fall. If the teacher grasps clearly and applies steadfastly these principles, some errors which might have disastrous consequences will be avoided. As the teacher, so is the school. No one is really a teacher of history, or of mathematics, or of any subject. All are teachers of pupils, all are builders of character. As such, the most important function of the teacher is to impart the moral guidance and spiritual training to which the child is entitled because of his nature. Therefore, it is the teacher's task to direct his pupils in such a way that they are aware of the fundamental purpose for which they were created, of the fact that they alone are responsible for the uses to which they put the endowments which they possess. The aim of constructive discipline is to help the child become true in thought and in word, pure in desire, faithful in act, upright in deed. The aim of constructive discipline must be self-discipline which is the foundation for successful living. The most important factors in constructive discipline are the content of courses and the quality of instruction. These factors which determine so thoroughly the interests, attitudes, ideals, and habits of the pupils, not only with reference to what takes place in the classroom but also toward life itself, must train the individual to achieve the power of self-discipline.

EXERCISES

1. Outline this chapter.
2. List and define the terms which you have learned from your study of this chapter.

---

[3] George V. Sheviakov and Fritz Redl, *Discipline for Today's Children and Youth,* revised by S. K. Richardson (Washington, D. C.: Department of Supervision and Curriculum Development, National Educational Association, 1956), pp. 9–16. Copyright 1944, 1956 by the Association for Supervision and Curriculum Development. Used by permission of the copyright owner.

3. Explain the nature of discipline.
4. List and discuss the basic principles of constructive discipline.
5. Distinguish between:
   a) Chastisement and discipline;
   b) Subjective and objective causes of discipline;
   c) Positive and correctional methods of discipline;
   d) The teacher's personal and scholastic qualifications;
   e) Obedience and authority.
6. Discuss:
   a) The teacher as a factor in discipline;
   b) The pupil as a factor in discipline;
   c) Method as a factor in discipline.
7. List and discuss the functions of constructive discipline.
8. Discuss the following statements:
   a) "The attainment of better disciplinary procedures will have the twofold effect of improving the mental health of the pupils and making the work of the teacher more enjoyable."
   b) "Discipline is as vital to effective living today as it has ever been."
   c) "Promoting good discipline becomes a matter of promoting desirable teaching-learning situations."
   d) "There is no specific formula for good discipline."
   e) "Avoid the use of children's fears as a basis for disciplinary measures."
   f) "Never use ridicule or sarcasm for disciplinary purposes."
9. *a*) Why is an understanding of the child's nature a factor of primary importance in good discipline?
   b) Why does the nature of the child make authority necessary?
   c) What is the relationship between authority and obedience?
10. What is the educational significance of constructive discipline?

SELECTED REFERENCES FOR STUDY AND READING

Bernard, H. W., *Mental Hygiene for Classroom Teachers,* 2 ed. (New York: McGraw-Hill Book Co., Inc., 1961), Chap. 10.

Bonney, M. E., *Mental Health in Education* (Boston: Allyn and Bacon, Inc., 1960), Chap. 4.

Brown, E. J., *Managing the Classroom,* 2 ed. (New York: The Ronald Press Co., 1961).

Burton, W. H., *The Guidance of Learning Activities,* 3 ed. (New York: Appleton-Century-Crofts, Inc., 1962), pp. 536–563.

Crow, L. D., and Crow, A., eds., *Mental Hygiene for Teachers: A Book of Readings* (New York: The Macmillan Co., 1963), Chap. 9.

Cutts, N. E., and Moseley, N., *Teaching Disorderly Pupils in Elementary and Secondary School* (New York: Longmans, Green and Co., 1957).

Hymes, J. L., *Behavior and Misbehavior* (Englewood Cliffs, N. J.: Prentice-Hall, Inc., 1955).

Jenkins, G. G., *Helping Children Reach Their Potential* (Chicago: Scott, Foresman and Co., 1961).

Phillips, E. L., Wiener, D. N., and Haring, N. G., *Discipline, Achievement and Mental Health* (Englewood Cliffs, N. J.: Prentice-Hall, Inc., 1960).

Prescott, D. J., *The Child in the Educative Process* (New York: McGraw-Hill Book Co., Inc., 1957).

Rivlin, H. N., *Teaching Adolescents in Secondary Schools,* 2 ed. (New York: Appleton-Century-Crofts, Inc., 1961), pp. 374–395.

Sheviakov, G. V., and Redl, F., *Discipline for Today's Children and Youth,* revised by S. K. Richardson (Washington, D. C.: Department of Supervision and Curriculum Development, National Educational Association, 1956).

Wittenberg, R. M., *Adolescence and Discipline: A Mental Hygiene Primer* (New York: Association Press, 1960).

Woodruff, A. D., "Discipline," in *Encyclopedia of Educational Research,* C. W. Harris, ed., 3 ed. (New York: The Macmillan Co., 1960), pp. 381–385.

chapter 19

Character Formation

The Definition of Character. In spite of the fact that there appears to be a general understanding of the meaning of character, it is not easily and readily definable in a formal way. Consequently, the term has acquired a variety of meanings; and, since there is no fundamental agreement concerning its meaning, the term lacks precision and its use as a technical term has not been standardized. Scores of definitions are available, but not one of these has yet proved to be acceptable to educators generally. However, among the many available definitions there seems to be a tendency for three factors to appear consistently. Practically all definitions recognize character as an aspect or quality of *personality.* Many definitions recognize that it connotes living according to *principles.* All definitions seem to recognize that character is expressed in *conduct.*

The term *character* has been derived from a Greek word which originally meant the impressions stamped upon a coin or the marks engraved upon a seal. The stamped impressions denoted the value and the worth of the coin, while the engraved marks constituted the seal a recognizable and understood sign. When applied to mankind the term *character* has a similar connotation; that is, it signifies differentiating marks or traits by which the quality of human conduct can be judged. It implies *the adherence to moral principles*[1] *which a person manifests consistently in his purposeful conduct. This conduct in turn constitutes a recognizable and understood sign of his moral worth as a human being.* Character may

[1] A complete understanding of character implies a knowledge of ethics as well as of psychology. "The early Christian theologians invested the term *character* with ethical, directional, and volitional meanings which give it its modern place among the larger concepts of human thought, will and action," V. E. Jones, "Character Education," *Encyclopedia of Educational Research,* C. W. Harris, ed., 3 ed. (New York: The Macmillan Co., 1960), p. 184.

be described as the intelligent direction and purposeful control of human conduct under the influence of moral principles which man chooses voluntarily and to which he adheres. In this significance Hull has defined character as "life dominated by principles as distinguished from life dominated by mere impulse from within and mere circumstances from without."[2] Another definition has stated that: "Character is personality evaluated; it is an ethical and social concept. Character is the aggregate of traits, mental and moral; comprising the personality as evaluated by a particular set of standards."[3]

In its educational significance, *character* denotes the intelligent direction and purposeful control of conduct through the recognition and acquisition of definite unchanging moral principles which are converted into standards of action and applied consistently in the complex and varied activities of life. In its educational significance, *character formation* denotes effort to improve the moral quality of human conduct and involves the training and guidance of the individual so that he will strive to achieve worthy ideals, to develop self-control through a disciplined will, to acquire suitable habits and proper attitudes, to attain emotional stability, and through the coordination of these to achieve moral integrity.

Factors in Character.[4] In defining character the terms *moral principles, human personality,* and *human conduct* have been used. Each of these terms in turn requires definition and explanation, since there is neither a general understanding of their meaning nor a common agreement in their use among psychologists and educators.

MORAL PRINCIPLES. *Morality* is the conformity of man's conduct, that is, his free volitional acts, to the rational nature of man considered in itself and in all its relations. These relations include man himself, his fellow men, the world about him, and his Creator. The true standard and sanction of morality is the Divine Will of God as expressed in the eternal and unchangeable natural moral law[5] and in supernatural revela-

[2] E. R. Hull, S.J., *The Formation of Character* (St. Louis: B. Herder Book Co., 1926), p. 18.

[3] Sister Annette Walters and Sister Kevin O'Hara, *Persons and Personality* (New York: Appleton-Century-Crofts, Inc., 1953), p. 6.

[4] It must be recognized that there are additional factors supernatural in nature, especially *Divine Grace,* which influence the development of character. However, that aspect has not been considered here, because it belongs more properly to the field of theology than to educational psychology.

[5] The moral law may be defined as those rules of action, mandatory in form, which reason itself reveals as established and promulgated by the Author of nature and imposed upon all men. "The natural law consists in practical universal judg-

tion. Insofar as human conduct conforms to that standard, it is morally right or good; insofar as human conduct deviates from that standard, it is morally wrong or evil.

Principles are judgments, accepted by the person, which become standards for directing his actions and behavior. They are rules or laws governing proper relationships in a given field. The application of these principles, consistently and habitually in life situations, gives constancy to human conduct.

Moral principles, then, are ethical standards, that is, laws and rules based upon the moral law and supernatural revelation, which become the sources for motivating and directing man's conduct. The acquisition and consistent application of moral principles to life situations are outcomes of the learning process.

HUMAN PERSONALITY. Character is considered to be the expression of personality. Consequently, it is essential to have a proper understanding of personality. Man in virtue of his nature is a person. He is a composite of a *body* which is sentient and material and of a *soul* which is spiritual and rational. Body and soul are united into one complete substance to form one self which is the subject of all the states and actions of complete life. This self is the person, that is, the whole being of man cooperating in the performance of every act. Long ago the Scholastics defined person as a "rational suppositum." By suppositum is meant "a singular complete substance subsisting in itself as something whole and entire." By adding the note of rationality it was indicated that the person is a complete individual substance endowed with reason and consequently responsible for its own acts. Hence, the person is a living, conscious, feeling, thinking, acting, willing substance distinct from everything and everyone else and responsible for its own actions. Physically the person is subject to all the laws of nature which govern life processes in general.

---

ments which man himself elicits. These express necessary and obligatory rules of human conduct which have been established by the Author of human nature as essential to the Divine purposes in the universe and have been promulgated by God solely through human reason," T. J. Higgins, S.J., *Man as Man* (Milwaukee: The Bruce Publishing Co., 1948), p. 88; "Man's freedom is not a blind freedom. He is given the power of reason by means of which he can discern the over-all order of things to which he *should* conform himself. The over-all order of things is the law of the universe, the law by which God regulates all creation. Man's law is to put himself through his free actions in conformity with what reason tells him is his true end. This is what is meant by the natural or moral law: man's rational and free participation in the over-all order established by God," D. J. Sullivan, *An Introduction to Philosophy*, rev. ed. (Milwaukee: The Bruce Publishing Co., 1964), p. 176.

Spiritually the person is made in the image and likeness of the Creator, is endowed with intellect, with free will, and is destined for eternal life.

Personality means the capacity for being a person. While person refers to the substance of man, personality has reference to the properties of man, his acts, habits, powers. It is an all-inclusive term for the total makeup of an individual, for all that a human being is, has, and can do, for that which constitutes one a person. Hence, *human personality* as used here means manifesting one's self, one's whole being through thought, word, and deed, in fact in every human activity in accordance with one's powers and capacities. Personality denotes all the characteristic qualities of man which form his total constitution as a human being. Differences in the development of these powers, capacities, and capabilities constitute the individual differences which exist among men and which distinguish each person from other human beings. However, human nature, though it varies in the concrete, is common to all men and is immutable in its essentials.

> Personality consists of the sum total of all the natural and acquired traits that an individual possesses. It includes, therefore, the body with its charm or lack of it; the mental powers of intelligence, imagination, and will; the emotional make-up; the impulses, tendencies, aspirations, habits, and attitudes which an individual has either inherited or formed through experience. Briefly, the personality embodies all the factors which a man externalizes in his behavior and thus makes manifest to others.[6]

Personality, then, involves the expression and manifestation of all the powers, capacities, and capabilities of the person through thought, word, deed, and feeling. Because character formation is the process of developing, directing, and guiding the complete person, the basic consideration in character formation must be a clear and adequate understanding of personality. The sacredness and dignity of human personality must be stressed, for upon the nature of personality hinge the rights, duties, and obligations of man. By virtue of his nature as a person, man belongs to four realms of being, namely, "the physical, the mental, the social, and the spiritual."[7] Modern education has been much concerned with

---

[6] R. C. McCarthy, S.J., *Safeguarding Mental Health* (Milwaukee: The Bruce Publishing Co., 1937), p. 262; see also M. B. Arnold and J. A. Gasson, S.J., *The Human Person* (New York: The Ronald Press Co., 1954), pp. 165–220; J. E. Royce, S.J., *Personality and Mental Health* (Milwaukee: The Bruce Publishing Co., 1955), pp. 40–49.

[7] R. Allers, *The Psychology of Character* (New York: Sheed & Ward, 1934), pp. 23–24.

the training of man for his place in the first three realms. Yet it has neglected and ignored completely the fourth and most important. It has failed to make any provision for the spiritual training of man. From this neglect and failure has arisen the major difficulty which at the present time is preventing adequate realization and achievement of the character aim. Modern education is based upon a distorted view of the nature and destiny of man, of the meaning and purpose of life, of the relation of man to God and to the Universe.

Character training is a process of developing, guiding, and forming the complete man. This includes the full range of man's nature, his physical, emotional, and social powers; his mental, moral, and volitional capacities. Man is so created and endowed that his character is deformed when his physical and social capabilities are developed to the neglect of his moral and spiritual powers. Character formation must provide for the direction of the powers, capacities, and capabilities of man to prepare him to lead an honorable, upright, and useful life in order that he may achieve the end for which he was created. Above all, character formation must develop in man an ever increasing capacity for moral excellence.

HUMAN CONDUCT. Character is manifested through conduct. It is gauged by deeds. *Human conduct* consists of those actions which man performs knowingly, willingly, and deliberately, and which he directs toward a known end with attention to the right and wrong of the end. Man's character is expressed in his conduct and is revealed by his actions and the motives and purposes for their performance. One's character is judged by his conduct, for, while principles are not in evidence, conduct is observable. From his conduct is inferred the motive for its performance. "Actions bespeak the man," and overt action is considered evidence of inward disposition. Conduct is the outcome of volition. The volitional activities of man are not haphazard and accidental results of impulse, but are directed and controlled by his purposes. Worthy human conduct involves correct reasoning, proper judgment, accurate evaluation of motives, and right decision. The character of a person is demonstrated most clearly in his deliberate acts of choice. Through the decisions he makes he shows of what he is capable. The simplest test of character is consistency of behavior.

The Nature of Character. Character is not something innate and inalienable. It is not the culmination of inborn traits. Character is not bestowed; it is not inherited; it does not just happen. Heredity plays a part in character formation, for each person must build his own character upon the foundation of his native endowment. Environment, however, plays a more important role in character formation than does heredity, because it provides the opportunity for the growth and development of hereditary capacities. Environment includes all the factors, surrounding conditions, influences, and forces which modify and influence the growth and development of hereditary capacities. Environment supplies the opportunities for the growth and development of native capacities. The chief environmental influences are provided by the home, the Church, the school, and the community. Peer culture, mass media of communication, and entertainment are also important conditioning environmental forces.

The child is not merely a passive recipient of the influences of environment. Rather is he an active participant in the effects of these forces, since by his very nature he possesses intellect and will which enable him to control many environmental factors. Heredity bestows capacity, environment presents opportunity, but it is the will which realizes inherited capacity and utilizes environmental opportunity. By his will man directs and restrains emotion, thought, and action. By his will he concentrates attention on his tasks and pursues his purposes. The will is the controlling factor in the direction of conduct. It is the guiding force of man's life. It is the integrating factor in his character. Barrett has described the part played by the will in character formation as follows:

> With all respect to the influence of heredity and environment, it is the exercise of the power of choice, in the last analysis, which plays the predominant part in the formation of character. *Every man is the architect of his own character*. If he yields to evil inclinations, and contracts bad habits, he becomes depraved and vicious. If, on the other hand, he controls his inordinate appetites and desires and learns to form good habits, he fashions for himself an upright, strong, and virtuous character. The will determines the manner and degree in which currents of thought and waves of emotion are initiated and controlled. For this reason the act of choice is the most important element in the cultivation of character. Firm, calm, certain, and determined choices reveal the strong man. Feeble, uncertain, hesitating, and painful choices stamp the weakling. Deliberate choices against evil impulses develop self-control; and it is by the constant exercise of self-control that character is eventually formed.[8]

[8] J. F. Barrett, *Elements of Psychology* (Milwaukee: The Bruce Publishing Co., 1931), p. 220.

Likewise Brennan has described character as *"The sum total of moral habits grouped around the axis of the will."*[9]

Character is man's own achievement. It is the result of one's own endeavors. It is the fruit of personal effort. Man forms his character as he gathers and organizes knowledge, as he learns to control his attention, as he establishes his habits, as he cultivates his memory, as he develops his imagery, as he directs his interests and desires, as he controls his emotions, as he forms his judgments, as he reasons out his decisions. Character is fashioned by every thought and by every volitional act. Character formation is the important business of life. It is the foundation upon which rests not only man's individual worth but also the general social welfare and strength of civilization. It is a significant aim of all education. The building of a business, the establishment of a professional reputation are the tasks of a lifetime, but a well-built, effective, and enduring character is the foundation upon which these must rest.

Character is not a mosaic or aggregate of specific traits.[10] Any number of individual traits does not make a character. Character is a whole, a unity. Character is the unity, the harmony, the integration of man's native endowment and of his acquired reactions functioning toward a morally good end under the guidance of intellect and will which direct and control his actions. Character is embedded in the total structure of personality. Furthermore, character is not fixed and unchangeable but transmutable. As Allers has pointed out, character is both in principle and in fact susceptible of change at all periods in life. Character is constantly undergoing changes for better or for worse, being improved or degraded. Every action, every thought, every feeling contributes to character for good or for evil. Finally, character is not to be considered as a distant or future culmination of one's education but as something to be achieved and realized at every step in the educational process.

The Need for Character Training. If the school is to serve the best interest of mankind, training for character must be a primary and essential function of all education. Character training is not a new branch, is not a new type of education. Every theory of education ever advanced, every system of education ever devised has included in its aims *training for right conduct*. The difficulty is that there has been no agree-

---

[9] R. E. Brennan, *op. cit.*, p. 292.

[10] R. Allers, *op. cit.*, p. 10.

ment among educators as to what constitutes right conduct. The modern *character-education movement* consists chiefly of an open and explicit acknowledgement of a definite and increasing responsibility on the part of the school for character as a primary objective and as a consciously sought outcome throughout the entire educational process.

There exists a general conviction that there has never been a greater need for character training than during modern times. The chaotic conditions which have characterized the critical periods, through which mankind has been and still is passing, have given additional consideration and new impetus to the character-education movement. Crises in political and economic spheres particularly have caused the development of a critical attitude concerning the results of education.

Among the conditions which educators recognize as indicative of an urgent need for the proper kind of character training are: a serious increase in juvenile delinquency and crime, the waning influence of the home, the breakdown of mental discipline in education, the demoralizing influence of licentious amusements and objectionable literature, including vicious "comics." Certain kinds of television entertainment and motion pictures, also, have an unwholesome influence.

The Bases of Character Formation. The formation of character is essentially an extended process of guided growth and directed development of all man's powers, capacities, and capabilities particularly during the formative years of childhood and youth, especially during the school years. All the factors that enter into character are capable of being formed by training, guidance, and direction, while the person is still *plastic* enough to be molded, guided, and directed. There exist no special courses, no scientific devices by which character can be developed analogous to those by which a child may be instructed in mathematics or language or history. The task in character formation is to strengthen the powers, capacities, and capabilities of the child by promoting all the factors which lead to worthy character and to prevent all those unhealthy and pernicious reactions which may become fixed in character. Success in the task of forming character requires a knowledge of the elements and factors which form the bases of character. These bases are:

1. The inculcation of ideals;
2. The establishment of volitional control;
3. The formation of proper habits;
4. The establishing of emotional stability;

5. The coordination of all these elements leading to the achievement of *moral integrity*.

The Inculcation of Ideals. Training for character must begin with the inculcation of true and worthy ideals of conduct, for without ideals there can be no character. In fact, man's character can be no better than the ideals which he cherishes. *An ideal is a type of excellence, which is desirable for personal imitation and toward which progress is possible.* An ideal is a worthy aspiration held as a guiding principle of action. Allers has described ideals as "those pictures fashioned by man of what he should be and how he should act."[11] Ideals are effective incentives for determining conduct, for ideals set a purpose for a composite of mental states involving feeling, thought, and volition. Ideals are embodied in a definite set of principles. Ideals are developed when ideas and attributes are made goals sufficiently worth striving for, that is, when they are set up as standards for determining conduct. They become effective motives for action when the idea is clearly recognized by the child, when he discovers values in it, and when he is able to act upon it with satisfactory results. Ideals are to be known, understood, and lived. To stimulate growth and development of character, knowledge of true and worthy ideals is necessary.

The mistake which the school so frequently makes is to believe that it suffices to present to students an ideal, or value concept, as an intellectual abstraction isolated from their lives, and forthwith they will strive to achieve that ideal. While right living involves a thorough knowledge of the right course of action, an ideal has no power in and by itself to modify conduct so long as one rests contented merely to contemplate it. Knowledge is not enough. The individual must be motivated. Ideals must become controlling incentives to action. In order that the school may train in moral thoughtfulness, it must provide an environment in which children may practice living up to the ideals which make for a better present and a still better future. Prudence must be used in setting ideals before the child in order that the values of the ideals may not conflict with his potentialities.[12] This means that it is not wise to place before the child ideal figures which represent conditions of life totally unlike those in which the child is placed. It is well also to avoid setting up artificial ideals. The aim is to set before the child

[11] *Ibid.*, p. 190.
[12] See *ibid.*, pp. 206–214.

the best and noblest ideals toward which progress may be made, although complete realization may not be possible. However, the school must take the child where it finds him and use as the starting point in character formation the most practical ideals which may be very basic. From this starting point it must guide the growth and development of the child to worth and worthiness, to the desire to strive for and to the intent to live up to the best and noblest ideals.

Precept and example are the means of actualizing ideals. Good rules do much, but good models do more. However, the child must understand the excellence of the model. Allers[13] has maintained that the primary sources of ideals are imitation and emulation. In this respect, it is well to remember that religion is rich in resources, supplying the highest motives, the most compelling ideals, the finest examples of morality.

Establishment of Volitional Control. The child in school cannot be considered with reference to his intellect alone. It is necessary to consider him as a personality composed of all of the mental and physical characteristics which he possesses, together with his hereditary influences and his reactions to environment. That the school is interested in the physical and mental factors and the part they play in molding character is evident from the fact that educators consult the physician, the dentist, the social worker, the psychologist, and the psychiatrist in order to seek out the strength and weakness of the child and to trace the causes thereof. Though this is excellent, it should be remembered that the fundamental method of approach in character formation should be through the child's mind. Above all, the school, in providing an environment wherein the child may be trained to react properly, should not overlook the fact that the child has a will which must also be trained. Will lies so deeply at the root of moral life that without it character would be nonexistent. Will is the source of all achievement. It keeps the intellect at work or lets it idle; it restrains passion and unseemly emotions or permits them to overwhelm the individual; it improves or neglects the opportunities which environment presents. The task of the school is to develop the will to meet situations where deliberation urges in opposite directions.

Whatever is voluntary is done on account of some real or apparent

[13] *Ibid.*, p. 191 ff.; also Sister M. Romana, "Means For Developing Christian Character," *Proceedings of the National Catholic Educational Association,* 51:515–523, 1954.

good to be derived from the action. The first motive of the will is the tendency to happiness. The desire for happiness is essential to man's nature. St. Thomas Aquinas stated that to desire happiness is "nothing else than to desire that the will be satisfied, and this every man desires." All do not agree on what constitutes the concrete realization of happiness. It is the task of the school to train pupils to distinguish happiness from mere pleasure, to realize that mere utility and temporal happiness are by no means the ultimate tests of what is good and honorable, to know that they are happiest who have best realized their capacities, who know the good through the intellect, cherish it in the will, and attain it in their actions. Since the will is the power to act deliberately, to be master of one's own actions, all teaching should be directed toward the training of the will, to act in conformity with correct principles. The will weaves into their fitting parts in life the factors of environment and heredity.

Since voluntary activity cannot be exercised without intellectual comprehension as a prerequisite, it is necessarily the task of the school to instill in the mind of the child a body of directive moral principles comprehensive enough to guide his voluntary activity and sufficiently strong to motivate him to choose freely, to think, to live, to act aright. Through repeated actions properly guided, self-control and self-discipline are to be developed, for any incompentency in this respect means individual and social disaster. The importance of the will lies in the influence which it exercises over the powers and capacities of man. It exercises both impelling and inhibiting influences. The will controls the manner and degree in which thoughts and emotions are initiated, guided, and controlled. Self-control or lack of self-control will determine what habits one acquires and whether these habits be virtues or vices. The will also presupposes proper evaluation of motives, and includes right decision, responsibility, and moral effort. It is the real integrating force in man's character, the guiding factor in the directing and fashioning of conduct.

The Formation of Proper Habits. The man of character is the man of reason, strength of will, and temperance in all things. To build character aright is to lay a foundation of safest hopes for future conduct. To accomplish this purpose it is necessary to establish firm, well-organized habits which will result in right ways of thinking and acting according to ideals and correct values in all of the conditions of life. Habits reveal the basic values which an individual has acquired. It is vital to realize that virtues as well as vices are habits. Not only knowledge and understanding but also effort of will is required to build correct habits and to live up to them in time of stress. It is the task of the school to make provisions for "a strong and decided initiative," to present situations which will stimulate the pupil to make use of every opportunity to respond in accordance with ideals — stimulate interest, which will lead to effort, which, in turn, will bring about exercise in the building of character. In habit formation, motive is of the highest importance. For good or for ill, character is being built all of the time. Education is for character, and habit formation is the basis of education. Habit is the tendency, conspicuous in the life of everyone, to acquire definite ways of reacting to situations. Habits are learned, that is, deliberately acquired. They are the results of choice. They are acquired through effort. To a considerable extent education consists in the forming of habits, a process which involves relationships making for mental economy and without which character would be impossible. Habit is a sort of second nature, stabilizing conduct, and is itself a mode of conduct. Habits growing out of true knowledge, fostered by religion, are in accord with morality. Habits signify stability of character. Persons of character possess a number of well-organized habits which help to fulfill the purpose of education — the establishing of *right ways of thinking, willing, and feeling.*

The Establishing of Emotional Stability. The great common sense of mankind has always held that the head must not be educated at the expense of the heart. Man is not all intellect, nor is he all will. One rarely has an experience entirely devoid of feeling; indeed, with most people conduct is more a matter of feeling than of intellect. Knowledge is bound up with the feelings regardless of whether or not the person is aware of these feelings. The very meaning which anything in the whole field of knowledge has for an individual is indicative of his feelings toward it. Since all thinking and doing are colored by feelings, the aim of education is to develop such feelings and emotions as will stimulate the intellect and motivate the will.

Emotional stability is a highly desirable accomplishment, necessary for a successful life. It implies emotional balance, resulting from a happy, reasonable control of the emotions. Emotions play an important role in life, for to some degree they enter into practically all action, behavior, and conduct. They furnish many of the motives, interests, and standards of life. They constitute one of the dynamics of life, giving to life not only its tone but also, in a large measure, its happiness or unhappiness. These facts, however, must not be overestimated, but neither can they be ignored. One of the most difficult problems in character training is the control of the emotions. It is impossible to deprive a normal person of his emotional experiences. It would be unfortunate if it were possible. Only when an emotion becomes sufficiently strong to disturb the functioning of the organism and to affect the powers of thought and decision does it become an evil force. The problem is for each individual to attain the proper balance between emotional expression and control. The task of the school in character formation is to direct educational motives and techniques so that they will make for such a healthy balance. Emotion which does not lead to right action is not only useless, it weakens character and becomes an excuse for neglect of effort.

Proper redirection of emotional activity keeps the emotions as helpful servants and prevents them from becoming masters. Such redirection is necessary, further, because uncontrolled emotions often lead to serious mental disturbances and behavior difficulties. The meaning and values of life depend largely upon the acquisition of proper emotional responses. This importance of the emotions in behavior has not been fully and properly appreciated.

One of the school's tasks in character formation is to endeavor by wise guidance to direct the emotions into constructive activities. The ideal should be to develop individuals whose emotions are under control, who derive their greatest pleasure from the higher and finer things of life. This ideal can be achieved by using the emotions as instruments of good and by preventing them from becoming instruments of evil. This ideal can be achieved by the avoidance of all those unhealthy and pernicious emotional reactions which may become fixed in character. The use of the will to control the emotions constitutes the essence of Christian spirit. The control of the emotions by the will is *self-control.* The way is direct and consists in setting clearly before the mind the desirability of acting from thought, from principles, from purposes rather than from impulses. This decision having been made, persistent and faithful adherence to it is required. Uncontrolled tendencies lead only to trouble, failure, and maladjustment.

Emotions also determine to a large extent the *attitude* of the individual toward his experiences, and attitudes in turn affect the emotions. One of the fundamental factors in character formation, which is often neglected, is the building of proper attitudes in children. Attitudes are essential to the development of character, for the fact that one possesses character is proved by the attitude[14] he exhibits when confronted by situations. Attitudes determine happiness and frequently health of mind as well as of body. In character building a great deal depends on the attitudes developed in school. One has character who has gained through his education the ability to know the right, who has been trained in self-control, and who has established attitudes that enable him to react habitually to the best and noblest ideals.

Attitudes cannot be assigned, nor can they be measured adequately. However, whether the teacher wills it or not, students in every class are learning much more than merely history or mathematics or other school subjects. They are developing attitudes in favor of or against the subject, the teacher, the methods of teaching, the school, and even life itself. Intelligence, knowledge, and skill are invaluable assets, the worth of which cannot be minimized, but in the last analysis it is the way in which these are used and the purposes which they are made to serve which determine the character of the individual. Not so much what one knows, but rather his attitude toward himself and others, is the mainspring of behavior. It would, therefore, be a great step forward if the school were to endeavor to handle the problems of behavior with the same energy that has characterized its efforts to understand and develop the intellectual and physical capacities of children.

Moral Integration. Knowledge of ideals, establishment of volitional control, formation of good habits, emotional stability must all be coordinated in order that moral integration will be achieved. It is impossible to guide the process of character formation without a basis of moral responsibility. Developing physical skill and mental efficiency through education without attaining moral integrity is necessarily fatal, both to the individual and to society. In fact, man's value to society is his moral

---

[14] The term *attitude* has been employed throughout the literature of both education and psychology with many connotations. The following definition seems to be in keeping with current usage and research. *Attitude is an enduring learned predisposition to behave in a consistent way toward a person or class of objects.* See H. B. English and A. C. English, *A Comprehensive Dictionary of Psychological and Psychoanalytical Terms* (New York: Longmans, Green and Co., 1958), p. 50. Courtesy of David McKay, Inc.

Perhaps an expansion of the above definition to include the sum total of an individual's feelings, inclinations, prejudices, preconceived notions, convictions which tend to create a disposition or readiness to act in a particular situation, may be more expressive.

value, because society can be no better than its constituent members. Morality involves something more than an external code for the orderly conduct of life. It provides the principles according to which life is to be lived. Furthermore, morality in any effective sense of the term cannot be divorced from religion. There is no satisfactory substitute for religious sanction in morality. Therefore, character cannot be formed adequately and effectively from any course of study which consists merely of poems, pledges, proverbs, stories, and the like. The purpose of character formation is the perfection of human nature. The basis of character formation must be systematic training in religion so that it may function dynamically in the life and activities of the individual. To this end all character education must be pervaded with instruction concerning the ground upon which rests the distinction between right and wrong, concerning the authority of moral law, concerning the sacredness of duty, concerning the inviolability of conscience, concerning respect for rights of others. Character formation must ultimately be bound up with religion.[15]

Character training must consist of something higher than a mere conditioning process. It must consist of training and guidance of the human being to make of him all that he can become. The supreme end of character training is spiritual. This means that character formation is a vital process, a furthering of life to develop the child in his entirety, to form a true man, to build a worthy and contented life. The only method of achieving these results is to adhere to the great principles which Christianity teaches, maintains, and sanctions. The cultivation of the intellect to know the good is the foundation. Since the physical has much to do with the moral, it is essential to develop a sound mind in a healthy body by building up ideals, habits, attitudes that result in good moral conduct. The most important factor, and the most neglected at present, is the real integrating force of man's character — his *will.*

Agencies of Character Training. The formation of character is necessarily an extended process. It begins at birth and continues throughout life. However, the formative years of childhood and youth are of prime importance in character training. It has been stated that "childhood shows the man as morning shows the day" or, more simply, "the child is father to the man." So also is the child's character the foundation of the adult's character. Throughout this chapter the tasks, the functions, and the importance of the school in the formation of character have

[15] See R. Allers, *op. cit.*, pp. 60, 61.

been stressed. Because the school influences a larger number of individuals than any other institution and because education is an indispensable mechanism of social control, society turns to the school for inspiration and guidance in character training. Likewise, since the child is intended for a supernatural destiny, the Church, from which alone he can learn the truths according to which he must live if he is to achieve that destiny, has provided a complete religious education for all her children. In addition, the Church has assumed the task of teaching also the secular branches in such a way that religion is the centralizing, unifying, and vitalizing force in the educational process. Still another important agency, in fact, the most basic and fundamental, in the formation of character, namely, *the home,* must be considered.

The home constitutes the greatest single factor in character formation largely because it is the first environment in which the child's character is shaped. The importance of the home is profound, its influence is extensive. As the "nursery for character," the home is the basic institutional unit in character formation; in fact, the home is so close to the child and has so large a control over him during the plastic years that it is really the principal character builder. Its potentialities for developing character are great. In the home the child receives the affection, security, and encouragement upon which will be laid the foundations of life. By surrounding the child with wholesome physical, mental, and moral environment, by precept and by example, the parents build the foundations of character. The child learns his first lessons, meets his first problems, has his first contacts with life, as a member of the family. The child's first impressions come from his parents, who are the child's models. The child will necessarily carry into life something of his parents' ideas about rights, duties, and obligations of man. Likewise the foundations of habits, of attitudes, and of emotional reactions are formed during the first years of life. Ways of acting, ideals, purposes, and self-control are in no small measure the products of early family experience. The importance of proper home environment and training from the outset of life cannot be stressed too strongly. It is the parent's task to prepare a suitable home environment which contains the essential incentives to virtue and self-control. Only the home can provide the intimate example, the consistent guidance, the constructive discipline essential for the molding of character.

The Aim of Character Training. Character formation must always be formative. It must mean something more than a tendency to establish purely relative codes of behavior in terms of personal well-being and social efficiency. It must mean the development of a greater capacity for the achievement of human excellence. True character training must involve the advancement of mankind in a knowledge of its fraility and dependence. It must involve the elevation of the mind to the infinite source of knowledge, the consecration of the will to the conquest of selfishness, and acquisition of virtuous habits, the achievement of emotional stability — all leading to moral integrity, all tending to assimilate man more closely with God. Allers has described the true aim of character training as "complete realization of all the potentialities inherent in the person."[16] Pius XI has expressed the aim of character training as follows:

> Since education consists essentially in preparing man for what he must do here below, in order to attain the sublime end for which he was created, it is clear that there can be no true education which is not wholly directed to man's last end. . . .
>
> It must never be forgotten that the subject of Christian education is man whole and entire, soul united to body in unity of nature, with all his faculties natural and supernatural, such as right reason and Revelation show him to be; man, therefore fallen from his original estate, but redeemed by Christ and restored to the supernatural condition of adopted son of God. . . .
>
> Every method of education founded, wholly or in part, on the denial or forgetfulness of original sin and of grace, and relying on the sole powers of human nature is unsound. . . .
>
> The proper and immediate end of Christian education is to cooperate with Divine grace in forming the true and perfect Christian, that is to form Christ Himself in those regenerated by Baptism. . . .
>
> Hence the true Christian, product of Christian education, is the supernatural man who thinks, judges, and acts consistently in accordance with right reason illumined by the supernatural light of the example and teaching of Christ; in other words, to use the current term, the true and finished man of character.[17]

Agreement on the method of attaining this aim is not to be expected while educators differ widely about the nature and destiny of man, about the meaning and purpose of life. The first step in the formation of character is recognition of the nature and destiny of the child. Education must consider the child in his entirety as a human being, composed of body and soul, endowed with intellect and free will, responsible for his conduct, destined for immortality. The child is a whole, and acts as

[16] R. Allers, *op. cit.*, p. 207.

[17] Pius XI, *Encyclical on the Christian Education of Youth* (New York: The America Press, 1936), pp. 19, 20, 32.

a unit, not by separate parts. Consequently, the educational process must consider the child according to his complete nature, not only the physical, the mental, and the social factors but the spiritual aspect as well. The whole child cannot be developed if his spiritual soul and immortal destiny are ignored.

The recognition of the spiritual element in man's nature is the very foundation of character formation. The fundamental element that underlies human existence consists in the dependence of man on God and his consequent obligations to God. This dependence continues every hour of life, and the obligations are expressed in every phase of life. This dependence, these obligations are expressed not only in formal worship and service but also as a way of living in accord with moral principles. Religion provides the ultimate principles for life and conduct. Consequently, all that enriches and enhances character is found in religion, and no true formation of character is possible without religion. It provides the only satisfactory sanction for morality. It is the only adequate source of motives, models, means, and methods of attaining character. To ignore religion is to lose the only solid motivating force in character training.

A general tendency in education has been to determine all objectives, curricula, and materials primarily in terms of the "good of society." This is at best a vague and tenuous method of avoiding a definite and absolute standard of conduct. Educators tend to realize this. To propose a line of conduct "worthy of society" it is necessary first to know and to appreciate the worth of the individual. The inherent worth and dignity of man, the intrinsic value of each individual in the sight of God must be taken into consideration. The rights, duties, and obligations of the individual must be recognized before he can be placed properly in society.

Furthermore, man is not merely a citizen of a particular state, a subject of a particular country. He is also a citizen and a subject "of the larger commonwealth of the kingdom of God." As such he is destined both for time and for eternity. Consequently, his education must prepare him for both. It must seek his best welfare in this life, his eternal happiness in the next. It must establish a scale of values in the things that are of concern to mankind, stressing in their proper order the spiritual, moral, mental, and, whenever possible, the physical perfection of man.

No successful method of training for character can ever be built upon the society in which man lives. It must be built upon the nature of man. Society does not make man what he is. Man makes society what it is. Man's actions ought to be governed by moral law and his value to society is his moral worth. Education is not merely a social investment, it is essentially a moral activity. Mere material readjustments of a social nature will be futile without moral bases. No mere addition of a course of instruction, no plan yet proposed will supply this need. In order that education may serve its proper function, morality must be the motive permeating and pervading the entire curriculum, the content of which must be organized and presented as moral in its essence and in its purpose.

There remains one more task, to determine the outcomes to be sought in character training and to interpret them in terms of objectives. This task must be accomplished satisfactorily in order that character education may not be merely something incidental to other phases of education, but will become the culminating goal of education to which all other phases will contribute. The best way of forming character strives, through resolute practice, to inculcate habits which constitute Christian motives. Love of God is, of course, the foundation. The groundwork for real human excellence consists of habits of prudence, justice, fortitude, temperance, and purity. The best way of forming character seeks also to instill those fine habits which distinguish a man of principles, namely:

1. Respect for lawful authority;
2. Dignity of bearing, modesty in manner, charity in speech;
3. Sense of honor, abhorrence of all smallness and meanness;
4. The angelic virtue of purity in thought and in action;
5. Wholesome interests;
6. Assumption of responsibilities and the conscientious fulfillment of obligations;
7. Realization of the purpose of existence and the end for which man was created;
8. Willingness to cooperate harmoniously with others;
9. Self-control and self-reliance.

The Methods and Means of Character Training. There is embodied in the various curricula of the school an abundance of material which by proper emphasis may be utilized in character training. Actually to be effective, character education must be integrated into every aspect of classroom activity. Science courses may be developed to demonstrate the reign of natural law and the consequences of violating this law. Through reading, art, composition, drama, and civics there may be received lasting impressions which aid in developing moral ideas. History provides bountiful examples of good and of evil conduct, and at the same time affords opportunities for training moral judgment. Likewise, since nobility of character tends to stimulate imitation, personalities that habitually exhibit nobility of character and devotion to ideals arouse admiration, strengthen and clarify the love of excellence, and motivate others to act in like manner. Literature, if it represents essentially accurate pictures of life, is necessarily a revelation of the real nature of right and wrong in conduct. Thus, the use of regular subject matter in the classroom represents an opportunity to teach character values.

Educators have recognized that no matter how valuable history, literature, and the other subjects of the curriculum may be as contributions to the knowledge of moral life, they do not form an adequate basis for the attainment of the ends of moral instruction. Since no one of these subjects is well adapted to serve as the basis of what is right and what is wrong, some educators have worked out plans whereby moral instruction may be given in a direct form. This has been designated as the *direct method.* They have realized that the child's incidental experiences cannot be relied upon to give him an insight into the basic principles underlying right conduct. They have maintained that the school cannot fulfill its responsibility by assuming that character has been attained as a by-product of the school program. They have become convinced that the pupil must have his mind focused specifically on the principles of right conduct by studying them as he would study history or science or literature. This *direct method* of teaching character has taken two forms.[18] In one form pupils study the virtues as so many chapters in character formation, and then indicate the applications of these virtues in their own lives. The other form of the direct method is to have children begin their study of character by discussing the conduct of individuals in specific situations, and then to build up the principles of right conduct which are involved. These principles become the ideals which serve as standards by which the pupils are to guide their own conduct when placed in a similar situation.

[18] V. E. Jones, *Character and Citizenship Education* (Washington, D. C.: National Educational Association, 1950); see also V. E. Jones, "Character Education," in C. W. Harris, ed., *Encyclopedia of Educational Research,* 3 ed. (New York: The Macmillan Co., 1960), pp. 184–191.

However, these direct methods of character training cannot be depended upon to give a real insight into moral life, and there has been a decline in the use of them. While such natural motivation is to be encouraged, nevertheless moral instruction without religion can have no higher basis than self-respect and social approval. The discussions of moral issues as they happen to be raised in school life are proper enough and to some extent effective, but they lack the basis of moral obligation. One who does right must first know what is right for him to do; he must recognize what is right and desire to do it. This means that the basis of character training must be systematic education in religion, which will result in thorough knowledge and constant practice of the essential means whereby true character is formed: namely, the sacraments and prayer. All moral teaching must be pervaded with instruction concerning the ground upon which the distinction between right and wrong rests, the authority of the moral law, the sacredness of duty, the inviolability of conscience. No plan or method, however well conceived or organized, will provide a substitute for religious sanction in morality. The only effective method and the most efficient means of achieving character is to base all activities of school upon the great principles which Christianity teaches, maintains, and sanctions.

The Character Aim in American Education. Although the formation of character as an aim of education has had a diverse and varied history in American education, three rather definite trends with regard to it can be distinguished. Throughout the Colonial and early National periods of American life, while religious principles and ideals were the motivating forces of education, its primary aim, naturally enough, was character formation. When, however, this religious influence had waned and Secularism became the guiding factor in education, character formation became an incidental aim. Now once again there exists a tendency to stress character as the product most to be sought in education. This modern trend has had a gradual development, dating back to the early years of the present century and has been given impetus both by the chaotic conditions of present-day life and by the realization that modern education lacks something essential in the preparation of youth to meet the exigencies of the times. A brief analysis of these three trends demonstrates that the character aim has been important in proportion to the recognition of the responsibility of education for providing moral and religious instruction and training.

The Colonists were men of sincere religious convictions. Consequently, when they established schools, it was natural that the primary purpose of these schools should be to instill a knowledge of the fundamentals of religion and to train the child according to principles of moral conduct. Thus the earliest American educational efforts were religious in nature and were directed toward the formation of moral character. It is significant that the earliest general school law in America, the Order of the General Court of Massachusetts, issued in 1647, not only provided for the establishment of schools but also emphasized the necessity of imparting religious and moral training as the reason for the existence of schools.

This religious influence was evident in all education throughout the Colonial period. Even where schools were established and financed by the community, they were religious both in content and in purpose. That the religious motive dominated education[19] is clearly demonstrated in the selection of subject matter and materials of instruction to fulfill the religious purpose of education, in the determination of qualifications of teachers who were licensed by the Church or other authority principally upon evidence of orthodoxy, in the content of textbooks, such as the *New England Primer,* which were largely scriptural and catechetical in content.[20] It is true, of course, that in the Colonies various forms of Protestantism were prescribed as the religion to be taught. This restriction constituted a serious barrier particularly to Catholics, a barrier which was removed only when the Federal Constitution established religious liberty, and the various states gradually rescinded the prejudicial laws.

The outstanding characteristic of early American education, then, was the recognition of the fact that character can only be formed by religious instruction and moral training. This idea of religion in education extended to the new units of the growing nation. In fact, the expression of this unification of religion, moral training, and education is best indicated in the Northwest Ordinance of 1787 in these words:

> Religion, morality, and knowledge being necessary to good government and the happiness of mankind, schools and the means of education shall forever be encouraged.

[19] E. W. Knight, *Education in the United States* (Boston: Ginn and Company, 1934), pp. 73–74; 124–125; also N. Edwards and H. C. Rickey, *The School in the American Social Order* (Boston: Houghton Mifflin Co., 1947), pp. 18–20.

[20] W. T. Kane, S.J., and J. J. O'Brien, *History of Education,* rev. ed. (Chicago: Loyola University Press, 1954), p. 374.

Likewise, Washington in his *Farewell Address* expressed the necessity of religion in democracy and stressed education as the means of securing religion and morality.

> Of all the dispositions and habits which lead to political prosperity, religion and morality are indispensable supports. In vain would that man claim the tribute of patriotism who should labor to subvert these great pillars of human happiness, these firmest props of the duties of men and citizens. . . . And let us with caution indulge the supposition that morality can be maintained without religion. Whatever may be conceded to the influence of refined education on minds of peculiar structure, reason and experience both forbid us to expect that national morality can prevail in the exclusion of religious principle.
>
> 'Tis substantially true that virtue or morality is a necessary spring of popular government. . . . Who that is a sincere friend to it can look with indifference upon attempts to shake the foundation of the fabric?
>
> Promote, then, as an object of primary importance, institutions for the general diffusion of knowledge.

Character formation continued to rank among the foremost aims in education during the first half century of America's existence as a nation. Education generally throughout this period was religious in content, while schools and instruction were denominational in control. Yet even during the formative years of the nation a gradual change to secular aims in education was becoming evident. Expansion, industrialization, urbanization, and consequent changing conditions of life finally brought about a definite change in the middle of the nineteenth century. As a result of agitation for nonsectarian schools the state assumed the task of providing free public schools for all children. These schools, separated from the control and influence of religion, became definitely and completely secular. Religion lost its place in the curriculum and was excluded from the formal training of the child. Character formation, no longer the chief goal of education, became something incidental. Educational machinery was not set up to produce it and it was not incorporated in the procedure. Since both the subject matter and influence of religion had been discarded, American education had deviated from its original purpose. The goals of education had become exclusively human and materialistic, developing specialized knowledge and techniques, but because the spiritual was entirely neglected it lacked compelling purpose or value to give meaning to life. Good citizenship, the goal which replaced character, was sought in an adverse and materialistic atmosphere. Guided by a materialistic educational philosophy, youth turned toward material goals.

Secularism in American education meant that the school completely ignored God, the supernatural, religion, and the value of religious training and ideals. This exclusion led to the substitution of naturalistic ends and human purposes. Education became preparation and training for this life alone, concentrated upon temporal affairs to the disregard of the hereafter. This divorce of religion from education resulted in a clash of essential values which is having so many unfortunate consequences at the present time. A distorted view of man, his nature and destiny, of the meaning and purpose of life has reacted upon men as members of society.

The elimination of religious instruction from the school has always been of concern to those who felt that the character education program could not proceed without the religious element. Consequently during the last decade of the nineteenth century such prominent educators as Harris and De Garmo called attention to the lack of moral education in the public school. They called attention to the fact that religious influence consisted chiefly of reading from the Bible at opening exercises and that was little more than a formality. They advocated the use of curriculum subjects, especially the social studies, to secure this training.

The early years of the twentieth century were marked by a gradual reawakening of interest in character formation as a significant goal of education. This interest was stimulated further by World War I and the subsequent economic depression. Formal recognition was given to this interest in 1918 when "ethical character" was included among the *Seven Cardinal Principles of Secondary Education.* This was followed within two decades by legal provisions in every state for incorporating the character aim and by specific programs in many states. In 1932 the *Yearbooks*[21] of the Department of Classroom Teachers and the Department of Superintendence both dealt with the problems of character education. Likewise, character formation was a topic of considerable significance in the proceedings of the various White House Conferences on Child Welfare. This interest was manifested further in a vast amount of psychological and sociological research, in experimentation with methods and practices for achieving character through various plans and a variety of subject matter. There has been for several decades a trend toward the recognition of character as a dominant aim of all education, and a realiza-

[21] *Character Education,* Tenth Yearbook, Department of Superintendence, Nation Educational Association, 1932; *The Classroom Teacher and Character Education,* Seventh Yearbook, Department of Classroom Teachers, National Educational Association, 1932.

tion that Secularism has alienated the traditions and fundamentals of education. This trend is laudable, but it has not yet progressed beyond the stage of acknowledgment that the school has a definite responsibility to seek character as a major objective of the entire educational process.

At the present time there seems to be a realization that the separation of all religious influence from education has created problems of an acute nature. This realization of the need for spiritual guidance and stability has been expressed in the programs for weekday religious instruction, for "released time" and similar plans for religious training. The general idea of released time is to permit the children of the public schools to attend religious instructions, with permission of their parents and under the supervision of the clergy of the church to which they belong. Released time is no new experiment. The movement began in 1912. Special legislation for released time during school hours for religious education has been enacted in some states while in others rulings of the attorney general authorize such release and in some others court decisions have permitted it. Still other states permit released time under opinions expressed by state boards of education and by state superintendents of instruction.

In addition to released time other plans for character training have been formulated and developed both by city and state school systems. Usually these plans have taken the form of bulletins, courses of study, and other types of published materials including outlines, courses, bibliographies of character, and guidance studies and references. There is, however, little uniformity in the contents of these programs, in the aims sought and in the methods used. In some instances the state plan has been made compulsory throughout all the schools of the state. In many other cases the cities have carried on their work in character practically free from state supervision. The effect of this absence of agreement on the manner and means of providing character has been to stimulate a wide variety of programs. This has resulted in many approaches to the problem and many suggestions for its solution.

In addition many organizations independent of the school have been founded especially for the development of good moral character. These include the C.Y.O., the Boy Scouts, the Girl Scouts, the 4-H Clubs, the Hi-Y, the Girl Reserves, and the Campfire Girls. The programs of these organizations include special modes of supplementary education. Their value consists in the ideals developed through participation in the activities and membership of the organization.

Within the school itself large numbers and varieties of scholastic and extracurricular activities have been devised to provide opportunities for training in character. Some of the more important and more widely recognized activities include: homeroom activities, assembly periods, debating, student government organizations, counseling techniques, and guidance services of various types, student clubs, athletics, and honor societies.

The very existence of all these provisions, programs, activities, and plans constitutes evidence of the fact that character formation requires something more than merely providing subject matter suited to individual needs, something above and beyond the techniques of teaching and guidance, something superior to wholesome classroom environment, something other than codes, slogans, pledges, and the many similar devices. The existence of such plans and programs manifests recognition of the need for inculcating the principles essential for living a truly Christian life. The existence of these plans and programs affords evidence that the function of the school and its program must be reinterpreted.

While education has become "character conscious," so far it has been seeking only the externals of character. The essentials have been overlooked. Modern education, though realizing its obligations and seeming convinced that there must be inaugurated a universal program for character training, really is uncertain concerning the very essentials of character, namely: the elements constituting it, the adequate means and methods of attaining it, the objectives to be sought.

The Measurement of Character.[22] There are many difficulties involved in the measurement of character. In fact, the task of measuring character precisely and accurately seems to be an almost impossible one because character is a complex combination of intellectual, volitional, and emotional factors. It seems evident that character as a unified whole cannot be measured or tested adequately. Yet, many various types of measuring instruments have been devised in an endeavor to evaluate character quantitatively and to predict behavior. However, it should be noted that a person's motives cannot be known by others with certainty, but only as a conjecture, which is a generalization based upon observation of external conduct and upon evidence of opinions and attitudes expressed.

The basic devices which have been utilized in the attempts to measure character are: (*a*) inventories or questionnaires in the forms of structural

---

[22] See O. K. Buros, *The Fifth Mental Measurements Yearbook* (Highland Park, N. J.: The Gryphon Press, 1959).

self-reports; (*b*) situational tests; (*c*) rating scales; (*d*) projective techniques.

The inventory type has been designed to measure such factors as dependability, emotional stability, social adaptability, home adjustment, and the like. Generally these instruments seek information concerning feelings, behavior, and attitudes. The value of these tests depends upon the cooperation and the truthfulness of the individual who makes the self-report. As a rule the inventory type is easy to score, but it has serious limitations since only slight claim can be made for high validity.

The situational tests for measuring character are of the paper and pencil type which attempt to determine the child's comprehension of what constitutes right conduct in certain situations. These are the *moral information and knowledge tests.* They are measures of ethical information and discrimination built around hypothetical situations. Usually such a test consists of a list of ethical terms to be defined together with a series of problem situations which call for the expression of moral judgment in determining solutions. Such tests investigate or measure only one phase of character. They are measures of *knowledge,* but not necessarily of practice. They reveal for example the child's knowledge of honesty, and whether or not his knowledge of what is honest in a particular situation is correct; but they do not reveal how honest the child actually is, or the specific ways in which he is honest. Yet such tests of moral information do serve an important purpose, for knowledge of right principles is a basic element in character formation. One who is well informed should be able to make correct decisions.

There have also been other attempts to measure character objectively through actual observation of the child's behavior when placed in definite situations within the classroom, or at least within the school setting. The most extensive of these attempts was the Character Education Inquiry conducted by Hartshorne and May.[23] To carry on the study, the investigators devised tests for the measurement of honesty, truthfulness, self-control, cooperativeness, and other traits.

The idea of isolating traits and constructing tests for each trait has not proved useful in character testing; for character is a unity, and, if the totality of character is missed, something of its essence is lacking. Another

[23] H. Hartshorne and M. A. May, *Studies in Deceit* (New York: The Macmillan Co., 1928); *Studies in Service and Self-Control* (New York: The Macmillan Co., 1929); *Studies in the Organization of Character* (New York: The Macmillan Co., 1930).

difficulty with this type is the fact that the results of character training may not be apparent for years. While tests assume that any phase of character can be measured, nevertheless there are no simple measures of character.

In addition to the situational tests of moral information there exists an older and more commonly used technique for appraising character: namely, the *rating scale*. Rating scales are not, as a rule, sufficiently exact to measure progress with any degree of accuracy. A number of forms of the rating scale have been developed. Some list traits to be checked for possession or nonpossession; others furnish space for a quantitative estimate, such as good, average, and poor. There are also *graphic rating scales* in which the rater checks the amount of the characteristic which he believes the person to possess, along a line extending theoretically at least from 0 to 100 percent, then the ratings are connected by lines which yield a trait profile or graph that portrays the pupil's strong or weak points.

These character rating scales have been more widely used in schools than the more objective measurement. As supplements to other measures of capacity, rating scales are valuable, but such ratings are always subjective and low in reliability. People differ markedly in their ability to make ratings. Frequently these scales measure the child's reputation with the teacher, and this reputation may or may not rest upon substantial evidence, may or may not be related to his character. It is worthy of note in this connection that school report cards, almost without exception, at the elementary school level and frequently at the secondary school level, contain teacher ratings and evaluations of a variety of character traits.

There exist also character rating scales upon which the child may rate himself for the possession or nonpossession of character traits. The purpose of such scales is to stimulate the child to think about his character and to motivate him to improve where his analysis of himself reveals weaknesses.

In addition, the use of *projective techniques* as a method for the measurement of the same aspects of character seems definitely to be on the increase. It is maintained that inferences may be drawn from responses made to these techniques which constitute valuable information concerning present organization and possible future development of character since these techniques seek to interpret motives, attitudes, and needs. However, these techniques should be employed only by a thoroughly trained and experienced clinical psychologist. Those which are used most frequently include: the *Thematic Apperception Test,* the *Children's Apperception Test,* and the *Rorschach Test.* Other projective tests designed specifically for children include: *The Blacky Pictures* and *The Driscoll Play Kit.*

In addition, *sociometric techniques* also seem to offer possibilities as methods of measuring character in a social setting. These techniques involve procedures for sampling the attitudes and behavior of members of a group toward each other. In a school situation this involves ordinarily an appraisal of personal and social adjustments by peers or children of similar age and grade status. Of these techniques the *sociogram* is the most widely used and most interesting. It is a graphic device for representing interpersonal relations within a group of pupils. *The Guess Who Test* employed in the Character Education Inquiry was one of the earliest and simplest of the sociometric devices. In addition to the various measures of character, it gives helpful character information and includes interviews, questionnaires, checklists, biographies, case studies, genetic records, school records, and the like.

It is quite likely that these tests which have been devised to measure character will be improved and refined. These tests and scales offer some aid in evaluating character, but they have not yet attained that degree of perfection where they can be considered as reliable and valid measures of character. This field of measurement is significant, since character is considered to be the most important aim and objective of all education, and the reliable measurement of the degree of attainment of that aim will be welcomed by educators.

Research Studies in Character. The *Character Education Inquiry* was an elaborate and intensive investigation sponsored by the Institute of Social and Religious Research and directed by Hartshorne and May. It extended over a period of five years from 1924 to 1929. Approximately 11,000 children of ages 8 to 16 years constituted the subjects. The findings of the investigation were reported in three volumes under the general title of *Studies in the Nature of Character.*[24] Because of the limitations of the paper and pencil tests, questionnaires, and checklists available at the time, the investigators sought to devise objective measures and techniques which involved concrete situations and tasks to which the subjects reacted in an individual manner. These measures were really performance tests, some of which involved classroom situations, others involved schoolwork done at home, and still others involved situations arising in athletic con-

[24] H. Hartshorne and M. A. May, *op. cit.*

tests and in party games. Such tests were formulated for the measurement of several aspects of moral behavior. The fundamental phase of the investigation was concerned with the measurement of *honesty.* Other aspects of the investigation sought to ascertain the extent to which the participating subjects possessed such moral qualities as *helpfulness, cooperativeness, persistence,* and *self-control.*

In the measurement of honesty three types of dishonest behavior were tested — cheating, lying, and stealing. These tests contained situations which presented opportunities for the subjects to cheat on classroom tests or exercises or in schoolwork done at home or in reporting achievement in athletic contests; to lie about whether or not the individual had cheated; to steal small sums of money or to take small articles utilized in test situations. The findings regarding this phase of the investigation indicated that the subjects manifested little tendency to be uniformly honest in all situations. Only a few subjects were consistently honest in all of the situations. There were also a few who utilized practically every opportunity to exhibit dishonest behavior. The great majority of the subjects manifested behavior which was honest in some situations and dishonest in others. When the same tests were administered a second time to the same subjects they displayed a tendency to act consistently in the specific test situations; that is, if they had cheated or lied or stolen on the original administration they tended to do so again on the repetition of the test. The findings revealed that the subjects were not consistently honest or dishonest in all types of situations. The child who consistently cheated in classroom tests was not likely to cheat in reporting achievement in athletic contests. The child who cheated on an arithmetic test might be perfectly honest when taking a spelling test in the same room under the same examiner. In like manner, the child who was dishonest in all classroom situations might be wholly honest in his dealings with his fellow pupils on the playground. The child who reported a false score on a test did not necessarily tell other lies. The conclusion drawn by the investigators was that *no general factor of honesty had been found,* that there were only honest and dishonest *actions,* not honest and dishonest *children.*

When the results of the tests utilized in the other phases of the investigation were analyzed, similar findings were reported. The investigators maintained that no evidence had been found to demonstrate the existence of such traits as helpfulness, cooperativeness, persistence, and self-control.

What had been ascertained in the investigation was that the subjects at times were helpful, at times acted cooperatively, at times manifested persistence and exhibited self-control. The general conclusion drawn from the investigation was that the qualities and traits tested were groups of specific habits rather than general traits;[25] that is, *ethical behavior is specific*. Considerable criticism was directed against the conclusions presented in the Character Education Inquiry.[26]

A more recent investigation of character development which explored individual patterns over a period of seven years was conducted by Peck and Havighurst.[27] This investigation was based upon extensive case studies of 34 subjects, 17 boys and 17 girls, who were studied from their tenth to seventeenth year, during the period of 1943 to 1950. The purpose of this intensive study with this small sample was to obtain information concerning motives, attitudes, and other personality traits which went into the formation of the individual's character. Full-time field workers and public school teachers assisted in the collection of data. Projective tests, sociometric devices largely of the "guess-who" type, and mental and achievement tests were administered to the subjects. Likewise fifteen questionnaires were administered during the period of the investigation. Reputation ratings were secured for each subject from parents, teachers, employers, and other adults. Interviews with the subject and the parents, as well as with others with whom the subjects had contact, constituted an important source of information. The subjects were tested and rated at ages 10, 14, and 17.

This study examined intensively the following factors: the structure of personality and character, family influence on personality and character, moral values and the peer group, sources of moral values in the social environment, the consistency of moral character through time. From an analysis of the findings the investigators concluded that there was "a persisting pattern of attitudes and motives which produce a rather

---

[25] *Ibid.*, Vol. III, p. 1; see also H. Hartshorne, *Character in Human Relations* (New York: Chas. Scribner's Sons, 1933), Chap. 16.

[26] See G. W. Allport, *Personality: A Psychological Interpretation* (New York: Holt, Rinehart and Winston, Inc., 1937), p. 252; G. W. Allport, *Pattern and Growth in Personality* (New York: Holt, Rinehart and Winston, Inc., 1961), pp. 316–317; F. L. Goodenough and L. E. Tyler, *Developmental Psychology*, 3 ed. (New York: Appleton-Century-Crofts, Inc., 1959), pp. 345–349.

[27] R. F. Peck and R. J. Havighurst, *The Psychology of Character Development* (New York: John Wiley & Sons, Inc., 1960).

predictable kind and quality of moral behavior."[28] In addition, the pattern of motives and actions manifested by each individual at the age of 10 years tended to persist through adolescence. In the major aspects of morality most individuals tended to maintain the same attitudes and motives through the years. It seemed possible and useful to define "basic character" in a series of types arranged on an ascending scale of psychological and moral maturity as follows: amoral, expedient, conforming, irrational conscientious, and rational altruistic. However, no one subject was entirely of one type. The dominant force in the structure and content of character was the intimate and powerful relationship between the child and the parents within the family. The peer group exerted a reinforcing influence rather than an instigating one on moral values and behavior. Likewise there was substantial qualitative evidence of the importance of a stable community code. The indirect influence of the Church, the school, the press, and other media constituted a consequential force for the maintenance of sound morality.[29]

The Educational Significance of Character Formation. The first essential for the successful conduct of life is character. The development of character has always engaged the attention and has directed the energy of those responsible for the education of children and youth, for they are ever seeking means for achieving that goal in the best and most efficacious way. Development of character is a very important responsibility of the educator. No aspect of education is of greater importance from the standpoint of the welfare of the individual and of society. It is character which is required for living a right life successfully, and the keynote of life is the measure of character, which renders possible the fulfillment of such high ideals as unselfish service. Since the most vital part of service is the inspiration of it, everyone turns to education for that inspiration and for guidance. There is a universal acceptance of the idea that the ultimate aim of all education is development of character. Men have come to realize that character training is not a new type of education, but rather that it is the consciousness of the true end of education, the recognition that the chief purpose of the school is to glorify right living.

Education through the school has a very important function to fulfill in character training. Education must help to control and direct the forces influencing human development. The direction in which education

[28] *Ibid.*, p. 165.

[29] *Ibid.*, pp. 164–188.

leads a man will greatly influence his future life. The most significant aims of education in training for character are the unfolding of personality and the development of efficiency. Such education consists essentially in building up in the individual an organization of knowledge and ideals, of habits and attitudes which will aid in fulfilling life's purposes.

The mere teaching of character platitudes is all but futile. Pupils should be guided in such a way as to produce satisfactory moral growth. Education is an active process; it is the doing of something; it is the cultivating and fertilizing of minds. Such education is possible only when basic virtues are embodied in the curriculum in such a way as to function directly in the conduct of pupils. The school must be a moral laboratory. It must stress moral values in its government, instruction, and activities. So, for character formation, the emphasis must be placed not only on lessons and information but also on guidance and activity. The best preparation for later development is present right living, and right conduct is the acid test of both right living and good citizenship.

Although strictly scientific knowledge in the field of character development is lacking, educational research is beginning slowly to investigate the learning processes and teaching techniques involved in character training. Even without adequate research it is apparent that training for character should be implicit in all activities of school life. It should not be something incidental, but a training for functional and dynamic moral citizenship. School is not merely preparation for adult life; it is also an integral part of child life. Education which is concerned with the growth, development, and adjustment of the child must determine very definitely the outcomes sought in terms of objectives that include character traits growing out of school experiences. Hence, the work of character training is a practical, everyday matter demanding constant attention and practical wisdom in its conduct. Training for character is worth just the difference it will make in the efficiency of the way in which one will meet all the aspects of all the experiences of life in all of its complex relationships.

EXERCISES

1. Outline this chapter.
2. List and define the terms which you have learned from your study of this chapter.

3. Explain the nature of character.
4. Discuss the following topics:
   a) The bases of character;
   b) The home as a factor in character development;
   c) Character implications in the various school subjects;
   d) Merits of the direct and indirect methods of character formation;
   e) Philosophy of life related to character;
   f) Tests and measures of character.
5. What influence on character is exerted by social institutions outside the home, the school, and the Church? How can these institutions be induced to cooperate with the basic social agencies in the program of character formation? What are some of the difficulties involved? How may these difficulties be overcome?
6. Discuss the following statements:
   a) "Every man is the architect of his own character."
   b) "Character is nothing more than a perfectly fashioned will."
   c) "Character is not a mosaic or aggregate of specific traits."
   d) "Character has been the *primary* end sought for through the educative process from the beginning of educational history."
   e) "A gem cannot be polished without friction, nor man's character perfected without trials."
7. Distinguish between:
   a) Personality and character;
   b) Habit and attitude;
   c) Principle and value;
   d) Ideal and virtue;
   e) Direct and indirect method of character formation.
8. *a*) List and discuss the conditions in present-day life which demonstrate an urgent need for character training.
   b) What is the present trend in curriculum construction with regard to character?
9. What is the relation of each of the following to character formation:
   a) Mental hygiene?
   b) Guidance?
   c) Discipline?
10. *a*) What types of tests are utilized to measure character?
   b) What is the significance and value of each type?
   c) Contrast the findings of the Character Education Inquiry and those of Peck and Havighurst.

FOR STUDY AND READING
SELECTED REFERENCES

Allers, R., *Psychology of Character* (New York: Sheed and Ward, 1934).

——— *Character Education in Adolescence* (New York: Joseph F. Wagner, Inc., 1940).

Allport, C. W., *Personality: A Psychological Interpretation* (New York: Holt, Rinehart and Winston, Inc., 1937).

——— *Becoming: Basic Considerations for a Psychology of Personality* (New Haven: Yale University Press, 1955).
——— *Pattern and Growth in Personality* (New York: Holt, Rinehart and Winston, Inc., 1961).
Arnold, M. B., and Gasson, J. A., *The Human Person* (New York: The Ronald Press Co., 1954), Chaps. 4, 5, and 6.
Donceel, J. F., *Philosophical Psychology,* 2 ed. (New York: Sheed and Ward, 1961).
Educational Policies Commission, *Moral and Spiritual Values in the Public Schools* (Washington, D. C.: National Education Association, 1951).
Havighurst, R. J., and Taba, H., *Adolescent Character and Personality* (New York: John Wiley & Sons, Inc., 1949).
Hull, E. R., *The Formation of Character* (St. Louis: B. Herder Book Co., 1926).
Jones, V. E., *Character and Citizenship Education* (Washington, D. C.: National Education Association, 1950).
——— "Character Development in Children: An Objective Approach," in *Manual of Child Psychology,* L. Carmichael, ed., 2 ed. (New York: John Wiley & Sons, Inc., 1954), Chap. 13.
——— "Character Formation," in *Encyclopedia of Educational Research,* C. W. Harris, ed., 3 ed. (New York: The Macmillan Co., 1960), pp. 184–191.
Kircher, C. J., *Character Formation Through Books,* 3 ed. (Washington, D. C.: The Catholic University of America Press, 1952).
Langdon, G., and Stout, I., *Teaching Moral and Spiritual Values* (New York: The John Day Co., 1962).
Ligon, E. M., *Dimensions of Character* (New York: The Macmillan Co., 1956).
Mouroux, J., *The Meaning of Man* (New York: Sheed and Ward, 1948).
Peck, R. F., and Havighurst, R. J., *The Psychology of Character Development* (New York: John Wiley & Sons, Inc., 1960).
Piaget, J., *The Moral Judgment of the Child* (Glencoe, Ill.: The Free Press, 1949).
Robach, A. A., *The Psychology of Character,* 3 ed. (Boston: Sci-Art Publisher, 1952).

Appendix

THE PREPARATION OF THE TERM PAPER OR REPORT

I. *Purposes of the term paper*

1. To supplement the student's knowledge by affording an opportunity to explore some phase of educational psychology in which he has developed a special interest.
2. To provide experience in locating and evaluating source materials.
3. To enable the student to become familiar with research procedures.
4. To give the student an opportunity to organize and present, in systematic fashion, a constructive and critical account of a phase of the field of educational psychology.

II. *Selecting a subject*

1. The subject of the term paper should:
   a) Be related to some aspect of educational psychology;
   b) Have the appeal of interest.
2. The subject should be analyzed and delimited to the restricted phase which is to be presented in the term paper.

III. *Gathering materials*

1. Prepare a bibliography which includes available references consisting of books, articles, and reports from professional journals, dissertations, monographs.
2. In selecting references:
   a) Consult the bibliography and footnotes in the textbook;
   b) Use the subject and author indexes in the library card catalogue;
   c) Consult such specialized sources as *Psychological Abstracts, Education Index, Review of Educational Research, Encyclopedia of Educational Research,* and the like.
3. Record on a card or slip each reference in the following manner:
   a) Name of author;
   b) Complete title;
   c) Publisher, place, and date of publication;
   d) Chapter or pages containing essential material;
   e) Annotation or comment concerning the value and use of the reference.

IV. *Outlining the report*

1. The purpose of the outline is to provide a logical and coherent plan to serve as a guide in the organization of the report.
2. Plan the outline carefully by indicating:
   a) The main divisions of the report by the use of principal headings;
   b) The subdivisions under each principal heading.
3. Arrange the bibliographical references under the appropriate headings and subheadings.

V. *Writing the report*
1. Follow the outline, developing points in order.
2. Write carefully and be clear in the presentation of materials.
3. The introduction should contain a brief, forceful, and interesting statement of the purpose and significance of the report.
4. End with a conclusion, summarizing essential points.
5. Follow the rules for the preparation of a good manuscript* with regard to typing, margins, footnotes, quotations, etc.

VI. *Guidance*
1. Obtain the instructor's approval of the subject or topic selected.
2. Submit the outline to the instructor for inspection, correction, and approval.
3. Submit the term paper on the date designated.
4. Devote sufficient time to the preparation of the report and do not postpone it until the last week of the course.

OUTLINE FOR BOOK REPORT

I. *Heading, which includes:*
1. Name of the author;
2. Title of the book;
3. Place of publication;
4. Publisher;
5. Date of Publication.

II. *A concise summary of the materials presented,* including the major facts, the order of topics considered, and the viewpoint expressed concerning various phases or problems of educational psychology.

III. *A critical evaluation stating:*
1. Whether or not the book is beneficial to the purposes and needs of Catholic education;
2. Whether or not the viewpoint of the author is in keeping with the Catholic concept of man;
3. The contribution made by the book to the field of educational psychology.

OUTLINE FOR REPORTING RESEARCH PRESENTED IN PROFESSIONAL JOURNALS

I. *Heading, which includes:*
1. Name of the investigator;
2. Title of the article;
3. The journal in which the article was published;
4. The volume number;
5. The pages;
6. The date of publication.

---

* See W. G. Campbell, *Form and Style in Thesis Writing* (Boston: Houghton Mifflin Co., 1954).

II. *The statement of the problem under investigation, including:*
   1. Definition of terms, where given;
   2. Significance of the problem;
   3. Limitations of the investigation.

III. *The subjects who participated in the investigation, including:*
   1. Number;
   2. Age range;
   3. Mental ability;
   4. Grade placement, etc.

IV. *The materials used, including:*
   Tests, inventories, and other devices.

V. *The procedures employed in conducting the investigation, including:*
   Description of matching techniques, etc.

VI. *The statistical devices employed in analyzing the data.*

VII. *The findings.*

VIII. *The conclusions.*

IX. *An evaluation.*

X. *Relationship of the investigation to educational psychology.*

A LIST OF MATERIALS USEFUL TO THE STUDENT OF EDUCATIONAL PSYCHOLOGY

I. *Professional journals and periodicals:*

American Psychologist
British Journal of Educational Psychology
Catholic Educational Review
Catholic Educator
Catholic School Journal
Child, The
Child Development
Childhood Education
Contemporary Psychology
Education
Educational and Psychological Measurement
Elementary School Journal
Exceptional Children
Genetic Psychology Monographs
Journal of Abnormal and Social Psychology
Journal of Applied Psychology
Journal of Clinical Psychology
Journal of Consulting Psychology
Journal of Counseling Psychology
Journal of Educational Psychology
Journal of Educational Research
Journal of Experimental Education
Journal of Experimental Psychology
Journal of General Psychology
Journal of Genetic Psychology

Journal of Personality
Journal of Psychology
Journal of Social Psychology
Mental Hygiene
Modern Schoolman
New Scholasticism
News letter (American Catholic Psychological Association)
Peabody Journal of Education
Personnel and Guidance Journal
Phi Delta Kappan
Psychological Bulletin
Psychological Monographs
Psychological Review
School and Society
School Review
Teachers College Record
Understanding the Child

II. *Indexes and digests:*
Annual Review of Psychology
Catholic Periodical Abstracts
Catholic Periodical Index
Child Development Abstracts and Bibliography
Education Digest
Education Index
Review of Educational Research

III. *Encyclopedias and handbooks:*
Encyclopedia of Child Guidance
Encyclopedia of Educational Research
Encyclopedia of Modern Education
Encyclopedia of Psychology
Encyclopedia of Vocational Guidance
Handbook of Applied Psychology
Handbook of Child Guidance
Handbook of Experimental Psychology
Manual of Child Psychology

IV. *Readings:*
Andrew, D. C., and Downing, L. N., *120 Readings in Guidance*
Brayfield, A. H., *Readings in Modern Methods of Counseling*
Buros, O. K., *The Mental Measurements Yearbooks*
Coladarci, A. P., *Educational Psychology: A Book of Readings*
Dennis, W., *Readings in Child Psychology*
——— *Readings in General Psychology*
——— *Readings in the History of Psychology*
Foff, A., and Grambs, J. D., *Readings in Education*
Hartley, E. L., *Outside Readings in Psychology*
Kuhlen, R. G., and Thompson, G. G., *Psychological Studies of Human Development*
Martin, W. E., and Stendler, C. B., *Readings in Child Development*

Seidman, J. M., *The Adolescent: A Book of Readings*
——— *Readings in Educational Psychology*
Skinner, C. E., and Associates, *Readings in Educational Psychology*
——— *Readings in Psychology*

V. *Dictionaries:*
Drever, J., *A Dictionary of Psychology*
English, H. B., *A Student's Dictionary of Psychological Terms*
Good, C. V., *Dictionary of Education*
Harriman, P. H., *The New Dictionary of Psychology*
Warren, H. C., *Dictionary of Psychology*

VI. *Yearbooks:*
Proceedings of the National Catholic Educational Association
Yearbooks of the National Society for the Study of Education

Index